ESSENTIALS
★ edition ★
12

We the People

An Introduction to American Politics

The 116th Congress, January 3, 2019–January 3, 2021

United States House of Representatives

Democrats: 233   Republicans: 200   Undecided: 2   **2018 Election Results: Democrats gained control of the House***

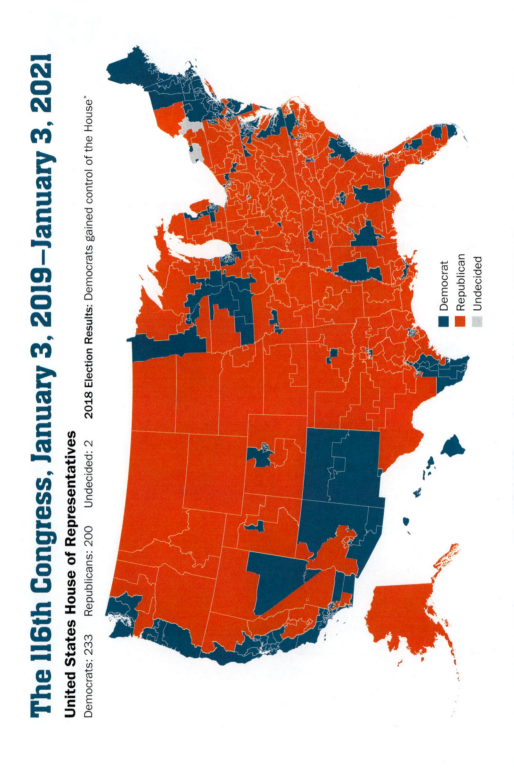

- ■ Democrat
- ■ Republican
- ▨ Undecided

United States Senate

Democrats: 45   Republicans: 52   Independents: 2   **2018 Election Results**: Republicans retained control of the Senate*

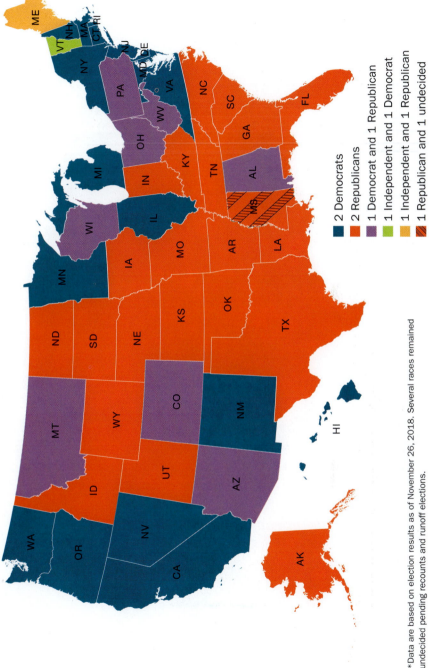

Legend:
- 2 Democrats
- 2 Republicans
- 1 Democrat and 1 Republican
- 1 Independent and 1 Democrat
- 1 Independent and 1 Republican
- 1 Republican and 1 undecided

*Data are based on election results as of November 26, 2018. Several races remained undecided pending recounts and runoff elections.

ESSENTIALS
★ *edition* ★
12

We the People

An Introduction to American Politics

★ **BENJAMIN GINSBERG**
THE JOHNS HOPKINS UNIVERSITY

★ **THEODORE J. LOWI**
LATE OF CORNELL UNIVERSITY

★ **MARGARET WEIR**
BROWN UNIVERSITY

★ **CAROLINE J. TOLBERT**
UNIVERSITY OF LOWA

★ **ANDREA L. CAMPBELL**
MASSACHUSETTS INSTITUTE OF
TECHNOLOGY

★ **ROBERT J. SPITZER**
SUNY CORTLAND

 W. W. NORTON & COMPANY
NEW YORK   LONDON

W. W. Norton & Company has been independent since its founding in 1923, when William Warder Norton and Mary D. Herter Norton first published lectures delivered at the People's Institute, the adult education division of New York City's Cooper Union. The firm soon expanded its program beyond the Institute, publishing books by celebrated academics from America and abroad. By mid-century, the two major pillars of Norton's publishing program—trade books and college texts—were firmly established. In the 1950s, the Norton family transferred control of the company to its employees, and today—with a staff of four hundred and a comparable number of trade, college, and professional titles published each year—W. W. Norton & Company stands as the largest and oldest publishing house owned wholly by its employees.

Editor: Peter Lesser

Project Editor: Christine D'Antonio

Assistant Editor: Anna Olcott

Manuscript Editor: Lynne Cannon

Managing Editor, College: Marian Johnson

Managing Editor, College Digital Media: Kim Yi

Production Manager, College: Ashley Horna

Media Editor: Spencer Richardson-Jones

Associate Media Editor: Michael Jaoui

Media Editorial Assistant: Tricia Vuong

Ebook Production Manager: Danielle Lehmann

Marketing Manager, Political Science: Erin Brown

Art Director: Rubina Yeh

Text Design: Jen Montgomery

Photo Editor: Stephanie Romeo

Photo Researcher: Elyse Rieder

Director of College Permissions: Megan Schindel

Permissions Associate: Elizabeth Trammell

Information Graphics: Kiss Me I'm Polish LLC, New York

Composition: Graphic World, Inc.

Manufacturing: TransContinental

Permission to use copyrighted material is included in the credits section of this book, which begins on page A83.

The Library of Congress has cataloged the full edition as follows:

Library of Congress Cataloging-in-Publication Data
Names: Ginsberg, Benjamin, author.
Title: We the people : an introduction to American politics / Benjamin
  Ginsberg, The Johns Hopkins University, Theodore J. Lowi, Cornell
  University, Margaret Weir, Brown University, Caroline J. Tolbert,
  University of Iowa, Andrea L. Campbell, Massachusetts Institute of
  Technology.
Description: Twelfth Edition. | New York : W.W. Norton & Company, [2018] |
  Includes bibliographical references and index.
Identifiers: LCCN 2018046033 | ISBN 9780393644326 (hardcover)
Subjects: LCSH: United States--Politics and government--Textbooks.
Classification: LCC JK276 .G55 2018 | DDC 320.473--dc23 LC record available at https://lccn.loc.gov/2018046033

ISBN 978-0-393-66464-5

W. W. Norton & Company, Inc., 500 Fifth Avenue, New York, NY 10110
wwnorton.com

W. W. Norton & Company Ltd., 15 Carlisle Street, London W1D 3BS

1 2 3 4 5 6 7 8 9 0

To:

Teresa Spitzer

Sandy, Cindy, and Alex Ginsberg

David, Jackie, Eveline, and Ed Dowling

Dave, Marcella, Logan, and Kennah Campbell

Contents

2 ★ The Founding and the Constitution 30

PART II   POLITICS

5 ★ Public Opinion   144

6 ★ The Media 176

7 ★ Political Parties, Participation, and Elections 204

PART III   INSTITUTIONS

10 ★ The Presidency   314

11 ★ Bureaucracy   346

12 ★ The Federal Courts   374

PART IV POLICY

13 ★ Domestic Policy 406

14 ★ Foreign Policy   444

Appendix

Preface

This book has been and continues to be dedicated to developing a satisfactory response to the question more and more Americans are asking: Why should we be engaged with government and politics? Through the first 11 editions, we sought to answer this question by making the text directly relevant to the lives of the students who would be reading it. As a result, we tried to make politics interesting by demonstrating that students' interests are at stake and that they therefore need to take a personal, even selfish, interest in the outcomes of government. At the same time, we realized that students needed guidance in how to become politically engaged. Beyond providing students with a core of political knowledge, we needed to show them how they could apply that knowledge as participants in the political process. The "Who Participates?" and "What You Can Do" sections in each chapter help achieve that goal.

As events from the last several years have reminded us, "what government does" inevitably raises questions about political participation and political equality. The size and composition of the electorate, for example, affect who is elected to public office and what policy directions the government will pursue. Hence, the issue of voter ID laws became important in the 2016 election, with some arguing that these laws reduce voter fraud and others contending that they decrease participation by poor and minority voters. Charges of Russian meddling in the 2016 election have raised questions about the integrity of the voting process. Fierce debates about the policies of the Trump administration have heightened students' interest in politics. Other recent events have underscored how Americans from different backgrounds experience politics. Arguments about immigration became contentious during the 2016 election as the nation once again debated the question of who is entitled to be an American and have a voice in determining what the government does. And charges that the police often use excessive violence against members of minority groups have raised questions about whether the government treats all Americans equally. Reflecting all of these trends, this new Twelfth Edition shows more than any other book on the market (1) how students are connected to government, (2) why students should think critically about government and politics, and (3) how Americans from different backgrounds experience and shape politics. To help us explore these themes, Professor Andrea Campbell has joined us as the most recent in a group of distinguished coauthors. Professor Campbell's scholarly work focuses on the ways in which government and politics affect the lives of ordinary citizens. Among her contributions are new chapter introductions that focus on stories of individuals and how government has affected them. Many Americans, particularly the young, can have difficulty seeing the role of government in their everyday lives. Indeed, that's a chief explanation of low voter participation among younger citizens. The new chapter openers profile various individuals and illustrate their interactions with government, from a rock band that gets its controversial name approved by the Supreme Court (Chapter 4), to a young mother who realizes the tap water in her Flint, Michigan, home is poisoning her children after local officials switched the source (Chapter 11), to teenagers protesting the end of net neutrality and the internet as they have known it (Chapter 6). The goal of these stories is to show students in a vivid way how government and politics mean something to their daily lives.

Several other elements of the book also help show students why politics and government should matter to them. These include:

- **A twenty-first-century perspective on demographic change** moves beyond the book's strong coverage of traditional civil rights content with expanded coverage of contemporary group politics.

- **"Who Participates?" infographics at the end of every chapter** show students how different groups of Americans participate in key aspects of politics and government. Each concludes with a "What You Can Do" section that provides students with specific, realistic steps they can take to act on what they've learned and get involved in politics.

- **"America Side by Side" boxes** in every chapter use data figures and tables to provide a comparative perspective. By comparing political institutions and behavior across countries, students gain a better understanding of how specific features of the American system shape politics.

- **Up-to-date coverage**, with more than 10 pages and numerous graphics on the 2016 and 2018 elections, including a five-page section devoted to analysis of these momentous elections in Chapter 8, as well as updated data, examples, and other information throughout the book.

- **"What Do We Want" chapter conclusions** step back and provide perspective on how the chapter content connects to fundamental questions about the American political system. The conclusions also reprise the important point made in the personal profiles that begin each chapter that government matters to the lives of individuals.

- **This Twelfth Edition is accompanied by InQuizitive**, Norton's award-winning formative, adaptive online quizzing program. The InQuizitive course for *We the People*, Essentials Edition, guides students through questions organized around the text's chapter learning objectives to ensure mastery of the core information and to help with assessment. More information and a demonstration are available at digital.wwnorton.com/wethepeople12ess.

We note with regret the passing of Theodore Lowi as well as Margaret Weir's decision to step down from the book. We miss them but continue to hear their voices and to benefit from their wisdom in the pages of our book. We also continue to hope that our book will itself be accepted as a form of enlightened political action. This Twelfth Edition is another chance. It is an advancement toward our goal. We promise to keep trying.

Acknowledgments

We are especially pleased to acknowledge the many colleagues who had a direct and active role in criticism and preparation of the manuscript. Our thanks go to:

First Edition Reviewers

Sarah Binder, Brookings Institution
Kathleen Gille, Office of Representative David Bonior
Rodney Hero, University of Colorado at Boulder
Robert Katzmann, Brookings Institution
Kathleen Knight, University of Houston
Robin Kolodny, Temple University
Nancy Kral, Tomball College
Robert C. Lieberman, Columbia University
David A. Marcum, University of Wyoming
Laura R. Winsky Mattei, State University of New York at Buffalo
Marilyn S. Mertens, Midwestern State University
Barbara Suhay, Henry Ford Community College
Carolyn Wong, Stanford University
Julian Zelizer, State University of New York at Albany

Second Edition Reviewers

Lydia Andrade, University of North Texas
John Coleman, University of Wisconsin at Madison
Daphne Eastman, Odessa College
Otto Feinstein, Wayne State University
Elizabeth Flores, Delmar College
James Gimpel, University of Maryland at College Park
Jill Glaathar, Southwest Missouri State University
Shaun Herness, University of Florida

William Lyons, University of Tennessee at Knoxville
Andrew Polsky, Hunter College, City University of New York
Grant Reeher, Syracuse University
Richard Rich, Virginia Polytechnic
Bartholomew Sparrow, University of Texas at Austin

Third Edition Reviewers

Bruce R. Drury, Lamar University
Andrew I. E. Ewoh, Prairie View A&M University
Amy Jasperson, University of Texas at San Antonio
Loch Johnson, University of Georgia
Mark Kann, University of Southern California
Robert L. Perry, University of Texas of the Permian Basin
Wayne Pryor, Brazosport College
Elizabeth A. Rexford, Wharton County Junior College
Andrea Simpson, University of Washington
Brian Smentkowski, Southeast Missouri State University
Nelson Wikstrom, Virginia Commonwealth University

Fourth Edition Reviewers

M. E. Banks, Virginia Commonwealth University
Lynn Brink, North Lake College
Mark Cichock, University of Texas at Arlington

Del Fields, St. Petersburg College

Nancy Kinney, Washtenaw Community College

William Klein, St. Petersburg College

Dana Morales, Montgomery College

Christopher Muste, Louisiana State University

Larry Norris, South Plains College

David Rankin, State University of New York at Fredonia

Paul Roesler, St. Charles Community College

J. Philip Rogers, San Antonio College

Greg Shaw, Illinois Wesleyan University

Tracy Skopek, Stephen F. Austin State University

Don Smith, University of North Texas

Terri Wright, Cal State, Fullerton

Fifth Edition Reviewers

Annie Benifield, Tomball College

Denise Dutton, Southwest Missouri State University

Rick Kurtz, Central Michigan University

Kelly McDaniel, Three Rivers Community College

Eric Plutzer, Pennsylvania State University

Daniel Smith, Northwest Missouri State University

Dara Strolovitch, University of Minnesota

Dennis Toombs, San Jacinto College–North

Stacy Ulbig, Southwest Missouri State University

Sixth Edition Reviewers

Janet Adamski, University of Mary Hardin–Baylor

Greg Andrews, St. Petersburg College

Louis Bolce, Baruch College

Darin Combs, Tulsa Community College

Sean Conroy, University of New Orleans

Paul Cooke, Cy Fair College

Vida Davoudi, Kingwood College

Robert DiClerico, West Virginia University

Corey Ditslear, University of North Texas

Kathy Dolan, University of Wisconsin, Milwaukee

Randy Glean, Midwestern State University

Nancy Kral, Tomball College

Mark Logas, Valencia Community College

Scott MacDougall, Diablo Valley College

David Mann, College of Charleston

Christopher Muste, University of Montana

Richard Pacelle, Georgia Southern University

Sarah Poggione, Florida International University

Richard Rich, Virginia Tech

Thomas Schmeling, Rhode Island College

Scott Spitzer, California State University–Fullerton

Robert Wood, University of North Dakota

Seventh Edition Reviewers

Molly Andolina, DePaul University

Nancy Bednar, Antelope Valley College

Paul Blakelock, Kingwood College

Amy Brandon, San Jacinto College

Jim Cauthen, John Jay College

Kevin Davis, North Central Texas College

Louis DeSipio, University of California–Irvine

Brandon Franke, Blinn College

Steve Garrison, Midwestern State University

Joseph Howard, University of Central Arkansas

Aaron Knight, Houston Community College

Paul Labedz, Valencia Community College

Elise Langan, John Jay College

Mark Logas, Valencia Community College

Eric Miller, Blinn College

Anthony O'Regan, Los Angeles Valley College

David Putz, Kingwood College

Chis Soper, Pepperdine University

Kevin Wagner, Florida Atlantic University

Laura Wood, Tarrant County College

Eighth Edition Reviewers

Brian Arbour, John Jay College, CUNY

Ellen Baik, University of Texas–Pan American

David Birch, Lone Star College–Tomball

Bill Carroll, Sam Houston State University

Ed Chervenak, University of New Orleans

Gary Church, Mountain View College

Adrian Stefan Clark, Del Mar College

Annie Cole, Los Angeles City College

Greg Combs, University of Texas at Dallas

Cassandra Cookson, Lee College

Brian Cravens, Blinn College

John Crosby, California State University–Chico
Scott Crosby, Valencia Community College
Courtenay Daum, Colorado State University, Fort Collins
Peter Doas, University of Texas–Pan American
John Domino, Sam Houston State University
Doug Dow, University of Texas–Dallas
Jeremy Duff, Midwestern State University
Heather Evans, Sam Houston State University
Hyacinth Ezeamii, Albany State University
Bob Fitrakis, Columbus State Community College
Brian Fletcher, Truckee Meadows Community College
Paul Foote, Eastern Kentucky University
Frank Garrahan, Austin Community College
Jimmy Gleason, Purdue University
Steven Greene, North Carolina State University
Jeannie Grussendorf, Georgia State University
M. Ahad Hayaud-Din, Brookhaven College
Alexander Hogan, Lone Star College–CyFair
Glen Hunt, Austin Community College
Mark Jendrysik, University of North Dakota
Krista Jenkins, Fairleigh Dickinson University
Carlos Juárez, Hawaii Pacific University
Melinda Kovács, Sam Houston State University
Boyd Lanier, Lamar University
Jeff Lazarus, Georgia State University
Jeffrey Lee, Blinn College
Alan Lehmann, Blinn College
Julie Lester, Macon State College
Steven Lichtman, Shippensburg University
Fred Lokken, Truckee Meadows Community College
Shari MacLachlan, Palm Beach Community College
Guy Martin, Winston-Salem State University
Fred Monardi, College of Southern Nevada
Vincent Moscardelli, University of Connecticut
Jason Mycoff, University of Delaware
Sugumaran Narayanan, Midwestern State University
Anthony Nownes, University of Tennessee, Knoxville
Elizabeth Oldmixon, University of North Texas

John Osterman, San Jacinto College–Central
Mark Peplowski, College of Southern Nevada
Maria Victoria Perez-Rios, John Jay College, CUNY
Sara Rinfret, University of Wisconsin, Green Bay
Andre Robinson, Pulaski Technical College
Susan Roomberg, University of Texas at San Antonio
Ryan Rynbrandt, Collin County Community College
Mario Salas, Northwest Vista College
Michael Sanchez, San Antonio College
Mary Schander, Pasadena City College
Laura Schneider, Grand Valley State University
Subash Shah, Winston-Salem State University
Mark Shomaker, Blinn College
Roy Slater, St. Petersburg College
Debra St. John, Collin College
Eric Whitaker, Western Washington University
Clay Wiegand, Cisco College
Walter Wilson, University of Texas at San Antonio
Kevan Yenerall, Clarion University
Rogerio Zapata, South Texas College

Ninth Edition Reviewers

Amy Acord, Lone Star College–CyFair
Milan Andrejevich, Ivy Tech Community College
Steve Anthony, Georgia State University
Phillip Ardoin, Appalachian State University
Gregory Arey, Cape Fear Community College
Joan Babcock, Northwest Vista College
Evelyn Ballard, Houston Community College
Robert Ballinger, South Texas College
Mary Barnes-Tilley, Blinn College
Robert Bartels, Evangel University
Nancy Bednar, Antelope Valley College
Annie Benifield, Lone Star College–Tomball
Donna Bennett, Trinity Valley Community College
Amy Brandon, El Paso Community College
Mark Brewer, The University of Maine
Gary Brown, Lone Star College–Montgomery

Joe Campbell, Johnson County Community College

Dewey Clayton, University of Louisville

Jeff Colbert, Elon University

Amanda Cook-Fesperman, Illinois Valley Community College

Kevin Corder, Western Michigan University

Kevin Davis, North Central Texas College

Paul Davis, Truckee Meadows Community College

Terri Davis, Lamar University

Jennifer De Maio, California State University, Northridge

Christopher Durso, Valencia College

Ryan Emenaker, College of the Redwoods

Leslie Feldman, Hofstra University

Glen Findley, Odessa College

Michael Gattis, Gulf Coast State College

Donna Godwin, Trinity Valley Community College

Precious Hall, Truckee Meadows Community College

Sally Hansen, Daytona State College

Tiffany Harper, Collin College

Todd Hartman, Appalachian State University

Virginia Haysley, Lone Star College–Tomball

David Head, John Tyler Community College

Rick Henderson, Texas State University–San Marcos

Richard Herrera, Arizona State University

Thaddaus Hill, Blinn College

Steven Holmes, Bakersfield College

Kevin Holton, South Texas College

Robin Jacobson, University of Puget Sound

Joseph Jozwiak, Texas A & M–Corpus Christi

Casey Klofstad, University of Miami

Samuel Lingrosso, Los Angeles Valley College

Mark Logas, Valencia College

Christopher Marshall, South Texas College

Larry McElvain, South Texas College

Elizabeth McLane, Wharton County Junior College

Eddie Meaders, University of North Texas

Rob Mellen, Mississippi State University

Jalal Nejad, Northwest Vista College

Adam Newmark, Appalachian State University

Stephen Nicholson, University of California, Merced

Cissie Owen, Lamar University

Suzanne Preston, St. Petersburg College

David Putz, Lone Star College–Kingwood

Auksuole Rubavichute, Mountain View College

Ronnee Schreiber, San Diego State University

Ronald Schurin, University of Connecticut

Jason Seitz, Georgia Perimeter College

Jennifer Seitz, Georgia Perimeter College

Shannon Sinegal, The University of New Orleans

John Sides, George Washington University

Thomas Sowers, Lamar University

Jim Startin, University of Texas at San Antonio

Robert Sterken, University of Texas at Tyler

Bobby Summers, Harper College

John Theis, Lone Star College–Kingwood

John Todd, University of North Texas

Delaina Toothman, The University of Maine

David Trussell, Cisco College

Ronald Vardy, University of Houston

Linda Veazey, Midwestern State University

John Vento, Antelope Valley Community College

Clif Wilkinson, Georgia College

John Wood, Rose State College

Michael Young, Trinity Valley Community College

Tyler Young, Collin College

Tenth Edition Reviewers

Stephen P. Amberg, University of Texas at San Antonio

Juan F. Arzola, College of the Sequoias

Thomas J. Baldino, Wilkes University

Christina Bejarano, University of Kansas

Paul T. Bellinger, Jr., University of Missouri

Melanie J. Blumberg, California University of Pennsylvania

Matthew T. Bradley, Indiana University Kokomo

Jeffrey W. Christiansen, Seminole State College

McKinzie Craig, Marietta College

Christopher Cronin, Methodist University

Jenna Duke, Lehigh Carbon Community College

Francisco Durand, University of Texas at San Antonio

Carrie Eaves, Elon University

Paul M. Flor, El Camino College Compton Center

Adam Fuller, Youngstown State University

Christi Gramling, Charleston Southern
University
Sally Hansen, Daytona State College
Mary Jane Hatton, Hawai'i Pacific University
David Helpap, University of
Wisconsin–Green Bay
Theresa L. Hutchins, Georgia Highlands College
Cryshanna A. Jackson Leftwich, Youngstown
State University
Ashlyn Kuersten, Western Michigan University
Kara Lindaman, Winona State University
Timothy Lynch, University of
Wisconsin–Milwaukee
Larry McElvain, South Texas College
Corinna R. McKoy, Ventura College
Eddie L. Meaders, University of North Texas
Don D. Mirjanian, College of Southern
Nevada
R. Shea Mize, Georgia Highlands College
Nicholas Morgan, Collin College
Matthew Murray, Dutchess Community
College
Harold "Trey" Orndorff III, Daytona State
College
Randall Parish, University of North Georgia
Michelle Pautz, University of Dayton
Michael Pickering, University of New Orleans
Donald Ranish, Antelope Valley College
Glenn W. Richardson, Jr., Kutztown
University of Pennsylvania
Jason Robles, Colorado State University
Ionas Aurelian Rus, University of Cincinnati–
Blue Ash
Robert Sahr, Oregon State University
Kelly B. Shaw, Iowa State University
Captain Michael Slattery, Campbell University
Michael Smith, Sam Houston State University
Maryam T. Stevenson, University of
Indianapolis
Elizabeth Trentanelli, Gulf Coast State
College
Ronald W. Vardy, University of Houston
Timothy Weaver, University of Louisville
Christina Wolbrecht, University of Notre
Dame

Eleventh Edition Reviewers

Maria J. Albo, University of North Georgia
Andrea Aleman, University of Texas at San
Antonio

Juan Arzola, College of the Sequoias
Ross K. Baker, Rutgers University
Lauren Balasco, Pittsburg State University
Daniel Birdsong, University of Dayton
Phil Branyon, University of North Georgia
Camille D. Burge, Villanova University
Matthew DeSantis, Guilford Technical
Community College
Sheryl Edwards, University of
Michigan–Dearborn
Lauren Elliott-Dorans, University of
Toledo
Heather Evans, Sam Houston State
University
William Feagin, Jr., Wharton County Junior
College
Glen Findley, Odessa College
Heather Frederick, Slipper Rock University
Jason Ghibesi, Ocean County College
Patrick Gilbert, Lone Star–Tomball
Rebecca Herzog, American River College
Steven Horn, Everett Community College
Demetra Kasimis, California State
University, Long Beach
Eric T. Kasper, University of Wisconsin–Eau
Claire
Jill Kirkham, Brigham Young University–
Idaho
Mary Linder, Grayson County College
Johnson Louie, California State University,
Stanislaus
Phil McCall, Portland State University
Patrick Novotny, Georgia Southern
University
Carolyn Myers, Southwestern Illinois
College–Belleville
Gerhard Peters, Citrus College
Michael A. Powell, Frederick Community
College
Robert Proctor, Santa Rosa Junior College
Allen K. Settle, California Polytechnic State
University
Laurie Sprankle, Community College of
Allegheny County
Ryan Lee Teten, University of Louisiana
at Lafayette
Justin Vaughn, Boise State University
John Vento, Antelope Valley College
Aaron Weinschenk, University of
Wisconsin–Green Bay
Tyler Young, Collin College

Twelfth Edition Reviewers

Craig Albert, Augusta University

Alexa Bankert, University of Georgia

Nathan Barrick, University of South Florida

Jeff Birdsong, Northeastern Oklahoma A&M College

Sara Butler, College of the Desert

Cory Colby, Lone Star College

Anthony Daniels, University of Toledo

Dennis Falcon, Cerritos College

Kathleen Ferraiolo, James Madison University

Patrick Gilbert, Lone Star College, Tomball

Matthew Green, Catholic University of America

Matt Guardino, Providence College

Barbara Headrick, Minnesota State University, Moorhead

Justin Hoggard, Three Rivers Community College

John Patrick Ifedi, Howard University

Cryshanna Jackson Leftwich, Youngstown State University

Douglas Kriner, Boston University

Thom Kuehls, Weber State University

Jennifer Lawless, American University

LaDella Levy, College of Southern Nevada

Timothy Lim, California State University, Los Angeles

Sam Lingrosso, Los Angeles Valley College

Mandy May, College of Southern Maryland

Suzanne Mettler, Cornell University

Michael Miller, Barnard College

Joseph Njoroge, Abraham Baldwin Agricultural College

Michael Petri, Santa Ana College

Christopher Poulios, Nassau Community College

Andrew Rudalevige, Bowdoin College

Amanda Sanford, Louisiana Tech University

Elizabeth Saunders, George Washington University

Kathleen Searles, Louisiana State University

Matthew Snyder, Delgado Community College

Steven Sylvester, Utah Valley University

Linda Trautman, Ohio University Lancaster

Donald Williams, Western New England University

Peter Yacobucci, Buffalo State College

We are also grateful to Melissa Michelson, of Menlo College, who contributed to the "Who Participates?" infographics for this edition; Holley Hansen, of Oklahoma State University, who contributed to the "America Side by Side" boxes.

Perhaps above all, we thank those at W. W. Norton. For its first five editions, editor Steve Dunn helped us shape the book in countless ways. Lisa McKay contributed smart ideas and a keen editorial eye to the Tenth Edition. Ann Shin carried on the Norton tradition of splendid editorial work on the Sixth through Ninth and Eleventh Editions. Peter Lesser brought intelligence and dedication to the development of this Twelfth Edition. For our InQuizitive course and other instructor resources, Spencer Richardson-Jones has been an energetic and visionary editor. Ashley Horna, Michael Jaoui, Tricia Vuong, and Anna Olcott also kept the production of the Eleventh Edition and its accompanying resources coherent and in focus. Lynne Cannon copyedited the manuscript, and our superb project editor Christine D'Antonio devoted countless hours to keeping on top of myriad details. We thank Elyse Rieder for finding new photos and our photo editor Stephanie Romeo for managing the image program. Finally, we thank Roby Harrington, the head of Norton's college department.

Benjamin Ginsberg
Caroline J. Tolbert
Andrea L. Campbell

October 2018

We the People

An Introduction to American Politics

Introduction: The Citizen and Government

WHAT GOVERNMENT DOES AND WHY IT MATTERS Meet two of the nation's youngest elected officials. Saira Blair became the youngest member of West Virginia's House of Delegates when she won election as an 18-year-old college freshman. The day after her victory party in November 2014, she was back in class at West Virginia University. In May 2017, Prairie View A&M senior Kendric D. Jones similarly achieved electoral victory, becoming the youngest city council member in the state of Texas. What got Blair and Jones involved in politics? Both had sources of political inspiration. Blair followed in the footsteps of her father, a West Virginia state senator, who she had accompanied to political events since childhood. Jones was inspired by the long history of activism at Prairie View, which was founded in 1876 during Reconstruction by some of the first African American members of the Texas state legislature. A further spur to action was President Obama's call in his 2017 farewell address to "grab a clipboard, get some signatures, and run for office yourself." Both also had strong commitments to issues. Blair believes

While Americans share a belief in the values of liberty, equality, and democracy, debates rage about how to live up to those values. To advocate for their beliefs, Republican Saira Blair (left) and Democrat Kendric Jones (right)—both college students—ran for office and won. What is the citizen's role in America's democratic system?

in limited government, lower taxes, and Second Amendment gun rights. Jones has a long history of working in the community, serving in student government, and founding a mentoring program for middle-school boys.

Both Blair and Jones also believe deeply in political participation, especially that of young people. As Jones said, "The students of Prairie View A&M University's voices have not been heard. Since I have been here, the city has been stagnant and has not made any progression—outside of the university. I feel as though a young, innovative mind can push this city forward." After participating in a mock government program in high school, Blair saw that young people were just as capable as lawmakers decades older: "When I saw how capable the students were of creating...legislation and really getting work done, it really made me realize that we really didn't need to wait."[1]

Blair and Jones's experiences show that citizens are at the center of democratic government. They ran for office because they care about public issues and want to have a hand in shaping policy outcomes. What are you passionate about? How does government affect your everyday life and that of your family, friends, and community? And how are differences in political views resolved in politics? Americans hold certain values dear, including liberty, equality, and democracy. In fact, if you asked Blair and Jones, they would almost certainly agree that these are critical values to uphold. However, Blair and Jones might emphasize one more than the other. And they might have major disagreements about what those values mean and what the government should do to shape and uphold them. What are your values? Do you see them reflected in government today? What do you want government to do?

CHAPTER GOALS

★ Define government and forms of government (pp. 5–7)

★ Describe the role of the citizen in politics (pp. 8–9)

★ Show how the social composition of the American population has changed over time (pp. 10–16)

★ Analyze whether the U.S. system of government upholds American political values (pp. 16–20)

★ Explore Americans' attitudes toward government (pp. 20–23)

Government

Government refers to the formal institutions and procedures through which a territory and its people are ruled. To govern is to rule. A government may be as simple as a town meeting in which community members make policy and determine budgets together or as complex as the vast establishments found in many large countries today, with their extensive procedures, laws, and bureaucracies. In the history of civilization, governments have not been difficult to establish. There have been thousands of them. The hard part is establishing a government that lasts. Even more difficult is developing a stable government that promotes liberty, equality, and democracy.

DIFFERENT FORMS OF GOVERNMENT ARE DEFINED BY POWER AND FREEDOM

Governments vary in their structure, in their size, and in the way they operate. Two questions are of special importance in determining how governments differ: Who governs? And how much government control is permitted?

In some nations, government power is held by a single individual, such as a king or dictator, or by a small group of powerful individuals, such as military leaders or wealthy landowners. Such a system of government normally pays little attention to popular preferences; it tends to hold power by violence or the threat of violence and is referred to as an **authoritarian** system, meaning that the government recognizes no formal limit but may nevertheless be restrained by the power of other social institutions. A system of government in which the degree of control is even greater is a **totalitarian** system, where the government recognizes no formal limits on its power and seeks to absorb or eliminate other social institutions that might challenge it. Nazi Germany under Adolf Hitler and the Soviet Union under Joseph Stalin are classic examples of totalitarian rule.

In contrast, a **democracy** is a political system that permits citizens to play a significant part in the governmental process, where they are vested with the power to rule themselves, usually through the election of key public officials. Under such a system, **constitutional government** is the norm, in that formal and effective limits are placed on the powers of the government. At times, an authoritarian government might bend to popular wishes, and democratic governments do not automatically follow the wishes of the majority. The point, however, is that these contrasting systems of government are based on very different assumptions and practices.

Americans have the good fortune to live in a nation in which limits are placed on what governments can do and how they can do it. By one measure, just 40 percent of the global population (those living in 86 countries) enjoy sufficient levels of political and personal freedom to be classified as living in a constitutional democracy.[2] And constitutional democracies were unheard of before the modern era. Prior to the eighteenth and nineteenth centuries, governments seldom sought (and rarely received) the support of their ordinary subjects.[3]

Beginning in the seventeenth century, in a handful of Western nations, two important changes began to take place in the character and conduct of government. First, governments began to acknowledge formal limits on their power. Second, a small number of governments began to provide the ordinary citizen with a formal voice in public affairs—through the vote. Obviously, the desirability of limits on government and the expansion of popular influence were at the heart of the American Revolution in 1776. "No taxation without representation" was hotly debated from the beginning of the Revolution through the adoption of the modern Constitution in 1789. But even before the Revolution, a tradition of limiting government and expanding citizen participation in the political process had developed throughout western Europe. Thus, to understand how the relationship between rulers and the ruled was transformed, we must broaden our focus to take into account events in Europe as well as in America. We will divide the transformation into its two separate parts. The first is the effort to put limits on government. The second is the effort to expand the influence of the people through access to government and politics.

LIMITS ON GOVERNMENTS ENCOURAGED FREEDOM

The key force behind the imposition of limits on government power was a new social class, the bourgeoisie. *Bourgeoisie* is a French word for "freeman of the city," or *bourg*. Being part of the bourgeoisie later became associated with being "middle class" and with involvement in commerce or industry. In order to gain a share of control of government, joining or even displacing the kings, aristocrats, and gentry who had dominated government for centuries, the bourgeoisie sought to change existing institutions—especially parliaments—into instruments of real political participation. Parliaments had existed for centuries but were generally controlled by the aristocrats. The bourgeoisie embraced parliaments as means by which they could exert the weight of their superior numbers and growing economic advantage against their aristocratic rivals. At the same time, the bourgeoisie sought to restrain the capacity of governments to threaten these economic and political interests by placing formal or constitutional limits on governmental power.

Although motivated primarily by the need to protect and defend their own interests, the bourgeoisie advanced many of the principles that became the central underpinnings of individual liberty for all citizens—freedom of speech, freedom of assembly, freedom of conscience, and freedom from arbitrary search and seizure. It is important to note here that the bourgeoisie generally did not favor democracy as we know it. They were advocates of electoral and representative institutions, but they favored property requirements and other restrictions so as to limit political participation to the middle and upper classes. Yet once these institutions of politics and the protection of the right to engage in politics were established, it was difficult to limit them to the bourgeoisie.

EXPANSION OF PARTICIPATION IN AMERICA CHANGED THE POLITICAL BALANCE

In America, the expansion of participation to ever-larger segments of society, seen mostly in the expansion of voting rights, occurred because competing segments of the bourgeoisie sought to gain political advantage by reaching out and mobilizing the support of working- and lower-class groups that craved the opportunity to take part in politics. To be sure, excluded groups often agitated for greater participation. But seldom was such agitation, by itself, enough to secure the right to participate. Usually, expansion of voting rights resulted from a combination of pressure from below and help from above.

This pattern of suffrage expansion by groups hoping to derive some political advantage has been typical in American history. After the Civil War, one of the chief reasons that the Republican Party moved to enfranchise newly freed slaves was to use the support of the former slaves to maintain Republican control over the defeated southern states. Similarly, in the early twentieth century, upper-middle-class Progressives advocated women's suffrage because they believed that women were likely to support the reforms espoused by the Progressive movement.

THE GOAL OF POLITICS IS HAVING A SAY IN WHAT HAPPENS

Expansion of participation means that more and more people have a legal right to take part in politics. *Politics* is an important term. In its broadest sense, it refers to conflicts over the character, membership, and policies of any organization to which people belong. As Harold Lasswell, a famous political scientist, once put it, politics is the struggle over "who gets what, when, how."[4] Although politics is a phenomenon that can be found in any organization, our concern in this book is narrower. Here, **politics** will be used to refer only to conflicts and struggles over the leadership, structure, and policies of governments. The goal of politics, as we define it, is to have a share or a say in the composition of the government's leadership, how the government is organized, or what its policies are going to be. Having a share is called **power** or influence.

Participation in politics can take many forms, including blogging and posting opinion pieces online, voting, sending emails to government officials, lobbying legislators on behalf of particular programs, and participating in protest marches and even violent demonstrations. A system of government in which the populace selects representatives, who play a significant role in governmental decision making, is usually called a **representative democracy**, or republic. A system that permits citizens to vote directly on laws and policies is often called a **direct democracy**. At the national level, America is a representative democracy in which citizens select government officials but do not vote on legislation. Some states and cities, however, have provisions for direct legislation through ballot initiative and popular referendum. In 2017, for example, voters in Maine approved by statewide vote to expand Medicaid under the Affordable Care Act after the governor had vetoed expansion multiple times.[5]

Citizenship Is Based on Political Knowledge and Participation

Describe the role of the citizen in politics

Citizen participation is the hallmark of the democratic form of government. "Government by the people" depends on lively citizen involvement in public discussion, debate, and activity designed to improve the welfare of one's community. The very legitimacy of democratic government depends on political participation, which takes a variety of forms, from the conventional—voting, contacting elected officials, working on campaigns, making political donations, attending political meetings—to the unconventional—protesting, boycotting, and signing petitions.

One key ingredient for political participation is **political knowledge** and information. Democracy functions best when citizens are informed and have the knowledge needed to participate in political debate. Indeed, our definition of **citizenship** derives from the ideal put forth by the ancient Greeks: *enlightened* political engagement.[6]

Citizens need political knowledge, which includes knowing the rules and strategies that govern political institutions and the principles on which they are based, to figure out how best to act in their own interests. For example, during the debate in 2017 about whether to repeal the Obama health care reform, one-third of Americans

Protests are a form of direct action citizens can take to influence policy outcomes. The Black Lives Matter movement used peaceful protests and marches to educate fellow citizens and lawmakers on the impact of police brutality on the African American community.

did not know that "Obamacare" and the "Affordable Care Act" are the same thing.[7] That meant that some Americans who had enrolled in "Obamacare" did not realize their access to health insurance would be affected if the ACA were repealed. Citizens need knowledge in order to assess their interests and to know when to act on them.

Effective participation requires knowledge. (It should come as no surprise, then, that people who have less knowledge of politics vote at lower rates than those with more knowledge.) Knowledge is the first prerequisite for achieving an increased sense of political efficacy.

As more and more of our social, workplace, and educational activities have migrated online, so too have opportunities for political knowledge and participation, creating a new concept of "digital citizenship." *Digital citizenship* is the ability to participate in society online, and it is increasingly important in politics. A 2015 survey found that over the previous year, 65 percent of Americans had used the internet—including visiting local, state, or federal government websites—to find data or information about government.[8] Digital citizens are more likely to be interested in politics and to discuss politics with friends, family, and coworkers than individuals who do not use online political information. They are also more likely to vote and participate in other ways in elections. Individuals without internet access or the skills to participate in politics and the economy online are being left further behind. Exclusion from participation online is referred to as the "digital divide." Lower-income and less educated Americans, racial and ethnic minorities, those living in rural areas, and the elderly are all less likely to have internet access.

POLITICAL EFFICACY MEANS PEOPLE CAN MAKE A DIFFERENCE

Another important trend in American views about government has been a declining sense of **political efficacy**, the belief that ordinary citizens can affect what government does. In 2015, 74 percent of Americans said that elected officials do not care what people like them think; in 1960, only 25 percent felt so shut out of government.[9] Accompanying this sense that ordinary people cannot be heard is a growing belief that government is not run for the benefit of all the people. In 2015, 76 percent of the public disagreed with the idea that the "government is really run for the benefit of all the people."[10] These views are widely shared across the age spectrum.

This widely felt loss of political efficacy is bad news for American democracy. Why bother to participate if you believe it makes no difference? Yet the belief that you can be effective is the first step needed to influence government. Research shows that the relationship between efficacy and participation is two-way: a feeling that one can make a difference leads to participation, but in addition, joining in can increase one's feeling of efficacy. Not every effort of ordinary citizens to influence government will succeed, but without any such efforts, government decisions will be made by a smaller and smaller circle of powerful people. Such loss of broad popular influence over government actions undermines the key feature of American democracy: government by the people. Most people do not want to be politically active every day of their lives, but it is essential to American political ideals that all citizens be informed and able to act.

The Identity of Americans Has Changed over Time

Show how the social composition of the American population has changed over time

While American democracy aims to give the people a voice in government, the meaning of "we the people" has changed over time. Who are Americans? Over the course of American history, politicians, religious leaders, prominent scholars, and ordinary Americans have puzzled over and fought about the answer to this fundamental question. It is not surprising that such a simple question could provoke so much conflict: the American population has increased over eighty-fold, from 3.9 million in 1790, the year of the first official census, to 327 million in 2018.[11] As the American population has grown, it has become more diverse in nearly every dimension imaginable.[12]

At the time of the Founding, when the United States consisted of 13 states arrayed along the Eastern seaboard, 81 percent of Americans counted by the census traced their roots to Europe, mostly England and northern Europe; nearly one in five were of African origin, the vast majority of whom were slaves.[13] There was also an unknown number of Native Americans, not counted by the census because the government did not consider them Americans.[14]

Fast-forward to 1900. The country, now stretched out across the continent, had a sharply altered racial and ethnic composition. Waves of immigrants, mainly from Europe, had boosted the population to 76 million. The black population stood at 12 percent. Residents who traced their origins to Latin America or Asia each accounted for less than 1 percent of the entire population.[15] Although principally of European origin, the American population had become much more ethnically diverse as immigrants, first from Germany, then from Ireland, and finally from southern and eastern Europe, made their way to the United States. The foreign-born population of the United States reached its height at 14.7 percent in 1910.[16]

IMMIGRATION AND INCREASING ETHNIC DIVERSITY HAVE LONG CAUSED INTENSE DEBATE

As the population grew more diverse, anxiety about Americans' ethnic identity mounted, and much as today, politicians and scholars argued about whether the country could absorb such large numbers of immigrants. The debate encompassed such issues as whether immigrants' political and social values were compatible with American democracy, whether they would learn English, and what diseases they might bring into the United States.

Immigrants' religious affiliations also aroused concern. The first immigrants to the United States were overwhelmingly Protestant, many of them fleeing religious persecution. The arrival of Germans and Irish in the mid-1800s meant increasing numbers of Catholics, and the large-scale immigration of the early twentieth century threatened to reduce the percentage of Protestants significantly: many eastern

In the 1900s many immigrants entered the United States through New York's Ellis Island, where they were checked for disease before being admitted.

European immigrants pouring into the country were Jewish, while the southern Europeans were mostly Catholic. A more religiously diverse country challenged the implicit Protestantism embedded in many aspects of American public life.

After World War I, Congress responded to the fears swirling around immigration with new laws that sharply limited the number of immigrants who could enter the country each year. Congress also established a new National Origins Quota System based on the nation's population in 1890 before the wave of immigrants from eastern and southern Europe arrived.[17] The new system set up a hierarchy of admissions: northern European countries received generous quotas for new immigrants, whereas eastern and southern European countries were granted very small quotas. These restrictions ratcheted down the numbers of immigrants so that by 1970 the foreign-born population in the United States reached an all-time low of 5 percent.

Official efforts to use racial and ethnic criteria to restrict the American population were not new. The very first census, as we have seen, did not count Native Americans; in fact, Native Americans were not granted the right to vote until 1924. Most people of African descent were not officially citizens until 1868, when the Fourteenth Amendment to the Constitution conferred citizenship on the freed slaves.

In 1790 the federal government had sought to limit the nonwhite population with a law stipulating that only free whites could become naturalized citizens. Not until 1870 did Congress lift the ban on the naturalization of nonwhites. Restrictions applied to Asians as well. The Chinese Exclusion Act of 1882 outlawed the entry of Chinese laborers to the United States, and additional barriers enacted after World War I meant that virtually no Asians entered the country as immigrants until 1943, when China became our ally in World War II and these provisions were lifted. People of Hispanic origin do not fit simply into the American system of racial classification. In 1930, for example, the census counted people of Mexican origin as nonwhite, but it reversed this decision a decade later. Not until 1970 did the census officially begin counting persons of Hispanic origin, noting that they could be any race.[18] As this history suggests, American citizenship has always been tied to "whiteness" even as the meaning of "white" shifted over time.

WHO ARE AMERICANS TODAY?

Race and Ethnicity By 2000 immigration had profoundly transformed the nation's racial and ethnic profile once again. The primary cause was Congress's decision in 1965 to lift the tight immigration restrictions of the 1920s, a decision that resulted, among other things, in the growth of the Latino population (see Figure 1.1). Census figures for 2016 show that the total Hispanic proportion of the population, who can be of any race, is now 17.8 percent, while the black, or African American, population is 12.7 percent of the total population. Asians make up 5.4 percent of the population. Non-Hispanic white Americans account for 61 percent of the population—their lowest share ever. Moreover, about 3.2 percent of the population now identifies itself as of "two or more races."[19] Although it is only a small percentage of the population, the multiracial category points toward a future in which the lines separating the traditional labels of racial identification may be blurring.

In 2016, 13.5 percent of the population was born outside the United States, a figure comparable to the rates of foreign-born at the turn of the previous century. About half of the foreign-born population came from Latin America and the Caribbean, with just over one-third from Central America (including Mexico). Those born in Asia constituted the next largest group, making up 31 percent of foreign-born residents. By 2016 just 10.9 percent of those born outside the United States came from Europe.[20] These figures represent only legally authorized immigrants, while estimates put the number of undocumented immigrants at 11.4 million, the majority of whom are from Mexico and Central America.[21]

Religion The new patterns of immigration combined with a number of other factors to alter the religious affiliations of Americans. In 1900, 80 percent of the population was Protestant; by 2016 only 44 percent of Americans identified themselves as Protestants.[22] Catholics made up 20 percent of the population, and Jews accounted for 2 percent. A small Muslim population had also grown, to nearly 1 percent of the population. One of the most important changes in religious affiliation during the latter half of the twentieth century was the percentage of people who professed no organized religion. In 2016, 23 percent of the population was not affiliated with an organized church. These changes suggest an important shift in American religious identity: although the United States thinks of itself as a "Judeo-Christian" nation—and indeed was 95 percent Protestant, Catholic, or Jewish from 1900 to 1968—by 2016 the numbers had fallen to under 70 percent of the adult population.[23]

FIGURE 1.1

Immigration by Continent of Origin*

Where did most immigrants come from at the start of the twentieth century? How does that compare with immigration in the twenty-first century?

*Less than 1 percent not shown.

SOURCE: Department of Homeland Security 2016 Yearbook of Immigration Statistics Table 2, November 2017, www.dhs.gov/immigration-statistics/yearbook/2016 (accessed 2/16/18). Figure shows those who have obtained "lawful permanent resident status" by continent of origin.

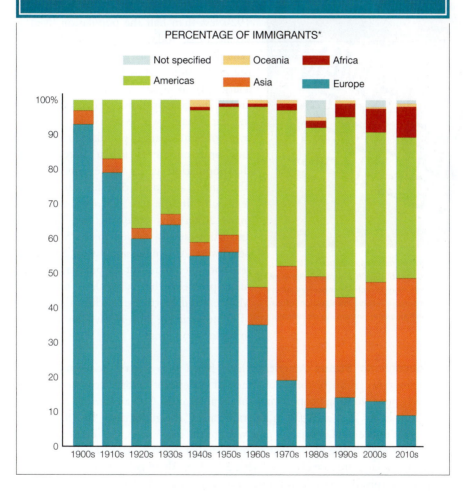

PERCENTAGE OF IMMIGRANTS*

Legend: Not specified, Oceania, Africa, Americas, Asia, Europe

Age As America grew and its population expanded and diversified, the country's age profile shifted with it. In 1900 only 4 percent of the population was over 65. As life expectancy increased, the number of older Americans grew with it: by 2016 nearly 15.2 percent of the population was over 65. The number of children under the age of 18 also changed; in 1900 this group comprised 40.5 percent of the American population; by 2016 it had fallen to 22.8 percent of the population.[24] An aging

Immigration remains a controversial issue in the United States. While many believe we should do more to protect our borders, others call for comprehensive immigration reform, including an easier pathway to citizenship.

population poses challenges to the United States. As the elderly population grows and the working-age population shrinks, questions arise about how we will fund programs for the elderly such as Social Security.

Geography Over the nation's history, Americans have changed in other ways as well, moving from mostly rural settings and small towns to large urban areas. Before 1920 less than half the population lived in urban areas; today 82 percent of Americans do.[25] Critics charge that the American political system, created when America was a largely rural society, underrepresents urban areas. The constitutional provision allocating each state two senators, for example, overrepresents sparsely populated rural states and underrepresents urban states, where the population is far more concentrated. The American population has also shifted regionally. In the past 50 years, especially, many Americans have left the Northeast and Midwest and moved to the South and Southwest. As congressional seats have been reapportioned to reflect the population shift, many problems that particularly plague the Midwest and Northeast, such as the decline of manufacturing jobs, receive less attention in national politics.

Socioeconomic Status Americans have fallen into diverse economic groups throughout American history. For much of American history most people were relatively poor working people, many of them farmers. A small wealthy elite, however, grew larger in the 1890s, in a period called "the gilded age." By 1928 nearly 25 percent of the total annual income went to the top 1 percent of earners; the top 10 percent took home 46 percent of total annual income. After the New Deal in the 1930s, a large middle class took shape, and the share going to those at the top dropped sharply. By 1976 the top 1 percent took home only 9 percent of the national annual income. Since then, however, economic inequality has once again widened as a tiny group of super-rich has emerged. By 2015 the top 1 percent earned 20.3 percent of annual income, and the top 10 percent took home almost 50 percent of the total national income.[26] At the same time, the incomes of the broad middle class have largely stagnated (see Figure 1.2).[27] And 12.7 percent of the population remains below the official poverty line. As the middle class has

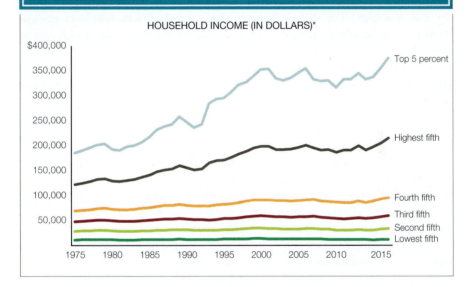

FIGURE 1.2

Income in the United States

This figure shows that while the income of most Americans has risen only slightly since 1975, the income of the richest Americans (the top 5 percent) has increased dramatically. What are some of the ways that this shift might matter for American politics? Does the growing economic gap between the richest groups and most other Americans conflict with the political value of equality?

*Dollar values are given in constant 2016 dollars, which are adjusted for inflation so that we can compare a person's income in 1975 with a person's income today.

SOURCE: U.S. Census Bureau, "Income and Poverty in the United States: 2016," Table A-2, www.census.gov/content/dam/Census/library/publications/2017/demo/P60-259.pdf (accessed 4/16/18).

HOUSEHOLD INCOME (IN DOLLARS)*

frayed around the edges, the numbers of poor and near poor have swelled to nearly one-third of the population.[28]

Population and Politics The shifting contours of the American people have regularly raised challenging questions about our politics and governing arrangements. Population growth has spurred politically charged debates about how the population should be apportioned among congressional districts and how they should be drawn. These conflicts have major implications for the representation of different regions of the country—for the balance of representation between urban and rural areas. The representation of various demographic and political groups may also be affected, as there is substantial evidence of growing geographic sorting of citizens by education, income, marriage rates, and party voting.[29] In addition, immigration and the cultural and religious changes it entails provoked heated debates 100 years ago and still do today. The different languages and customs that immigrants bring to the

United States trigger fears among some that the country is changing in ways that may undermine American values and alter fundamental identities. Yet a changing population has been one of the constants of American history.

America Is Built on the Ideas of Liberty, Equality, and Democracy

Analyze whether the U.S. system of government upholds American political values

A few fundamental values underlie the American system. These values are reflected in such Founding documents as the Declaration of Independence, the Constitution, and the Bill of Rights. The three values on which the American system of government is based are liberty, equality, and democracy. Most Americans find it easy to affirm all three values in principle. In practice, however, matters are not always so clear. Americans, moreover, are sometimes willing to subordinate liberty to security and have frequently tolerated significant departures from the principles of equality and democracy.

LIBERTY MEANS FREEDOM

No idea is more central to American values than liberty. The Declaration of Independence defined three inalienable rights: "Life, Liberty and the pursuit of Happiness." The preamble to the Constitution likewise identified the need to secure "the Blessings of Liberty" as one of the key reasons for which the Constitution was drawn up. For Americans, **liberty** means freedom from government control as well as economic freedom. Both are closely linked to the idea of **limited government**, meaning that powers are defined and limited by a constitution.

The Constitution's first 10 amendments, known collectively as the Bill of Rights, above all preserve individual personal liberties and rights. In fact, liberty has come to mean many of the freedoms guaranteed in the Bill of Rights: freedom of speech and writing, the right to assemble freely, and the right to practice religious beliefs without interference from the government. Over the course of American history, the scope of personal liberties has expanded as laws have become more tolerant and as individuals have successfully used the courts to challenge restrictions on their individual freedoms. Far fewer restrictions exist today on the press, political speech, and individual moral behavior than in the early years of the nation. Even so, conflicts persist over how personal liberties should be extended and when personal liberties violate community norms.

In addition to personal freedom, the American concept of liberty means economic freedom. Since the Founding, economic freedom has been linked to capitalism, free markets, and the protection of private property. Free competition, the unfettered movement of goods, and the right to enjoy the fruits of one's labor are all essential aspects of economic freedom and American capitalism.[30] In the first century of the Republic, support for capitalism often meant support for the doctrine of laissez-faire

Global Diversity

How does the racial and ethnic diversity of the United States compare to that of other countries around the world, and why are some countries more diverse than others?

As a "nation of immigrants," the United States is more diverse than many Western countries, but some former colonies are even more diverse than the United States. Many countries in sub-Saharan Africa were colonized by empires whose governments often drew borders that encompassed multiple ethnic groups in the region. State-building and nationalism are new to these regions, meaning that local identities often remain stronger than national ones.

In contrast, many western European and Asian countries have histories of past conflict and strong state-building efforts, resulting in less diversity either by eliminating rival groups or forcibly assimilating them. Japan's geographic isolation has created a racially homogeneous society, which was reinforced by the government's use of isolationism as a means to consolidate power.[a] Modern policies limiting immigration continue these historic trends. France has historically pursued both political and cultural assimilation, using its schools to socialize its citizens into a common identity. Recent immigration, however, has highlighted potential problems with this policy.[b]

How might the degree of diversity shape political values in specific countries? What types of values and policies would we expect to see in countries with a high degree of diversity versus those with less diversity?

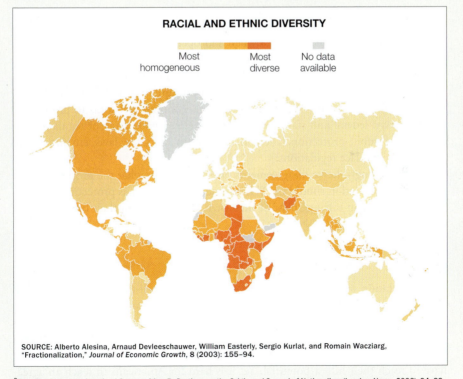

RACIAL AND ETHNIC DIVERSITY

SOURCE: Alberto Alesina, Arnaud Devleeschauwer, William Easterly, Sergio Kurlat, and Romain Wacziarg, "Fractionalization," *Journal of Economic Growth*, 8 (2003): 155–94.

[a]Benedict Anderson, *Imagined Communities: Reflections on the Origin and Spread of Nationalism* (London: Verso, 2006), 94–99.
[b]John R. Bowen, *Why the French Don't Like Headscarves: Islam, the State, and Public Space* (Princeton, NJ: Princeton University Press, 2007).

Economic freedom lies at the heart of many conflicts in American life. While supporters of the Tea Party movement protest against economic regulation and higher taxes and support smaller government, many Americans feel it is the government's responsibility to regulate economic activity to benefit the majority of Americans.

(literally, "let do" in French), an economic system in which the means of production and distribution are privately owned and operated for profit with minimal or no government interference. **Laissez-faire capitalism** allowed very little room for the national government to regulate trade or restrict the use of private property, even in the public interest. Americans still strongly support capitalism and economic liberty, but they now also endorse some restrictions on economic freedoms to protect the public. Today, federal and state governments deploy a wide array of regulations in the name of public protection. These include health and safety laws, environmental rules, and workplace regulations.

Not surprisingly, fierce disagreements often erupt over what the proper scope of government regulation should be. What some people regard as protecting the public, others see as an infringement of their own freedom to run their businesses and use their property as they see fit.

EQUALITY MEANS TREATING PEOPLE FAIRLY

The Declaration of Independence declares as its first "self-evident" truth that "all men are created equal." As central as it is to the American political creed, however, equality has been a less well-defined ideal than liberty because people interpret "equality" in different ways. Most Americans share the ideal of **equality of opportunity** wherein all people should have the freedom to use whatever talents and wealth they have to reach their fullest potential. Yet it is hard for Americans to reach an agreement on what constitutes equality of opportunity. Must a group's *past* inequalities be remedied in order to ensure equal opportunity in the *present*? Should inequalities in the legal, political, and economic spheres be given the same weight? In contrast to liberty, which requires limits on the role of government, equality implies an *obligation* of the government to the people.[31]

Americans do make clear distinctions between political equality and social or economic equality. **Political equality** refers to the right to participate in politics equally, based on the principle of "one person, one vote." Beginning from a very restricted definition of political community, which originally included only propertied white men, the United States has moved much closer to an ideal of political equality. Broad support for this ideal has helped expand the American political community and extend the right to participate to all. Although considerable conflict remains over whether the political system makes it harder for some people to participate and easier for others, and about whether the role of money in politics has drowned out the public voice, Americans agree that all citizens should have an equal opportunity to participate and that government should enforce that right.

In part because Americans believe that individuals are free to work as hard as they choose, they have always been less concerned about social or economic inequality. Many Americans regard economic differences as the consequence of individual choices, virtues, or failures. Because of this, Americans tend to be less supportive than most Europeans of government action to ensure economic equality. Since the recession of 2008, however, income inequality has risen on the political agenda. In 2015 two-thirds of Americans said the distribution of wealth and money is not fair and should be more evenly distributed; in 2017, 63 percent of Americans said upper-income people pay too little in taxes, and 67 percent said corporations pay too little.[32]

DEMOCRACY MEANS THAT WHAT THE PEOPLE WANT MATTERS

The essence of democracy is the participation of the people in choosing their rulers and the people's ability to influence what those rulers do. In a democracy, political power ultimately comes from the people. The principle of democracy in which political authority rests ultimately in the hands of the people is known as **popular sovereignty**. In the United States, popular sovereignty and political equality make politicians accountable to the people. Ideally, democracy envisions an engaged citizenry prepared to exercise its power over rulers. As we noted earlier, the United States is a representative democracy, meaning that the people do not rule directly but instead exercise power through elected representatives. Forms of participation in a democracy vary greatly, but voting is a key element of the representative democracy that the American Founders established.

American democracy rests on the principle of **majority rule** with **minority rights**, the democratic principle that a government follows the preferences of the majority of voters but protects the interests of the minority. Majority rule means that the wishes of the majority determine what government does. The House of Representatives—a large body elected directly by the people—was designed in particular to ensure majority rule. But the Founders feared that popular majorities could turn government into a "tyranny of the majority" in which individual liberties would be violated. Concern for individual rights has thus been a part of American democracy from the beginning. The rights enumerated in the Bill of Rights and enforced through the courts provide an important check on the power of the majority.

Government Affects Our Lives Every Day

Explore Americans' attitudes toward government

Since the United States was established as a nation, Americans have been reluctant to grant government too much power, and they have often been suspicious of politicians. But over the course of the nation's history, Americans have also turned to government for assistance in times of need and have strongly supported the government in periods of war. In 1933 the power of the government began to expand to meet the crises created by the stock market crash of 1929, the Great Depression, and the run on banks. Congress passed legislation that brought the government into the businesses of home mortgages, farm mortgages, credit, and relief of personal distress. More recently, when the economy fell

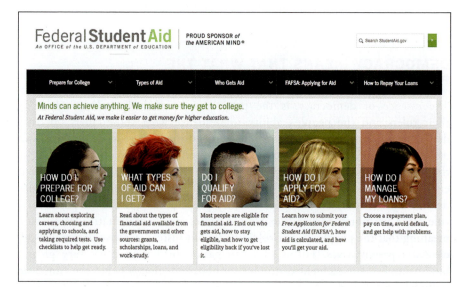

The federal government maintains a large number of websites that provide useful information to citizens on such topics as loans for education, civil service job applications, the inflation rate, and how the weather will affect farming. These sites are just one way in which the government serves its citizens.

into a recession in 2008 and 2009, the federal government took action to shore up the financial system, oversee the restructuring of the ailing auto companies, and inject hundreds of billions of dollars into the faltering economy. Today, the national government is an enormous institution with programs and policies reaching into every corner of American life. It oversees the nation's economy, it is the nation's largest employer, it provides citizens with a host of services, it controls the world's most formidable military establishment, and it regulates a wide range of social and commercial activities.

Much of what citizens have come to depend on and take for granted—as, somehow, part of the natural environment—is in fact created by government. Take the example of a typical college student's day, throughout which that student relies on a host of services and activities organized by national, state, and local government agencies. The extent of this dependence on government is illustrated by Table 1.1.

TRUST IN GOVERNMENT HAS DECLINED

Ironically, even as popular dependence on government has grown, the American public's view of government has turned more sour. Public trust in government has declined, and Americans are now more likely to feel that they can do little to influence the government's actions. Different groups vary somewhat in their levels of trust: African Americans and Latinos express more confidence in the federal government than do whites. But even among the most supportive groups, more than half do not trust the government.[33] These developments are important because politically engaged citizens and public confidence in government are vital for the health of a democracy. In the early 1960s three-quarters of Americans said they trusted government most of the time or always. By 2017 only 18 percent of Americans expressed such trust in government.[34] Trust hit a high point after the September 11, 2001, terrorist attacks, but fell to pre-attack levels within three years, and the trend continued its downward path. Distrust of government greatly influenced the presidential primary elections in 2015 and 2016, when a number of "outsider" candidates—most notably

While levels of participation in politics are relatively low for young Americans, the presidential primary campaigns of 2008 and 2016 saw the highest levels of youth turnout—to volunteer and to vote—in decades. What factors might have energized young people to become involved in these campaigns?

TABLE 1.1

The Presence of Government in the Daily Life of a Student at "State University"

TIME	SCHEDULE
7:00 A.M.	Wake up. Standard time set by the national government.
7:10 A.M.	Shower. Water courtesy of local government, either a public entity or a regulated private company. Brush your teeth with toothpaste whose cavity-fighting claims have been verified by a federal agency.
7:30 A.M.	Have a bowl of cereal with milk for breakfast. "Nutrition Facts" on food labels are a federal requirement, pasteurization of milk required by state law, recycling the empty cereal box and milk carton enabled by state or local laws.
8:30 A.M.	Drive or take public transportation to campus. Air bags and seat belts required by federal and state laws. Roads and bridges paid for by state and local governments, speed and traffic laws set by state and local governments, public transportation subsidized by all levels of government.
8:45 A.M.	Arrive on campus of large public university. Buildings are 70 percent financed by state taxpayers.
9:00 A.M.	First class: Chemistry 101. Tuition partially paid by a federal loan (more than half the cost of university instruction is paid for by taxpayers), chemistry lab paid for with grants from the National Science Foundation (a federal agency).
Noon	Eat lunch. College cafeteria financed by state dormitory authority on land grant from federal Department of Agriculture.
2:00 P.M.	Second class: American Government 101 (your favorite class!). You may be taking this class because it is required by the state legislature or because it fulfills a university requirement.
4:00 P.M.	Third class: Computer Science 101. Free computers, software, and internet access courtesy of state subsidies plus grants and discounts from IBM and Microsoft, the costs of which are deducted from their corporate income taxes; internet built in part by federal government.
6:00 P.M.	Eat hamburger for dinner. Meat inspected by federal agencies.
7:00 P.M.	Work at part-time job at the campus library. Minimum wage set by federal, state, or local government; books and journals in library paid for by state taxpayers.
8:15 P.M.	Check the status of your application for a federal student loan (FAFSA) on the Department of Education's website at studentaid.ed.gov.
10:00 P.M.	Go home. Street lighting paid for by county and city governments, police patrols by city government.
10:15 P.M.	Watch TV. Networks regulated by federal government, cable public-access channels required by city law. Weather forecast provided to broadcasters by a federal agency.

Donald Trump and Bernie Sanders, who were critical of government and eager to depart from business as usual in Washington—attracted wide support.

Does it matter if Americans trust their government? For the most part, the answer is yes. Most Americans rely on government for a wide range of services and laws that they simply take for granted. But long-term distrust in government can result in public refusal to pay the taxes necessary to support such widely approved public activities. Low levels of confidence may also make it difficult for government to attract talented and effective workers to public service.[35] The weakening of government as a result of prolonged levels of distrust may ultimately harm the capacity of the United States to defend its national interest in the world economy and may jeopardize its national security. Likewise, a weak government can do little to assist citizens who need help in weathering periods of sharp economic or technological change.

American Political Culture
WHAT DO WE WANT?

Americans express mixed views about government. Almost everyone complains about government, and general trust in government has declined significantly. Despite mounting distrust, when asked about particular government activities or programs, a majority of Americans generally support the activities that government undertakes. These conflicting views reflect the tensions in American political culture: there is no perfect balance between liberty, equality, and democracy. In recent years, finding the right mix of government actions to achieve these different goals has become especially troublesome. Some charge that government initiatives designed to promote equality infringe on individual liberty, while others point to the need for government to take action in the face of growing inequality. Sharp political debate over competing goals alienates many citizens, who react by withdrawing from politics. Yet, in contrast to totalitarian and authoritarian forms of government, democracy rests on the principle of popular sovereignty. No true democracy can function properly without knowledgeable and engaged citizens. The stories of Saira Blair and Kendric Jones at the beginning of this chapter show that people often turn frustration with government into political action. But running for office is only one way to participate in politics. The "**Who Participates?**" feature on page 25 shows who voted in the 2016 presidential election.

The remarkable diversity of the American people represents a great strength for American democracy as well as a formidable challenge. The shifting religious, racial, ethnic, and immigration statuses of Americans throughout history have always provoked fears about whether American values could withstand such dramatic shifts. The changing face of America also sparks hopes for an America that embodies its fundamental values more fully.

Demographic changes will continue to raise tough new questions. For example, as the American population grows older, programs for the elderly will take up an increasing share of the federal budget. Yet, to be successful, a nation must invest in its young people. And, as any college student knows, the cost of college has risen in recent years. Many students drop out as they discover that the cost of college is too high. Or they graduate and find themselves saddled with loans that will take decades to pay back. Yet, in a world of ever-sharper economic competition, higher education has become increasingly important for individuals seeking economic security. Moreover, an educated population is critical to the future prosperity of the country as a whole. Are there ways to support the elderly and the young at the same time? Is it fair to cut back assistance to the elderly, who have worked a lifetime for their benefits? If we decrease assistance to the elderly, will they stay in the labor market and make the job hunt for young people even more difficult? As these trade-offs suggest, there are no easy answers to these demographic changes.

Who Voted in 2016?

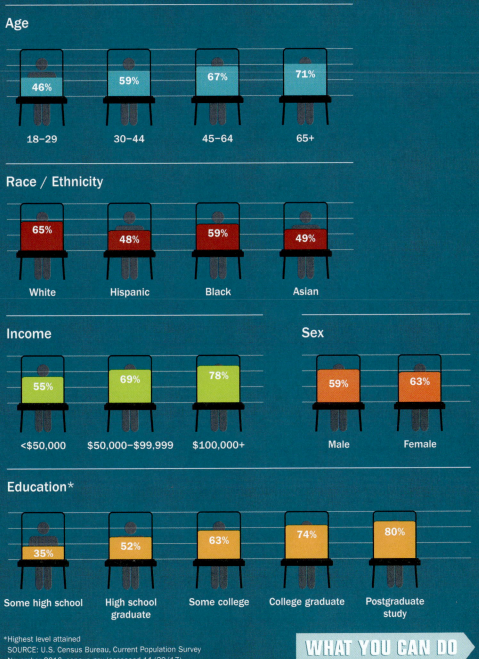

Age

46% — 18–29
59% — 30–44
67% — 45–64
71% — 65+

Race / Ethnicity

65% — White
48% — Hispanic
59% — Black
49% — Asian

Income

55% — <$50,000
69% — $50,000–$99,999
78% — $100,000+

Sex

59% — Male
63% — Female

Education*

35% — Some high school
52% — High school graduate
63% — Some college
74% — College graduate
80% — Postgraduate study

*Highest level attained
SOURCE: U.S. Census Bureau, Current Population Survey
November 2016, census.gov (accessed 11/20/17).

WHAT YOU CAN DO

WHAT YOU CAN DO ★

Vote

 Register to vote. See page 242.

 Find out what's on the ballot in upcoming elections in your state and district by entering your address at **www.vote411.org** (a website from the League of Women Voters).

✔ Cast your vote on Election Day. Consider encouraging others to vote too. Research shows that people are more likely to turn out to vote if a friend or family member asks them to.

★ STUDY GUIDE ★

Practice Quiz

1. What is the difference between a totalitarian government and an authoritarian government? *(p. 5)*
   a) Authoritarian governments require popular participation while totalitarian governments do not.
   b) Totalitarian governments are generally based on religion, while authoritarian governments are not.
   c) Authoritarian governments are often restrained by the power of social institutions, while totalitarian governments are not.
   d) Totalitarian governments acknowledge strict limits on their power, while authoritarian governments do not.
   e) There is no difference between these two kinds of government.

2. In a constitutional government *(p. 5)*
   a) the government recognizes no formal limits on its power.
   b) presidential elections are held every four years.
   c) governmental power is held by a single individual.
   d) formal and effective limits are placed on the powers of government.
   e) the government follows the wishes of the majority.

3. A state that permits its citizens to vote directly on laws and policies is practicing a form of *(p. 7)*
   a) representative democracy
   b) direct democracy
   c) pluralism
   d) laissez-faire capitalism
   e) republicanism

4. *Political efficacy* is the belief that *(p. 9)*
   a) government operates efficiently.
   b) government has grown too large.
   c) government cannot be trusted.
   d) ordinary citizens can influence what government does.
   e) government is wasteful and corrupt.

5. What is digital citizenship? *(p. 9)*
   a) a new government initiative to expand online voter registration
   b) the ability to vote online
   c) an online certification program that allows immigrants to become American citizens
   d) the ability to participate in society online
   e) a new government initiative to provide daily legislative updates online

6. The percentage of foreign-born individuals living in the United States *(pp. 11–12)*
   a) has increased significantly since reaching its low point in 1970.
   b) has decreased significantly since reaching its high point in 1970.
   c) has remained the same since 1970.
   d) has never been less than the percentage of native-born individuals living in the United States.
   e) has not been studied since 1970.

7. In 2016, Latinos were approximately what percent of the American public? *(p. 13)*
   a) 67 percent
   b) 52 percent
   c) 31 percent
   d) 18 percent
   e) 6 percent

8. Which of the following statements best describes the changes in America's age profile since 1900? *(p. 13)*
   a) The percentage of adults over the age of 65 has declined dramatically.
   b) The percentage of adults over the age of 65 has increased dramatically.
   c) The percentage of adults over the age of 65 has remained constant.
   d) The percentage of children under the age of 18 has increased dramatically.
   e) The percentage of children under the age of 18 has remained constant.

9. What percent of Americans live in urban areas today? *(p. 14)*
   a) less than 10 percent
   b) about 20 percent
   c) about 40 percent
   d) about 60 percent
   e) about 80 percent

10. Which of the following statements best describes the history of income inequality in the United States? *(p. 14)*
    a) The top 1 percent has never earned more than 10 percent of the nation's annual income.
    b) The top 1 percent has never earned less than 10 percent of the nation's annual income.
    c) Income inequality has remained fairly constant since the late 1970s.
    d) Income inequality has increased considerably since the late 1970s.
    e) Income inequality has decreased considerably since the late 1970s.

11. The phrase "Life, Liberty and the pursuit of Happiness" appears in *(p. 16)*
    a) the preamble to the Constitution.
    b) the Bill of Rights.
    c) the Declaration of Independence.
    d) the Magna Carta.
    e) the Gettysburg Address.

12. An economic system in which the means of production and distribution are privately owned and operated for profit with minimal or no government interference is referred to as *(p. 18)*
    a) socialism.
    b) communism.
    c) laissez-faire capitalism.
    d) corporatism.
    e) feudalism.

13. The principle of political equality can be best summed up as *(p. 19)*
    a) "equality of results."
    b) "equality of opportunity."
    c) "one person, one vote."
    d) "equality between the sexes."
    e) "leave everyone alone."

14. Americans' trust in their government *(p. 21)*
    a) has risen steadily since the 1960s.
    b) has remained relatively constant since the 1960s.
    c) increased between 1960 and 2008 but has declined since.
    d) increased after the September 11, 2001, terrorist attacks but has declined since.
    e) declined after the September 11, 2001, terrorist attacks but has increased since.

Key Terms

authoritarian government *(p. 5)* a system of rule in which the government recognizes no formal limit but may nevertheless be restrained by the power of other social institutions

citizenship *(p. 8)* informed and active membership in a political community

constitutional government *(p. 5)* a system of rule in which formal and effective limits are placed on the powers of the government

democracy *(p. 5)* a system of rule that permits citizens to play a significant part in the governmental process, usually through the election of key public officials

direct democracy *(p. 7)* a system of rule that permits citizens to vote directly on laws and policies

equality of opportunity *(p. 18)* a widely shared American ideal that all people should have the freedom to use whatever talents and wealth they have to reach their fullest potential

government *(p. 5)* institutions and procedures through which a territory and its people are ruled

laissez-faire capitalism *(p. 18)* an economic system in which the means of production and distribution are privately owned and operated for profit with minimal or no government interference

liberty *(p. 16)* freedom from government control

limited government *(p. 16)* a principle of constitutional government; a government whose powers are defined and limited by a constitution

majority rule/minority rights *(p. 19)* the democratic principle that a government follows the preferences of the majority of voters but protects the interests of the minority

political efficacy *(p. 9)* the ability to influence government and politics

political equality *(p. 19)* the right to participate in politics equally, based on the principle of "one person, one vote"

political knowledge *(p. 8)* possessing information about the formal institutions of government, political actors, and political issues

politics *(p. 7)* conflict over the leadership, structure, and policies of governments

popular sovereignty *(p. 19)* a principle of democracy in which political authority rests ultimately in the hands of the people

power *(p. 7)* influence over a government's leadership, organization, or policies

representative democracy (republic) *(p. 7)* a system of government in which the populace selects representatives, who play a significant role in governmental decision making

totalitarian government *(p. 5)* a system of rule in which the government recognizes no formal limits on its power and seeks to absorb or eliminate other social institutions that might challenge it

For Further Reading

Dahl, Robert. *How Democratic Is the American Constitution?* New Haven, CT: Yale University Press, 2002.

Dalton, Russell. *The Good Citizen: How a Younger Generation Is Reshaping American Politics*. 2nd ed. Washington, DC: CQ Press, 2015.

Delli Carpini, Michael X., and Scott Keeter. *What Americans Know about Politics and Why It Matters*. New Haven, CT: Yale University Press, 1996.

Hochschild, Jennifer L. *Facing Up to the American Dream: Race, Class, and the Soul of the Nation*. Princeton, NJ: Princeton University Press, 1995.

Lasswell, Harold. *Politics: Who Gets What, When, How*. New York: Meridian Books, 1958.

McCarty, Nolan, Keith T. Poole, and Howard Rosenthal. *Polarized America: The Dance of Ideology and Unequal Riches*. Cambridge, MA: MIT Press, 2008.

Mettler, Suzanne. *The Submerged State: How Invisible Government Policies Undermine American Democracy*. Chicago: University of Chicago Press, 2011.

Nye, Joseph S., Jr., Philip D. Zelikow, and David C. King, eds. *Why People Don't Trust Government*. Cambridge, MA: Harvard University Press, 1997.

Page, Benjamin I., and Lawrence R. Jacobs. *Class War? What Americans Really Think about Economic Inequality*. Chicago: University of Chicago Press, 2009.

Tocqueville, Alexis de. *Democracy in America*. Translated by Phillips Bradley. New York: Knopf, Vintage Books, 1945. First published 1835.

The Founding and the Constitution

WHAT GOVERNMENT DOES AND WHY IT MATTERS One of the worries of the framers of the U.S. Constitution was the concentration of government powers and the possible infringement on individual liberties. One solution was to divide the executive, legislative, and judicial powers of government across different institutions with separate powers, each checking the other. Governmental power was further divided between the national and state governments. Sometimes this constitutional system and its effect on average Americans comes vividly to life.

Jim Obergefell was a real estate agent and IT consultant in Cincinnati, Ohio, in 1992 when he met and fell in love with John Arthur.[1] Although their relationship would last for decades, they were unable to marry. In 1996, Congress passed and President Clinton signed the Defense of Marriage Act (DOMA), a federal law defining marriage as between one man and one woman. States could still permit same-sex marriage, but the marriages would not be recognized for federal purposes such as filing taxes or earning Social Security survivor benefits. The law also permitted states to refuse to recognize same-sex marriages

From America's founding to today, debates over the role of the United States government in citizens' lives have persisted. After the historic decision to rule same-sex marriage a right guaranteed by the Constitution, Jim Obergefell holds a photo of his late husband on the steps of the Supreme Court to celebrate his bittersweet victory.

performed in other states. Then the state of Ohio enacted its own DOMA in 2004, prohibiting same-sex marriage and refusing to recognize those performed elsewhere.

Thus Obergefell and Arthur were unable to marry due to the actions of two branches of the federal government—the executive and legislative—and their state. The issue became more acute when Arthur was diagnosed with ALS, or Lou Gehrig's disease—a progressive, debilitating disease. Obergefell served as Arthur's primary caregiver, and the couple traveled to Maryland in 2013 and wed on the airport tarmac. Then they filed a lawsuit with the state of Ohio for Obergefell to be recognized as the surviving spouse on Arthur's imminent death certificate. Arthur passed away three months later.

The case made it to the Supreme Court. In 2015 the Court ruled in *Obergefell v. Hodges* that the fundamental right to marry is guaranteed to same-sex couples by the Due Process and Equal Protection Clauses of the Fourteenth Amendment to the U.S. Constitution.[2] Thus the Court secured a civil right that the executive and legislative branches and a number of states had denied.

The U.S. Constitution lays out the purpose of government: to promote justice, to maintain peace at home, to defend the nation from foreign foes, to provide for the welfare of the citizenry, and, above all, to secure the "blessings of liberty" for Americans. It also spells out a plan for achieving these objectives, including provisions for the exercise of legislative, executive, and judicial powers and a recipe for the division of powers among the federal government's branches and between the national and state governments. Jim Obergefell's quest to marry the love of his life intersected with all three branches and both levels of government.

His story also shows that although many Americans believe strongly in the long-standing values of liberty, equality, and democracy, how those values are defined and implemented by the political institutions that the Constitution created are a source of considerable controversy. The framers believed that a good constitution created a government with the capacity to act forcefully. But they also believed that government should be compelled to take a variety of interests and viewpoints into account when it formulates policies. Sometimes the deliberation and compromise encouraged by the constitutional arrangements of "separated institutions sharing powers" can result in policymaking that is slow or even gridlocked.[3] Public policy is always a product of political bargaining. But so was the Constitution itself. As this chapter will show, the Constitution reflects high principle as well as political self-interest and defines the relationship between American citizens and their government.

CHAPTER GOALS

- ★ Describe the events that led to the Declaration of Independence and the Articles of Confederation (pp. 33–38)
- ★ Analyze the reasons many Americans thought a new Constitution was needed, and assess the obstacles to a new Constitution (pp. 38–43)
- ★ Explain how the Constitution attempted to improve America's governance, and outline the major institutions established by the Constitution (pp. 43–51)
- ★ Present the controversies involved in the struggle for ratification (pp. 51–56)
- ★ Trace how the Constitution has changed over time through the amendment process (pp. 56–60)

The First Founding: Ideals, Interests, and Conflicts

Describe the events that led to the Declaration of Independence and the Articles of Confederation

The government created by the country's Founders was the product of British legal and political traditions, colonial experience, and new ideas about governance that gained currency in the century before America broke with Britain. While America's leaders were first and foremost practical politicians, they also read political philosophy and were influenced by the important thinkers of their day, including Hobbes, Locke, and Montesquieu.

The seventeenth-century British philosopher Thomas Hobbes (1588–1679) was no advocate of democratic government, but he wrote persuasively in *Leviathan* about the necessity of a government authority as an antidote to human existence in a government-less state of nature, where life was "solitary, poor, nasty, brutish, and short." He also believed that governments should have limits on the powers they exercised and that political systems are based on the idea of "contract theory"—that the people of a country voluntarily give up some freedom in exchange for an ordered society. The monarchs who rule that society derive their legitimacy from this contract, not from a God-given right to rule.

Another British political thinker, John Locke (1632–1704), advanced the principles of republican government by arguing not only that monarchical power was not absolute, but that such power was dangerous and should therefore be limited. In a break with Hobbes, Locke argued that the people retain rights despite the social contract they make with the monarch. Preserving safety in society is not enough; people's lives, liberty, and property also require protection. Further, Locke wrote in his *Second Treatise of Civil Government* that the people of a country have a right to overthrow a government they believe to be unjust or tyrannical. This key idea shaped the thinking of the Founders, including Thomas Jefferson, the primary author of the Declaration of Independence, who said that the document was "pure Locke." Locke advanced the important ideas of limited government and consent of the governed.

Baron de la Brède et de Montesquieu (1689–1755) was a French political thinker who advocated the idea that power needed to be balanced by power as a bulwark against tyranny. The way in which this could be achieved was through the separation of governing powers. This idea was already in practice in Britain, where legislative and executive powers were divided between Parliament and the monarch. In *The Spirit of the Laws*, Montesquieu argued for the separation and elevation of judicial power, which in Britain was still held by the monarch. Montesquieu did not argue for a pure separation of powers; rather, basic functions would be separated, but there would also be some overlap of functions. These ideas were central in shaping the three-branch system of government that America's Founders outlined in the Constitution of 1787.

NARROW INTERESTS AND POLITICAL CONFLICTS SHAPED THE FIRST FOUNDING

The American Revolution and the U.S. Constitution were outgrowths of a struggle among competing economic and political forces within the colonies. Five sectors of society had interests that were important in colonial politics: (1) New England merchants; (2) southern planters; (3) "royalists"—holders of royal lands, offices, and patents (licenses to engage in a profession or business activity); (4) shopkeepers, artisans, and laborers; and (5) small farmers. Throughout the eighteenth century, these groups were in conflict over issues of taxation, trade, and commerce. For the most part, however, the southern planters, the New England merchants, and the royal office and patent holders—groups that together made up the colonial elite—were able to maintain a political alliance that held in check the more radical forces representing shopkeepers, laborers, and small farmers. After 1760, however, by seriously threatening the interests of New England merchants and southern planters, British tax and trade policies split the colonial elite, permitting radical forces to expand their political influence, and set in motion a chain of events that culminated in the American Revolution.[4]

BRITISH TAXES HURT COLONIAL ECONOMIC INTERESTS

During the first half of the eighteenth century, Britain ruled its American colonies with a light hand. Evidence of British rule was hardly to be found outside the largest towns, and the enterprising colonists had found ways of evading most of the taxes levied by the distant British government. Beginning in the 1760s, however, debts and other financial problems faced by the British government forced it to search for new revenue sources. This search rather quickly led to the Crown's North American colonies, which, on the whole, paid remarkably little in taxes to their parent country. Much of Britain's debt arose from the expenses it had incurred in defense of the colonies during the recent French and Indian War (1756–63), as well as from the continuing protection that British forces were giving the colonists from Indian attacks and that the British navy was providing for colonial shipping. Thus, during the 1760s, Great Britain sought to impose new, though relatively modest, taxes on the colonists.

Like most governments of the period, the British regime had limited ways in which to collect revenues. In the mid-eighteenth century, governments relied mainly on tariffs, duties, and other taxes on commerce; and it was to such taxes, including the Stamp Act, that the British turned during the 1760s.

The Stamp Act and other taxes on commerce, such as the Sugar Act of 1764, which taxed sugar, molasses, and other commodities, most heavily affected the two groups in colonial society whose commercial interests and activities were most extensive—the New England merchants and the southern planters. United under the famous slogan "No taxation without representation," the merchants and planters sought to organize opposition to these new taxes. In the course of the struggle against British tax measures, the planters and merchants broke with their royalist allies and turned to their former adversaries—the shopkeepers, laborers, artisans, and small farmers—for help. With the assistance of these groups, the merchants and planters organized demonstrations and a boycott of British goods that ultimately forced the Crown to rescind most of its hated new taxes.

From the perspective of the merchants and planters, this was a victorious conclusion to their struggle with the parent country. They were anxious to end the unrest they had helped to arouse, and they supported the British government's efforts to restore order. Indeed, most respectable Bostonians supported the actions of the British soldiers involved in the Boston Massacre (1770), when those soldiers killed five colonists while attempting to repel an angry mob moving against a government building. In their subsequent trial, the soldiers were defended by John Adams, a pillar of Boston society and a future president of the United States. Adams asserted that the soldiers' actions were entirely justified, provoked as they were by "a motley rabble of saucy boys, negroes and mulattoes, Irish teagues and outlandish Jack tars." All but two of the soldiers were acquitted.[5]

Yet political strife persisted. The more radical forces representing shopkeepers, artisans, laborers, and small farmers, who had been mobilized and energized by the struggle over taxes, continued to agitate for political and social change. These radicals, whose leaders included Samuel Adams, a cousin of John Adams, asserted that British power supported an unjust political and social structure within the colonies and began to advocate an end to British rule.[6]

POLITICAL STRIFE RADICALIZED THE COLONISTS

The political strife within the colonies was the background for the events of 1773–74. In 1773 the British government granted the politically powerful but ailing East India Company a monopoly on the export of tea from Britain, eliminating a lucrative form of trade for colonial merchants. To add insult to injury, the East India Company sought to sell the tea directly in the colonies instead of working through the colonial merchants. Tea was an extremely important commodity in the 1770s, and these British actions posed a serious threat to the New England merchants. Together with their southern allies, the merchants once again called upon the radicals for support. The most dramatic result was the Boston Tea Party of 1773, when anti-British radicals, led by Samuel Adams (some of them "disguised" as Mohawk Indians), boarded three vessels anchored in Boston Harbor and threw the entire cargo of 342 chests of tea into the harbor.

This event was of decisive importance in American history. The merchants had hoped to force the British government to rescind the Tea Act, but they did not support any demands beyond this one. They certainly did not seek independence from Britain. Samuel Adams and the other radicals, however, hoped to provoke the British government to take actions that would alienate its colonial supporters and pave the way for a rebellion. This was precisely the purpose of the Boston Tea Party, and it succeeded. By dumping the East India Company's tea into Boston Harbor, Adams and his followers goaded the British into enacting a number of harsh reprisals that closed the port of Boston to commerce, changed the provincial

The British helped radicalize colonists through policy decisions in the years before the Revolution. For example, Britain gave the East India Company a monopoly on the tea trade in the American colonies, which colonists feared would hurt colonial merchants' business.

government of Massachusetts, provided for the removal of accused persons to Britain for trial, and, most important, restricted movement to the West—further alienating the southern planters, who depended upon access to new western lands. These acts of retaliation confirmed the worst criticisms of British rule and helped radicalize Americans. Radicals such as Samuel Adams had been agitating for more violent measures against the British. But ultimately it was Britain's political repression that fanned support for independence.

Thus, the Boston Tea Party set in motion a cycle of provocation and retaliation that in 1774 resulted in the convening of the First Continental Congress—an assembly of delegates from all parts of the colonies that called for a total boycott of British goods and, under the prodding of the radicals, began to consider the possibility of independence from British rule. The eventual result was the Declaration of Independence.

THE DECLARATION OF INDEPENDENCE EXPLAINED WHY THE COLONISTS WANTED TO BREAK WITH GREAT BRITAIN

In 1776, more than a year after open warfare had commenced in Massachusetts, the Second Continental Congress appointed a committee consisting of Thomas Jefferson of Virginia, Benjamin Franklin of Pennsylvania, Roger Sherman of Connecticut, John Adams of Massachusetts, and Robert Livingston of New York to draft a statement of American independence from British rule. The Declaration of Independence, written by Jefferson and adopted by the Second Continental Congress, was an extraordinary philosophical and political document. Philosophically, the Declaration was remarkable for its assertion that certain rights, called "unalienable rights"—including life, liberty, and the pursuit of happiness—could not be abridged by governments. In the world of 1776, a world in which some kings still claimed to rule by divine right, this was a dramatic statement.

Politically, the Declaration was remarkable because it focused on grievances, aspirations, and principles that might unify the various colonial groups that were otherwise divided economically, philosophically, and by region. The Declaration was an attempt to identify and articulate a history and set of principles that might help to forge national unity.[7] It also explained to the rest of the world why American colonists were attempting to break away from Great Britain.

The purpose of the Declaration of Independence was to explain to the world why the colonists had rebelled against the British and sought self-government. Every year, Americans celebrate the signing of the Declaration on the Fourth of July.

THE ARTICLES OF CONFEDERATION CREATED AMERICA'S FIRST NATIONAL GOVERNMENT

Having declared their independence, the colonies needed to establish a governmental structure. In November 1777 the Continental Congress adopted the **Articles of Confederation**, the United States' first written constitution. Although it was not ratified by all the states until 1781, it was the country's operative constitution until the final months of 1788.

The Articles of Confederation were concerned primarily with limiting the powers of the central government. The central government, first of all, was based entirely in a Congress. Since it was not intended to be a powerful government, it was given no executive branch. Execution of its laws was to be left to the individual states. Second, the Congress had little power. Its members were not much more than delegates or messengers from the state legislatures. They were chosen by the state legislatures, their salaries were paid out of the state treasuries, and they were subject to immediate recall by state authorities. In addition, each state, regardless of its size, had only a single vote.

The Congress was given the power to declare war and make peace, to make treaties and alliances, to coin or borrow money, and to regulate trade with the

Native Americans. It could also appoint the senior officers of the U.S. Army. But it could not levy taxes or regulate commerce among the states. Moreover, the army officers it appointed had no army to serve in because the nation's armed forces were composed of the state militias. And in order to amend the Articles, all 13 states had to agree—a virtual impossibility. Probably the most unfortunate part of the Articles of Confederation was that the central government could not prevent one state from discriminating against other states in the quest for foreign commerce.

The relationship between the Congress and the states under the Articles of Confederation was one in which the states retained virtually all governmental powers. It was properly called a **confederation** (a system of government in which states retain sovereign authority except for the powers expressly delegated to the national government) because, as provided under Article II, "each state retains its sovereignty, freedom and independence, and every Power, Jurisdiction and right, which is not by this confederation expressly delegated to the United States, in Congress assembled." Not only was there no executive, there also was no judicial authority and no other means of enforcing the Congress's will. If there was to be any enforcement at all, the states would do it for the Congress.[8]

The Failure of the Articles of Confederation Made the "Second Founding" Necessary

> **Analyze the reasons many Americans thought a new Constitution was needed, and assess the obstacles to a new Constitution**

The Declaration of Independence and the Articles of Confederation were not sufficient to hold the new nation together as an independent and effective nation-state. From almost the moment of armistice with the British in 1783, moves were afoot to reform and strengthen the Articles of Confederation.

Competition among the states for foreign commerce posed a special problem to the new country because it allowed the European powers to play the states against one another, which not only made America seem weak and vulnerable abroad but also created confusion on both sides of the Atlantic. At one point during the winter of 1786–87, John Adams of Massachusetts, a leader in the independence struggle, was sent to negotiate a new treaty with the British, one that would cover disputes left over from the war. The British government responded that, because the United States under the Articles of Confederation was unable to enforce existing treaties, it would negotiate with each of the 13 states separately.

At the same time, well-to-do Americans—in particular the New England merchants and southern planters—were troubled by the influence that "radical" forces exercised in the Continental Congress and in the governments of several of the states. As a result of the Revolution, one key segment of the colonial elite—the royal land office, and patent holders—was stripped of its economic and political privileges. And while the pre-Revolutionary elite were weakened, the pre-Revolutionary radicals were better organized than ever and now controlled such states as Pennsylvania and Rhode Island, where they pursued economic and political policies that struck terror into the hearts of the pre-Revolutionary political establishment. Of course, the central government under the Articles of Confederation was powerless to intervene.

THE ANNAPOLIS CONVENTION WAS KEY TO CALLING A NATIONAL CONVENTION

The continuation of international weakness and domestic economic turmoil led many Americans to consider whether their newly adopted form of government might not already require revision. In the fall of 1786, many state leaders accepted an invitation from the Virginia legislature for a conference of representatives of all the states, to be held in Annapolis, Maryland. Delegates from only five states actually attended, so nothing substantive could be accomplished. Still, this conference was the first step toward what is now known as the second founding. The one positive thing that came out of the Annapolis convention was a carefully worded resolution calling on the Congress to send commissioners to Philadelphia at a later time "to devise such further provisions as shall appear to them necessary to render the Constitution of the Federal Government adequate to the exigencies of the Union."[9] But the resolution did not necessarily imply any desire to do more than improve and reform the Articles of Confederation.

The government under the Articles did enact some important measures, including the Land Ordinance of 1785 and the Northwest Ordinance of 1787. The Land Ordinance established the principles of land surveying and landownership that governed America's westward expansion, and under the Northwest Ordinance the states agreed to surrender their western land claims, which opened the way for the admission of new states to the Union. Still, the young nation's political and economic position deteriorated during the 1780s, and something had to be done.

SHAYS'S REBELLION SHOWED HOW WEAK THE GOVERNMENT WAS

It is quite possible that the Constitutional Convention of 1787 in Philadelphia would never have taken place at all except for a single event that occurred during the winter following the Annapolis convention: Shays's Rebellion.

Daniel Shays, a former army captain, led a mob of farmers in a rebellion against the government of Massachusetts, which had levied heavy taxes against them. The purpose of the rebellion was to prevent foreclosures on farmers' debt-ridden land by keeping the county courts of western Massachusetts from sitting until after the next election. A militia force, organized by the Governor of Massachusetts and privately

In 1787, Daniel Shays led a makeshift army against the federal arsenal at Springfield to protest heavy taxes levied by the Massachusetts legislature. The rebellion proved the Articles of Confederation were too weak to protect the fledgling nation.

funded by a group of prominent merchants, dispersed the mob, but for several days in February 1787, Shays and his followers terrified the state government by attempting to capture the federal arsenal at Springfield, provoking an appeal to the Congress to help restore order. Within a few days, the state government regained control and captured 14 of the rebels. (All were eventually pardoned.) Later that year, a newly elected Massachusetts legislature granted some of the farmers' demands.

George Washington summed up the effects of this incident: "I am mortified beyond expression that in the moment of our acknowledged independence we should by our conduct verify the predictions of our transatlantic foe, and render ourselves ridiculous and contemptible in the eyes of all Europe."[10]

The Congress under the Confederation had been unable to act decisively in a time of crisis. This provided critics of the Articles of Confederation with precisely the evidence they needed to push the Annapolis resolution through the Congress. Thus, the states were asked to send representatives to Philadelphia to discuss constitutional revision. Delegates were eventually sent by every state except Rhode Island.

THE CONSTITUTIONAL CONVENTION DIDN'T START OUT TO WRITE A NEW CONSTITUTION

The delegates who convened in Philadelphia in May 1787 had political strife, international embarrassment, national weakness, and local rebellion fixed in their minds. Recognizing that these issues were symptoms of fundamental flaws in the Articles of Confederation, the delegates soon abandoned the plan to revise the Articles and committed themselves to a second founding—a second, and ultimately successful, attempt to create a legitimate and effective national system of government. This effort would occupy the convention for the next five months.

A Marriage of Interest and Principle For years, scholars have disagreed about the motives of the Founders in Philadelphia. Among the most controversial views of the framers' motives is the "economic interpretation" put forward by historian Charles Beard and his disciples.[11] According to Beard's account, America's Founders were a collection of securities speculators and property owners whose only aim was personal enrichment. From this perspective, the Constitution's lofty principles are little more than sophisticated masks behind which the most venal interests sought to enrich themselves.

The opposing view is that the framers of the Constitution *were* concerned with philosophical and ethical principles. Indeed, the framers did try to devise a system of government consistent with the dominant philosophical and moral principles of the day. But, in fact, these two views belong together; the Founders' interests were reinforced by their principles. The convention that drafted the American Constitution was chiefly organized by the New England merchants and southern planters. Although the delegates representing these groups did not all hope to profit personally from an increase in the value of their securities, as Beard would have it, they did hope to benefit in the broadest political and economic sense by breaking the power of their radical foes and establishing a system of government more compatible with their long-term economic and political interests. Thus, the framers sought to create a new government capable of promoting commerce and protecting property from radical state legislatures and populist forces hostile to the interests of the commercial and propertied classes.

The Great Compromise The proponents of a new government fired their opening shot on May 29, 1787, when Edmund Randolph of Virginia offered a resolution that proposed corrections and enlargements in the Articles of Confederation. The proposal, reflecting the strong influence of James Madison, was no simple motion; rather, it provided for an entirely new government.

The portion of Randolph's motion that became most controversial was called the **Virginia Plan**. This plan provided for a system of representation in the national legislature based upon the population of each state or the proportion of each state's revenue contribution to the national government or both. (Randolph also proposed a second chamber of the legislature, to be elected by the members of the first chamber.) Since the states varied enormously in size and wealth, the Virginia Plan was heavily biased in favor of the large states.

While the convention was debating the Virginia Plan, opposition to it began to mount as more delegates arrived in Philadelphia. William Paterson of New Jersey introduced a new resolution known as the **New Jersey Plan**, which called for equal state representation in the national legislature regardless of population. Its main proponents were delegates from the less populous states, including Delaware, New Jersey, Connecticut, and New York, who asserted that the more populous states, such as Virginia, Pennsylvania, North Carolina, Massachusetts, and Georgia, would dominate the new government if representation were determined by population. The smaller states argued that each state should be equally represented in the new regime regardless of the state's population.

The issue of representation was one that threatened to wreck the entire constitutional enterprise. Delegates conferred, factions maneuvered, and tempers flared. James Wilson of Pennsylvania told the small-state delegates that if they wanted to disrupt the union, they should go ahead. The separation, he said, could "never happen on better grounds." Small-state delegates were equally blunt. Gunning Bedford of Delaware declared that the small states might, if forced, look elsewhere for friends. "The large states," he said, "dare not dissolve the confederation. If they do the small ones will find some foreign ally of more honor and good faith, who will take them by the hand and do them justice." These sentiments were widely shared.

The union, as Luther Martin of Maryland put it, was "on the verge of dissolution, scarcely held together by the strength of a hair."[12]

The outcome of this debate was the Connecticut Compromise, also known as the **Great Compromise.** Under the terms of this compromise, in the first chamber of Congress, the House of Representatives, the representatives would be apportioned according to the population in each state. This, of course, was what delegates from the large states had sought. But in the second chamber, the Senate, each state would have equal representation regardless of its population; this provision addressed the concerns of the small states. This compromise was not immediately satisfactory to all the delegates. Indeed, two of the most vocal members of the small-state faction, John Lansing and Robert Yates of New York, were so incensed by the concession that their colleagues had made to the large-state forces that they stormed out of the convention. In the end, however, most of the delegates preferred compromise to the breakup of the Union, and the plan was accepted.

The Question of Slavery: The Three-Fifths Compromise Many of the conflicts that emerged during the Constitutional Convention were reflections of the fundamental differences between the slave and the nonslave states—differences that pitted the southern planters against New England merchants. This was one example of the conflict that would later almost destroy the Republic.

More than 90 percent of the country's slaves resided in five states—Georgia, Maryland, North Carolina, South Carolina, and Virginia—where they accounted for 30 percent of the total population. In some places, slaves outnumbered nonslaves by as many as 10 to 1. For the Constitution to embody any principle of national supremacy, some basic decisions would have to be made about the place of slavery in the general scheme. James Madison observed, "It seemed now to be pretty well understood that the real difference of interests lay, not between the large and small but between the northern and southern states. The institution of slavery and its consequences formed the line of discrimination."[13]

The issue of slavery was the most difficult one faced by the framers, and it nearly destroyed the Union. Although some delegates believed slavery to be morally wrong, an evil and oppressive institution that made a mockery of the ideals and values espoused in the Constitution, morality was not the issue that caused the framers to support or oppose the Three-Fifths Compromise. Whatever they thought of the institution of slavery, most delegates from the northern states opposed counting slaves in the distribution of congressional seats. James Wilson of Pennsylvania, for example, argued that if slaves were citizens, they should be treated and counted like other citizens. If, on the other hand, they were property, then why should not other forms of property be counted toward the apportionment of representatives? But southern delegates made it clear that if the northerners refused to give in, they would never agree to the new government. William R. Davie of North Carolina heatedly asserted that the people of North Carolina would never enter the Union if slaves were not counted as part of the basis for representation. Without such agreement, he asserted ominously, "the business was at an end." Even southerners such as Edmund Randolph of Virginia, who conceded that slavery was immoral, insisted on including slaves in the allocation of congressional seats. Eventually the North and South compromised on the issue of slavery and representation. Indeed, northerners

Despite the Founders' emphasis on liberty, the new Constitution allowed slavery. In this 1792 painting, *Liberty Displaying the Arts and Sciences*, the books, instruments, and classical columns at the left contrast with the kneeling slaves at the right—illustrating the divide between America's rhetoric of liberty and equality and the realities of slavery.

even agreed to permit a continuation of the odious slave trade until 1808 in order to keep the South in the Union. Eventually, the disparate interests of the North and the South could no longer be reconciled, and a bloody civil war was the result.

Northerners and southerners eventually reached agreement through the **Three-Fifths Compromise**. The seats in the House of Representatives would be apportioned according to a "population" in which only three-fifths of slaves would be counted. The slaves would not be allowed to vote, of course; but the number of representatives would be apportioned accordingly.

The Constitution Created Both Bold Powers and Sharp Limits on Power

Explain how the Constitution attempted to improve America's governance, and outline the major institutions established by the Constitution

The political significance of the Great Compromise and the Three-Fifths Compromise was to reinforce the unity of the mercantile and planter forces that sought to create a new government. The Great Compromise reassured those in both groups who feared that this new governmental framework would reduce the importance of their own local or regional influence. The Three-Fifths Compromise temporarily defused the rivalry between the merchants and planters. Their unity secured, members of the alliance supporting the establishment of a new government moved to fashion a constitutional framework consistent with their economic and political interests.

In particular, the framers sought a new government that, first, would be strong enough to promote commerce and protect property from radical state legislatures such as Rhode Island's. This became the constitutional basis for national control over commerce and finance and for the establishment of national judicial supremacy and the effort to construct a strong presidency. (See Table 2.1 for a comparison of the Articles of Confederation to the Constitution.) Second, the framers sought to prevent what they saw as the threat posed by the "excessive democracy" of the state and national governments under the Articles of Confederation. This led to such constitutional principles as a **bicameral** legislature (a legislative assembly composed of two chambers or houses), **checks and balances** (mechanisms through which each branch of government is able to participate in and influence the activities of the other branches), staggered terms in office with longer terms for senators, and indirect election (selection of the president not by voters directly but by an **electoral college**; senators also were chosen indirectly, by state legislatures). Third, the framers, lacking the power to force the states or the public at large to accept the new form of government, sought to identify principles that would help to secure support. This became the basis of the constitutional provision for direct popular election of representatives and, subsequently, for the addition of the **Bill of Rights** (the first 10 amendments to the Constitution, ratified in 1791; they ensure certain rights and liberties to the people). Finally, the framers wanted to be certain that the government they created did not pose an even greater threat to its citizens' liberties and property rights than did the radical state legislatures they feared and despised. To prevent the new government from abusing its power, the framers incorporated principles such as the **separation of powers** (the division of governmental power among several institutions that must cooperate in decision-making) and **federalism** (a system of government in which power is divided, by a constitution, between a central government and regional governments) into the Constitution.

THE LEGISLATIVE BRANCH WAS DESIGNED TO BE THE MOST POWERFUL

In Article I, Sections 1–7, the Constitution provides for a Congress consisting of two chambers: a House of Representatives and a Senate. Members of the House of Representatives were given two-year terms in office and were to be elected directly by the people. Members of the Senate were to be appointed by the state legislatures (this was changed in 1913 by the Seventeenth Amendment, which instituted direct election of senators) for six-year terms. These terms were staggered so that the appointments of one-third of the senators would expire every two years. The Constitution assigned somewhat different tasks to the House and Senate. Although the approval of each body was required for the enactment of a law, the Senate alone

TABLE 2.1

Comparing the Articles of Confederation and the Constitution

MAJOR PROVISIONS	ARTICLES	CONSTITUTION
Executive branch	None	President of the United States
Judiciary	No federal court system. Judiciary exists only at state level.	Federal judiciary headed by the Supreme Court
Legislature	Unicameral legislature with equal representation for each state. Delegates to the Congress of the Confederation were appointed by the states.	Bicameral legislature consisting of Senate and House of Representatives. Each state is represented by two senators, while apportionment in the House is based on state population. Senators are chosen by the state legislatures (changed to popular election in 1913) and House members by popular election.
Fiscal and economic powers	The national government is dependent upon the states to collect taxes. The states are free to coin their own money, print paper money, and sign commercial treaties with foreign governments.	Congress given the power to levy taxes, coin money, and regulate commerce. States prohibited from coining money or entering into treaties with other nations.
Military	The national government is dependent upon state militias and cannot form an army during peacetime.	The national government is authorized to maintain an army and navy.
Legal supremacy	State constitutions and state law are supreme.	National Constitution and national law are supreme.
Constitutional amendment	Must be agreed upon by all states.	Must be agreed upon by three-fourths of the states.

was given the power to ratify treaties and approve presidential appointments. The House, on the other hand, was given the sole power to originate revenue bills.

The structure of the legislative branch reflected the framers' major goals. The House of Representatives was designed to be directly responsible to the people in order to encourage popular consent for the new Constitution and to help enhance the power of the new government. At the same time, to guard against "excessive democracy," the Constitution checks the power of the House of Representatives with that of the Senate, whose members were to be appointed by the states for long terms rather than elected directly by the people. The purpose of this provision, according to Alexander Hamilton, was to avoid "an unqualified complaisance to every sudden breeze of passion, or to every transient impulse which the people may receive."[14] Staggered terms of service in the Senate, moreover, were intended to make that body even more resistant to popular pressure. Since only one-third of the senators would be selected at any given time, the composition of the institution would be protected from changes in popular preferences transmitted by the state legislatures. This would prevent what James Madison called "mutability in the public councils arising from a rapid succession of new members."[15] Thus, the structure of the legislative branch was designed to contribute to governmental power, to promote popular consent for the new government, and at the same time to place limits on the popular political currents that many of the framers saw as a radical threat to the economic and social order.

The issues of power and consent were important throughout the Constitution. Section 8 of Article I specifically listed the powers of Congress, which include the authority to collect taxes, borrow money, regulate commerce, declare war, and maintain an army and navy. By granting Congress these powers, the framers indicated very clearly that they intended the new government to be far more powerful than its predecessor. At the same time, by defining the new government's most important powers as belonging to Congress, the framers sought to promote popular acceptance of this critical change by reassuring citizens that their views would be fully represented whenever the government exercised its new powers.

As a further guarantee to the people that the new government would pose no threat to them, the Constitution seems to say that any powers not listed are not granted at all. Specific powers granted to Congress in the Constitution are **expressed powers**. But the framers intended to create an active and powerful government, so they also included the necessary and proper clause, sometimes known as the **elastic clause**, which declared that Congress could write laws needed to carry out its expressed powers. This clause indicated that the expressed powers could be broadly interpreted as a source of strength for the national government, not a limitation on it. In response to the charge that they intended to give the national government too much power, the framers adopted language in the Tenth Amendment stipulating that powers not specifically granted by the Constitution to the federal government were reserved to the states or to the people. As we will see in Chapter 3, the resulting tension between the elastic clause and the Tenth Amendment has been at the heart of constitutional struggles between federal and state powers.

THE EXECUTIVE BRANCH CREATED A BRAND NEW OFFICE

The Articles of Confederation had not provided for an executive branch, and the framers viewed this as a source of weakness, so the Constitution provides for the establishment of the presidency in Article II. As Hamilton commented, the presidential article aimed toward "energy in the Executive." It did so in an effort to overcome the natural tendency toward stalemate that was built into the bicameral legislature as well as into the separation of powers among the three branches. The Constitution affords the president a measure of independence from the people and from the other branches of government—particularly the Congress.

In line with the framers' goal of increased power to the national government, the president is granted the unconditional power to receive ambassadors from other countries—this amounts to the power to "recognize" other countries—as well as the power to negotiate treaties, although their acceptance requires the approval of two-thirds of the Senate. The president is also given the unconditional right to grant reprieves and pardons, except in cases of impeachment, and the powers to appoint major departmental personnel, to convene Congress in special session, and to veto congressional enactments. The veto power is formidable, but it is not absolute, since Congress can override it by a two-thirds vote, reflecting the framers' concern with checks and balances.

The framers hoped to create a presidency that would make the federal government rather than the states the agency capable of timely and decisive action to deal with public issues and problems. At the same time, however, the framers sought to help the presidency withstand excessively democratic pressures by creating a system of indirect rather than direct election through an electoral college.

THE JUDICIAL BRANCH WAS A CHECK ON TOO MUCH DEMOCRACY

In establishing the judicial branch in Article III, the Constitution reflects the framers' preoccupation with nationalizing governmental power and checking radical democratic impulses while preventing the new national government from interfering with liberty and property.

Under the provisions of Article III, the framers created a court that was to be literally a supreme court of the United States and not merely the highest court of the national government. The most important expression of this intention was granting the Supreme Court the power to resolve any conflicts that might emerge between federal and state laws. In particular, the Supreme Court is given the right to determine whether a power is exclusive to the national government, concurrent with the states, or exclusive to the states. In addition, the Supreme Court is assigned jurisdiction over controversies between citizens of different states. The long-term significance of this provision was that as the country developed a national economy, it came to rely increasingly on the federal judiciary, rather than on the state courts, for the resolution of disputes.

Federal judges are given lifetime appointments in order to protect them from popular politics and from interference by the other branches. This, however, does not mean that the judiciary remains totally impartial to political considerations or to the other branches, for the president is to appoint the judges and the Senate to approve the appointments. Congress also has the power to create inferior (lower) courts, change the jurisdiction of the federal courts, add or subtract federal judges, and even change the size of the Supreme Court.

No explicit mention is made in the Constitution of **judicial review**, the power of the courts to review and, if necessary, declare actions of the legislative and executive branches invalid or unconstitutional. The Supreme Court asserted this power in *Marbury v. Madison* (1803).[16] Its assumption of this power, as we shall see in Chapter 12, was based not on the Constitution itself but on the politics of later decades and the membership of the Court.

NATIONAL UNITY AND POWER SET THE NEW CONSTITUTION APART FROM THE OLD ARTICLES

Various provisions in the Constitution address the framers' concern with national unity and power, including Article IV's provisions for comity (reciprocity) among states and among citizens of all states. Each state is prohibited from discriminating against the citizens of other states in favor of its own citizens, and the Supreme Court is charged with deciding in each case whether a state has discriminated against goods or people from another state. The Constitution restricts the power of the states in favor of ensuring enough power to the national government to give the country a free-flowing national economy.

The framers' concern with national supremacy was also expressed in Article VI, in the **supremacy clause**, which provides that national laws and treaties "shall be the supreme Law of the Land" and superior to all laws adopted by any state or any subdivision. This means that states are expected to respect all laws made under the "Authority of the United States." The supremacy clause also binds the officials of all state and local governments as well as the federal government to take an oath of office to support the national Constitution. This means that every action taken by the U.S. Congress has to be applied within each state as though the action were in fact state law.

THE CONSTITUTION ESTABLISHES THE PROCESS FOR AMENDMENT

The Constitution establishes procedures for its own revision in Article V. Its provisions are so difficult that the document has been successfully amended only 17 times since 1791, when the first 10 amendments were adopted. Thousands of other amendments have been proposed in Congress, but fewer than 40 of them have even come close to fulfilling the Constitution's requirement of a two-thirds vote in Congress.

THE CONSTITUTION SETS FORTH RULES FOR ITS OWN RATIFICATION

The rules for the ratification of the Constitution are set forth in Article VII. Nine of the 13 states have to ratify, or agree to, the terms in order for the Constitution to be formally adopted.

THE CONSTITUTION LIMITS THE NATIONAL GOVERNMENT'S POWER

As we have indicated, although the framers sought to create a powerful national government, they also wanted to guard against possible misuse of that power. To that end, the framers incorporated two key principles into the Constitution: the separation of powers and federalism. A third set of limitations, the Bill of Rights, was added to the Constitution in the form of 10 amendments proposed by the first Congress and ratified by the states in 1791. Most of the framers had thought a Bill of Rights to be unnecessary but accepted the idea during the debates over the Constitution's ratification.

The Separation of Powers No principle of politics was more widely shared at the time of the 1787 Founding than the principle that power must be used to balance power. As mentioned earlier in the chapter, Montesquieu believed that this balance was an indispensable defense against tyranny. His writings, especially his major work, *The Spirit of the Laws*, "were taken as political gospel" at the Philadelphia convention.[17] Although the principle of the separation of powers is not explicitly stated in the Constitution, the entire structure of the national government is built precisely on Article I (the legislature), Article II (the executive), and Article III (the judiciary; see Figure 2.1).

However, separation of powers is nothing but mere words on parchment without a method to maintain that separation. The method became known by the popular label

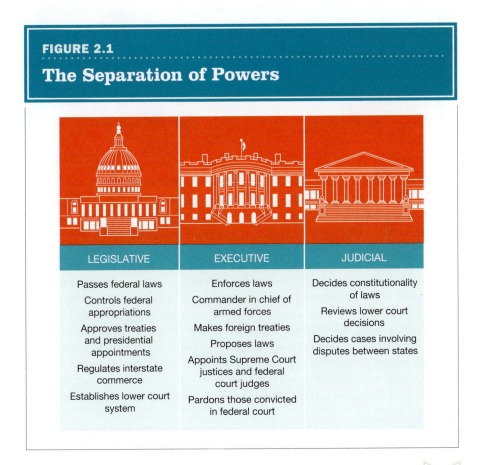

FIGURE 2.1
The Separation of Powers

LEGISLATIVE	EXECUTIVE	JUDICIAL
Passes federal laws	Enforces laws	Decides constitutionality of laws
Controls federal appropriations	Commander in chief of armed forces	Reviews lower court decisions
Approves treaties and presidential appointments	Makes foreign treaties	Decides cases involving disputes between states
Regulates interstate commerce	Proposes laws	
Establishes lower court system	Appoints Supreme Court justices and federal court judges	
	Pardons those convicted in federal court	

FIGURE 2.2

Checks and Balances

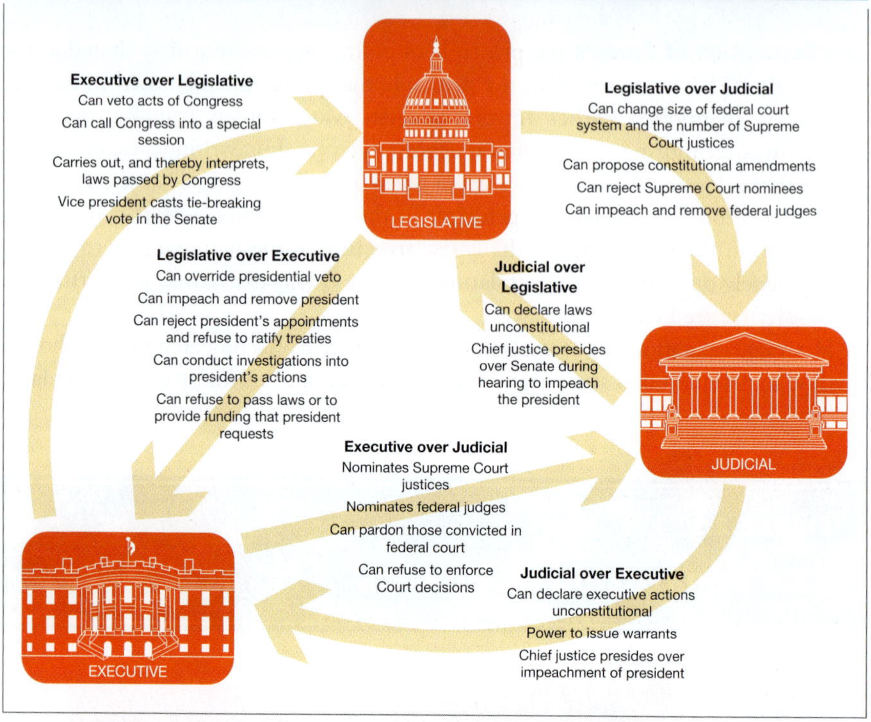

Executive over Legislative
Can veto acts of Congress
Can call Congress into a special session
Carries out, and thereby interprets, laws passed by Congress
Vice president casts tie-breaking vote in the Senate

Legislative over Judicial
Can change size of federal court system and the number of Supreme Court justices
Can propose constitutional amendments
Can reject Supreme Court nominees
Can impeach and remove federal judges

Legislative over Executive
Can override presidential veto
Can impeach and remove president
Can reject president's appointments and refuse to ratify treaties
Can conduct investigations into president's actions
Can refuse to pass laws or to provide funding that president requests

Judicial over Legislative
Can declare laws unconstitutional
Chief justice presides over Senate during hearing to impeach the president

Executive over Judicial
Nominates Supreme Court justices
Nominates federal judges
Can pardon those convicted in federal court
Can refuse to enforce Court decisions

Judicial over Executive
Can declare executive actions unconstitutional
Power to issue warrants
Chief justice presides over impeachment of president

LEGISLATIVE

JUDICIAL

EXECUTIVE

"checks and balances" (see Figure 2.2). Each branch is given not only its own powers but also some power over the other two branches. Among the most familiar checks and balances are the president's veto as a power over Congress and Congress's power over the president through its control of appointments to high executive posts and to the judiciary. Congress also has power over the president with its control of appropriations (the spending of government money) and the right of approval of treaties (by the Senate). The judiciary has the power of judicial review over the other two branches.

Another important feature of the separation of powers is the principle of giving each of the branches a distinctly different constituency. Theorists such as Montesquieu called this a "mixed regime," with the president chosen indirectly by electors, the House by popular vote, the Senate (originally) by state legislature, and the judiciary by presidential appointment. By these means, the occupants of each branch would tend to develop very different outlooks on how to govern, different definitions of the public interest, and different alliances with private interests.

Federalism Compared to the confederation principle of the Articles of Confederation, federalism was a step toward greater centralization of power. The delegates agreed that they needed to place more power at the national level, without completely undermining the power of the state governments. Thus, they devised a system of two sovereigns—the states and the nation—with the hope that competition between the two would be an effective limitation on the power of both.

The Bill of Rights Late in the Philadelphia convention of 1787, a motion was made to include a list of citizens' rights in the Constitution. After a brief debate in which hardly a word was said in its favor and only one speech was made against it, the motion was almost unanimously defeated. Most delegates sincerely believed that since the federal government was already limited to its expressed powers, further protection of citizens was not needed. The delegates argued that the states should adopt bills of rights because their greater powers needed greater limitations. But almost immediately after the Constitution was ratified, there was a movement to adopt a national bill of rights. This is why the Bill of Rights, adopted in 1791, comprises the first 10 amendments to the Constitution rather than being part of the body of it. (We will have a good deal more to say about the Bill of Rights in Chapter 4.)

Ratification of the Constitution Was Difficult

> **Present the controversies involved in the struggle for ratification**

The first hurdle facing the proposed Constitution was ratification by state conventions of delegates elected by the people of each state. This struggle for ratification was carried out in 13 separate campaigns. Each involved different people, moved at a different pace, and was influenced by local and national considerations. Two sides faced off throughout the states, however; the two sides called themselves Federalists and Antifederalists (see Table 2.2).

The Federalists (who more accurately should have called themselves "Nationalists" but who took their name to appear to follow in the Revolutionary tradition) supported the constitution proposed at the American Constitutional Convention of 1787 and preferred a strong national government. The Antifederalists favored strong state governments and a weak national government and opposed the document produced at the Constitutional Convention. They preferred a federal system of government that was decentralized; they took their name by default, in reaction to their better-organized opponents. The Federalists were united in their support of the Constitution, while the Antifederalists were divided over possible alternatives to the Constitution.

During the struggle over ratification of the Constitution, Americans argued about great political principles. How much power should the national government be given? What safeguards would most likely prevent the abuse of power? What institutional arrangements could best ensure adequate representation for all Americans? Was tyranny to be feared more from the many or from the few?

TABLE 2.2

Federalists versus Antifederalists

	FEDERALISTS	ANTIFEDERALISTS
Who were they?	Property owners, creditors, merchants	Small farmers, frontiersmen, debtors, shopkeepers, some state government officials
What did they believe?	Believed that elites were most fit to govern; feared "excessive democracy"	Believed that government should be closer to the people; feared concentration of power in hands of the elites
What system of government did they favor?	Favored strong national government; believed in "filtration" so that only elites would obtain governmental power	Favored retention of power by state governments and protection of individual rights
Who were their leaders?	Alexander Hamilton, James Madison, George Washington	Patrick Henry, George Mason, Elbridge Gerry, George Clinton

FEDERALISTS AND ANTIFEDERALISTS FOUGHT BITTERLY OVER THE WISDOM OF THE NEW CONSTITUTION

During the ratification struggle, thousands of essays, speeches, pamphlets, and letters were written in support of and in opposition to the proposed Constitution. The best-known pieces supporting ratification of the Constitution were the 85 essays written, under the name of "Publius," by Alexander Hamilton, James Madison, and John Jay between the fall of 1787 and the spring of 1788—known today as the *Federalist Papers*. They not only defended the principles of the Constitution but also sought to dispel fears of a strong national authority. The Antifederalists published essays of their own, arguing that the new Constitution betrayed the Revolution and was a step toward monarchy. Among the best of the Antifederalist works were the essays, usually attributed to New York Supreme Court justice Robert Yates, that were written under the name of "Brutus" and published in the *New York Journal* at the same time the *Federalist Papers* appeared. The Antifederalist view was also ably presented in the pamphlets and letters written by a former delegate to the Continental Congress and future U.S. senator, Richard Henry Lee of Virginia, using the pen name "The Federal Farmer." These essays highlight the major differences of opinion between Federalists and Antifederalists. Federalists appealed to basic principles of government in support of their nationalist vision. Antifederalists cited equally fundamental precepts to support their vision of a looser confederacy of small republics. Three areas of disagreement were representation, majority tyranny, and governmental power.

Representation The Antifederalists believed that the best and most representative government was closest to the people, what we would think of as local and state governments. These smaller, more homogeneous governing units would provide "a true picture of the people...[possessing] the knowledge of their circumstances and their wants."[18] A strong national government could not represent the interests of the nation as effectively, the Antifederalists argued, because the nation as a whole was simply too large and diverse.

The Federalists, on the other hand, thought that some distance between the people and their representatives might be a good thing because it would encourage the selection of a few talented and experienced representatives to serve in a national legislature who could balance the wishes of the people with their own considered judgment. In James Madison's view, representatives would not simply mirror society; rather, they must be "[those] who possess [the] most wisdom to discern, and [the] most virtue to pursue, the common good of the society."[19]

Tyranny Both Federalists and Antifederalists feared **tyranny**, oppressive and unjust government that employs cruel and arbitrary use of power and authority. But each painted a different picture of what kind of tyranny to fear.

The Antifederalists feared that tyranny would arise from the tendency of all governments to become more "aristocratic," wherein a few individuals in positions of authority would use their positions to gain more and more power over the people. For this reason, Antifederalists were sharply critical of those features of the Constitution that limited direct popular influence over the government, including the election of senators by state legislatures, election of the president by the electoral college, and selection of federal judges by the president and the Senate. Judges, who are appointed for life, were seen as an especially dire threat: "I wonder if the world ever saw...a court of justice invested with such immense powers, and yet placed in a situation so little responsible," protested Brutus.[20]

For the Federalists, tyranny in a republic was less likely to come from aristocrats and more likely to come from the majority. They feared that a popular majority, "united and actuated by some common impulse of passion, or of interest, adverse to the rights of other citizens," would attempt to "trample on the rules of justice."[21] Those features of the Constitution opposed by the Antifederalists were the very ones that the Federalists defended as the best hope of avoiding tyranny. The sheer size and diversity of the American nation, as represented in the two houses of Congress, would provide a built-in set of balances that would force competing interests to moderate and compromise.

Governmental Power A third difference between Federalists and Antifederalists was over the matter of governmental power. Both sides agreed on the principle of **limited government**, meaning a government whose powers are defined and limited by a constitution; but they differed on how best to limit the government.

Antifederalists wanted the powers of the national government to be carefully specified and limited. Otherwise, the federal government would "swallow up all the

Debates over how much power the national government should have continue today. After the San Bernardino shooting in 2015, the FBI demanded Apple unlock the perpetrator's iPhone for details into his criminal activity. Here, a group protests the FBI's infringement on the right to privacy.

power of the state governments." Antifederalists bitterly attacked the supremacy clause and the elastic clause of the Constitution, saying that these provisions gave the national government dangerously unlimited grants of power. They also insisted that a bill of rights be added to the Constitution to place limits on the government's power over citizens.

Federalists favored a national government with broad powers to defend the nation from foreign threats, guard against domestic strife and insurrection, promote commerce, and expand the nation's economy. Federalists agreed that such power could be abused but believed that the best safeguard against such abuse was through the Constitution's internal checks and controls, not by keeping the national government weak. As Madison put it, "The power surrendered by the people is first divided between two distinct governments [federal and state], and then the portion allotted to each subdivided among distinct and separate departments. Hence, a double security arises to the rights of the people. The different governments will control each other, at the same time that each will be controlled by itself."[22] The Federalists considered a bill of rights to be unnecessary, although this Antifederalist demand was eventually embraced by Federalists, including Madison.

Comparing Systems of Government

There is tremendous variation across the world's democracies. All democracies possess some form of an executive, a legislature, and a judiciary; but the amount of power that each branch has varies. Note that in some systems, no one branch has very much power. In the United States, that is because of the system of checks and balances among the branches. Israel and the United Kingdom, which lack written constitutions, have branches with even less power than in the United States.

COUNTRY	WRITTEN CONSTITUTION?	FEDERAL OR UNITARY SYSTEM	STRENGTH OF EXECUTIVE	STRENGTH OF LEGISLATURE	JUDICIAL INDEPENDENCE
Brazil	Yes	Federal	High	Medium	High
France	Yes	Unitary	High	Low	Low
India	Yes	Federal	Medium	Low	Medium
Israel	No	Unitary	Low	Low	Medium
South Africa	Yes	Unitary	Medium	Low	High
Tunisia	Yes	Unitary	High	Medium	Low
United States	Yes	Federal	Low	Medium	High*
United Kingdom	No	Unitary	High*	Low	Medium

*Although the Comparative Constitutions Project classifies the formal powers of both the American presidency and the judicial branch, as originally provided for in the Constitution, as relatively weak, we have classified both here as strong, based on the greater powers that have developed over time.

SOURCE: Comparative Constitutions Project, "CCP Rankings," http://comparativeconstitutionsproject.org/ccp-rankings/ (accessed 7/16/15).

BOTH FEDERALISTS AND ANTIFEDERALISTS CONTRIBUTED TO THE SUCCESS OF THE NEW SYSTEM

In general, the Federalist vision of America triumphed. The Constitution adopted in 1789 creates the framework for a powerful national government that for more than 200 years has defended the nation's interests, promoted its commerce, and maintained national unity. In one notable instance, the national government fought and won a bloody war to prevent the nation from breaking apart. And despite this powerful government, the system of internal checks and balances has functioned reasonably well, as the Federalists predicted, to prevent the national government from tyrannizing its citizens.

Although they were defeated in 1788, the Antifederalists present us with an important picture of a road not taken and of an America that might have been. Would Americans in the eighteenth century have been worse off if they had been governed by a confederacy of small republics linked by a national administration with severely limited powers? Were the Antifederalists correct in predicting that a government given great power in the hope that it might do good would, through "insensible progress," inevitably turn to evil purposes?

Changing the Constitution

Trace how the Constitution has changed over time through the amendment process

The Constitution has endured for more than two centuries as the framework of government because it has changed over time.

AMENDMENTS: MANY ARE CALLED; FEW ARE CHOSEN

The inevitable need for change was recognized by the framers of the Constitution, and the provisions for **amendment** (a change added to a bill, law, or constitution) were incorporated into Article V. The Constitution has proven to be extremely difficult to amend. Since 1789, more than 11,000 amendments have been formally offered in Congress. Of these, Congress officially proposed only 29, and 27 of these were eventually ratified by the states.

Four methods of amendment are provided for in Article V:

1. Passage in House and Senate by two-thirds vote, then ratification by majority vote of the legislatures of three-fourths (now 38) of the states.

2. Passage in House and Senate by two-thirds vote, then ratification by conventions called for the purpose in three-fourths of the states.

3. Passage in a national convention called by Congress in response to petitions by two-thirds of the states, then ratification by majority vote of the legislatures of three-fourths of the states.

4. Passage in a national convention, as in method 3, then ratification by conventions called for the purpose in three-fourths of the states.

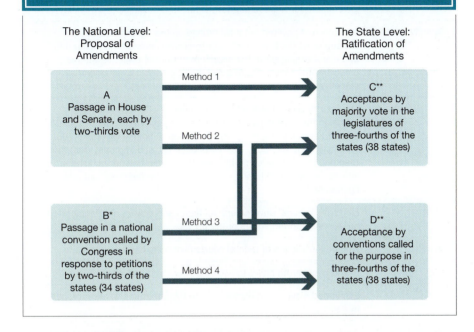

FIGURE 2.3

Four Ways the Constitution Can Be Amended

*This method of proposal has never been employed. Thus, amendment routes 3 and 4 have never been attempted.
**For each amendment proposal, Congress has the power to choose the method of ratification, the time limit for consideration by the states, and other conditions of ratification. The movement to repeal Prohibition in the Twenty-First Amendment was the only occasion in which route 2 was used successfully.

The National Level:
Proposal of
Amendments

The State Level:
Ratification of
Amendments

Method 1

A
Passage in House
and Senate, each by
two-thirds vote

Method 2

C**
Acceptance by
majority vote in the
legislatures of
three-fourths of the
states (38 states)

B*
Passage in a national
convention called by
Congress in
response to petitions
by two-thirds of the
states (34 states)

Method 3

Method 4

D**
Acceptance by
conventions called
for the purpose in
three-fourths of the
states (38 states)

Figure 2.3 illustrates each of these possible methods. Since no amendment has ever been proposed by national convention, routes 3 and 4 have never been employed. And route 2 has only been employed once (the Twenty-First Amendment, which repealed the Eighteenth Amendment, or Prohibition). Thus, route 1 has been used for all the others.

Now it should be clear why it has been so difficult to amend the Constitution. The requirement of a two-thirds vote in the House and the Senate means that any proposal for an amendment in Congress can be killed by only 34 senators or 136 members of the House. What is more, if the necessary two-thirds vote is obtained, the amendment can still be killed by the refusal or inability of only 13 out of 50 state legislatures to ratify it. Since each state has an equal vote regardless of its population, the 13 holdout states may represent a very small fraction of the total American population.

THE AMENDMENT PROCESS REFLECTS "HIGHER LAW"

Most efforts to amend the Constitution have failed because they were simply attempts to use the Constitution as an alternative to legislation for dealing directly with a specific public problem. Successful amendments, on the other hand, are concerned with the structure or composition of government (see Table 2.3; the

TABLE 2.3

Amendments to the Constitution

AMENDMENT	PURPOSE
I	Congress is not to make any law establishing a religion or abridging free exercise of religion, speech, press, assembly, or petitioning the government for redress of grievances.
II, III, IV	No branch of government may infringe on the right of people to keep arms (II), is not arbitrarily to occupy homes for a militia (III), and is not to engage in the search or seizure of evidence without a court warrant swearing to belief in the probable existence of a crime (IV).
V, VI, VII, VIII	The courts* are not to hold trials for serious offenses without provision for a grand jury (V), a petit (trial) jury (VII), a speedy trial (VI), presentation of charges (VI), confrontation of hostile witnesses (VI), immunity from testimony against oneself (V), and immunity from more than one trial for the same offense (V). Neither bail nor punishment can be excessive (VIII), and no property can be taken without just compensation (V).
IX, X	*Limits on National Government:* All rights and powers not enumerated are reserved to the states or the people.
XI	Limited jurisdiction of federal courts over suits involving the states.
XII	Provided separate ballot for vice president in the electoral college.
XIII	Eliminated slavery and eliminated the right of states to allow property in persons.**
XIV	Asserted the principle of national citizenship and prohibited the states from infringing upon the rights of citizens of the nation, no matter that they happened to live in that state. Also prohibited states from denying voting rights to male citizens over the age of 21.†
XV	Extended voting rights to all races.
XVI	Established national power to tax incomes.
XVII††	Provided direct election of senators.
XIX	Extended voting rights to women.
XX	Eliminated "lame-duck" session of Congress.
XXII	Limited presidential term.
XXIII	Extended voting rights to residents of the District of Columbia.
XXIV	Extended voting rights to all classes by abolition of poll taxes.
XXV	Provided presidential succession in case of disability.

TABLE 2.3

Amendments to the Constitution—cont'd

AMENDMENT	PURPOSE
XXVI	Extended voting rights to citizens aged 18 and over.†
XXVII	Limited Congress's power to raise its own salary.

* These amendments also impose limits on the law-enforcement powers of federal (and especially) state and local executive branches.

** The Thirteenth Amendment was proposed January 31, 1865, and adopted less than a year later, on December 18, 1865.

† In defining *citizenship*, the Fourteenth Amendment actually provided the constitutional basis for expanding the electorate to include all races, women, and residents of the District of Columbia. Only the "18-year-olds' amendment" should have been necessary since it changed the definition of citizenship. The fact that additional amendments were required following the Fourteenth suggests that voting is not considered an inherent right of U.S. citizenship. Instead, it is viewed as a privilege.

†† The Eighteenth Amendment, ratified in 1919, outlawed the sale and transportation of liquor. It was repealed by the Twenty-First Amendment, ratified in 1933.

‡ The Twenty-Sixth Amendment holds the record for speed of adoption. It was proposed on March 23, 1971, and adopted on July 5, 1971.

first 10 amendments will be discussed in Chapter 4). This is consistent with the dictionary, which defines *constitution* as the makeup or composition of something. And it is consistent with the concept of a constitution as "higher law" because the whole point and purpose of a higher law is to establish a framework within which government and the process of making ordinary law can take place. Even those who would have preferred more changes to the Constitution have to agree that there is great wisdom in this principle. A constitution ought to enable legislation and public policies to be enacted, but it should not determine what that legislation or those public policies ought to be.

For those whose hopes for change center on the Constitution, it must be emphasized that the amendment route to social change is, and always will be, extremely limited. Through a constitution it is possible to establish a working structure of government and basic rights of citizens by placing limitations on the powers of that government. Once these goals have been accomplished, the next problem is how to extend rights to those people who do not already enjoy them. Of course, the Constitution cannot enforce itself. But it can and does have a real influence on everyday life because a right or an obligation set forth in the Constitution can become a cause of action in the hands of an otherwise powerless person.

Private property is an excellent example. Property is one of the most fundamental and well-established rights in the United States, but it is well established not because it is recognized in so many words in the Constitution but because legislatures and courts have made it a crime for anyone, including the government, to trespass or to take away property without compensation.

A constitution is good if it produces the cause of action that leads to good legislation, good court decisions, and appropriate police behavior. A constitution cannot eliminate power. But its principles can be a citizen's dependable defense against the abuse of power.

The Constitution
WHAT DO WE WANT?

The Constitution's framers placed individual liberty ahead of all other political values, a concern that led many of the framers to distrust both democracy and equality. They feared that democracy could degenerate into a majority tyranny in which the populace, perhaps led by rabble-rousing demagogues, trampled on liberty. As for equality, the framers were products of their time and place; our contemporary ideas of racial and gender equality would have been foreign to them. The basic structure of the Constitution—separated powers, internal checks and balances, and federalism—was designed to safeguard liberty, and the Bill of Rights created further safeguards for liberty. At the same time, however, many of the Constitution's other key provisions, such as indirect election of senators and the president and the appointment of judges for life, were designed to limit democracy and, hence, the threat of majority tyranny.

By championing liberty, however, the framers virtually guaranteed that democracy and even a measure of equality would sooner or later evolve in the United States. The "**Who Participates?**" feature on the facing page traces the expansion of the United States from the founding to today. Where they have liberty, more and more people, groups, and interests will engage in politics and gradually overcome whatever restrictions might have been placed on participation. They will fight for their rights and interests, and in doing, may achieve greater equality, as Jim Obergefell did in securing marriage equality for same-sex couples. By granting citizens the freedom to exercise voice, liberty is over time conducive to democracy.

Who Gained the Right to Vote through Amendments?

Adult Citizens Eligible to Vote in National Elections*

1789

The Founding:
White men of property,
age 21+

27.9%

1869

15th Amendment:
All men, age 21+

31.7%

1920

19th Amendment:
All men and women,
age 21+

92.6%

1971

26th Amendment:
All men and women,
age 18+

99.9%

*Percentages are of the adult (18+) population. These figures are approximate
for 1789 and 1869. The votings rights of convicted felons are restricted in
some states and of noncitizens in all states.

SOURCES: U.S. Census of Population and Housing, 1790–2010,
www.census.gov/prod/www/decennial.html (accessed 9/28/15);
United States Elections Project, www.electproject.org/national-1789–present
(accessed 9/27/15).

WHAT YOU CAN DO

Know Your Constitutional Rights

 Review your rights as outlined in the Constitution, a copy of which is reproduced in the appendix of this book.

 Find out what voting rights are retained by individuals who have been convicted of a felony. Go to **www.ncsl.org** and search "felon voting rights" for more information.

 Find out what voting rights are retained by individuals with mental illness. Go to **www.bazelon.org** and search "voting" for more information.

Should noncitizens (such as longtime permanent legal residents) have the right to vote? Go to **www.latimes.com/citizenship** to read more and to join the conversation online.

★ STUDY GUIDE ★

Practice Quiz

1. How did the British attempt to raise revenue in the North American colonies? *(p. 34)*
   a) income taxes
   b) tariffs, duties, and other taxes on commerce
   c) expropriation and sale of Native American lands
   d) licensing fees for the mining of natural resources
   e) requests for voluntary donations

2. In their fight against British taxes such as the Stamp Act and the Sugar Act of 1764, New England merchants and southern planters allied with which of the following groups? *(pp. 34–35)*
   a) shopkeepers, small farmers, laborers, and artisans
   b) shopkeepers only
   c) laborers only
   d) artisans only
   e) shopkeepers and laborers only

3. The first governing document in the United States was *(p. 37)*
   a) the Declaration of Independence.
   b) the Articles of Confederation.
   c) the Constitution.
   d) the Bill of Rights.
   e) the Virginia Plan.

4. Who was responsible for executing laws passed by the national government under the Articles of Confederation? *(p. 37)*
   a) the presidency
   b) the Congress
   c) the states
   d) the federal judiciary
   e) the federal bureaucracy

5. Which event led directly to the Constitutional Convention by providing evidence that the government created under the Articles of Confederation was unable to act decisively in times of national crisis? *(pp. 39–40)*
   a) the Boston Massacre
   b) the Boston Tea Party
   c) Shays's Rebellion
   d) the Annapolis Convention
   e) the War of 1812

6. Which state's proposal embodied a principle of representing states in the Congress according to their size and wealth? *(p. 41)*
   a) Connecticut
   b) Maryland
   c) New Jersey
   d) Rhode Island
   e) Virginia

7. The agreement reached at the Constitutional Convention that determined that every five slaves would be counted as three free persons for the purposes of taxation and representation in the House of Representatives was called the *(pp. 42–43)*
   a) Virginia Plan.
   b) New Jersey Plan.
   c) Connecticut Compromise.
   d) Three-Fifths Compromise.
   e) Great Compromise.

8. Which of the following mechanisms were in the Congress to guard against "excessive democracy"? *(p. 44)*
   a) bicameralism
   b) staggered terms in office

   c) appointment of senators for long terms
   d) indirect election of the president
   e) all of the above

9. Which of the following best describes the Supreme Court as understood by the Founders? *(p. 47)*
   a) the body that would choose the president
   b) the principle check on presidential power
   c) arbiter of disputes within the Congress
   d) a figurehead commission of elders
   e) the highest court of both the national government and the states

10. Theorists such as Montesquieu referred to the system of giving each branch of government a distinctly different constituency as *(p. 50)*
    a) a mixed regime.
    b) a confederation.
    c) a bicameral structure.
    d) a limited government.
    e) a federalist arrangement.

11. Which of the following were the Antifederalists most concerned with? *(p. 51)*
    a) interstate commerce
    b) the protection of property
    c) the distinction between principles and interests
    d) the potential for tyranny in the central government
    e) abolishing slavery

12. Which of the following best describes the process of amending the Constitution? *(p. 56)*
    a) It is difficult and has rarely been used successfully to address specific public problems.
    b) It is difficult and has frequently been used successfully to address specific public problems.
    c) It is easy and has rarely been used successfully to address specific public problems.
    d) It is easy and has frequently been used successfully to address specific public problems.
    e) It is easy, but it has never been used for any purpose.

Key Terms

amendment *(p. 56)* a change added to a bill, law, or constitution

Antifederalists *(p. 51)* those who favored strong state governments and a weak national government and were opponents of the constitution proposed at the American Constitutional Convention of 1787

Articles of Confederation *(p. 37)* America's first written constitution; served as the basis for America's national government until 1789

bicameral *(p. 44)* having a legislative assembly composed of two chambers or houses; distinguished from *unicameral*

Bill of Rights *(p. 44)* the first 10 amendments to the Constitution, ratified in 1791; they ensure certain rights and liberties of the people

checks and balances *(p. 44)* mechanisms through which each branch of government is able to participate in and influence the activities of the other branches. Major examples include the presidential veto power over congressional legislation, the power of the Senate to approve presidential appointments, and judicial review of congressional enactments

confederation *(p. 38)* a system of government in which states retain sovereign authority except for the powers expressly delegated to the national government

elastic clause *(p. 46)* Article I, Section 8, of the Constitution (also known as the *necessary and proper clause*), which declares that Congress can write laws needed to carry out its expressed powers, providing Congress with the authority to make all laws "necessary and proper" to do so

electoral college *(p. 44)* the electors from each state who meet after the popular election to cast ballots for president and vice president

expressed powers *(p. 46)* specific powers granted by the Constitution to Congress (Article I, Section 8) and to the president (Article II)

federalism *(p. 44)* a system of government in which power is divided, by a constitution, between the central (national) government and regional (state) governments

Federalist Papers *(p. 52)* a series of essays written by James Madison, Alexander Hamilton, and John Jay supporting the ratification of the Constitution

Federalists *(p. 51)* those who favored a strong national government and supported the constitution proposed at the American Constitutional Convention of 1787

Great Compromise *(p. 42)* the agreement reached at the Constitutional Convention of 1787 that gave each state an equal number of senators regardless of its population but linked representation in the House of Representatives to population

judicial review *(p. 47)* the power of the courts to review and, if necessary, declare actions of the legislative and executive branches invalid or unconstitutional. The Supreme Court asserted this power in *Marbury v. Madison* (1803)

limited government *(p. 53)* a principle of constitutional government; a government whose powers are defined and limited by a constitution

New Jersey Plan *(p. 41)* a framework for the Constitution, introduced by William Paterson, that called for equal state representation in the national legislature regardless of population

separation of powers *(p. 44)* the division of governmental power among several institutions that must cooperate in decision-making

supremacy clause *(p. 48)* Article VI of the Constitution, which states that laws passed by the national government and all treaties "shall be the supreme law of the land" and superior to all laws adopted by any state or any subdivision

Three-Fifths Compromise *(p. 43)* the agreement reached at the Constitutional Convention of 1787 that stipulated that for purposes of the apportionment of congressional seats only three-fifths of slaves would be counted

tyranny *(p. 53)* oppressive and unjust government that employs cruel and unjust use of power and authority

Virginia Plan *(p. 41)* a framework for the Constitution, introduced by Edmund Randolph, that called for representation in the national legislature based on the population of each state

For Further Reading

Ackerman, Erin, and Benjamin Ginsberg. *A Guide to the United States Constitution*. 4th ed. New York: W. W. Norton, 2019.

Beeman, Richard. *Plain, Honest Men: The Making of the American Constitution*. New York: Random House, 2009.

Chernow, Ron. *Alexander Hamilton*. New York: Penguin Books, 2005.

Ellis, Joseph. *The Quartet: Orchestrating the Second American Revolution*. New York: Knopf, 2015.

Gerstle, Gary. *Liberty and Coercion: The Paradox of American Government from the Founding to the Present*. Princeton, NJ: Princeton University Press, 2015.

Hamilton, Alexander, James Madison, and John Jay. *The Federalist Papers*. Edited by Isaac Kramnick. New York: Viking, 1987.

Jensen, Merrill. *The Articles of Confederation*. Madison: University of Wisconsin Press, 1963.

Paulson, Michael S, and Luke Paulson. *The Constitution: An Introduction*. New York: Basic Books, 2017.

Storing, Herbert, ed. *The Complete Anti-Federalist*. 7 vols. Chicago: University of Chicago Press, 1981.

Wood, Gordon S. *Empire of Liberty: A History of the Early Republic*. New York: Oxford University Press, 2011.

Federalism

WHAT GOVERNMENT DOES AND WHY IT MATTERS

Decades of work as a commercial fisherman and long-haul truck driver left Larry Harvey with severe pain. The 70-year-old grandfather found one thing that helped: medical marijuana, which was legalized in the state of Washington in 1998. He and his wife included cannabis among the many herbs they grew on their property outside a little town some 80 miles north of Spokane.

One hot August day in 2012, armed federal agents stormed the Harveys' home. Harvey was handcuffed and sent to jail, despite his poor health and advanced age. Prosecutors said guns had been found along with the marijuana. A judge released him 17 days later, but the lack of health care in jail caused his gout to flare up and left him unable to walk more than short distances.[1]

Washington State, along with 32 other states and the District of Columbia, protect qualified medical marijuana patients from arrest and prosecution (as of 2018, 10 states permit the use of recreational marijuana as well).[2]

Federalism is at the center of a national debate over marijuana policy: while marijuana remains illegal under federal law, some states permit marijuana for medicinal or recreational use. Larry Harvey, pictured here, was prosecuted under federal law for growing marijuana though Washington state allowed the practice.

Yet under federal law marijuana is classified as a Schedule I controlled substance, in the same category as heroin, LSD, and MDMA ("ecstasy"). Users are subject to arrest and prosecution by the federal Drug Enforcement Administration. Thus medical marijuana patients like Harvey are caught in a clash between state and federal law. States can legalize medical marijuana, and medical marijuana defenses can be mounted in state courts, but federal law considers marijuana a dangerous drug with no medical value; evidence about the medical necessity of marijuana for patient-defendants cannot even be admitted in federal court.[3]

The federal response to the states has shifted over time. As state laws began to loosen restrictions on marijuana starting in the late 1990s, the federal government at first sought to assert its authority, raiding marijuana clinics and individual homes like Harvey's. In 2005 the Supreme Court ruled that these federal actions were constitutional. By 2013, however, the Justice Department under President Obama stated that it would not challenge state laws so long as the states maintained a close watch over their marijuana markets. Instead the federal government would focus its enforcement efforts on specific issues, including trafficking by gangs, sales to minors, and selling across state lines. It remains to be seen whether marijuana will be a focus of a possibly renewed War on Drugs in the Trump administration.[4]

Larry Harvey's situation and the debates about marijuana policy engage some of the oldest questions in American government: What is the responsibility of the federal government, and what is the responsibility of the states? When should there be uniformity across the states, and when is it better to let the states adopt their own laws based on the preferences of their population, which may result in a diverse set of laws across the nation? The United States is a federal system, in which the national government shares power with lower levels of government. Throughout American history, lawmakers, politicians, and citizens have wrestled with questions about how responsibilities should be allocated across the different levels of government. Some responsibilities, such as foreign policy, clearly lie with the federal government. Others, such as divorce laws, are controlled by state governments. Many government responsibilities are shared in American federalism and require cooperation among local, state, and federal governments. The debate about "who should do what" remains one of the most important discussions in American politics.

CHAPTER GOALS

★ **Describe what the Constitution says about the powers of the national government and of the states (pp. 69–72)**

★ **Trace developments in the federal framework leading to a stronger national government (pp. 73–84)**

★ **Analyze the changing role of states in the federal framework (pp. 85–89)**

Federalism Shapes American Politics

The Constitution has had a profound influence on American life through **federalism**, the division of powers and functions between the national government and the state governments. Governments can organize power in a variety of ways. One of the most important distinctions is between unitary and federal governments. In a **unitary system**, the central government makes the important decisions and lower levels of government have little independent power. In such systems, lower levels of government primarily implement decisions made by the central government. In France, for example, the central government was once so involved in the smallest details of local activity that the minister of education boasted that by looking at his watch he could tell what all French schoolchildren were learning at that moment because the central government set the school curriculum. In a **federal system**, by contrast, the central government shares power or functions with lower levels of government, such as regions or states. Nations with diverse ethnic or language groupings, such as Switzerland and Canada, are most likely to have federal arrangements. In federal systems, lower levels of government often have significant independent power to set policy in some areas, such as education and social programs, and to impose taxes. Yet the specific ways in which power is shared vary greatly: no two federal systems are exactly the same.

FEDERALISM COMES FROM THE CONSTITUTION

The United States was the first nation to adopt federalism as its governing framework. With federalism, the framers sought to limit the national government by creating a second layer of state governments. American federalism thus recognized two sovereigns in the original Constitution by granting a few "expressed powers" to the national government and reserving the rest to the states.

The Powers of the National Government As we saw in Chapter 2, the **expressed powers** granted to the national government are found in Article I, Section 8, of the Constitution. These 17 powers include the powers to collect taxes, coin money, declare war, and regulate commerce. Article I, Section 8, also contains another important source of power for the national government: the **implied powers** that enable Congress "to make all Laws which shall be necessary and proper for carrying into Execution the foregoing Powers." Such powers are not specifically expressed but are *implied* through the expansive interpretation of delegated powers. Not until several decades after the Founding did the Supreme Court allow Congress to exercise the power granted in this **necessary and proper clause**, but as we shall see later in this chapter, this doctrine allowed the national government to expand considerably the scope of its authority, although the process was a slow one.

Aside from these powers, the federal government operates with one other advantage over the states: as mentioned in the last chapter, Article VI of the Constitution says that whenever there is a conflict between a national law and a state law, the national law shall prevail. This doctrine of *national supremacy* says that "[t]his Constitution, and the Laws of the United States . . . and all Treaties made . . . shall be the supreme Law of the Land," even extending to state courts and constitutions.

The Powers of State Government One way in which the framers sought to preserve a strong role for the states was through the Tenth Amendment to the Constitution. The Tenth Amendment states that the powers that the Constitution does not delegate to the national government or prohibit to the states are "reserved to the States respectively, or to the people." The Antifederalists, who feared that a strong central government would encroach on individual liberty, repeatedly pressed for such an amendment as a way of limiting national power. The Federalists agreed to the amendment because they did not think it would do much harm, given the powers of the Constitution already granted to the national government. The Tenth Amendment is also called the "**reserved powers** amendment" because it aims to reserve powers to the states.

The most fundamental power that the states retain is that of coercion—the power to develop and enforce criminal codes, to administer health and safety rules, and to regulate the family via marriage and divorce laws. The states have the power to regulate individuals' livelihoods; if you're a doctor or a lawyer or a plumber or a hairstylist, you must be licensed by the state. Even more fundamentally, the states have the power to define private property—private property exists because state laws against trespass define who is and is not entitled to use a piece of property. If you own a car, your ownership isn't worth much unless the state is willing to enforce your right to possession by making it a crime for anyone else to drive your car without your permission. These laws are essential to citizens' everyday lives, and the powers of the states regarding such domestic issues are much greater than the powers of the national government.

A state's authority to regulate the health, safety, and morals of its citizens is commonly referred to as the **police power** of the state. Policing is what states do—they coerce you in the name of the community in order to maintain public order. And this was exactly the type of power that the Founders intended the states, rather than the federal government, to exercise.

In some areas, the states share **concurrent power** (authority possessed by *both* state and national governments) with the national government, whereby they retain and share some power to regulate commerce and to affect the currency—for example, by being able to charter banks, grant or deny corporate charters, grant or deny licenses to engage in a business or practice a trade, and regulate the quality of products or the conditions of labor. Wherever there is a direct conflict of laws between the federal and the state levels, the issue will most likely be resolved in favor of national supremacy.

States' Obligations to One Another The Constitution also creates obligations among the states. These obligations, spelled out in Article IV, were intended to promote national unity. By requiring the states to recognize actions and decisions taken in other states as legal and proper, the framers aimed to make the states less like independent countries and more like parts of a single nation.

Article IV, Section 1, establishes the **full faith and credit clause**, stipulating that each state is normally expected to honor the "public Acts, Records, and judicial Proceedings" that take place in any other state. So, for example, if a person has a restraining order placed on a stalker or batterer in one state, the other states are required to enforce that order as if they had issued it.

Until recently, the full faith and credit clause was embroiled in the controversy over same-sex marriage. In 2004, Massa-

Previously a state-level policy, same-sex marriage was declared a fundamental right nationwide by the Supreme Court in 2015. The decision prompted a brief backlash when clerks in some states, such as Kim Davis from Kentucky, pictured here, refused to issue marriage licenses to same-sex couples.

chusetts became the first state to legalize gay marriage. By 2015, 37 states plus the District of Columbia had legalized gay marriage, and 13 states had either state constitutional amendments or laws that barred same-sex marriage.[5] The principle of full faith and credit would seem to suggest that states without same-sex marriage would be obliged to recognize such unions in their states, just as they would recognize heterosexual marriages performed in other states. But to forestall this possibility, in 1996, Congress passed the Defense of Marriage Act (DOMA), which declared that states did not have to recognize same-sex marriage even if it were legal in other states. DOMA also said that the federal government would not recognize same-sex marriage, even if legal in some states, and that same-sex partners were not eligible for federal benefits such as Medicare and Social Security. In 2013, however, the Supreme Court in *United States v. Windsor* struck down part of the DOMA, ordering that same-sex married couples receive equal treatment on issues relating to taxes, inheritance, and other federal laws.[6] It also opened the door for same-sex couples to receive federal social benefits on the same terms as heterosexual married couples. The court did not rule on whether states have to recognize same-sex marriages in other states.

On the second anniversary of the *Windsor* ruling, the Supreme Court, in a historic and long-awaited decision, ruled that the Fourteenth Amendment guaranteed a fundamental right to same-sex marriage. The case, *Obergefell v. Hodges*, combined four lawsuits by same-sex couples challenging their home states' refusals to grant same-sex marriage licenses or recognize same-sex marriages performed out of state. While 37 states recognized same-sex marriage on the eve of the *Obergefell* announcement, the Court's 5–4 decision immediately required that all 50 states must offer marriage licenses to two people of the same sex and recognize same-sex marriages licensed out of state. In one stroke, same-sex marriage turned from a state-level policy choice to a nationally recognized right. In the aftermath of the *Obergefell* decision, several of the 13 states that were mandated to lift their bans on same-sex marriage protested the ruling. However, such resistance ebbed as it became clear that the courts would enforce the constitutional right to same-sex marriage.

Article IV, Section 2, known as the "comity clause," also seeks to promote national unity. This clause provides that citizens enjoying the "**privileges and immunities**" of one state should be entitled to similar treatment in other states. What this has come to mean is that a state cannot discriminate against someone from another state or give special privileges to its own residents. For example, in the 1970s, when Alaska passed a law that gave residents preference over nonresidents in obtaining work on the state's oil and gas pipelines, the Supreme Court ruled the law illegal because it discriminated against citizens of other states.[7] The comity clause also regulates criminal justice among the states by requiring states to return fugitives to the states from which they have fled. Thus, in 1952, when an inmate escaped from an Alabama prison and sought to avoid being returned to Alabama on the grounds that he was being subjected to "cruel and unusual punishment" there, the Supreme Court ruled that he must be returned according to Article IV, Section 2.[8]

Local Government and the Constitution Local government occupies a peculiar but very important place in the American system (Table 3.1). In fact, the status of American local government is probably unique in world experience. First, local government has no status in the U.S. Constitution and is therefore an authority or function under the control of the states. *State* legislatures created local governments, and *state* constitutions and laws permit local governments to take on some of the responsibilities of the state governments. Most states amended their constitutions to give their larger cities **home rule**, powers delegated by the state to a local unit of government to manage its own affairs. Local governments have always been creatures of the states.[9] In recent years, some local governments have passed laws making policy on matters from minimum wage to public broadband, only to have state legislatures preempt, or remove, that authority, illustrating the degree to which local governments are creations of the state.

TABLE 3.1

90,107 Governments in the United States

TYPE	NUMBER
National	1
State	50
County	3,031
Municipal	19,519
Townships	16,360
School districts	12,880
Other special districts	38,266

SOURCE: U.S. Census Bureau, www2.census.gov/govs/cog/g12_org.pdf (accessed 11/02/13).

The Definition of Federalism Has Changed Radically over Time

> **Trace developments in the federal framework leading to a stronger national government**

Many of the fiercest political controversies in American history have revolved around competing views of federalism. The best way to understand these disputes, and how federalism has been redefined throughout American history, is to examine how its conception has changed over time. From 1789 to 1937, the political scales clearly favored the states over the federal government. Then, from the New Deal period of the 1930s to the present, some important limits were placed on state governments and the federal government exerted far more power than it had under the traditional system. Over the last 80 years, even as the trend has been toward centralization of government power, the states have asserted themselves at certain times and in certain policy areas, sometimes aided by the courts. At other moments a crisis shifts power toward the national government again, as during the September 11, 2001, terror attacks and the fiscal crisis that began in 2008.

FEDERALISM UNDER THE "TRADITIONAL SYSTEM" GAVE MOST POWERS TO THE STATES

The prevailing view of national government–state government relations under the traditional system was one of **dual federalism**. During this time, the states possessed a vast amount of governing power, and virtually all of the important policies affecting the lives of Americans were made by the state governments. For evidence, look at Table 3.2, which lists the major types of public policies by which Americans were governed for the first century and a half under the Constitution. Under this traditional system, the national government was quite small by comparison both with the state governments and with the governments of other Western nations. It was also very narrowly specialized in the functions it performed. The national government built or sponsored the construction of roads, canals, and bridges (internal improvements). It provided cash subsidies to shippers and shipbuilders and distributed free or low-priced public land to encourage western settlement and business ventures. It placed relatively heavy taxes on imported goods (tariffs), not only to raise revenues but also to protect "infant industries" from competition from the more advanced European enterprises. It protected patents and provided for a common currency, which encouraged and facilitated enterprises and helped to expand markets.

What do these functions of the national government reveal? First, virtually all the national government's functions were aimed at assisting commerce. Second, virtually none of the national government's policies directly coerced citizens. The emphasis of governmental programs was on assistance, promotion, and encouragement—the allocation of land or capital to meet the needs of economic development.

TABLE 3.2

The Federal System: Specialization of Governmental Functions, 1789–1937

NATIONAL GOVERNMENT POLICIES (DOMESTIC)	STATE GOVERNMENT POLICIES	LOCAL GOVERNMENT POLICIES
Internal improvements	Property laws (including slavery)	Adaptation of state laws to local conditions
Subsidies	Estate and inheritance laws	
Tariffs	Commerce laws	Public works
Public land disposal	Banking and credit laws	Contracts for public works
Patents	Corporate laws	
Currency	Insurance laws	Licensing of public accommodation
	Family laws	
	Morality laws	Zoning and other land-use regulation
	Public health laws	
	Education laws	Basic public services
	General penal laws	
	Eminent domain laws	
	Construction codes	
	Land-use laws	
	Water and mineral laws	
	Criminal procedure laws	
	Electoral and political party laws	
	Local government laws	
	Civil service laws	
	Occupations and professions laws	

Meanwhile, state legislatures were also actively involved in economic regulation during the nineteenth century. In the United States, then and now, private property exists only in state laws and state court decisions regarding property, trespass, and real estate. American capitalism took its form from state property and trespass laws and from state laws and court decisions regarding contracts, markets, credit, banking, incorporation, and insurance. Laws concerning slavery were a subdivision of property law in states where slavery existed. The practice of important professions, such as law and medicine, was (and is) illegal except as provided for by state law. Most criminal laws, from trespass to murder, have been state laws, as are requirements regarding the education of children. Thus, most of the fundamental governing in the United States was done by the states.

Ultimately, the fundamental impact of federalism on the way the United States is governed comes not from any particular provision of the Constitution but from the framework itself, which has determined the flow of government functions and, through that, the political development of the country. By allowing state governments to do most of the fundamental governing, the Constitution saved the national government from many policy decisions that might have proved too divisive for a large and very young country. In helping the national government remain small and apart from the most divisive issues of the day, federalism contributed significantly to the political stability of the young nation, even as the social, economic, and political systems of many of the states and regions of the country were undergoing tremendous, profound, and sometimes violent change.[10] As we shall see, some important aspects of federalism have changed, but the federal framework has survived over two centuries and through a devastating civil war.

THE SUPREME COURT PAVED THE WAY FOR THE END OF THE EARLY FEDERAL SYSTEM

As the nation grew, disputes arose about the powers of the federal government versus the powers of the states. In the first several decades after the Founding, the Supreme Court decided several critical cases that expanded federal powers and facilitated trade across the states. These decisions removed barriers to trade in the new nation and laid the groundwork for a national economy. However, by the end of the nineteenth century, as reformers began to enact laws regulating businesses through such measures as child labor restrictions, the Court took a much more restrictive view of federal power. Not until well into the New Deal, in 1937, did the federal government gain the expansive powers it exercises today.

Article I, Section 8, of the Constitution delegates to Congress the power "to regulate Commerce with foreign Nations, and among the several States and with the Indian Tribes." For most of the nineteenth century, the Supreme Court consistently interpreted this **commerce clause** in favor of national power over the economy. The first and most important such case was *McCulloch v. Maryland* (1819), which involved the question of whether Congress had the power to charter a national bank as such an explicit grant of power was nowhere to be found in Article I, Section 8.[11] Chief Justice John Marshall answered that this power could be "implied" from other powers that were expressly delegated to Congress, such as the "powers to lay and collect taxes; to borrow money; to regulate commerce; and to declare and conduct a war."

By allowing Congress to use the necessary and proper clause to interpret its delegated powers expansively, the Supreme Court created the potential for an unprecedented increase in national government power. Marshall also concluded that whenever a state law conflicted with a federal law (as in the case of *McCulloch v. Maryland*), the state law would be deemed invalid since the Constitution states that "the Laws of the United States...shall be the supreme Law of the Land." Both parts of this great case are pro-national, including the verification of the principle of "national supremacy," yet Congress did not immediately seek to expand the policies of the national government.

Another major case, *Gibbons v. Ogden* (1824), reinforced this nationalistic interpretation of the Constitution. The important but relatively narrow issue was whether the state of New York could grant a monopoly to Robert Fulton's steamboat company to operate an exclusive service between New York and New Jersey. Chief Justice Marshall argued that New York State did not have the power to grant this particular monopoly. In reaching this decision, Marshall had to define what Article I, Section 8, meant by "commerce among the several states." He insisted that the definition was "comprehensive," extending to "every species of commercial intercourse." However, this comprehensiveness was limited "to that commerce which concerns more states than one." *Gibbons* is important because it established the supremacy of the national government in all matters affecting what later came to be called "interstate commerce."[12] But the precise meaning of interstate commerce would remain uncertain during several decades of constitutional discourse. Backed by the implied powers and national supremacy decision in *McCulloch* and by the broad definition of "interstate commerce" in *Gibbons*, Article I, Section 8, was a source of power for the national government as long as Congress sought to facilitate commerce through subsidies, services, and land grants.

Later in the nineteenth century, though, the Supreme Court declared any effort of the national government to *regulate* commerce in such areas as fraud, the production of substandard goods, the use of child labor, or the existence of dangerous working conditions or long hours to be unconstitutional as a violation of the concept of interstate commerce. Such legislation meant that the federal government was entering the factory and the workplace—local areas—and was attempting to regulate goods that had not yet passed into interstate commerce. To enter these local workplaces was to exercise police power—a power reserved to the states. No one questioned the power of the national government to regulate businesses that intrinsically involved interstate commerce, such as railroads, gas pipelines, and waterway transportation. But well into the twentieth century, the Supreme Court used the concept of interstate commerce as a barrier against most efforts by Congress to regulate local conditions.

This interpretation of federalism gave the American economy a freedom from federal government control that closely approximated the ideal of free enterprise. The economy was never entirely free, of course; in fact, entrepreneurs themselves did not want complete freedom from government. Between the Civil War and the 1930s, the federal government aided business by providing law and order; a stable currency; roads, canals, and railroads; and the courts and police necessary to enforce contracts and prevent trespass. But federalism, as interpreted by the Supreme Court for 70 years after the Civil War, made it possible for business to have its cake and eat it, too. Entrepreneurs enjoyed the benefits of national policies facilitating commerce but were shielded by the courts from policies that regulate commerce by protecting the rights of consumers and workers.[13] In addition, the Tenth Amendment was used to bolster arguments about **states' rights**, the principle that the states should oppose the increasing authority of the national government. This principle was most popular in the period before the Civil War.

In the early twentieth century, however, the Tenth Amendment appeared to lose its force as reformers began to press for national regulations to limit the power of large corporations and to protect the health and welfare of citizens, as we shall see next.

FDR'S NEW DEAL REMADE THE GOVERNMENT

The New Deal of the 1930s marked a major change in how the courts interpreted national power. The door to increased federal action opened when states proved unable to cope with the demands brought on by the Great Depression. Before the depression, states and localities took responsibility for addressing the needs of the poor, usually through private charity. But the extent of the depression quickly exhausted local and state capacities. By 1932, 25 percent of the workforce was unemployed. The jobless lost their homes and settled into camps all over the country, called "Hoovervilles" after President Herbert Hoover. Elected in 1928, the year before the depression hit, Hoover steadfastly maintained that there was little the federal government could do to alleviate these people's misery caused by the depression. It was a matter for state and local governments, he said.

Yet demands mounted for the federal government to take action. When Franklin Delano Roosevelt took office in 1933, he energetically threw the federal government into the business of fighting the depression through a number of proposals known collectively as the New Deal. He proposed a variety of temporary measures to provide federal relief and work programs. Most of the programs he proposed were to be financed by the federal government but administered by the states. In addition to these temporary measures, Roosevelt presided over the creation of several important federal programs designed to provide future economic security for Americans. The New Deal signaled the rise of a more active national government.

For the most part, the new national programs that the Roosevelt administration developed did not directly take power away from the states. Instead, Washington typically redirected states by offering them grants-in-aid, programs through which Congress provided money to state and local governments on the condition that the funds be employed for purposes defined by the federal government.

Franklin Roosevelt did not invent the idea of grants-in-aid, but his New Deal vastly expanded the range of grants-in-aid to include social programs, providing grants to the states for financial assistance to poor children. Congress added more grants after World War II, creating new programs to help states fund activities such as providing school lunches and building highways. Sometimes the national government required state or local governments to match the national contribution dollar for dollar, but in some programs,

John C. Calhoun, one of the most prominent advocates of states' rights, argued that states should have the right to veto any federal law they found to be unconstitutional.

The New Deal expanded the scope of the federal government. One of the largest and most effective New Deal programs, the Works Progress Administration, employed millions of Americans in public-works projects such as constructing highways, bridges, and public parks.

such as the development of the interstate highway system, the congressional grants provided 90 percent of the cost.

These types of federal grants-in-aid are called **categorical grants** because they are given to states and localities by the national government on the condition that expenditures be limited to a problem or group specified by law. For the most part, the categorical grants created before the 1960s simply helped the states perform their traditional functions.[14] In the 1960s, however, the national role expanded and federal funding in the form of categorical grants increased dramatically (see Figure 3.1). The grants authorized during the 1960s addressed national purposes much more strongly than did earlier grants. One of the most important—and expensive—was the federal Medicaid program, which provides states with grants to pay for medical care for the poor, the disabled, and many nursing home residents. Over time the value of categorical grants has risen dramatically, increasing from $2.3 billion in 1950 to an estimated $675 billion in 2017.

CHANGING COURT INTERPRETATIONS OF FEDERALISM HELPED THE NEW DEAL WHILE PRESERVING STATES' RIGHTS

In a dramatic change beginning in 1937, the Supreme Court threw out the old distinction between interstate and intrastate commerce on which it had relied in the late 1800s and early 1900s. It converted the commerce clause from a source of limitations to a source of power for the national government. The Court began to refuse to review appeals that challenged acts of Congress protecting the rights of employees to organize and engage in collective bargaining, regulating the amount of farmland in cultivation, extending low-interest credit to small businesses and farmers, and restricting the activities of corporations dealing in the stock market; it upheld many other laws that contributed to the construction of the modern "welfare state."[15]

The Court also reversed its position on the Tenth Amendment, which it had used to strike down national laws as violations of state power. Instead, the Court

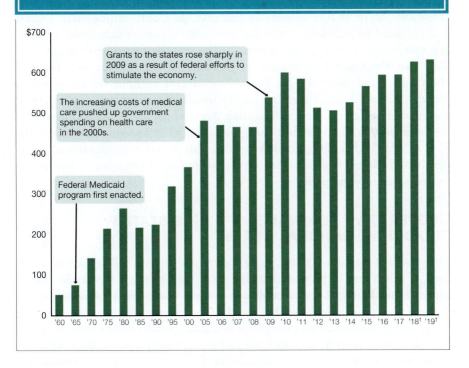

FIGURE 3.1

Historical Trend of Federal Grants-in-Aid,*
1960–2019 (in billions of dollars)**

Spending on federal grants-in-aid to the states and local governments has grown dramatically since 1990. These increases reflect the growing public expectations about what government should do. What has been the most important cause of the steady increase in these grants?

*Excludes outlays for national defense and international affairs.
**Data in constant (fiscal year 2009) dollars.
†Data for 2018 and 2019 are estimated.

SOURCE: Office of Management and Budget, U.S. Budget for Fiscal Year 2019, Historical Tables: Table 12.1, Summary Comparison of Total Outlays for Grants to State and Local Governments: 1940-2023, www.whitehouse.gov/omb/historical-tables/ (accessed 6/8/18).

Grants to the states rose sharply in 2009 as a result of federal efforts to stimulate the economy.

The increasing costs of medical care pushed up government spending on health care in the 2000s.

Federal Medicaid program first enacted.

approved numerous expansions of national power, to such an extent that the Tenth Amendment appeared irrelevant. In fact, in 1941, Justice Harlan Fiske Stone declared that the Tenth Amendment was simply a "truism" that had no real meaning.[16]

Yet the idea that some powers should be reserved to the states did not go away. Indeed, in the 1950s southern opponents of the civil rights movement revived the idea of states' rights. In 1956, 96 southern members of Congress issued a "Southern Manifesto" in which they declared that southern states were not constitutionally bound by Supreme Court decisions outlawing racial segregation. They believed that states' rights should override individual rights to liberty and formal equality. With the triumph of the civil rights movement, the slogan of "states' rights" became tarnished by its association with racial inequality.

The 1990s saw a revival of interest in the Tenth Amendment and important Supreme Court decisions limiting federal power. Much of the interest in the Tenth Amendment stemmed from conservatives who believe that a strong federal government encroaches on individual liberties. They believed such freedoms were better protected by returning more power to the states through the process of **devolution**, whereby a program is removed from one level of government by delegating it or passing it down to a lower level of government, such as from the national government to the state and local governments. In 1996, Republican presidential candidate Bob Dole carried a copy of the Tenth Amendment in his pocket as he campaigned, pulling it out to read at rallies.[17]

The Supreme Court's 1995 ruling in *United States v. Lopez* fueled further interest in the Tenth Amendment. In that case, the Court, stating that Congress had exceeded its authority under the commerce clause, struck down a federal law that barred handguns near schools.[18] This was the first time since the New Deal that the Court had limited congressional powers in this way. In 1997 the Court again relied on the Tenth Amendment to limit federal power in *Printz v. United States*.[19] The decision declared unconstitutional a provision of the Brady Handgun Violence Prevention Act that required state and local law-enforcement officials to conduct background checks on handgun purchasers. The Court declared that this provision violated state sovereignty guaranteed in the Tenth Amendment because it required state and local officials to administer a federal regulatory program.

COOPERATIVE FEDERALISM PUSHES STATES TO ACHIEVE NATIONAL GOALS

The growth of categorical grants, along with favorable court rulings, created a new kind of federalism. If the traditional system of two sovereigns performing highly different functions could be called dual federalism, historians of federalism suggest that the system since the New Deal could be called **cooperative federalism**, in which grants-in-aid have been used strategically to encourage states and localities to pursue nationally defined goals, with national and state governments sharing powers and resources via intergovernmental cooperation. One political scientist characterized this as a move from "layer cake federalism" to "marble cake federalism,"[20] in which intergovernmental cooperation and sharing have blurred a once-clear distinguishing line, making it difficult to say where the national government ends and the state and local governments begin (see Figure 3.2).

For a while in the 1960s, it appeared as if the state governments would become increasingly irrelevant to American federalism. Many of the new federal grants bypassed the states and instead sent money directly to local governments and even to local nonprofit organizations. The theme heard repeatedly in Washington was that the states simply could not be trusted to carry out national purposes.[21]

FIGURE 3.2

Dual versus Cooperative Federalism

In layer-cake federalism, the responsibilities of the national government and state governments are clearly separated. In marble-cake federalism, national policies, state policies, and local policies overlap in many areas.

DUAL FEDERALISM

National Government

State Governments

"Layer Cake"

Cooperate on some policies

COOPERATIVE FEDERALISM

National Government

State Governments

"Marble Cake"

One of the reasons that Washington distrusted the states was the way African American citizens were treated in the South. The southern states' forthright defense of segregation, justified on the grounds of states' rights, tarnished the image of the states as the civil rights movement gained momentum. The national officials who planned the War on Poverty during the 1960s pointed to the racial exclusion practiced in the southern states as a reason for bypassing state governments. Political scientist James Sundquist described their thinking: "In the drafting of the Economic Opportunity Act, an 'Alabama syndrome' developed. Any suggestion within the poverty task force that the states be given a role in the administration of the act was met with the question, 'Do you want to give that kind of power to [then–Alabama governor] George Wallace?'"[22] (Wallace at the time was nationally known for his virulent opposition to the civil rights movement.)

Yet even though many national policies of the 1960s bypassed the states, other new programs, such as Medicaid, relied on state governments for their implementation. In addition, as the national government expanded existing programs run by the states, states had to take on more responsibilities. These new responsibilities meant that the states were now playing a critical role in the federal system.

NATIONAL STANDARDS HAVE BEEN ADVANCED THROUGH FEDERAL PROGRAMS

Over time, the Supreme Court has pushed for greater uniformity in rules and procedures across the states. In addition to legal decisions, the national government uses two other tools to create similarities across the states: grants-in-aid and regulations.

Grants-in-aid, as we have seen, are incentives: Congress provides an incentive by giving money to state and local governments if they agree to spend it for the purposes Congress specifies. But as Congress in the 1970s began to enact legislation in new areas, such as environmental policy, it resorted to another tool: regulated federalism.[23] The national government began to set standards of conduct or to require the states to set standards that met national guidelines. The effect of these national standards is that state and local policies in the areas of environmental protection, social services, and education are more uniform from coast to coast than are other nationally funded policies.

Some national standards require the federal government to take over areas of regulation formerly overseen by state or local governments. Such **preemption** (the principle that allows the national government to override state or local actions in certain policy areas) occurs when state and local actions are found to be inconsistent with federal requirements. If this occurs, all regulations in the preempted area must henceforth come from the national government. In many cases, the courts determine the scope of the federal authority to preempt. For example, in 1973 the Supreme Court struck down a local ordinance prohibiting jets from taking off from the airport in Burbank, California, between 11 P.M. and 7 A.M. It ruled that the federal Civil Aeronautics Act granted the Federal Aviation Administration all authority over flight patterns, takeoffs, and landings and that local governments could not impose regulations in this area.

As federal regulations increased after the 1970s, Washington increasingly preempted state and local action in many different policy areas. After 1994, when Republicans retook control of Congress, the federal government used its preemption power in business's favor, limiting the ability of states to tax and regulate industry. For example, in 1998, Congress passed a law that prohibited states and localities from taxing internet access services. The 1996 Telecommunications Act reduced local control by giving broadcasters and digital companies broad discretion over where they could erect digital television and cellular phone towers even if local citizens objected.[24]

In 2009, after only a few months in office, President Obama reversed the Bush administration's use of federal regulations to limit state laws. Under the new policy, federal regulations should preempt state laws only in extraordinary cases. The president directed agency leaders to review the regulations that had been put in place over the previous 10 years and consider amending them if they interfered with the "legitimate prerogatives of the states."[25] But the Obama administration did use its power of preemption to challenge state immigration laws, charging that states were making laws in a domain reserved for federal authority.

The growth of national standards has created some new problems and has raised questions about how far federal standardization should go. One problem that emerged in the 1980s was the increase in **unfunded mandates**—regulations or new conditions for receiving grants that impose costs on state and local governments for which they are not reimbursed by the national government. The growth of unfunded mandates was the product of a Democratic Congress, which wanted to achieve liberal social objectives, and Republican presidents who opposed increased social spending. Between 1983 and 1991, Congress mandated standards in many policy areas, including social services and environmental regulations, without providing additional funds to

Cooperative Federalism: Competition or a Check on Power?

While the United States has evolved into a system of cooperative federalism, some democracies began that way. Germany's constitution, adopted in 1949, was designed to use a cooperative federal system to help prevent the abuses of central government power seen in Hitler's Germany. For example, the upper house of the German parliament comprises delegates from the Länder ("states") governments, giving the states an official check on all national policy.

The most interesting blending of power, however, is in taxation and spending. Unlike U.S. states, German states and local governments have no taxation powers, making them fully dependent on federal funding. However, German states are responsible for implementing most government policy. As a result, almost two-thirds of German government spending is carried out by states and local governments, compared to less than half of U.S. spending. This emphasis on local spending includes the running of Germany's extensive social security program, a complex system carried out at the national, state, and local levels. In the United States, comparable social spending is done by the national government or is left to Americans to pay out of pocket.

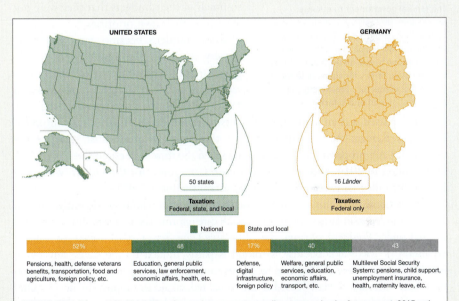

UNITED STATES

50 states

Taxation:
Federal, state, and local

GERMANY

16 *Länder*

Taxation:
Federal only

■ National ■ State and local

52%	48
Pensions, health, defense veterans benefits, transportation, food and agriculture, foreign policy, etc.	Education, general public services, law enforcement, economic affairs, health, etc.

17%	40	43
Defense, digital infrastructure, foreign policy	Welfare, general public services, education, economic affairs, transport, etc.	Multilevel Social Security System: pensions, child support, unemployment insurance, health, maternity leave, etc.

SOURCE: OECD, "Figure 2.42. Distribution of general government expenditures across levels of government, 2015 and 2016," Government at a Glance 2017, www.oecd-ilibrary.org/governance/government-at-a-glance-2017_gov_glance-2017-en; "Regional Policy Profile: United States," www.oecd.org/regional/regional-policy/profile-United-States.pdf and "Regional Policy Profile: Germany," www.oecd.org/regional/regional-policy/profile-Germnay.pdf (accessed 6/7/18).

2443

The federal government frequently passes laws that impose mandates on the states, such as the 1990 Americans with Disabilities Act, which protects against discrimination based on disability. States were required to pay for changes to meet federal standards for accessibility in public transportation and public facilities.

meet those standards. Altogether, Congress enacted 26 laws that imposed new regulations or required states to expand existing programs.[26] For example, the 1973 Rehabilitation Act prohibited discrimination against the disabled in programs that were partly funded by the federal government. The new law required state and local governments to make public transit accessible to disabled people with wheelchair lifts in buses, elevators in train stations, and special transportation systems where needed. These requirements were estimated to cost state and local governments $6.8 billion over 30 years.[27] But Congress did not supply additional funding to help states meet these new requirements; the states had to shoulder the increased financial burden themselves. States complained that mandates took up so much of their budgets that they were not able to set their own priorities.[28]

These burdens became part of a rallying cry to reduce the power of the federal government—a cry that took center stage when a Republican Congress was elected in 1994. One of the first measures the new Congress passed was an act to limit the cost of unfunded mandates, the Unfunded Mandates Reform Act (UMRA). Under this law, Congress must estimate the expense for any proposal it believes would exceed the threshold established in UMRA ($76 million in 2014, adjusted for inflation). Congress must then identify funding sources for bills that exceed the threshold established in UMRA.

New national problems inevitably raise the question of who pays. Recently, concern about unfunded mandates arose around health care reform. The major health care reform enacted under President Obama, the Affordable Care Act of 2010, called for a major expansion of Medicaid. Because Medicaid is partly funded by the states, any major increase in the number of Medicaid recipients could impose a significant fiscal burden on the states. Although the law provided additional federal aid to support the new requirements, the Medicaid provisions became a target for state challenges to the health care law. One of the central claims in the 26 states' lawsuits charged that the federal government did not have the power to withhold Medicaid funds from states that did not implement the new expansions. The Supreme Court ultimately ruled that states could decline to expand Medicaid coverage without losing their existing Medicaid funds. After the Court's decision, some Republican governors announced that they would not implement the expanded coverage. By late 2018, 36 states plus the District of Columbia had decided to expand Medicaid, and 14 had decided to not expand.

New Federalism Means More State Control

Analyze the changing role of the states in the federal framework

Since the 1970s, as states have become more capable of administering large-scale programs, the idea of devolution—transferring responsibility for policy from the federal government to the states and localities—has become popular.

Proponents of more state authority have looked to **block grants** as a way of reducing federal control. Block grants are federal grants-in-aid that allow states considerable discretion in how the funds are spent. Richard Nixon led the first push for block grants in the early 1970s. Nixon's approach consolidated programs in the areas of job training, community development, and social services into three large block grants. These grants imposed some conditions on states and localities as to how the money should be spent but avoided the narrow regulations contained in the categorical grants discussed earlier. In addition, Congress approved a fourth block grant called **general revenue sharing**, whereby the federal government provided money to local governments and counties with no strings attached; localities could spend the money as they wished. In enacting revenue sharing, Washington acknowledged both the critical role that state and local governments play in implementing national priorities and their need for increased funding and enhanced flexibility in order to carry out that role (see Figure 3.3). Ronald Reagan's version of **New Federalism**

The debate over national versus state control of speed limits arose in 1973, when gas prices skyrocketed and supplies became scarce. Drivers nationwide were forced to wait in long lines at gas stations. The federal government responded to the gas crisis by instituting a national 55-mile-per-hour speed limit.

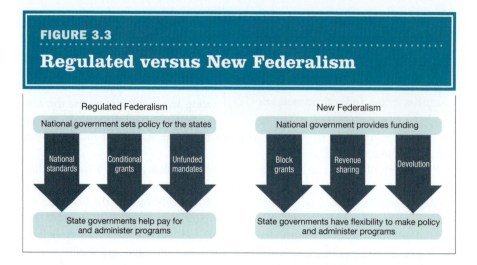

FIGURE 3.3

Regulated versus New Federalism

Regulated Federalism

National government sets policy for the states

National standards | Conditional grants | Unfunded mandates

State governments help pay for and administer programs

New Federalism

National government provides funding

Block grants | Revenue sharing | Devolution

State governments have flexibility to make policy and administer programs

(returning power to the states through block grants) similarly aimed to reduce the national government's control. In all, Congress created 12 new block grants between 1981 and 1990.[29]

But this new approach, like those that preceded it, has not provided magic solutions to the problems of federalism. For one thing, there is always a trade-off between accountability—that is, whether the states are using funds for the purposes intended—and flexibility. If the objective is to have accountable and efficient government, it is not clear that state bureaucracies are any more efficient or more capable than national agencies. In Mississippi, for example, the state Department of Human Services spent money from the child care block grant for office furniture and designer salt and pepper shakers that cost $37.50 a pair. As one Mississippi state legislator said, "I've seen too many years of good ol' boy politics to know they shouldn't [transfer money to the states] without stricter controls and requirements."[30] Even after block grants were created, Congress reimposed regulations in order to increase the states' accountability.

At times the federal government has also moved to limit state discretion over spending in cases where it thinks states are too generous. For example, in 2007, President Bush issued regulations that prevented states from providing benefits under the State Child Health Insurance Program (SCHIP) to children in families well above the poverty line. The Bush administration also barred states from providing chemotherapy to undocumented immigrants, who are guaranteed emergency medical treatment under Medicaid.[31]

THERE IS NO SIMPLE ANSWER TO FINDING THE RIGHT NATIONAL–STATE BALANCE

As Figure 3.4 indicates, federalism has changed dramatically over the course of American history, even over just the past several decades. Finding the right balance among states and the federal government is a persistent challenge for American democracy.

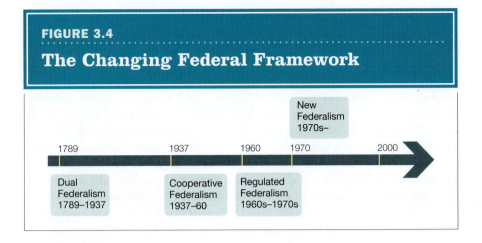

FIGURE 3.4

The Changing Federal Framework

New Federalism 1970s–

| 1789 | 1937 | 1960 | 1970 | 2000 |

Dual Federalism 1789–1937

Cooperative Federalism 1937–60

Regulated Federalism 1960s–1970s

In recent years, many of the most controversial issues in American politics—including the appropriate size of public social spending, the rights and benefits of immigrants (legal as well as undocumented), what government should do in response to climate change, and whether and how government should regulate business and moral behavior—have been fought out through the federal system. Politicians of all stripes regularly turn to the federal government to override decisions made by states. Likewise, when the federal government proves unable or unwilling to act, activists and politicians try to achieve their goals in states and localities. In many cases, it is up to the courts to decide which level of government should have the final say.

Although conservatives proclaim their preference for a small federal government and their support for more state autonomy, in fact, they often expand the federal government and limit state autonomy. President George W. Bush, for example, expanded federal control and increased spending in various policy areas. The 2001 No Child Left Behind Act, passed with Democratic support, introduced unprecedented federal intervention in public education, traditionally a state and local responsibility. New detailed federal testing requirements stipulating how states should treat failing schools were major expansions of federal authority in education. When a number of states threatened to defy some of the new federal requirements, Bush's Department of Education relaxed its tough stance and became more flexible in enforcing the act. But the administration did not back down entirely, leading to several legal challenges to different aspects of the law.

In the Supreme Court, too, many decisions supported a stronger federal role over the states. Decisions to uphold the federal Family and Medical Leave Act and the Americans with Disabilities Act asserted federal authority against state claims of immunity from the acts. In one important 2005 case, the Court upheld the right of Congress to ban medical marijuana, even though 11 states had legalized its use. Overturning a lower court ruling that said Congress did not have authority to regulate marijuana when it had been grown for noncommercial purposes in a single state, the Supreme Court ruled that the federal government did have the power to regulate use of all marijuana under the commerce clause. Even so, as we saw in the chapter opener, by 2018, 32 states and the District of Columbia had legalized medical marijuana, and 10 states have now gone further to legalize its recreational use. Although the federal government has not endorsed these laws, it has made prosecution of marijuana in these states a low priority.

The most significant Obama law to affect the states was the 2010 health care overhaul. One controversial part of that legislation required states to expand their Medicaid programs to cover more low-income residents and to offer them additional services. As we saw earlier, the Supreme Court's 2012 ruling in *National Federation of Independent Business v. Sebelius* that the federal government could not impose all-or-nothing conditions on the states—implement the expansion or lose all Medicaid funding—represented a new limit on the national government's power. The ruling mostly upheld the law but also gave the states more leeway. The other controversial provision of the Affordable Care Act was the "individual mandate," the requirement that individuals without health care insurance be required to purchase such insurance. The 26 states suing the federal government charged that Congress had no power to force individuals to purchase a product and that it had exceeded its power under the commerce clause. In defending the law, the federal government argued the opposite: that the complex interactions of the health care market made the individual mandate constitutional under the commerce clause.[32] From the moment a person is born, he or she is part of the health care economy. Even if a person does not have health insurance, federal law requires that hospitals provide treatment in an emergency. Those costs are borne by all of the people who do pay for health insurance.

Taking a more narrow view of the health care market, the Court rejected this argument on the grounds that the federal government cannot regulate economic *in*activity, that is, the failure to purchase health insurance. Instead, it found that the Affordable Care Act was constitutional based on Congress's power to tax. The law requires individuals who do not receive insurance from their employers or their parents and are not eligible for Medicaid to purchase insurance or pay a penalty. The Court reasoned that the penalty could be considered a tax and, for that reason, was constitutional. At the end of 2017, however, Congress passed a sweeping tax bill that included a provision to eliminate the individual mandate.

The Affordable Care Act survived another challenge in 2015 when the Supreme Court ruled that federal subsidies to help pay for insurance should be available to residents in states that offered insurance only through the federal exchange as well as in states that had formed their own state insurance marketplaces. The outcome of *King v. Burwell* ensured that subsidies would be available in all states.[33]

In other policy areas, states and localities have forged their own policies because the federal government has not acted. One of the most controversial of these issues is immigration legislation. In the first half of 2013, for example, state legislatures enacted 377 laws and resolutions related to immigration.[34] Many state and local laws that govern immigration are not controversial, but some raise critical questions about the federal government's role as opposed to the responsibilities of state and local governments. In 2010, Arizona enacted an extremely controversial immigration measure requiring immigrants to carry identity documents and requiring police to ask about immigration status when they stop drivers they suspect of being undocumented immigrants. The federal Department of Justice joined several other groups in challenging the law. In the words of then–attorney general Eric Holder, "It is clearly unconstitutional for a state to set its own immigration policy."[35] In 2012 the Supreme Court ruled that Arizona's law did not preempt federal authority to make immigration law.[36] The court's decision in *Arizona v. United States* did overturn three of four provisions in Arizona's law, but it ruled in favor of the most controversial provision, which allows state police to check the immigration status of anyone stopped or arrested.

Since the Trump administration's announcement of the phaseout of the DACA program put in place by the Obama administration, the legislative branch on the federal level has failed to implement a solution. State-level challenges to the termination of the policy, however, have been successful in protecting those covered by the program.

Immigration policy once again became embroiled in federal–state conflict after 2014. Frustrated by congressional inaction on immigration, President Obama issued executive memoranda in 2012 to provide temporary legal status and work permits to undocumented children who had been brought to the United States, termed the "Dreamers." However, when Obama moved to expand this Deferred Action for Childhood Arrivals program (DACA) in 2014 and extend legal status to some parents of U.S. citizens and legal residents (called Deferred Action for Parents of Americans, or DAPA), 26 states, led by Texas, challenged the executive order in court. They charged that the expansion exceeded executive authority and would impose unreasonable costs on states. The expansion was never implemented because the Supreme Court, in the wake of the death of Justice Antonin Scalia, deadlocked in a 4–4 decision, leaving in place lower-court decisions that sided with the states.[37] The Trump administration began a six-month phaseout of the DACA program in September 2017, giving Congress until March 2018 to devise a legislative solution.[38] Congressional action failed, but as of mid-2018, DACA remained in place due to two federal judges' rulings.

President Donald Trump campaigned promising more rigorous immigration enforcement. In 2017 he signed an executive order increasing the number of immigrants considered a priority for deportation, from those convicted of serious crimes such as felonies or multiple misdemeanors as under Obama to those accused or convicted of minor crimes as well.[39] A growing number of cities, counties, and states declared themselves "sanctuaries," which limit cooperation with national government enforcement of immigration law. President Trump pledged to cancel funding for sanctuary cities and states, but in 2017 a federal judge temporarily blocked the Trump administration from withholding federal grants from these jurisdictions because of sanctuary policies.[40] The Department of Homeland Security rescinded the DACA expansion in 2017, but the original program remained. Claiming sympathy for the "Dreamers," Trump asked Congress to resolve the matter through legislation.[41]

As the cases of health care and immigration show, federalism operates like ping-pong, with the federal and state governments reacting to the actions, or inactions, of the other. It is easy to see how confusing and ever-changing federal–state relations can be.

Federalism
WHAT DO WE WANT?

In recent years, sharp differences in Americans' views on many economic and social issues have been reflected in the federal system. Until 2015, when the Supreme Court ruled that state-level bans on same-sex marriage were unconstitutional, 37 states allowed same-sex marriage and 13 did not. Today, over half of the 50 states have legalized medical marijuana, while 10 and Washington, D.C., have gone further and legalized recreational marijuana. More states are likely to change their laws on marijuana, but differences across the states are likely to persist for many years. Half of the states welcomed the expansion of Medicaid, the program that provides medical assistance to the poor. The other half, concerned about costs and the growing role of government in the economy, initially declined to implement the expansion. Some states actively welcome immigrants and seek to opt out of restrictive federal laws; other states go beyond the federal government in enacting restrictive immigration laws. Yet while states have the authority to devise their own laws on a variety of important issues, Americans' participation in state and local politics remains low (see the "**Who Participates?**" feature on the facing page).

As described in the opening of this chapter, Larry Harvey's arrest for using medical marijuana, legal in his state but illegal under federal law, raises questions about the promise, conflict, and ambiguity inherent in a federal system of government. Our history of federalism means that we are comfortable with the idea that states should have the freedom to enact laws that best serve their residents, within the bounds set by Congress and the courts. We expect states to act as "laboratories of democracy" that try out new policies. But the great variation across the states today poses questions that will have to be answered in the coming decades. Is the federal government endangering people by allowing states to legalize marijuana? Or is the federal government endangering critically ill people by prosecuting medical marijuana use even in states with legalization? Is it fair that a transgender person in California can legally change the sex on her birth certificate, but a transgender person in Tennessee would be denied the same? Is it reasonable that a gun owner can openly carry a handgun in Georgia but not in Florida? Each generation confronts a different set of questions about how much variation across the states is appropriate. Are some of the issues on which the states differ fundamental rights that should be uniform across the country? Is it important to preserve state choice on most matters? As today's youth help to answer these questions in the coming decades, they will be remaking American federalism.

Thus, American federalism remains a work in progress. As public problems shift and as local, state, and federal governments change, questions about the relationship between American values and federalism naturally emerge. The different views that people bring to this discussion suggest that federalism will remain a central issue in American democracy.

Who Participates in State and Local Politics?

Turnout in Recent Gubernatorial Elections

Percentage of voting-eligible population*

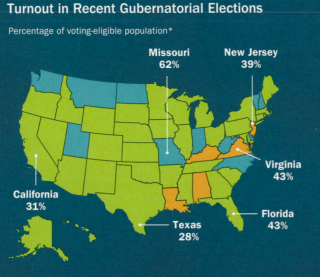

Missouri
62%

New Jersey
39%

California
31%

Texas
28%

Virginia
43%

Florida
43%

Median % of voters to turn out in the following years:

Non-presidential, non-congressional
2015, 2017

39%

Non-presidential, congressional
2014

40%

Presidential
2016

65%

Turnout in Most Recent Municipal Election

Percentage of voting-age population in selected cities*

Seattle	Washington, D.C.	Chicago	Detroit
43%	38%	33%	27%

Denver	Houston	San Antonio	New York City
24%	22%	10%	7%

*The voting-eligible population excludes noncitizens and people who are institutionalized or not allowed to vote in some states because they are ex-felons. The voting-age population includes everyone over 18.

NOTE: Oregon had an additional election in 2016 to fill a vacancy.

SOURCES: Elect Project, electproject.org; Voter Turnout, elect.ky.gov; Post Election Statistics, electionstatistics.sos.la.gov; 2017 Results, state.nj.us; 2017 Results Report, elections.virginia.gov (accessed 3/10/18).

WHAT YOU CAN DO ▶

★ WHAT YOU CAN DO ★

Get Involved in State and Local Politics

 Attend a board of supervisors, city council, planning commission, or other local government meeting. Agendas and minutes will usually be available on county and city websites.

 Visit the state capitol. If you make an appointment, you might be able to meet with your local representative. Committee meetings and hearings are generally open to the public, as are meetings of the legislature.

 Attend a session of your local or state judiciary. Cases on the docket are available online, as are rules for attendance and behavior when the court is in session.

★ STUDY GUIDE ★

Practice Quiz

1. Which term describes the division of powers between the national government and the state governments? *(p. 69)*
   a) separation of powers
   b) federal system
   c) checks and balances
   d) expressed powers
   e) implied powers

2. Which amendment to the Constitution stated that the powers not delegated to the national government or prohibited to the states were "reserved to the states"? *(p. 70)*
   a) First Amendment
   b) Fifth Amendment
   c) Tenth Amendment
   d) Fourteenth Amendment
   e) Twenty-Sixth Amendment

3. A state government's authority to regulate the health, safety, and morals of its citizens is frequently referred to as *(p. 70)*
   a) the reserved power.
   b) the expressed power.
   c) the police power.
   d) the concurrent power.
   e) the implied power.

4. Which constitutional clause requires that states normally honor the public acts and judicial decisions of other states? *(p. 71)*
   a) privileges and immunities clause
   b) necessary and proper clause
   c) interstate commerce clause
   d) preemption clause
   e) full faith and credit clause

5. Many states have amended their constitutions to guarantee that large cities will have the authority to manage local affairs without interference from state government. This power is called *(p. 72)*
   a) home rule.
   b) preemption.
   c) devolution.
   d) states' rights.
   e) New Federalism.

6. The relationship between the states and the national government from 1789 to 1937 is known as *(p. 73)*
   a) dual federalism.
   b) regulated federalism.
   c) states' rights.
   d) cooperative federalism.
   e) New Federalism.

7. In which case did the Supreme Court create the potential for increased national power by ruling that Congress could use the necessary and proper clause to interpret its delegated powers broadly? *(p. 75)*
   a) *United States v. Lopez*
   b) *Printz v. United States*
   c) *Loving v. Virginia*
   d) *McCulloch v. Maryland*
   e) *Gibbons v. Ogden*

8. The process of returning more of the responsibilities of governing from the national level to the state level is known as *(p. 80)*
   a) dual federalism.
   b) devolution.
   c) preemption.
   d) home rule.
   e) incorporation.

9. The principle that allows the federal government to take over areas of regulation formerly overseen by states or local governments is called *(p. 82)*
   a) regulated federalism.
   b) preemption.
   c) devolution.
   d) "layer cake" federalism.
   e) exemption.

10. When state and local governments must conform to costly regulations or conditions in order to receive grants but do not receive reimbursements for their expenditures from the federal government it is called *(p. 82)*
    a) states' rights.
    b) block grants.
    c) general revenue sharing.
    d) an unfunded mandate.
    e) redistributive programs.

11. To what does the term *New Federalism* refer? *(pp. 85–86)*
    a) the era of federalism initiated by President Roosevelt during the late 1930s
    b) the national government's regulation of state action through grants-in-aid
    c) the type of federalism that uses categorical grants to influence state action
    d) efforts to return more policy-making discretion to the states through the use of block grants
    e) the recent emergence of local governments as important political actors

12. The Supreme Court's decision in *National Federation of Independent Business v. Sebelius* was significant because *(p. 88)*
    a) it affirmed the federal government's absolute power to impose all-or-nothing conditions on state governments attempting to receive federal funding.
    b) it limited the federal government's power to impose all-or-nothing conditions on state governments attempting to receive federal funding.
    c) it struck down the individual mandate of the Affordable Care Act as a violation of the interstate commerce clause.
    d) it eliminated the federal government's ability to provide subsidies for health insurance coverage.
    e) it invalidated the educational standards and testing requirements imposed by the 2001 No Child Left Behind Act.

Key Terms

block grants *(p. 85)* federal grants-in-aid that allow states considerable discretion in how the funds are spent

categorical grants *(p. 78)* congressional grants given to states and localities on the condition that expenditures be limited to a problem or group specified by law

commerce clause *(p. 75)* Article I, Section 8, of the Constitution, which delegates to Congress the power "to regulate Commerce with foreign Nations, and among the several States and with the Indian Tribes"; this clause was interpreted by the Supreme Court in favor of national power over the economy

concurrent powers *(p. 70)* authority possessed by both state and national governments, such as the power to levy taxes

cooperative federalism *(p. 80)* a type of federalism existing since the New Deal era in which grants-in-aid have been used strategically to encourage states and localities (without commanding them) to pursue nationally defined goals; also known as "intergovernmental cooperation"

devolution *(p. 80)* a policy to remove a program from one level of government by delegating it or passing it down to a lower level of government, such as from the national government to the state and local governments

dual federalism *(p. 73)* the system of government that prevailed in the United States from 1789 to 1937 in which most fundamental governmental powers were shared between the federal and state governments

expressed powers *(p. 69)* specific powers granted by the Constitution to Congress (Article I, Section 8) and to the president (Article II)

federal system *(p. 69)* a system of government in which the national government shares power with lower levels of government such as states

federalism *(p. 69)* a system of government in which power is divided, by a constitution, between the central (national) government and regional (state) governments

full faith and credit clause *(p. 71)* provision from Article IV, Section 1, of the Constitution requiring that the states normally honor the public acts and judicial decisions that take place in another state

general revenue sharing *(p. 85)* the process by which one unit of government yields a portion of its tax income to another unit of government, according to an established formula; revenue sharing typically involves the national government providing money to state governments

grants-in-aid *(p. 77)* programs through which Congress provides money to state and local governments on the condition that the funds be employed for purposes defined by the federal government

home rule *(p. 72)* power delegated by the state to a local unit of government to manage its own affairs

implied powers *(p. 69)* powers derived from the necessary and proper clause of Article I, Section 8, of the Constitution; such powers are not specifically expressed but are implied through the expansive interpretation of delegated powers

necessary and proper clause *(p. 69)* provision from Article I, Section 8, of the Constitution providing Congress with the authority to make all laws necessary and proper to carry out its expressed powers

New Federalism *(p. 85)* attempts by presidents Nixon and Reagan to return power to the states through block grants

police power *(p. 70)* power reserved to the state government to regulate the health, safety, and morals of its citizens

preemption *(p. 82)* the principle that allows the national government to override state or local actions in certain policy areas; in foreign policy, the willingness to strike first in order to prevent an enemy attack

privileges and immunities clause *(p. 72)* provision, from Article IV, Section 2, of the Constitution, that a state cannot discriminate against someone from another state or give its own residents special privileges

reserved powers *(p. 70)* powers, derived from the Tenth Amendment to the Constitution, that are not specifically delegated to the national government or denied to the states

states' rights *(p. 76)* the principle that the states should oppose the increasing authority of the national government; this principle was most popular in the period before the Civil War

unfunded mandates *(p. 82)* regulations or conditions for receiving grants that impose costs on state and local governments for which they are not reimbursed by the federal government

unitary system *(p. 69)* a centralized government system in which lower levels of government have little power independent of the national government

For Further Reading

Derthick, Martha. *Keeping the Compound Republic: Essays on American Federalism.* Washington, DC: Brookings Institution Press, 2001.

Elazar, Daniel. *American Federalism: A View from the States.* 3rd ed. New York: Harper & Row, 1984.

Gerston, Larry N. *American Federalism: A Concise Introduction.* Armonk, NY: M. E. Sharpe, 2007.

Johnson, Kimberly S. *Governing the American State: Congress and the New Federalism, 1877–1929.* Princeton, NJ: Princeton University Press, 2007.

Kettl, Donald. *The Regulation of American Federalism.* Baltimore: Johns Hopkins University Press, 1987.

Mettler, Suzanne. *Dividing Citizens: Gender and Federalism in New Deal Public Policy.* Ithaca, NY: Cornell University Press, 1998.

Michener, Jamila. *Fragmented Democracy: Medicaid, Federalism, and Unequal Politics.* New York: Cambridge University Press, 2018.

Peterson, Paul E. *The Price of Federalism.* Washington, DC: Brookings Institution Press, 1995.

Pierceson, Jason. *Same-Sex Marriage in the United States: The Road to the Supreme Court.* Lanham, MD: Rowman and Littlefield, 2014.

Robertson, David Brian. *Federalism and the Making of America.* New York: Routledge, 2011.

Van Horn, Carl E. *The State of the States.* 4th ed. Washington, DC: CQ Press, 2005.

Zimmerman, Joseph. *Contemporary American Federalism.* 2nd ed. Albany: SUNY Press, 2009.

Civil Liberties and Civil Rights

WHAT GOVERNMENT DOES AND WHY IT MATTERS

In Portland in 2006, Simon Tam founded what Oregon Music News called the first and only all Asian American dance-rock band, or "Chinatown Dance Rock," as the band prefers. The various members of the band are of Chinese, Taiwanese, Vietnamese, and Filipino descent. In addition to playing at anime conventions and cultural festivals, they are known for their community involvement battling Asian stereotypes and supporting young Asian people.[1]

They are also known for a First Amendment case over the band's name, The Slants. The name has three sources. The first two reference the members' "slant" on life and the guitar chords they use: "It actually sounds like a fun, '80s, New Wave kind of band. And it's a play on words. We can share our personal experiences about what it's like being people of color—our own slant on life, if you will. It's also a musical reference. There are slant guitar chords that we use in our music," Tam said. The third source was a reclaiming and repurposing of the old ethnic slur about Asian people. "We grew up and the notion of having slanted eyes was always considered a negative thing," Tam

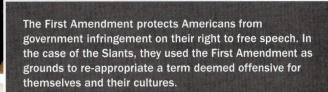

The First Amendment protects Americans from government infringement on their right to free speech. In the case of the Slants, they used the First Amendment as grounds to re-appropriate a term deemed offensive for themselves and their cultures.

said. "Kids would pull their eyes back in a slant-eyed gesture to make fun of us… I wanted to change it to something that was powerful, something that was considered beautiful or a point of pride instead."

The U.S. Patent and Trademark Office had a different view. Tam's application for a trademark on the band's name was rejected as a violation of the Disparagement Clause of the Lanham Act of 1946, which prohibits trademarks that disparage a racial or ethnic group. The denial stated that although the "applicant, or even the entire band, may be willing to take on the disparaging term as a band name, in what may be considered an attempt…to wrest 'ownership' of the term," that "does not mean that all [Asian Americans] share the applicant's view." The case ultimately went to the Supreme Court, which in 2017 ruled unanimously that the disparagement clause violated the First Amendment's free speech clause. The band could keep the name.

Free speech, along with the freedoms of assembly, religion, and privacy, are among the civil liberties contained in the Bill of Rights and elsewhere in the Constitution. Thomas Jefferson said that a bill of rights "is what people are entitled to against every government on earth." Note the wording: *against government.* Civil liberties are *protections from* improper government action. Civil rights, on the other hand, are positives—what the government *must* do to guarantee equal citizenship and protect citizens from discrimination. Civil rights regulate *who* can participate in the political process and civil society and *how* they can participate: for example, who can vote, who can hold office, who can have a trial or serve on juries, and when and how citizens can petition the government to take action. Civil rights also define how people are treated in employment, education, and other aspects of American society.

Liberties are limits on government action, and the courts are the institution best situated to tell Congress, the president and state governments what they may not do. Civil rights, though, involve the government's obligation to act and the evolution of civil rights required much more action on the part of Congress and the president.

CHAPTER GOALS

★ **Explain the origins and evolution of the civil liberties in the Bill of Rights as they apply to the federal government and the states (pp. 99–103)**

★ **Describe how the First Amendment protects freedom of religion, speech, and the press (pp. 103–11)**

★ **Explore whether the Second Amendment means people have a right to own guns (pp. 112–13)**

★ **Explain the major rights that people have if they are accused of a crime (pp. 113–19)**

★ **Assess whether people have a right to privacy under the Constitution (pp. 119–20)**

★ **Trace the legal developments and social movements that expanded civil rights (pp. 120–30)**

★ **Describe how different groups have fought for and won protection of their civil rights (pp. 130–37)**

The Origin of the Bill of Rights Lies in Those Who Opposed the Constitution

Explain the origins and evolution of the civil liberties in the Bill of Rights as they apply to the federal government and the states

Since the early 1960s the Supreme Court has expanded considerably the scope of **civil liberties**, defined as individual rights and personal freedoms with which governments may not interfere; that is, they are protections for Americans *from* the government. These liberties are constantly subject to judicial interpretation, and their provisions need to be safeguarded vigilantly, especially during times of war or a threat to national security, such as in the aftermath of the terrorist attacks of September 11, 2001.

Civil rights—protections of citizen equality provided *by* the government—have also expanded dramatically since the middle of the twentieth century, when the African American struggle for equal rights took center stage. Many goals of the civil rights movement that once aroused bitter controversy are now widely accepted as part of the American commitment to equal rights. But even today the question of what is meant by "equal rights" is hardly settled. To what extent can states mandate racial preferences in college admissions? Do transgender individuals have the right to use a public restroom based on their gender identification rather than their physical characteristics? What rights do undocumented immigrants possess? Although the United States was founded on the ideals of liberty, equality, and democracy, its history of civil rights reveals a gap between these principles and actual practice.

When the first Congress under the newly ratified Constitution met in April 1789, the most important item of business was the proposal to add a bill of rights to the Constitution. Such a proposal had been turned down with little debate in the waning days of the Philadelphia Constitutional Convention in 1787, not because the delegates were against rights but because—as the Federalists, led by Alexander Hamilton, later argued—such a bill was "not only unnecessary in the proposed Constitution but would even be dangerous."[2] First, according to Hamilton, a bill of rights would be irrelevant to a national government that was given only delegated powers in the first place. To put restraints on "powers which are not granted" could provide a pretext for governments to claim more powers than were in fact granted: "For why declare that things shall not be done which there is no power to do?"[3] Second, the Constitution was to Hamilton and the Federalists a bill of rights in itself, containing provisions that amounted to a bill of rights without requiring additional amendments (see Table 4.1). For example, Article I, Section 9, included the right of **habeas corpus**, a court order demanding that an individual in custody be brought into court and shown the reason for detention. This prohibits the government from depriving a person of liberty without explaining the reason before a judge.

Despite the power of Hamilton's arguments, when the Constitution was submitted to the states for ratification, Antifederalists, most of whom had not been delegates in Philadelphia, picked up on the argument of Thomas Jefferson (who also had

TABLE 4.1

Rights in the Original Constitution (Not in the Bill of Rights)

CLAUSE	RIGHT ESTABLISHED
Article I, Section 9	Guarantee of habeas corpus
Article I, Section 9	Prohibition of **bills of attainder**
Article I, Section 9	Prohibition of **ex post facto laws**
Article I, Section 9	Prohibition against acceptance of titles of nobility, etc., from any foreign state
Article III	Guarantee of trial by jury in state where crime was committed
Article III	Treason defined and limited to the life of the person convicted, not to the person's heirs

not been a delegate) that the omission of a bill of rights was a major imperfection of the new Constitution. The Federalists conceded that for the document to gain ratification they would have to make an "unwritten but unequivocal pledge" to add a bill of rights.

The Bill of Rights might well have been titled the "Bill of Liberties" because the provisions that were incorporated in it were seen as defining a private sphere of personal liberty, free from governmental restrictions.[4] As Jefferson put it, a bill of rights "is what people are entitled to against every government on earth." Note the wording: *against* government. Civil liberties are *protections of citizens from* improper government action. Some of these restraints are substantive liberties, which put limits on *what* the government shall and shall not have power to do—such as establishing a religion, quartering troops in private homes without consent, or seizing private property without just compensation. Other restraints are procedural liberties, which are restraints on *how* the government is supposed to act. These procedural liberties are usually grouped under the general category of **due process of law**, which is the right of every citizen to be protected against arbitrary action by national or state governments. It first appears in the Fifth Amendment provision that "no person shall be...deprived of life, liberty, or property, without due process of law." For example, even though the government has the substantive power to declare certain acts to be crimes and to arrest and imprison persons who violate criminal laws, it may not do so without meticulously observing procedures designed to protect the accused person. The best-known procedural rule is that an accused person is presumed innocent until proven guilty. This rule does not question the government's power to punish someone for committing a crime; it questions only the way the government determines who committed the crime. Substantive and procedural restraints together identify the realm of civil liberties.

In contrast, civil rights are the obligations imposed on government to *take positive action* to protect citizens from any illegal actions by government agencies and by other private citizens. Civil rights did not become part of the Constitution until 1868, with the adoption of the Fourteenth Amendment, which sought to provide for each citizen "the equal protection of the laws."

THE FOURTEENTH AMENDMENT NATIONALIZED THE BILL OF RIGHTS THROUGH INCORPORATION

In the first 70 years of the country's history, the Bill of Rights was understood to apply only to the national government and not to the states. This meant that the actions of state governments were restricted only by their own state constitutions as interpreted by their own courts. In fact, the Supreme Court said this in a decision in 1833, *Barron v. Baltimore.*[5] But the Civil War cast new light on the large question of state versus national governmental power. After the war, the Fourteenth Amendment was added to the Constitution. Part of the amendment reads as though it were meant to tell the states that they must now adhere to the Bill of Rights:

> No State shall make or enforce any law which shall abridge the privileges or immunities of citizens of the United States; nor shall any State deprive any person of life, liberty, or property, without due process of law; nor deny to any person within its jurisdiction the equal protection of the laws.

This language sounds like an effort to extend the Bill of Rights to all citizens, wherever they might reside.[6] Yet this was not the Supreme Court's interpretation of the amendment for nearly 100 years. Within five years of ratification of the Fourteenth Amendment, the Court was making decisions as though the amendment had never been adopted.[7]

The first change in civil liberties following the adoption of the Fourteenth Amendment came in 1897, when the Supreme Court held that the due process clause of the Fourteenth Amendment did in fact prohibit states from taking property for a public use without just compensation (a protection found in the Fifth Amendment), overruling the *Barron* case.[8] However, the Supreme Court had selectively "incorporated" under the Fourteenth Amendment only the property protection provision of the Fifth Amendment and no other clause of the Fifth or any other amendment of the Bill of Rights. In other words, although according to the Fifth Amendment "due process" applied to the taking of life and liberty as well as property, only property was incorporated into the Fourteenth Amendment as a limitation on state power.

No further expansion of civil liberties via the Fourteenth Amendment occurred until 1925, when the Supreme Court held that freedom of speech is "among the fundamental personal rights and 'liberties' protected by the due process clause of the Fourteenth Amendment from impairment by the states."[9] In 1931 the Court added freedom of the press to that short list protected by the Bill of Rights from state action; by 1939 it had added freedom of assembly and petitioning the government for redress of grievances.[10] But that was as far as the Court was then willing to go.

As Table 4.2 shows, **selective incorporation**—the process by which different protections in the Bill of Rights were incorporated or applied to the states, part by part, using the Fourteenth Amendment, thus guaranteeing citizens' protection from state as well as national government—continued to occur gradually until 2010. The final provision of the Bill of Rights to be incorporated by the Supreme Court was the Second Amendment, which protects the right to bear arms.[11] (Incorporation is also sometimes referred to as the "absorption" or the "nationalizing" of the Bill of Rights.)

TABLE 4.2

Incorporation of the Bill of Rights into the Fourteenth Amendment

SELECTED PROVISIONS AND AMENDMENTS	INCORPORATED	KEY CASE
Eminent domain (V)	1897	*Chicago, Burlington, and Quincy R.R. v. Chicago*
Freedom of speech (I)	1925	*Gitlow v. New York*
Freedom of press (I)	1931	*Near v. Minnesota*
Free exercise of religion (I)	1934	*Hamilton v. Regents of the University of California*
Freedom of assembly (I) and freedom to petition the government for redress of grievances (I)	1937	*DeJonge v. Oregon*
Freedom of assembly (I)	1939	*Hague v. CIO*
Nonestablishment of state religion (I)	1947	*Everson v. Board of Education*
Freedom from unnecessary search and seizure (IV)	1949	*Wolf v. Colorado*
Freedom from warrantless search and seizure (IV; "exclusionary rule")	1961	*Mapp v. Ohio*
Freedom from cruel and unusual punishment (VIII)	1962	*Robinson v. California*
Right to counsel in any criminal trial (VI)	1963	*Gideon v. Wainwright*
Right against self-incrimination and forced confessions (V)	1964	*Malloy v. Hogan; Escobedo v. Illinois*
Right to counsel and to remain silent (V)	1966	*Miranda v. Arizona*
Right against double jeopardy (V)	1969	*Benton v. Maryland*
Right to bear arms (II)	2010	*McDonald v. Chicago*

To make clear that "selective incorporation" should be narrowly interpreted, Justice Benjamin Cardozo, writing for an 8–1 majority in 1937, asserted that although many rights have value and importance, some rights do not represent a "principle of justice so rooted in the traditions and conscience of our people as to be ranked as fundamental." So, until 1961, only the First Amendment and one clause of the Fifth Amendment had been clearly incorporated into the Fourteenth Amendment as binding on the states as well as on the national government.[12]

The best way to examine the Bill of Rights today is the simplest way: to take each of the major provisions one at a time. Some of these provisions are settled areas of law; others are not.

The First Amendment Guarantees Freedom of Religion, Speech, and the Press

Describe how the First Amendment protects freedom of religion, speech, and the press

Congress shall make no law respecting an establishment of religion, or prohibiting the free exercise thereof; or abridging the freedom of speech, or of the press; or the right of the people peaceably to assemble, and to petition the Government for a redress of grievances.

FREEDOM OF RELIGION

The Bill of Rights begins by guaranteeing freedom of religion, and the First Amendment provides for that freedom in two distinct clauses: "Congress shall make no law (1) respecting an establishment of religion, or (2) prohibiting the free exercise thereof." The first clause is called the "establishment clause," and the second is called the "free exercise clause."

Separation between Church and State Comes from the First Amendment
The **establishment clause** and the idea of "no law" regarding the establishment of religion can be interpreted in several ways. One interpretation, which probably reflects the views of many of the First Amendment's authors, is that the government is prohibited from establishing an official church. Official state churches, such as the Church of England, were common in the eighteenth century and were viewed by many Americans as inconsistent with a republican form of government. Indeed, many American colonists had fled Europe to escape persecution for having rejected state-sponsored churches. A second interpretation is the view that the government may not take sides among competing religions but may provide assistance to religious institutions or ideas as long as it shows no favoritism. The United States accommodates religious beliefs in a variety of ways, from the reference to God on U.S. currency to the prayer that begins every session of Congress. These forms of establishment have never been struck down by the courts.

The third view regarding religious establishment, the most commonly held today, is the idea of a "wall of separation" between church and state—Jefferson's formulation—that cannot be breached by the government. For two centuries, Jefferson's words have had a powerful impact on our understanding of the proper relationship between church and state in America.

Despite the seeming absoluteness of the phrase "wall of separation," there is ample room to disagree on how high or strong this wall is. For example, the Court has been consistently strict in the area of public education in cases of school prayer, striking down such practices as Bible reading,[13] nondenominational prayer,[14] reading prayers over a public address system during a football game,[15] and even a moment of silence for meditation.[16] In each of these cases, the Court reasoned that school-sponsored religious observations, even if nondenominational, are highly suggestive of school sponsorship and therefore violate the prohibition against establishment of religion. On the other hand, the Court has been quite permissive (and some would say inconsistent) about the public display of religious symbols, such as city-sponsored Nativity scenes in commercial or municipal areas.[17] And although the Court has consistently disapproved of government financial support for religious schools, even when the purpose has been purely educational and secular, it has permitted certain direct aid to students of such schools in the form of busing, for example.

The difficulty in defining what religious establishment means is evident from two cases in 2005 involving government-sponsored displays of religious symbols. In *Van Orden v. Perry*, the Court decided by a 5–4 margin that a display of the Ten Commandments at the Texas State Capitol did not violate the Constitution.[18] However, in *McCreary v. ACLU of Kentucky*, decided at the same time and also by a 5–4 margin, the Court determined that a display of the Ten Commandments inside two Kentucky courthouses was unconstitutional.[19] Justice Stephen Breyer, the swing vote in the two cases, said that the displays in *Van Orden* had a secular purpose, whereas the displays in *McCreary* had a purely religious purpose. The key difference between the two cases is that the Texas display had been exhibited in a large park for 40 years with other monuments related to the development of American law without any objections raised until this case, whereas the Kentucky display was erected much more recently and initially by itself, suggesting to some justices that its posting had a religious purpose. But most observers saw little difference between the two cases. Clearly, the issue of government-sponsored displays of religious symbols has not been settled.

Free Exercise of Religion Means You Have a Right to Your Beliefs The **free exercise clause** protects the citizen's right to believe and to practice any religion; it also protects the right to choose not to practice a religion. The precedent-setting case involving free exercise is *West Virginia State Board of Education v. Barnette* (1943), which involved the children of a family of Jehovah's Witnesses who refused to salute and pledge allegiance to the American flag on the grounds that their religious faith did not permit it. Three years earlier, the Court had upheld such a requirement and had permitted schools to expel students for refusing to salute the flag. But the entry of the United States into a war to defend democracy, coupled with the ugly treatment to which the Jehovah's Witnesses children had been subjected, induced the Court to reverse itself and to endorse the free exercise of religion even when it may be offensive to the beliefs of the majority.[20]

In recent years, the principle of free exercise has been bolstered by statutes prohibiting religious discrimination by public and private entities in a variety of realms including hiring, land use, and the treatment of prison inmates. Two recent cases illustrating this point are *Holt v. Hobbs* and *Burwell v. Hobby Lobby Stores*.[21] The *Holt* case involved a Muslim prisoner in an Arkansas jail. The prisoner, Gregory Holt, asserted that his religious beliefs required him to grow a beard. Thus, according to Holt, an Arkansas prison policy prohibiting beards was a violation of his ability to exercise his religion. The Court held that the prison policy was a violation of the free exercise clause and violated a federal statute designed to protect the ability of prisoners to worship as they pleased. The Hobby Lobby case involved the owners of a chain of craft stores who claimed that a section of the Affordable Care Act requiring employers to provide their female employees with free contraceptive coverage violated their religious beliefs as protected by the Religious Freedom Restoration Act. This law requires the government to prove a "compelling interest" for requiring individuals to obey a law that violates their religious beliefs. The Supreme Court ruled in favor of Hobby Lobby.

Does religious freedom lead to discrimination on the basis of religion? Here, senior counsel for Hobby Lobby Stores speaks to supporters after the Supreme Court ruled that businesses were not required to provide free contraceptive coverage if they find it in violation of their religious beliefs.

THE FIRST AMENDMENT AND FREEDOM OF SPEECH AND OF THE PRESS ENSURE THE FREE EXCHANGE OF IDEAS

Congress shall make no law…abridging the freedom of speech, or of the press.

Freedom of speech and of the press have a special place in American political thought. To begin with, democracy depends upon the ability of individuals to talk to one another and to disseminate information. A democratic nation could not function without free and open debate. Such debate, moreover, is seen as an essential mechanism for determining the quality or validity of competing ideas. As Justice Oliver Wendell Holmes said, "The best test of truth is the power of the thought to get itself accepted in the competition of the market…that at any rate is the theory of our Constitution."[22] What is sometimes called the "marketplace of ideas" receives a good deal of protection from the courts. In 1938 the Supreme Court held that any legislation that attempts to restrict these fundamental freedoms "is to be subjected to a more exacting judicial scrutiny…than are most other types of legislation."[23] This higher standard of judicial review came to be called **strict scrutiny**.

The doctrine of strict scrutiny places a heavy burden of proof on the government if it seeks to regulate or restrict speech. Americans are assumed to have the right to speak and to broadcast their ideas unless some compelling reason can be identified to stop them. But strict scrutiny does not mean that speech can never be regulated. According to the courts, although virtually all speech is protected by the Constitution, some forms of speech are entitled to a greater degree of protection than others.

POLITICAL SPEECH IS CONSISTENTLY PROTECTED

Over the past 200 years the courts have scrutinized many different forms of speech and constructed different principles and guidelines for each. And of all forms of speech, political speech is the most consistently protected.

Political speech was the activity of greatest concern to the framers of the Constitution, even though some found it the most difficult provision to tolerate. Within seven years of the ratification of the Bill of Rights in 1791, Congress adopted the infamous Alien and Sedition Acts, which, among other things, made it a crime to say or publish anything that might tend to defame or bring into disrepute the government of the United States. Quite clearly, the acts' intentions were to criminalize the very thing protected by the First Amendment—political speech. Fifteen violators, including several newspaper editors, were indicted; and a few were actually convicted before the relevant portions of the acts were allowed to expire.

The first modern free speech case arose immediately after World War I. It involved persons who had been convicted under the federal Espionage Act of 1917 for opposing U.S. involvement in the war. The Supreme Court upheld the Espionage Act and refused to protect the speech rights of the defendants on the grounds that their activities—appeals to draftees to resist the draft—constituted a **"clear and present danger"** to national security.[24] This is the first and most famous, though since discarded, "test" for when government intervention or censorship can be permitted.

It was only after the 1920s that real progress toward a genuinely effective First Amendment was made. Since then, the courts have consistently protected political speech even when it has been deemed "insulting" or "outrageous."

SYMBOLIC SPEECH, SPEECH PLUS, ASSEMBLY, AND PETITION ARE HIGHLY PROTECTED

The First Amendment treats the freedoms of religion and political speech as equal to the freedoms of assembly and petition—speech associated with action. Freedom of speech and freedom of assembly are closely related by the "public forum doctrine." In the 1939 case of *Hague v. Committee for Industrial Organization*, the Court declared that the government may not prohibit speech-related activities such as demonstrations or leafleting in public areas traditionally used for that purpose, though, of course, the government may impose rules designed to protect the public safety so long as these rules do not discriminate against particular viewpoints.[25]

Generally, the Supreme Court has protected actions that are designed to send a political message. Thus, the Court held unconstitutional a California statute making it a felony to display a red Communist flag "as a sign, symbol or emblem of opposition to organized government."[26]

Another example is the burning of the American flag as a symbol of protest. In 1984, at a political rally held during the Republican National Convention in Dallas, Texas, a political protester burned an American flag, thereby violating a Texas law that prohibited desecration of a venerated object. The Supreme Court declared the Texas law unconstitutional on the grounds that flag burning was expressive conduct protected by the First Amendment.[27]

In the 2011 case of *Snyder v. Phelps*, the Court continued to protect symbolic speech. Members of the Westboro Baptist Church had frequently demonstrated at military funerals, claiming that the deaths of soldiers were a sign that God disapproved of acceptance of homosexuality in the United States. They carried signs that included slogans like "Thank God for dead soldiers." The father of a soldier killed in Iraq brought suit against the church and its pastor, claiming that the demonstrators had caused him and his family severe emotional distress. The Supreme Court ruled, however, that the First Amendment protected this form of speech in a public place against such suits.[28]

Should the First Amendment's protection of free speech apply even when that speech is seen as offensive? The Supreme Court ruled that members of the Westboro Baptist Church had a right to picket soldiers' funerals to demonstrate what they take as a sign of God's disapproval of homosexuality.

Closer to the original intent of the assembly and petition clause is the category of "speech plus"—speech accompanied by conduct or physical activity such as sit-ins, picketing, and demonstrating; protection of this form of speech under the First Amendment is conditional, and restrictions imposed by state or local authorities are acceptable if properly balanced by considerations of public order. Courts consistently protect such assemblies under the First Amendment; state and local laws regulating such activities are closely scrutinized and frequently overturned. But the same assembly on private property is quite another matter and can in many circumstances be regulated. For example, the directors of a shopping center can lawfully prohibit an assembly protesting a war or supporting a ban on abortion. Assemblies in public areas can also be restricted in some circumstances, especially when the assembly or demonstration jeopardizes the health, safety, or rights of others. This condition was the basis of the Supreme Court's decision to uphold a lower-court order that restricted the access abortion protesters had to the entrances of abortion clinics.[29]

Speech by Public School Students One group that seems to enjoy only a limited right of free speech is public school students. In 1986 the Supreme Court upheld the punishment of a high school student for making sexually suggestive speech. The Court opinion held that such speech interfered with the school's goal of teaching students the limits of socially acceptable behavior.[30] Two years later, the Supreme Court restricted student speech and press rights even further by defining them as part of the educational process, not to be treated with the same standard as adult speech in a regular public forum.[31] In the 2007 case of *Morse v. Frederick*, the Court held that a principal did not violate a student's free speech rights by suspending him for displaying a banner proclaiming "BONG HiTS 4 JESUS."[32] The decision affirmed that school officials can censor student speech that advocates or celebrates the use of illegal drugs.

FREEDOM OF THE PRESS IS BROAD

For all practical purposes, freedom of speech implies and includes freedom of the press. With the exception of the broadcast media, which are subject to federal regulation, the press is protected under the doctrine against **prior restraint** (efforts by a governmental agency to block the publication of material it deems libelous or harmful in some other way; otherwise known as "censorship"). Beginning with the landmark 1931 case of *Near v. Minnesota*, the U.S. Supreme Court has held that, except under the most extraordinary circumstances, the First Amendment of the Constitution prohibits government agencies from seeking to prevent newspapers or magazines from publishing whatever they wish.[33] In the case of *New York Times v. United States* (1971), the so-called Pentagon Papers case, the Supreme Court ruled that the government could not block publication of secret Defense Department documents given to the *New York Times* by an opponent of the Vietnam War who had obtained the documents illegally.[34]

Another press freedom issue is the question of whether journalists can be compelled to reveal their sources of information. Journalists assert that if they cannot promise to keep the confidentiality of their sources, the flow of information will be reduced and press freedom effectively curtailed. Government agencies, however, assert that the names of news sources may be relevant to criminal or even national security investigations. Nearly all states have "shield laws" that to varying degrees protect journalistic sources. There is, however, no federal shield law, and the Supreme Court has held that the press has no constitutional right to withhold information in court.[35] In 2005, Judith Miller, a *New York Times* reporter, was jailed for contempt of court for refusing to tell a federal grand jury the name of a confidential source in a case involving the leaked identity of the CIA analyst Valerie Plame. Plame's husband, Joseph Wilson, had been critical of the Bush administration's Iraq policies.

SOME SPEECH HAS ONLY LIMITED PROTECTION

At least four categories of speech fall outside the guarantees of the First Amendment and therefore outside the realm of absolute protection: (1) libel and slander, (2) obscenity and pornography, (3) fighting words, and (4) commercial speech. It should be emphasized once again that these types of speech still enjoy considerable protection by the courts.

Libel and Slander If a written statement is made in "reckless disregard of the truth" and is considered damaging to the victim because it is "malicious, scandalous, and defamatory," it can be punished as **libel**. If an oral statement of such a nature is made, it can be punished as **slander**.

Today, most libel suits involve freedom of the press, and the realm of free press is enormous. Historically, newspapers were subject to the law of libel, which provided that newspapers that printed false and malicious stories could be compelled to pay damages to those they defamed. In recent years, however, American courts have greatly narrowed the meaning of libel and made it extremely difficult, particularly for politicians or other public figures, to win a libel case against a newspaper. In the important 1964 case of *New York Times v. Sullivan*, the Court held that to be deemed libelous, a story about a public official not only had to be untrue but also had to result from "actual malice" or "reckless disregard" for the truth.[36] In other words, the newspaper had to print false and malicious material *deliberately*. In practice, this is a very difficult legal standard to meet.

With the emergence of the internet as an important communications medium, the courts have had to decide how traditional libel law applies to internet content. In 1995 the New York courts held that an online bulletin board could be held responsible for the libelous content of material posted by a third party. To protect internet service providers, Congress subsequently enacted legislation absolving them of responsibility for third-party posts. The federal courts have generally upheld this law and declared that service providers are immune from suits regarding the content of material posted by others.[37]

Obscenity and Pornography If libel and slander cases can be difficult because of the problem of determining the truth of statements and whether those statements are malicious and damaging, cases involving pornography and obscenity can be even trickier. Not until 1957 did the Supreme Court confront these issues, and it did so with a definition of *obscenity* that may have caused more confusion than it cleared up. Justice William Brennan, in writing the Court's opinion, defined *obscenity* as speech or writing that appeals to the "prurient interest"—that is, whose purpose is to excite lust as this appears "to the average person, applying contemporary community standards." Even so, Brennan added, the work should be judged obscene only when it is "utterly without redeeming social importance."[38] In 1964, Justice Potter Stewart confessed that, although he found *pornography* impossible to define, "I know it when I see it."[39]

An effort was made to strengthen the restrictions in 1973, when the Supreme Court expressed its willingness to define *pornography* as a work that (1) as a whole, is deemed prurient by the "average person" according to "community standards"; (2) depicts sexual conduct "in a patently offensive way"; and (3) lacks "serious literary, artistic, political, or scientific value." This definition meant that pornography would be determined by local rather than national standards. Thus, a local bookseller might be prosecuted for selling a volume that was a best-seller nationally but that was deemed pornographic locally.[40] This new definition of standards did not help much either, and not long after 1973 the Court began again to review all such community antipornography laws, reversing most of them.

In recent years, the battle against obscene speech has targeted "cyberporn," pornography on the internet. Opponents of this form of expression argue that it should be banned because of the easy access children have to the internet. The first major effort to regulate the content of the internet occurred in 1996, when Congress passed the Communications Decency Act (CDA), designed to regulate the online transmission of obscene material. The constitutionality of the CDA was immediately challenged in court by a coalition of interests led by the American Civil Liberties Union (ACLU). In the 1997 Supreme Court case of *Reno v. ACLU*, the Court struck down the CDA, ruling that it suppressed speech that "adults have a constitutional right to receive," saying that "the level of discourse reaching the mailbox simply cannot be limited to that which would be suitable for a sandbox." Supreme Court justice John Paul Stevens described the internet as the "town crier" of the modern age and said that the internet was entitled to the greatest degree of First Amendment protection possible.[41] By contrast, radio and television are subject to more control than the internet. In 2008 the Supreme Court upheld a law that made it a crime to sell child pornography on the internet.[42]

In 2000 the Supreme Court extended the highest degree of First Amendment protection to cable (not broadcast) television. In *United States v. Playboy Entertainment Group*, the Court struck down a portion of the 1996 Telecommunications Act that required cable TV companies to limit the broadcast of sexually explicit programming to late-night hours. In its decision, the Court noted that the law already provided parents with the means to restrict access to sexually explicit cable channels through various blocking devices. Moreover, such programming could come into the home only if parents decided to purchase such channels in the first place.[43]

Closely related to the issue of obscenity is the matter of violent broadcast content. Here, too, the Court has generally upheld freedom of speech. For example, in the 2011 case of *Brown v. Entertainment Merchants Association* the Court struck down a California law banning the sale of violent video games to children, saying that the law violated the First Amendment.[44]

Fighting Words Speech can also lose its protected position when it moves toward the sphere of action. "Expressive speech," for example, is protected until it moves from the symbolic realm to the realm of actual conduct—to direct incitement of damaging conduct with the use of so-called **fighting words**. In 1942 a man called a police officer a "goddamned racketeer" and "a damn Fascist" and was arrested and convicted of violating a state law forbidding the use of offensive language in public. When his case reached the Supreme Court, the arrest was upheld on the grounds that the First Amendment provides no protection for such offensive language because such words "are no essential part of any exposition of ideas."[45] This decision was reaffirmed in the important 1951 case of *Dennis v. United States*, in which the Supreme Court held that there is no substantial public interest in permitting certain kinds of utterances: the lewd and obscene, the profane, the libelous, and the insulting or "fighting" words—those which by their very utterance inflict injury or tend to incite an immediate breach of the peace.[46] Since that time, however, the Supreme Court has reversed almost every conviction based on arguments that the speaker had used "fighting words."

Commercial Speech Commercial speech, such as newspaper or television advertisements, has only partial First Amendment protection because it cannot be considered political speech. Initially considered to be entirely outside the protection of the First Amendment, commercial speech is subject to regulation, although it is also recognized and protected for the part it plays in the free flow of information. For example, prohibition of false and misleading advertising by the Federal Trade Commission is an old and well-established power of the federal government. The Supreme Court long ago approved the constitutionality of laws prohibiting electronic media from carrying cigarette advertising.[47] It has also upheld city ordinances prohibiting the posting of all signs on public property (as long as the ban is total so that there is no hint of censorship).[48]

However, the gains outweigh the losses in the effort to expand the protection of commercial speech under the First Amendment. For example, in 1996 the Court struck down Rhode Island laws and regulations banning the advertisement of liquor prices,[49] and in 2001 the Court overturned a Massachusetts ban on all cigarette advertising as violations of the First Amendment.[50] These instances of commercial speech indicate the breadth and depth of the freedom today to direct appeals to a large public, to sell goods and services, and to mobilize people for political purposes.

The Second Amendment Now Protects an Individual's Right to Own a Gun

Explore whether the Second Amendment means people have a right to own guns

The Second Amendment was included in the Bill of Rights to provide for "well-regulated" militias to enforce the "security of a free State," which were to be the backing of the government for the maintenance of local public order and national defense. *Militia* was understood to be a military or police resource for state and the national governments; militias were distinguished from professional armies, which came within the sole constitutional jurisdiction of Congress. While the right of the people "to keep and bear Arms" was linked to citizen service in militias, many have argued that the Second Amendment also establishes an individual right to bear arms.

A 1939 Supreme Court case upheld a federal gun law in which the Court concluded that the Second Amendment pertained to "the preservation or efficiency of a well regulated militia,"[51] but the Court made no further Second Amendment decisions for nearly 70 years. Thus, states and localities across the country have very different gun ownership standards. For instance, in Wyoming there is no ban on any type of gun and no permit is required for carrying a concealed weapon. In California, by contrast, the possession of assault weapons is banned and a permit is required to carry a concealed weapon. Figure 4.1 shows the background check requirements to purchase a firearm across the country.

The Court's silence on the application of the Second Amendment ended in 2008, when it made the first of two rulings in favor of expansive rights of gun ownership by individuals. The case of *District of Columbia v. Heller* challenged a Washington, D.C., law that banned handguns. In a 5–4 decision, the Court ruled that the Second Amendment provides a constitutional right to keep a loaded handgun at home for self-defense. The dissenting opinion asserted that the Second Amendment only protects the rights of individuals to bear arms as part of a militia force, not in an individual capacity.[52] Because the District of Columbia is an entity of the federal government, the ruling did not apply to state firearm laws. However, in the 2010 case of *McDonald v. Chicago*, the Court applied the Second Amendment to the states, making this decision the first new incorporation decision by the Court in 40 years (see Table 4.2). The case concerned a Chicago ordinance that made it extremely difficult to own a gun within city limits, and the Court's ruling had the effect of overturning the law.[53]

Despite these rulings, the debate over gun control continues to loom large. A series of tragic shootings in recent years—including the killing of 20 elementary school students in Newtown, Connecticut; 50 people at a gay nightclub in Orlando, Florida; 59 people at a concert in Las Vegas, Nevada; and 17 people at a high school in Parkland, Florida—has kept the issue of gun laws firmly on the national agenda. Proponents of gun control point to these shootings as evidence of the need to restrict the availability of firearms, while opponents of gun control say that shooting incidents demonstrate that Americans are not safe and should be free to carry guns for self-protection.

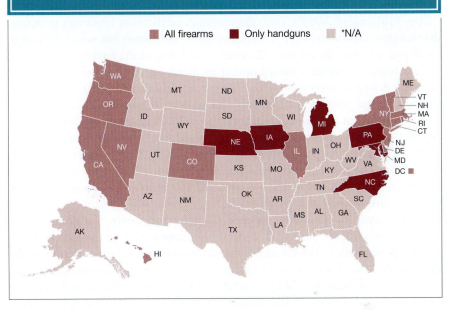

FIGURE 4.1

Background Checks on Firearm Sales

Although state gun laws must conform to the Second Amendment as interpreted by the U.S. Supreme Court, laws concerning gun sales and ownership vary widely from state to state. It is much more difficult to buy a gun in, say, New York or California than in Texas or Kentucky. This map shows states that require criminal background checks for the sale of all firearms, only handguns, or none when purchasing firearms. While federal law requires background checks when purchasing a firearm from a licensed seller, only 21 states require them from unlicensed sellers as well.

*An answer of N/A indicates the state does not require criminal background checks for gun sales by unlicensed sellers.

SOURCE: Background Checks, Gun Law Navigator, www.everytownresearch.org/ (accessed 6/12/18).

Legend: ■ All firearms ■ Only handguns ■ *N/A

Rights of the Criminally Accused Are Based on Due Process of Law

> **Explain the major rights that people have if they are accused of a crime**

Except for the First Amendment, most of the battle to apply the Bill of Rights to the states was fought over the various protections granted to individuals who are accused of a crime, who are suspects in the commission of a crime, or who are brought before the court as a witness to a crime. The Fourth, Fifth, Sixth, and Eighth amendments, taken together, are the essence of the due process of law, even though this key phrase does not appear until the very last words of the Fifth Amendment.

THE FOURTH AMENDMENT PROTECTS AGAINST UNLAWFUL SEARCHES AND SEIZURES

> The right of the people to be secure in their persons, houses, papers, and effects, against unreasonable searches and seizures, shall not be violated, and no Warrants shall issue, but upon probable cause, supported by Oath or affirmation, and particularly describing the place to be searched, and the persons or things to be seized.

The purpose of the Fourth Amendment is to guarantee the security of citizens against unreasonable (that is, improper) searches and seizures. In 1990 the Supreme Court summarized its understanding of the Fourth Amendment brilliantly and succinctly: "A search compromises the individual interest in privacy; a seizure deprives the individual of dominion over his or her person or property."[54] But how are we to define what is reasonable and what is unreasonable?

The 1961 case of *Mapp v. Ohio* illustrates one of the most important principles that has grown out of the Fourth Amendment: the **exclusionary rule**, which is the ability of courts to exclude evidence obtained in violation of the Fourth Amendment, such as barring evidence obtained during an illegal search from being introduced in a trial. Acting on a tip that Dollree Mapp was harboring a suspect in a bombing incident, several police officers forcibly entered Mapp's house claiming they had a warrant to look for the bombing suspect. The police did not find the bombing suspect but did find some materials connected to the local numbers racket (an illegal gambling operation) and a quantity of "obscene materials," in violation of an Ohio law banning possession of such materials. Although no warrant was ever produced, the evidence that had been seized was admitted by a court and Mapp was convicted for illegal possession of obscene materials.

By the time Mapp's appeal reached the Supreme Court, the question was whether any evidence produced under the circumstances of the search of her home was admissible. The Court's opinion affirmed the exclusionary rule: under the Fourth Amendment (applied to the states through the Fourteenth Amendment), "all evidence obtained by searches and seizures in violation of the Constitution . . . is inadmissible."[55] This means that even people who are clearly guilty of the crime of which they are accused must not be convicted if the only evidence for their conviction was obtained illegally.

The exclusionary rule is the most dramatic restraint imposed by the courts on police behavior because it rules out precisely the evidence that produces a conviction; it frees those people who are *known* to have committed the crime of which they have been accused because the evidence was obtained improperly, though few convictions are actually lost because of excluded evidence. Because it works so dramatically in favor of persons known to have committed a crime, the Court has since softened the application of the rule. In recent years, the federal courts have relied upon a discretionary use of the exclusionary rule, whereby they make a judgment as to the "nature and quality of the intrusion." It is thus difficult to know ahead of time whether a defendant will or will not be protected from an illegal search under the Fourth Amendment.[56] Several recent cases have imposed strict interpretations of a reasonable search. In 2013 the Court held that the use of a drug-sniffing dog on the front porch of a home constituted an improper search in the absence of consent or a warrant.[57]

Changes in technology have also had an impact on Fourth Amendment jurisprudence. In the 2012 case of *United States v. Jones*, the Court held that prosecutors violated Jones's rights when they attached a Global Positioning System device to his Jeep and monitored his movements for 28 days.[58] On the other hand, in *Maryland v. King*, the Court upheld DNA testing of arrestees without the need for individualized suspicion. The Court characterized DNA testing as an administrative tool for identifying the arrestee and thus as legally indistinguishable from photographing and fingerprinting.[59] In the 2014 case of *Riley v.*

Under what circumstances can the police search an individual's car? The Fourth Amendment protects against "unreasonable searches and seizures," but the Supreme Court has had to interpret what is unreasonable.

California, the Court held that the police were constitutionally prohibited from seizing and searching the digital contents of a cell phone during an arrest.[60] As new technologies develop, the Court will continue to face the question of what constitutes a reasonable search. In 2016 the Federal Bureau of Investigation (FBI) sought to compel the Apple Corporation to unlock the cell phone used by Syed Farook, an alleged terrorist who, along with his wife Tashfeen Malik, killed 14 people in San Bernardino, California. Apple asserted that creating new software to enable the FBI to unlock the phone would allow the agency to invade the privacy of millions of iPhone users. The case became moot when the FBI was able to unlock the phone without Apple's help.

Finally, the Fourth Amendment places limits on government surveillance of individuals, an ongoing and controversial issue in the United States today. For example, a federal judge in Washington, D.C., recently ruled that a National Security Agency (NSA) program that collected millions of records of telephone calls was impermissible under the Fourth Amendment.[61]

THE FIFTH AMENDMENT COVERS COURT-RELATED RIGHTS

No person shall be held to answer for a capital, or otherwise infamous crime, unless on a presentment or indictment of a Grand Jury, except in cases arising in the land or naval forces, or in the Militia, when in actual service in time of War or public danger; nor shall any person be subject for the same offence to be twice put in jeopardy of life or limb; nor shall be compelled in any criminal case to be a witness against himself, nor be deprived of life, liberty, or property, without due process of law; nor shall private property be taken for public use, without just compensation.

Grand Juries The first clause of the Fifth Amendment sets forth the right to a **grand jury** to determine whether a trial is warranted; grand juries do not rule on the accused's guilt or innocence. Grand juries play an important role in federal criminal cases. However, the provision for a grand jury is the one important civil liberties provision of the Bill of Rights that was not incorporated by the Fourteenth Amendment to apply to state criminal prosecutions. Thus, some states operate without grand juries. In such states, the prosecuting attorney simply files a "bill of information," affirming that there is sufficient evidence available to justify a trial. If the accused person is to be held in custody, the prosecutor must take the available information before a judge to determine that the evidence shows probable cause.

Double Jeopardy "Nor shall any person be subject for the same offence to be twice put in jeopardy of life or limb" is the constitutional protection from **double jeopardy**, a protection to prevent a person from being tried more than once for the same crime. The protection from double jeopardy was at the heart of the *Palko v. Connecticut* case in 1937. In that case, a Connecticut court had found Frank Palko guilty of second-degree murder and sentenced him to life in prison. Unhappy with the verdict, the state of Connecticut appealed the conviction to its highest state court, won the appeal, got a new trial, and then succeeded in getting Palko convicted of first-degree murder. Palko appealed to the Supreme Court on what seemed an open-and-shut case of double jeopardy. Yet, although the majority of the Court agreed that this could indeed be considered a case of double jeopardy, they decided that double jeopardy was not one of the provisions of the Bill of Rights incorporated in the Fourteenth Amendment as a restriction on the powers of the states.[62] Palko was executed for the crime in 1938, because he lived in Connecticut rather than in a state whose constitution included a guarantee against double jeopardy. It took more than 30 years for the Court to nationalize the constitutional protection against double jeopardy, when the court overruled *Palko* and declared that double jeopardy now applied to the states (see Table 4.2).

Self-Incrimination Perhaps the most significant liberty found in the Fifth Amendment, and the one most familiar to many Americans who watch television crime shows, is the guarantee that no citizen "shall be compelled in any criminal case to be a witness against himself." The most famous case concerning self-incrimination involved 23-year-old Ernesto Miranda, who was sentenced to between 20 and 30 years in prison for the kidnap and rape of an 18-year-old woman. The woman had identified him in a police lineup, and, after two hours of questioning, Miranda confessed, subsequently signing a statement that his confession had been made voluntarily, without threats or promises of immunity. This confession was admitted into evidence and served as the basis for Miranda's conviction. After his conviction, Miranda argued that his confession had not been truly voluntary and that he had not been informed of his right to remain silent or his right to consult an attorney. The Supreme Court agreed and overturned the conviction.[63] Following one of the most intensely and widely criticized decisions ever handed down by the Supreme Court, Miranda's case produced the rules the police must follow before questioning an arrested criminal suspect. The reading of a person's "*Miranda* rights" became a standard scene in every police station and on virtually every dramatization of police action on television and in the movies. *Miranda* advanced the civil liberties of accused persons not only by expanding the scope of the Fifth Amendment clause covering coerced confessions and self-incrimination but also by confirming the right to counsel (discussed later). Subsequent Supreme Courts considerably softened the *Miranda* restrictions, but the **Miranda rule** (as set out in *Miranda v. Arizona*) that persons under arrest must be informed prior to police interrogation of their rights to remain silent and to have the benefit of legal counsel, still stands as a protection against egregious police abuses of arrested persons.

Eminent Domain The other fundamental clause of the Fifth Amendment is the "takings clause," which extends to each citizen a protection against the "taking" of private property by the government "without just compensation." The power of any government to take private property for public use is called **eminent domain**. The Fifth Amendment puts limits on that inherent power through procedures that require a showing of a public purpose and the provision of fair payment for the government's taking of someone's property.

THE SIXTH AMENDMENT'S RIGHT TO COUNSEL IS CRUCIAL FOR A FAIR TRIAL

In all criminal prosecutions, the accused shall enjoy the right to a speedy and public trial, by an impartial jury of the State and district wherein the crime shall have been committed, which district shall have been ascertained by law, and to be informed of the nature and the cause of the accusation; to be confronted with the witnesses against him; to have compulsory process for obtaining witnesses in his favor, and to have the Assistance of Counsel for his defence.

Like the exclusionary rule of the Fourth Amendment and the self-incrimination clause of the Fifth Amendment, the "right to counsel" provision of the Sixth Amendment is notable for sometimes freeing defendants who seem to the public to be guilty as charged. Other provisions of the Sixth Amendment, such as the right to a speedy trial and the right to confront witnesses before an impartial jury, are not very controversial.

Gideon v. Wainwright (1963) is the perfect case study because it involved a disreputable person who seemed patently guilty of the crime of which he was convicted. In and out of jails for most of his 51 years, Clarence Earl Gideon received a five-year sentence for breaking and entering a poolroom in Panama City, Florida. While serving time in jail, Gideon became a fairly well-qualified "jailhouse lawyer," made his own appeal on a handwritten petition, and eventually won the landmark ruling on the right to counsel in all felony cases. After the Supreme Court's decision, Gideon was granted a new trial. This time, represented by an attorney, he was found not guilty.[64] The right to counsel was later expanded, beyond just serious crimes, to any trial, with or without a jury, that holds the possibility of imprisonment.

THE EIGHTH AMENDMENT BARS CRUEL AND UNUSUAL PUNISHMENT

> Excessive bail shall not be required, nor excessive fines imposed, nor cruel and unusual punishment inflicted.

Virtually all the debate over Eighth Amendment issues focuses on the last clause of the amendment: the protection from "cruel and unusual punishment." One of the greatest challenges in interpreting this provision consistently arises over the death penalty. In 1972 the Supreme Court overturned several state death penalty laws, not because they were cruel and unusual but because they were being applied unevenly—that is, blacks were much more likely than whites to be sentenced to death, the poor more likely than the rich, and men more likely than women.[65] Very soon after that decision, a majority of states revised their capital punishment provisions to meet the Court's standards, and the Court reaffirmed that the death penalty could be used if certain standards were met.[66] Since 1976 the Court has consistently upheld state laws providing for capital punishment, although it also continues to review death penalty appeals each year.

Between 1976 and April 2017, states executed 1,448 people. Most of those executions occurred in southern states, with Texas leading the way at 542. As of 2018, 30 states had statutes providing for capital punishment for specified offenses, a policy supported by a majority of Americans, according to polls. On the other hand, 19 states bar the death penalty; and since the end of the 1990s both the number of death sentences and the number of executions have declined annually.

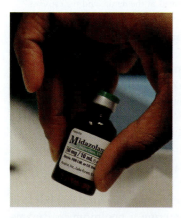

Opponents argue that the death penalty constitutes cruel and unusual punishment. In recent years, the use of lethal injection drugs including Midazolam has come under scrutiny after troubling executions where the process was drawn out and painful. In 2015 the Supreme Court upheld the use of lethal injection.

Many death penalty supporters assert it deters other would-be criminals. Although studies of capital crimes usually fail to demonstrate any direct deterrent effect, this failure may be due to the lengthy delays (typically years and even decades) between convictions and executions. A system that eliminates undue delays might enhance deterrence.

Death penalty opponents are quick to counter that the death penalty has not been proven to deter crime, either in the United States or abroad. In fact, America is the only Western nation that still executes criminals. If the government is to serve as an example of proper behavior, say foes of capital punishment, it has no business sanctioning killing when incarceration also protects society. Furthermore, execution is time-consuming and expensive—more expensive than life imprisonment—precisely because the government must make every effort to ensure that it is not executing an innocent person. Curtailing legal appeals would increase the possibility of a mistake. Race also intrudes in death penalty cases: people of color are disproportionately more likely than whites charged with identical crimes to be given the ultimate punishment.

In recent years, the Court has issued a number of death penalty opinions, declaring that death was too harsh a penalty for the crime of raping a child[67] and invalidating a death sentence for a black defendant when the prosecutor had improperly excluded African Americans from the jury.[68] In 2015 the Court upheld lethal injection as a mode of execution, despite arguments that this form of execution was likely to cause considerable pain.[69]

The Right to Privacy Means the Right to Be Left Alone

Assess whether people have a right to privacy under the Constitution

Although the word *privacy* never appears in the Bill of Rights, there is general agreement that a right to privacy emanates from the first 10 amendments—even though judges and legal scholars continue to disagree about where the right comes from. The idea behind the right to privacy is simple: people have a right to be left alone from government or other persons' interference in certain personal areas.

The sphere of privacy was drawn by the Supreme Court in 1965, when it ruled that a Connecticut statute forbidding the use of contraceptives violated the right of marital privacy. Estelle Griswold, the executive director of the Planned Parenthood League of Connecticut, was arrested by the state of Connecticut for providing information, instruction, and medical advice about contraception to married couples. She and her associates were found guilty as accessories to the crime and fined $100 each. The Supreme Court reversed the lower-court decisions and declared the Connecticut law unconstitutional because it violated "a right of privacy older than the Bill of Rights—older than our political parties, older than our school system."[70] Justice William O. Douglas, author of the majority decision in the *Griswold v. Connecticut* case, argued that this right of privacy is also grounded in the Constitution because it fits into a "zone of privacy" created by a combination of the Third, Fourth, and Fifth amendments. A concurring opinion, written by Justice Arthur Goldberg, attempted to strengthen Douglas's argument by adding that "the concept of liberty...embraces the right of marital privacy though that right is not mentioned explicitly in the Constitution [and] is supported by numerous decisions of this Court...and *by the language and history of the Ninth Amendment* [emphasis added]."[71]

The right to privacy was confirmed and extended in 1973 in an important but controversial privacy decision: *Roe v. Wade*. This decision established a woman's right to seek an abortion and prohibited states from making abortion a criminal act

One of the most important cases related to the right to privacy was *Roe v. Wade*, which established a woman's right to seek an abortion. However, the decision has remained highly controversial, with opponents arguing that the Constitution does not guarantee this right.

prior to the point at which the fetus becomes viable, which, in 1973, was the twenty-seventh week.[72] It is important to emphasize that the preference for privacy rights and for their extension to include the rights of women to control their own bodies was not something invented by the Supreme Court in a vacuum. Most states did not regulate abortions in any fashion until the 1840s, at which time only 6 of the 26 existing states had any regulations governing abortion. In addition, many states had begun to ease their abortion restrictions well before the 1973 *Roe* decision. In recent years, a number of states have reinstated some restrictions on abortion, including lowering the viability standard to 20 weeks (Texas), 12 weeks (Arkansas), and 6 weeks (North Dakota). While the Supreme Court has continued to affirm a woman's right to seek an abortion, it has limited the right, approving restrictions as long as they do not pose an "undue burden."

Like any important principle, once privacy was established as an aspect of civil liberties protected by the Bill of Rights through the Fourteenth Amendment, it took on a life of its own. In a number of important decisions, the Supreme Court and the lower federal courts sought to protect rights that could not be found in the text of the Constitution but could be discovered through a study of the philosophic sources of fundamental rights. Right-to-privacy claims have been made by those attempting to preserve the right to obtain legal abortions, by those seeking to obtain greater rights for gay people, and by supporters of physician-assisted suicide (also known as the "right-to-die" movement). In the case of gay people, the Supreme Court extended privacy protections to them in 2003 when it ruled that they are "entitled to respect for their private lives" in the case of *Lawrence v. Texas*.[73] The case overturned a Texas law banning certain sexual acts among same-sex partners. The Court concluded, "Petitioners are entitled to respect for their private lives. The State cannot demean their existence or control their destiny by making their private sexual conduct a crime." For the first time, gay men and lesbians could claim right-to-privacy protection.

Civil Rights Are Protections by the Government

Trace the legal developments and social movements that expanded civil rights

With the adoption of the Fourteenth Amendment in 1868, civil rights became part of the Constitution, guaranteed to each citizen through "equal protection of the laws."

Together with the Thirteenth Amendment, which abolished slavery, and the Fifteenth Amendment, which guaranteed voting rights for black men, it seemed to provide a guarantee of civil rights for the newly freed black slaves. But the general language of the Fourteenth Amendment meant that its support for civil rights could be even more far-reaching. The very simplicity of the **equal protection clause** of the Fourteenth Amendment left it open to interpretation:

> No State shall make or enforce any law which shall . . . deny to any person within its jurisdiction the equal protection of the laws.

These words launched a century of political movements and legal efforts to press for racial equality. The African American quest for civil rights in turn inspired many other groups, including members of other racial and ethnic groups, women, the disabled, and gay men, lesbians, and transgender individuals, to seek new laws and constitutional guarantees of their civil rights.

PLESSY V. FERGUSON ESTABLISHED "SEPARATE BUT EQUAL"

The Supreme Court was initially no more ready to enforce the civil rights aspects of the Fourteenth Amendment than it was to enforce the civil liberties provisions. Resistance to equality for African Americans in the South led Congress to adopt the Civil Rights Act of 1875, which attempted to protect blacks from discrimination by proprietors of hotels, theaters, and other public accommodations. But the Court declared the Civil Rights Act of 1875 unconstitutional on the grounds that it sought to protect blacks against discrimination by *private* businesses, while the Fourteenth Amendment, according to the Court's interpretation, was intended to protect individuals only from discrimination that arose from actions by *public* officials of state and local governments.

In the infamous case of *Plessy v. Ferguson* (1896), the Court went still further by upholding a Louisiana statute that *required* segregation of the races on trolleys and other public carriers (and, by implication, in all public facilities, including schools). Homer Plessy, a man defined as "one-eighth black," sat in a trolley car reserved for whites and was found guilty of violating a Louisiana law that provided for "equal but separate accommodations" on trains and a $25 fine for any white passenger who sat in a car reserved for blacks or any black passenger who sat in a car reserved for whites. The Supreme Court held that the Fourteenth Amendment's "equal protection of the laws" was not violated by laws requiring segregation of the races in public accommodations as long as the facilities were equal, thus establishing the **"separate but equal" rule** that prevailed through the mid-twentieth century.[74] White people generally pretended that segregated accommodations were equal as long as some accommodation for blacks existed. Thus, racial inequality in the guise of the separate but equal doctrine persisted for decades.

The 1896 Supreme Court case of *Plessy v. Ferguson* upheld legal segregation and created the "separate but equal" rule, which fostered national segregation. Overt discrimination in public accommodations was common.

LAWSUITS TO FIGHT FOR EQUALITY CAME AFTER WORLD WAR II

The Supreme Court had begun to change its position on racial discrimination before World War II by being stricter about the criterion for equal facilities in the "separate but equal" rule. In 1938, for example, the Court rejected Missouri's policy of paying the tuition of qualified blacks to out-of-state law schools rather than admitting them to the University of Missouri Law School.[75] Similar rulings in the 1940s and '50s began to chip away at "separate but equal."

Although none of those pre-1954 cases confronted "separate but equal" and the principle of racial discrimination head-on, they gave black leaders encouragement to believe that recent legal precedent might change the constitutional framework itself. Much of this legal work was done by the Legal Defense and Educational Fund of the National Association for the Advancement of Colored People (NAACP). Formed in 1909 to fight discrimination against African Americans, the NAACP was the most important civil rights organization during the first half of the twentieth century.

In the fall of 1952 the Court had on its docket cases from Delaware, the District of Columbia, Kansas, South Carolina, and Virginia challenging the constitutionality of school segregation. Of these, the case filed in Kansas became the chosen one by the NAACP. It seemed to be ahead of the pack in its district court, and it had the special advantage of being located in a state outside the Deep South, which would minimize local opposition to a favorable decision.[76]

Oliver Brown, the father of three girls, lived "across the tracks" in a low-income, racially mixed Topeka neighborhood. Every school day morning, Linda Brown took the school bus to the Monroe School for black children about a mile away but had to walk through a dangerous railroad switchyard to get to the stop—all this, even though a white school was closer to their home. In September 1950, Oliver Brown took Linda to the closer all-white Sumner School to enter her into the third grade in defiance of state law and local segregation rules. When they were refused, Brown took his case to the NAACP; and soon thereafter *Brown v. Board of Education* was born.

In deciding the *Brown* case, the Court, to the surprise of many, rejected as inconclusive historical evidence about the intent and the history of the Fourteenth Amendment and committed itself instead to considering only the consequences of segregation:

> Does segregation of children in public schools solely on the basis of race, even though the phys-ical facilities and other "tangible" factors may be equal, deprive the children of the minority group of equal educational opportunities? We believe that it does. ... We conclude that in the field of public education the doctrine of "separate but equal" has no place. Separate educational facilities are inherently unequal.[77]

The *Brown* decision altered the constitutional framework by concluding that racial discrimination violated the Constitution.

THE CIVIL RIGHTS STRUGGLE ESCALATED AFTER *BROWN V. BOARD OF EDUCATION*

Brown v. Board of Education withdrew all constitutional authority to use race as a criterion for exclusion, and it signaled more clearly the Court's determination to use the strict scrutiny test in cases related to racial discrimination. This meant that the burden of proof would fall on the government to show that the law in question *was* constitutional—not on the challengers to show the law's *un*constitutionality.[78] But the historic decision in *Brown v. Board of Education* was merely a small open-ing move. First, most states refused to cooperate until sued, and many ingenious schemes were employed to delay obedience (such as states paying the tuition for white students to attend newly created "private" academies). Second, while school boards began to cooperate by eliminating legally enforced school segregation (what is referred to as *de jure* segregation, meaning literally "by law" or legally enforced practices), extensive actual segregation remained (what is referred to as *de facto* seg-regation, meaning literally "by fact," wherein races are still segregated even though the law does not require it). Thus, school segregation in the North as well as in the South remained as a consequence of racially segregated housing patterns that were untouched by the 1954–55 *Brown* principles. Third, discrimination in employment, public accommodations, juries, voting, and other areas of social and economic activity was not directly touched by *Brown*.

Social Protest and Congressional Action Ten years after *Brown*, fewer than 1 percent of black school-age children in the Deep South were attending schools with whites.[79] A decade of frustration made it fairly obvious to all observers that

"Massive resistance" among white southerners attempted to block the desegregation efforts of the national government. For example, at Little Rock Central High School in 1957, an angry mob of white southerners prevented black students from entering the school.

adjudication alone would not succeed. The goal of "equal protection" required positive, or affirmative, action by Congress and by federal agencies. And given massive southern resistance and a generally negative national public opinion toward racial integration, progress would not be made through courts, Congress, or federal agencies without intense, well-organized support. Organized civil rights demonstrations began to mount slowly but surely after *Brown v. Board of Education*. Only a year after Brown, black citizens in Montgomery, Alabama, challenged the city's segregated bus system with a yearlong boycott. The boycott began with the arrest of Rosa Parks, who refused to give up her bus seat for a white man. A seamstress who worked with civil rights groups, Parks eventually became a civil rights icon, as did one of the ministers leading the boycott: Martin Luther King, Jr. After a year of private carpools and walking, Montgomery's bus system desegregated but only after the Supreme Court ruled the system unconstitutional.

By the 1960s the many organizations that made up the civil rights movement had accumulated experience and built networks capable of launching massive direct-action campaigns against southern segregationists. The Southern Christian Leadership Conference, the Student Nonviolent Coordinating Committee, and many other organizations had built a movement that stretched across the South, using the media to attract nationwide attention and support. The image of protesters being beaten, attacked by police dogs, and set upon with fire hoses did much to win broad sympathy for the cause of black civil rights and to discredit state and local governments in the South. In the massive March on Washington in 1963, the Reverend Martin Luther King, Jr., staked out the movement's moral claims in his famous "I Have a Dream" speech.

Protests against discriminatory practices toward African Americans did not end in the 1960s. Beginning in 2012, a variety of protests coalesced under the banner Black Lives Matter to focus attention on allegations of police misconduct directed at African Americans. The movement took off after the shooting of an unarmed black teenager by a white police officer in Ferguson, Missouri, in 2014 and spread across the nation as the media, including social media, carried reports, photos, and videos of police violence against blacks around the country. African Americans have long asserted that they are often victims of racial profiling and more likely than whites to be harassed or arrested by the police. Police departments have replied that blacks are more likely than whites to be engaged in criminal activity.

THE CIVIL RIGHTS ACTS MADE EQUAL PROTECTION A REALITY

The right to equal protection of the laws could be established and, to a certain extent, implemented by the courts. But after a decade of very frustrating efforts, the courts and Congress ultimately came to the conclusion that the federal courts alone were not adequate to the task of changing the social rules and that legislation and administrative action would be needed.

Congress used its legislative powers to help make equal protection of the laws a reality by passing the Civil Rights Act of 1964, prohibiting major forms of discrimination against racial, ethnic, national and religious minorities, and women in voting registration, schools, public accommodations, and the workplace. The act seemed bold at the time, but it was enacted 10 years after the Supreme Court had declared racial discrimination "inherently unequal" and long after blacks had demonstrated that discrimination was no longer acceptable.

Public Accommodations After the passage of the 1964 Civil Rights Act, public accommodations quickly removed some of the most visible forms of racial discrimination. Signs defining "colored" and "white" restrooms, water fountains, waiting rooms, and seating arrangements were removed and a host of other practices that relegated black people to separate and inferior arrangements were ended. In addition, the federal government filed more than 400 antidiscrimination suits in federal courts against hotels, restaurants, taverns, gas stations, and other "public accommodations."

Many aspects of legalized racial segregation, such as using separate Bibles to swear in black and white witnesses in the courtroom, seem like ancient history today. But the issue of racial discrimination in public settings is by no means over. In 1993 six African American Secret Service agents filed suit after a Denny's restaurant in Annapolis, Maryland, failed to serve them. Similar charges citing discriminatory service at Denny's restaurants surfaced across the country. Faced with evidence of a pattern of systematic discrimination and numerous lawsuits, Denny's paid $45 million in damages to plaintiffs in Maryland and California in what is said to be the largest settlement ever in a public accommodation case.[80] In addition to the settlement, the chain vowed to expand employment and management opportunities for minorities in Denny's restaurants.

School Desegregation The 1964 Civil Rights Act also declared discrimination by private employers and state governments (school boards, etc.) illegal, then went further by providing for administrative agencies to help the courts implement these laws. The act, for example, authorized the executive branch, through the Justice Department, to implement federal court orders to desegregate schools and to do so without having to wait for individual parents to bring complaints. The act also provided that federal grants-in-aid to state and local governments for education be withheld from any school system practicing racial segregation.

In recent years, a series of court rulings have slowed race-based integration efforts. In 2007 the Supreme Court's ruling in *Parents Involved in Community Schools v.*

Seattle School District No. 1 limited the measures that can be used to promote school integration.[81] The case involved school assignment plans voluntarily initiated by the cities of Seattle, Washington, and Louisville, Kentucky. By making race one factor in assigning students to schools, the cities hoped to achieve greater racial balance across the public schools. The Court ruled that these plans, even though they were voluntarily adopted by cities, were unconstitutional because it assigned some students to schools based on race (in violation of *Brown*). Still, some described the decision as the end of the Brown era because it eliminated one of the few public strategies left to promote racial integration.[82]

Outlawing Discrimination in Employment The federal courts and the Justice Department also fought employment discrimination through the Civil Rights Act of 1964, which outlawed job discrimination by all private and public employers, including governmental agencies (such as fire and police departments) that employed more than 15 workers.[83] The 1964 act makes it unlawful to discriminate in employment on the basis of color, religion, sex, or national origin, as well as race.

In order to enforce fair employment practices, the national government could revoke public contracts for goods and services and refuse to engage in contracts with any private company that could not guarantee that its rules for hiring, promotion, and firing were nondiscriminatory.

But one problem was that the complaining party had to show that deliberate discrimination was the cause of the failure to get a job or a training opportunity. Rarely, of course, does an employer explicitly admit discrimination on the basis of race, sex, or any other illegal reason. Recognizing this, the courts have allowed aggrieved parties (the plaintiffs) to make their case if they can show that an employer's hiring practices had the *effect* of exclusion, even if they cannot show the *intention* to discriminate.

Voting Rights Although 1964 was the most important year for civil rights legislation, it was not the only important year. In 1965, Congress significantly strengthened legislation protecting voting rights by barring literacy and other tests as a condition for voting in six southern states,[84] by making it a crime to interfere with voting, and by providing for the replacement of local registrars with federally appointed registrars in counties designated by the attorney general as significantly resistant to registering eligible blacks to vote. The right to vote was further strengthened with ratification in 1964 of the Twenty-Fourth Amendment, which abolished the poll tax, and later with legislation permanently outlawing literacy tests and mandating bilingual ballots or oral assistance for Spanish, Chinese, Japanese, and Korean speakers, and Native Americans. This 1965 law finally led to a dramatic increase in voting by African Americans, meaning that it took almost 100 years to carry out the Fifteenth Amendment.

In the long run, the laws extending and protecting voting rights could prove to be the most effective of all the great civil rights legislation because the progress in black political participation produced by these acts has altered the shape of American politics. In 1965, in the seven states of the Old Confederacy covered by the Voting Rights Act, 29.3 percent of the eligible black residents were registered to vote, compared with 73.4 percent of the white residents (see Table 4.3). In 1967, a mere two years after implementation of the voting rights laws, 52.1 percent of the eligible blacks in the seven states were registered. By 1972 the gap between black and white registration in the seven states was only 11.2 points.

A new area of controversy in the realm of voting rights concerns so-called voter ID laws. Some 34 states have enacted legislation requiring voters to show positive identification at the polls. As of 2018, seven of these states required photo ID, like a driver's license, in order to vote. Republicans generally support such laws, arguing that they deter voter fraud. Democrats generally oppose such laws, countering that

TABLE 4.3

Registration by Race and State in Southern States Covered by the Voting Rights Act (VRA)

The VRA had a direct impact on the rate of black voter registration in the southern states, as measured by the gap between white and black voters in each state. Further insights can be gained by examining changes in white registration rates before and after passage of the VRA and by comparing the gaps between white and black registration. Why do you think registration rates for whites increased significantly in some states and dropped in others? What impact could the increase in black registration have had on public policy?

	BEFORE THE ACT*			AFTER THE ACT* 1971–72		
	WHITE (%)	BLACK (%)	GAP** (%)	WHITE (%)	BLACK (%)	GAP (%)
Alabama	69.2	19.3	49.9	80.7	57.1	23.6
Georgia	62.6	27.4	35.2	70.6	67.8	2.8
Louisiana	80.5	31.6	48.9	80.0	59.1	20.9
Mississippi	69.9	6.7	63.2	71.6	62.2	9.4
North Carolina	96.8	46.8	50.0	62.2	46.3	15.9
South Carolina	75.7	37.3	38.4	51.2	48.0	3.2
Virginia	61.1	38.3	22.8	61.2	54.0	7.2
AVERAGE	73.4	29.3	44.1	67.8	56.6	11.2

*Available registration data as of March 1965 and 1971–72.
**The gap is the percentage-point difference between white and black registration rates.

SOURCE: U.S. Commission on Civil Rights, Political Participation (1968), Appendix VII: Voter Education Project, attachment to press release, October 3, 1972.

they are particularly burdensome to poor, young, and minority voters, who they say are less likely to possess such IDs. Critics also note that virtually no documented cases of voter ID fraud exist, despite intensive efforts to uncover them. In 2017 the Trump administration established an election integrity commission to look into charges of illegal voting in the 2016 elections. The Commission was blasted by Democrats as another effort to discourage voting.

Housing The Civil Rights Act of 1964 did not address housing, but in 1968, Congress passed another civil rights act specifically to outlaw housing discrimination. Called the Fair Housing Act, the law prohibited discrimination in the sale or rental of most housing, eventually covering nearly all of the nation's housing. Housing was among the most controversial of discrimination issues because of deeply entrenched patterns of residential segregation across the United States.

Although it pronounced sweeping goals, the Fair Housing Act had little effect on housing segregation because its enforcement mechanisms were so weak. Individuals believing they had been discriminated against had to file suit themselves. The burden was on the individual to prove that housing discrimination had occurred, even though such discrimination is often subtle and difficult to document. Although local fair-housing groups emerged to assist individuals in their court claims, the procedures for proving discrimination created a formidable barrier to effective change. These procedures were not altered until 1988, when Congress passed the Fair Housing Amendments Act. This new law put more teeth in the enforcement procedures and allowed the Department of Housing and Urban Development to initiate legal action in cases of discrimination.[85]

Another kind of discrimination, related to discriminatory home mortgage–lending practices, remained significant. So-called predatory lending—offering loans with interest rates that are higher than prevailing market rates, including "subprime mortgages"—led to charges that such loans were offered to African Americans and Latinos, while whites with similar incomes were offered loans with lower interest rates. These charges received extensive national attention when the economic downturn of 2008–09 led to widespread mortgage defaults, with many people losing their homes.[86] Lawsuits over these practices have resulted in the largest financial settlements ever issued for lending discrimination.

AFFIRMATIVE ACTION ATTEMPTS TO RIGHT PAST WRONGS

Over the past half-century, the relatively narrow goal of equalizing opportunity by eliminating discriminatory barriers developed toward the far broader goal of **affirmative action,** government policies or programs that seek to redress past injustices against specified groups by making special efforts to provide members of these groups with access to educational and employment opportunities. An affirmative action policy uses two novel approaches: (1) positive or benign discrimination in which race or some other status is counted as a positive rather than negative factor and (2) compensatory action to favor members of the disadvantaged group who themselves may never have been the victims of discrimination.

Affirmative action also took the form of efforts by the agencies in the Department of Health, Education, and Welfare to shift their focus from "desegregation" to "integration."[87] Federal agencies required school districts to present plans for busing children across district lines, for closing certain schools, and for redistributing faculties as well as students or face the loss of aid from the federal government. The guidelines constituted preferential treatment to compensate for past discrimination, leading to a dramatic increase in the numbers of black children attending integrated classes.

The Supreme Court Shifts the Burden of Proof in Affirmative Action Efforts by the government to shape the meaning of affirmative action today tend to center on one key issue: What is the appropriate level of review in affirmative action cases— that is, on whom should the burden of proof be placed: the plaintiff, to show that discrimination has not occurred, or the defendant, to show that discrimination has occurred? The reason this question is difficult is because the cases in which the Court struck down racially discriminatory laws all involved historically disadvantaged racial minority groups. The Court struck down those laws partly because it concluded they were motivated by racial hostility and partly because the Court concluded that disadvantaged minority groups were effectively unable to use the political process to challenge laws that harmed them. The new cases, however, rather than being motivated by racial hostility, were enacted with the objective of assisting victims of past injustice. And instead of harming minority groups, they disadvantaged members of the dominant majority racial group. Yet critics argued that discriminating against *any* individual because of their race violated the Equal Protection clause.

This question was addressed by the Supreme Court in the case of *Regents of the University of California v. Bakke*. Allan Bakke, a white male, brought suit against the University of California at Davis Medical School in 1973 on the grounds that it denied him admission on the basis of his race. (That year the school had reserved 16 of its 100 available slots for minority applicants.) Bakke argued that his grades and test scores had ranked him well above many students who had been accepted at the school and that the only possible explanation for his rejection was that he was white, whereas those others accepted were black or Latino. In 1978, Bakke won his case before the Supreme Court and was admitted to the medical school, but he did not succeed in getting affirmative action declared unconstitutional. The Court accepted the argument that achieving "a diverse student body" was "a compelling public purpose," but it ruled that the method of a rigid quota of student slots assigned on the basis of race was incompatible with the Fourteenth Amendment's equal protection clause. Thus, the Court permitted universities and other hiring authorities to continue to take minority status into consideration but barred the use of quotas.[88]

This ambiguous status of affirmative action was how things stood in 2003, when the Supreme Court took two cases against the University of Michigan. In *Grutter v. Bollinger*, the Court upheld the affirmative action program used by Michigan's law school, finding it in keeping with the standard set in the *Bakke* case.[89] Michigan's undergraduate affirmative action program was declared unconstitutional, however, in *Gratz v. Bollinger* because its ranking system for admissions gave specific points to African American, Latino, and Native American applicants.[90] This approach was barred for resembling too closely the specific numerical quota system struck down by *Bakke*. In 2013 the Court indicated in *Fisher v. University of Texas* that a school's affirmative action program of admissions that seems to discriminate in favor of black students must be subjected to the same "strict scrutiny" as a program that seems to discriminate against black students and sent the case back to the lower courts for consideration.[91] The Court heard the case again in 2016, and declared that some intrusion on equal protection was warranted by the importance of creating a diverse student body.[92]

The Civil Rights Struggle Was Extended to Other Disadvantaged Groups

Describe how different groups have fought for and won protection of their civil rights

Even before equal employment laws began to have a positive effect on the economic situation of blacks, something far more dramatic began to happen: the universalization of civil rights. The right not to be discriminated against was being successfully claimed by the other groups listed in the 1964 Civil Rights Act (those defined by sex, religion, or national origin) and eventually by still other groups (defined by age or sexual orientation). This extension of civil rights became the new frontier of the civil rights struggle, and women emerged with the greatest prominence in this new struggle.

AMERICANS HAVE FOUGHT GENDER DISCRIMINATION

In many ways the Civil Rights Act fostered the growth of the women's movement (although critics noted that this movement largely benefited white women). The first major campaign of the National Organization for Women (NOW) involved picketing the Equal Employment Opportunity Commission for its refusal to ban sex-segregated employment advertisements. NOW also sued the *New York Times* for continuing to publish such ads after the passage of the act. Another organization, the Women's Equity Action League, pursued legal action on a wide range of sex-discrimination issues, filing lawsuits against law schools and medical schools for discriminatory admission policies, for example.

Building on these victories and the growth of the women's movement, feminist activists sought to add an "Equal Rights Amendment" (ERA) to the Constitution. The proposed amendment was short; it stated that "equality of rights under the law shall not be denied or abridged by the United States or by any State on account of sex." The amendment's supporters believed that such a sweeping guarantee of equal rights was a necessary tool for ending all discrimination against women and for making gender roles more equal. Opponents charged that it would be socially disruptive and would introduce changes (such as unisex restrooms) that most

Americans did not want. The amendment easily passed Congress in 1972 and won quick approval in many state legislatures, but it fell 3 states short of the 38 needed to ratify it by the 1982 deadline.[93]

Despite the failure of the ERA, efforts to stop gender discrimination expanded dramatically as an area of civil rights law. In the 1970s the conservative Burger Court (under Chief Justice Warren Burger) helped establish gender discrimination as a major and highly visible civil rights issue. Although the Supreme Court refused to treat gender discrimination as the equivalent of racial discrimination,[94] it did make it easier for plaintiffs to file and win suits on the basis of gender discrimination.

Courts began to find sexual harassment a form of sex discrimination during the late 1970s. Most of the law on sexual harassment has been developed by courts through interpretation of Title VII of the Civil Rights Act of 1964. In 1986 the Supreme Court recognized two forms of sexual harassment: the quid pro quo type, which involves an explicit or strongly implied threat that submission is a condition of continued employment, and the hostile environment type, which involves offensive or intimidating employment conditions amounting to sexual intimidation.[95]

Another major step was taken in 1992, when the Court decided in *Franklin v. Gwinnett County Public Schools* that violations of Title IX of the 1972 Education Act could be remedied with monetary damages.[96] Title IX forbade gender discrimination in education, but it initially sparked little litigation because of its weak enforcement provisions. The Court's 1992 ruling that monetary damages could be awarded for gender discrimination opened the door for more legal action in the area of education. The greatest impact has been in the areas of sexual harassment (the subject of the *Franklin* case) and in equal treatment of women's athletic programs. The potential for monetary damages has made universities and public schools take the problem of sexual harassment more seriously.

In 1996 the Supreme Court made another important decision by putting an end to all-male schools supported by public funds. It ruled that the policy of the Virginia Military Institute (VMI) not to admit women was unconstitutional.[97] Along with The Citadel, an all-male military college in South Carolina, VMI had never admitted women in its 157-year history. VMI argued that the unique educational experience it offered—including intense physical training and the harsh treatment of freshmen—would be destroyed if women were admitted. The Court, however, ruled that the male-only policy denied "substantial equality" to women. Two days after the Court's ruling, The Citadel announced that it would accept women.

Women have also pressed for civil rights in employment. In particular, women have fought against pay discrimination, which occurs when a male employee is paid more than a female employee of equal qualifications in the same job. In the 1960s pay discrimination was common. After the Equal Pay Act of 1963 made such discrimination illegal, women's pay slowly moved toward the level of men's pay. In 2007 this movement received a setback when the Supreme Court ruled against a claim of pay discrimination. The case, *Ledbetter v. Goodyear Tire and Rubber Co.*, involved a female supervisor named Lily Ledbetter, who learned late in her career that she was being paid up to 40 percent less than male supervisors, including those with less seniority. Ledbetter filed a grievance with the EEOC, charging sex discrimination.[98]

Political equality did not end discrimination against women in the workplace or in society at large. In 2009, President Obama signed the Lily Ledbetter Fair Pay Act in an effort to reinstate fair pay protections for women.

The Supreme Court denied her claim, ruling that, according to the law, workers must file their grievance 180 days after the discrimination occurs. Many observers found the ruling unfair because workers often do not know about pay differentials until well after the initial decision to discriminate has been made. In 2009 the Lily Ledbetter Fair Pay Act became the first bill that President Obama signed into law, giving workers expanded rights to sue in cases such as Ledbetter's when an employee learns of discriminatory treatment well after it has started.

In recent years, laws and court decisions designed to deal with discrimination against women have been used by groups representing transgender individuals to press for equal rights, especially in the realm of employment. For example, Title VII of the 1964 Civil Rights Act makes it unlawful to discriminate in employment on the basis of color, religion, sex, national origin, or race. Pressed by groups representing transgender workers, in 2015 President Obama issued an executive order prohibiting federal contractors from discriminating against workers based on their sexual orientation or gender identity. Two months later the EEOC filed its first-ever lawsuits to protect transgender workers under Title VII. Later that year Attorney General Eric Holder announced that the Justice Department would consider discrimination against transgender people as covered by the Civil Rights Act's prohibition of sex discrimination.[99] Nonetheless, attempts have been made to pass legislation requiring transgender individuals to use public bathrooms that correspond to the gender designated on their birth certificates. In 2016, North Carolina enacted such a law. After the federal Department of Justice warned the state that the law violated the Civil Rights Act, the state and the department filed opposing lawsuits over the issue. As the legal standoff continued, many companies pulled conventions and other events out of the state, costing North Carolina's economy millions of dollars. Bowing to pressure, North Carolina repealed the ordinance in 2017. Also in 2017, President Trump tweeted that transgender people would be barred from military service. The president's tweet caused confusion and consternation with Pentagon officials, saying they had neither been consulted nor received any formal directive. On the heels of a court decision pausing the enactment of any ban, the military said that transgender enlistments would be allowed in 2018.[100]

LATINOS AND ASIAN AMERICANS FIGHT FOR RIGHTS

Although the Civil Rights Act of 1964 outlawed discrimination on the basis of national origin, persistent discrimination plus limited English proficiency kept many Asian Americans and Latinos from full participation in American life. Two developments in the 1970s, however, established rights for language minorities. In 1974 the Supreme Court ruled in *Lau v. Nichols* that school districts have to provide education for students whose English is limited.[101] It did not mandate bilingual education, but it established a duty to provide instruction that the students could understand. And as mentioned earlier the 1970 amendments to the Voting Rights Act permanently outlawed literacy tests in all 50 states and mandated bilingual ballots or oral assistance for those who speak Spanish, Chinese, Japanese, Korean, or Native American languages.

Asian Americans and Latinos have also been concerned about the impact of immigration laws on their civil rights. Many Asian American and Latino organizations opposed the Immigration Reform and Control Act of 1986 because it imposed sanctions on employers who hire undocumented workers. Such sanctions, they feared, would lead employers to discriminate against Latinos and Asian Americans. These suspicions were confirmed in a 1990 report by the General Accounting Office that found employer sanctions had created a "widespread pattern of discrimination" against Latinos and others who appear foreign.[102]

As we saw in Chapter 3, a number of states have recently passed very strict immigration laws. Arizona's 2010 law provided the inspiration for these far-reaching state measures. Arizona's law required immigrants to carry identity documents with them at all times, made it a crime for an undocumented immigrant to apply for a job, gave

Immigration is one of today's most controversial issues. President Trump campaigned on a promise to build a protective wall on the U.S.-Mexico border. Supporters of stricter immigration policies believe they will help protect jobs for American citizens. Others support the rights of undocumented people—especially young people brought to the United States by their parents, so-called Dreamers—and believe that they should have a path to American citizenship.

the police greater powers to stop anyone they suspected of being an unauthorized immigrant, and required the police to check the immigration status of a person they detain if they suspect that person is an unauthorized immigrant. The Justice Department challenged the law on the grounds that the federal government was responsible for making immigration law, not the states. In 2012 the Court struck down three parts of the Arizona law: the provision that immigrants carry identity papers, that undocumented immigrants cannot apply for jobs, and that police can stop persons they suspect of being undocumented immigrants. But the Court let stand the provision that required local police to check the immigration status of an individual detained for other reasons, if they had grounds to suspect that the person was in the country illegally.[103]

In 2014, President Obama issued executive orders granting quasi-legal status and work permits to millions of individuals who entered the United States illegally as children or who have children who are American citizens. The Supreme Court challenged Obama's authority to issue the executive order, and in 2016, with only eight members on the Court after the death of Justice Scalia, the Court issued a 4–4 tie.[104] The stalemate let stand a lower-court decision striking down Obama's order. The lower-court decision, however, did not establish a binding national precedent, and the administration seemed likely to ignore it.

NATIVE AMERICANS HAVE SOVEREIGNTY BUT STILL LACK RIGHTS

Native Americans occupy a unique place in the American equality landscape. An early Supreme Court decision referred to native peoples as "domestic dependent nations"—they were not considered American citizens, but they were also placed firmly under the power of the national government. Native peoples were forcibly removed from lands, attacked in sustained military campaigns, and subject to extensive and explicit discrimination across the country.

In 1924 native peoples were collectively naturalized by Congress. In 1975 they were granted federal voting-rights protections in the amendments to the Voting Rights Act. The *Lau* decision established the right of Native Americans to be taught in their own languages. This marked quite a change from the period when Native American children attended boarding schools run by the Bureau of Indian Affairs, where they were forbidden from speaking their own languages and otherwise forced to assimilate to the dominant culture. Native Americans have also sought to expand their rights on the basis of their sovereign status. Since the 1920s and '30s, Native American tribes have sued the federal government for illegally seizing land, seeking monetary reparations and land. Both types of damages have been awarded in such suits but only in small amounts. Native American tribes have been more successful in winning federal recognition of their sovereignty. Most significant economically was a 1987 Supreme Court decision that freed Native American tribes from most state regulations prohibiting gambling. The establishment of casino gambling on Native American lands has brought a substantial flow of new income into some desperately poor reservations.

Civil Liberties around the World

Elections are only a small part of what makes a democracy a democracy. *Liberal democracies* also have extensive civil rights and civil liberties.

Freedom House, an independent watchdog organization focusing on freedom and democracy around the world, collects data on political rights and civil liberties from each country. They measure freedom of expression and belief, respect for the "rule of law,"[a] the right to organize and form associations, and personal autonomy and individual rights to rank countries as free, partly free, and not free (shown below).

All countries vary in how they prioritize specific liberties. The United States is generally comparable to other democracies when it comes to the freedom of expression and belief and the right to organize and form associations, but the United States places exceptionally high emphasis on personal autonomy and individual rights. In comparison, Latvia is ranked slightly higher on the right to organize and form associations, but concerns regarding the treatment of women and minorities mean its individual rights score is lower.

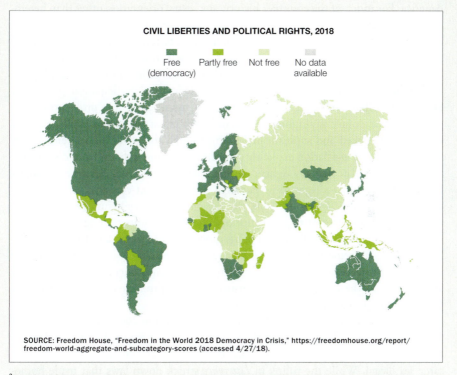

CIVIL LIBERTIES AND POLITICAL RIGHTS, 2018

Free (democracy) Partly free Not free No data available

SOURCE: Freedom House, "Freedom in the World 2018 Democracy in Crisis," https://freedomhouse.org/report/freedom-world-aggregate-and-subcategory-scores (accessed 4/27/18).

[a]A legal principle that laws should govern a country—including its leaders—rather than having decisions made arbitrarily by individuals in the government.

DISABLED AMERICANS WON A GREAT VICTORY IN 1990

The concept of rights for the disabled began to emerge in the 1970s as the civil rights model spread to other groups. The seed was planted in a little-noticed provision of the 1973 Rehabilitation Act, which outlawed discrimination against individuals on the basis of disabilities. As in many other cases, the law itself helped give rise to the movement demanding rights for the disabled.[105] Modeling it on the NAACP's Legal Defense Fund, the disability movement founded the Disability Rights Education and Defense Fund to press its legal claims. The movement achieved its greatest success with the passage of the Americans with Disabilities Act of 1990, which guarantees equal employment rights and access to public businesses for the disabled and bars discrimination in employment, housing, and health care. The EEOC is a body that considers claims of discrimination in violation of this act. The impact of the law has been far-reaching as businesses and public facilities have installed ramps, elevators, and other devices to meet the act's requirements.[106]

LGBTQ AMERICANS

In less than 50 years, the lesbian, gay, bisexual, transgender, and queer (LGBTQ) movement has become one of the largest civil rights movements in contemporary America. For much of the country's history, any sexual orientation other than hetero-sexuality was considered "deviant," and many states criminalized sexual acts considered to be "unnatural." Gay people were often afraid to reveal their sexual orientation for fear of reprisals, including being fired from their jobs; and the police in many cities raided bars and other establishments where it was believed that gay people gathered. While no formal restrictions existed on their political participation, gay people faced the possibility of ostracism, discrimination, assault, and even prosecution.[107]

The contemporary gay rights movement began in earnest in the 1960s, growing into a well-financed and sophisticated lobby, though there was no Supreme Court ruling or national legislation explicitly protecting gays and lesbians from discrimination until 1996. The first gay rights case that the Court decided, *Bowers v. Hardwick* (1986), ruled against a right to privacy that would protect consensual homosexual activity.[108] After the *Bowers* decision, the gay and lesbian rights movement sought suitable legal cases to test the constitutionality of discrimination against gay men and lesbians, much as the black civil rights movement did in the late 1940s and '50s. In 1996 the Supreme Court, in *Romer v. Evans*, explicitly extended fundamental civil rights protections to gays and lesbians by declaring unconstitutional a 1992 amendment to the Colorado state constitution that prohibited local governments from passing ordinances to protect gay rights.[109]

The gay community won another major victory in the 2003 case of *Lawrence v. Texas* (mentioned earlier), in which the Supreme Court overturned *Bowers* and struck down a Texas law that made certain sexual conduct between consenting partners of the same sex illegal. While the ruling in *Lawrence* struck down laws that made homosexual acts a crime, it did not change federal and state laws that deprived gay people of full civil rights, including the right to marry. In 2013 the Supreme Court struck down a federal law (the Defense of Marriage Act) that barred benefits to married same-sex couples and let stand a California law recognizing same-sex marriage. The federal government subsequently expanded recognition of same-sex marriages for the purpose of federal benefits and legal proceedings, such as survivor benefits, bankruptcies, tax purposes, and immigration.

In 2015 the Supreme Court clarified the law concerning same-sex marriage. In the landmark case of *Obergefell v. Hodges*, the Court ruled that the Constitution's equal protection clause and the Fourteenth Amendment's due process clause guarantee same-sex couples the right to marry in all states and required states to recognize same-sex marriages performed in other jurisdictions.[110] Though the Court was divided in the case, its decision actually reflected a dramatic shift in public opinion in favor of same-sex unions and their right to wed.

In 2013 the Supreme Court struck down the portion of the Defense of Marriage Act denying federal benefits to married same-sex couples. This decision paved the way for the Court decision two years later legalizing same-sex marriage nationwide. The Obama administration showed its support by illuminating the White House in rainbow light.

Another significant victory at the national level occurred in 2009, when new legislation extended the definition of hate crimes to include crimes against gays and transgender people. Such legislation had been sought since the 1998 murder of Matthew Shepard, a Wyoming college student who was brutally slain because of his sexual orientation. The 2009 law allows for tougher penalties when a crime is designated a hate crime. In another important victory for the gay rights movement, an executive order signed by President Obama in 2011 repealed the U.S. military's "Don't Ask, Don't Tell" policy, a 20-year-old rule that expelled gays and lesbians from the military if they made their sexual orientation known. The new policy allows gays to serve openly in the military.

Civil Liberties and Civil Rights
WHAT DO WE WANT?

The prominent place of civil liberties is one of the hallmarks of American government. The freedoms enshrined in the Constitution and its amendments help define the relationship between government and citizens by limiting what government can do to individuals.

But these freedoms also come with trade-offs. As we saw in the chapter opener, the freedom to reimagine an ethnic slur as a term of empowerment was afforded to the Slants rock band. In a further twist, this decision undermined Native Americans' efforts to revoke the Washington Redskins' team name, as they found it to be an offensive ethnic term, and the groups were unable to establish a legal basis to sue the team. The Slants' free speech was protected to their joy, but so was the Redskins' free speech to the disappointment of Native Americans. Issues related to free speech, privacy, and religious freedom (see the "**Who Participates?**" feature on the facing page) are unlikely to go away anytime soon.

The civil rights revolution, a revolution that began with African Americans, has broadened to include women and Latinos and to address such matters as sexual orientation, sexual identification, and immigration status. As our nation becomes more and more diverse, equal protection of the laws will become more and more important. If we are to succeed and prosper as a nation, we must be inclusive. The tumultuous history of civil rights in America demonstrates that exclusion is a recipe for national calamity, and that struggles for civil rights often take a long time, beginning with political action by a small group of committed individuals and often ending with legislation and legal decisions from the highest court in the country. What civil rights battles now appear on the country's horizon? What can and should be done to remedy past wrongs that have current consequences, such as when past discrimination results in an economic underclass for a racial or ethnic minority? And, most fundamentally, how does a country based on the democratic principle of majority rule ensure that the civil rights of minorities are protected?

Religious Affiliation and Freedom of Religion

Percentage of American Adults in Each Religious Tradition

Under the First Amendment, Americans enjoy the freedom to practice (or not practice) the religion of their choice. Most Americans identify with and participate in some form of religion.

- Protestant **44%**
- Catholic **20%**
- Other Christian **3%**
- Jewish **2%**
- Muslim **1%**
- Buddhist **1%**
- Hindu **1%**
- Other faiths **1%**
- Nothing in particular **17%**
- Agnostic **3%**
- Atheist **3%**
- Don't know **4%**

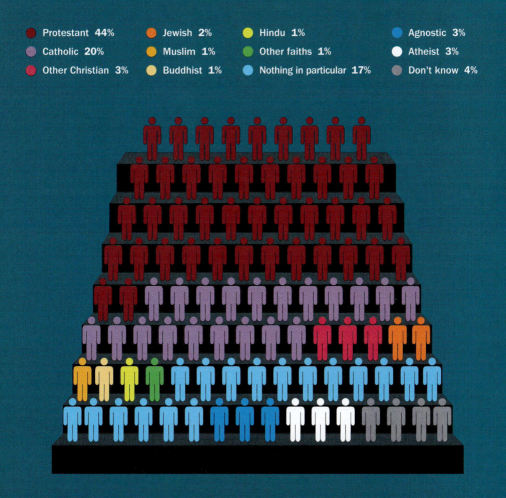

SOURCE: Robert P. Jones and Daniel Cox, *America's Changing Religious Identity*, 2016, www.prri.org/ (accessed 11/4/17).

WHAT YOU CAN DO ➤

Know Your First Amendment Rights

 Learn more about freedom of religion from a variety of legal scholars at **www.constitutioncenter.org**.

✓ Share your opinion about the First Amendment and religion on campus with your school newspaper. Find information about students' religious rights at **www.thefire.org**.

✓ Learn more about your other First Amendment rights, such as free speech on the internet, at **www.eff.org**.

★ STUDY GUIDE ★

Practice Quiz

1. Which of the following rights was *not* included in the original Constitution? *(p. 100)*
   a) prohibition of bills of attainder
   b) prohibition of ex post facto laws
   c) guarantee of habeas corpus
   d) guarantee of trial by jury in state where crime was committed
   e) prohibition of warrantless search and seizure

2. When did civil rights first become part of the Constitution? *(p. 101)*
   a) in 1789 at the Founding
   b) with the adoption of the Fourteenth Amendment in 1868
   c) when Barack Obama was elected president
   d) with the adoption of the Nineteenth Amendment in 1920
   e) in the 1954 *Brown v. Board of Education* case

3. The process by which some of the liberties in the Bill of Rights were applied to the states is known as *(p. 102)*
   a) selective incorporation.
   b) judicial activism.
   c) civil liberties.
   d) establishment.
   e) preemption.

4. The judicial doctrine that places a heavy burden of proof on the government when it seeks to regulate or restrict speech is called *(pp. 105–6)*
   a) judicial restraint.
   b) judicial activism.
   c) habeas corpus.
   d) prior restraint.
   e) strict scrutiny.

5. Which of the following describes a written statement made in "reckless disregard of the truth" that is considered damaging to a victim because it is "malicious, scandalous, and defamatory"? *(p. 109)*
   a) slander
   b) libel
   c) speech plus
   d) fighting words
   e) expressive speech

6. In *District of Columbia v. Heller*, the Supreme Court ruled that *(p. 112)*
   a) states can require citizens to own firearms.
   b) federal grants can be used to support the formation of state militias.
   c) felons can be prevented from purchasing assault rifles.
   d) the Second Amendment applies to states as well as the federal government.
   e) the Second Amendment applies only to the federal government and not to states.

7. The Fourth, Fifth, Sixth, and Eighth amendments, taken together are the essence of *(p. 113)*
   a) due process of law.
   b) free speech.
   c) the right to bear arms.
   d) civil rights of minorities.
   e) freedom of religion.

8. In *Mapp v. Ohio*, the Supreme Court ruled that *(p. 114)*
   a) evidence obtained from an illegal search could not be introduced in a trial.
   b) the government must provide legal counsel for defendants who are too poor to provide for themselves.
   c) persons under arrest must be informed prior to police interrogation of their rights to remain silent and to have the benefits of legal counsel.
   d) the government has the right to take private property for public use if just compensation is provided.
   e) a person cannot be tried twice for the same crime.

9. In which case did the Supreme Court rule that state governments no longer had the authority to make private sexual behavior a crime? *(p. 120)*
   a) *Webster v. Reproductive Health Services*
   b) *Gonzales v. Oregon*
   c) *Lawrence v. Texas*
   d) *Bowers v. Hardwick*
   e) *Texas v. Johnson*

10. Which of the following declared that "equality of rights under the law shall not be denied or abridged by the United States or by any State on account of sex"? *(p. 129)*
    a) the Lily Ledbetter Fair Pay Act
    b) Title IV of the 1964 Civil Rights Act
    c) the DREAM Act
    d) the Equal Rights Amendment
    e) *Obergefell v. Hodges*

11. In *Bakke v. Board of Regents,* the Supreme Court ruled *(p. 129)*
    a) race can never be used as a factor in university admissions.
    b) achieving "adiverse student body" was a "compelling public purpose" but a rigid quota system based on race was incompatible with the Fourteenth Amendment's equal protection clause.
    c) achieving "a diverse student body" was a "compelling public purpose," but the method of a rigid quota of student slots assigned on the basis of race was incompatible with the Fourteenth Amendment's equal protection clause.
    d) achieving "a diverse student body" was a "compelling public purpose," but affirmative action policies can only be used to give preferences to African Americans.
    e) achieving "a diverse student body" was a "compelling public purpose," but affirmative action policies can only be used to give preferences to Asian Americans.

Key Terms

affirmative action *(p. 128)* government policies or programs that seek to redress past injustices against specified groups by making special efforts to provide members of these groups with access to educational and employment opportunities

bill of attainder *(p. 100)* a law that declares a person guilty of a crime without a trial

Brown v. Board of Education *(p. 123)* the 1954 Supreme Court decision that struck down the "separate but equal" doctrine as fundamentally unequal; this case eliminated state power to use race as a criterion for discrimination in law and provided the national government with the power to intervene by exercising strict regulatory policies against discriminatory actions

civil liberties *(p. 99)* areas of personal freedom constitutionally protected from government interference

civil rights *(p. 99)* obligation imposed on government to take positive action to protect citizens from any illegal action of government agencies and of other private citizens

"clear and present danger" test *(p. 106)* test to determine whether speech is protected or unprotected, based on its capacity to present a "clear and present danger" to society

double jeopardy *(p. 116)* the Fifth Amendment right providing that a person cannot be tried twice for the same crime

due process of law *(p. 100)* the right of every citizen against arbitrary action by national or state governments

eminent domain *(p. 117)* the right of government to take private property for public use

equal protection clause *(p. 121)* provision of the Fourteenth Amendment guaranteeing citizens "the equal protection of the laws"; this clause has served as the basis for the civil rights of African Americans, women, and other groups

establishment clause *(p. 103)* the First Amendment clause that says that "Congress shall make no law respecting an establishment of religion"; this law means that a "wall of separation" exists between church and state

exclusionary rule *(p. 114)* the ability of courts to exclude evidence obtained in violation of the Fourth Amendment

ex post facto laws *(p. 100)* laws that declare an action to be illegal after it has been committed

fighting words *(p. 111)* speech that directly incites damaging conduct

free exercise clause *(p. 104)* the First Amendment clause that protects a citizen's right to believe and practice whatever religion he or she chooses

grand jury *(p. 116)* jury that determines whether sufficient evidence is available to justify a trial; grand juries do not rule on the accused's guilt or innocence

habeas corpus *(p. 99)* a court order demanding that an individual in custody be brought into court and shown the cause for detention

libel *(p. 109)* a written statement made in "reckless disregard of the truth" that is considered damaging to a victim because it is "malicious, scandalous, and defamatory"

Miranda rule *(p. 117)* the requirement, articulated by the Supreme Court in *Miranda v. Arizona* (1966), that persons under arrest must be informed prior to police interrogation of their rights to remain silent and to have the benefit of legal counsel

prior restraint *(p. 108)* an effort by a governmental agency to block the publication of material it deems libelous or harmful in some other way; censorship; in the United States, the courts forbid prior restraint except under the most extraordinary circumstances

selective incorporation *(p. 102)* the process by which different protections in the Bill of Rights were incorporated into the Fourteenth Amendment, thus guaranteeing citizens protection from state as well as national governments

"separate but equal" rule *(p. 121)* doctrine that public accommodations could be segregated by race but still be considered equal

slander *(p. 109)* an oral statement made in "reckless disregard of the truth" that is considered damaging to the victim because it is "malicious, scandalous, and defamatory"

strict scrutiny *(p. 105)* a test used by the Supreme Court in racial discrimination cases and other cases involving civil liberties and civil rights that places the burden of proof on the government rather than on the challengers to show that the law in question is constitutional

For Further Reading

Abraham, Henry J., and Barbara A. Perry. *Freedom and the Court: Civil Rights and Liberties in the United States*. 8th ed. Lawrence: University Press of Kansas, 2004.

Ash, Timothy Garton. *Free Speech*. New Haven, CT: Yale University Press, 2017.

Chen, Anthony S. *The Fifth Freedom: Jobs, Politics, and Civil Rights in the United States, 1941–1972*. Princeton, NJ: Princeton University Press, 2009.

Eisgruber, Christopher. *Religious Freedom and the Constitution*. Cambridge, MA: Harvard University Press, 2010.

King, Desmond, and Rogers M. Smith. *Still a House Divided: Race and Politics in Obama's America*. Princeton, NJ: Princeton University Press, 2011.

Lee, Sonia Song-Ha. *Building a Latino Civil Rights Movement*. Chapel Hill: University of North Carolina Press, 2014.

Lewis, Anthony. *Freedom for the Thought That We Hate: A Biography of the First Amendment*. New York: Basic Books, 2010.

Nichols, Walter. *The Dreamers: How the Undocumented Youth Movement Transformed the Immigrant Rights Debate*. Stanford, CA: Stanford University Press, 2013.

Orth, John. *Due Process of Law: A Brief History*. Lawrence: University Press of Kansas, 2003.

Richards, Neil. *Intellectual Privacy: Rethinking Civil Liberties in the Digital Age*. New York: Oxford University Press, 2015.

Solove, Daniel. *Nothing to Hide: The False Tradeoff between Privacy and Security*. New Haven, CT: Yale University Press, 2011.

Spitzer, Robert J. *Saving the Constitution from Lawyers: How Legal Training and Law Reviews Distort Constitutional Meaning*. New York: Cambridge University Press, 2008.

Spitzer, Robert J. *Guns across America: Reconciling Gun Rules and Rights*. New York: Oxford University Press, 2015.

Waldman, Michael. *The Fight to Vote*. New York: Simon & Schuster, 2016.

Public Opinion

WHAT GOVERNMENT DOES AND WHY IT MATTERS

Americans can have quite different opinions on important issues, even citizens who have had similarly vivid, harrowing experiences. In 1991, Suzanna Hupp was eating lunch in a Texas restaurant when a man drove his truck through the window and began shooting people. Hupp had often carried a handgun in her purse, but had recently taken it out because Texas did not allow concealed carry at the time, and she was afraid she would lose her license as a chiropractor if caught. "Could I have hit the guy? He was fifteen feet from me....Could I have missed? Yeah, it's possible. But the one thing nobody can argue with is that it would have changed the odds." The gunman killed 23 people, including her parents. She has become a strong proponent of gun rights since then. "One of my bugaboos is gun laws. Anytime we list a place where you can't carry guns, to me, that's like a shopping list for a madman....If you think about nearly every one of these mass shootings, they have occurred at places where guns weren't allowed. That's frustrating to me, particularly when you talk about schools. Where do these madmen go? They go to schools and slaughter people."[1]

Suzanna Hupp (left) and Justin Gruber (right) were both present during episodes of gun violence. These events pushed Hupp to advocate for more gun rights, and Gruber to speak out for more restrictive gun laws. How do political opinions form? And how do government officials respond to shifts in public opinion?

Fifteen-year-old Justin Gruber also survived a terrible shooting incident, in a school: the shooting at the Marjory Stoneman Douglas High School in Parkland, Florida, in February 2018. The incident left seventeen students and teachers dead. But Gruber and many of his schoolmates reached the opposite view of Suzanna Hupp, arguing for greater gun control, such as assault weapons bans and increased age limits for purchase. Objecting to one suggestion raised after the shooting, Gruber said that arming teachers is a "terrible idea." "Adding guns to solve a gun problem will increase the possible negative outcomes," he said. "Teachers shouldn't have to be trained to carry weapons. They are supposed to mold the minds of the next generation."[2] Some students formed a group, Never Again MSD, known by the hashtag #NeverAgain, to advocate for tighter gun control.

The "consent of the governed"—demanded in the Declaration of Independence—is critical for the functioning of a democracy. We expect government to pay attention to the people. But whose opinion gets represented in public policy, particularly on issues such as gun rights and gun control where there are strong divides among the public? What is the role of public opinion compared to that of other political actors, such as organized interests? How well informed are people, and by what channels can individuals have their voices heard? As we will see in this chapter, research shows that public opinion does indeed have a significant impact on public policy. But there are debates among scholars about whether the public is sufficiently informed about politics, as well as whether elected officials represent the interests of all Americans or only some Americans.

CHAPTER GOALS

★ Define public opinion, and identify broad types of values and beliefs Americans have about politics (pp. 147–52)

★ Explain the major factors that shape specific individual opinions (pp. 152–57)

★ Explore when and why public opinion changes and the role that political knowledge plays (pp. 157–60)

★ Describe the major forces that shape public opinion (pp. 160–63)

★ Describe basic survey methods and other techniques researchers use to measure public opinion (pp. 163–69)

Public Opinion Represents Attitudes about Politics

Define public opinion, and identify broad types of values and beliefs Americans have about politics

The term **public opinion** refers to the attitudes citizens have about political issues, leaders, institutions, and events. It is useful to distinguish between values and beliefs, on the one hand, and attitudes and opinions, on the other. **Values (or beliefs)** are the basic principles that shape a person's opinions about political issues and events. They constitute a person's basic orientation to politics. Values underlie deep-rooted goals, aspirations, and ideals that shape an individual's perceptions of political issues and events. Liberty, equality of opportunity, and democracy, for example, are basic political values held by most Americans.

An **attitude (or opinion)** is a specific preference on a particular issue. An individual may have an attitude toward American policy in the Middle East or an opinion about economic inequality in the United States. The attitude or opinion may have emerged from a broad belief about the purpose of military intervention or about the role of government in the economy, but the opinion itself is very specific. Some attitudes may be short-lived and can change based on changing circumstances or new information.

Factors such as race, gender, income, age, religion, and region—which not only affect individuals' interests but also shape their experiences and upbringing—influence Americans' beliefs and opinions. For example, blacks and whites often have different views on issues that touch upon civil rights and race relations, such as affirmative action, presumably reflecting differences of interest and historical experience. Views expressed by men and by women often vary as well, especially on foreign policy questions, where women appear to be much more concerned with the dangers of war.

Political attitudes are increasingly influenced by partisanship (Republicans versus Democrats) and ideology (conservatives versus liberals). For example, shortly after taking office in January 2017, President Trump signed an executive order immediately halting the U.S. refugee program and banning immigration to the United States from a half dozen predominantly Muslim countries, including Syria. The Supreme Court upheld the travel ban as constitutional, despite legal challenges. Opinion polls show 45 percent of Americans overall believe that refugees from Syria and Iraq pose a serious threat to the well-being of the United States. But 63 percent of Republicans say refugees from the Middle East are a threat compared to 30 percent of Democrats.[3]

Opinions about issues and politics have strong emotional underpinnings as well.[4] Emotions are traditionally measured by survey questions asking if a candidate, politician, event, or issue makes the respondent feel fearful, anxious, angry, or enthusiastic. Donald Trump's 2016 presidential campaign, for example, benefited from high enthusiasm from his supporters. Similarly high positive emotions may have given Barack Obama an advantage as the first African American president in

Dramatic events, and the emotions they stir, can alter public opinion. In the aftermath of the violence erupting at a white nationalist rally in Charlottesville, Virginia, in 2017, seemingly everyone had an opinion of the state of race relations in America.

2008, overcoming racial resentment among some citizens.[5] Contrary to the idea that public opinion is purely rational, feelings are complicated and often irrational; once individuals become emotionally attached to particular beliefs, they tend to hold on to those beliefs even in the face of contradictory information. Using emotions as a guide, individuals form opinions quickly in response to current events.[6]

AMERICANS SHARE COMMON POLITICAL VALUES

Most Americans share a common set of values, including a belief in the principles, if not always the actual practice, of liberty, equality, and democracy. The United States was founded on the principle of individual **liberty**, or freedom. Since the birth of our nation, Americans have always voiced strong support for the idea of liberty and typically support the notion that governmental interference in individuals' lives and property should be kept to a minimum.

Similarly, **equality of opportunity** has always been an important theme in American society. Most Americans believe that all individuals should be allowed to seek personal and material/economic success. Moreover, Americans generally believe that such success should be the result of individual effort and ability, rather than family connections or other forms of special privilege. Quality public education is one of the most important mechanisms for obtaining equality of opportunity in that it allows individuals, regardless of personal or family wealth, a chance to get ahead. Today, the internet is an important example of equality of

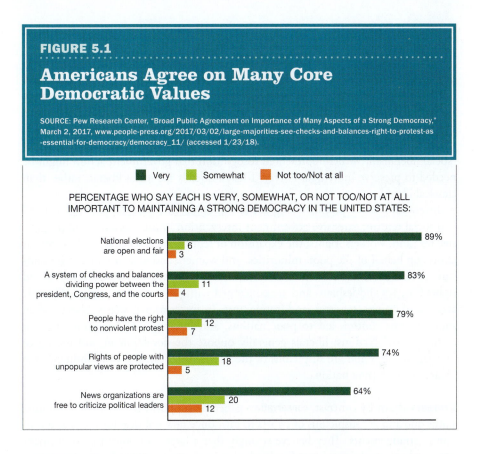

FIGURE 5.1

Americans Agree on Many Core Democratic Values

SOURCE: Pew Research Center, "Broad Public Agreement on Importance of Many Aspects of a Strong Democracy," March 2, 2017, www.people-press.org/2017/03/02/large-majorities-see-checks-and-balances-right-to-protest-as-essential-for-democracy/democracy_11/ (accessed 1/23/18).

■ Very   ■ Somewhat   ■ Not too/Not at all

PERCENTAGE WHO SAY EACH IS VERY, SOMEWHAT, OR NOT TOO/NOT AT ALL IMPORTANT TO MAINTAINING A STRONG DEMOCRACY IN THE UNITED STATES:

National elections are open and fair — 89%, 6, 3

A system of checks and balances dividing power between the president, Congress, and the courts — 83%, 11, 4

People have the right to nonviolent protest — 79%, 12, 7

Rights of people with unpopular views are protected — 74%, 18, 5

News organizations are free to criticize political leaders — 64%, 20, 12

opportunity by providing online access to news, politics, jobs, and other benefits of digital citizenship.[7]

Most Americans also believe in **democracy**. They believe that every citizen should have the opportunity to take part in the nation's governmental and policy-making processes and to have some say in determining how he or she is governed, including the right to vote in elections.[8] Figure 5.1 shows there is consensus among Americans on fundamental values.

Obviously, the principles that Americans espouse have not always been put into practice. For 200 years, Americans embraced the principles of individual liberty and equality of opportunity while denying them in practice to generations of African Americans. Yet the strength of the principles ultimately helped overcome practices that deviated from those principles.

AMERICA'S DOMINANT POLITICAL IDEOLOGIES ARE LIBERALISM AND CONSERVATISM

The application of America's shared values to specific policies varies quite a bit. The set of underlying orientations, ideas, and beliefs through which we come to understand and interpret politics is called a **political ideology**. In the United States today, a variety of ideologies compete for attention and support, but two are dominant: liberalism and conservatism.

Liberalism In classical political theory, a *liberal* was someone who favored individual initiative and was suspicious of governments and their ability to manage economic and social affairs—a definition akin to that of today's libertarian. The proponents of a larger and more active government called themselves *progressives*. In the early twentieth century, many liberals and progressives coalesced around the doctrine of "social liberalism," which represented recognition that government action might be needed to preserve individual liberty. Today's liberals are social liberals rather than classical liberals.

In contemporary politics being **liberal** has come to imply supporting political and social reform; extensive government intervention in the economy and progressive taxation; workers' rights; the expansion of federal social services; more vigorous efforts on behalf of the poor, minorities, and women; and greater concern for consumers and the environment. Liberals generally support reproductive rights and rights for gays and lesbians and are concerned with protecting the rights of people accused of crimes, refugees, and immigrants. In international affairs, liberals often support arms control, aid to poor nations, and international organizations such as the United Nations; liberals generally oppose the development and testing of nuclear weapons and are suspicious of the use of American troops to influence the affairs of developing nations.

Conservatism By contrast, **conservatives** generally support the social and economic status quo and are suspicious of efforts to introduce new political formulae and economic arrangements. They believe strongly that a large and powerful government poses a threat to the freedom of individual citizens. Ironically, today's conservatives support the views of classical liberalism. Today, in the domestic arena, conservatives generally oppose the expansion of governmental activity and support finding solutions to social and economic problems in the private sector, local communities, or by religious organizations. Conservatives particularly oppose efforts to impose government regulation on business and the environment, maintaining that regulation frequently leads to economic inefficiency, is costly, and can ultimately lower the entire nation's standard of living. In terms of social policy, many conservatives support school prayer and traditional family arrangements and are concerned about law and order; conservatives generally oppose abortion, same-sex marriage, drug legalization, and seek to reduce immigration to the United States. In international affairs, conservatism has come to mean support for military intervention and the maintenance of American military power as well as a desire to restrict immigration.

Other political ideologies also influence American politics. **Libertarians**, for example, argue that government interferes with freedom of expression, free markets, and society and thus should be limited to as few spheres of activity as possible (national defense being a notable exception). Libertarians prefer government to be even smaller than that favored by conservatives. While libertarians believe in less government intervention in economic and social realms, **socialists** and the Green Party argue that more government is necessary to promote justice and to reduce economic inequality. 2016 Democratic presidential candidate Bernie Sanders calls himself a "democratic socialist"; Sanders wants government to ensure more equality of opportunity for citizens through free public college, single-payer health care, and increased taxation on the very affluent. He also supports government policies to protect workers' rights and unions. Socialists are more to the ideological left than the mainstream Democratic Party.

Americans' Ideologies Today Although many Americans subscribe to libertarianism, socialism, or other ideologies in part, most describe themselves as either liberals, conservatives, or moderates. Figure 5.2 shows that the percentage of Americans who consider themselves moderates, liberals, or conservatives has remained relatively constant since the 1990s. Gallup surveys indicate that as of 2017 35 percent of Americans considered themselves conservatives, 35 percent moderates, and 25 percent liberals. These numbers have remained virtually unchanged since the 1990s. But among young people aged 18–33, trends are different: just 15 percent identify as conservatives, while 41 percent identify as liberals and 44 percent as moderates (and independent from the political parties).[9]

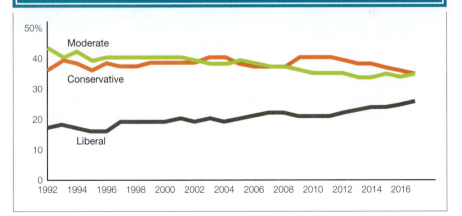

FIGURE 5.2

Americans' Ideology

More Americans identify themselves as "conservatives" than "liberals." During the period shown in this figure, however, Americans have had two Democratic presidents and have several times elected Democratic majorities to a house of Congress. What might account for this apparent discrepancy? What role do moderates play in the electorate? How stable is Americans' ideology over time?

SOURCE: Lydia Saad, "Conservative Lead in U.S. Ideology Down to Single Digits," Gallup, January 11, 2018, https://news.gallup.com/poll/225074/conservative-lead-ideology-down-single-digits.aspx (accessed 10/10/18).

AMERICANS EXHIBIT LOW TRUST IN GOVERNMENT

One of the most important measures of public opinion in a democracy is trust in government. High levels of political trust create legitimacy for democratic government, whereas very low levels can cause concern. Many scholars and political pundits argue that Americans are becoming more and more disenchanted with traditional political institutions; public approval of Congress reached a low of only 10 percent in 2014.[10]

Why does public opinion in the form of trust matter? Declining trust has been linked to declines in political participation and voting. Low confidence in government and elected officials is related to the perception that the government is unable to solve problems, spend money in an effective or efficient way, or represent the interests and policy preferences of average voters.[11]

The Pew Research Center has tracked trust in the federal government from 1958 to 2017 by asking this question on national surveys: "How much of the time do you trust the government in Washington?"[12] The percentage of Americans who indicate they trust the government "just about always or most of the time" has fallen from 73 percent in 1960 to just 15 percent in 2017. These trends span party lines. In 2017, 22 percent of Republicans indicated they trusted government all or most of the time compared with 12 percent of independents and 15 percent of Democrats.

Political Socialization Shapes Public Opinion

> **Explain the major factors that shape specific individual opinions**

People's attitudes about political issues and elected officials tend to be shaped by underlying political beliefs and values. For example, an individual who has negative feelings about government intervention in America's economy and society would probably oppose the development of new social and health care programs. Similarly, someone who distrusts the military would likely be suspicious of any call for the use of U.S. troops. The processes through which these underlying political beliefs and values are formed are collectively called **political socialization**.

Probably no nation, and certainly no democracy, could survive if its citizens did not share some fundamental beliefs. If Americans had few common values or perspectives, it would be very difficult for them to reach agreement on particular issues. In contemporary America, some elements of the socialization process tend to produce differences in outlook, whereas others promote similarities. The **agents of socialization** that shape political beliefs are the family and social networks, social groups and race, political party affiliation, education, and political environment.

The Family and Social Networks Most people acquire their initial orientation to politics from their families. As might be expected, differences in family background tend to produce divergent political perspectives. Although relatively few parents spend much time directly teaching their children about politics, political conversations occur in many households, and children tend to absorb the political views of parents and other caregivers, often without realizing it. Studies find, for example, that political party preferences are initially acquired at home. Children raised in households in which the primary caregivers are Democrats tend to become Democrats, whereas children raised in homes where their caregivers are Republicans tend to favor the Republican Party.[13] Similarly, children reared in politically liberal households are more likely than not to develop a liberal outlook, whereas children raised in politically conservative settings are likely to see the world through conservative lenses. Family, friends, coworkers, and neighbors are an important source of political orientation for nearly everyone.

Online social networks such as Facebook and Twitter may increase the role of peers in shaping public opinion. For example, after the 2015 Supreme Court decision legalizing same-sex marriage nationwide, Facebook launched a "Celebrate Pride" tool that enabled users to give their profile pictures a rainbow-tinted background to show their support for gay rights, signaling to friends and family their opinion on this issue. In the 72 hours following the Court's decision, 26 million individuals added this filter to their profile picture.[14] This phenomenon was associated with upticks in public support for same-sex marriage rights.[15]

Education Often thought of as a great equalizer, education is also an important source of differences in political perspectives. Governments use public education to try to teach all children a common set of civic values; it is mainly in school that Americans acquire their basic beliefs in liberty, equality, and democracy. In history classes, students are taught that the Founders fought for the principle of liberty (freedom). In studying such topics as the Constitution, the Civil War, and the civil rights movement, students are taught the importance of equality. Research finds education to be a strong predictor of tolerance for racial, ethnic, and religious minorities.[16] Through participation in class elections and student government, students are taught the virtues of democracy. These lessons are repeated in every grade and in many contexts.

At the same time, differences in formal education are strongly associated with differences in political outlook. In particular, those who attend college are often exposed to modes of thought that will distinguish them from their friends and neighbors who do not pursue college diplomas. One of the major differences between college graduates

The family is one of the largest influences on a person's political views. Children raised in conservative or liberal families, usually, but not always, hold those same views later in life.

and other Americans is that higher levels of education are associated with greater involvement in politics. College graduates are more likely to vote, join campaigns, take part in protests, and generally make their voices heard.[17]

Social Groups and Public Opinion Another important source of political values is the social groups to which individuals belong. Social groups include those that individuals haven't chosen (national, religious, gender, and racial groups, for example) and those they join willingly (such as political parties, labor unions, the military, and environmental, educational, and occupational groups). Group membership gives individuals experiences and perspectives that shape their views of political and social life.

Race and Ethnicity Among the most important of these is race. Blacks, for example, are a minority and have been victims of persecution and discrimination throughout American history. Blacks and whites thus often have different occupational opportunities, live in separate communities, and may attend separate schools. Such differences tend to produce distinctive political outlooks. That black and white Americans have different views is reflected in public perception of fair treatment across racial groups in the United States (see Figure 5.3).

In 2009, 80 percent of African Americans said blacks and other minorities do not get equal treatment under the law; the number of whites giving this response was just 40 percent.[18] In the past few years, however, widely publicized incidents of excessive use of police force against African Americans around the country, often resulting in their deaths, have begun to cause a shift in public opinion on this issue. By 2015, 90 percent of African Americans agreed that blacks and whites are not treated equally by police and 54 percent of whites felt the same way, showing that while there is still a racial divide on this issue, opinions on it have changed significantly over the past few years.[19] Strikingly, half of all Americans now agree that racism is a big problem, compared to only 26 percent in 2009.[20]

Ethnicity also affects policy attitudes. Latinos are the fastest-growing minority population in the United States. Latinos' shared Hispanic ethnicity contributes to a group consciousness that shapes opinions. Unsurprisingly, immigration is one of the most important policy issues among Latinos, with significant majorities of Latinos concerned about restrictive immigration politics and the threat of deportation. With respect to ideology, Latinos typically are supportive of government policy to improve the lives of citizens and to reduce prevailing inequality, which includes favoring public funding for education, health, and welfare. While Latinos tend to be fairly religious, Latino Decision surveys find they do not allow their religious beliefs to dictate their political decisions—they are thus less likely to vote for conservative politicians because of social issues.[21] This helps explain why a majority of Latinos supported Democratic candidate Hillary Clinton for president in 2016.

Gender Men and women have important differences of opinion as well. Reflecting differences in social roles and occupational patterns, women tend to oppose military

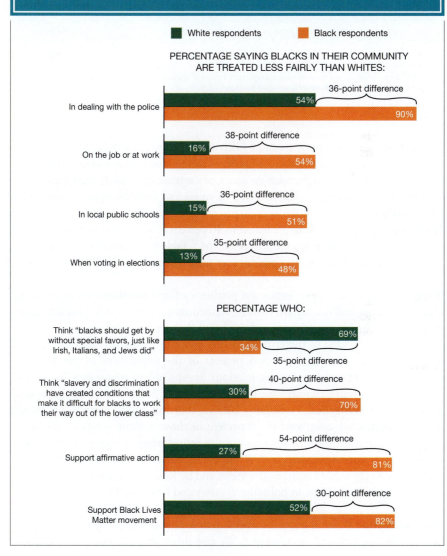

FIGURE 5.3

Perception of Fair Treatment across Racial Groups

In the United States, racial groups may not perceive race relations in precisely the same way. How, according to the data in this figure, do blacks and whites differ in their views on race relations? Which group is more likely to think that race relations are good? What factors help to account for these differences in perception?

SOURCE: Brakkton Booker, "How Equal Is American Opportunity? Survey Shows Attitudes Vary by Race," National Public Radio, September 21, 2015, www.npr.org/sections/thetwo-way/2015/09/21/442068004/how-equal-is -american-opportunity-survey-shows-attitudes-vary-by-race (accessed 3/11/16); Samantha Neal, "Views of Racism as a Major Problem Increase Sharply, Especially among Democrats," Pew Research Center, August 29, 2017, www.pewresearch.org (accessed 5/23/18).

■ White respondents   ■ Black respondents

PERCENTAGE SAYING BLACKS IN THEIR COMMUNITY ARE TREATED LESS FAIRLY THAN WHITES:

In dealing with the police — 54% / 90% — 36-point difference

On the job or at work — 16% / 54% — 38-point difference

In local public schools — 15% / 51% — 36-point difference

When voting in elections — 13% / 48% — 35-point difference

PERCENTAGE WHO:

Think "blacks should get by without special favors, just like Irish, Italians, and Jews did" — 69% / 34% — 35-point difference

Think "slavery and discrimination have created conditions that make it difficult for blacks to work their way out of the lower class" — 30% / 70% — 40-point difference

Support affirmative action — 27% / 81% — 54-point difference

Support Black Lives Matter movement — 52% / 82% — 30-point difference

TABLE 5.1

Disagreements among Men and Women on Public Policy Issues

On many policy issues, there is an approximately 5- to 20-point gap between the opinions of men and women. What might explain this consistent difference?

POLICY	MEN	WOMEN	GENDER GAP
Support cutting defense spending	38	43	5 points
Support cutting domestic spending	43	34	9 points
Favor raising the minimum wage	68	81	13 points
Favor background checks to purchase guns	82	92	10 points
Support banning assault rifles	51	71	20 points

SOURCE: Brian Schaffner and Stephen Ansolabehere, "CCES Common Content, 2014," Harvard Dataverse, V2, http://dx.doi.org/10.7910/DVN/XFXJVY (accessed 5/4/16).

intervention more than men, are more likely than men to favor policies to protect the environment, and are more likely to support government education and social programs. Perhaps because of these differences on issues, women are more likely than men to vote for Democratic candidates. This tendency of men's and women's opinions to differ is known as the **gender gap**. In 2018, only 30 percent of women approved of the job Donald Trump was doing as president, compared to 46 percent of men. This 16 percent gender gap is wider than for any other modern president.[22] Table 5.1 shows that across different policy areas, men's and women's opinions vary from a 5- to 20-point difference.

Religion Religion is a more important predictor of opinion than previously recognized. Religious individuals are usually defined in surveys by religious affiliation, frequency of church attendance, and the belief that religion and prayer are important in their lives. One of the fastest-growing groups in America are those without religious affiliation, rising from 5–6 percent of the population in the 1990s to almost 25 percent today.[23] Among religious groups, white evangelical Protestants tend to be even more conservative than Catholics. A 2014 study found that only 32 percent of evangelical Protestants believe abortion rights for women should always be permitted, compared to 75 percent of those without religious affiliation. Similarly sharp differences in opinion are also found when it comes to other social issues, such as same-sex marriage.[24] White evangelicals and weekly churchgoers are much more likely to hold conservative views and be Republican, while the religiously unaffiliated are more likely to hold liberal views and favor the Democratic Party.

Party Affiliation Political party membership or loyalty is one of the most important factors affecting political orientation.[25] We can think of partisanship as red-tinted (referring to the Republican Party) or blue-tinted (referring to the Democratic Party) glasses that color opinion on a vast array of issues. Partisans tend to rely on party leaders and the media for cues on the appropriate positions to take on major political issues.[26]

According to recent studies, differences between Democratic and Republican partisans on a variety of political and policy questions are greater today than during any other period for which data are available. For example, 72 percent of Republicans oppose granting legal citizenship to immigrants with jobs in the United States, but only 34 percent of Democrats do. Seventy-six percent of Democrats strongly favor government policies to protect the environment compared to 30 percent of Republicans.[27] Wide differences in public opinion exist based on partisanship involving energy, income inequality, infrastructure, job creation, immigration, climate change, national defense, budget deficit, taxes, terrorism, trade, and much more. Democrats and Republicans also have different policy priorities.

Political Environment The conditions and events that exist when individuals and groups enter political life shape their political attitudes and values. Although political beliefs are influenced by family background and group membership, the content and character of these views are, to a large extent, determined by political circumstances. For example, the baby-boom generation that came of age in the 1960s was exposed both to the Vietnam War and to widespread antiwar protests, which has made that generation suspicious of foreign wars. The September 11, 2001, terrorist attacks and the war on terrorism contributed to shaping the political lives of those who came of age during that time, making them more concerned about security and safety and less opposed to foreign wars.

Political Knowledge Is Important in Shaping Public Opinion

Explore when and why public opinion changes and the role that political knowledge plays

What best explains whether citizens are generally consistent in their political views or inconsistent and open to the influence of others? In general, knowledgeable citizens are better able to evaluate new information and determine if it is relevant to and consistent with their beliefs and opinions.[28] As a result, better-informed individuals can recognize their political interests and act consistently to further those interests. But political knowledge is generally low in America. In one widely reported survey, 71 percent of Americans could not name their own member of Congress.[29]

This raises the question of how much political knowledge is necessary for one to act as an effective citizen. In an important study of political knowledge in the United States, researchers found that the average American exhibits little knowledge of political institutions, processes, leaders, and policy debates.[30] They also found that political knowledge is not evenly distributed throughout the population. Those with higher education, income, and occupational status and who are members of social or political organizations are more likely to know about and be active in politics. Do these gaps or advantages in political knowledge matter? An interest in politics reinforces an individual's sense of political efficacy (the belief that their actions and opinions matter) and provides an incentive to acquire additional knowledge and information about politics. As a result, individuals with higher income and education also have more knowledge and influence and thus are better able to get what they want from government. For less-informed individuals, the media and political leaders may play a larger role in influencing public opinion. Low-informed individuals are more susceptible to fake news, partisan news, and political propaganda than more informed individuals.

Shortcuts and Cues Because being politically informed requires a substantial investment of time and energy, most Americans seek to acquire political information and to make political decisions "on the cheap," making use of shortcuts for political evaluation and decision-making rather than engaging in a lengthy process of information-gathering. Researchers have found that individuals rely on cues and information from party elites and the media to aid them in attitude formation.[31] Other "inexpensive" ways to become informed include taking cues from trusted friends, social networks and social media, relatives, colleagues, or religious leaders.[32] By means of these informational shortcuts, average citizens can form political opinions that are, in most instances, consistent with their underlying preferences. Studies show that even individuals with low levels of political knowledge are able to make relatively informed political choices by relying on these voter cues.

The public's reliance on elite cues has taken on new significance in today's era of party polarization. As the political parties and elected officials have become increasingly polarized, has this change affected the way that citizens arrive at their opinions? Researchers have found stark evidence that polarized political environments fundamentally change how citizens make decisions and form opinions. Notably, polarization between the parties means that party endorsements (such as of an issue or candidate) have a larger impact on public opinion formation than they used to. At the same time, polarization decreases the impact of other information on public opinion—that is, party polarization may actually reduce levels of political knowledge. Thus, elite polarization may have negative implications for public-opinion formation.[33]

Skim and Scan Another factor affecting political knowledge is the *form* in which people consume information. The transformation of political information in the digital era has had a profound effect on the way the news is reported and how citizens learn about politics, as more Americans get political news and information online. Recent research also indicates a trend in journalism toward shorter articles and flashier headlines. Americans today are likely to read the news by scanning and skimming multiple headlines online, in bits and bytes, rather than by reading long news articles.[34] Today, tweets from elected officials are an increasingly important source of news; Donald Trump relies on Twitter far more extensively than other elected officials, typically tweeting multiple times a day.

Political knowledge matters because it may protect individuals from exposure to misinformation than can distort public opinion. While social media has created new platforms for discussing politics and organizing, it has been associated with increased misinformation. Fake news on Facebook—with a billion users globally—was extensive in the 2016 election. A study found that the top 10 fake news stories circulated on Facebook were shared more widely than the top 10 authentic news stories about the election. Additionally, Russian Twitter "bot" accounts have been linked to the posting of many of the fake news stories benefiting Trump and attacking Clinton. Since the election both Google and Facebook have implemented new protocols to block content from deceptive outlets, and Twitter deleted thousands of fake accounts. Misinformation from elected officials and online news has encouraged more Americans to seek websites such as PolitiFact.com, FactCheck.org, and Snopes.com to verify the content of political information. It has also encouraged more Americans to turn to established media outlets, such as the *Washington Post*, *Wall Street Journal*, or the *New York Times*, for news.

Costs to Democracy? If political scientists are correct in their findings that many citizens base their opinions (and votes) on inadequate knowledge, fake news sources, and an overreliance on cues from political elites, this raises a critical question: If political knowledge is necessary for effective citizenship, how does a general lack of such knowledge affect the way we govern ourselves?

Although understandable and perhaps inevitable, low levels of political knowledge and engagement weaken American democracy in two ways. First, those who lack political information cannot effectively defend their own political interests and can easily become losers in political struggles. The presence of large numbers of politically inattentive or ignorant individuals means that political power can more easily be manipulated by political elites, the media, and wealthy special interests. But other research has shown that individuals are quite stable and rational in their policy formation. Notice that even when public opinion has shifted, as in the case of same-sex marriage, the shifts have been relatively steady; we don't see dramatic jumps up and down.

Second, if knowledge is power, then a lack of knowledge can contribute to growing political and economic

After political opinions form, they remain relatively stable. The most knowledgeable people are generally able to discern whether or not new information fits or contradicts their previously held beliefs. Do you think the people in this protest (top) would change their opinions about tax cuts after seeing President Trump's tweet (bottom)?

inequality. When individuals are unaware of their interests or how to pursue them, it is virtually certain that political outcomes will not favor them.

The Media and Government Mold Opinion

Describe the major forces that shape public opinion

When individuals attempt to form opinions about particular political issues, events, or personalities, they seldom do so in isolation. Typically, they are confronted with—sometimes bombarded by—the efforts of a host of individuals and groups seeking to persuade them to adopt a particular point of view. During the 2016 presidential election, someone trying to decide what to think about Hillary Clinton or Donald Trump could hardly avoid an avalanche of opinions expressed through the media, in meetings, or in conversations with friends. The **marketplace of ideas** is the interplay of opinions and views that occurs as competing forces attempt to persuade as many people as possible to accept a particular position on a particular issue. Given this constant exposure to the ideas of others, it is virtually impossible for most individuals to resist some modification of their own beliefs. Three forces that play important roles in shaping opinions in the marketplace are the government, private groups, and the news media.[35]

THE GOVERNMENT LEADS PUBLIC OPINION

All governments try to influence, manipulate, or manage their citizens' beliefs. But the extent to which public opinion is actually affected by governmental public relations can be limited. Often, governmental claims are disputed by the media, by interest groups, and at times even by opposing forces within the government itself.

This hasn't stopped modern presidents from focusing a great deal of attention on shaping public opinion to boost support for their policy agendas. Franklin Delano Roosevelt promoted his policy agenda directly to the American people through his famous "fireside chat" radio broadcasts. The George W. Bush administration developed an extensive public-relations program to bolster popular support for its policies, including its war against terrorism. These efforts included presidential speeches, media appearances by administration officials, numerous press conferences, and thousands of press releases presenting the administration's views.[36] Using the runway of an aircraft carrier as his stage, a confident Commander in Chief Bush, dressed in a flight suit, proclaimed the end of the Iraq War in 2003. His statement was premature by eight years but was effective at maintaining public support for the Iraq War. Like his predecessors, President Obama was effective in shaping public opinion. He built support for his administration's initiatives in domestic and foreign policy. But Obama's White House was unique in using social media to promote the president's policy agenda. Hourly posts on Facebook promoted Obama's policies and campaign and served to personalize the president. Obama was the first to make use of Twitter, with 77 million followers.

Though Obama used Twitter, Donald Trump is the nation's first Twitter president; he uses it promote his policy agenda, make government announcements, attack opponents, defend himself, vent his dismay, and shape public opinion. Often tweeting in the early morning hours, Trump communicates his sentiments on politics like no other president in modern history. Laced with emotions and frequent typos, his tweets are authentic, if not always factually correct. New scholarship argues political leaders like Trump prefer social media to traditional media because it allows them to control the content unfiltered by the mainstream press.[37]

PRIVATE GROUPS ALSO SHAPE PUBLIC OPINION

Important political ideas in political life are developed and spread not only by government officials but also by important economic and political groups searching for issues that will advance their causes. One especially notable example is abortion, which has inflamed American politics over the past 40 years. The notion of a fetal "right to life," whose proponents seek to outlaw abortion and overturn the Supreme Court's 1973 *Roe v. Wade* decision, was developed by conservative politicians who saw the issue of abortion as a means of uniting Catholic and Protestant conservatives and linking both groups to the Republican Party, along with various right-to-life groups.[38] Catholic and evangelical Protestant religious leaders organized to denounce abortion from their church pulpits and, increasingly, from their television, radio, and internet pulpits, including the Christian Broadcasting Network. Religious leaders have also organized demonstrations, pickets, and disruptions at abortion clinics throughout the nation.[39] These efforts have helped win the enactment of stricter abortion laws in many states.

THE NEWS MEDIA'S MESSAGE AFFECTS PUBLIC OPINION

The media are among the most powerful forces operating in the marketplace of ideas. As we shall see in Chapter 6, the mass media are not simply neutral messengers for ideas developed by others. Instead, they are very much opinion makers and have an enormous impact on popular attitudes. For example, since the publication of the Pentagon Papers by the *New York Times* and the exposure of the Watergate scandal led by the *Washington Post* in the early 1970s, the national news media have relentlessly investigated personal and official wrongdoing on the part of politicians and public officials. The continual media presentation of corruption in government has undoubtedly contributed to the general attitude of cynicism and distrust that prevails in much of the general public.

At the same time, the ways in which media coverage interprets or "frames" specific events can have a major impact on popular responses and opinions about these events (see Chapter 6). For example, President George W. Bush went to great lengths to persuade the media to follow its lead in their coverage of America's response to terrorism in the months following the September 11, 2001, attacks. The media mostly went along, presenting the administration's military campaigns in Afghanistan and Iraq, as well as its domestic antiterrorist efforts, in a positive light. Even supposedly liberal newspapers such as the *New York Times*, which had strongly opposed Bush in the 2000 election, praised his leadership and published articles supportive of the president's bellicose rhetoric against the Iraqi regime prior to March 2003, when President Bush ordered the invasion of Iraq. From the time Congress authorized military action in late 2002 to the invasion of Iraq in March 2003, months of presidential messages and media coverage focused on the threat of terrorism boosted public support from 50 percent to over 70 percent.[40]

GOVERNMENT POLICIES ALSO RESPOND TO PUBLIC OPINION

Studies generally suggest that elected officials pay attention to the preferences of the public.[41] For example, one study explored the relationship between changes in opinion toward various political issues and the policy outcomes that most closely correspond to the issues.[42] The results show that shifts in public opinion on particular issues do in fact tend to lead to changes in public policy. One such example is in health care. A July 2009 Pew survey found that 65 percent of Americans favored a law "requiring all Americans to have health insurance, and government aid for those unable to afford it."[43] The federal government adopted the Affordable Health Care Act in 2010, which required health insurance for all citizens.

However, there is reason to question whether prevailing public opinion causes politicians to make policies that reflect the general will or whether government policy in fact causes changes in public opinion. The relationship between government policy and opinion may be dynamic, wherein policy responds to opinion but opinion also shifts based on new government policies.[44] Studies of whether government policy can affect public opinion have found it to have an effect in various policy areas, such as the environment, health care, welfare reform, the death penalty, and smoking bans.

To what extent do political leaders listen to the opinions of their constituents? To what extent *should* they listen? Is Calvin's father right that leaders should do what they believe is right, not what the public wants?

Of course, sometimes public opinion and policy do not align, and officials may act on their own preferences or judgment if they believe it will benefit government or society.[45] The bailout of the banks in 2008, for example, was carried out despite polls showing that a majority of Americans opposed this policy. When elected officials pursue policies not aligned with centrist opinion, it is often because they view particular groups of the electorate as more important than others. Inevitably, loyal voting blocs or interest groups that regularly contribute to a candidate may have their interests more closely represented than those of the general public.[46]

Measuring Public Opinion Is Crucial to Understanding What It Is

> **Describe basic survey methods and other techniques researchers use to measure public opinion**

Today public officials make extensive use of **public-opinion polls** to help them decide whether to run for office, what policies to support, how to vote on important legislation, and what types of appeals to make in their campaigns. All recent presidents and other major political figures have worked closely with polls and pollsters, as do major media outlets and other private organizations.

PUBLIC-OPINION SURVEYS ARE ACCURATE IF DONE PROPERLY

It is not feasible to interview the more than 300 million Americans residing in the United States on their opinions of who should be the next president or what should be done about important policy issues. Instead, pollsters take a **sample** of the population and use it to make inferences (e.g., extrapolations and educated guesses) about the preferences of the population as a whole. For a political survey to be an accurate representation of the population, it must meet certain requirements, including an appropriate sampling method, a sufficient sample size, and the avoidance of selection bias.[47]

Representative Samples One way to obtain a representative sample is what statisticians call a **simple random sample (or probability sample)**, in which every individual in the population has an equal probability of being selected as a respondent. Since we don't have a complete list of all Americans, pollsters use census data, lists of households, and telephone numbers to create lists, drawing samples from regions and then neighborhoods within regions. Just as in a simple random sample, everyone has an equal chance of being selected for the survey. Rolls of registered voters are often used in political surveys designed to predict the outcome of an election.

Another method for drawing samples of the national population is a technique called **random digit dialing** of home landline and cell phone numbers. In this method,

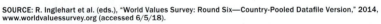

Confidence in Democratic Institutions

Parliaments, political parties, and the press are three institutions that play an important role in making democracy work. Parliament is the branch of government that most directly represents the voters; it serves as a major forum for policy debate and prevents abuse of executive power. Political parties offer different ideological goals, thereby helping to organize government, mobilize voters, and ensure political competition and accountability. Finally, the press plays an important "watchdog" role in politics, informing voters and helping them hold their leaders accountable for their actions.

While these institutions are important to all democracies, we do notice that Americans tend to be much less confident in these institutions than are citizens in other democracies. This raises two important questions: Why are the U.S. scores so low, and what does it mean for politics when a large percentage of a population loses confidence in the institutions that keep its democracy functioning?

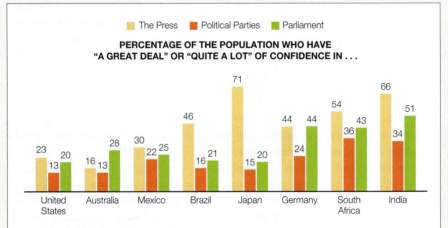

PERCENTAGE OF THE POPULATION WHO HAVE "A GREAT DEAL" OR "QUITE A LOT" OF CONFIDENCE IN . . .

Legend: The Press · Political Parties · Parliament

Country	The Press	Political Parties	Parliament
United States	23	13	20
Australia	16	13	28
Mexico	30	22	25
Brazil	46	16	21
Japan	71	15	20
Germany	44	24	44
South Africa	54	36	43
India	66	34	51

SOURCE: R. Inglehart et al. (eds.), "World Values Survey: Round Six—Country-Pooled Datafile Version," 2014, www.worldvaluessurvey.org (accessed 6/5/18).

respondents are selected at random from a list of 10-digit telephone numbers, with every effort made to avoid bias in the construction of the sample. A computer random-number generator is used to produce a list of 10-digit telephone numbers. Given that 98 percent of Americans have telephones (cell phones or landlines), this technique usually results in a random national sample. Telephone surveys are fairly accurate, cost-effective, and flexible in the type of questions that can be asked; but many people refuse to answer political surveys, and response rates—the percent of those called who actually answer the survey—have been falling steadily and average less than 15 percent.[48]

Sample Size A sample must be large enough to provide an accurate representation of the population. Surprisingly, though, the size of the population being measured doesn't matter, only the size of the *sample*. A survey of 1,000 people is just as effective for measuring the opinions of all Texans, a state with 28 million residents, as the opinions of all Americans, with over 325 million residents.

Flipping a coin shows how this works. After tossing a coin 10 times, the number of heads and tails may not be close to 5 and 5. After 100 tosses of the coin, though, the percentage of heads should be close to 50 percent, and after 1,000 tosses, very close to 50 percent. In fact, after 1,000 tosses, there is a 95 percent chance that the number of heads will be somewhere between 46.9 percent and 53.1 percent. This 3.1 percent variation from 50 percent is called the **sampling error (or margin of error)**—a polling error that arises based on the small size of the sample. That is, it is the amount of error we can expect with a typical 1,000-person survey. Normally, samples of 1,000 people are considered sufficient for accurately measuring public opinion through the use of surveys. When the media refer to a "scientific poll" conducted by a highly respected polling firm, they actually mean a poll that has followed the steps just outlined: a poll based on a random (representative) sample of the population that is sufficiently large and avoids selection bias.

Survey Design and Question Wording Even with a good sample design, surveys may fail to reflect the true distribution of opinion within a target population. One frequent source of measurement error is the wording of survey questions. The precise words used in a question can have an enormous impact on the answers that question elicits. The reliability of survey results can also be adversely affected by poor question format, faulty ordering of questions, poor vocabulary, ambiguity of questions, or questions with built-in biases.

Often, seemingly minor differences in the wording of a question can convey vastly different meanings to respondents and, thus, produce quite different response patterns (see Box 5.1). For example, for many years the University of Chicago's National Opinion Research Center has asked respondents whether they think the federal government is spending too much, too little, or about the right amount of money on "assistance for the poor." Answering the question posed this way, about two-thirds of all respondents seem to believe that the government is spending too little. However, the same survey also asks whether the government spends too much,

It Depends on How You Ask

THE SITUATION
The public's desire for tax cuts can be hard to measure. In 2000, pollsters asked what should be done with the nation's budget surplus and got different results depending on the specifics of the question.

THE QUESTION
President Clinton has proposed setting aside approximately two-thirds of an expected budget surplus to fix the Social Security system. What do you think the leaders in Washington should do with the remainder of the surplus?

VARIATION 1
Should the money be used for a tax cut, or should it be used to fund new government programs?

VARIATION 2
Should the money be used for a tax cut, or should it be spent on programs for education, the environment, health care, crime fighting, and military defense?

SOURCE: Pew Research Center, reported in the *New York Times*, January 30, 2000, WK 3.

too little, or about the right amount for "welfare." When the word *welfare* is substituted for *assistance for the poor*, about half of all respondents indicate that too much is being spent.[49] Today, pollsters are increasingly turning to the use of online surveys, often using similar techniques to those of telephone surveys. But while internet surveys can be more efficient, less costly, and can have much larger samples, many online surveys do not use probability sampling (random sampling) and thus are not representative of the American population.

WHY ARE SOME POLLS WRONG?

The history of polling over the past century contains many instances of getting it wrong and learning valuable lessons in the process. As a result, polling techniques have grown more and more sophisticated, and pollsters have a more and more nuanced understanding of how public opinion is formed and how it is revealed.

Social Desirability Effects Political scientists have found that survey results can be inaccurate when the survey includes questions about sensitive issues for which individuals do not wish to share their true preferences. For example, respondents tend to overreport voting in elections and the frequency of their church attendance. Why? These activities are deemed socially appropriate, so even if the respondents do not vote or attend church regularly, they may feel social pressure to do so and thus may respond inaccurately on a survey. This is called the **social desirability effect**, whereby respondents report what they expect the interviewer wishes to hear or whatever they think is socially acceptable rather than what they actually believe or know to be true.[50] On other topics, such as questions about income or alcohol and drug use, respondents may feel self-conscious and so choose not to answer.

Many questioned the accuracy of public opinion polls during the 2016 presidential election, when Donald Trump performed better at the ballot box than in the polls. Because Trump is a polarizing and controversial figure, some people may have been reluctant to tell interviewers they supported Trump or his policies. The fact that Hillary Clinton won nearly 3 million more votes than Trump nationwide suggests that the 2016 election polls were right after all, but polls did fail to predict that several key swing states would go to Trump.

Questions that ask directly about race or gender are particularly problematic. "Social desirability" makes it difficult to learn voters' true opinions about touchy subjects such as racial attitudes because respondents hide their preferences from the interviewer for fear of social retribution. However, surveys can be designed to tap respondents' latent or hidden feelings about sensitive issues without directly asking them to express overt opinions.

Selection Bias The importance of accurate sampling was brought home early in the history of political polling when a 1936 *Literary Digest* poll predicted that the Republican presidential candidate, Alf Landon, would defeat the Democratic incumbent, Franklin Delano Roosevelt, in that year's presidential election. The actual election ended in a Roosevelt landslide. The main problem with the survey was what is called **selection bias** in drawing the sample. The pollsters had relied on telephone directories and automobile registration rosters to produce the survey sample. During the Great Depression, though, only wealthier Americans owned telephones and automobiles. Thus, the millions of working-class Americans who constituted Roosevelt's base of support were excluded from the sample.

Selection bias was also at play in preelection polls in the 2016 presidential election. As noted above, although most polls predicted the direction of the popular vote correctly in Hillary Clinton's favor, they failed to predict the size of the vote margin. Additional reasons for the polling inaccuracies included the use of "likely voter models," which left out some groups that ended up voting at higher-than-usual rates, such as rural, non-college-educated, blue-collar voters who supported Trump in large numbers. Selection bias may have been at play, as well as nonresponse bias, where Trump supporters were less likely to respond to surveys.

In recent years, the issue of selection bias has been complicated by the fact that growing numbers of individuals refuse to answer pollsters' questions, or they use such devices as voicemail and caller ID to screen unwanted callers. If pollsters could be certain that those who responded to their surveys simply reflected the views of those who refused to respond, there would be no problem. Studies suggest that the views of respondents and nonrespondents can differ, especially along social class

Though public opinion is important, it is not always easy to interpret, and polls often fail to predict how Americans will vote. In 1948 election-night polls showed Thomas Dewey defeating Harry S. Truman for the presidency, which caused the *Chicago Daily Tribune* to incorrectly print a banner announcing Dewey's win. In 2016 polls considerably favored Hillary Clinton over Donald Trump, causing many to doubt the possibility of Trump winning the election.

lines. Additionally, women are significantly more likely to answer telephone surveys than men. This can lead to incorrect inferences of public opinion.

Push Polling Push polls are not scientific polls and are not intended to yield accurate information about a population. Instead, they involve asking a respondent a loaded question about a political candidate designed to elicit the response sought by the pollster and, simultaneously, to shape the respondent's perception of the candidate in question. One of the most notorious uses of push polling occurred in the 2000 South Carolina Republican presidential primary, in which George W. Bush defeated John McCain and went on to win the presidency. Callers working for Bush supporters asked conservative white voters if they would be more or less likely to vote for McCain if they knew he had fathered an illegitimate black child. Because McCain often campaigned with a daughter whom he and his wife had adopted from Mother Teresa's orphanage in Bangladesh, many voters accepted the premise of the "poll." The purpose of such push polls is not to solicit opinions as much as to plant negative ideas about the opposing candidate—to, in this case, "push" McCain voters away from him.

The Bandwagon Effect Sometimes polling can even create its own reality. The so-called **bandwagon effect** occurs when polling results convince people to support a candidate marked as the probable victor. This is especially true in the presidential nomination process, where there may be multiple candidates within one party vying to be the party's nominee. A candidate who has "momentum"—that is, one who demonstrates a lead in the polls—usually finds it considerably easier to raise campaign funds than a candidate whose poll standing is low. And with these additional funds, poll leaders can often afford to pay for television time and other campaign activities that will generate positive media attention and thus cement their advantage. Wanting to highlight the momentum he felt he had in the 2016 election, Trump frequently cited his lead in the polls to mobilize his base and give them confidence that he would win.

Public Opinion
WHAT DO WE WANT?

A major purpose of democratic government, with its participatory procedures and representative institutions, is to ensure that political leaders will heed the public will. And, indeed, a good deal of evidence suggests that they do.[51] However, it is not always clear what the public will is. Mass shootings heighten the preferences of supporters of both gun control and gun rights. Whose preferences prevail when attitudes differ among groups? Or when they differ between the public and elites? Or between the affluent and the poor? Some political scientists argue, however, that government policy is much less responsive to public opinion on the issues that really count and that when the interests of elites are at stake, government officials are much more likely to represent the opinions of the affluent than of the poor.[52] People in lower-income groups are less likely to actively seek out ways to express their political opinions than are wealthier people (see the "**Who Participates?**" feature on p. 171).

New technology may be able to help. The migration of politics online has greatly expanded the amount of information available and the ease of becoming informed. Given this new media environment, we might expect public opinion to be more accurate, even about the nuances of public policy. Digital citizenship offers the promise of a more informed electorate, with citizens having multiple venues in which to translate their opinions into political action and demand improved representation from political leaders. The use of social media by students from the Marjory Stoneman Douglas High School to argue for greater gun regulations shows digital citizenship in action.

At the same time, social media raises concerns about the accuracy and consistency of public opinion. Some research finds that the gap between the haves and the have-nots in terms of political knowledge actually increases with the availability of more information. The implications are significant, given the explosion of political coverage online. The research suggests that with more information, public opinion may actually be less consistent.[53]

Of course, technological change will continue; the media of 2040 will not be the same as the media of 2020. Young adults will face a changing media environment, just as their parents did. Such technological evolution may bring yet further changes to our understanding of the relationship between public opinion, government, and the media. New media may make it easier than ever for citizens to stay informed (or easier to be misled) about the actions of their elected leaders or for leaders to learn about their constituents' preferences. What can citizens do to stay informed and make their views known amid a changing media and political environment?

Who Expresses Their Political Opinions?

By income group ● < $20,000 ● $20,000–$39,999 ● $40,000–$74,999 ● $75,000+

Attended a town or city council meeting

26%   25%   28%   35%

Signed a petition

19%   24%   24%   28%

Attended a protest march

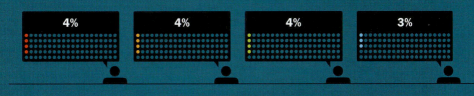

4%   4%   4%   3%

Tried to contact a member of Congress

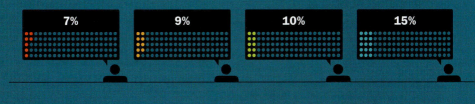

7%   9%   10%   15%

SOURCE: American National Election Study 2016 time series,
www.electionstudies.org (accessed 11/4/17).

WHAT YOU CAN DO

★ WHAT YOU CAN DO ★

Be an Informed Consumer of Opinion Polls

 When you encounter information from opinion polls, consider the source of the poll, the question wording, and whether individuals were randomly selected to participate. Learn more at **www.umich.edu/~numbers/polls**.

 Go to **www.realclearpolitics.com** to see polls about the same issues from different sources. Note the margins of error, and notice how aggregating polls makes a difference.

✓ If asked, consider responding to an opinion poll—or take the initiative and express your views through one of the actions above.

★ STUDY GUIDE ★

Practice Quiz

1. The term *public opinion* is used to describe *(p. 147)*
   a) the collected speeches and writings made by a president during his or her term in office.
   b) the analysis of events broadcast by news reporters during the evening news.
   c) the beliefs and attitudes that people have about issues, events, elected officials, and policies.
   d) decisions of the Supreme Court.
   e) any political statement that is made by a citizen outside of his or her private residence or place of employment.

2. Today, the term _____ refers to someone who generally supports the social and economic status quo and is suspicious of efforts to introduce new political formulas and economic arrangements. *(p. 150)*
   a) libertarian
   b) liberal
   c) conservative
   d) democrat
   e) Whig

3. *Socialism* refers to *(p. 151)*
   a) a political ideology that emphasizes social ownership, strong government, and reducing economic inequality.

b) a political ideology that emphasizes freedom and voluntary association with small government.

c) a political ideology that argues for the need to place strict limitations on voting rights and civil liberties.

d) a political ideology that argues a single ruler should have total control over every aspect of people's lives.

e) a political ideology that argues governments are inherently repressive and should be abolished entirely.

4. The process by which Americans learn political beliefs and values is called *(p. 152)*
   a) brainwashing.
   b) propaganda.
   c) indoctrination.
   d) political socialization.
   e) political development.

5. Which of the following is *not* an agent of socialization? *(p. 152)*
   a) the family
   b) social groups
   c) education
   d) the political environment
   e) All of the above are agents of socialization.

6. The fact that women tend to oppose military intervention more than men do is an example of *(p. 156)*
   a) the rally around the flag effect.
   b) partisan polarization.
   c) the peace paradox.
   d) the bandwagon effect.
   e) the gender gap.

7. Which of the following are the most important external influences on how political opinions are formed in the marketplace of ideas? *(p. 160)*
   a) the government, private groups, and the news media
   b) the unemployment rate, the Dow Jones Industrial Average, and the NASDAQ composite
   c) random digit dialing surveys, push polls, and the bandwagon effect

d) the Constitution, the Declaration of Independence, and *The Federalist Papers*
e) the legislative branch, the executive branch, and the judicial branch

8. Which statement best describes the relationship between public opinion and government policy? *(p. 163)*
   a) Public opinion almost never influences government policy.
   b) Government policy almost never influences public opinion.
   c) The relationship between government policy and public opinion is dynamic, wherein government policy responds to public opinion but public opinion also shifts based on new government policies.
   d) Public opinion always influences government policy because lawmakers are legally bound to enact the majority's preferences.
   e) Government policy never influences public opinion because most Americans pay very little attention to politics.

9. Which of the following is the term used in public-opinion polling to denote the small group representing the opinions of the whole population? *(p. 163)*
   a) control group
   b) sample
   c) micropopulation
   d) respondents
   e) median voters

10. A *push poll* is a poll in which *(p. 168)*
    a) the questions are designed to shape the respondent's opinion rather than measure the respondent's opinion.
    b) the questions are designed to measure the respondent's opinion rather than shape the respondent's opinion.
    c) the questions are designed to reduce measurement error.
    d) the sample is chosen to include only undecided or independent voters.
    e) the sample is not representative of the population it is drawn from.

11. A familiar polling problem is the "bandwagon effect," which occurs when (p. 169)
   a) the same results are used over and over again.
   b) polling results influence people to support the candidate marked as the probable victor in a campaign.
   c) polling results influence people to support the candidate who is trailing in a campaign.
   d) background noise makes it difficult for a pollster and a respondent to communicate with each other.
   e) a large number of people refuse to answer a pollster's questions.

Key Terms

agents of socialization (p. 152) social institutions, including families and schools, that help to shape individuals' basic political beliefs and values

attitude (or opinion) (p. 147) a specific preference on a particular issue

bandwagon effect (p. 169) a shift in electoral support to the candidate whom public-opinion polls report as the front-runner

conservative (p. 150) today this term refers to those who generally support the social and economic status quo and are suspicious of efforts to introduce new political formulae and economic arrangements; conservatives believe that a large and powerful government poses a threat to citizens' freedom

democracy (p. 149) a system of rule that permits citizens to play a significant part in the governmental process, usually through the election of key public officials

equality of opportunity (p. 148) a widely shared American ideal that all people should have the freedom to use whatever talents and wealth they have to reach their fullest potential

gender gap (p. 156) a distinctive pattern of voting behavior reflecting the differences in views between women and men

liberal (p. 150) today this term refers to those who generally support social and political reform, governmental intervention in the economy, more economic equality, the expansion of federal social services, and greater concern for consumers and the environment

libertarian (p. 150) someone who emphasizes freedom and believes in voluntary association with small government

liberty (p. 148) freedom from governmental control

marketplace of ideas (p. 160) the public forum in which beliefs and ideas are exchanged and compete

political ideology (p. 149) a cohesive set of beliefs that forms a general philosophy about the role of government

political socialization (p. 152) the induction of individuals into the political culture; learning the underlying beliefs and values on which the political system is based

public opinion (p. 147) citizens' attitudes about political issues, leaders, institutions, and events

public-opinion polls (p. 163) scientific instruments for measuring public opinion

push polling (p. 168) a polling technique in which the questions are designed to shape the respondent's opinion

random digit dialing (p. 163) a polling method in which respondents are selected at random from a list of 10-digit telephone numbers, with every effort made to avoid bias in the construction of the sample

sample *(p. 163)* a small group selected by researchers to represent the most important characteristics of an entire population

sampling error (or margin of error) *(p. 165)* polling error that arises based on the small size of the sample

selection bias (surveys) *(p. 167)* polling error that arises when the sample is not representative of the population being studied, which creates errors in overrepresenting or underrepresenting some opinions

simple random sample (or probability sample) *(p. 163)* a method used by pollsters to select a representative sample in which every individual in the population has an equal probability of being selected as a respondent

social desirability effect *(p. 167)* the effect that results when respondents in a survey report what they expect the interviewer wishes to hear rather than what they believe

socialist *(p. 151)* someone who generally believes in social ownership, strong government, free markets, and reducing economic inequality

values (or beliefs) *(p. 147)* basic principles that shape a person's opinions about political issues and events

For Further Reading

Asher, Herbert. *Polling and the Public: What Every Citizen Should Know*. 9th ed. Washington, DC: CQ Press, 2016.

Bartels, Larry. *Unequal Democracy: The Political Economy of the New Gilded Age*. Princeton, NJ: Princeton University Press, 2008.

Berinsky, Adam. *Silent Voices: Public Opinion and Political Participation in America*. Princeton, NJ: Princeton University Press, 2005.

Bishop, George. *The Illusion of Public Opinion*. New York: Rowman and Littlefield, 2004.

Clawson, Rosalee, and Zoe Oxley. *Public Opinion: Democratic Ideals and Democratic Practice*. 2nd ed. Washington, DC: CQ Press, 2012.

Erikson, Robert, and Kent Tedin. *American Public Opinion*. 9th ed. New York: Routledge, 2014.

Fiorina, Morris. *Culture War: The Myth of a Polarized America*. New York: Longman, 2005.

Gallup, George. *The Pulse of Democracy*. New York: Simon and Schuster, 1940.

Ginsberg, Benjamin. *The American Lie: Government by the People and Other Political Fables*. Boulder, CO: Paradigm, 2007.

Jacobs, Lawrence R., Fay Lomax Cook, and Michael X. Delli Carpini. *Talking Together*. Chicago: University of Chicago Press, 2009.

Lee, Taeku. *Mobilizing Public Opinion*. Chicago: University of Chicago Press, 2002.

Lippman, Walter. *Public Opinion*. New York: Harcourt, Brace, 1922.

Norrander, Barbara, and Clyde Wilcox. *Understanding Public Opinion*. Washington, DC: CQ Press, 2009.

Zaller, John. *The Nature and Origins of Mass Opinion*. New York: Cambridge University Press, 1992.

The Media

WHAT GOVERNMENT DOES AND WHY IT MATTERS When the chairman of the Federal Communications Commission, Ajit Pai, proposed to end "net neutrality" in 2017, teenagers across the country leapt into action. Many had lived their entire lives in an era of neutrality, aspects of which began in 2006 and were codified by President Barack Obama in 2015. Under net neutrality, internet service providers were regulated like a utility. They could not block websites, slow some data transmission while imposing fees for fast transmission, or charge consumers to connect to certain sites. Chairman Pai asserted that such rules overregulated the internet. But many teenagers, who get the majority of their news and information from the internet, disagreed. They used social media to coordinate letter-writing, tweet, and protest efforts.

Sixteen-year-old student Will Howes led a protest in front of a Verizon store in Sioux Falls, South Dakota (Pai formerly worked for Verizon), arguing, "They can throttle your Netflix, they can change your Google results. The right to access information online is threatened." His fellow protesters worried that

Net neutrality—the principle that all data and content on the web must be treated equally and not blocked or slowed for certain users—has been a hot-button issue. Anooha Dasari is just one of many young people who have spoken out and organized in support of net neutrality.

rural South Dakotans might get priced out of internet service, which was already limited there. Teen protesters in front of a Keene, New Hampshire, Verizon store had similar concerns about the price and availability of high-speed internet, holding signs asking, "Hey Siri, how much does this sentence cost?" As high school senior Harrison Hicks said, "The internet is imperative to my education, and it's really hard to be a self-starter and to teach yourself the information you need without the internet especially since we're the first generation who's grown up with the internet having been around our entire lives." Anooha Dasari, a high school junior from Mundelein, Illinois, who sent classmates links for emailing the FCC, said, "For research, for news, to communicate with friends, the internet is a big part of my life. It has formulated my personality, opinions and political ideology. If it is controlled, my generation of students could be inclined to be just on one part of the spectrum. That's dangerous." In December 2017, Chairman Pai cast the deciding vote to end the neutrality rules. Dasari vowed to continue to fight: "I will tweet and email and call and stay in the process."

The sharing of information, whether via traditional or digital media, is an essential component of American democracy. So central is information to citizen participation that the Constitution's First Amendment guarantees freedom of the press, and most Americans believe that a free press is an essential condition for both liberty and democratic politics. Today, as the means of communication has expanded, the media continue to play a central role in American politics, not only in setting the agenda of topics that Americans think about and discuss but also in shaping public opinion on political issues and politicians. The political implications of this media system are significant. Politics is increasingly defined by the individuals and groups who are best able to blend older and newer media—using, for example, both television and digital media to promote their message.

Discussing the right of press freedom, Thomas Jefferson wrote, "The basis of our government being the opinion of the people, the very first object should be to keep that right; and were it left to me to decide whether we should have a government without newspapers or newspapers without a government, I should not hesitate a moment to prefer the latter."[1] As the nature of media has evolved, its centrality to government and politics has never waned. In fact, in an era when politicians accuse each other and media members of promoting "Fake News," and people fight for or against control of internet communications, a full understanding of America's dynamic media landscape may be more important than ever.

CHAPTER GOALS

★ **Describe the key roles the media play in American political life (pp. 179–82)**

★ **Discuss how digital media have transformed how citizens learn about politics (pp. 182–90)**

★ **Analyze the ways the media can influence public opinion and politics (pp. 191–97)**

Media Have Always Mattered in a Democracy

Freedom of the press is protected under the First Amendment to the U.S. Constitution, along with the most cherished individual rights in American democracy, including freedom of speech and religion. The freedom to speak one's mind in public is one of the most cherished of American political values.

Freedom of the press is the right to circulate information and opinions in print and digital media without censorship by the government. In the United States citizens and private companies have the right to publish newspapers, magazines, and other forms of digital media with few government restrictions. In many authoritarian countries there is no freedom of the press and the government controls the news and political information through state-sponsored media.

The **media** serve three important roles in American democracy: to help inform the public about current political issues and events; to provide a forum through which candidates, politicians, and the public can debate policies and issues; and to act as a watchdog on the actions of the government and political actors.

Without the work of journalists and the media, democracy and self-government would not be possible. Individuals learn about politics, current events, government policy, and political candidates and parties from the news media. The information presented by the media allows citizens to cast informed decisions in elections and to form opinions about policy issues. This communication ensures that elected officials adopt policies consistent, for the most part, with the preferences of the citizens and serves as a counterweight to communication among elites, the wealthy, and corporations.

Perhaps most important, the media serve as a watchdog for the public, scrutinizing the actions of elected officials on behalf of citizens, most of whom do not have the opportunity to closely follow the actions of politicians and government. The media are like an alarm system for a home—notifying the public of actions taken by government that may harm them. Important political news is reported on page 1 of print newspapers or in news alerts on your mobile phone. The media prioritize covering major decisions by the government. They inform the public about important policy issues and expose those individuals and groups that exert power in politics, including their tactics and strategies. They reveal scandalous and illegal behavior of politicians, and therefore serve as a check on political power.

JOURNALISTS ARE NEWS-GATHERING PROFESSIONALS

Most practicing journalists receive training in schools of journalism and mass communication. Journalists are guided by standards in reporting the news in the public interest, known as the principles of journalism. Above all the news media seek to report the truth via fact-checking, verification of sources, and investigative journalism. This includes reporting factual claims by relying on legitimate sources, and citing people with credible positions, eyewitnesses and participants in events, and documents associated with recognizable and credible institutions. The traditional news media aim to balance coverage of current events by providing objective treatment of opposing sides and avoiding including personal views of reporters or editors.

THE PROFIT MOTIVE DRIVES THE NEWS BUSINESS

The media are sometimes referred to as the fourth branch of government, as they provide a check on the power of government and political leaders.

Public broadcasting refers to television, radio, and digital media that receive funding from the public through license fees, subsidies, or tax dollars. In most other democratic countries public broadcasting plays a major role in informing the public about politics and current events. In contrast, public broadcasting in the United States—such as National Public Radio or PBS—plays a very small role in the media system, at just 2 percent of market share, compared to 35 percent in France, 40 percent in Germany, and 65 percent in Denmark.

For-profit private companies dominate U.S. political media. Media companies earn most of their revenue from advertising, rather than subscriptions, although revenue from subscriptions has been increasing. This means media actors—from journalists to editors to the owners of media companies—are motivated by what audiences want, because higher ratings generate more advertising revenue. Because of the need to reach wide audiences to sell advertisements, the U.S. media are more focused on soft news—such as entertainment, sports, and celebrity news—than are European media, which provide more hard news coverage of politics and civic events. And when it comes to political news, American media tend to focus increasingly on dramatic, highly conflictual events and issues. Sensational stories of scandals or candidate attacks often generate more interest—and thus revenue—than the stories of everyday governing and details of public policy. Nonetheless, objectivity is still the goal, and standard practice is that news, opinion, and ads should be separate and distinct; that is why the opinions of editors are reserved for the opinion pages.

The profit motive of the news industry may have contributed to Donald Trump's unexpected victory in the 2016 election. Due to the novelty of a television celebrity running for president, Trump's campaign was a financial boon for the media industry. His candidacy received double the media coverage of his Democratic opponent Hillary Clinton and his Republican challengers in the primaries. CBS head Les Moonves said the Trump phenomenon "may not be good for America, but it's damn good for CBS...." The money to the television station was "rolling in."[2]

MORE MEDIA OUTLETS ARE OWNED BY FEWER COMPANIES

A key feature of the traditional media in the United States is the concentration of its ownership. A small number of giant corporations control a wide swath of media holdings, including television networks, movie studios, record companies, cable channels and local cable providers, book publishers, magazines, newspapers, and increasingly online and digital media outlets. Large global corporations own much of the media offline and online.[3] Media monopolies, such as that of The Walt Disney Company, have prompted questions about whether enough competition exists among traditional media to produce a truly diverse set of views on political matters.[4] In 2019, for example, Disney purchased 21st Century Fox to become the third largest media company in the United States. As major newspapers, television stations, and radio networks fall into fewer hands, the risk increases that politicians and citizens who express less popular or minority viewpoints will have difficulty finding a public forum.

The actual number of traditional news-gathering sources operating nationally is actually quite small—several wire services, four broadcast networks, a few elite print newspapers, and a smattering of other sources, such as a few large local papers and several small, independent radio networks. More than three-fourths of the daily print newspapers in the United States are owned by large media conglomerates such as the Hearst, McClatchy, and Gannett corporations. Much of the national news that is published by local newspapers is provided by one wire service, the Associated Press. More than 500 of the nation's television stations are affiliated with one of just four networks and carry that network's evening news programs.

The trend in concentration of traditional media ownership occurred in large part due to the relaxation of government regulations in the 1980s and '90s. The

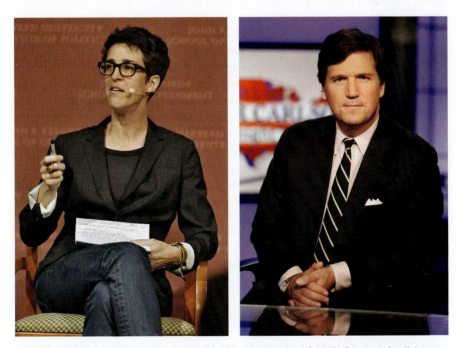

Though the media generally attempt to remain unbiased, a number of media figures and outlets are distinctly left- or right-leaning, such as Rachel Maddow of MSNBC and Tucker Carlson of Fox News. Consumers are increasingly turning to partisan media, reflecting a tendency to self-select information that already conforms with their beliefs, making it more difficult to objectively evaluate information.

enactment of the 1996 Telecommunications Act opened the way for additional consolidation in the media industry, and a wave of mergers and consolidations has further reduced the field of independent media across the country. But as more digital-only news sources come online, these trends toward concentration in media ownership may reverse.

The Media Today

> **Discuss how digital media have transformed how citizens learn about politics**

The past three decades have resulted in a massive transformation of the U.S. news media. New competition from free digital sources has put pressure on traditional subscription-based news sources as Americans have migrated to reading the news online. Today 93 percent of adults have read the news online.[5] This picture is very different from the early 2000s, when most Americans said that after television, print newspapers were their main source for news, and less than 20 percent read the news online.[6] Though not replacing losses in subscription and traditional advertising revenue, digital advertising revenue continues to grow.[7]

Despite the digital transformation of the news media, much of what makes the media important in American politics remains the same. Major newspapers and TV networks—even if their content is increasingly delivered in digital form—remain popular and important sources of news. Political leaders are successful in making headline news and setting the news agenda. And journalists trained in professional schools create and develop much of what we consume as news, including original reporting.

But more and more, the media are online companies facing an environment where anyone with access to an internet connection can publish the news. There are still only a small number of organizations that have credibility and the largest audiences, however.[8] The leading newspapers in the United States, such as the *New York Times*, the *Wall Street Journal*, and the *Washington Post*, receive some of the highest traffic online.

Before the internet, journalism organizations largely controlled the news through original reporting, writing and production, packaging and delivery, and selecting editors. Over time, technology companies like Facebook, Apple, Google, and Amazon have become major players in the content and delivery of the news. These companies are partners in the business of journalism, from the financial side to how the news is produced and delivered to consumers. They report the news using advanced technology, engineering, and market research to push specific news alerts to specific people, based on their interests and preferences. And it seems to be working: Facebook and Google, for example, generate the most digital advertising revenue for newspapers.[9]

The interdependence between technology and media companies continues to grow, representing a major change in the industry. In one of the latest trends, technology companies and their CEOs have been purchasing or developing major news media companies, such as the creation of the *Intercept* by Ebay founder Pierre

Omidyar, or the purchase of the *Washington Post* by Amazon CEO Jeff Bezos. Both the *Intercept* and the *Washington Post* have a reputation for forceful investigative journalism and original reporting. And at Facebook, editors control trending topics in the news on the global platform, a key editorial role in what makes the headline news.

Beyond making the news profitable again, these high-tech collaborations are changing how Americans learn about current events. The tech world has long valued transparency, networked environments, and participation.[10] This is evident in the growing number of Americans who read news by using social network platforms, such as Twitter or Facebook. How citizens read the news has changed in the digital age, but the role of the media in politics remains as important today as during the founding of our nation.

Americans get their news from (1) newspapers and magazines; (2) **broadcast media** (radio and television); and, increasingly, (3) digital media. Each of these three sources—newspapers, broadcast, and digital—has distinctive characteristics.

NEWSPAPERS STILL SET THE STANDARD FOR NEWS REPORTING

Newspapers are the oldest medium for the dissemination of the news, though most Americans read digital versions of print media today. Newspapers have an especially influential audience because they help set the political agenda for the nation. Their audience of political elites relies on the detailed coverage provided by professional journalists to inform their views about public matters.

The emergence of newspapers (and later radio and television networks) as mass-production businesses driven primarily for profit had major implications for the role of the media in politics in the late nineteenth and early twentieth centuries. The development of standardized reporting and writing practices emphasizing objectivity in political news coverage was motivated in part as a way to generate revenue for media organizations. The owners of large newspaper companies determined that the best way to make a profit was to appeal to as broad an audience as possible, which meant not alienating potential readers who held liberal or conservative political views. This, in turn, required methods to train and "discipline" reporters to produce a standardized, seemingly neutral news product. In contrast, some native digital news is much less likely to be value neutral like journalism from legacy media outlets.

These journalistic practices were successful in attracting audiences, and for a long time, most cities and towns in the country had their own newspaper. However, for most traditional newspapers, recent decades have been financially challenging. Competition from broadcast media and free content online, combined with simultaneous declines in advertising revenue and circulation levels, have undermined the traditional business model of newspapers.[11] In 2018 there were roughly 39,210 working journalists, down from a high of 60,000 a decade before.[12] Estimates indicate daily newspaper print circulation has declined by over 30 percent over the past 20 years.[13] Lower circulation leads to lower advertising revenue.

Following the 2016 election, however, some major U.S. newspapers reported a sharp increase in digital subscriptions.[14] The *New York Times* added more than 500,000 digital subscriptions in 2016—a 47 percent increase from the previous year—while the *Wall Street Journal* had a 23 percent increase over the previous year and the *Chicago Tribune* a 76 percent increase. The newspaper industry as a whole, however, continues to face declines in circulation and ad revenue. The *New York Times* saw a 9 percent decline in advertising revenue but a 3 percent rise in circulation revenue, for an overall revenue decline of 2 percent in 2016.[15]

For most newspapers today, non-ad revenue comes mainly from digital subscriptions rather than print circulation. This model allows a certain number of free visits before requiring users to pay and appears to be a viable business model for the digital press. Digital subscription models have not been as viable for many smaller or midsized local, regional, and even big-city papers, however. Legacy newspapers face the greatest competition from digital-only news outlets, such as Bloomberg News, the Drudge Report, and a host of others. And the pace of technological change in the news media shows no signs of slowing down.[16]

BROADCAST MEDIA ARE STILL POPULAR

Television news reaches more Americans than any other single news source (Figure 6.1). It is estimated that over 95 percent of Americans have a television, and tens of millions of people watch national and local news programs every day. Television news, however, generally covers relatively few topics and provides little depth of coverage. It serves the important function of alerting viewers to issues and events—headline news—via brief quotes and short characterizations of the day's events. Furthermore, broadcast media do very little of their own reporting, instead relying on leading newspapers or digital media to set their news agenda. Print and digital media, as written text, also provide more detailed and complete information than radio or television media, offering a better context for analysis.

Because they are aware of the character of television news coverage, politicians and others often seek to manipulate the news by providing the media with sound bites that will dominate news coverage. Sound bites can work for or against politicians. During the 2016 presidential election, calls for deporting undocumented immigrants were a frequent sound bite topic from candidates such as Donald Trump.

Twenty-four-hour cable news stations such as MSNBC, CNN, and Fox News offer more detail and commentary than the half-hour evening news shows found on the three broadcast news stations—ABC, NBC, and CBS. Pew reports that combined average viewership for the ABC, CBS, and NBC evening newscasts remained stable in 2016 at about 24 million.[17]

Politicians generally consider local broadcast news a friendlier venue than the national news. National reporters are often inclined to criticize and question, whereas local and state reporters are more likely to accept the pronouncements of national leaders at face value. Local TV continues to be a major source of news, especially for older Americans, though its importance as a news source is decreasing among the younger generation in favor of social media such as Facebook.

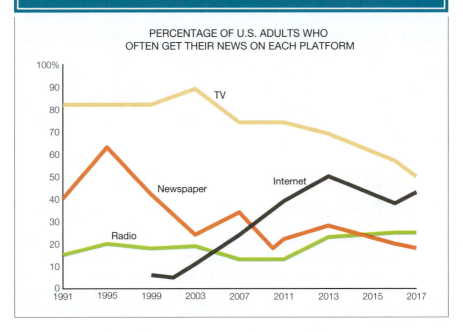

FIGURE 6.1

Americans' Main Sources for News

The media landscape for news has seen remarkable shifts in a short period of time. Twenty years ago, more than 80 percent of Americans watched news on television and more than half read news in a newspaper. Today, fewer Americans watch news on TV and just over one-quarter read the newspaper. What media source has gained rather than lost its audience?

SOURCE: "Americans' Online News Use Is Closing in on TV News Use," Pew Research Center, September 5, 2017, www.pewresearch.org (accessed 5/23/18).

PERCENTAGE OF U.S. ADULTS WHO
OFTEN GET THEIR NEWS ON EACH PLATFORM

Generally, however, Americans' reliance on television does not appear to be going away.

RADIO HAS ADAPTED TO MODERN HABITS

Radio is another broadcast news source that has evolved with the popularity of podcasting. In the 1990s talk radio became an important source of commentary as well as entertainment. Conservative radio hosts, such as Rush Limbaugh and Sean Hannity, have huge audiences and have helped to mobilize support for conservative political causes and candidates. In the political center or center left, National Public Radio (NPR) is a coveted source for in-depth political reporting. In recent years radio news listening has experienced significant growth; in 1990 there were 400 radio stations, a number that has grown to over 2,000 today.

Broadcast radio includes traditional AM/FM radio and digital formats such as online radio and podcasting. While AM/FM radio reaches almost all Americans and remains steady in its revenue, online radio and podcasting have expanded rapidly in the past decade, steadily growing to 64 percent of Americans who tuned in during the last month of 2018, up from 12 percent in 2007. While public broadcasting has a much smaller share of the total media market in the United States than in other countries, National Public Radio is still popular and an important way for people to learn about politics. In 2017 there were 5.4 million unique downloads of NPR podcasts every week, a number that continues to grow.[18] Mobile devices, including satellite radio and cell phones, have triggered a growth in radio use as online radio listening can occur nearly anywhere. Listening to radio news while commuting is a primary way many Americans become informed about politics.[19]

Comedy Comedy talk shows with political content, such as *The Daily Show, The Late Show,* and *Saturday Night Live,* attract millions of television viewers. These shows use humor, sarcasm, and social criticism to discuss serious topics, generally covering almost every major political event. Pew surveys have shown that these talk shows are important sources of political news, especially for young people and liberals, and that followers of comedic talk shows are well informed about politics.[20]

DIGITAL MEDIA HAVE TRANSFORMED MEDIA HABITS

The impact of the internet in mass communication in the twenty-first century parallels that of the printing press in nineteenth-century America, which saw the rise of the **penny press** and widespread literacy.[21] Today, even as the print newspaper business has consolidated, readership of online news has soared. Digital media have become the media of choice for all age groups below 50. In 2000 just 35 percent of adult internet users said they looked for news or information about politics or the upcoming campaigns online.[22] As of 2016 that number had risen to 9 in 10 Americans.[23]

News aggregators, such as Google News, Reddit, and RealClearPolitics, generally compile and repackage stories that were created by other sources, and then deliver them online to consumers in convenient formats. They serve as a platform that allows users to share and comment on the news. Some of this content is produced by digital-only news organizations, mainstream media, social movement organizations, ordinary users, and other "amateurs," as well as powerful political groups, governments, candidates, nonprofits, corporations, and professional media organizations. News aggregators cover thousands of news stories each day, as well as the latest public-opinion polls and their own synthesis of the headline news.

Rather than merely providing a forum to connect with friends and family, social media are spaces for learning about politics and now a primary source for news—a dramatic change from just a few years ago. A majority of American adults— 67 percent—gets news on social media (Figure 6.2).[24] The trend in using social media for political information continues to grow at a rapid rate across all demographic groups.

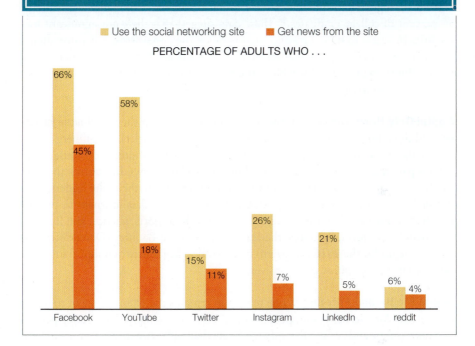

FIGURE 6.2

Social Media and the News

Many Americans who use social media use those sites as a way to obtain political news. This graph shows the percentage of American adults who use each social media site compared with the percentage who report getting news from that site. What are the advantages of getting news on social media, and what are some potential drawbacks?

SOURCE: Jeffrey Gottfried and Elisa Shearer, "News Use across Social Media Platforms 2017," Pew Research Center, September 7, 2017, www.journalism.org/2016/05/26/news-use-across-social-media-platforms-2017/ (accessed 5/15/18).

■ Use the social networking site   ■ Get news from the site

PERCENTAGE OF ADULTS WHO . . .

	Facebook	YouTube	Twitter	Instagram	LinkedIn	reddit
Use the social networking site	66%	58%	15%	26%	21%	6%
Get news from the site	45%	18%	11%	7%	5%	4%

Online media are more diverse and have created a more participatory press, one in which citizens and nonprofit organizations now play a prominent role, and journalists regularly interact with readers via social media, especially Twitter. Readers can now post comments online, upload videos, and participate in a community, providing feedback on almost all online news articles. Digital media have created more information and a more vibrant media environment.

The term *digital citizenship* refers to the ability to participate in culture and politics online. In much the same way that education and literacy promoted democracy and economic growth in the nineteenth century, today's internet has the potential to benefit society as a whole by facilitating political participation and social inclusion through greater access to political information and news.[25] The internet helps provide the information and skills needed for democratic engagement and economic opportunity.[26]

However, regular and effective use of the internet requires high-speed access and digital literacy to evaluate and use information online.[27] Individuals without access or the skills to use the internet may be increasingly uninformed and excluded from the world of politics online. In 2018, 73 percent of Americans were **digital citizens**, individuals with home high-speed access and the technology and literacy skills to use it. Access to the internet is also shaped by income and education. While only half of the working poor (those earning less than $20,000 a year) had home broadband, 85 percent of those earning more than $100,000 a year did. Sixty-three percent of high school graduates have home broadband compared with almost 90 percent of college graduates.[28] These data suggest that there are significant inequalities in access to digital media, what is called the **digital divide**.[29] Because digital media are essential to participation in society, some argue that government has a responsibility to provide affordable and universal access, as provided by most other democratic countries.

Digital-Only News Organizations The last decade has seen the rise of **niche journalism** and digital-only publications, or "born digital" news outlets. Bloomberg News, one of the most successful specialty online sources, has hundreds of thousands of readers paying an annual fee for detailed business-related news. In politics, the Hill, the Blaze, Vice, Vox, BuzzFeed, and the Drudge Report are the niche leaders, with detailed political reporting. FiveThirtyEight specializes in data journalism, providing election forecasts but also broad coverage including sports, science, and lifestyle. Breitbart News, formerly under the leadership of Steve Bannon (Donald Trump's chief strategist for the 2016 campaign) has become a key source of political information for far-right populist conservatives.

Social Media and Filtering While television remains the main source of news for one in two Americans, young people ages 18–33 increasingly learn about politics and news online and are significantly less likely than older Americans to turn to local TV. Seventy-eight percent of people under age 50 get their news from social media. What factors might account for these generational differences?

Social media, such as Twitter and Facebook, tend to be a secondary source for news after television for many Americans, but are a primary source for the young. The high rate of exposure to political news via social media is notable since young Americans overall are less engaged in politics—just 46 percent of people ages 18–29 voted in the 2016 election compared to 59 percent for the 30–44 age group.[30] As the web becomes an increasingly important source for political news, young people may become more engaged in politics.

Because they are more personalized and interactive than anonymous news organizations, social media allow Americans to learn about politics and political news from each other. Growing use of social media for news is evident across *all* demographic groups, including older people, women and men, and groups defined by race, education, and income. Two-thirds of Americans use social media.[31] With President Trump tweeting multiple times per day, as well as its use by congressional leaders and other politicians, social media have become news sources in their own right, as well as forums to share news published in the mainstream media.

Facebook provides a more interactive forum for learning about politics than does Twitter, with users more likely to post and respond to news about government and politics. Twitter's strength is in providing news coverage as it happens, focusing on live events. More than two-thirds of users of both sites say they have posted about news at least at some point. Compared to passively watching television or reading the news, this is a high rate of engagement.[32]

Social media also provide a platform for citizens to be directly engaged with political candidates and elected officials, who have been quick to adopt Facebook and Twitter as means of communicating with their supporters and filtering the daily news for them. In their book *Tweeting to Power*, Jason Gainous and Kevin Wagner argue that using social media is how citizens learn about politics: "Social media alters the political calculus in the United States by filtering who controls information, who consumes information, and how that information is distributed." Because the networks operate outside of traditional media and users can pick their own friend networks and avoid disagreeable ideas and information, parties, groups, and political candidates are able to directly dictate the content of these information networks. Their study finds individuals who are more active politically online and read the news using social media hold stronger partisan opinions. This means using social media for reading the news can exaggerate party polarization among the mass public.[33]

CITIZEN JOURNALISM GIVES PEOPLE NEWS POWER

Digital news is creating a new generation of whistle-blowers, enhancing the media's traditional role as a watchdog for the people against government corruption. A distinguishing feature of this phenomenon is the development of **citizen journalism**, which is interactive and participatory. Citizen journalism includes news reporting and political commentary by ordinary citizens and even crisis coverage from eyewitnesses on the scene, thus involving a wider range of voices in gathering news and interpreting political events. The near-universal availability of cameras on cell phones gives millions of Americans the capacity to photograph or record events, thus providing eyewitness accounts. At the same time, social media permit users to upload videos that can be viewed by hundreds of thousands of subscribers or relayed by the mainstream media for even wider dissemination.

Citizen journalism supplements the work of professional journalists in many important ways. The diversity of online media has created new opinion leaders and new voices and has even, at times, improved information. In recent years, for example, bloggers have uncovered major factual errors in media reports and forced the networks and newspapers to issue corrections. Furthermore, because bloggers and social media users do not have editorial boards, they can post a story within minutes. This ability to scoop the mainstream media means bloggers can frame stories about political candidates before those stories break in the mainstream media.[34] By sharply lowering the technological and financial barriers that previously prevented all but a few individuals from reaching mass audiences, blogs increase the ability of ordinary people to engage in effective political action. On the other hand, the freewheeling nature of blogging and social media often means that there is no quality control like that employed by professional journalists and traditional media.[35]

CONCERNS ABOUT ONLINE NEWS

While online news holds significant promise for improving access to political information, the shift toward online media has also given rise to several major concerns. These potential disadvantages include a decline in investigative journalism, uneven quality in news content, and negative effects on knowledge and tolerance. Two primary concerns dominate the debate about online news: fake news, and the impact on tolerance.

Fake News Political candidates and political leaders are particularly susceptible to attack when negative stories go viral and spread quickly without fact-checking and respect for the privacy of public figures. In contrast to legitimate new stories, *fake news* are false stories circulated to generate ad revenue or to benefit one political candidate or party over another. The most widely publicized fake news story in the 2016 election, the top fake news story circulated on Facebook, was that the Pope had endorsed Trump for president (he did not). Circulation of the top 10 fake news stories on Facebook was more widespread than circulation of the top real news stories about the election. A study published by Stanford University found fake news stories on social media in the 2016 presidential election disproportionately favored Trump over Hillary Clinton, and there is growing evidence that the Russian government was involved in generating many of the fake news stories in order to discredit Clinton and her campaign. Websites such as FactCheck.org, Snopes.com, and PolitiFact.com are devoted exclusively to checking the veracity of political claims.

Knowledge Up, Tolerance Down? The variety of online news may actually *lower* tolerance for social, religious, and political diversity, leading to more partisan polarization and societal conflict. Digital media often do not abide by traditional media's principle of objective journalism. Instead, the specialization of information online and on cable television means that liberals and conservatives alike can self-select media that are consistent with their underlying assumptions and avoid exposure to information that might challenge their preconceived beliefs.[36] The natural tendency to select news that conforms with our own beliefs is exacerbated by the way search engines cater to our individual preferences—called the "filter bubble," or "self-selection bias"—which screens out exposure to information that might challenge or broaden our worldview.[37]

The Media Affect Power Relations in American Politics

The content and character of news and public affairs programming—what the media choose to present and how they present it—can have far-reaching political consequences. The media can shape and modify, if not fully form, the public's perception of events, issues, and institutions. Media coverage can rally support for, or intensify opposition to, national policies on important matters such as health care, the economy, and international wars.

THE MEDIA INFLUENCE PUBLIC OPINION THROUGH AGENDA-SETTING, FRAMING, AND PRIMING

Traditional and digital media influence American politics in a number of important ways. The power of the media lies in their ability to shape what issues Americans think about (setting the agenda) and what opinions Americans hold about those issues (framing and priming).

Agenda-Setting and Selection Bias The first source of media power is **agenda-setting**—that is, the power of the media to bring public attention to particular issues and problems. Groups and forces that wish to bring their ideas before the public in order to generate support for policy proposals or political candidacies must secure media coverage. If the media are persuaded that an idea is newsworthy, they may declare it an "issue" that must be confronted or a "problem" to be solved, thus clearing the first hurdle in the policy-making process. If, on the other hand, an idea lacks or loses media appeal, its chance of resulting in new programs or policies is diminished.

For example, in the lead-up to the 2016 election, the mainstream media and Donald Trump focused extensively on Hillary Clinton's use of a private email server during her tenure as Secretary of State, and its possible risk of jeopardizing government secrets. Clinton's email use dominated the media agenda, especially in the 10 days before the election when FBI director James Comey reopened the investigation into her email server.

Through agenda setting, the media have the power to influence which issues the public pays attention to. After FBI director James Comey released a letter indicating the reopening of the investigation into Hillary Clinton's use of a private email server days before the 2016 election, the media's intense coverage of the investigation caused the Clinton campaign to respond to the letter publicly.

Because the media are businesses and because the media seek to attract the largest possible audiences, they naturally tend to cover stories with dramatic or entertainment value, giving less attention to important stories that are less compelling. News coverage thus often focuses on crimes and scandals, especially those involving prominent individuals. This **selection bias**—the tendency to focus news coverage on only one aspect of an event or issue, avoiding coverage of other aspects—means that the media may provide less information about important political issues. The age-old journalistic instinct for sensational stories to tell often trumps the media's responsibility to inform the public about what really matters— and the public's responsibility to demand that from the media.

What the mainstream media decide to report on and what they ignore have important implications. For example, the mainstream media provided little coverage of the Bush tax cuts of 2001 and 2003 (or their extension under President Obama in 2009), although they dramatically increased the federal budget deficit and widened the gap between the super-rich and most other Americans in terms of wealth.[38] It is not surprising that public-opinion polls showed that 40 percent of Americans had no opinion on whether they favored the massive tax cuts in 2001.

Framing Framing is the media's ability to influence how the American people interpret events and policies. Politicians take care to choose language that presents their ideas in the most favorable light possible. Public opinion on politics naturally changes with facts, but few citizens read legislation; so when forming opinions about policy and politics, the public relies on media coverage. This means that arguments made by elected officials and other political actors, or "frames," are critical to the process of forming opinions. For example, during the 2016 presidential campaign, Donald Trump framed Hillary Clinton as a criminal for her use of a private email server even though no charges were ever brought.

Priming Another source of media influence on opinion, related to framing, is **priming**. Priming involves "calling attention to some matters while ignoring others."[39] As a result, the public will be *primed* to use certain criteria when evaluating a politician or an issue and to ignore other criteria. In the lead-up to the 2008 presidential election, for example, the serious economic recession took much of the spotlight. As a result, the economy—far more than other issues— was a more important lens through which the public evaluated the candidates rather than national security.

In the case of political candidates, the media have considerable influence over whether a particular individual will receive public attention and whether a particular individual will be taken seriously as a viable contender. Thus, if the media find a candidate interesting, they may treat him or her as a serious contender despite possible weaknesses and shortcomings. For example, the media were criticized in the 2016 presidential race for covering Donald Trump—a reality TV star known for his inflammatory comments and disdain for political correctness—much more than other candidates. Many people believed that Trump's unexpected victory in the Republican primaries was due in part to widespread media coverage.

News media are not alone in agenda-setting, framing, and priming; elected officials, interest groups, and other political players compete over all three in hopes of influencing public opinion.

LEAKED INFORMATION CAN COME FROM GOVERNMENT OFFICIALS OR INDEPENDENT SOURCES

The media may report information that is leaked by government officials. A *leak* is the disclosure of confidential information to the news media. Leaks may emanate from a variety of sources, including whistle-blowers or lower-level officials who hope to publicize what they view as their bosses' improper activities. In 1971, for example, a minor Defense Department staffer named Daniel Ellsberg sought to discredit official justifications for U.S. involvement in Vietnam by leaking top-secret documents to the press. The Pentagon Papers—the Defense Department's own secret history of the war, differing widely from the Pentagon's public pronouncements—were published by the *New York Times* and the *Washington Post* after the U.S. Supreme Court ruled that the government could not block their release.[40] Pentagon credibility was severely damaged, hastening the erosion of public support for the war.

Most leaks, though, originate not with low-level whistle-blowers but rather with senior government officials, prominent politicians, and political activists. These individuals cultivate long-term relationships with journalists, to whom they regularly leak confidential information, knowing that it is likely to be published on a priority basis in a form acceptable to them. In turn, of course, journalists are likely to regard high-level sources of confidential information as valuable assets whose favor must be retained.

Digital media has taken leaks to a new level. WikiLeaks, an independent nonprofit organization dedicated to publishing classified information, posts leaked documents to its website and uses an anonymous system so that leakers cannot be identified. In recent years, WikiLeaks has released thousands of secret government documents involving instances of government corruption, such as war crimes in Afghanistan and Iraq. During the 2016 presidential campaign, WikiLeaks released thousands of stolen emails from Democratic candidate Hillary Clinton's campaign. WikiLeaks shares its treasure trove of leaked government documents with major international papers, including the *New York Times*.

In 2013, Edward Snowden, a former employee of the Central Intelligence Agency (CIA) and contractor for the National Security Agency (NSA), disclosed thousands of classified digital documents to journalists and international media. The leaks disclosed widespread global surveillance programs by the U.S. government working with telecommunication companies. The world learned the NSA was searching millions of email and instant messaging contact lists and tracking and mapping the locations of cell phones. For revealing the mass surveillance programs, Snowden has been called a hero, a whistle-blower, a dissident, and a traitor. The leaks garnered intense media attention and

sparked heated public debate over government surveillance and privacy of information for individuals.

Critics of WikiLeaks and Snowden argue that posting government documents online is not journalism, that governments must have some secrets, and that the release of some government documents may jeopardize national security as well as American soldiers and their local allies by revealing their identities.

ADVERSARIAL JOURNALISM HAS RISEN IN RECENT YEARS

The political power of the news media vis-à-vis the government has greatly increased in recent years through the growing prominence of "adversarial journalism," an aggressive form of investigative journalism that attempts to expose and antagonize the status quo.

The national media's aggressive use of the techniques of investigation, publicity, and exposure allow them to inform the public about major news stories. Without such aggressive media coverage, we might never have known of Bill Clinton's extramarital affair or of Richard Nixon's Committee to Re-elect the President's illegal break-in to the Democratic Party headquarters in the Watergate building. We might never have known that Iraq did not have weapons of mass destruction, despite claims to the contrary by then-president George W. Bush. Without aggressive media coverage, would we know about Russian interference in the 2016 elections? It is easy to criticize the media for their aggressive tactics, but would our democracy function effectively without the critical role of the press? Independent media are needed as the watchdogs of American politics. Digital technology has provided a new means by which the media can be watchdogs.

Leaks of classified information have sparked significant debate over what the government should classify as "secret" and what deserves to be public knowledge. After Edward Snowden leaked thousands of classified documents, he fled the United States in order to escape arrest and prosecution. His actions have been both defended and denounced.

BROADCAST MEDIA ARE REGULATED, BUT NOT PRINT MEDIA

In many countries, such as China, the government controls media content. In other countries, the government owns the broadcast media (for example, the BBC in Britain) but does not tell the media what to say.

In the United States, the print media are essentially free from government interference. The broadcast media, on the other hand, are subject to federal regulation. American radio and television are regulated by the Federal Communications

Commission (FCC), an independent regulatory agency established in 1934. Radio and TV stations must have FCC licenses, which must be renewed every five years. Licensing provides a mechanism for allocating radio and TV frequencies to prevent broadcasts from interfering with and garbling one another.

Through regulations prohibiting obscenity, indecency, and profanity, the FCC has also sought to prohibit radio and television stations from airing explicit sexual and excretory references between 6 A.M. and 10 P.M., the hours when children are most likely to be in the audience. Generally speaking, FCC regulation applies only to the "over-the-air" broadcast media. It does not apply to cable television, the internet, or satellite radio.

In 1996, Congress passed the Telecommunications Act, a broad effort to do away with most regulations in effect since 1934. The legislation loosened restrictions on media ownership and allowed telephone companies, cable television providers, and broadcasters to compete with one another for telecommunication services. Following the passage of the act, several mergers between telephone and cable companies and among different segments of the entertainment media produced an even greater concentration of media ownership than had been possible since regulation of the industry began in 1934.

Though the act loosened many regulations, it did include an attempt to regulate the content of material transmitted over the internet. This law, known as the Communications Decency Act, made it illegal to make "indecent" sexual material on the internet accessible to those under 18 years old. The act was immediately denounced by civil libertarians and became the subject of lawsuits. The case reached

The debate over net neutrality highlights fundamental questions about democracy. If the media are intended to be a marketplace of ideas, what should the government do to regulate that marketplace? Should any single entity be allowed to exert more influence or control, or should everyone be allowed to participate equally?

The Internet and Global Democracy

The internet and social media play an increasing role in elections, as demonstrated in this chapter. Critics of this trend have raised concerns that a lack of "quality control" allows the spreading of fake news by unscrupulous groups.[a] A number of foreign and domestic actors have used the open nature of this media to manipulate campaign rhetoric for political gain. The British government opened investigations into the spread of false news during the "Brexit" vote on leaving the European Union,[b] and Russia used internal techniques to manipulate elections in the United States and Europe.[c]

Supporters, however, point out that the internet and social media have allowed voters to connect better with their political systems. In Kenya, biometric voter registration has made it more difficult for people to cast multiple ballots, and real-time texting has improved oversight on election counts, helping to combat voter fraud.[d]

While internet and social media are certainly transforming politics, it is important to remember that not all global citizens are part of this trend. If the future of politics is online, then many poor and older people around the world may be increasingly left behind.

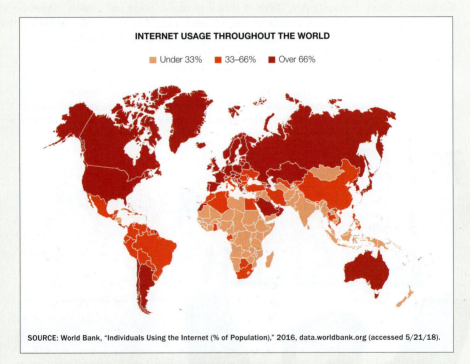

INTERNET USAGE THROUGHOUT THE WORLD

Under 33%   33–66%   Over 66%

SOURCE: World Bank, "Individuals Using the Internet (% of Population)," 2016, data.worldbank.org (accessed 5/21/18).

[a] Thomas B. Edsall, "Opinion: Democracy, Disrupted," March 2, 2017, *New York Times*, www.nytimes.com/2017/03/02/opinion/how-the-internet-threatens-democracy.html (accessed 5/21/18).

[b] "What Are the Links between Cambridge Analytica and a Brexit Campaign Group?" Reuters, March 21, 2018, www.reuters.com/article/us-facebook-cambridge-analytica-leave-eu/what-are-the-links-between-cambridge-analytica-and-a-brexit-campaign-group-idUSKBN1GX2IO (accessed 5/21/18).

[c] Constanze Stelzenmüller, "Testimony: The Impact of Russian Interference on Germany's 2017 Election," June 28, 2017, www.brookings.edu/testimonies/the-impact-of-russian-interference-on-germanys-2017-elections/ (accessed 5/21/18).

[d] Loren Treisman, "How Kenyans Are Using Tech to Stop Election Fraud," August 3, 2017, CNN, www.cnn.com/2017/07/27/africa/kenya-elections-technology/index.html (accessed 5/21/18).

the Supreme Court in 1997, and the act was ruled an unconstitutional infringement of the First Amendment's right to freedom of speech (see Chapter 4).

Although the government's ability to regulate the content of electronic media on the internet has been questioned, the federal government has used its licensing power to impose several regulations that can affect the political content of radio and TV broadcasts. The first of these is the **equal time rule**, under which broadcasters must provide candidates for the same political office equal opportunities to communicate their messages to the public. Under the terms of the Telecommunications Act, during the 45 days before an election, broadcasters are required to make time available to candidates at the lowest rate charged for that time slot.

The second regulation affecting the content of broadcasts is the **right of rebuttal**, which requires that individuals be given the opportunity to respond to personal attacks made on a radio or television broadcast. In the 1969 case of *Red Lion Broadcasting Company v. Federal Communications Commission*, for example, the U.S. Supreme Court upheld the FCC's determination that a radio station was required to provide a liberal author with an opportunity to respond to a conservative commentator's attack that the station had aired.[41]

For many years, a third important federal regulation was the *fairness doctrine*. Under this doctrine, broadcasters who aired programs on controversial issues were required to provide time for opposing views. In 1987, however, the FCC revoked the fairness doctrine on the grounds that there were so many radio and television stations—to say nothing of newspapers and newsmagazines—that in all likelihood many different viewpoints were already being presented without each station's being required to try to present all sides of an argument.

The rise of online media challenges our thinking about regulation of the media as it is more difficult—some say impossible—to regulate political content online. In 2011 the United Nations declared that access to the internet is a human right.[42] While this came in response to threats by authoritarian governments against internet access, the UN's position demonstrates the significance of information technology in modern life.

The Media
WHAT DO WE WANT?

The freedom of the press is essential to democratic government. Ordinary citizens depend on the media to investigate wrongdoing, publicize and explain governmental policy, evaluate politicians, and bring to light matters that might otherwise be known to only a handful of governmental insiders. In short, without free and active media, democratic government would be virtually impossible. Citizens would have few means through which to know or assess the government's actions—other than the claims or pronouncements of the government itself. Moreover, without active (indeed, aggressive) media, citizens would be hard-pressed to make informed choices among competing candidates at the polls. That is one reason that the teenaged defenders of net neutrality we discussed at the beginning of the chapter hoped to keep the internet open as a source of information on public affairs.

Today's media are not only adversarial but also increasingly partisan. Blogs, digital-only news websites, social media, and others can be unabashedly partisan. To some extent, increasing ideological and partisan stridency is an inevitable result of the expansion and proliferation of news sources. When the news was dominated by three networks and a handful of national papers, each sought to appeal to the entire national audience. This required a moderate and balanced tone so that consumers would not be offended and transfer their attention to a rival network or newspaper. Today, there are so many news sources that few can aim for a broad-based national audience. Instead, many target a partisan or ideological niche and aim to develop a strong relationship with consumers in that audience segment by catering to their biases and predispositions.

The rise of digital media has fundamentally changed how political information is gathered and distributed. News today is participatory and involves citizens as well as professional journalists. Wikipedia, the free online encyclopedia founded by Jimmy Wales, has millions of pages compiled by legions of volunteers and provides relatively unbiased content on virtually every political topic imaginable. Social media, Wikipedia, and all Wiki-type sites involve people working collaboratively to write and create information and transmit knowledge. Social media also enable citizens to express their political opinions. (The "**Who Participates?**" feature on the facing page shows some of the ways Americans participate in politics via social media.) Is such a system the future of the news media?

The media can make or break reputations, help to launch or destroy political careers, and build support for or rally opposition to programs and institutions.[43] Wherever there is so much power, at least the potential exists for its abuse or overly zealous use. All things considered, free media are so critically important to the maintenance of a democratic society that Americans must be prepared to take the risk that the media will occasionally abuse their power. Governmental controls that would prevent the media from misusing their power would also limit freedom. The ultimate beneficiaries of free and active media are the American people.

Civic Engagement in the Digital Age

In the last 12 months, did you send a message on Facebook or Twitter about political issues?

Percentage who said "yes" to this question

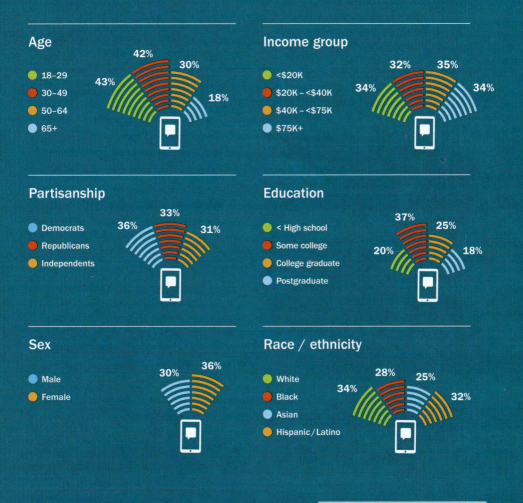

Age
- 18–29
- 30–49
- 50–64
- 65+

43% | 42% | 30% | 18%

Income group
- <$20K
- $20K – <$40K
- $40K – <$75K
- $75K+

34% | 32% | 35% | 34%

Partisanship
- Democrats
- Republicans
- Independents

36% | 33% | 31%

Education
- < High school
- Some college
- College graduate
- Postgraduate

20% | 37% | 25% | 18%

Sex
- Male
- Female

30% | 36%

Race / ethnicity
- White
- Black
- Asian
- Hispanic/Latino

34% | 28% | 25% | 32%

SOURCE: American National Election Study 2016 time series, www.electionstudies.org (accessed 11/4/17).

WHAT YOU CAN DO

★ WHAT YOU CAN DO ★

Be an Informed Consumer of Media

 Gather information from a variety of news sources rather than relying on just one. You can set up a news aggregator with a variety of free downloadable apps, including Flipboard (**www.flipboard.com**) and Feedly (**www.feedly.com**).

 Check media watchdog organizations such as the Columbia Journalism Review (**www.cjr.org**), Fairness & Accuracy in Reporting (**www.fair.org**), and Accuracy in Media (**www.aim.org**) for reports of media bias and censorship.

 For information on the factual accuracy of what is said by political players, go to **www.factcheck.org**. For investigative journalism in the public interest, go to **www.propublica.org**. For reporting on the accuracy of news rumors, go to **www.snopes.com**.

★ STUDY GUIDE ★

Practice Quiz

1. Public broadcasting outlets that receive government funding through license fees, subsidies, or tax dollars *(p. 180)*
   a) are prohibited by the Constitution from operating in the United States.
   b) account for less than 5 percent of media market share in the United States.
   c) account for nearly one-third of media market share in the United States.
   d) account for approximately half of media market share in the United States.
   e) account for more than two-thirds of media market share in the United States.

2. More than three-fourths of daily print newspapers are owned by *(p. 181)*
   a) large media conglomerates.
   b) the national government.
   c) small local companies.
   d) private individuals.
   e) the employees who run them.

3. Digital citizenship requires *(p. 188)*
   a) a subscription to one or more online newspapers.
   b) high-speed internet access and the technical and literacy skills to evaluate and use information online.
   c) high-speed internet access only.
   d) a social media account, such as Facebook or Twitter.
   e) maintaining a political blog.

4. The fact that almost 90 percent of college graduates have home broadband access but only 63 percent of high school graduates do is an example of *(p. 188)*
   a) the "college chasm."
   b) the "online opening."
   c) the "download disparity."
   d) the "digital divide."
   e) the "BA bump."

5. Which of the following is *not* a reason that many Americans appear to prefer online news? *(p. 190)*
   a) the depth of the information available online
   b) the diversity of online viewpoints
   c) the convenience of getting news online
   d) the accuracy and objectivity compared to traditional media outlets
   e) the up-to-the-minute currency of the information available online

6. Media's powers to bring public attention to a particular issue or problem is known as *(p. 191)*
   a) agenda-setting.
   b) framing.
   c) priming.
   d) adversarial journalism.
   e) selection bias.

7. Most leaks originate with *(p. 191)*
   a) low-level government whistle-blowers.
   b) senior government officials, prominent politicians, and political activists.
   c) members of the public who witness misbehavior.
   d) ambassadors from foreign countries.
   e) members of the media.

8. *Adversarial journalism* refers to *(p. 194)*
   a) the recent shift in American society away from general-purpose sources of information and toward narrowly focused niche sources.
   b) an era in American history when political parties provided all of the financing for newspapers.
   c) an aggressive form of journalism that attempts to expose and antagonize the status quo.

   d) a form of reporting in which the media adopt an accepting and friendly posture toward the government and public officials.
   e) the process of preparing the public to take a particular view of an event or political actor.

9. In general, FCC regulations apply only to *(p. 195)*
   a) cable television.
   b) internet websites.
   c) over-the-air broadcast media.
   d) satellite radio.
   e) newspapers and magazines.

10. In *Red Lion Broadcasting Company v. Federal Communications Commission*, the Supreme Court ruled that a radio station *(p. 197)*
    a) could not legally charge Democratic and Republican gubernatorial candidates different prices for commercials aired at the same time of day.
    b) could legally charge Democratic and Republican gubernatorial candidates different prices for commercials aired at the same time of day.
    c) was required to provide a liberal author with an opportunity to respond to a personal attack broadcast by one of the station's conservative commentators.
    d) was not required to provide a liberal author with an opportunity to respond to a personal attack broadcast by one of the station's conservative commentators.
    e) was not required to secure a license from the FCC if it accepted no money in grants or tax credits from the federal government.

11. The now-defunct requirement that broadcasters provide time for opposing views when they air programs on controversial issues was called *(p. 197)*
    a) the equal time rule.
    b) the fairness doctrine.
    c) the right of rebuttal.
    d) the response rule.
    e) the free speech doctrine.

Key Terms

agenda-setting *(p. 191)* the power of the media to bring public attention to particular issues and problems

broadcast media *(p. 183)* television, radio, or other media that transmit audio and/or video content to the public

citizen journalism *(p. 189)* news reported and distributed by citizens, rather than by professional journalists and for-profit news organizations

digital citizen *(p. 188)* a daily internet user with high-speed home internet access and the technology and literacy skills to go online for employment, news, politics, entertainment, commerce, and other activities

digital divide *(p. 188)* the gap in access to the internet among demographic groups based on education, income, age, geographic location, and race/ethnicity

equal time rule *(p. 197)* the requirement that broadcasters provide candidates for the same political office equal opportunities to communicate their messages to the public

framing *(p. 192)* the power of the media to influence how events and issues are interpreted

media *(p. 179)* print and digital forms of communication, including television, newspapers, radio, and the internet, intended to convey information to large audiences

news aggregator *(p. 186)* an application or feed that collects web content such as news headlines, blogs, podcasts, online videos, and more in one location for easy viewing

niche journalism *(p. 188)* news reporting devoted to a targeted portion (subset) of a journalism market sector or for a portion of readers or viewers based on content or ideological presentation

penny press *(p. 186)* cheap, tabloid-style newspaper produced in the nineteenth century, when mass production of inexpensive newspapers first became possible due to the steam-powered printing press; a penny press newspaper cost one cent compared with other papers, which cost more than five cents

priming *(p. 192)* process of preparing the public to take a particular view of an event or political actor

right of rebuttal *(p. 197)* a Federal Communications Commission regulation giving individuals the right to have the opportunity to respond to personal attacks made on a radio or television broadcast

selection bias *(p. 192)* the tendency to focus news coverage on only one aspect of an event or issue, avoiding coverage of other aspects

social media *(p. 188)* web-based and mobile-based technologies that are used to turn communication into interactive dialogue between organizations, communities, and individuals; social media technologies take on many different forms including blogs, Wikis, podcasts, pictures, video, Facebook, and Twitter

For Further Reading

Boydstun, Amber E. *Making the News: Politics, the Media, and Agenda Setting*. Chicago: University of Chicago Press, 2013.

Campbell, Richard, Christopher Martin, and Bettina Fabos. *Media and Culture*. New York: St. Martin's Press, 2009.

Carr, Nicholas. *The Shallows: What the Internet Is Doing to Our Brains*. New York: W. W. Norton, 2011.

Fenton, Tom. *Bad News: The Decline of Reporting, the Business of News, and the Danger to Us All*. New York: HarperCollins, 2005.

Fox, Richard, and Jennifer Ramos. *iPolitics: Citizens, Elections and Governing in the New Media Era*. New York: Cambridge University Press, 2011.

Graber, Doris, and Johanna Dunaway. *Mass Media and American Politics*, 9th ed. Washington, DC: CQ Press, 2014.

Iyengar, Shanto. *Media Politics: A Citizen's Guide*, 3rd ed. New York: W. W. Norton, 2015.

Iyengar, Shanto, and Donald Kinder. *News That Matters: Television and American Public Opinion*. Chicago: University of Chicago Press, 2010.

Jenkins, Henry. *Convergence Culture: Where Old and New Media Collide*. New York: New York University Press, 2008.

MacArthur, John. *Second Front: Censorship and Propaganda in the 1991 Gulf War*. Berkeley and Los Angeles: University of California Press, 2004.

Spitzer, Robert J., ed. *Media and Public Policy*. Westport, CT: Praeger, 1993.

West, Darrell M. *Air Wars: Television Advertising and Social Media in Election Campaigns, 1952–2016*, 7th ed. Washington, DC: CQ Press, 2017.

Political Parties, Participation, and Elections

WHAT GOVERNMENT DOES AND WHY IT MATTERS

Political parties play a variety of important roles in American democracy. They mobilize people to participate in the political arena and to vote. They convey information about what policies candidates support. And they are broader than interest groups, which generally seek narrow policy objectives. Political parties are capable of mobilizing many more voters to win control of government.

For all their important mobilizing and information conveying functions, parties, like other aspects of government and politics, can seem far from ordinary people. But ordinary people can have a big impact in political parties. Early in 2009, before the term "Tea Party" was coined, Keli Carender was a conservative blogger in Seattle. She became concerned that the stimulus bill that Congress was considering to address the financial crisis and ensuing recession was simply more of "big government" trampling on her "freedom and liberty." After calls and emails to her congressional representative were ignored, she organized a "Porkulus Protest" in Seattle without support from any national organization. "I just got fed up and planned it. . . . I had

Individuals can have profound effects on political parties. Keli Carender took her belief in limited government and her anger over excessive government spending and started the Tea Party movement, which has strongly influenced the direction of the Republican Party.

120 people show up, which is amazing for the bluest of blue cities I live in, and on only four days' notice!! This was due to me spending the entire four days calling and emailing every person, think tank, policy center, university professors (that were sympathetic), etc. in town, and not stopping until the day came." She also contacted conservative author Michelle Malkin, who publicized the rally on her blog. At a second rally later that month, twice as many people showed up, in part because Carender had collected email addresses at the first rally. Her advice to other would-be organizers: "Number one: just get it done. Do you need a permit? Find out and then just get it. Do you want a guest speaker? Get on the phone and call anyone you can think of and get them there. You will need to alert the media, so just get that done. . . . Let people help you. Almost immediately I had two women email me and say, what can I do? And boom, I had two other organizers to start helping me with the next event."[1]

Carender's protests were among the first events in what became known as the Tea Party movement, which gained steam when CNBC business analyst

Rick Santelli called for a "tea party" protest of the Obama administration's plans for addressing the Great Recession. Many political candidates associated with the Tea Party gained office beginning in the 2010 midterm elections, and Donald Trump courted Tea Party supporters during his presidential campaign in 2016. As we will see in this chapter, political parties and elections are all about who controls the government; participation is about who gets involved and why. Revolts against the political parties by rank-and-file members occur very rarely in American history. But sometimes, parties are shaken up by grassroots activity like Keli Carender's. Her story, and others like it, show that individuals can make a difference if they participate. The key is to "just get it done."

CHAPTER GOALS

★ Explain the roles that parties play in American elections and government (pp. 207–10)

★ Describe the American party system and how it has changed over time (pp. 210–20)

★ Describe the major forms of traditional and digital participation in politics (pp. 220–27)

★ Examine the factors that influence voters' decisions (pp. 227–29)

★ Explain the major rules, levels, and types of elections in the United States (pp. 229–32)

★ Analyze the strategies, issues, and outcomes of the 2016 and 2018 elections (pp. 232–36)

★ Describe how candidates raise the money they need to run (pp. 237–39)

Parties and Elections Have Been Vital to American Politics and Government

Political parties, like interest groups (see Chapter 8), are organized groups that seek influence over the government. A party seeks to control the entire government by electing its members to office. Interest groups, by comparison, don't control the operation of government and its personnel but rather try to influence government policies, often through lobbying elected officials and campaign contributions.

POLITICAL PARTIES AROSE FROM THE ELECTORAL PROCESS

Although the Founders did not envision the rise of political parties and George Washington was elected the nation's first president without association with a political party, parties quickly became a core feature of the American political system. Historically, parties form in one of two ways. The first, which could be called "internal mobilization," occurs when political conflicts prompt officials and competing factions within government to mobilize popular support. This is precisely what happened during the early years of the American Republic. Competition in Congress between northeastern merchants and southern farmers led first the southerners and then the northeasterners to attempt to organize their supporters. The result was the foundation of America's first national parties: the Jeffersonians, or Antifederalists, whose primary base was in the South, and the Federalists, whose strength was greatest in the New England states.

The second way that parties form is called "external mobilization," which takes place when a group of politicians outside government organizes popular support to win governmental power. For example, during the 1850s, a group of state politicians who opposed slavery, especially the expansion of slavery in America's territorial possessions, built what became the Republican Party by constructing party organizations and mobilizing popular support in the Northeast and West.

America's two major parties now, of course, are the Democratic Party and the Republican Party. Both trace their roots back over 150 years, and both have evolved over time. Since they were formed, the two major parties have undergone significant shifts in their policy positions and their membership. These changes have been prompted both by issues and events (economic change, the civil rights movement, immigration, etc.) and by demographic and social developments in the United States.

Political parties play an important role in elections. They recruit candidates to run for office, get their loyal party members out to vote, and work in a variety of ways to promote the causes and issues of the party. In earlier times the parties had near total control over the electoral process. In recent decades, however, they have lost their monopoly to candidates who decide not to work within the party, to **political action committees (PACs)** that raise and distribute millions of dollars for candidates, and to direct appeals through the media.

PARTIES RECRUIT CANDIDATES

One of the most important party activities is the recruitment of candidates to run for office. Where they do not have an incumbent running for re-election, party leaders attempt to identify strong candidates and to interest them in entering the campaign.

An ideal candidate will have a strong leadership record and the capacity to raise enough money to mount a serious campaign. Party leaders are usually not willing to provide financial backing to candidates who are unable to raise substantial funds on their own. For a U.S. House seat, this can mean several hundred thousand dollars; for a Senate seat, a serious candidate must be able to raise several million dollars. Presidential candidates raise hundreds of millions of dollars, an amount that continues to rise with every election cycle.

Often, party leaders have difficulty finding attractive candidates and persuading them to run. Candidate recruitment has become particularly difficult in an era in which **incumbents** (candidates running for re-election to positions that they already hold) are hard to beat. Over 20 percent of races for the House of Representatives, for example, are uncontested (meaning there is only one candidate from one party on the ballot) because challenging incumbents in the House and winning is so difficult. On average, incumbents in the House have more than double the money for their political campaigns than challengers, while Senate incumbents have on average 50 percent more. Other barriers to recruiting quality candidates include lengthy political campaigns that often involve mudslinging, and the fact that candidates must assume that their personal lives will be intensely scrutinized on social media, in the press, and in negative campaign ads run by their opponents.[2]

PARTIES ORGANIZE NOMINATIONS

Nomination is the process by which a party selects a single candidate to run for each elective office. The party nomination process varies from state to state and office to office, but it usually involves a primary election among multiple candidates from the same party. Voters in the primary election select just one candidate to go on to general election. Scholars have found that although the nomination process appears democratic in that average citizens have a say, party elites play an outsized role in selecting the candidates nominated by their party for president of the United States. In 2016, however, the Republican Party insiders had less control over the process; outsider businessman and reality-TV star Donald Trump secured the nomination despite the fact that many members of the party emphatically opposed him.

PARTIES HELP GET OUT THE VOTE

The formal general election begins immediately after the nominations conclude. Throughout American history, the general election competition is a time of heightened partisanship, when popular support for the political parties is high. All the paraphernalia of party committees—from signs, bumper stickers, and buttons to social media slogans and YouTube ads—are on display, and all the committee members are activated into local party workforces.

The first step involves voter registration. Party workers collaborate with nonprofit organizations, local community groups, and other organizations to turn out the vote. The parties and candidate campaigns still mail notices, call voters, organize voter-registration drives on college campuses, and knock on doors to ensure citizens are registered.

The next step is turning out the vote: after all, it doesn't matter which party has more support if that party's voters stay home on Election Day. Convincing voters to actually show up and vote on Election Day is one of the hardest tasks that the parties face, as it usually involves getting individuals to go to the polls, stand in line, and vote for the party's candidates. If they are voting by mail—one in three Americans now vote by absentee ballots or mail voting—voters still have to request the ballot, fill it out, and return it. Voter mobilization, once an art, has now become a science. Research has shown that face-to-face, in-person contacts are much more effective than mailings, robocalls, or TV advertising in mobilizing voters. Campaigns now organize large-scale voter-mobilization drives and field offices with hundreds of thousands of party workers and volunteers contacting millions of voters. In recent years, parties have developed extensive databases of

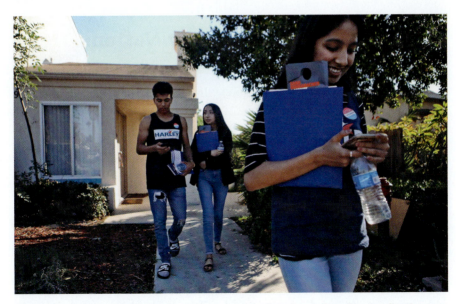

People are more likely to turn out to vote if someone asks them face to face. Direct mail and impersonal phone calls are less likely to have an effect on turnout.

over 240 million potential adult voters. Modern political campaigns can predict who you will vote for and are extremely effective at turning out the voters who are most likely to vote for their candidates. One way campaigns use this data is through **micro-targeting**. Micro-targeting involves tailoring campaign messages to individuals in small, homogenous groups (e.g., suburban stay-at-home mothers or fans of NASCAR) and emphasizing specific issues, rather than a one-size-fits-all campaign message. This technique enables political parties to target candidates' strategies and messages to these very specific groups.

PARTIES ORGANIZE POWER IN CONGRESS

Congress depends more on the party system than is generally recognized. For one thing, power in Congress is organized along party lines. The speakership of the House is essentially a party office because the Speaker is chosen by the **majority party**—that is, the party that holds the majority of seats in the House or Senate. (The other party is known as the **minority party**.) When the majority party presents a nominee to the entire House, its choice is usually ratified in a straight vote along party lines.

The committee system of both houses of Congress is also a product of the two-party system; the party with the most seats chairs the congressional committees, setting the policy agenda. Each party is also assigned a quota of members for each committee, depending on the percentage of total seats held by the party. As we will see in Chapter 9, the assignment of individual members to committees is a party decision. Granting a member of Congress permission to transfer to another committee is also a party decision, as is advancement up the committee ladder toward serving as committee chair.

America Is One of the Few Nations with a Two-Party System

> **Describe the American party system and how it has changed over time**

In his 1796 Farewell Address, President George Washington warned his countrymen to shun partisan politics. Nonetheless, a **two-party system**—a political system in which only two parties have a realistic opportunity to compete effectively for control of the government—emerged early in the history of the new Republic. Beginning with the Federalists and the Jeffersonian Republicans in the late 1780s, two major parties have dominated national politics, although which particular two parties they have been has changed with the times and issues.

However, the term *party system* refers to more than just the number of parties competing for power or the set of parties that are important at any given time. It also includes the organization of the parties, the balance of power between and within party coalitions, the parties' social and institutional bases, and the issues and policies around which party competition is organized. Seen from this broader perspective, the character of a nation's party system can change even if the number of parties remains the same and even when the same two parties seem to be competing for power. Today's American party system is very different from the country's party system of 100 years ago, but the Democrats and Republicans continue to be the two major competing forces. Over the course of American history, changes in political forces and alignments have produced six distinctive party systems (see Figure 7.1).

The First Party System: Federalists and Jeffersonian Republicans The first party system emerged in the 1790s and pitted the Federalists, who favored a strong national government, against the Jeffersonian Republicans, or Antifederalists, who favored a weak national government and strong states. The Federalists were the establishment party at the time, and the Antifederalists were the outsiders. The Federalists represented New England merchants and supported a program of protective tariffs to encourage manufacturing, forgiving states' Revolutionary War debts, the creation of a national bank, and commercial ties with Britain. The Jeffersonians, led by southern agricultural interests, opposed these policies and instead favored free trade, the promotion of agricultural over commercial interests, and friendship with France. Over the years the Federalists gradually weakened and disappeared altogether, especially after the pro-British sympathies of some Federalist leaders during the War of 1812 led to charges of treason against the party.

From the collapse of the Federalists until the 1830s, America had only one political party, the Jeffersonian Republicans, who gradually came to be known as the Democrats. This period of one-party politics had an absence of party competition. Throughout this period, however, there was intense factional conflict within the Democratic Party, particularly between the supporters and opponents of General Andrew Jackson, America's great military hero of the War of 1812. Jackson was the first populist president with a wide base of mass support; he sought to give rank-and-file members more say in party politics. Jackson's opponents denied him the presidency in 1824, but Jackson won election in 1828 and again in 1832. Jackson's base of support was in the South and the West, and he espoused a program of free trade and other policies that appealed to those regions. During the 1830s groups opposing Jackson united to form a new political force, the Whig Party, thus giving rise to the second American party system.

The Second Party System: Democrats and Whigs Both the Democrats and the Whigs built party organizations throughout the nation, and both sought to enlarge their bases of support by expanding the right to vote. They increased the number of eligible voters—though only white males—through the elimination of property restrictions and other barriers to voting. Support for the new Whig Party was stronger in the Northeast than in the South and West and among merchants than among small farmers. Hence, in some measure, the Whigs were the successors of the Federalists. Yet conflict between the two parties revolved more around personalities than policies. The Whigs were a diverse group, united more by opposition to the Democrats than by agreement on programs. In 1840 the Whigs won their first presidential election by nominating a military hero, General William Henry

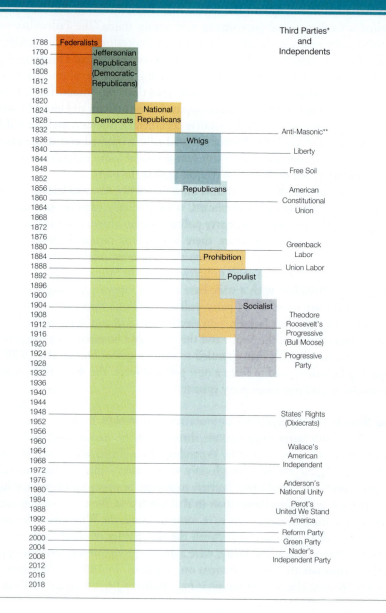

FIGURE 7.1

How the Party System Evolved

During the nineteenth century, the Democrats and the Republicans emerged as the two dominant parties in American politics. As the American party system evolved, many third parties emerged, but few of them remained in existence for very long.

*Or in some cases, fourth parties; most of these parties lasted through only one term.

**The Anti-Masonics had the distinction of being not only the first third party but also the first party to hold a national nominating convention and the first to announce a party platform.

Third Parties* and Independents

1788 — Federalists
1790 — Jeffersonian
1804 — Republicans
1808 — (Democratic-
1812 — Republicans)
1816
1820
1824 — National
1828 — Democrats — Republicans
1832 — Anti-Masonic**
1836 — Whigs
1840 — Liberty
1844
1848 — Free Soil
1852
1856 — Republicans — American
1860 — Constitutional
1864 — Union
1868
1872
1876
1880 — Greenback
1884 — Prohibition — Labor
1888 — Union Labor
1892 — Populist
1896
1900
1904 — Socialist
1908 — Theodore
1912 — Roosevelt's
1916 — Progressive
1920 — (Bull Moose)
1924 — Progressive
1928 — Party
1932
1936
1940
1944
1948 — States' Rights
1952 — (Dixiecrats)
1956
1960
1964 — Wallace's
1968 — American Independent
1972
1976 — Anderson's
1980 — National Unity
1984 — Perot's
1988 — United We Stand
1992 — America
1996 — Reform Party
2000 — Green Party
2004 — Nader's
2008 — Independent Party
2012
2016
2018

Harrison. The Whig campaign carefully avoided issues—since the party could agree on almost none—and emphasized the personal qualities and heroism of the candidate. The Whigs also invested heavily in campaign rallies and entertainment to win over voters. The 1840 campaign came to be called the "hard cider" campaign because of the practice of using food and especially drink to win votes.

During the late 1840s and early 1850s, conflicts over slavery produced sharp divisions within both the Whig and the Democratic parties. By 1856 the Whig Party had all but disintegrated under the strain, and many Whig politicians and voters, along with antislavery Democrats, joined the new Republican Party, which pledged to ban slavery from the western territories. In 1860 the Republicans nominated Abraham Lincoln for the presidency. Lincoln's victory strengthened southern calls for secession from the Union and, soon thereafter, for all-out civil war.

The Civil War and Post–Civil War Party System: Republicans and Democrats
During the course of the war, President Lincoln depended heavily on Republican governors and state legislatures to raise troops, provide funding, and maintain popular support for a long and bloody military conflict. The secession of the South had stripped the Democratic Party of many of its leaders and supporters, but the Democrats remained politically competitive throughout the war and nearly won the 1864 presidential election against Republican Lincoln because of northern war weariness. With the defeat of the Confederacy in 1865, some Republicans sought to use Reconstruction to grant the vote to newly freed slaves in order to create a large pro-Republican voting bloc. This Reconstruction program failed in part because of violent resistance by southern whites. With the end of Reconstruction, the former Confederate states regained full membership in the Union and full control of their internal affairs. Throughout the South, African Americans were deprived of hard-won political rights, including the right to vote, despite post–Civil War constitutional guarantees to the contrary. The post–Civil War South was solidly Democratic in its political affiliation because of its resentment of Lincoln's Republican Party, and with a firm southern base, the national Democratic Party was able to confront the Republicans on a more or less equal basis. From the end of the Civil War to the 1890s, the Republican Party remained the party of the North, with strong business and middle-class support, while the Democrats were the party of the South, with support also from northern working-class and immigrant groups.

The System of 1896: Republicans and Democrats
During the 1890s profound and rapid social and economic changes led to the emergence of a variety of protest parties, including the Populist Party, which appealed mainly to small farmers, western mining interests, and urban workers. In the 1892 presidential election, the Populist Party carried four states and elected governors in eight. In 1896 the Populist Party effectively merged with the Democrats, who nominated William Jennings Bryan, a Democratic senator with pronounced Populist sympathies, for the presidency. The Republicans nominated the conservative senator William McKinley. In the ensuing campaign, northern and midwestern businesses made an all-out effort

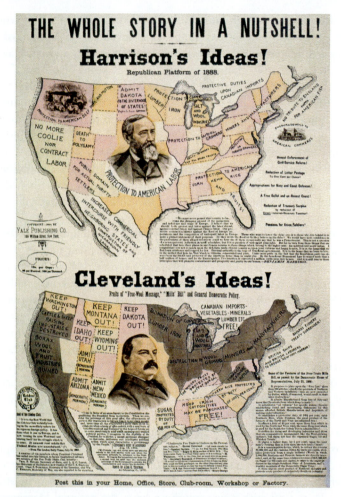

Following the Civil War, the Republican Party remained dominant in the North. This poster supporting Republican Benjamin Harrison in the 1888 election promises protective tariffs and other policies that appealed to the industrial states in the North.

to defeat what they saw as a radical threat from the Populist–Democratic alliance. By the time the dust settled, the Republicans had won a resounding victory and confined the Democrats to their smaller bases of support in the South and far West. For the next 36 years, the Republican Party was the nation's majority party, carrying seven of nine presidential elections and controlling both houses of Congress in 15 of 18 contests. The Republican Party was pro business, advocating low taxes, high tariffs on imports, and a minimum of government regulation.

The New Deal Party System: Reversal of Fortune Soon after the Republican presidential candidate Herbert Hoover won the 1928 presidential election, the nation's economy collapsed. The Great Depression, which produced unprecedented economic hardship, stemmed from many causes; but from the perspective of millions of Americans, the Republican Party did not do enough to promote economic recovery. In 1932, Americans elected Franklin Delano Roosevelt (FDR) and a solidly Democratic Congress. FDR developed a program for economic recovery that he dubbed the "New Deal," under which the size and reach of America's national government increased substantially. The federal government took responsibility for economic management and social welfare to an extent that was unprecedented in American history. FDR designed many of his programs specifically to expand the political base of the Democratic Party. He rebuilt and revitalized the party around a nucleus of unionized workers, upper-middle-class intellectuals and professionals, southern farmers, Jews, Catholics, and African Americans—the so-called New Deal coalition that made the Democrats the nation's majority party for the next 36 years. Groping for a response to the New Deal, Republicans often wound up supporting popular New Deal programs such as Social Security in what was sometimes derided as "me-too" Republicanism. Even the relatively conservative administration of Dwight D. Eisenhower in the 1950s left the principal New Deal programs intact.

The New Deal coalition was severely strained during the 1960s by conflicts over civil rights and the Vietnam War. The struggle over civil rights divided northern Democrats who supported the civil rights cause from white southern Democrats who defended the system of racial segregation. The struggle over the Vietnam War further divided the Democrats, with upper-income liberal Democrats strongly opposing the Johnson administration's decision to greatly expand the numbers of U.S. troops fighting in Southeast Asia. These schisms provided an opportunity for the Republicans' "Grand Old Party," or GOP, which returned to power in 1968 under the leadership of Richard Nixon.

The Contemporary American Party System Although the number of Americans identifying as Democrats remained higher than those identifying as Republicans in the 1960s and '70s, the Republican Party widened its appeal in the second half of the twentieth century (see Figure 7.2). In 1964, for example, the conservative Republican presidential candidate Barry Goldwater argued in favor of substantially reduced levels of taxation and spending, less government regulation of the economy, and the elimination of many federal social programs. Though Goldwater was defeated by Lyndon Johnson, his ideas continued to be major themes for the Republican Party. It took Richard Nixon's "southern strategy" to give the GOP the votes it needed to end Democratic control of national politics. Nixon appealed to disaffected white southerners, and with the help of the independent candidate and former Alabama governor George Wallace, he sparked the shift of voters that gave the Republican Party a strong position in all the states of the former Confederacy. During the 1980s, under the leadership of President Ronald Reagan, Republicans added two important groups to their coalition. The first were religious conservatives, who were offended by Democratic support for abortion and gay rights and who felt the Democrats were not protecting traditional cultural and religious values. The second were working-class whites, who were drawn to Reagan's tough

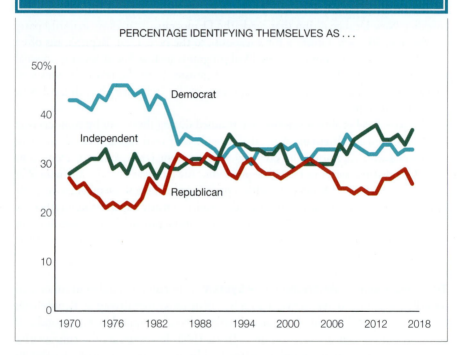

PERCENTAGE IDENTIFYING THEMSELVES AS . . .

approach to foreign policy and his positions against affirmative action. Many Republicans consider Reagan's tenure in office as a "golden era" that saw deregulation of many industries, reduced government intervention in the economy, and strong economic growth.

While Republicans built a political base around economic and social conservatives and white southerners, the Democrats appealed strongly to Americans concerned with inequality, abortion rights, gay rights, women's rights, the environment, and other progressive social causes.

In 2008, Democrats won the presidency and maintained control of Congress for the first time since 1995. Democrat Barack Obama, the nation's first African American president, united racial and ethnic minorities, the youth, and liberals with older white moderates in a powerful national coalition, winning popular majorities in the 2008 and 2012 elections. Democrats lost control of the House in 2010, however, and the Senate in 2014. And in 2016 Republicans retained both chambers and Donald Trump captured the presidency in a tight race, signaling that sharp partisan differences and intense party conflict would continue to characterize American politics.

PARTIES HAVE INTERNAL DISAGREEMENTS

While party polarization, or the depth of divisions between Republicans and Democrats, is at an all-time high, the divisions *within* each political party may be nearly as important. Political parties are diverse and represent many people with competing interests for power and influence. For leaders in Congress and state legislatures, keeping these different groups working toward shared goals can be difficult. And when this effort is not successful, a party's internal divisions can weaken it.

The Republican Party today is divided in four ways. Pro-business conservatives are traditional Republicans, generally a relatively affluent group that supports small government and lower corporate taxes but also favors global free trade. Far-right conservatives tend to be social conservatives who are opposed to immigration and U.S. involvement in the global economy and institutions like the United Nations. Religious conservatives are primarily driven by their socially conservative values, such as opposition to abortion and gay marriage. Finally, libertarians believe in small government and reduced government regulations, and emphasize individual freedom.

The 2016 presidential election also revealed serious divides within the Democratic Party between its liberal wing (whose members supported Bernie Sanders) and traditional Democrats, who supported Hillary Clinton and who tend to be older and hold a mix of moderate and liberal values. Such divisions within the Party may have contributed to the Democrats losing the White House and Congress in 2016.

ELECTORAL REALIGNMENTS DEFINE PARTY SYSTEMS IN AMERICAN HISTORY

Transitions between party systems in American history are sometimes called **electoral realignments**, the points in history when a new party replaces the ruling party, becoming in turn the dominant political force. During these periods, the coalitions that support the parties and the balance of power between the parties are redefined. In historical terms, realignments occur when new issues, combined with economic or political crises, mobilize new voters and persuade large numbers of voters to permanently shift their support from one party to another.

There is general agreement that five realignments have occurred since the Founding. The first took place around 1790–1800, when the Jeffersonian Republicans defeated the Federalists and became dominant. The second realignment occurred in about 1828, when the Jacksonian Democrats took control of the White House and the Congress.

In the third period of realignment, centered on the 1860 election, the newly founded Republican Party, led by Abraham Lincoln, won power and in the process destroyed the Whig Party. Many northern voters who had supported the Whigs or the Democrats on the basis of their economic policies shifted their support to the Republicans as slavery replaced tariffs and economic concerns as the central issue on the nation's political agenda. Many southern Whigs shifted their support to the Democrats.

In the fourth realignment, the Republican candidate, William McKinley, emphasizing business, industry, and urban interests, defeated the Democrat, William Jennings Bryan, in 1896, who spoke for sectional interests, farmers, and miners. Republican dominance lasted until the fifth realignment, during the period 1932–36, when the Democrats, led by Franklin Delano Roosevelt, took control of the White House and Congress. Despite sporadic interruptions, the Democrats maintained control of both through the 1960s. Since that time, American party politics has been characterized primarily by party polarization and by **divided government**, wherein the presidency is controlled by one party while the other party controls one or both houses of Congress.

Major partisan realignments are rare in the United States, occurring on average about once every 50 years. There are frequent false alarms, when pundits describe elections as realignments and they turn out not to be. When realignments do occur, it is often the result of new issues or societal problems, coupled with economic or political crises that weaken the established political elite and allow new groups of politicians to create coalitions capable of capturing the reins of governmental power. In the 2016 presidential election, significant factions of the Republican Party were in disagreement over Donald Trump's candidacy, leading some observers to question whether the election was the beginning of a new party realignment. Many high-profile Republican politicians refused to support Trump, but in his first two years congressional Republicans have generally supported Trump's agenda.

AMERICAN THIRD PARTIES SOMETIMES CHANGE THE MAJOR PARTIES AND ELECTION OUTCOMES

Although the United States has a two party–dominant system, the country has always had more than two parties. Typically, **third parties** in the United States (parties that organize to compete against the two major American political parties) have represented social and economic interests that, for one reason or another, were not given voice by the two major parties.[3] Such parties often provide new ideas and even party realignment. The Populists, a party centered in the rural areas of the West and Midwest, and the Progressives, spokespeople for the urban middle classes in the late nineteenth and early twentieth centuries, are the most important examples in the past 100 years. The most successful recent third-party candidate was H. Ross Perot, who ran in 1992 for president as an independent and in 1996 as the Reform Party's nominee. Perot won the votes of almost one in five Americans in 1992. In the extremely close 2000 presidential election, third-party candidate Ralph Nader won just 3 percent of the popular vote; but that was enough to swing the election to

TABLE 7.1

Parties and Candidates in 2016

CANDIDATE	PARTY	VOTE TOTAL*	PERCENTAGE OF VOTES
Hillary Clinton	Democratic	65,853,652	48%
Donald Trump	Republican	62,985,134	46
Gary Johnson	Libertarian	4,489,235	3
Jill Stein	Green	1,457,226	1
Other candidates		1,186,153	0.9

*Preliminary counts as of December 1, 2016.

SOURCE: U.S. Election Atlas, "2016 Presidential General Election Results," www.uselectionatlas.org/RESULTS/national.php?year=2016&minper=0&f=0&off=0&elect=0 (accessed 7/16/18).

Republican George W. Bush. Table 7.1 lists the top presidential candidates in 2016. Third-party candidates fared better in 2016 than in the last three presidential elections, leading some observers to suggest that third parties were one reason Clinton lost key battleground states and thus the election.

Although the Republican Party was the only American third party ever to make itself permanent (by replacing the Whigs), some third parties have enjoyed influence far beyond their electoral size. This was because large parts of their programs were adopted by one or both of the major parties, who sought to appeal to the voters mobilized by the new party to expand their own electoral strength. The Democratic Party, for example, became a great deal more liberal when it adopted most of the Progressive program early in the twentieth century. Many Socialists felt that FDR's New Deal had adopted most of their party's program, including old-age pensions, unemployment compensation, an agricultural marketing program, and laws guaranteeing workers the right to organize into unions.

Some proponents of election reform argue that two major parties are not sufficient to represent the varied interests of America's 325 million people and that more political parties would improve representation. Many nations have **proportional representation.** Under this kind of system, many competing political parties field multiple candidates in each district and are awarded legislative seats in rough proportion to the percentage of popular votes that each party wins. A party that wins, say, 20 percent of the popular vote receives roughly 20 percent of the seats in the parliament or other representative body. Unlike a plurality system, a party's candidates need not come in first to win seats.

In the United States, state ballot-access laws are often a major impediment for third parties, imposing barriers such as registration fees or petition requirements in which a certain number of voters must sign a petition for a third-party or independent candidate to gain ballot access. States with lower access hurdles, such as Minnesota, have more third-party candidates. Supporters of the current two-party system contend that it creates stability in governing and prevents the need for coalition government, where multiple small parties work together to form a majority to govern.

GROUP AFFILIATIONS ARE BASED ON VOTERS' PSYCHOLOGICAL TIES TO ONE OF THE PARTIES

One reason parties are so important is that many voters develop **party identification**—an individual voter's psychological ties to one party or another. Party identification has been compared to wearing blue- or red-tinted glasses; it colors voters' understanding of politics in general and is the most important cue as to how to vote in elections. That is, most Republicans vote for Republican Party candidates, and most Democrats vote for Democratic Party candidates. Although it is an emotional tie, party identification also has a rational component. Voters generally form attachments to parties that reflect their views and interests. Once those attachments are formed, however, they are likely to persist and even to be handed down to children, unless some very strong factors convince individuals that their party is no longer an appropriate object of their affections. Figure 7.3 indicates the relationship between party identification and a number of social characteristics.

Political Participation Takes Both Traditional and Digital Forms

Describe the major forms of traditional and digital participation in politics

Political participation refers to activities designed to influence government, politics, and policy. These activities include traditional forms of participation, such as voting and volunteering, as well as newer online forms of participation.

VOTING IS THE MOST IMPORTANT FORM OF TRADITIONAL PARTICIPATION

Elections are the hallmark of political participation in a democracy. For most citizens today, voting is the most common form of participation in politics. In addition to voting, citizens can give money to politicians or political organizations, volunteer in campaigns, contact political officials, sign petitions, attend public meetings, join organizations, display campaign signs and pins, write letters to the editor, publish articles, attend rallies, or lobby their representatives in Congress. They can also join interest groups (see Chapter 8). These other forms of political action generally require more time, effort, or money than voting.

Who Identifies with Which Party?

Party identification varies by income, race, and gender. For example, as these statistics from 2016 show, Americans with higher incomes are more supportive of the Republican Party than are Americans with lower incomes. Women are significantly more likely than men to identify with the Democratic Party, whereas more men identify as independents.

NOTE: Percentages do not add to 100 because the category "Other/Don't know" is omitted.

SOURCE: American National Election Study 2016 time series, www.electionstudies.org (accessed 11/4/17).

	Democrat	Independent	Republican
Men	28%	40%	31%
Women	39	34	27
Age 18–29	35	41	24
Age 30–49	34	41	25
Age 50–64	34	34	32
Age 65+	34	37	29
White, non-Hispanic	28	37	35
Black, non-Hispanic	73	23	4
Asian	34	39	27
Hispanic	46	39	16
High school diploma or less	35	39	26
Some college	31	39	30
College graduate	31	34	35
Postgraduate	44	33	24
Income <$20K	40	40	20
Income $20–40K	38	39	23
Income $40–75K	32	37	31
Income $75K+	32	35	34

DIGITAL POLITICAL PARTICIPATION IS SURGING

Digital political participation is rapidly changing the way Americans experience politics. The internet and social media give citizens greater access to political inform-ation about candidates and campaigns, and a greater role in politics, than ever before. Many forms of online participation build on traditional forms of participation, but the internet makes many of these activities easier and gives them greater poten-tial as community-building tools. Online participation in elections includes dis-cussing issues or mobilizing supporters through email and social media, posting comments on blogs and online news stories, contributing money to candidates, visiting candidate and political party websites, creating and viewing online campaign ads, campaigning on social networking sites, and organizing face-to-face neighborhood meetings through social media.

Digital media's effectiveness works through emotional appeals, immediacy, personal networks, and social pressure. Social connections are much more important in political participation than was previously understood. Research reveals that individual factors such as income and education are imperfect predictors of turnout, but one's social network *is* strongly predictive of political participation. When members of a social network indicate they have voted in an election or contributed to a candidate, for example, that can motivate others to do the same. Peer social pressure allows members of a social network to model and mimic actions of other members of their group.[4]

Social media in particular has become a key networking tool for politics and a preferred platform of candidates and political organizations. Sixty-two percent of Americans get news on social media.[5] One in three social media users have encouraged others to vote, and roughly the same percentage have shared their own thoughts or comments on politics or government using social media.[6] Social media is characterized by tiny acts of political participation—sharing, following a candidate or organization, liking a post, commenting—that can scale up to dramatic changes, leading to real world political protests, voter mobilization drives, and the election of candidates and parties to government.[7] Small acts of political participation made possible by social media may give those uninterested in politics or who are rarely engaged a way of getting involved easily, which can than encourage them to do more.[8]

Politicians, too, make much use of social media. In 2016 every serious presidential candidate had a Facebook page and Twitter account, with millions of fans who received frequent updates from the campaigns and candidates. These fans, in turn, signaled to their "friends" which candidates they supported for elected office, making politics part of everyday discussion. Donald Trump's supporters receive emails from his organization, follow him on Twitter and Facebook, and turn out for rallies and campaign events. While Twitter is how Trump talks to the people, Facebook was how his campaign won the election. Based on a survey analysis of 65,000 registered voters and holding all other demographic factors constant, frequent social media users were more likely to vote for Trump than any other candidate in 2016.[9]

Unlike traditional social movements that gain momentum slowly over time, digital politics, and the use of social media especially, can create punctuated explosive bursts of collective action. For example, Bernie Sanders's supporters relied heavily on Reddit to organize rallies and rock concerts during the 2016 presidential primaries on behalf of the Vermont senator.

An important question is whether online political participation influences offline participation, especially voting. A growing body of research finds that online activities such as reading digital news, commenting on blogs, and using email or social media for politics increases the likelihood of voting. Digital politics is associated with contributing to political campaigns, volunteering on behalf of candidates, and even contacting elected officials. Online participation is also linked with discussing politics with friends or family, developing an interest in politics in general, and being politically knowledgeable.

VOTER TURNOUT IN AMERICA IS LOW

Today, voting rights are granted to all American citizens aged 18 and older, although some states revoke this right from those who have committed a felony or are mentally impaired. Despite granting the right to vote, or **suffrage**, to women, racial minorities, and young adults, however, the percentage of eligible individuals who actually vote in America, or **turnout**, is low. Only 6 in 10 eligible Americans vote in presidential elections, and turnout for midterm elections (elections that fall between presidential elections) is typically lower, about one-third of eligible voters; for local elections, turnout is even lower[10] (see Figure 7.4). Turnout in state and local races that do not

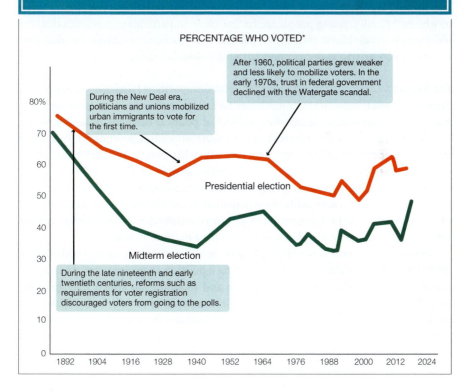

FIGURE 7.4

Voter Turnout in Presidential and Midterm Elections, 1892–2018

Since the 1890s, participation in elections has declined substantially. One pattern is consistent across time: more Americans tend to vote in presidential election years than in years when only congressional and local elections are held. What are some of the reasons that participation rose and fell during the last century?

*Percentage of voting-eligible population

SOURCES: Erik Austin and Jerome Clubb, *Political Facts of the United States since 1789* (New York: Columbia University Press, 1986); United States Election Project, www.electproject.org (accessed 11/9/18).

PERCENTAGE WHO VOTED*

During the New Deal era, politicians and unions mobilized urban immigrants to vote for the first time.

After 1960, political parties grew weaker and less likely to mobilize voters. In the early 1970s, trust in federal government declined with the Watergate scandal.

Presidential election

Midterm election

During the late nineteenth and early twentieth centuries, reforms such as requirements for voter registration discouraged voters from going to the polls.

coincide with national contests is typically much lower. In most European countries and other Western democracies, by contrast, national voter turnout is usually between 70 and 90 percent.[11]

WHY DO PEOPLE VOTE?

Three factors organize our understanding of voting in elections: (1) a person's social and demographic background and attitudes about politics, (2) the political environment in which elections take place and whether an election is contested among at least two political candidates, and (3) the state electoral laws that shape the political process.

Social Background Americans with higher levels of education, more income, and higher-level occupations—collectively, what social scientists call higher **socioeconomic status**—participate much more in politics than do those with less education and less income.[12] Education level is the single most important factor in predicting whether an individual will vote or engage in most other kinds of participation. Unsurprisingly, income is an important factor when it comes to people making campaign contributions. Those with money, time, and capacity to participate effectively in the political system are more likely to do so.[13] Other individual characteristics also affect participation. For example, African Americans, Asian Americans, and Latinos are less likely to participate than are whites, although when differences in education and income are taken into account, African Americans participate at similar levels to whites.[14] Finally, young people are far less likely to participate in politics than are older people. Individuals with strong partisan ties to one of the major political parties are more likely to vote than nonpartisans or independents.

The Political Environment, Mobilization, and Competition Political environments—defined by social networks, communities and neighborhoods, states, and region—matter a great deal in understanding individual political behavior. Whether or not people feel engaged or are recruited to participate in politics depends on their social setting—their friends and family, where they live, what associations they belong to. A critical aspect of political environments is whether people are mobilized—by parties, candidates, campaigns, interest groups, and social movements. A recent comprehensive study of the decline in political participation in the United States found that half of the drop-off could be accounted for by reduced **mobilization** efforts—the process by which large numbers of people are organized for a political activity.[15]

An additional factor is whether elections are competitive—that is, whether there are at least two candidates actively contesting a position in government.[16] Competitive elections, and the campaign spending and mobilization efforts that go along with them, directly affect turnout rates.[17] To be motivated to vote, individuals must be interested in the election and knowledgeable about the candidates. In competitive elections, when candidates and political parties spend more effort and money to compete for an elected office, more information becomes available to voters in the form of media ads, news coverage, door-to-door campaigns, online campaigns, and more. Electoral competition reduces the cost to individuals of becoming informed, leading to higher turnout. Conversely, if elections are uncompetitive, or uncontested, they generate little political information. Limited exposure to competitive elections may be one reason for the lower levels of turnout recorded since the 1960s.

Convenience voting, such as early voting and voting by mail, removes the need to stand in a potentially long line to cast a vote and may result in increased voter turnout.

State Electoral Laws State electoral laws, which vary widely from state to state, create formal barriers to voting that can reduce participation. In most other democratic nations, where voting rates are higher, citizens are automatically registered to vote; but the United States generally requires a two-step process: registering to vote and then voting. (Thirteen states plus Washington, D.C., have adopted automatic voter registration, whereby eligible residents are automatically registered to vote.) Eighteen states and D.C. allow voters to register and cast a ballot on the same day, but most states require registration in advance of Election Day. Registration requirements particularly reduce voting by the young, those with low education, and those with low incomes because registration requires higher political involvement, planning, and effort than does the act of voting itself. Those with relatively little education may become interested in politics once the issues of a particular campaign become salient, but by then it may be too late for them to register, especially if they live in states that require registration up to a month before the election. And because young people tend to change residences more often than older people, registration requirements place a greater burden on them. (Information on registering to vote in your state is provided in the back of the book.)

In addition to registration, other election regulations have an impact on turnout. For example, in most other nations elections are held on weekends, when most people are not working, or their election day is treated as a holiday. The United States holds elections during the work week. Many states maintain residency requirements that result in citizens' losing their registration if they move their residences even short distances. Most states purge their voter-registration rolls of voters who fail to vote for a given period of time. America holds many different elections, often at staggered times throughout the year, such as primary elections and elections for local offices and school budget votes, rather than consolidating elections at a single time. A relatively recent barrier is a requirement that voters provide proof of identity. As of 2018, 34 states require all voters to show some form of ID before voting. Seven of these states require a photo ID, while another 10 request photo ID but may count the vote with nonphoto ID under some circumstances. In the remaining states, nonphoto forms of ID are acceptable.[18] Voter ID laws in the states may disproportionately reduce voter turnout of certain groups: racial minorities, the elderly, and the poor.[19]

Voter Turnout in Comparison

Over the past 20 years, voter turnout in U.S. national elections has hovered around 45 percent of the voting-age population. While the number is significantly higher in presidential elections than in midterm elections (in the 2018 midterm elections, turnout was roughly 49 percent),[a] voting rates in the United States still lag behind those in many other democratic countries.

Why does voter turnout vary so much from country to country?

One explanation relates to the rules governing elections. In many democracies, citizens are automatically registered to vote when they reach a certain age; in contrast, U.S. citizens generally must register themselves, reregister if they move, and, in many states, register a certain number of days before the election. Many countries hold their elections on a Sunday, send their ballots through the mail, or declare their election day a national holiday. Voting is also compulsory in many countries. Australia, for instance, charges a $20 fine (about US$16) unless a citizen can provide a good excuse for why she did not vote.[b]

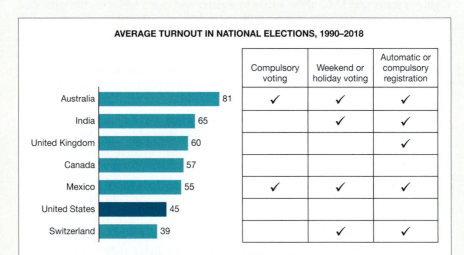

AVERAGE TURNOUT IN NATIONAL ELECTIONS, 1990–2018

		Compulsory voting	Weekend or holiday voting	Automatic or compulsory registration
Australia	81	✓	✓	✓
India	65		✓	✓
United Kingdom	60			✓
Canada	57			
Mexico	55	✓	✓	✓
United States	45			
Switzerland	39		✓	✓

SOURCES: International Institute for Democracy and Electoral Assistance (IDEA) voter turnout database, www.idea.int/vt/viewdata.cfm, and the ACE Electoral Knowledge Network, www.aceproject.org/epic-en/CDMap?question=VR008&f= (accessed 3/27/18).

[a]International Institute for Democracy and Electoral Assistance (IDEA), Voter Turnout Database, www.idea.int/data-tools/data/voter-turnout (accessed 4/12/18).

[b]Nicole Hasham, "Election 2016: Voter Turnout Lowest since Compulsory Voting Began in 1925," *The Sydney Morning Herald*, August 8, 2016, www.smh.com.au/politics/federal/election-2016-voter-turnout-lowest-since-compulsory-voting-began-in-1925-20160808-gqnij2.html (accessed 4/12/18).

Some states have taken steps to make voting easier, such as same-day and automatic registration discussed above. Additionally, some western states use an all-mail voting system, thus eliminating polling places altogether. Many states now offer early voting, which allows registered voters to cast a ballot at their regular polling place up to 40 days before the election.

Voters Decide Based on Party, Issues, and Candidate

> **Examine the factors that influence voters' decisions**

Three key factors influence voters' decisions at the polls: party loyalty, issue and policy concerns, and candidate characteristics. The prominence of these three bases for electoral choice varies from contest to contest and voter to voter.

PARTY LOYALTY IS IMPORTANT

Partisan identification predisposes voters in favor of their party's candidates and opposes those of the other party (see Figure 7.5). At the level of the presidential contest, issues and candidate personalities may become very important, although even here many Americans support presidential candidates primarily because of party loyalty. But partisanship is more likely to be a factor in the less visible races, where issues and the candidates are not as well known. State legislative races, for example, are often decided by voters' party ties. Once formed, voters' partisan loyalties seldom change. Voters tend to keep their party affiliations unless some crisis causes them to reexamine the bases for their loyalty and decide to support a different party, such as happened at the beginning of the New Deal era, between 1932 and 1936, when millions of former Republicans transferred their allegiance to FDR and the Democrats.

After the 1960s, many analysts expressed concern that American parties had become too weak to play their role in converting popular political participation into effective government. These scholars noted such trends as a decline in partisan attachment within the electorate, a growth in the number of voters identifying as independents, and a rise in so-called split-ticket voting. This overall trend, sometimes termed "dealignment," was seen as a product of growing social diversity and educational attainment, which made voters less reliant on parties to guide their political decision-making. The growth of the mass media, particularly television, also seemed to reduce the role of parties in elections as television tends to focus on the personalities of individual candidates rather than the "institution" of the party. Today, party loyalties in America continue to be in a state of flux. On the one hand, the percentage of voters who declare no party loyalty remains at an all-time high.[20] On the other hand, party identification among a large number of the most active voters has grown stronger.[21]

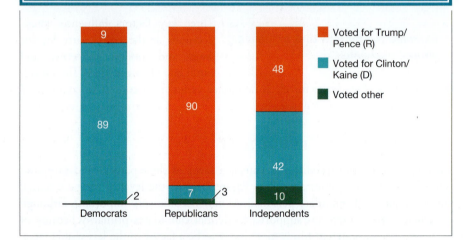

The Effect of Party Identification on the Vote, 2016

In 2016 about 90 percent of Democrats and Republicans supported their party's presidential candidate. Should candidates devote their resources to converting voters who identify with the opposition or to winning more support among independents? What factors might make it difficult for candidates to simultaneously pursue both courses of action?

Legend:
- Voted for Trump/Pence (R)
- Voted for Clinton/Kaine (D)
- Voted other

Democrats: 9, 89, 2
Republicans: 90, 7, 3
Independents: 48, 42, 10

ISSUES CAN SHAPE AN ELECTION

Issues and policy preferences are a second factor influencing voters' choices at the polls. Voters may cast their ballots for the candidate whose position on economic issues they believe to be closest to their own or the candidate who has what they believe to be the best record on foreign policy or immigration. Issues are more important in some races than in others.

In 2016, for example, Donald Trump made curbing immigration and building a wall along the U.S.-Mexico border a key issue of the presidential campaign. Democratic candidate Hillary Clinton, on the other hand, supported comprehensive immigration reform, including an easier path to full and equal citizenship and ending family detention. If candidates actually do "take issue" with one another—that is, articulate and publicize very different positions on important public questions—voters are more likely to be able to identify and act on whatever policy preferences they may have.

Voters' issue choices usually involve a mix of their judgments about the past behavior of competing parties and candidates and their hopes and fears about candidates' future behavior. Political scientists call choices that focus on future behavior *prospective voting*, whereas those based on past performance are called *retrospective voting*. Retrospective economic voting, in which voters evaluate candidates on the strength of the economy, has been found to be more important than prospective voting.

CANDIDATE CHARACTERISTICS ARE MORE IMPORTANT IN THE MEDIA AGE

Candidates' personal attributes always influence voters' decisions. The important candidate characteristics that affect voters' choices include race, ethnicity, religion, gender, geography, and social background. In general, voters may be proud to see someone of their ethnic, religious, or geographic background in a position of leadership, and they may presume that such candidates are likely to have views and perspectives close to their own. This is why, for many years, politicians sought to "balance the ticket," making certain that their party's ticket included members of as many important groups as possible.

Just as candidates' personal characteristics may attract some voters, they may repel others. Many voters are prejudiced against candidates of certain ethnic, racial, or religious groups. And for many years voters were reluctant to support the candidacies of women, although this appears to be slowly changing. Indeed, that the 2008 Democratic candidate was a black man, the 2012 Republican presidential candidate a Mormon, and the 2016 Democratic candidate a woman indicates the increasing diversity of candidates for public office.

Voters also pay attention to candidates' personality characteristics, such as "decisiveness," "honesty," and "vigor." In recent years integrity has become a key election issue. In the 2016 presidential election, many Americans questioned the trustworthiness of both Hillary Clinton and Donald Trump. Nonetheless, Trump supporters saw their candidate as unafraid to speak his mind. Clinton supporters, on the other hand, admired her ambition, toughness, and discipline.

The Electoral Process Has Many Levels and Rules

Explain the major rules, levels, and types of elections in the United States

Three types of elections are held in the United States: primary elections, general elections, and initiative and referendum elections; the last are where proposed laws are placed on the ballot for a popular vote.

Primary elections are elections within a political party to select each party's candidates for the general election. In the case of local and statewide offices, the winners of primary elections face one another as their parties' nominees in the general election. At the presidential level, however, primary elections are indirect because they are used to select state delegates to the national conventions, at which the major party presidential candidates are chosen. The United States is one of the few nations in the world to use primary elections. In most countries, nominations are controlled by party officials. The primary system was introduced at the turn of the twentieth century by Progressive reformers who hoped to weaken the power of party leaders; the introduction of primary elections for the first time enabled voters, rather than party elites, to pick the candidates to compete in the general election.

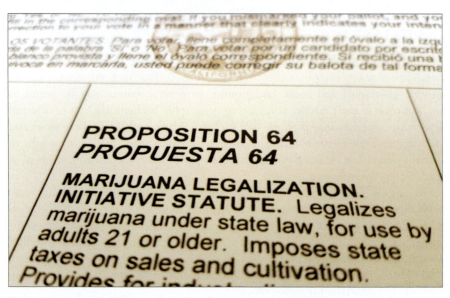

Voters often turn out in higher numbers when there are controversial initiatives on the ballot. In 2016, Californians voted on a total of 18 ballot measures, including whether to legalize recreational marijuana, which ultimately passed.

Under the laws of most states, only registered members of a political party may vote in a primary election to select that party's candidates. This is called a **closed primary**. Other states allow all registered voters to choose on the day of the primary in which party's primary they will participate. This is called an **open primary**. In nominating presidential candidates, though most states hold primary elections, about one-third use **caucuses** instead, which are essentially party business meetings held to select candidates.

The primary is followed by the **general election**, a regularly scheduled election involving most districts in the nation or state, in which voters decide who wins office; in the United States, general elections for national office and most state and local offices are held on the first Tuesday following the first Monday in November in even-numbered years (every four years for presidential elections).

Beyond presidential and congressional elections, 24 states also provide for the initiative process. **Ballot initiatives** allow citizens to circulate petitions to place policy change or proposed laws directly on the ballot for a popular vote. If a ballot measure receives majority support, it becomes law. In recent years voters in several states have voted to raise taxes on the wealthy, prohibit social services for undocumented immigrants, end affirmative action, provide universal health care, create nonpartisan redistricting, protect open space and the environment, and prevent offshore drilling. At the turn of the twentieth century, ballot initiatives were used to grant women suffrage (the right to vote), prevent child labor, limit the workday to eight hours, adopt progressive taxes, and allow voters to elect U.S. senators directly (rather than having them chosen by state legislatures).

All 50 states have the legislative **referendum**, in which the state legislature refers certain laws to the voters for a popular vote. Ballot measure campaigns often involve high spending by proponents and opponents and mass media campaigns that can rival those of congressional and presidential candidates within a state.

The general referendum and initiative are called direct democracy because they allow voters to govern directly without intervention by government officials or the political parties. The validity of ballot measure results, however, is subject to judicial action. If a court finds that an initiative violates the state or national constitution, it can overturn the result. This happened in the case of a 1995 California initiative curtailing social services to undocumented aliens and again in 2012 when the federal courts overturned California's Proposition 8 banning same-sex marriage.[22] Hundreds of initiatives and referenda appear on state election ballots every two years.

Eighteen states also have legal provisions for **recall** elections, which allow voters to remove governors and other state officials from office prior to the expiration of their terms. Generally, a recall effort begins with a petition campaign. In California, for example, if 12 percent of those who voted in the last general election sign petitions demanding a special recall election, one must be held. In 2003 many California voters blamed Governor Gray Davis for the state's $38-billion budget deficit, and he was turned out of office in a recall election. Federal officials, such as the president and members of Congress, are not subject to recall.

THE ELECTORAL COLLEGE STILL ORGANIZES PRESIDENTIAL ELECTIONS

In the early history of popular voting, nations often made use of indirect elections. In these elections, voters would choose the members of an intermediate body. These members would, in turn, select public officials. The assumption underlying such processes was that ordinary citizens were not really qualified to choose their leaders and could not be trusted to do so directly. The last vestige of this procedure in America is the **electoral college**, the group of electors who formally select the president and vice president of the United States.

When Americans go to the polls on Election Day, they are technically not voting directly for presidential candidates, even though they mark ballots as such; they are instead choosing among slates of electors selected by each state's party and pledged, if elected, to support that party's presidential candidate. Electors are allocated to each state based on the size of the state's congressional delegation (senators and House members); larger-population states thus have more votes in the electoral college. North Dakota, for example, has 3 votes in the electoral college (based on its 2 senators plus 1 representative), while California has 55 (2 senators plus 53 representatives).

The presidential candidate who receives a majority of the electoral college's 538 votes (a majority is 270) becomes president—not necessarily the candidate with the most votes from the people. This is in part because the electoral college and most elections in the United States are governed by plurality, or winner-take-all, rules. With only two exceptions, each state awards *all* of its electors to the candidate who receives the most votes in the state.[23] Thus, Trump received all 29 of Florida's electoral votes, though he won only 49 percent of the votes in the state.

Only four times in the nation's history has the winner in the electoral college not won the popular vote. Since electoral votes are won on a state-by-state basis, it is mathematically possible for a candidate who receives a nationwide popular plurality to fail to carry states whose electoral votes would add up to a majority. Thus, in 1876, Rutherford B. Hayes was the winner in the electoral college despite receiving fewer popular votes than his rival, Samuel Tilden. In 1888, Grover Cleveland received more popular votes than Benjamin Harrison but fewer electoral votes, so Harrison was elected. In 2000 a lengthy legal battle over recounting votes in Florida ultimately ended with the Supreme Court's decision in *Bush v. Gore* that handed George W. Bush the presidency.[24] But while Bush had won a majority in the electoral college, Democratic candidate Al Gore had won more votes nationwide. In 2016, Hillary Clinton won almost 3 million more votes, but Donald Trump won in the electoral college. These controversial elections generated new calls for electoral reform.

The 2016 and 2018 Elections

Analyze the strategies, issues, and outcomes of the 2016 and 2018 elections

In 2016, Democrat Hillary Clinton faced Republican Donald Trump in a dramatic and bitterly fought presidential race. Despite media predictions of Democratic success, Trump won a surprise victory with a majority of votes in the electoral college, though Clinton won the popular vote, receiving 2.9 million more votes than Trump. The GOP also retained control of both houses of Congress. In the 2018 midterm elections, Democrats won control of the House of Representatives for the first time since 2010. Republicans, however, were able to expand their majority in the U.S. Senate.

THE 2016 ELECTIONS

After closely contested and often rancorous nomination battles, former first lady, senator, and secretary of state Hillary Clinton and real estate mogul, reality TV star, and first-time candidate Donald Trump faced one another in the general election. Clinton seemed to possess several advantages, especially her experience in public office and the Democrats' seeming advantage in the electoral college. Based on voting patterns in recent elections, states with a total of roughly 217 electoral votes were considered "blue states," either safely Democratic or favorable to the Democrats. States with another 32 electoral votes leaned toward the Democrats, potentially putting the Democratic candidate within 21 of the 270 votes needed to win. The Republicans, by contrast, could generally only count on around 191 electoral votes from reliably "red" states. Democratic candidates, moreover, usually receive support from the most rapidly growing segments of the electorate—namely, minority voters—along with women and young people.

The Trump campaign was confident it could overcome the Democrats' advantages. Trump believed his appeal to blue-collar white voters, especially men, would make him competitive in Democratic strongholds in Midwestern states. He also calculated that he would increase Republican support among white voters sufficiently to offset the Democratic edge among nonwhite voters. Moreover, Trump hoped that his provocative style would continue to encourage extensive free media coverage, offsetting Clinton's fund-raising advantage and ability to spend freely on paid campaign ads.

Gender played a significant, though ultimately not decisive, role in 2016. Not only did this election see the first female presidential candidate representing a major party, but gender issues were also headline news throughout much of the election. Donald Trump made comments about women that many people deemed offensive and similar past comments of his were unearthed. The Trump campaign countered that Clinton's husband had also treated women inappropriately. Nonetheless, by November, exit polls showed a gender gap of 13 percentage points, with 54 percent of women supporting Clinton compared with 41 percent of men.

The media played an outsized role in 2016. In the general election, Trump received more than double Clinton's free media attention.[25] He excelled on the campaign trail, tweeting his daily campaign messages and effectively writing his own headline news. At the same time, some people, including Trump himself, believed that the news media's political bias favored Clinton. Trump began declaring that the mainstream media published and broadcast "fake news" and should be ignored.

Lastly, money mattered—and it didn't. Clinton raised and spent twice as much as the Trump campaign and had superior organization, with more field offices than Trump in almost every state. However, Trump's enormous free media coverage (estimated to be worth as much as $2 billion) more than offset Clinton's financial edge. Almost every morning, a new and ever more outrageous Trump tweet or Facebook post would dominate the news, leaving little space for Clinton to set the media agenda.

UNDERSTANDING THE 2016 RESULTS

In the end, the 2016 presidential election was a historic upset in which the national media and the polling forecasts were mistaken. Many Americans who had been following the opinion polls and media analyses before the election were stunned by Trump's surprise win and by the Republicans' success in retaining control of both houses of Congress. Trump's unexpected success in the northern industrial states of Michigan, Pennsylvania, and Wisconsin—all of which had gone to Obama in 2012—ultimately tipped the balance, leading to his victory in the electoral college (see Figure 7.6). For only the fourth time in U.S. history, the candidate who won a majority in the electoral college did not win the popular vote. Republicans also retained control of both houses of Congress as well as a majority of the state legislatures.

Russian Hackers Meddled in the 2016 Elections Soon after the conclusion of the campaign, Democrats charged that Trump had been helped by Russian hacking of the Democratic National Committee and Clinton emails and "trolls" mounting

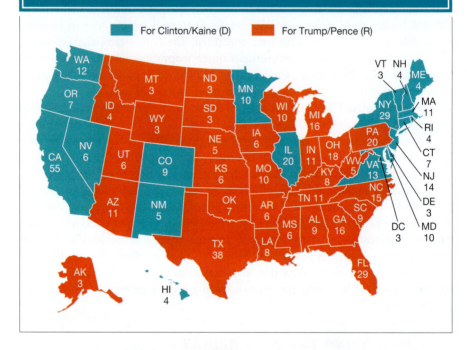

FIGURE 7.6

Distribution of Electoral Votes in the 2016 Election

NOTE: Maine and Nebraska allocate electoral college votes by congressional district. Donald Trump won one of Maine's four electoral votes.

SOURCE: "Presidential Election Results: Donald J. Trump Wins," *New York Times*, www.nytimes.com/elections/results/president (accessed 11/18/16).

For Clinton/Kaine (D)   For Trump/Pence (R)

a social media campaign aimed at defeating Clinton. Multiple reports from the national intelligence agencies confirmed the Russian government did seek to intervene in the 2016 election. For example, in October 2018, Twitter released millions of tweets from some 3,400 accounts linked to a Russian "troll farm" known as the Internet Research Agency run by the Kremlin.[26] At this agency, approximately 1,000 Russian agents, working 24 hours a day spent more than a million dollars a week creating thousands of social media accounts impersonating Americans. These agents also purchased thousands of political ads promoting their posts on Facebook and other platforms. Russian groups also organized campaign rallies in the United States on behalf of Donald Trump and sought to discredit Hillary Clinton, portraying her as a criminal and untrustworthy.

The fact that the Russians meddled in the 2016 election raised questions about whether the Trump campaign had knowledge of Russian efforts or in any way worked with the Russians. To answer these questions, a probe led by Special

Counsel and former FBI director Robert Mueller was launched in May 2017. As a result of the Mueller probe, a half dozen Trump campaign officials have been indicted for various federal crimes and violations of campaign laws. President Trump has vehemently denied allegations of impropriety and denounced the Mueller probe as a "witch hunt" organized by his political foes. At the time of this writing the relationship between the Trump campaign and the Russian government remains unclear.

THE 2018 ELECTION: A BLUE WAVE MEETS A RED WALL

The 2018 election, more than most midterm contests, revolved around the president. Trump's outsized personality and frequent inflammatory rhetoric inspired anger on the part of some voters and fierce loyalty on the part of others. Between 2016 and 2018, across the nation, hundreds of thousands of Democrats who had never previously been much involved in politics, especially women and young people, entered the political arena to oppose Donald Trump. These Democrats engaged in political activity by signing petitions, attending rallies and protests, and contacting public officials. In addition, an unusually large number of women launched campaigns for national and state office. These women saw the GOP, and President Trump in particular, as insufficiently attentive to issues of sexual harassment. This view was underscored by Republican support for Brett Kavanaugh's nomination to the Supreme Court despite allegations of sexual assault made against him.

While Democrats mobilized their blue wave, the Republicans also planned their campaigns. President Trump made the Kavanaugh fight along with such other hot-button issues as Trump's determination to stop a caravan of Central American immigrants from crossing the U.S. border, major themes as he crisscrossed the country speaking to large and usually raucous Republican rallies. In 2016, Trump had promised to build a wall on America's southern border to hold back immigrants. That wall was never built, but now President Trump was attempting to build a red wall around GOP strongholds to hold back the Democrats' blue wave.

After the 2018 elections there will be a record number of female members of Congress, most of them Democrats. Here, Sharice Davids (left) celebrates after ousting Republican Kevin Yoder. With this victory, Davids became Kansas' first openly gay member of Congress and the first Native American woman elected to Congress. (She shares the latter distinction with New Mexico's Deb Haaland, another Native American Democrat elected to Congress in 2018.)

The Outcome On November 6, 2018, the blue wave crashed against Trump's red wall with mixed results. Democrats won control of the U.S. House of Representatives for the first time since 2010, Republicans expanded their majority in the Senate, and Democrats defeated Republican incumbents in seven governor's races.[27] The 2018 elections saw 49 percent voter turnout—the highest level since 1966 and a strong increase over recent midterm elections. Youth voter turnout, which is historically very hard to increase, soared by 10 percentage points to 31 percent of voters aged 18–29. Women were critical to Democratic victories. Women made up more than half the 2018 electorate and supported Democratic candidates by margins of as much as 20 percentage points. The new 116th Congress would include over 100 women in the House and more than 20 in the Senate, an all-time record. In the Senate, two seats previously held by Republicans went to the Democrats, but the GOP won other critical races and extended their control over the chamber.

THE 2018 ELECTION AND AMERICA'S FUTURE

The mixed results of the 2018 election were something of a disappointment to Democrats who thought they would hand President Trump a crushing defeat. As Democrats had hoped, however, voter turnout increased sharply in 2018. Some 114 million Americans or 49 percent of the nation's eligible voters participated. In the last midterm election in 2014, voter turnout was only 36 percent. A majority of the nation's voters, according to exit polls, saw the election as a referendum on President Trump's performance in office. Given Trump's low levels of public approval, this should have helped the Democrats and, indeed, many more voters said they cast their votes to oppose Trump than voted to support him. On a national basis, Democrats received a clear majority of the votes cast in congressional elections, approximately 5 million more than were cast for Republicans.

Despite losses in the Senate, taking control of the House of Representatives was an important achievement. With control of the House, Democrats are in a position to block Trump's legislative efforts and to conduct investigations into the president's conduct as well as the activities of Trump appointees in the executive branch. The president will almost certainly feel compelled to rely ever more heavily on executive orders and other forms of executive action that bypass the Congress. With the Senate firmly in Republican hands, Trump will continue to use his appointment powers to reshape the bureaucracy and the courts. The stage seems set for two more years of the partisan struggle that characterizes American democratic politics.

The 2018 elections also made clear that if the Republican Party is to remain competitive nationally it must develop a message that appeals to voters outside its current base of older white men in America's small towns and rural areas. The Democrats have built a coalition that includes women, minorities, and young people. It is no accident that the first Muslim and Native American women elected to Congress along with the first openly gay governor are all Democrats. The Democratic electorate is growing while the GOP's base represents a shrinking percentage of the national electorate and even of the electorate in rapidly growing red states like Texas where as formidable a Republican politician as Senator Ted Cruz had to scramble to avoid defeat. If the Republican Party cannot find a way to expand its constituency, 2018 may be the last time the red wall can hold back the blue wave.

Money Is Critical to Campaigns

> **Describe how candidates raise the money they need to run**

Modern national political campaigns are fueled by enormous amounts of money. The 2016 election shattered previous records for campaign spending. Combined spending by candidates, parties, and interest groups on the congressional and presidential races was $6.5 billion in 2016 compared with $6.2 billion in 2012 and $5.3 billion in 2008. Of the $6.5 billion, $4.3 billion was spent on congressional races and $2.6 billion on the presidential race.

CAMPAIGN FUNDS COME FROM DIRECT APPEALS, THE RICH, PACS, AND PARTIES

According to the Center for Responsive Politics, the $6.5 billion spent in 2016 included money from leadership PACs, Super PACs, and 501(c)(4) "dark money" groups (who can shield donor identities). The two presidential candidates raised $1.3 billion combined, including about $500 million by Hillary Clinton's campaign and $190 million from outside groups supporting her. Donald Trump raised only about $250 million with another $59 million from outside groups.[28]

Individual Donors Politicians spend a great deal of time asking people for money. Money is solicited via direct mail, through the internet, over the phone, and in numerous face-to-face meetings. Under federal law, individuals may donate as much as $2,700 per candidate per election, $5,000 per PAC per calendar year, $33,400 per national party committee per calendar year, and $10,000 to state and local committees per calendar year. There is no limit on the number of candidates that an individual can give to, however.[29]

Political Action Committees PACs are organizations established by corporations, labor unions, or interest groups to channel the contributions of their members and employees into political campaigns. Under the terms of the 1971 Federal Election Campaign Act, which governs campaign finance in the United States, PACs are permitted to make larger contributions to any given candidate than individuals are allowed to make. Moreover, allied or related PACs often coordinate their campaign contributions, greatly increasing the amount of money a candidate actually receives from the same interest group. More than 4,600 PACs are registered with the Federal Election Commission, which oversees campaign finance practices in the United States. Nearly two-thirds of all PACs represent corporations, trade associations, and other business and professional groups. Alliances of bankers, lawyers, doctors, and merchants all sponsor PACs.

Outside Spending—Super PACs and Dark Money 527 committees (Super PACs) and 501(c)(4)s (dark money) are independent groups that are not covered by the campaign-spending restrictions imposed in 2002 by the Bipartisan Campaign

Reform Act, but now raise much of the money used for political campaigns. These groups, named for the sections of the tax code under which they are organized, can raise and spend unlimited amounts so long as their efforts are not coordinated with those of any candidate's campaign. As a result, each presidential campaign raises millions from sympathetic outside groups. A 527 is a group established specifically for the purpose of political advocacy and is required to report to the IRS. A 501(c)(4) is a nonprofit group that also engages in campaign advocacy but may not spend more than half its revenues for political purposes. Unlike a 527, a 501(c)(4) is not required to disclose where it gets its funds or exactly what it does with them. As a result, its funding has earned the name "dark money" and has raised growing concern that the lack of transparency in campaign funding threatens fair elections. Indeed, it has become a common practice for wealthy and corporate donors, as well as foreigners, to route campaign contributions through 501(c)(4)s to avoid the legal limits on contributions through other channels.

Super PACs came about after the Supreme Court's 2010 decision in *Citizens United v. Federal Election Commission* that the government could not restrict independent expenditures by corporations or unions to political campaigns. Following that decision, *SpeechNow v. FEC* permitted individuals and organizations to form committees that could raise unlimited amounts of money to run advertising for and against candidates so long as their efforts were not coordinated with those of the candidates.[30]

In 2014 the Supreme Court removed additional limits on individuals' campaign contributions in its decision in *McCutcheon et al. v. Federal Election Commission*.[31] Outside spending via 527s and 501(c)(4)s played an unprecedented role in the 2012 and 2016 presidential races as groups ran extensive television ads. Super PACs on both sides relied on very large contributions. In 2016, Super PACs supporting candidates' campaigns spent a total of $594 million. A growing concern is that elections in the United States can be bought with big money from corporations and wealthy donors, who will then hold significant influence when that candidate is elected.

Public Funding The Federal Election Campaign Act also provides for public funding of presidential campaigns. As they seek a major-party presidential nomination, candidates become eligible for public funds by raising at least $5,000 in individual contributions of $250 or less in each of 20 states. Candidates who reach this threshold may apply for federal funds to match, on a dollar-for-dollar basis, all individual contributions of $250 or less that they receive. In 2016 candidates who accepted matching funds could spend no more than $48.7 million, including matching funds, in their presidential primary campaigns. The funds are drawn from the Presidential Election Campaign Fund. Taxpayers can contribute $3 to this fund, at no additional cost to themselves, by checking a box on the first page of their federal income tax returns. Major-party presidential candidates receive a lump sum (about $96 million in 2016, although neither Clinton nor Trump accepted this money) during the summer prior to the general election, and they must meet all their general expenses from this money. Third-party candidates are eligible for public funding only if they received at least 5 percent of the vote in the previous presidential race.

Under current law, no candidate is required to accept public funding for either the nominating races or the general presidential election. Candidates who do not accept public funding are not bound by any expenditure limits. In 2008, John McCain accepted public funding for the general-election campaign, receiving $84 million, but Barack Obama declined, choosing to rely on his own fund-raising prowess. Obama ultimately outspent McCain by a wide margin. The 2008 race was the last time that major-party presidential candidates limited their own fund-raising in favor of public funding. Neither major party candidate accepted public funding in 2012 or 2016.

The Candidates Themselves On the basis of the Supreme Court's 1976 decision in *Buckley v. Valeo*, the right of individuals to spend their *own* money to campaign for office is a constitutionally protected matter of free speech and is not subject to limitation.[32] Thus, extremely wealthy candidates often contribute millions of dollars to their own campaigns. The only exception to the *Buckley* rule concerns presidential candidates who accept federal funding for their general-election campaigns. Such individuals are limited to $50,000 in personal spending.

In 2014, Shaun McCutcheon successfully challenged the federal limit on the amount of money any one individual can donate to political campaigns and candidates. Many people worry that recent Supreme Court decisions overturning campaign spending limits reinforce the influence of the very affluent in American politics at the expense of everyone else.

Political Parties, Elections, and Participation
WHAT DO WE WANT?

While party leaders exercise great control over party platforms, the party message, candidate funding, who holds elected office, and who wins the nomination for president, many aspects of party politics have been turned upside-down with the digital revolution in communication and by "outsider" candidates running for president who have exploited digital platforms to advance their campaigns. Four resources that political parties use to contest and win elections (time, money, expertise, and organization) have all been altered by the internet. New media are decentralizing party power as citizens like Keli Carender (described at the beginning of this chapter) can volunteer, communicate, and give money to the party of their choice or even start their own group without ever being contacted by a party official. Online fund-raising allows millions of donors to give small contributions to parties, and new media allow the party to spread its message far and wide online. This is beneficial for parties because more people are involved, but there are more divergent opinions that must be recognized and appeased. At the same time, huge contributions from a handful of very wealthy individuals have increased. Will the ability of the mass public to make their desires known to party leaders mean that party leaders pay more attention to these preferences? Is the two-party system the optimal system for American politics, or should electoral reforms encourage more parties to form and, hence, provide more choice for voters?

The important role played by private funds in American elections affects the balance of power among contending economic groups. Politicians need large amounts of money to campaign successfully for major offices. This fact inevitably ties their interests to the interests of the groups and forces that can provide this money: the affluent. In a nation as large and diverse as the United States, to be sure, campaign contributors represent many different groups and, often, clashing interests. The fact remains, however, that those with more money will be able to give more and speak with a louder voice. Since 2000 a series of highly competitive presidential elections has spurred political campaigns to pay more attention to drawing greater numbers of voters from a variety of backgrounds into the political process; even so, many Americans still do not participate in politics. The "**Who Participates?**" feature shows who participated in the 2016 election.

Who Participated in the 2016 Presidential Election?

Age group ● 18–24 ● 25–44 ● 45–64 ● 65+

Percentage of each age group who...

Voted

70.4%   82.3%   88.6%   93.9%

Displayed a campaign button, lawn sign, or bumper sticker

14.3%   11.0%   12.2%   13.3%

Gave money to a candidate, party, or other group

6.7%   7.1%   10.8%   20.1%

Talked about voting for or against a candidate or party

46.2%   45.3%   52.6%   54.4%

Went to political meetings, rallies, or speeches

9.4%   8.0%   6.3%   6.3%

SOURCE: American National Election Study, 2016 Time Series, www.electionstudies.org (accessed 12/20/17).

WHAT YOU CAN DO ▶

Register to Vote

 In most states you can register to vote using the National Mail Voter Registration Form found at **www.eac.gov**. The Election Assistance Commission website also includes various tips about registering and voting.

 Find out when you need to register in order to vote in the next election. Visit **www.usa.gov/register-to-vote** for a list of registration deadlines.

 Many states allow online registration. Go to **www.ncsl.org** and search "online voter registration" to find a list of these states with links to their websites.

 If you've moved to attend college or for another reason, you can register with your new address.

★ STUDY GUIDE ★

Practice Quiz

1. A political party is different from an interest group in that a political party *(p. 207)*
   a) seeks to control the government by nominating candidates and electing its members to office.
   b) is constitutionally exempt from taxation.
   c) is entirely nonprofit.
   d) has a much larger membership.
   e) has a much smaller membership.

2. Which party was formed in the 1830s in opposition to Andrew Jackson's presidency? *(p. 211)*
   a) American Independent
   b) Federalist
   c) Jacksonian Republican
   d) Democratic
   e) Whig

3. The so-called New Deal coalition was severely strained *(p. 215)*
   a) during the 1860s by conflicts over slavery and southern secession.
   b) during the 1890s by conflicts over the gold standard.
   c) during the 1930s by conflicts over the Great Depression and America's involvement in World War II.
   d) during the 1960s by conflicts over civil rights and the Vietnam War.
   e) during the 1990s by conflicts over abortion and affirmative action.

4. The periodic episodes in American history in which an "old" dominant political party is replaced by a "new" dominant political party are called *(p. 217)*
   a) constitutional revolutions.
   b) divided governments.
   c) unified governments.
   d) dealignments.
   e) electoral realignments.

5. In a _____ electoral system, political parties are awarded legislative seats in rough approximation to the percentage of popular votes that each party wins. *(p. 219)*
   a) plurality
   b) proportional representation
   c) split-ticket
   d) straight-ticket
   e) open primary

6. Which of the following factors is *not* currently an obstacle to voting in the United States? *(p. 225)*
   a) registration requirements
   b) that elections occur on weekdays
   c) the restriction of voting rights for people who have committed a felony
   d) literacy tests
   e) voter identification laws

7. An open primary is a primary election in which *(p. 230)*
   a) one's vote is made public.
   b) only registered members of the party may vote.
   c) all registered voters are allowed to choose on the day of the primary which party's primary they will participate in.
   d) there are no limits on campaign spending.
   e) only superdelegates are allowed to vote.

8. If a state has 10 members in the U.S. House of Representatives, how many votes in the electoral college does that state have? *(p. 231)*
   a) 2
   b) 10
   c) 12
   d) 20
   e) The number of votes cannot be determined from this information.

9. The main difference between a 527 committee and a 501(c)(4) is that *(p. 237)*
   a) a 527 is not legally required to disclose where it gets its money, while a 501(c)(4) is legally required to do so.
   b) a 501(c)(4) is not legally required to disclose where it gets its money, while a 527 is legally required to do so.
   c) a 527 can only contribute to one campaign, while a 501(c)(4) can contribute to many.
   d) a 501(c)(4) can only contribute to one campaign, while a 527 can contribute to many.
   e) a 527 can legally coordinate its spending with a candidate's campaign, while a 501(c)(4) cannot.

10. Public funding of presidential campaigns was *(p. 238)*
    a) outlawed by the Federal Election Campaign Act.
    b) declared unconstitutional by the Supreme Court in *McCutcheon et al. v. Federal Election Commission*.
    c) accepted by both major-party presidential candidates in 2016.
    d) rejected by all four major-party presidential candidates in 2012 and 2016.
    e) limited to only $25 million in 2008, 2012 and 2016.

11. In *Buckley v. Valeo*, the Supreme Court ruled that *(p. 239)*
    a) PAC donations to campaigns are constitutionally protected.
    b) candidates cannot spend any of their own money to run for office.
    c) the right of individuals to spend their own money to campaign is constitutionally protected.
    d) there is no limit to the number of candidates that an individual can contribute money to.
    e) the Bipartisan Campaign Reform Act is unconstitutional.

Key Terms

ballot initiative *(p. 230)* a proposed law or policy change that is placed on the ballot by citizens or interest groups for a popular vote

caucus (political) *(p. 230)* a normally closed political party business meeting of citizens to select candidates, elect officers, plan strategy, or make decisions regarding legislative matters

closed primary *(p. 230)* a primary election in which voters can participate in the nomination of candidates but only of the party in which they are enrolled for a period of time prior to primary day

divided government *(p. 218)* the condition in American government wherein the presidency is controlled by one party while the opposing party controls one or both houses of Congress

electoral college *(p. 231)* the electors from each state who meet after the popular election to cast ballots for president and vice president

electoral realignment *(p. 217)* the point in history when a new party supplants the ruling party, becoming in turn the dominant political force

501(c)(4)s (dark money) *(p. 237)* politically active nonprofits; under federal law, these nonprofits can spend unlimited amounts on political campaigns and not disclose their donors as long as their activities are not coordinated with the candidate campaigns and political activities are not their primary purpose

527 committees (Super PACs) *(p. 237)* non-profit independent groups that receive and disburse funds to influence the nomination, election, or defeat of candidates; named after Section 527 of the Internal Revenue Code, which defines and provides tax-exempt status for nonprofit advocacy groups

general election *(p. 230)* a regularly sched-uled election involving most districts in the nation or state, in which voters decide who wins office; in the United States, general elections for national office and most state and local offices are held on the first Tuesday following the first Monday in November in even-numbered years (every four years for presidential elections)

incumbent *(p. 208)* a candidate running for re-election to a position that he or she already holds

majority party *(p. 210)* the party that holds the majority of legislative seats in either the House or the Senate

micro-targeting *(p. 210)* when political campaigns tailor messages to individuals in small homogenous groups based on their group interests to support a candidate or policy issue

minority party *(p. 210)* the party that holds the minority of legislative seats in either the House or the Senate

mobilization *(p. 224)* the process by which large numbers of people are organized for a political activity

nomination *(p. 208)* the process by which political parties select their candidates for election to public office

open primary *(p. 230)* a primary election in which the voter can wait until the day of the primary to choose which party to enroll in to select candidates for the general election

party identification *(p. 220)* an individual voter's psychological ties to one party or another

political action committee (PAC) *(p. 208)* a private group that raises and distributes funds for use in election campaigns

political parties *(p. 207)* organized groups that attempt to influence the government by electing their members to important government offices

primary elections *(p. 229)* elections within a political party to select the party's candid-ate for the general election

proportional representation *(p. 219)* a multiple-member district system in which many competing political parties are awarded legislative seats in rough proportion to the percentage of popular votes that each party wins.

recall *(p. 231)* a procedure to allow voters to remove state officials from office before their terms expire by circulating petitions to call a vote

referendum *(p. 231)* the practice of referring a measure proposed or passed by a legislature to the vote of the electorate for approval or rejection

socioeconomic status *(p. 224)* status in society based on level of education, income, and occupational prestige

suffrage *(p. 223)* the right to vote; also called *franchise*

third parties *(p. 218)* parties that organize to compete against the two major American political parties

turnout *(p. 223)* the percentage of eligible individuals who actually vote

two-party system *(p. 210)* a political system in which only two parties have a realistic opportunity to compete effectively for control of the government

For Further Reading

Aldrich, John H., et al. *Change and Continuity in the 2016 Elections,* Washington, DC: CQ Press, 2018.

Brewer, Mark D., and L. Sandy Maisel. *Parties and Elections in America.* 7th ed. Lanham, MD: Rowman & Littlefield, 2015.

Cohen, Marty, David Karol, Hans Noel, and John Zaller. *The Party Decides: Presidential Nominations before and after Reform.* Chicago: University of Chicago Press, 2008.

Ginsberg, Benjamin, and Martin Shefter. *Politics by Other Means: Institutional Conflict and the Declining Significance of Elections in America.* New York: W. W. Norton, 1999.

Maisel, L. Sandy. *Political Parties and Elections: A Very Short Introduction.* New York: Oxford University Press, 2007.

McCarty, Nolan, Keith Poole, and Howard Rosenthal. *Polarized America: The Dance of Ideology and Unequal Riches.* Cambridge, MA: MIT Press, 2006.

Milkis, Sidney. *The President and the Parties: The Transformation of the American Party System since the New Deal.* New York: Oxford University Press, 1993.

Patterson, Thomas E. *The Vanishing Voter: Public Involvement in an Age of Uncertainty.* New York: Vintage Books, 2003.

Wayne, Stephen. *Is This Any Way to Run a Democratic Election?* 6th ed. New York: Routledge, 2018.

West, Darrell. *The Next Wave.* Washington, DC: Brookings Institution Press, 2011.

Interest Groups

WHAT GOVERNMENT DOES AND WHY IT MATTERS After graduating from college with a degree in physics, 25-year-old Ben Brown was working in New York City in the energy business when he read a newspaper article quoting former senator Alan Simpson, Republican of Wyoming. Simpson asserted that young people would lack political power until a young person "could walk into his office and say, 'I'm from the American Association of Young People. We have 30 million members, and we're watching you, Simpson.'"[1] He was referencing the political clout of AARP, formerly known as the American Association of Retired Persons, the largest membership organization in the country. AARP is known for its formidable defense of Social Security, Medicare, and other issues of interest to older Americans.

In contrast, young Americans have not had a broad-based membership group representing their interests, and in 2016 Brown decided to found one. Individuals can join the Association of Young Americans for $20 per year and enjoy discounts on transportation and movies, much as AARP members have long enjoyed travel and insurance services. While those benefits are intended

Interest groups have a strong influence in American political life, but whose interests do these groups serve? Young people have struggled to have a strong voice in politics, but Ben Brown founded the Association for Young Americans to change that.

to entice members, the real purpose of AYA is to lobby on issues such as preserving net neutrality, stopping unpaid internships, and protecting student debt repayment programs. The organization has a weekly newsletter and provides a "Contact Our Reps" tool to "make it easy for anyone to connect with their elected officials" and make their preferences known. "We work to insert the voices of the 80 million Americans ages 18 to 35 into everyday politics," the group's website says.[2]

Tens of thousands of organized groups have formed in the United States, ranging from civic associations to huge nationwide organizations such as the National Rifle Association (NRA), whose chief cause is opposition to restrictions on gun ownership, and Common Cause, a public interest group that advocates for such issues as limits on campaign spending. Despite the array of interest groups in American politics, however, not all interests—like those of young people— are represented equally, and the results of competition among various interests are not always consistent with the common good. Indeed, Alexis de Tocqueville, a famous nineteenth-century French writer, once wrote that America was "a nation of joiners."[3] This defining characteristic of American political life has not changed since Tocqueville made his observation. Americans are much more likely to join political and social organizations than people in other countries, and America has more organized interest groups than other nations.

Many believe this unique trend has a positive impact on democracy. But others worry that the power and money wielded by these groups can dominate Congress, the president, and the political process—such as elections—at the expense of average citizens and the public welfare. Another concern is that despite the array of interest groups in American politics, not all interests—like those of young people—are represented equally, and the results of competition among various interests are not always consistent with the common good. In this chapter we will examine the nature and consequences of interest group politics in the United States.

CHAPTER GOALS

★ Describe the major types of interest groups and whom they represent (pp. 249–54)

★ Describe how groups organize (pp. 254–58)

★ Analyze why the number of interest and advocacy groups has grown in recent decades (pp. 258–59)

★ Explain how interest groups try to influence government (pp. 259–67)

Interest Groups Form to Advocate for Different Interests

Describe the major types of interest groups and whom they represent

The framers of the U.S. Constitution feared the power that could be wielded by organized interests. Yet they believed that interest groups thrived because of liberty—the freedom that all Americans have to organize and express their views. In the eighteenth and nineteenth centuries, organized groups were called "associations." The Federalists and the Antifederalists themselves were organized groups of political elites that had different views about how to create America's new democracy. Both the Federalists and Antifederalists agreed that if the government were given the power to regulate, restrict, or forbid efforts by organized interests to impose themselves in the political process, it would in effect have the power to suppress individual liberty. The solution to this dilemma was presented by James Madison in the *Federalist Papers*, no. 10:

> Take in a greater variety of parties and interests [and] you make it less probable that a majority of the whole will have a common motive to invade the rights of other citizens.... [Hence the advantage] enjoyed by a large over a small republic.[4]

According to the Madisonian theory, a good government encourages multitudes of interests so that no single interest can ever dominate the others. The basic assumption is that many competing interests will regulate one another, producing a kind of balance.[5] Today, this Madisonian principle of regulation is called **pluralism**. According to pluralist theory, all interests are and should be free to compete for political influence. While an interest group may lose on one issue, it may win on the next; and overall the majority of society will be represented in government. Moreover, according to the theory of pluralism, the outcome of this competition is compromise and moderation since no group is likely to be able to achieve any of its goals without accommodating itself to some of the views of its many competitors.[6] Another assumption of pluralism is that all groups have equal access to the political process and that achieving an outcome favorable to a particular group depends only upon that group's strength and resources, not upon biases inherent in the political system. But, as we shall see, group politics has worked and continues to work more to the advantage of some types of interests than others.

Critics of pluralism point out that not all interests are equally represented in the competition for political influence. Some interests speak with loud voices (for example, large corporations), while others can barely make themselves heard (for example, Midwest farmers). Pluralism does not guarantee political equality. Indeed, important research indicates that economic elites have considerably more influence than mass-based forces in the American political process. This version of pluralism is called elite pluralism and more accurately describes American politics.

An **interest group** is a group of individuals who organize to influence the government's programs and policies. This definition includes membership organizations composed of average citizens but also businesses, corporations, labor unions, universities, and other institutions that restrict membership to particular occupational groups or other categories of persons. Individuals form groups in order to increase the chance that their views will be heard and their interests treated favorably by the government.

Interest groups are sometimes referred to as "lobbies" or "special interests." They are also sometimes confused with **political action committees (PACs)**, which are private groups that raise and distribute funds for use in election campaigns. Many interest groups create PACs in their name to be the money-giving arm of the interest group. The purpose of PACs is to influence elections rather than to influence the elected. Another distinction is that interest groups are also different from political parties: interest groups tend to focus on the *policies* of government; parties tend to concern themselves with the *personnel* of government. Parties organize to win elected office and interest groups do not, although interest groups are increasingly engaged in political campaigns and seek to help candidates supportive of their policy goals win elections.

WHAT INTERESTS ARE REPRESENTED?

Economic Groups Interest groups come in as many shapes and sizes as the interests they represent. The most obvious are groups with a direct economic interest in government policy. Businesses and corporations make up over a third of those with lobbying offices in Washington; trade associations comprise another 23 percent and labor unions just 2 percent of groups registered to lobby.[7] Trade associations are generally supported by groups of producers or manufacturers in a particular economic sector, such as the National Association of Manufacturers and the American Farm Bureau Federation. Combined, over 6 in 10 groups lobbying in Washington represent businesses, corporations, or trade associations. Trade associations spent more than $716 million to lobby the federal government and Congress in 2017.[8] Some of the biggest spenders included the U.S. Chamber of Commerce, Blue Cross Blue Shield, the American Medical Association, Boeing, and AT&T.

Labor Groups Labor organizations are also active in lobbying government. The American Federation of Labor and Congress of Industrial Organizations (AFL-CIO), the United Mine Workers, and the Teamsters are all groups that lobby on behalf of organized labor. Other groups have organized to further the interests of public employees, such as the American Federation of State, County and Municipal Employees, which has 1.4 million members. However, as mentioned above, labor unions represent just 2 percent of the total number of registered lobby groups in Washington.[9] Despite being out-lobbied, labor unions continue to exercise influence in Washington. Union members vote, and organized labor can have a significant impact on elections.

Professional Associations Professional lobbies such as the American Bar Association and the American Medical Association have been particularly successful at

Although public school teachers are a minority of the total population, they are an influential interest group in many states because they are highly informed and act as a group in support of issues related to their profession, including teachers' salaries.

furthering their members' interests in Congress and state legislatures. Accountants, real estate agents, dentists, teachers, and even college faculty have professional associations. Financial institutions, represented by organizations such as the American Bankers Association and the National Savings and Loan League, although often less visible than other lobbies, also play an important role in shaping legislative policy. These groups comprise just over 10 percent of all lobby groups in Washington.

Public Interest Groups Recent years have witnessed the growth of a powerful "public interest" lobby, purporting to represent the general good rather than its own economic interests. **Public interest groups** have been most visible in the consumer protection and environmental policy areas, although public interest groups cover a broad range of issues. The Natural Resources Defense Council, the Sierra Club, and Common Cause are all examples of citizen groups. Citizen groups comprise 20 percent of groups with lobbying offices in Washington. Claims to represent only the public interest should be viewed with caution, however: it is not uncommon to find decidedly private interests hiding behind the term *public interest*. For example, the benign-sounding Partnership to Protect Consumer Credit is a coalition of credit card companies fighting for less federal regulation of credit abuses.[10]

Ideological Groups Closely related to and overlapping public interest groups are ideological groups, organized in support of a particular political or philosophical

Civil Society around the World

Political scientists who study democracy around the world emphasize the important role society may play in shaping democracy. Interest groups are part of what is known more broadly as civil society: organizations outside the state that help people define and promote their interests. These groups play an important role in maintaining the overall health of democracy. Countries with an active civil society may be more likely to transition to democracy. South Africa's strong civil society played a major role in protesting for democracy against a repressive Apartheid regime. In contrast, civil society membership was heavily co-opted by authoritarian regimes in Germany and Japan; rebuilding the independence and engagement of these groups remains a major democratic challenge to this day. So, while de Tocqueville may have been writing about the United States as a "nation of joiners," many other democracies have also joined this club.

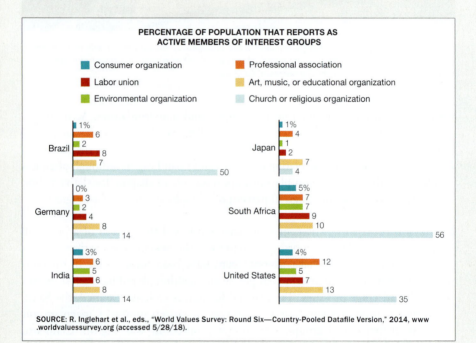

PERCENTAGE OF POPULATION THAT REPORTS AS ACTIVE MEMBERS OF INTEREST GROUPS

Legend:
- Consumer organization
- Labor union
- Environmental organization
- Professional association
- Art, music, or educational organization
- Church or religious organization

Brazil: Consumer organization 1%, Professional association 6, Environmental organization 2, Labor union 8, Art, music, or educational organization 7, Church or religious organization 50

Germany: Consumer organization 0%, Professional association 3, Environmental organization 2, Labor union 4, Art, music, or educational organization 8, Church or religious organization 14

India: Consumer organization 3%, Professional association 6, Environmental organization 5, Labor union 6, Art, music, or educational organization 8, Church or religious organization 14

Japan: Consumer organization 1%, Professional association 4, Environmental organization 1, Labor union 2, Art, music, or educational organization 7, Church or religious organization 4

South Africa: Consumer organization 5%, Professional association 7, Environmental organization 7, Labor union 9, Art, music, or educational organization 10, Church or religious organization 56

United States: Consumer organization 4%, Professional association 12, Environmental organization 5, Labor union 7, Art, music, or educational organization 13, Church or religious organization 35

SOURCE: R. Inglehart et al., eds., "World Values Survey: Round Six—Country-Pooled Datafile Version," 2014, www .worldvaluessurvey.org (accessed 5/28/18).

perspective. The National Right to Life Committee and the Christian Coalition focus on conservative social goals, such as opposing abortion. The National Taxpayers Union and Americans for Tax Reform campaign to reduce the size of the federal government. Liberal-leaning groups, including EMILY's List and MoveOn. org, support causes such as protecting national parks and public lands, climate action, free college, and increasing the minimum wage.

Public-Sector Groups The perceived need for representation on Capitol Hill has generated a public-sector lobby in the past several years, including the National League of Cities, the National Conference on State Legislatures, and the "research" lobby. This latter group includes universities and think tanks that have an interest in obtaining government funds for research and support, such as Harvard University and the American Enterprise Institute. These groups represent about 10 percent of Washington lobby groups.

SOME INTERESTS ARE NOT REPRESENTED

It is difficult to categorize unrepresented interests precisely because they are not organized and are not able to present to governments their identity and their demands. The political scientist David Truman referred to these interests as "potential interest groups."[11] He is undoubtedly correct that at any time, as long as there is freedom, it is possible that any interest shared by a lot of people can develop through "voluntary association" into a genuine interest group that can demand some representation. But the fact remains that many interests—including some very widely shared interests—do not get organized and recognized. Two such groups are the homeless and the poor.[12] Both groups have shared interests in policy outcomes, such as job programs and affordable housing, but lack organization through which to push for government policy to address these concerns.[13]

GROUP MEMBERSHIP HAS AN UPPER-CLASS BIAS

Despite the benefits of interest groups in terms of mobilizing and educating the public and the arguments in favor of pluralism, there are concerns about the influence of special interests in the United States. One long-standing critic is E. E. Schattschneider, who argued in a famous quote that "the flaw in the pluralist heaven is that the heavenly chorus sings with a strong upper-class accent."[14] Critics contend that interest group politics is heavily skewed in favor of corporate, business, and upper-class groups, leaving those with lower socioeconomic status less able to participate in and influence politics.

This is because people with higher incomes, more education, and management or professional occupations are much more likely to become members of groups than those who occupy the lower rungs on the socioeconomic ladder.[15] Well-educated, upper-income business- and professional people are more likely to have the time, money, information, and skills that are needed to play a role in a group or association. Moreover, for business- and professional people, group membership may provide personal contacts and access to information that can help advance their careers. At the same time, of course, corporations and businesses usually have ample resources to form or participate in groups that seek to advance their interests.

The result of this elitist tendency is that interest group politics in the United States has a very pronounced class bias. Certainly, there are many interest groups and political associations that have a working- or lower-class membership (labor organizations or welfare rights organizations, for example), but the great majority of interest group members are drawn from the middle and upper-middle classes. Even when interest groups take opposing positions on issues and policies, the conflicting positions they take on policy issues usually reflect divisions among upper-income strata rather than conflicts between the upper and lower classes. Many policy issues critical to working and middle-class people—quality public education, efficient transportation, affordable housing, safe neighborhoods—are often ignored by government. Thus, when the political system is run by interest groups, democracy will be unequal and many issues important to average Americans will be ignored.

The Organizational Components of Groups Include Money, Offices, and Members

> **Describe how groups organize**

Although interest groups are many and varied, most share certain key organizational components. These include leadership, money, an agency or office, and members.

Leadership and decision-making structure is vital for group organization. For some groups, this structure is very simple. For others, it can be quite elaborate and involve hundreds of local chapters that are melded into a national apparatus. Political entrepreneurs initially organize and lead groups. Later, these leaders are replaced by a paid professional staff. For example, MoveOn.org initially formed in 1998 as an email group by software entrepreneurs Joan Blades and Wes Boyd to oppose the impeachment of President Bill Clinton. Beginning as a ragtag band of liberal activists, MoveOn.org in the past two decades has raised millions of dollars for candidates and progressive policy issues such as legislation protecting consumers, the environment, immigrants, and the working class. Today MoveOn.org has millions of members and 250 local chapters in every state.

Today every group needs a social media strategy. Both progressive and conservative online advocacy groups often have a streamlined staff structure with little bureaucracy. As computer scientist Clay Shirky explains in *Here Comes Everybody*, the internet has given rise to a proliferation of online organizations without formal organizing structures.[16] Examples include Wikipedia, whose content is provided by volunteers from around the world. But the real impact of the digital media revolution is the advent of new forms of organization. Leadership remains a priority for online organizations. Entrepreneurship and leadership are important for all interest groups but especially so for those with little staff and formal organization as the leader holds the organization together.

A second key organizational component of interest groups is a financial structure capable of sustaining an organization and funding the group's activities, although the costs of maintaining an online organization are lower. Most interest groups rely on membership dues and voluntary contributions from sympathizers. Many also sell services or benefits to members, such as insurance and vacation tours. In addition, most groups establish an agency that carries out the group's tasks, which may be a research organization, a public-relations office, or a lobbying office in Washington or a state capital.

Finally, all interest groups must attract and keep members. Somehow, groups must persuade individuals to invest the money, time, energy, or effort required to take part in the group's activities. Members play a larger role in some groups than in others. In **membership associations**, group members play a substantial role, serving on committees and engaging in group projects. In the case of labor unions, members pay dues and may march on picket lines; and in the case of political or ideological groups, members may participate in demonstrations and protests. In another set of groups, **staff organizations**, a professional staff conducts most of the group's activities. Members are called upon only to pay dues and make other contributions. Among well-known public interest groups, some, such as the National Organization for Women (NOW), are membership groups, whereas others, such as Defenders of Wildlife and the Children's Defense Fund, are staff organizations.

The "Free-Rider" Problem Whether they need individuals to volunteer or merely to write checks, interest groups need to recruit and retain members. Yet many groups find this task difficult, even when it comes to recruiting members who agree strongly with the group's goals. Why? As economist Mancur Olson explains, the benefits of a group's success are often broadly available and cannot be denied to nonmembers.[17] Such benefits are called **collective goods**. Following Olson's own example, suppose a number of private property owners live near a mosquito-infested swamp. Each owner wants this swamp cleared. But if only a few of the owners were to clear the swamp, their actions would benefit all the other owners as well, without any effort on the part of those other owners. Each of the inactive owners would be a **free rider** on the efforts of the ones who cleared the swamp; they would enjoy the benefits of collective goods but without having participated in acquiring them. Thus, there is a disincentive for any of the owners to undertake the job alone.

Since the number of concerned owners is small in this particular case, they might eventually be able to organize themselves to share the costs as well as enjoy the benefits of clearing the swamp. But suppose the number of interested people increases. Suppose the common concern is not the neighborhood swamp but polluted air or groundwater involving thousands of residents in a region or millions of residents in a whole nation. National defense is the most obvious collective good whose benefits are shared by all residents, regardless of the taxes they pay or the support they provide. As the size of the group increases, the free-rider problem becomes greater. Individuals do not have much incentive to become active members and supporters of a group if they are already benefiting from the group's activities.

Why Join Groups? To overcome the free-rider problem, interest groups offer numerous incentives to join. Most important, they make "selective benefits" available only to group members. These benefits can be information-related, material, solidary, or purposive—or a combination of benefits. Table 8.1 gives some examples of the range of benefits in each of these categories.

Informational benefits are the most widespread and important category of selective benefits offered to group members. Information is provided through conferences, training programs, online communications, newsletters, and other periodicals sent automatically to those who have paid membership dues.

Material benefits include anything that can be measured monetarily, such as special goods, services, and even money, provided to members of groups to entice others to join. These benefits often include discount purchasing, shared advertising, and, perhaps most valuable of all, health and retirement insurance.

Another option identified in Table 8.1 is that of solidary benefits. These are selective benefits of group membership that include friendship, networking, and consciousness-raising, which provide the satisfaction of working toward a common goal with like-minded individuals. One example of the latter are the claims of many women's organizations that active participation conveys to each female

TABLE 8.1
Selective Benefits of Interest Group Membership

CATEGORY	BENEFITS
Informational benefits	Conferences Professional contacts Training programs Publications Coordination among organizations Research Legal help Professional codes Collective bargaining
Material benefits	Travel packages Insurance Discounts on consumer goods
Solidary benefits	Friendship Networking opportunities
Purposive benefits	Advocacy Representation before government Participation in public affairs

SOURCE: Adapted from Jack Walker, Jr., *Mobilizing Interest Groups in America: Patrons, Professions, and Social Movements* (Ann Arbor: University of Michigan Press, 1991), 86.

member of the organization an enhanced sense of her own value and a stronger ability to advance individual as well as collective rights. Members of associations based on ethnicity, race, or religion also derive solidary benefits from interacting with individuals they perceive as sharing their own backgrounds, values, and perspectives.

A fourth type of benefit involves the appeal of the purpose of an interest group. These **purposive benefits** emphasize the purpose and accomplishments of the group. For example, people join religious, consumer, environmental, or other civic groups to pursue goals important to them.

Many of the most successful interest groups of the past 20 years have been citizen groups or public interest groups, whose members are brought together largely around shared ideological goals, including government reform, election and campaign reform, civil rights, economic equality, "family values," and even opposition to government itself.

AARP and the Benefits of Membership One group that has been extremely successful in recruiting members and mobilizing them for political action is AARP (formerly called the American Association of Retired Persons). AARP was founded in 1958 as a result of the efforts of a retired California high school principal, Ethel Percy Andrus, to find affordable health insurance for herself and the thousands of members of the National Retired Teachers Association.

Today, AARP is a large and powerful organization with 38 million members and an annual income of $900 million. In addition, the organization receives $90 million in federal grants. Its national headquarters in Washington, D.C., staffed by nearly 3,000 full-time employees, is so large that it has its own zip code.

How did this large organization overcome the free-rider problem and recruit 38 million older people as members? First, no other organization has ever provided more successfully the selective benefits necessary to overcome the free-rider problem. It helps that AARP began as an organization to provide affordable health insurance for aging members rather than as an organization to influence public policy. But that fact only strengthens the argument that members need short-term individual benefits if they are to invest effort in a longer-term and less concrete set of benefits. As AARP evolved into a political interest group, its leadership added more selective benefits for members. They provided guidance against consumer fraud, offered low-interest credit cards, evaluated and endorsed products that were deemed of best value to members, and provided auto insurance and a discounted mail-order pharmacy. The membership fee is only $16 (or less with a multi-year membership).

THE INTERNET HAS CHANGED THE WAY INTEREST GROUPS FOSTER PARTICIPATION

Digital communication is changing how interest groups foster participation in politics and sustained collective action by citizens. For example, liberal-leaning MoveOn.org and conservative-leaning Americans for Prosperity have arisen over the past two decades to play an increasingly important role in citizen participation in politics. These grassroots online activist organizations have redefined membership and fund-raising practices via innovative methods for communicating with their members, measuring the opinions of their members, and moving their members into action—in terms of both influencing public opinion and working on behalf of the organization.

Traditional interest groups are expensive to organize (which is one reason group membership has an upper-class bias), and they rely on professional advocates and direct mail. They are also slow to change. By contrast, today's advocacy groups are quick to adapt to an ever-changing world of politics and have lower costs than traditional interest groups because they have fewer staff, who often work from virtual offices. This less expensive staff structure engages in different work routines that prioritize communication with members through email, Twitter, and other digital platforms.

Today's advocacy groups employ grassroots strategies to pressure elected officials, including using social media to organize rallies, and generate news headlines, fund-raising events, letter-writing campaigns, boycotts, and protests. In the aftermath of a mass shooting at a high school in Parkland, Florida, in February 2018, for example, students there used social media, including Twitter, Instagram, Facebook, and Snapchat, to mobilize Americans across the nation in support of stronger gun laws. Under the label "March for Our Lives," these students successfully coordinated a mass rally in Washington, D.C., and subsequent rallies around the country. Largely as a result of their efforts, and those of supporters they attracted, several states enacted tougher gun laws.[18] Online advocacy groups may improve representation for citizens, counteracting the disproportionate influence of business and corporate interests in Washington. Both liberal and conservative groups alike, as well as economic interest groups, have been better able to organize and affect government policy in the past decade with the help of the internet and social media.

The Number of Groups Has Increased in Recent Decades

> **Analyze why the number of interest and advocacy groups has grown in recent decades**

Over the past several decades, there has been an enormous increase both in the number of interest groups seeking to play a role in the American political process and in the extent of their influence over that process. This explosion of interest group activity has two basic origins: first, the expansion of the role of government during this period and, second, the coming-of-age of a new dynamic set of political forces in the United States—forces that have relied heavily on public interest groups to advance their causes.

THE EXPANSION OF GOVERNMENT HAS SPURRED THE GROWTH OF GROUPS

Modern governments' extensive economic and social programs have powerful politicizing effects, often sparking the organization of new groups and interests. In other words, interest groups often form as the result of, or in response to, government actions, rather than groups pressing the government to take on new responsibilities. For example, during the 1970s, expanded federal regulation of the automobile, oil, gas, education, and health care industries impelled each of these interests to increase substantially its efforts to influence the government's behavior. These efforts, in turn, spurred the organization of other groups, either to support or to oppose the activities of the first.[19] Similarly, federal social programs have sparked political organization and action by affected groups. For example, federal programs and court decisions in such areas as abortion, school prayer, and same-sex marriage helped spur the rise of fundamentalist religious groups. Thus, the expansion of government in recent decades has also stimulated increased group activity and organization.

PUBLIC INTEREST GROUPS GREW IN THE 1960S AND '70S

The second factor accounting for the explosion of interest group activity was the emergence of a new set of forces in American politics that can collectively be called the "New Politics" movement.

The **New Politics movement** is made up of upper-middle-class professionals and intellectuals for whom the civil rights and anti–Vietnam War movements of the 1960s were formative experiences. The crusade against racial discrimination and the Vietnam War led these young men and women to see themselves as a political force, focusing their attention on such issues as environmental protection, women's rights, and nuclear disarmament. In recent years, these citizens have focused attention on issues such as environmental protection, economic inequality, and rights for the LGBTQ community.

Members of the New Politics movement founded or bolstered public interest groups such as Common Cause, the Sierra Club, the Environmental Defense Fund, Physicians for Social Responsibility, NOW, and the various organizations formed by consumer activist Ralph Nader. Through these groups, New Politics forces were able to influence the media, Congress, and the courts, and enjoyed a remarkable degree of success, playing a major role in gaining the passage of environmental, consumer, and occupational health and safety legislation. Today, the internet and digital platforms, including social media and blogs, reduce the cost and increase the reach of organizing activities.

Interest Groups Use Different Strategies to Gain Influence

Explain how interest groups try to influence government

As we have seen, interest groups work to improve the likelihood that their interests will be heard and treated favorably by the government.

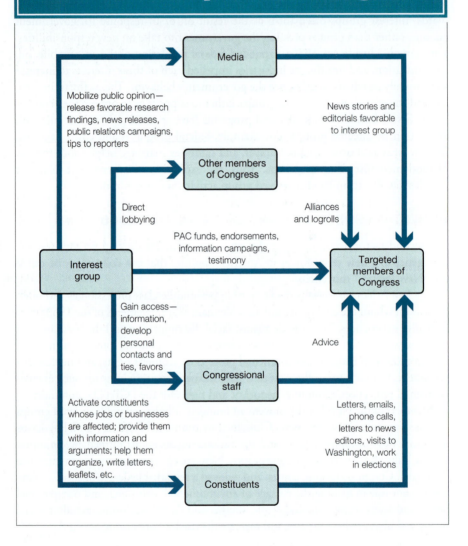

FIGURE 8.1

How Interest Groups Influence Congress

Media

Mobilize public opinion—
release favorable research
findings, news releases,
public relations campaigns,
tips to reporters

News stories and
editorials favorable
to interest group

Other members
of Congress

Direct
lobbying

Alliances
and logrolls

PAC funds, endorsements,
information campaigns,
testimony

Interest
group

Targeted
members of
Congress

Gain access—
information,
develop
personal
contacts and
ties, favors

Advice

Congressional
staff

Activate constituents
whose jobs or businesses
are affected; provide them
with information and
arguments; help them
organize, write letters,
leaflets, etc.

Letters, emails,
phone calls,
letters to news
editors, visits to
Washington, work
in elections

Constituents

The quest for political influence or power takes many forms, but among the most frequently used strategies or "tactics of influence" (see Figure 8.1) are lobbying, gaining access to key decision makers, using the courts, mobilizing public opinion, and using electoral politics. Many groups employ a mix of insider and outsider strategies.

DIRECT LOBBYING COMBINES EDUCATION, PERSUASION, AND PRESSURE

Lobbying is a strategy by which organized interests seek to influence the passage of legislation or other public policy by exerting direct pressure on members of the legislature. Lobbying encompasses a wide range of activities that groups engage in with all sorts of government officials and the public as a whole.

Lobbyists first and foremost provide information to lawmakers about their interests and the legislation at hand.[20] They often testify on behalf of their clients at congressional committee and agency hearings. Lobbyists talk to reporters, place ads in newspapers, and organize letter-writing and email campaigns. They also play an important role in fund-raising, helping to direct clients' contributions to members of Congress and presidential candidates.

Traditionally, the term *lobbyist* referred mainly to individuals who sought to influence the passage of legislation in the Congress. The First Amendment to the Constitution provides for the right to "petition the Government for a redress of grievances." But as early as the 1870s, *lobbying* became the common term for "petitioning." And since petitioning cannot take place on the floor of the House or Senate, petitioners must confront members of Congress in the lobbies of the legislative chamber—hence the term *lobbying*. Although interest groups do not necessarily buy votes, they do buy time, expertise, and influence. Studies have found that those interest groups providing the most money to representatives are more likely to be consulted by that representative and asked to provide information and expertise in discussing a bill pertaining to that group's area of interest. This, in essence, gives interest groups a voice in shaping how legislation is written, and while it cannot ensure votes for laws preferred by the group, it is an effective means for organized interests to influence policy.

The influence of lobbyists, in many instances, is based on personal relationships and the behind-the-scenes services they are able to perform for lawmakers. Many of Washington's top lobbyists have close ties to important members of Congress or are themselves former members of Congress, thus virtually guaranteeing that their clients will have direct access to congressional leaders.

What happens to interests that do not engage in extensive lobbying? They often find themselves "Microsofted"; that is, marginalized in the political process. In 1998 the software giant was facing antitrust action from the Justice Department and had few friends in Congress. One member of the House, Representative Billy Tauzin (R-La.), told Microsoft's chair, Bill Gates, that without an extensive investment in lobbying, the corporation would continue to be "demonized." Gates responded by quadrupling Microsoft's lobbying expenditures and hiring lobbyists with strong ties to Congress. The result was congressional pressure on the Justice Department that led to a settlement of the Microsoft suit on terms favorable to the company.[21]

CULTIVATING ACCESS MEANS GETTING THE ATTENTION OF DECISION MAKERS

In many areas, interest groups, government agencies, and congressional committees routinely work together for mutual benefit. The interest group provides campaign contributions for members of Congress, lobbies for larger budgets for the agency, and provides policy expertise to lawmakers. The agency, in turn, provides government contracts for the interest group and constituency services for friendly members of Congress. The congressional committee or subcommittee, meanwhile, supports the agency's budgetary requests and the programs the interest group favors. This so-called **iron triangle** has one angle in an executive branch program, another angle in a Senate or House legislative committee or subcommittee, and a third angle in some highly stable and well-organized interest group. The angles in the triangular relationship are mutually supporting, especially if a committee member has seniority in Congress. Figure 8.2 illustrates one of the most important iron triangles in recent American political history: that of the defense industry. Iron triangles explain how interest groups have influence over

FIGURE 8.2

The Iron Triangle in the Defense Sector

Defense contractors are powerful actors in shaping defense policy; they act in concert with defense committees and subcommittees in Congress and executive agencies concerned with defense.

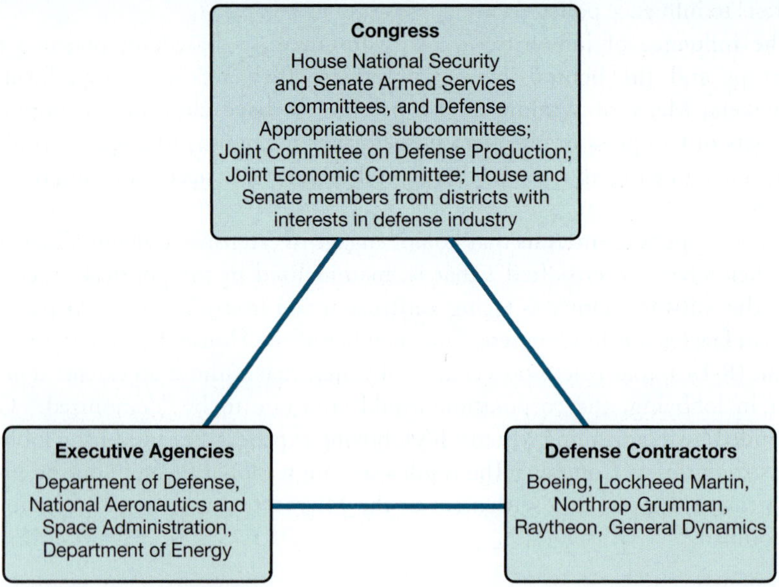

Congress

House National Security and Senate Armed Services committees, and Defense Appropriations subcommittees; Joint Committee on Defense Production; Joint Economic Committee; House and Senate members from districts with interests in defense industry

Executive Agencies

Department of Defense, National Aeronautics and Space Administration, Department of Energy

Defense Contractors

Boeing, Lockheed Martin, Northrop Grumman, Raytheon, General Dynamics both Congress and the government agency directly regulating their interests in many policy areas.

A number of important policy domains, such as environmental and tax policies, are controlled not by highly structured iron triangles but by a jumble of issue networks. These networks consist of like-minded politicians, consultants, public officials, political activists, and interest groups having some concern with the issue in question. Activists and interest groups recognized as being involved in the area (the "stakeholders") are customarily invited to testify before congressional committees or give their views to government agencies considering action in their domain.

Regulating Lobbying Lobbyists' extensive access to members of Congress has led to repeated calls for reform. In 2007 congressional Democrats secured the enactment of a new package of ethics rules designed to bring an end to lobbying abuses. The new rules prohibited lobbyists from paying for most meals, trips, parties, and gifts for members of Congress. Lobbyists were also required to disclose the amounts and sources of small campaign contributions they collected from clients and "bundled" into large contributions. And interest groups were required to disclose the funds they used to rally voters to support or oppose legislative proposals. According to the *Washington Post*, however, within a few weeks lobbyists had learned how to circumvent many of the new rules, and lobbying firms were as busy as ever.[22]

USING THE COURTS (LITIGATION) CAN BE HIGHLY EFFECTIVE

Interest groups sometimes turn to litigation when they lack access or when they feel they have insufficient influence to change a law or policy. Interest groups can use the courts to affect public policy in at least three ways: (1) by bringing suit directly on behalf of the group itself, (2) by financing suits brought by individuals, and (3) by filing a companion brief as an *amicus curiae* (literally "friend of the court") to an existing court case.

Among the best-known illustrations of using the courts as a strategy for political influence is found in the history of the National Association for the Advancement of Colored People (NAACP). The most important of such court cases was *Brown v. Board of Education of Topeka, Kansas* (1954), in which the U.S. Supreme Court held that legal segregation of the schools was unconstitutional.[23] Later, extensive litigation spearheaded the women's rights movement of the 1960s and the rights of gays and lesbians since the 1990s.

The 1973 Supreme Court case of *Roe v. Wade*, which took away a state's power to ban abortions, sparked a controversy that brought conservatives to the fore on a national level.[24] Since 1973, conservative groups have made extensive and successful use of the courts to whittle away at the scope of the privacy doctrine upon which the ruling in *Roe v. Wade* was based. They won rulings, for example, that prohibit the use of federal funds to pay for voluntary abortions. In 1989, right-to-life groups were able to use the case of *Webster v. Reproductive Health Services* to restore the right of states to place restrictions on abortion, thus partly undermining the *Roe v. Wade* decision (see Chapter 4).[25] The *Webster* case brought more than 300 interest groups on both sides of the abortion issue to the Supreme Court's door. The movement to extend rights for gays and lesbians also found success in the courts. In 2015, in the case of *Obergefell v. Hodges*, the Supreme Court declared that the Fourteenth Amendment prohibited states from refusing to issue marriage licenses to same-sex couples.[26]

Litigation involving large businesses is voluminous in such areas as taxation, antitrust, interstate transportation, and product quality and standardization. Often a business is brought to litigation against its will by virtue of initiatives taken against it by other businesses or by government agencies. But many individual businesses bring suit themselves in order to influence government policy.

MOBILIZING PUBLIC OPINION BRINGS WIDER ATTENTION TO AN ISSUE

Going public is a strategy that attempts to mobilize the widest and most favorable climate of opinion and is a favored strategy of public interest groups, membership groups, or online advocacy groups. Many groups consider it imperative to maintain political pressure at all times. Online advocacy groups rely heavily on mobilizing their members via social media, Twitter campaigns, and targeted email messages on short notice. On any given day a new viral media story may become headline news, and in most cases an interest group is behind the story. Such groups span the ideological spectrum, from liberal to conservative, and can wield significant pressure on elected officials to act.

Institutional Advertising One of the best-known ways of going public is the use of institutional advertising—advertising designed to create a positive image of an organization. A casual scanning of important mass-circulation magazines, newspapers, and television provides numerous examples of expensive and well-designed ads by the major oil and gas companies, automobile and steel companies, other large corporations, and trade associations. The ads attempt to show how much these organizations are doing for the country. Their purpose is to create and maintain a strongly positive public image in the hope of drawing on these favorable feelings as needed for specific political campaigns later on.

Protests and Demonstrations Many groups resort to going public because they lack the resources, the contacts, or the experience to use other political strategies. The sponsorship of boycotts, sit-ins, mass rallies, and marches by Martin Luther King, Jr.'s Southern Christian Leadership Conference and related organizations in the 1950s and '60s is one of the most significant and successful cases of going public to create a more favorable climate of opinion by calling attention to abuses. The success of these events inspired similar efforts by women's groups.

The 2010 Republican takeover of the House of Representatives began with the spontaneous self-organization of the Tea Party movement in 2009 as an angry response to the Obama administration's health care initiatives. In 2011

Seeking to reform the criminal justice system and call attention to continued racism in the United States, the Black Lives Matter movement formed in 2013 and earned national attention following a series of high-profile shootings of African Americans by white police officers.

the Occupy Wall Street movement sparked demonstrations across America and around the world by those who were outraged by economic inequality. In 2014 the Black Lives Matter movement gained momentum after the shooting of a black teenager by a white police officer in Ferguson, Missouri. Shootings of black people by police across the country have led to major demonstrations under the banner of the movement.

Grassroots Mobilization Another form of going public is **grassroots mobilization**. In such a campaign, a lobby group mobilizes its members throughout the country to contact government officials in support of the group's position.

Among the most effective users of the grassroots lobby effort in contemporary American politics is the religious right. Networks of evangelical churches have the capacity to generate hundreds of thousands of letters and phone calls to Congress and the White House. Similarly, the NRA maintains a powerful grassroots lobbying effort, spending more on mobilization of its members than on professional lobbyists. The NRA's 3.5 million dues-paying members can be mobilized to flood congressional offices with letters and phone calls, and few members of Congress are eager to pick a fight with the group.[27] As discussed earlier, the interests of the NRA were seriously challenged in 2018 when high school students and teachers gained national attention and garnered massive support by launching the March for Our Lives movement to demand stricter regulations on gun ownership after a string of school shootings.

GROUPS OFTEN USE ELECTORAL POLITICS

In addition to the techniques already discussed, interest groups seek to use the electoral process to elect sympathetic legislators in the first place and to ensure that those who are elected will owe them a debt of gratitude for their support. While groups invest far more resources in lobbying than in electoral politics, financial support and campaign activism can be important tools for organized interests.

Political Action Committees and Super PACs By far the most common electoral strategy employed by interest groups is that of giving financial support to political parties or to candidates running for office. But such support can easily cross the threshold into outright bribery. Therefore, Congress has occasionally attempted to regulate this strategy, but with limited success. The Federal Election Campaign Act of 1971 (amended in 1974) limits campaign contributions and requires that each candidate or campaign committee itemize the full name and address, occupation, and principal business of each person who contributes more than $100. These provisions create an open record of which organizations and individuals fund the campaigns of candidates for public office.

Reaction to campaign spending abuses in the 1972 Watergate scandal produced further legislation on campaign finance in 1974 and 1976, but the effect has been to restrict individual rather than interest group campaign activity. In the 2017–18 election cycle, individuals could contribute no more than $2,700 to any candidate for federal office in any primary or general election. A PAC, however, can contribute $5,000, provided it contributes to at least five different federal candidates each year. Beyond this, the laws permit corporations, unions, and other interest groups to form PACs and to pay the costs of soliciting funds from private citizens for the PACs.

The flurry of reform legislation in the 1970s attempted to reduce the influence that interest groups had over elections, but the effect has been the exact opposite. Electoral spending by interest groups has been increasing dramatically. The number of PACs has also increased significantly—from 480 in 1972 to over 7,000 in 2016. Opportunities for legally influencing campaigns are now widespread.

Given the enormous costs of television commercials, polls, computers, and other elements of the new political technology, most politicians are eager to receive PAC contributions and are at least willing to give a friendly hearing to the needs and interests of contributors. Most politicians do not simply sell their votes to the interests that fund their campaigns. But there is considerable evidence to support the contention that interest groups' campaign contributions do influence the overall pattern of political behavior in Congress and in the state legislatures.

Concern about PACs grew through the 1980s and '90s, creating a constant drumbeat for reform of federal election laws. This resulted in the enactment of the "McCain-Feingold bill" (the Bipartisan Campaign Reform Act of 2002). When it was originally proposed, the bill was aimed at reducing or eliminating PACs. But in a stunning about-face, when the act was adopted, it did not restrict PACs in any significant way.

In addition, several court rulings, including the Supreme Court's *Citizens United* case in 2010, struck down limits on corporate political spending which gave rise to so-called **Super PACs**.[28] Super PACs cannot donate to candidates or parties directly, but they can spend unlimited sums of money on campaigns to influence an election in favor of candidates or parties, as long as their activity (for example, campaign ads or mobilization efforts) is not coordinated with the candidates or parties. Because there are no limits on the amount of money Super PACs may raise from corporations, unions, interest groups, and individuals to then spend to influence elections, they have become more important than PACs and have had the effect of strengthening interest groups. These organizations' expenditures are viewed as "issue advocacy" and are protected by the First Amendment. *Citizens United* dramatically increased the flow of money from Super PACs by removing restrictions on corporate and union political spending, freeing the Super PAC to back whatever politicians it chooses.[29]

In the 2016 presidential election, independent expenditures totaled about $1.3 billion, of which $594 million came from Super PACs. Candidates Hillary Clinton and Donald Trump raised $1.5 billion total, and the Super PACs supporting them raised $618 million, according to the Center for Responsive Government.[30] In 2016, Super PACs spent more than $1.1 billion on House and Senate races.[31] In the 2018 election there were 2,224 Super PACs, which together spent $815 million.[32] Super PACs now account for a major amount of the money spent in elections. The unlimited money raised and spent by independent political committees makes the formal regulations on PACs and individual contributions almost irrelevant.

The Initiative Another political tactic sometimes used by interest groups is sponsorship of ballot initiatives at the state level. The initiative, a device adopted by a number of states around 1900, allows proposed laws to be placed on the general-election ballot and submitted directly to the state's voters, bypassing the state legislature and governor. The initiative was originally promoted by late nineteenth-century Populists and Progressives as a mechanism that would allow the people to govern directly—an antidote to interest group influence in the legislative process.

Some studies have suggested that, ironically, many initiative campaigns today are actually sponsored by interest groups seeking to circumvent legislative opposition to their goals. In recent years, for example, initiative campaigns have been sponsored by the insurance industry, trial lawyer associations, and tobacco companies.[33] Liberal activists have developed their own issue campaigns to promote issues such as increasing the minimum wage, promoting clean energy, strengthening environmental protection laws, and decriminalizing of marijuana.

Groups and Interests
WHAT DO WE WANT?

We would like to think that government policies are products of legislators representing the public interest. The truth of the matter is that few programs and policies ever reach the public agenda without the vigorous efforts of important national interest groups. In the realm of economic policy, social policy, and international trade policy, the activity of interest groups is of critical importance.

James Madison wrote that "liberty is to faction as air is to fire."[34] By this he meant that the organization and proliferation of interests are inevitable in a free society. As long as competition among different interests was free, open, and vigorous—that is, as long as pluralism thrived—there would be some balance of power among them, and no one interest would be able to dominate the political or governmental process.

Indeed, there is considerable competition among organized groups in the United States. Prochoice and antiabortion forces, for example, continue to be locked in a bitter struggle, as are the NRA and gun control groups. Nevertheless, interest group politics is not as balanced as Madison's theory and pluralism might suggest. Although the weak and poor do occasionally become organized to assert their interests, interest group politics is generally a form of political competition best suited to the wealthy and powerful.

Moreover, although groups sometimes organize to promote broad public concerns, they more often represent relatively narrow, selfish interests. Small groups seeking narrow interests can be organized much more easily than large and diffuse collectives. The members of relatively small groups—say, bankers or hunting enthusiasts—are usually able to recognize their shared interests and the need to pursue them in the political arena. Members of large and diffuse groups—say, consumers or the unemployed—often find it difficult to recognize their shared interests or the need to engage in collective action to achieve them.[35] Whether Ben Brown's new Association of Young Americans (discussed at the start of the chapter) can grow and achieve legislative success remains to be seen, as younger Americans' activism may be undercut by the diverse array of interests they have and by the many immediate concerns that dominate their time (school, work, and family, among others).

Organized interest groups sometimes seem to have a greater impact than voters on the government's policies and programs, especially through lobbying and financial contributions to political candidates. (The "**Who Participates?**" feature on the facing page shows how much major groups spend on lobbying activities.) Yet, before we decide that we should do away with interest groups, we should think carefully: If there were no organized interests, would the government pay more attention to ordinary voters? Would young people be better or worse off if there were no interest groups in the United States? Or would the government simply pay less attention to everyone? In his work *Democracy in America*, Alexis de Tocqueville argued that the proliferation of groups promoted democracy by encouraging governmental responsiveness. Does group politics foster democracy or impede democracy? It does both.

How Much Do Major Groups Spend?

Lobbying Expenditures, 2016 (top spenders)

= $1,000,000

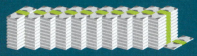

$103,950,000
U.S. Chamber of Commerce

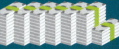

$64,821,111
National Association of Realtors

$25,006,109
Blue Cross/Blue Shield

$22,006,109
American Hospital Association

$19,730,000
Pharmaceutical Research & Manufacturers of America

$19,410,000
American Medical Association

$17,020,000
Boeing Co.

$16,438,000
National Association of Broadcasters

$16,370,000
AT&T Inc.

$15,700,000
Business Roundtable

$15,430,000
Alphabet Inc.

$14,330,000
Comcast Corp.

$13,900,000
Southern Co.

$13,635,982
Dow Chemical

$13,615,811
Lockheed Martin

$13,420,000
The Internet & Television Association (NCTA)

$12,541,000
FedEx Corp.

$12,050,000
Northrop Grumman

$11,840,000
ExxonMobil

$11,354,000
Amazon.com

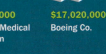

SOURCE: Center for Responsive Politics, www.opensecrets.org/lobby (accessed 11/21/17).

WHAT YOU CAN DO

★ WHAT YOU CAN DO ★

Get Involved with Interest Groups and Lobbying

✓ Find an interest group that appeals to you at **votesmart.org/interest-groups**, then follow that group on Facebook or Twitter.

✓ Find out which groups give the most money to your representatives in Congress by clicking "Congress" at **www.opensecrets.org/politicians**. You can look up your representatives by zip code.

✓ Contact your Center for Campus Life to find out if groups you're interested in have chapters on your campus. Many groups will gladly help students start campus chapters.

★ STUDY GUIDE ★

Practice Quiz

1. The theory that competition among organized interests will produce balance, with all the interests regulating one another, is called *(p. 249)*
   a) pluralism.
   b) elite power politics.
   c) democracy.
   d) socialism.
   e) libertarianism.

2. The Natural Resources Defense Council, the Sierra Club, the National Civic League, and the Common Cause are all examples of *(p. 251)*
   a) membership associations.
   b) citizen groups.
   c) professional associations.
   d) ideological groups.
   e) public-sector groups.

3. Benefits sought by groups that are broadly available and cannot be denied to nonmembers are called *(p. 255)*
   a) purposive benefits.
   b) informational benefits.
   c) solidary benefits.
   d) material benefits.
   e) collective goods.

4. Discount purchasing and health insurance are examples of *(p. 256)*
   a) purposive benefits.
   b) informational benefits.
   c) solidary benefits.
   d) material benefits.
   e) member dues.

5. Friendship and networking are examples of *(p. 256)*
   a) purposive benefits.
   b) informational benefits.
   c) solidary benefits.
   d) material benefits.
   e) member dues.

6. Which of the following is an important reason for the enormous increase in the number of groups seeking to influence the American political system? *(p. 258)*
   a) the decrease in the size and activity of government during the last few decades
   b) the increase in the size and activity of government during the last few decades
   c) the increase in the amount of soft money in election campaigns in recent decades
   d) the increase in legal protection provided to interest groups as a result of the Supreme Court's evolving interpretation of the First Amendment
   e) the increase in the number of people identifying themselves as an independent in recent decades

7. The term "Microsofted" refers to *(p. 261)*
   a) an individual having their identity stolen as a result of a data breach at a major technology company.
   b) a company becoming marginalized in the political process as a result of insufficient efforts to lobby policy makers.
   c) a member of Congress accepting monetary bribes in exchange for protecting a company's monopoly status.
   d) interest groups filing lawsuits against privately owned companies in order to promote social change.
   e) wealthy business people, such as Bill Gates, using their wealth to finance the creation and lobbying efforts of public interest groups.

8. A stable, cooperative relationship between a congressional committee, on administrative agency, and one or more supportive interest groups is called *(p. 262)*
   a) an issue network.
   b) a public interest group.
   c) a political action committee.
   d) pluralism.
   e) an iron triangle.

9. Which of the following best describes the federal government's rules regarding lobbying? *(pp. 261–3)*
   a) Federal rules allow lobbying but only on issues related to taxation.
   b) Federal rules allow lobbying but only if the lobbyists receive no monetary compensation for their lobbying.
   c) Federal rules strictly prohibit any form of lobbying.
   d) Federal rules require all lobbyists to disclose the amounts and sources of small campaign contributions they collect from clients and "bundle" into large contributions.
   e) There are no rules regulating lobbying because the federal government has never passed any legislation on the legality of the activity.

10. Which of the following is a way that interest groups use the courts to influence public policy? *(p. 263)*
    a) supplying judges with solidary benefits
    b) joining an issue network
    c) creating an iron triangle
    d) forming a political action committee
    e) filing amicus briefs

11. Which of the following are examples of the "going public" strategy? *(pp. 264–5)*
    a) free riding, pluralism, and issue networking
    b) donating money to political parties, endorsing candidates, and sponsoring ballot initiatives
    c) institutional advertising, grassroots advertising, and protests and demonstrations

d) providing informational benefits, providing solidary benefits, and providing material benefits

e) filing an amicus brief, bringing a lawsuit, and financing those who are filing a lawsuit

12. One of the major differences between PACs and Super PACs is that *(p. 266)*

a) a PAC has a maximum contribution limit of $500 per candidate in each election cycle while a Super PAC has a maximum contribution limit of $1,000.

b) a PAC has a maximum contribution limit of $1,000 per candidate in each election cycle while a Super PAC has a maximum contribution limit of $5,000.

c) a PAC has a maximum contribution limit of $5,000 per candidate in each election cycle while a Super PAC has a maximum contribution limit of $10,000.

d) a PAC has a maximum contribution limit of $5,000 per candidate in each election cycle while a Super PAC cannot donate to candidates directly.

e) a Super PAC has a maximum contribution limit of $5,000 per candidate in each election cycle while a PAC cannot donate to candidates directly.

Key Terms

collective goods *(p. 255)* benefits, sought by groups, that are broadly available and cannot be denied to nonmembers

free riders *(p. 255)* those who enjoy the benefits of collective goods but did not participate in acquiring them

grassroots mobilization *(p. 265)* a lobbying campaign in which a group mobilizes its membership to contact government officials in support of the group's position

informational benefits *(p. 256)* special newsletters, periodicals, training programs, conferences, and other information provided to members of groups to entice others to join

institutional advertising *(p. 264)* advertising designed to create a positive image of an organization

interest group *(p. 249)* individuals who organize to influence the government's programs and policies

iron triangle *(p. 262)* the stable, cooperative relationships that often develop among a congressional committee, an administrative agency, and one or more supportive interest groups; not all of these relationships

are triangular, but the iron triangle is the most typical

lobbying *(p. 261)* a strategy by which organized interests seek to influence the passage of legislation or other public policy by exerting direct pressure on members of the legislature

material benefits *(p. 256)* special goods, services, or money provided to members of groups to entice others to join

membership association *(p. 255)* an organized group in which members actually play a substantial role, sitting on committees and engaging in group projects

New Politics movement *(p. 259)* a political movement that began in the 1960s and '70s, made up of professionals and intellectuals for whom the civil rights and antiwar movements were formative experiences; the New Politics movement strengthened public interest groups

pluralism *(p. 249)* the theory that all interests are and should be free to compete for influence in the government; the outcome of this competition is compromise and moderation

political action committee (PAC) *(p. 250)* a private group that raises and distributes funds for use in election campaigns

public interest groups *(p. 251)* groups that claim they serve the general good rather than only their own particular interest

purposive benefits *(p. 257)* selective benefits of group membership that emphasize the purpose and accomplishments of the group

solidary benefits *(p. 256)* selective benefits of group membership that

emphasize friendship, networking, and consciousness-raising

staff organization *(p. 255)* type of membership group in which a professional staff conducts most of the group's activities

Super PACs *(p. 266)* an independent political action committee that may raise unlimited sums of money from corporations, unions, and individuals but is not permitted to contribute to or coordinate directly with parties or candidates

For Further Reading

Ainsworth, Scott. *Analyzing Interest Groups*. New York: W. W. Norton, 2002.

Baumgartner, Frank, Jeffrey M. Berry, Beth L. Leech, David C. Kimball, and Marie Hojnacki. *Lobbying and Policy Change: Who Wins, Who Loses, and Why*. Chicago: University of Chicago Press, 2009.

Berry, Jeffrey M., and Clyde Wilcox. *Interest Group Society*. 5th ed. New York: Routledge, 2008.

Cigler, Allan J., and Burdett A. Loomis, eds. *Interest Group Politics*. 9th ed. Washington, DC: CQ Press, 2015.

Drutman, Lee. *The Business of America Is Lobbying: How Corporations Became Politicized and Politics Became More Corporate*. New York: Oxford University Press, 2015.

Goldstein, Kenneth. *Interest Groups, Lobbying, and Participation in America*. New York: Cambridge University Press, 2008.

Herrnson, Paul, and Christopher Deering. *Interest Groups Unleashed*. Washington, DC: CQ Press, 2012.

Karpf, David. *The MoveOn Effect: The Unexpected Transformation of American Political Advocacy*. New York: Oxford University Press, 2012.

Lowi, Theodore J. *The End of Liberalism*. New York: W. W. Norton, 1979.

Olson, Mancur, Jr. *The Logic of Collective Action: Public Goods and the Theory of Groups*. Cambridge, MA: Harvard University Press, 1971.

Strolovitch, Dara. *Affirmative Advocacy: Race, Class, and Gender in Interest Group Politics*. Chicago: University of Chicago Press, 2007.

★ *chapter* ★

09

Congress

WHAT GOVERNMENT DOES AND WHY IT MATTERS As the nation's chief legislative body, Congress affects Americans every day with its decisions. Guy Berkebile, founder of the Guy Chemical Company of Somerset, Pennsylvania, was thrilled with the Tax Cut and Jobs Act passed by Congress in late 2017. The bill lowers taxes for both large corporations and small businesses like Guy Chemical, which manufactures silicone and epoxy adhesives. Berkebile noted that high business taxes had presented a challenge for him as a small business owner. "I did not draw a salary from my company for five years when I started it because the survival of my business in paying my employees was always more important than how much I was making at the time," noted Berkebile, who mortgaged his house seven times to help finance the business. He will face a lower tax rate under the new law.[1]

Congressional *inaction* affects Americans as well. Hazel Hoffman is a 5-year-old Illinois girl who suffers from a severe form of epilepsy, which frequently sends her to the hospital with powerful seizures and which requires expensive medications. Adding Hazel to her mother's health insurance at work

Guy Berkebile
Founder / CEO – Guy Chemical

Congress's actions—or lack of action—deeply affect the lives of everyday Americans. Taxes and children's health insurance are two issues that Congress has tackled recently.

would cost $6,000 per year and would only cover half her health care costs. Instead, Hazel is enrolled in the Children's Health Insurance Program (CHIP), created in 1997 to cover children in families with incomes too high for Medicaid but who can't afford private coverage. It has widely been viewed as a success, insuring nearly 9 million children for $13.6 billion in 2016[2] (in contrast, Medicare for older people and the permanently disabled insures 57 million people for $588 billion—six times the people for 43 times the cost).[3] CHIP was due for renewal in September 2017, but Congress declined to take action for months, unable to agree on a spending bill and contemplating a federal government shutdown. With CHIP money running out, officials in a number of states were forced to draft letters to families terminating their coverage. Finally, in January 2018, Congress broke its logjam and reauthorized CHIP for six years, but not before sending families into a panic about what they would do for health insurance if CHIP collapsed.

Congress has vast authority over many aspects of American life. Laws related to federal spending, taxing, regulation, and federal judicial appointments all pass through Congress. While the debates over these laws may seem hard to follow because they are often complex and technical or because heated, partisan struggles distract from the substance of the issue, it is important for the American people to learn about what Congress is doing. Actions taken—or not taken—in Congress affect the everyday experiences we take for granted. With its power to spend and tax, Congress also affects the choices that people face and the opportunities they can expect in life. Making laws is a complex and often messy process. Even so, it is vital for citizens to monitor what Congress does. With so much information about Congress available on the internet, it is not hard to get beyond the heated rhetoric and simplistic headlines and ask your own questions about a proposed law. How will it affect my life and the lives of people I care about? What is the impact on my country?

CHAPTER GOALS

★ Describe who serves in Congress and how they represent their constituents (pp. 277–88)

★ Explain how party leadership, the committee system, and the staff system help structure congressional business (pp. 288–93)

★ Outline the steps in the process of passing a law (pp. 293–97)

★ Analyze the factors that influence which laws Congress passes (pp. 297–303)

★ Describe Congress's influence over other branches of government (pp. 303–5)

Congress Represents the American People

Congress is the most important representative institution in American government. Each member's primary responsibility in theory is to the district, to the **constituency** (the residents in the area from which an official is elected), not to the congressional leadership, a party, or even Congress itself. Yet the task of representation is not a simple one. Views about what constitutes fair and effective representation differ, and constituents can make very different kinds of demands on their representatives. Members of Congress must consider these diverse views and demands as they represent their districts.

> **Describe who serves in Congress and how they represent their constituents**

THE HOUSE AND SENATE OFFER DIFFERENCES IN REPRESENTATION

The framers of the Constitution provided for a **bicameral** legislature—that is, a legislative body consisting of two chambers or houses. The 435 members of the House are elected from districts apportioned according to population; the 100 members of the Senate are elected in a statewide vote, with two senators from each. Senators have much longer terms in office and usually represent much larger and more diverse constituencies than do their counterparts in the House (see Table 9.1).

Both formal and informal factors contribute to differences between the two chambers of Congress. Differences in the length of terms and requirements for holding office specified by the Constitution in turn generate differences in how members of each body develop their constituencies and exercise their powers of office. The small size and relative homogeneity of their constituencies and the frequency with

TABLE 9.1

Differences between the House and the Senate

	HOUSE	SENATE
Minimum age of member	25 years	30 years
U.S. citizenship	At least 7 years	At least 9 years
Length of term	2 years	6 years
Number representing each state	1–53 per state (depends on population)	2 per state
Constituency	Local	Local and statewide

which they must seek re-election—every two years—make House members more attuned to the legislative needs of local interest groups. The result is that members of the House most effectively and frequently serve as the agents of well-organized local interests with specific legislative agendas—for instance, used-car dealers seeking relief from regulation or farmers looking for higher subsidies. Because House members seek re-election every two years, they are interested in doing what their constituents want right *now*.

Senators, on the other hand, serve larger and more heterogeneous constituencies. As a result, they are somewhat better able than members of the House to serve as the agents for groups and interests organized on a statewide or national basis. Moreover, with longer terms in office (six years), senators have the luxury of considering "new ideas" or seeking to bring together new coalitions of interests rather than simply serving existing ones.

REPRESENTATION CAN BE SOCIOLOGICAL OR AGENCY

We have become so accustomed to the idea of representative government that we tend to forget what a peculiar concept representation really is. A representative claims to act or speak for some other person or group. But how can one person be trusted to speak for another? How do we know that those who call themselves our representatives are actually speaking on our behalf rather than simply pursuing their own interests?

There are two circumstances under which one person reasonably might be trusted to speak for another. The first of these occurs if the two individuals are so similar in background, character, interests, and perspectives that anything said by one would very likely reflect the views of the other as well. This principle is at the heart of what is sometimes called **sociological representation**—a type of representation in which representatives have the same racial, gender, ethnic, religious, or educational backgrounds as their constituents. The assumption is that sociological similarity helps promote good representation; thus, the composition of a properly constituted representative assembly should mirror the composition of society.

The second circumstance under which one person might be trusted to speak for another occurs if the two are formally bound together so that the representative is in some way accountable to those she purports to represent. If representatives can somehow be punished or held to account for failing to represent their constituents properly, then they have an incentive to provide good representation even if their own personal backgrounds, views, and interests differ from those of the people they represent. This principle is called **agency representation**—the sort of representation that takes place when constituents have the power to hire and fire their representatives.

Both sociological and agency representation play a role in the relationship between members of Congress and their constituencies.

The Social Composition of the U.S. Congress The extent to which the U.S. Congress is representative of the American people in a sociological sense can be seen by examining the distribution of important social characteristics in the House and Senate today.

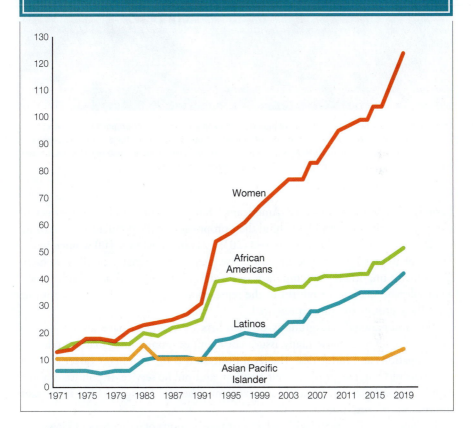

FIGURE 9.1

Diversity in Congress, 1971–2019

Congress has become much more socially diverse since the 1970s. How closely does the number of female, African American, and Latino representatives reflect their proportion of the total U.S. population?

SOURCES: Harold W. Stanley and Richard G. Niemi, eds., *Vital Statistics on American Politics 2003–2004* (Washington, DC: CQ Press, 2003), 207, Table 5–2; Jennifer E. Manning, *Membership of the 113th Congress: A Profile*, Congressional Research Service 7-5700, January 13, 2014, www.fas.org/sgp/crs/misc/R42964.pdf (accessed 2/24/14); Jennifer E. Manning, *Membership of the 114th Congress: A Profile*, Congressional Research Service, 7-5700, September 17, 2015, www.fas.org/sgp/crs/misc/R43869.pdf; R. Eric Petersen, *Representatives and Senators: Trends in Member Characteristics since 1945*, Congressional Research Service 7-5700, February 17, 2012, www.fas.org/sgp/crs/misc/R42365.pdf (accessed 9/28/15), 2019 data were calculated by the authors.

African Americans, women, Latinos, and Asian Americans have increased their congressional representation in the past two decades (see Figure 9.1); but for most of American history, these groups had no representatives in Congress. Even now, their representation in Congress is not comparable to the proportions in the general population. After the 2018 elections, Congress was 9 percent African American, 8 percent Latino, and 2 percent Asian American. By contrast, the American population was far more diverse, with 13.3 percent African Americans, 17.6 percent

To more effectively promote a legislative agenda addressing issues that disproportionately affect racial and ethnic minority groups, members of Congress from those groups have formed caucuses. Here, Michelle Lujan Grisham (D-N. Mex.), former chair of the Congressional Hispanic Caucus, speaks out about Donald Trump's proposed changes to immigration policies.

Latinos, and 5.6 percent Asian Americans.[4] Similarly, the number of women in Congress continues to trail far behind their proportion of the population. Following the 2018 elections, the 116th Congress (2019–21) included over 100 women in the House of Representatives and at least 23 women in the Senate, an all-time high. Since many important contemporary issues do cut along racial and gender lines, a considerable clamor for reform in the representative process is likely to continue until these groups are fully represented.

The occupational backgrounds of members of Congress have always been a matter of interest because many issues cut along economic lines that are relevant to occupations and industries. The legal profession is the dominant career of most members of Congress prior to their election, and public service or politics is also a significant background. In addition, many members of Congress have important ties to business and industry.[5]

Is Congress still able to legislate fairly or take account of a diversity of views and interests if it is not a sociologically representative assembly?

Representatives as Agents A good deal of evidence indicates that whether or not members of Congress share their constituents' sociological characteristics, they do work very hard to speak for their constituents' views and serve their constituents' interests in the governmental process. The idea of representative as agent is similar to the relationship of lawyer and client. True, the relationship between the

House member and an average of 710,767 "clients" in the district, or the senator and millions of "clients" in the state, is very different from that of the lawyer and client. But the criteria of performance are comparable. One expects at the very least that each representative will constantly be seeking to discover the interests of the constituency and will take those interests into account.[6] Whether members of Congress always represent the interests of their constituents is another matter, as we will see later in this chapter.

There is constant communication between constituents and congressional offices, and the volume of email from constituents and advocacy groups has grown so large so quickly that congressional offices have struggled to find effective ways to respond in a timely manner.[7] At the same time, members of Congress have found new ways to communicate with constituents. They have created websites describing their achievements, established a presence on social networking sites, and issued e-newsletters that alert constituents to current issues. Many have also set up blogs and Twitter accounts to establish a more informal style of communication with constituents.

The seriousness with which members of the House behave as representatives can be seen in the amount of time spent on behalf of their constituents. Well over one-quarter of their time and nearly two-thirds of the time of their staff members is devoted to constituency service (called "casework"). This service includes talking to constituents, providing them with minor services, presenting special bills for them, attempting to influence decisions by regulatory commissions on their behalf, helping them apply for federal benefits such as Social Security and Small Business Administration loans, and assisting them with immigration cases.[8]

In many districts there are two or three issues that are top priorities for constituents and, therefore, for the representatives. For example, representatives from districts that grow wheat, cotton, or tobacco will likely give legislation on these subjects great attention. In oil-rich states such as Oklahoma, Texas, and California, senators and members of the House are likely to be leading advocates of oil interests. For one thing, representatives are probably fearful of voting against their district interests; for another, the districts are unlikely to have elected representatives who would *want* to vote against them. On the other hand, on many issues, constituents do not have very strong views, so representatives are free to act as they think best. Foreign policy issues often fall into this category.

The influence of constituencies is so pervasive that both parties generally agree that members should not be pressured to vote against their constituencies if doing so would endanger the re-election chances of any member. Party leaders obey this rule fairly consistently by not asking any member to vote in a way that might conflict with a district interest.

THE ELECTORAL CONNECTION HINGES ON INCUMBENCY

The sociological composition of Congress and the activities of representatives once they are in office are very much influenced by electoral considerations. Two factors related to the U.S. electoral system affect who gets elected and what they do once in office. The first factor is that of incumbency advantage. The second is the way congressional district lines are drawn, which can greatly affect the outcome of an election. Let us examine more closely the impact that these considerations have on representation.

Incumbency—holding a political office for which one is running—plays a very important role in the American electoral system and in the kind of representation citizens get in Washington. Once in office, members have access to an array of tools that they can use to aid their re-election. The most important of these is constituency service—taking care of the problems and requests of individual voters. Congressional offices will intervene on behalf of constituents when they have problems with federal programs or agencies, in such areas as Social Security benefits, veterans' benefits, and passports. When congressional offices contact federal agencies dealing with such matters, the offices usually respond with extra speed, knowing that members of Congress can embarrass or penalize an agency that doesn't do its job properly. Through such services and through regular e-newsletters, the incumbent seeks to establish a "personal" relationship with the constituents. The success of this strategy is evident in the high rates of re-election for congressional incumbents, which are as high as 98 percent for House members and 90 percent for members of the Senate in recent years (see Figure 9.2). It is also evident in what is called "sophomore surge"—the tendency for incumbent candidates to win a higher percentage of the vote when seeking future terms in office.

The precarious economy and the backlash against the party in power made 2008 and 2010 difficult election years for some incumbents, particularly Democrats, given that their party controlled the presidency and both houses of Congress in a year when economic woes contributed to strong anti-incumbent sentiment.[9] In 2016, Trump's surprise victory in the presidential race benefited Republican incumbents, who had appeared to be in danger of losing their seats.

Incumbency can also help a candidate by scaring off potential challengers. In many races, potential candidates may decide not to run because they fear that the incumbent simply has too much money or is too well liked or too well known. Potentially strong challengers may also decide that a district's partisan leanings are too unfavorable. The efforts of incumbents to raise funds to ward off potential challengers start early. In addition to incumbents' own efforts, each political party makes a special effort to reelect incumbents viewed as especially vulnerable. The Democratic Congressional Campaign Committee (DCCC) places vulnerable incumbents in its "Frontline" program to receive extra funding, choice committee assignments, and high-profile speaking engagements. For the 2018 midterm elections, the DCCC placed 19 incumbents on its Frontline list, many of whom had won in 2016 in districts carried by Trump. For its part, the Republican Congressional Campaign Committee (RCCC) named ten members to its own incumbent protection program.[10] In 2018, approximately 93 percent of incumbents in the House and 86 percent in the Senate were re-elected. Seventy-six of the 435 House races were decided by a margin of less than 10 percent. Five incumbents in the Senate, and 20 in the House lost their seats in 2018.

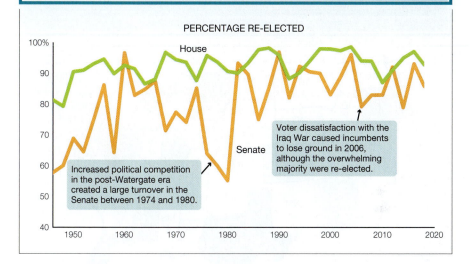

FIGURE 9.2

The Power of Incumbency

Members of Congress who run for re-election have a very good chance of winning. Has the incumbency advantage generally been greater in the House or in the Senate? What are the consequences of the incumbency advantage for who serves in Congress?

SOURCE: Norman J. Ornstein et al., eds., *Vital Statistics on Congress, 1999–2000* (Washington, DC: AEI Press, 2000), 57–58; "Reelection Rates over the Years," opensecrets.org.

PERCENTAGE RE-ELECTED

House

Senate

Increased political competition in the post-Watergate era created a large turnover in the Senate between 1974 and 1980.

Voter dissatisfaction with the Iraq War caused incumbents to lose ground in 2006, although the overwhelming majority were re-elected.

The advantage of incumbency thus tends to preserve the status quo in Congress. This fact has implications for the social composition of Congress. Women who run for open seats (that is, seats for which there are no incumbents) are just as likely to win as male candidates.[11] However, the incumbency advantage makes it harder for women to increase their numbers in Congress because most incumbents are men. Supporters of **term limits** (legally prescribed limits on the number of terms an elected official can serve) argue that such limits are the only way to get new faces into Congress.

Apportionment and Redistricting Another major factor that affects who wins a seat in the House of Representatives is the way congressional districts are drawn (senators, on the other hand, represent entire states). Every 10 years, state legislatures must redraw election districts and redistribute legislative representatives to reflect population changes or in response to legal challenges to existing districts. Because the number of congressional seats has been fixed at 435 since 1929, redistricting is a zero-sum process; for one state to gain a seat, another must lose one. The process of allocating congressional seats among the 50 states is called **apportionment**. Over the past several decades, the shift of the American population to the South

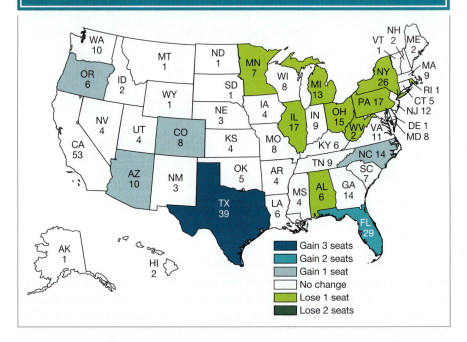

and the West has greatly increased the size of the congressional delegations from those regions. This trend continued after the 2010 census and will likely continue after 2020 (see Figure 9.3). Texas is likely to gain three seats (after gaining four after 2010), and Florida will likely gain two. States in the Northeast and "rust belt" are likely to lose seats. Latino voters are nearly three times as prevalent in states that gained seats than in states that lost seats, suggesting that the growth of the Latino population is a major factor in the American political landscape.[12]

States that gain or lose seats must then redraw their congressional district borders. This is a highly political process: districts are shaped to create an advantage for the party with a majority in the state legislature, which controls the **redistricting** process. In this complex process, those charged with drawing districts use sophisticated computer technologies to come up with the most favorable district boundaries. Redistricting can create open seats and pit incumbents of the same party against one

Redrawing legislative districts is a difficult task because it has implications for who will be elected. Here, the attorney for Arizona's Independent Redistricting Commission discusses a possible layout with a city council member from Casa Grande. Arizona gained one congressional seat following the 2010 census.

another, ensuring that one of them will lose. Redistricting can also give an advantage to one party by clustering voters with certain ideological or sociological characteristics in a single district or by diluting the influence of voter blocs by separating those voters into two or more districts. The manipulation of electoral districts to serve the interests of a particular group is known as **gerrymandering**.

Since the passage of the 1982 amendments to the 1964 Civil Rights Act, race has become a major (and controversial) consideration in drawing voting districts. These amendments, which encouraged the creation of districts in which members of racial minorities have decisive majorities, have greatly increased the number of minority representatives in Congress. After the 1990 redistricting cycle, the number of predominantly minority districts doubled, rising from 26 to 52. Among the most fervent supporters of the new minority districts were white Republicans, who used the opportunity to create more districts dominated by white Republican voters. These developments raise thorny questions about representation. Some analysts argue that the system may grant minorities greater sociological representation, but it has made it more difficult for them to win substantive policy goals, while others dispute this argument.[13]

In the case of *Miller v. Johnson* (1995), the Supreme Court limited racial redistricting by ruling that race could not be the predominant factor in creating electoral districts.[14] The distinction between race being a "predominant" factor and its being one factor among many is hazy. As a result, concerns about redistricting and representation persist.[15] Questions about minority representation emerged in 2011 in Texas, which gained four seats as a result of reapportionment. The Republican legislature drew a map that advantaged Republicans in three of those districts. But the plan drew a legal challenge on the grounds that it underrepresented Hispanic voters, who accounted for most of the state's population growth. Although federal judges drew a map more favorable to minorities (and Democrats), the Supreme Court ruled that the state did not have to use the map drawn by judges. The state ultimately agreed to a map that added two Latino-dominated districts. However, federal courts ruled that this map also weakened Latino and African American political power by creating too few minority districts.

The future of race in redistricting became more uncertain after the 2013 Supreme Court decision in *Shelby County v. Holder*. That decision invalidated a section of the Voting Rights Act requiring that the Justice Department approve the redistricting plans of jurisdictions with a history of racial discrimination.[16] Many Democrats expressed disappointment with the decision, fearing that the previously covered states, several of which are controlled by Republican majorities, might try to redraw district lines to partisan ends and further bias districts toward Republicans.[17] In 2015, Alabama's black legislators challenged that state's redistricting under the Voting Rights Act. They charged that the Republican legislature had diluted the vote of African Americans by packing black voters into districts that already had strong minority representation, thus enhancing the chances of white Republican candidates in the remaining districts. The legislature claimed, on the contrary, that it was acting in accordance with the Voting Rights Act by concentrating black voters. Although the Supreme Court did not declare the districting unconstitutional, it ruled that the lower court had erred in approving the districts.[18] The ruling signaled that state legislatures would not be able to use the Voting Rights Act to justify packing minority voters into districts.

DIRECT PATRONAGE MEANS BRINGING HOME THE BACON

Members of Congress have numerous opportunities to provide direct benefits, or **patronage**, for their constituents. The most important such opportunity for direct patronage is in so-called **pork-barrel legislation (or pork)**—appropriations made by legislative bodies for local projects that may not be needed but that are created to help local representatives win re-election in their home districts. This type of legislation specifies a project to be funded within a particular district. Many observers of Congress argue that pork-barrel bills are the only ones that some members are serious about moving toward actual passage because they are seen as so important to members' re-election bids.

A common form of pork-barreling is the "earmark," the practice through which members of Congress insert into bills language that provides special benefits for their own constituents. When Democrats took over Congress in 2007, they vowed to limit the use of earmarks, which had grown from 1,439 per year in 1995 to 15,268 in 2006. More troubling, earmarks were connected to congressional scandals. For example, Republican House member Randy "Duke" Cunningham (R-Calif.) was sent to jail in 2005 for accepting bribes by companies hoping to receive earmarks in return.[19] The House passed a new rule requiring that those representatives supporting each earmark identify themselves and guarantee that they have no personal financial stake in the requested project. An ethics law applied similar provisions to the Senate. Though the new requirements appeared to have had some impact, in the midst of the sharp economic downturn in 2009, Congress passed a bill designed to stimulate the economy that contained more than 8,000 earmarks. In his 2010 State of the Union address, President Obama called for Congress to publish a list of all earmark requests on a single website. Congress not only failed to enact such legislation, in 2010 it set a new record by passing 11,320 earmarks, worth $32 billion. But in 2011 the House and the Senate agreed to a two-year moratorium on earmarks in spending bills and renewed the ban for the 113th and 114th Congresses.[20] In 2018, President Trump suggested to Congress that it should consider restoring earmarks as a way of enhancing congressional power vis à vis the bureaucracy and to help "grease" the legislative wheels by giving members an incentive to support legislative programs. Trump's comments were greeted favorably by many congressional leaders.[21]

Some analysts claim that the lack of earmarks contributes to congressional gridlock. They argue that earmarks provide congressional leaders with incentives to promote compromise among members. Supporters of this position contend that earmarks are not inherently an abuse of power and note that they often support legitimate district projects, such as transportation and parks.[22]

There are a few other types of direct patronage (see Figure 9.4). One important form of constituency service is intervention with federal administrative agencies on behalf of constituents. Members of the House and Senate and their staffs spend a great deal of time seeking to secure favorable treatment for constituents and supporters. For example, members of Congress can assist senior citizens who are having Social Security or Medicare benefit eligibility problems. A small but related form of patronage is securing an appointment to one of the military academies for the child of a constituent. Traditionally, these appointments are allocated one to a district.

A different form of patronage is the **private bill**—a bill in Congress to provide a specific person with some kind of relief, such as a special exemption from immigration quotas. It is distinguished from a public bill, which is supposed to deal with general rules and categories of behavior, people, and institutions. As many as 75 percent of all private bills introduced (and one-third of those that pass) are concerned with obtaining citizenship for foreign nationals who cannot get permanent visas to the United States because the immigration quota for their country is filled or because of something unusual about their particular situation.[23] Other private bills address a diverse set of issues involving a claim against the federal government, such as problems with veterans' benefits or taxation. Private legislation is a congressional privilege that can be abused, but it is impossible to imagine members of Congress completely giving up one of the easiest, cheapest, and most effective forms of patronage available to them. It can be defended as an indispensable part of the process by which members of Congress seek to fulfill their role as representatives.

FIGURE 9.4

How Members of Congress Represent Their Districts

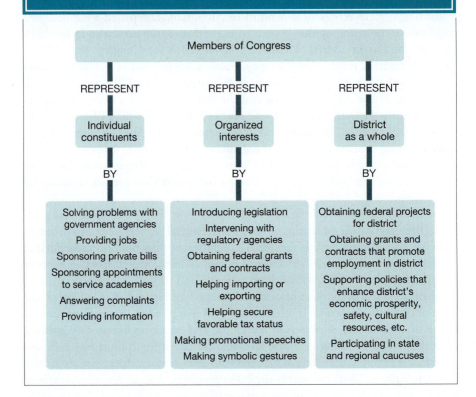

Members of Congress		
REPRESENT	REPRESENT	REPRESENT
Individual constituents	Organized interests	District as a whole
BY	BY	BY
Solving problems with government agencies Providing jobs Sponsoring private bills Sponsoring appointments to service academies Answering complaints Providing information	Introducing legislation Intervening with regulatory agencies Obtaining federal grants and contracts Helping importing or exporting Helping secure favorable tax status Making promotional speeches Making symbolic gestures	Obtaining federal projects for district Obtaining grants and contracts that promote employment in district Supporting policies that enhance district's economic prosperity, safety, cultural resources, etc. Participating in state and regional caucuses

The Organization of Congress Is Shaped by Party

Explain how party leadership, the committee system, and the staff system help structure congressional business

The U.S. Congress is not only a representative assembly but also a legislative body. To exercise its power to make laws, Congress must first bring about something close to an organizational miracle. The building blocks of congressional organization include the political parties, the committee system, congressional staff, the caucuses, and the parliamentary rules of the House and Senate. Each of these factors plays a key role in the organization of Congress and in the process through which Congress formulates and enacts laws.

PARTY LEADERSHIP IN THE HOUSE AND THE SENATE ORGANIZES POWER

Every two years, at the beginning of a new Congress, the members of each party in the House of Representatives gather to elect their leaders. House Republicans call their gathering the **conference**. House Democrats call theirs the **caucus**. The elected leader of the majority party is later proposed to the whole House and is elected to the position of **Speaker of the House**, with voting along straight party lines, although in recent speaker elections some members of the speaker's party have voted against their own candidate for the job to indicate their dissatisfaction with party leadership. The Speaker is the most important party and House leader and can influence the legislative agenda, the fate of individual pieces of legislation, and members' positions within the House. The House majority conference or caucus then also elects a **majority leader**. (In the House, the majority leader is subordinate in the party hierarchy to the Speaker of the House.) The minority party goes through the same process and selects the **minority leader**. Both parties also elect assistants to their party leaders, called **whips**, who are responsible for coordinating the party's legislative strategy, building support for key issues, and counting votes.

Next in line of importance for each party after the Speaker and majority or minority leader is what Democrats call the Steering and Policy Committee—Republicans have a separate Steering Committee and a separate Policy Committee—whose tasks are to assign new legislators to committees and to deal with the requests of incumbent members for transfers from one committee to another.

Generally, members of Congress seek assignments that will allow them to influence decisions of special importance to their districts. Representatives from farm districts, for example, may request seats on the Agriculture Committee.[24] Seats on powerful committees such as Ways and Means, which is responsible for tax legislation, and Appropriations are especially popular.

Within the Senate, the majority party usually designates a member of the majority party with the greatest seniority to serve as president pro tempore, a position of primarily ceremonial leadership. Real power is in the hands of the majority leader and minority leader, each elected by party conference. Together they control the Senate's calendar, or agenda, for legislation. Each party also elects a Policy Committee, which advises the leadership on legislative priorities. In recent years, party leaders in both chambers have gone around the committees to directly control the content and direction of important legislation.

THE COMMITTEE SYSTEM IS THE CORE OF CONGRESS

The committee system is central to the operation of Congress. At each stage of the legislative process, Congress relies on committees and subcommittees to do the hard work of sorting through alternatives and writing legislation. There are several different kinds of congressional committees; these include standing committees, select committees, joint committees, and conference committees.

Standing committees are very important arenas of congressional policy making. These permanent committees remain in existence from one session of Congress to

After Democrats took control of the House of Representatives in November 2018, former House minority leader Nancy Pelosi (D-Calif.) was poised to take over the role of Speaker of the House from retiring Speaker Paul Ryan (R-Wisc.). She had previously served in the same position from 2007–11.

the next; they have the power to propose and write legislation. The jurisdiction of each standing committee covers a particular subject matter, such as finance or agriculture, which in most cases parallels the major departments or agencies in the executive branch. Among the most important standing committees are those in charge of finances. The House Ways and Means Committee and the Senate Finance Committee are powerful because of their jurisdiction over taxes, trade, and expensive entitlement programs such as Social Security and Medicare. The Senate and House Appropriations committees also play important ongoing roles because they decide how much funding various programs will actually receive; they also determine exactly how the money will be spent. A seat on the Appropriations Committee allows a member the opportunity to direct funds to a favored program—perhaps one in his home district.

Except for the House Rules Committee, all standing committees receive proposals for legislation and process them into official bills. The House Rules Committee decides the order in which bills come up for a vote on the House floor and determines the specific rules that govern the length of debate and opportunity for amendments. The Senate, which has less formal organization and fewer rules, does not have a similarly powerful rules committee.

Select committees are usually temporary and normally do not have the power to present legislation to the full Congress but rather are set up to highlight or investigate a particular issue or address an issue not within the jurisdiction of existing committees. (The House and Senate Select Intelligence committees are permanent, however, and do have the power to report legislation, which means they can send legislation to the full House or Senate for consideration.) These committees may hold hearings and serve as focal points for the issues they are charged with considering. Congressional leaders form select committees when they want to take up issues that fall between the jurisdictions of existing committees, to highlight an issue, or to investigate a particular problem. For example, the Senate set up the Senate Watergate Committee in 1973 to investigate the Watergate break-in and cover-up. More recently, the House Select Committee on Benghazi was established to investigate the 2012 attack on the U.S. Embassy in Benghazi, Libya. In 2015 the committee held hearings to investigate Hillary Clinton's use of a private email server during her tenure as secretary of state. Select committees set up to highlight ongoing issues have included the House Select Committee on Hunger, established in 1984, and the House Select Committee on Energy Independence and Global Warming, created in 2007 but abolished in 2011, when Republicans assumed control of the House.

Joint committees are formed of members of both the Senate and the House. There are four such committees: economic, taxation, library, and printing. These joint committees are permanent, but they do not have the power to report legislation. The Joint Economic Committee and the Joint Taxation Committee have often played important roles in collecting information and holding hearings on economic and financial issues. Finally, **conference committees** are temporary joint committees whose members are appointed by the Speaker of the House and the presiding officer of the Senate. These committees are charged with working out a compromise on legislation that has been passed by the House and the Senate but in different versions. Conference committees can play an extremely important role in determining what laws are actually passed because they must reconcile any differences in the legislation passed by the House and Senate.

When control of Congress is divided between two parties, each is guaranteed significant representation in conference committees. When a single party controls both houses, the majority party is not obligated to offer such representation to the minority party. In 2003, Democrats complained that Republicans took this power to the extreme by excluding them and adding new provisions to legislation at the conference committee stage. Democrats even prevented several conference committees from convening to protest their near exclusion from conference committees on major energy, health care, and transportation laws. After the Democrats returned to power in 2007, they largely bypassed the conference committees; when their early efforts to reach compromises in the conference were derailed by partisan differences, the Democrats began making closed-door agreements between top leaders in the House and the Senate. Although the process facilitated compromises across the two chambers, it meant that important changes to bills were made in private, without the transparency that would have been part of the conference committee process. After 2010, Congress continued to avoid conference committees. Instead, the Republican House and Democratic Senate leaders exchanged amendments as they sought to reach agreement on the final version of a bill, a practice known informally as "ping-ponging."[25]

Within each committee, hierarchy is based on seniority. **Seniority** is the ranking given to an individual on the basis of length of continuous service on a committee in Congress. In general, each committee is chaired by the most senior member of the majority party. But the principle of seniority is not absolute. Both Democrats and Republicans have violated it on occasion. In 1995, when the Republicans won control of the House, then-Speaker Newt Gingrich instituted a new practice of frequent seniority violations, often selecting committee chairs based on loyalty or fund-raising abilities, a practice that subsequent Republican leaders have maintained. In 2007 the Democrats returned to the seniority principle to select committee chairs but altered traditional practices in other ways by offering freshman Democrats choice committee assignments to increase their chances of re-election.[26]

THE STAFF SYSTEM IS THE POWER BEHIND THE POWER

The congressional institution second in importance only to the committee system is the staff system. Every member of Congress employs a large number of staff members, whose tasks include handling constituent requests and, to a large

Women's Parliamentary Representation Worldwide

April 2018 marked the first time in U.S. history that women comprised 20 percent of Congress, with 19.3 percent of the House and 23 percent of the Senate being women.[a] When we look around the world however, we find that the United States ranks 102 out of 188 countries in women's parliamentary representation.

Why? Research suggests women candidates benefit from gender quotas instituted (in several countries) and may be at a disadvantage in "winner-take-all" elections like those in the United States.[b] In Rwanda, women comprise 61 percent of parliament, and there is both a gender quota (30 percent of the legislature is required to be women) and proportional representation (election rules where parties receive seats based on the percentage of the vote they received).

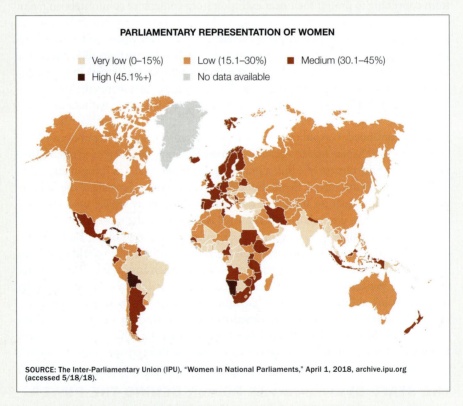

PARLIAMENTARY REPRESENTATION OF WOMEN

Very low (0–15%) Low (15.1–30%) Medium (30.1–45%)
High (45.1%+) No data available

SOURCE: The Inter-Parliamentary Union (IPU), "Women in National Parliaments," April 1, 2018, archive.ipu.org (accessed 5/18/18).

[a] The Center for American Women and Politics (CAWP), "With Election of Debbie Lesko (AZ-08), Record Number of Women in Congress," April 24, 2018, cawp.rutgers.edu/sites/default/files/resources/18.4.24_pr_lesko_az08.pdf (accessed 5/18/18).
[b] Lena Wängnerud, "Women in Parliaments: Descriptive and Substantive Representation," *Annual Review of Political Science* 12 (2009): 51–69.

and growing extent, dealing with legislative details and the activities of administrative agencies. Increasingly, staffers bear the primary responsibility for formulating and drafting proposals, organizing hearings, dealing with administrative agencies, and negotiating with lobbyists. Indeed, legislators typically deal with one another through staff rather than through direct, personal contact. Today, staffers develop policy ideas, draft legislation, and have a good deal of influence over the legislative process.

Representatives and senators together employ over 12,000 staffers in their Washington and home offices. In addition, Congress employs more than 2,000 committee staffers. These individuals make up the permanent staff, who stay attached to every House and Senate committee regardless of turnover in Congress and who are responsible for organizing and administering the committee's work, including researching, scheduling, organizing hearings, and drafting legislation. Committee staffers also play key roles in the legislative process.

Rules of Lawmaking Explain How a Bill Becomes a Law

> **Outline the steps in the process of passing a law**

The institutional structure of Congress is one key factor that helps shape the legislative process. A second and equally important set of factors is the rules of congressional procedure. These rules govern everything from the introduction of a **bill** (a proposed law that has been sponsored by a member of Congress and submitted to the clerk of the House or Senate) through its submission to the president for signing (see Figure 9.5). Not only do these regulations influence the fate of each and every bill but they also help determine the distribution of power in the Congress.

THE FIRST STEP IS COMMITTEE DELIBERATION

Even if a member of Congress, the White House, or a federal agency has spent months developing and drafting a piece of legislation, it does not become a bill until it is submitted officially by a senator or representative to the clerk of the House or Senate and referred to the appropriate committee for deliberation. Bills can originate in the House or the Senate, but only the House can introduce "money bills": those that spend or raise revenues. The framers inserted this provision in the Constitution because they believed that the chamber closest to the people should exercise greater authority over taxing and spending. No floor action on any bill can take place until the committee with jurisdiction over it has taken all the time it needs to deliberate. During the course of its deliberations, the committee typically refers the bill to one of its subcommittees, which may hold hearings, listen to expert testimony, and amend the proposed legislation before referring the bill to the full committee for consideration. The full committee may accept the recommendation of the subcommittee or hold its own hearings and prepare its own amendments. Or,

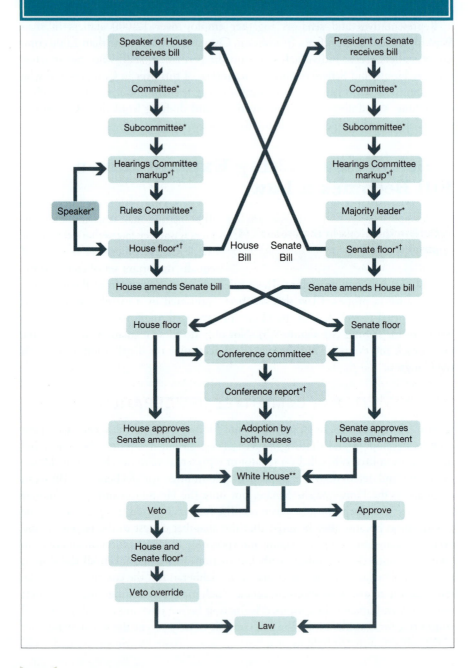

FIGURE 9.5

How a Bill Becomes a Law

*Points at which a bill can be amended.
**If the president neither signs nor vetoes a bill within 10 days, it automatically becomes law.
†Points at which a bill can die.

Speaker of House receives bill → Committee* → Subcommittee* → Hearings Committee markup*† → Rules Committee* → House floor*†

President of Senate receives bill → Committee* → Subcommittee* → Hearings Committee markup*† → Majority leader* → Senate floor*†

Speaker*

House Bill

Senate Bill

House amends Senate bill

Senate amends House bill

House floor

Senate floor

Conference committee*

Conference report*†

House approves Senate amendment

Adoption by both houses

Senate approves House amendment

White House**

Veto

Approve

House and Senate floor*

Veto override

Law

even more frequently, the committee and subcommittee may do little or nothing with a bill that has been submitted to them. Many bills are simply allowed to "die in committee" without serious consideration given to them. In a typical congressional session, 80–90 percent of the roughly 10,000 bills introduced die in committee—an indication of the power of the congressional committee system.

In the House, the relative handful of bills that are reported out of committee must, in the House, pass one additional hurdle within the committee system: the Rules Committee, which determines the rules that will govern action on the bill on the House floor. In particular, the Rules Committee allots the time for debate and decides to what extent amendments to the bill can be proposed from the floor. In recent years, the Rules Committee has become less powerful because the House leadership exercises so much influence over its decisions.

DEBATE IS LESS RESTRICTED IN THE SENATE THAN IN THE HOUSE

In the House, virtually all the time allotted for debate on a given bill is controlled by the bill's sponsor and by its leading opponent. In almost every case, these two people are the committee chair and the ranking minority member of the committee that processed the bill—or those they designate. These two participants are, by rule and tradition, granted the power to allocate most of the debate time in small amounts to members who are seeking to speak for or against the measure. Preference in the allocation of time goes to the members of the committee whose jurisdiction covers the bill.

The Filibuster In the Senate, the leadership has much less control over floor debate. Indeed, the Senate is unique among the world's legislative bodies for its commitment to unlimited debate. Once given the floor, a senator may speak as long as she wishes. On a number of memorable occasions, senators have used the right to talk without interruption for as long as they want to prevent action on legislation they opposed. Through this tactic, called the **filibuster**, members of the Senate can prevent action on legislation they oppose by continuously holding the floor and speaking until the majority backs down (or the filibustering senator gives up). A vote of three-fifths of the Senate, or 60 votes, is required to end a filibuster. This procedure to end a filibuster is called **cloture**. For much of American history, senators only rarely used the filibuster, though during the 1950s and '60s, opponents of civil rights legislation often used filibusters to block its passage. In the last 20 years, the filibuster (or the mere threat of a filibuster) has become so common that observers routinely note that it takes 60 votes to get anything passed in the Senate. The 113th Congress (2013–15) set a new record, with 218 cloture votes (the vote to end a filibuster). The number fell to 192 in the 115th Congress (2017–19).[27]

In 2013 the Democratic Senate leader Harry Reid (Nev.) mobilized his party to alter the filibuster rules for the first time in many decades. Frustrated by the repeated failure of the Senate to vote on many of President Obama's nominees to fill positions in the executive branch, as well as judgeships to important federal courts, Reid invoked what senators had come to call "the nuclear option," a change to the filibuster rules in the middle of the session by simple majority vote. Under the new rules, nominees for executive branch appointments and federal court nominees—except the Supreme Court—cannot be filibustered, meaning that they can be approved by a simple majority vote. (Filibusters of legislation were still allowed.) Not surprisingly, the two parties had different views on the decision. Reid defended it as necessary, due to what he called "unbelievable, unprecedented obstruction." Republicans denounced the new rule, stating, in the words of Pat Roberts (R-Kans.), "We have weakened this body permanently."[28] After winning control of both houses of Congress and the White House in 2016, however, Republicans expanded Reid's rule to include Supreme Court justices and so were able to secure the appointment of Justice Neil Gorsuch, who would undoubtedly have been blocked by Senate Democrats under the old rules. Legislation is still subject to filibuster, though some Republicans, along with President Trump, have declared that it is time to bring an end to the filibuster altogether.

Voting Once debate is concluded on the floor of the House and the Senate, the leaders schedule it for a vote on the floor of each chamber. By this time, congressional leaders know what the vote will be; leaders do not bring legislation to the floor unless they are fairly certain it is going to pass. As a consequence, it is unusual for the leadership to lose a bill on the floor. On rare occasions, the last moments of the floor vote can be very dramatic as each party's leadership puts its whip organization into action to make sure that wavering members vote with the party.

In 2015 the House of Representatives failed to pass a spending bill to fund the Department of Homeland Security, hours before the agency was to run out of money and begin to shut down. Despite having a majority in the chamber and an early vote that suggested that the bill would pass easily, House GOP leaders failed to prevent the most conservative members of the party from suddenly abandoning the bill over objections that it left out provisions to block President Obama's executive actions on immigration. As midnight approached, the House agreed on a one-week extension to keep the department open.[29] Leaders later secured sufficient support to enact longer-term funding for Homeland Security. The importance of being able to attract wavering members with "pork" for their districts is one reason President Trump urged Congress in 2018 to restore earmarks, which have been banned since 2011.

CONFERENCE COMMITTEES RECONCILE HOUSE AND SENATE VERSIONS OF LEGISLATION

Getting a bill out of committee and through both houses of Congress is no guarantee that it will be enacted into law. Before a bill can be sent to the president, both houses must pass it in the identical form. Frequently, bills that began with similar provisions in both chambers emerge with little resemblance to each other. Alternatively, a bill may be passed by one chamber but undergo substantial revision in the other chamber. In such a case, a conference committee composed of the senior members of the committees or subcommittees that initiated the bill from both houses may be convened to iron out differences between the two pieces of legislation.

When a bill comes out of conference, it faces one more hurdle. Before it can be sent to the president for signing, the House–Senate conference committee's version of the bill must be approved on the floor of each chamber. Usually such approval is given quickly. Occasionally, however, a bill's opponents use this round of approval as one last opportunity to defeat a piece of legislation. In recent years, polarization in Congress has led to much less reliance on conference committees. Instead, leaders exchange amendments in hopes of reaching agreement.

THE PRESIDENT'S VETO CONTROLS THE FLOW OF LEGISLATION

Once adopted by the House and Senate, a bill goes to the president, who may choose to sign it into law or **veto** it. If the president neither signs nor vetoes it within 10 days and Congress is in session, the bill automatically becomes law. The veto is the president's constitutional power to reject a piece of legislation. To veto a bill, the president returns it unsigned within 10 days to the house of Congress in which it originated. If Congress adjourns during the 10-day period, such that congressional adjournment prevents the president from returning the bill to Congress, the bill is also considered to be vetoed. This latter method is known as the **pocket veto**. Unlike a regular or return veto, a pocket-vetoed bill cannot be overridden; the bill simply dies. The possibility of a presidential veto affects how willing members of Congress are to push for different pieces of legislation at different times. If they think a proposal is likely to be vetoed, they might shelve it for a later time or alter it to suit the president's preferences.

A presidential veto may be overridden by a two-thirds vote in both the House and the Senate. Successful overrides are rare but are a blow to the president.

Several Factors Influence How Congress Decides

> **Analyze the factors that influence which laws Congress passes**

What determines the kinds of legislation that Congress ultimately produces? According to the simplest theories of representation, members of Congress respond to the views of their constituents. In fact, creating a legislative agenda, drawing up a list of possible measures, and deciding among them is a complex process in which a variety of influences from inside and outside government play important roles. External influences include a legislator's constituency and various interest groups. Influences from inside government include party leadership, congressional colleagues, and the president. Let us examine each of these influences individually and then consider how they interact to produce congressional policy decisions.

CONSTITUENTS MATTER

Because members of Congress, for the most part, want to be re-elected, we would expect the views of their constituents to be a primary influence on the decisions those legislators make. Yet most constituents pay little attention to politics and often do not even know what policies their representatives support. Nonetheless, members of Congress spend a lot of time worrying about what their constituents think because these representatives realize that the choices they make may be scrutinized in a future election and used as ammunition by an opposing candidate. Because of this possibility, members of Congress do try to anticipate their constituents' policy views.[30] In 2017, despite a personal effort by President Trump to persuade dissident Republicans, the House GOP leadership could not muster enough Republican votes to pass a measure that would have repealed Obamacare. Some Republicans from swing districts feared upsetting constituents who favored Obamacare, while more conservative Republicans thought the bill did not go far enough in dismantling government-sponsored health insurance.

INTEREST GROUPS INFLUENCE CONSTITUENTS AND CONGRESS

Interest groups are another important external influence on congressional policies. Members of Congress pay close attention to interest groups for a number of reasons: interest groups can mobilize constituents, serve as watchdogs on congressional action, and supply candidates with money. When members of Congress are making voting decisions, those interest groups that have some connection to constituents or that can mobilize followers in particular members' districts are most likely to be influential.

Interest groups also have substantial influence in setting the legislative agenda and helping craft specific language in legislation. Today, sophisticated lobbyists win influence by providing information about policies, as well as campaign contributions, to busy members of Congress. The $1.1 trillion end-of-year spending bill passed at the end of 2014 included an amendment exempting many financial transactions from federal regulation under the Dodd-Frank Act. The amendment language was taken from a bill originally written by Citigroup lobbyists, with 70 of 85 lines of the bill directly copying Citigroup's language.[31] After further lobbying by the banking industry, legislation enacted in 2018 loosened a number of Dodd-Frank rules and exempted regional banks from a number of remaining rules. In recent years, interest groups have also begun to build broader coalitions and comprehensive campaigns around particular policy issues. These coalitions do not rise from the grass roots but instead

Representatives spend a lot of time meeting with constituents in their districts to explain how they have helped their district and learn what issues their constituents care about. Such meetings are often informal events at local restaurants or fairs, or town halls where constituents can ask questions. Here, Senator Chuck Grassley (R-Iowa) meets with constituents.

are put together by Washington lobbyists who launch comprehensive lobbying campaigns that combine simulated grassroots activity with information and campaign funding for members of Congress.

Concerns that special interests exert too much influence led Congress to enact new ethics legislation in 2007. Now lobbyists are required to disclose the names of the individual contributors to these political donations. Although the new law provides additional transparency, it does not fundamentally alter the fact that wealthy interest groups continue to exercise tremendous influence in Congress.

Moreover, the large sums of cash raised by Super PACs (political action committees)—discussed in Chapter 7—have introduced a whole new set of questions about the role of special interests in politics, especially because donors to Super PACs can remain anonymous. Although they cannot openly coordinate with candidates, Super PACs can endorse candidates by name and are often run by people close to the candidates they support. In 2016, Super PACs poured unprecedented sums of money into the race for president, but they also targeted key congressional contests in an effort to affect the balance of power between the parties in Congress.

PARTY LEADERS RELY ON PARTY DISCIPLINE

In both the House and the Senate, party leaders have a good deal of influence over the behavior of their party members. This influence, sometimes called "party discipline," was once so powerful that it dominated the lawmaking process. In the 1800s party leaders could often command the allegiance of more than 90 percent of their members. A vote in which half or more of the members of one party take one position while at least half of the members of the other party take the opposing position is called a **party unity vote**. At the beginning of the twentieth century, nearly half of all **roll-call votes** (votes in which each legislator's yes-or-no vote is recorded as the clerk calls the names of the members alphabetically) in the House of Representatives were party votes. While party voting is rarer today than a century ago, in the last decade it has been fairly common to find at least a majority of the Democrats opposing a majority of the Republicans on any given issue.

Typically, party unity is greater in the House than in the Senate. House rules give more power to the majority party leaders, which gives them more influence over House members. In the Senate, however, the leadership has few controls over its members. Party unity has been on the rise in recent years because the divisions between the parties have deepened on many high-profile issues such as abortion, affirmative action, the minimum wage, and school vouchers (see Figure 9.6) and because the majority–minority party difference has been small. In 2016, House Democrats voted with the majority 96 percent of the time, marking an all-time high, at least in modern times. Senate Democrats voted with their caucus 92 percent of the time. Republicans were also very united. In 2016, House Republicans voted with their party 96 percent of the time, a record high; Senate Republicans voted with their party 86 percent of the time, only five points below the record set in 2015.[32]

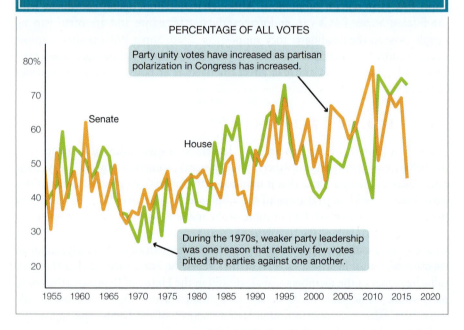

FIGURE 9.6

Party Unity Votes by Chamber

Party unity votes are roll-call votes in which a majority of one party lines up against a majority of the other party. Party unity votes increase when the parties are polarized and when the party leadership can enforce discipline. Why did the percentage of party unity votes decline in the 1970s? Why has it risen in recent years?

SOURCES: "CQ Roll Call's Vote Studies—2013 in Review," http://media.cq.com/votestudies (accessed 6/9/14); Eliza Newlin Carney, "Standing Together against Any Action," *CQ Weekly* (March 16, 2015); and "2015 Vote Studies: Party Unity Remained Strong," *CQ Weekly* (February 8, 2016); Vital Statistics, "Table 8-3 Party Unity Votes in Congress, 1953-2016," Brookings, May 21, 2018, www.brookings.edu/multi-chapter-report/vital-statistics-on-congress/ (accessed 11/9/18).

PERCENTAGE OF ALL VOTES

Party unity votes have increased as partisan polarization in Congress has increased.

Senate

House

During the 1970s, weaker party leadership was one reason that relatively few votes pitted the parties against one another.

Although party organization has weakened since the turn of the twentieth century, today's party leaders still have resources to reward loyal members who vote with the party: (1) leadership PACs, (2) committee assignments, (3) access to the floor, (4) the whip system, (5) logrolling, and (6) the presidency.

Leadership PACs Leaders have increased their influence over members in recent years with aggressive use of leadership PACs. Leadership PACs are organizations that members of Congress use to raise funds that they then distribute to other members of their party running for election. Republican congressional leaders pioneered the aggressive use of leadership PACs to win their congressional majority in 1995, and the practice has spread widely since that time. Money from leadership PACs can be directed to the most vulnerable candidates or to candidates who are having trouble raising money. They can also be used to influence primary elections. For example, New York Democratic senator Kirsten Gillibrand has used her leadership PAC to promote Democratic women candidates running for Congress. In 2016 the PAC, which she named Off the Sidelines, supplied funds to 61 candidates running for seats in the House and 10 for the Senate, all of them women.[33]

Committee Assignments Party leaders can create debts among members by helping them get favorable committee assignments. These assignments are made early in the congressional careers of most members and normally are not taken from them if they later go against party discipline (although this does happen occasionally to punish disloyalty). Nevertheless, if the leadership goes out of its way to get the right assignment for a member, this effort is likely to create a bond of obligation that can be called upon without any other payments or favors. This is one reason the Republican leadership gave freshmen favorable assignments when the Republicans took over Congress in 1995. When the Democrats won control of Congress in 2007, House Speaker Nancy Pelosi gave desirable and prestigious committee assignments to Democratic House members who faced competitive re-election races, to assist them in their home districts and increase their loyalty.

Access to the Floor The most important everyday resource available to the parties is control over access to the floor. With thousands of bills awaiting passage and most members clamoring for access in order to influence a bill or to publicize themselves, floor time is precious. Floor time is allocated in both houses of Congress by the majority and minority leaders. More important, the Speaker of the House and the majority leader in the Senate possess the power of recognition—that is, they decide who may and may not speak on the floor. This authority is quite formidable and can be used to stymie a piece of legislation completely or to frustrate a member's attempts to speak on a particular issue. Because the power is significant, members of Congress usually attempt to stay on good terms with the Speaker and the majority leader in order to ensure that they will continue to be recognized.

The Whip System Some influence accrues to party leaders through the whip system, which is primarily a communications network in each house of Congress for conveying the leaders' wishes and plans to the members. Between 12 and 20 assistant and regional whips are selected to operate at the direction of the majority or minority leader and the whip. They take polls of all the members to learn their intentions on specific bills, enabling the leaders to know whether they have enough support to allow a vote as well as whether the vote is so close that they need to put pressure on undecided members. In those instances, the Speaker or a lieutenant will go to a few party members who have indicated they will switch if their vote is essential—an expedient that the leaders try to limit to a few times per session.

The whip system helps maintain party unity in both houses of Congress, but it is particularly critical in the House of Representatives because of the large number of legislators whose positions and votes must be accounted for. The majority and minority whips and their assistants must be adept at inducing compromise among legislators who hold widely differing viewpoints.

Since 2010, when Republicans retook control of the House, the whip operation has been faced with significant challenges from conservative members. In 2015 a small group of conservative Republicans, organized into the House Freedom Caucus, regularly disputed the positions of the party leadership. Frustrated with the lack of discipline, House Majority Whip Steve Scalise (R-La.) expelled several members from his whip team for failing to support party positions.[34] Indeed, conflict with these rebellious Republicans prompted Speaker John Boehner to make the stunning announcement in September 2015 of his retirement from the speakership and from the House. In 2017, Republican House Speaker Paul Ryan (Wisc.) found that he sometimes needed Democratic votes to pass measures because Freedom Caucus members would not vote with the rest of the Republicans.

Logrolling A legislative practice wherein agreements are made between legislators in voting for or against a bill is called **logrolling**. Unlike with bargaining, legislators who are logrolling have nothing in common but their desire to exchange support. The agreement states, in effect, "You support me on bill X, and I'll support you on bill Y." Since party leaders are the center of the communications networks in the two chambers, they can help members create large logrolling coalitions. Hundreds of logrolling deals are made each year, and it is the job of the leader and whips to keep track of who owes what to whom.

The Presidency Of all the influences that maintain the clarity of party lines in Congress, the influence of the presidency is probably the most important. Indeed, the office is a touchstone of party discipline in Congress. Since the late 1940s, under President Harry Truman, presidents each year have identified a number of bills to be considered part of their administration's program. By the mid-1950s, both parties in Congress began to look to the president for these proposals, which became the most significant part of Congress's agenda. The president's support is an important criterion for party loyalty, and party leaders are able to use it to rally some members. Though President Trump was personally unpopular with many members of Congress, legislators still looked to him to set the agenda and most of the major legislative initiatives of 2017 and 2018, including border security, immigration, the repeal of Obamacare, and tax cuts originated in the White House.

In 2015 the most conservative factions of the Republican Party in Congress, frustrated that Speaker of the House John Boehner hadn't been more effective against the Obama administration, pressured him to resign.

PARTISANSHIP HAS THWARTED THE ABILITY OF CONGRESS TO DECIDE

Recent congresses have been notable for their inability to pass laws. The 114th Congress (2015–17), 113th Congress (2013–15), and the 112th Congress (2011–13) were the three least productive Congresses in modern history.[35] In November 2013, Congress received the lowest levels of approval ever recorded in public opinion polls: 9 percent approval, when many high-profile bills failed to pass.[36]

In 2018, President Trump and congressional leaders agreed on a spending bill that provided for increased defense and domestic social spending. Though the bill was opposed by Republican "deficit hawks" and by some Democrats who demanded legislation to protect undocumented immigrants, a majority of Republicans and more than 73 House Democrats supported the legislation. In the Senate, Rand Paul (R-Ky.) briefly filibustered the bill, but it was ultimately passed by a large majority and signed into law. By increasing overall spending levels, Trump and congressional leaders provided funding for programs that each party supported. The GOP got more money for the military and the Democrats won more money for domestic programs. It was the sort of classic logroll hated by ideological purists but necessary in a democratic legislature.

Congressional Polarization Congress's frequent inability to decide reflects the deep ideological differences that separate the two parties. Efforts to measure the ideological distance between the two parties show that since the mid-1970s Republicans and Democrats have been diverging sharply and are now more polarized than at any time in the last century. Democrats have become more liberal and Republicans have become more conservative on issues related to the economy and the role of government.[37] The Republican Party has experienced the greatest ideological shift, becoming sharply more conservative. Moreover, because congressional districts are increasingly homogeneous in their ideology—in part due to gerrymandering but mainly because of natural clustering of the population—most members of Congress are in safe seats. Their constituents will not punish them for failing to compromise. Additionally, active mobilization by organizations on the right, such as the Club for Growth, means that Republican members of Congress who support compromises might be punished. These outside organizations have financed alternative candidates to challenge members who vote against the organizations' positions.

Much Congressional Energy Goes to Tasks Other Than Lawmaking

Describe Congress's influence over other branches of government

In addition to the power to make the law, Congress has at its disposal an array of other instruments through which to influence the process of government. The Constitution gives the Senate the power to approve treaties and appointments. And Congress has a number of other powers through which it can share with the other branches the capacity to administer the laws.

CONGRESS OVERSEES HOW LEGISLATION IS IMPLEMENTED

Oversight refers to the effort by Congress, through hearings, investigations, and other techniques, to exercise control over the activities of executive agencies. Oversight is carried out by committees or subcommittees of the Senate or the House, which conduct hearings and investigations to analyze and evaluate bureaucratic agencies and the effectiveness of their programs. Their purpose may be to locate inefficiencies or abuses of power, to explore the relationship between what an agency does and what a law intends, or to change or abolish a program. Most programs and agencies are subject to some oversight every year during the course of hearings on **appropriations**—that is, the amounts of money approved by Congress in statutes (bills) that each unit or agency of government can spend.

Committees or subcommittees have the power to subpoena witnesses, administer oaths, cross-examine, compel testimony, and bring criminal charges for contempt (refusing to cooperate) and perjury (lying). Hearings and investigations resemble each other in many ways, but they differ on one fundamental point. A hearing is usually held on a specific bill, and the questions asked there are usually intended to build a record with regard to that bill. In an investigation, the committee or subcommittee does not begin with a particular bill but examines a broad area or problem and then concludes its investigation with one or more proposed bills.

Oversight hearings can serve as political tools. When party control between Congress and the president is divided, Congress is more likely to investigate the executive branch than when party control is unified. The Select Committee on Benghazi, for example, formed in 2014 to investigate the deaths of four American diplomats in Libya, became enmeshed in partisan contention after Hillary Clinton—secretary of state during the attacks—announced that she would run for president. In 2015, as revelations emerged that Clinton had used a private email server during her tenure as secretary of state, the committee began to investigate whether appropriate procedures had been followed and whether national security was compromised.[38] When the FBI undertook an investigation into the matter in 2016, FBI director James Comey recommended no criminal charges against Clinton but also questioned her judgment and called her actions "extremely careless."[39] Almost as soon as Donald Trump took office in 2017, Democrats called for investigations into allegations that the Trump administration had colluded with Russian operatives to help Trump win the 2016 election. Democrats demanded the appointment of a special counsel. Over the course of the investigation, the special counsel indicted several close Trump aides for improper contacts with Russian officials. Four of Trump's former aides pleaded guilty to crimes related to the investigation.

SPECIAL SENATE POWERS INCLUDE ADVICE AND CONSENT

The Constitution has given the Senate a special power, one that is not based on law-making. The president has the power to make treaties and to appoint top executive officers, ambassadors, and federal judges—but only "with the Advice and Consent of the Senate" (Article II, Section 2). For treaties, two-thirds of senators present must concur; for appointments, a simple majority is required.

The power to approve or reject presidential requests includes the power to set conditions. The Senate only occasionally exercises its power to reject treaties and appointments, and usually that is when opposite parties control the Senate and the White House.

IMPEACHMENT IS THE POWER TO REMOVE TOP OFFICIALS

The Constitution also grants Congress the power of **impeachment** over the president, vice president, top executive branch officials, and judicial officials. To impeach means the House of Representatives charges a government official (president or otherwise) with "Treason, Bribery, or other high Crimes and Misdemeanors" and brings that person before Congress to determine guilt. Impeachment is thus like a criminal indictment in which the House of Representatives acts like a grand jury, voting (by simple majority) on whether the accused ought to be impeached. If a majority of the House votes to impeach, an impeachment trial is conducted in and by the Senate, which acts like a trial jury by voting whether to convict and remove the person from office (this vote requires a two-thirds majority of the Senate).

Controversy over Congress's impeachment power has arisen over the grounds for impeachment, especially the meaning of "high Crimes and Misdemeanors." It is generally understood that an impeachable offense could include commission of a crime, but also a non-criminal offense that constitutes an abuse of the powers of office. Some also note that "an impeachable offense is whatever the majority of the House of Representatives considers it to be at a given moment in history."[40] In other words, impeachment, especially impeachment of a president, is a political decision.

The political nature of impeachment was very clear in the two instances of presidential impeachment that have occurred in American history. In 1867, President Andrew Johnson, a southern Democrat who had battled a congressional Republican majority over Reconstruction, was impeached by the House but saved from conviction by one vote in the Senate. In 1998 the House of Representatives approved two articles of impeachment against President Bill Clinton, accusing him of lying under oath and obstructing justice during the investigation of his affair with White House intern Monica Lewinsky. The vote was highly partisan, with only five Democrats voting for impeachment on each charge. In the Senate, where a two-thirds majority was needed to convict the president, only 45 senators voted to convict on the first count of lying and 50 voted to convict on the second charge of obstructing justice. As in the House, the vote for impeachment was highly partisan, with all Democrats and only five Republicans supporting the president's ultimate acquittal.

Congress
WHAT DO WE WANT?

Much of this chapter has described the major institutional components of Congress and has shown how they work as Congress makes policy. But what do these institutional features mean for how Congress represents the American public? As we saw with Guy Berkebile and Hazel Hoffman at the beginning of the chapter, congressional actions—and inaction—have profound effects on Americans' lives. Does the organization of Congress promote the equal representation of all Americans? Or are there institutional features of Congress that allow some interests more access and influence than others? What can we learn from a tax cut that passes Congress and a CHIP reauthorization that almost fails?

When Congress is ineffective, American democracy suffers. As we have seen in this chapter, prolonged stalemates in Congress have led to a reduction in America's credit rating and a costly government shutdown. Moreover, Americans have lost confidence in Congress as it has lurched from crisis to crisis. Is it time for some major changes to make Congress work better? Disillusionment with congressional gridlock has led some to say that the United States should become a parliamentary system, where the winning party can enact the legislation it promised in its party platform. Such a system is more accountable to voters and less prone to stalemate. But Americans would have to jettison the presidency and become a unicameral body to operate as a true parliamentary system, like that of Britain.

Changes in the way Congress conducts its business could also promote more bipartisan decision-making. For example, former House Speaker John Boehner decided that he would only bring legislation to the floor if a majority of Republicans supported it. Speaker Paul Ryan also followed the same practice. The "Hastert rule," as this practice is called could easily be abandoned, allowing bipartisan majorities to enact legislation. Another significant change—eliminating the filibuster in the Senate—would heighten partisan differences but ease gridlock. As we have seen, the Senate voted to eliminate the filibuster for executive branch appointments and judicial candidates (except for the Supreme Court) in 2013. Abandoning the filibuster altogether would allow legislation to move more smoothly through the Senate. Will any of these changes—or other measures—be adopted? Each carries risks to political parties and to politicians. Yet, gridlock also carries political risks, as the public grows frustrated with congressional inaction on important policy areas. What areas of public policy might suffer if Congress continues its inability to decide? How politicians weigh these different choices will shape how—and whether—Congress fills its central position in American democracy.

Gridlock and bitter disagreements in Congress turn some Americans off to politics. However, as the core representative institution of government, Congress is supposed to represent all Americans. As the "**Who Participates?**" feature on the facing page shows, the electorate that turns out to vote for Congress is on average older, whiter, and more affluent than the average American.

Who Elects Congress?

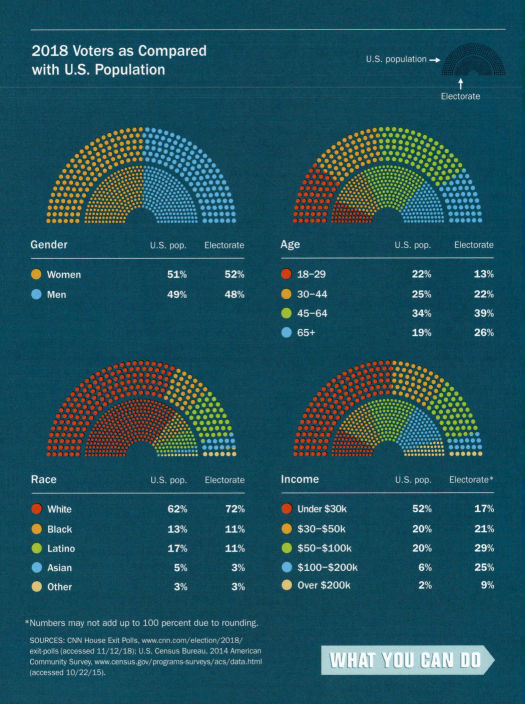

2018 Voters as Compared with U.S. Population

U.S. population →
↑ Electorate

Gender

	U.S. pop.	Electorate
🟠 Women	51%	52%
🔵 Men	49%	48%

Age

	U.S. pop.	Electorate
🔴 18–29	22%	13%
🟠 30–44	25%	22%
🟢 45–64	34%	39%
🔵 65+	19%	26%

Race

	U.S. pop.	Electorate
🔴 White	62%	72%
🟠 Black	13%	11%
🟢 Latino	17%	11%
🔵 Asian	5%	3%
🟡 Other	3%	3%

Income

	U.S. pop.	Electorate*
🔴 Under $30k	52%	17%
🟠 $30–$50k	20%	21%
🟢 $50–$100k	20%	29%
🔵 $100–$200k	6%	25%
🟡 Over $200k	2%	9%

*Numbers may not add up to 100 percent due to rounding.

SOURCES: CNN House Exit Polls, www.cnn.com/election/2018/exit-polls (accessed 11/12/18); U.S. Census Bureau, 2014 American Community Survey, www.census.gov/programs-surveys/acs/data.html (accessed 10/22/15).

WHAT YOU CAN DO ▶

★ WHAT YOU CAN DO ★

Know Your Members of Congress

 Vote in the next congressional election. If you haven't registered, see page 242 for instructions on how to do so.

 Discover what bills are currently under consideration in Congress by visiting **www.congress.gov**.

 Contact your member of Congress to state your opinion. Go to **www.house.gov** and enter your ZIP code to find your representative. Go to **www.senate.gov** and find your state in the drop-down menu to find your two U.S. senators.

★ STUDY GUIDE ★

Practice Quiz

1. Which of the following is a way in which the House and the Senate are different? *(p. 278)*
   a) Senators are more interested in doing what their constituents want right now, while members of the House have more time to consider "new ideas" and bring together new coalitions of interests.
   b) Members of the House are more interested in doing what their constituents want right now, while senators have more time to consider "new ideas" and to bring together new coalitions of interests.
   c) Senators serve smaller and more homogeneous constituencies than members of the House.
   d) Senators are often more attuned to the legislative needs of local interest groups than members of the House.
   e) There are no important differences between the House and the Senate.

2. Which type of representation is described when constituents have the power to hire and fire their representative? *(p. 278)*
   a) agency representation
   b) sociological representation
   c) philosophical representation
   d) ideological representation
   e) economic representation

3. Which of the following statements best describes the social composition of the U.S. Congress? *(pp. 279–80)*
   a) The majority of representatives do not have university degrees.
   b) Men and women are equally represented in Congress.
   c) Most members of Congress do not affiliate with any specific religion.
   d) The legal profession is the dominant career of most members of Congress prior to their election.
   e) The number of African American, Latino, and Asian American representatives has decreased over the last 20 years.

4. Which of the following is an advantage that incumbents have in winning re-election? *(p. 282)*
   a) Challengers are not legally allowed to spend more money campaigning than incumbents.
   b) Incumbents can provide constituency services during their tenure in office.
   c) Term limits for incumbents mean they always know when an election will be their last.
   d) The Supreme Court has ruled that a district cannot be redrawn while an incumbent remains in office.
   e) Incumbents have no advantage over challengers in winning office.

5. The Supreme Court has ruled that *(p. 285)*
   a) only the House of representatives has the constitutional authority to redraw congressional district lines
   b) race can be the predominant factor in drawing congressional districts.
   c) race cannot be the predominant factor in drawing congressional districts.
   d) states can forgo the redistricting process if they lose more than 10 percent of their population between censuses.
   e) only the Senate has the constitutional authority to redraw congressional district lines

6. An "earmark" is *(p. 286)*
   a) a rule in the House of Representatives that limits who can be heard during legislative debates.
   b) a congressional district drawn to advantage candidates from a certain racial or ethnic group.
   c) a law that grants some special privilege or exemption to a single individual.
   d) language inserted into a bill by a member of Congress that provides special benefits for the member of Congress's constituents.
   e) a weekly, informal meeting between members of Congress and their constituents.

7. Which of the following types of committees includes members of both the House and the Senate on the same committee? *(p. 291)*
   a) standing committee
   b) conference committee
   c) select committee
   d) All committees include both House members and senators.
   e) No committees include both House members and senators.

8. Which of the following statements about the filibuster is most accurate? *(p. 295)*
   a) The filibuster was first used in 1975.
   b) The votes of 67 senators are currently required to end a filibuster.
   c) The filibuster was used far more frequently in the 1930s and 1940s than it has been in the last two decades.
   d) Nominees for positions in the executive branch and the federal courts cannot currently be filibustered.
   e) Filibusters were declared unconstitutional by the Supreme Court in 2013.

9. Members of Congress take their constituents' views into account because *(p. 298)*
   a) the Supreme Court can invalidate laws passed without majority support in the public.
   b) interest groups are forbidden from lobbying during legislative votes.

c) most constituents pay close attention to what's going on in Congress at all times.

d) they worry that their voting record will be scrutinized at election time.

e) they can be impeached if they go against their constituents' policy preferences.

10. Which of the following is *not* a resource that party leaders in Congress use to create party discipline? *(p. 299)*
   a) leadership PACs
   b) committee assignments
   c) access to the floor
   d) the whip system
   e) party unity votes

11. An agreement between members of Congress to trade support for each other's bills is known as *(p. 302)*
   a) oversight.
   b) filibuster.
   c) logrolling.
   d) patronage.
   e) cloture.

12. Congressional polarization *(p. 303)*
   a) has decreased since the mid-1970s.
   b) has increased since the mid-1970s.
   c) has remained the same since the mid-1970s.
   d) has been driven entirely by Democrats becoming more liberal since the mid-1970s.
   e) has not been measured since the mid-1970s.

13. When Congress conducts an investigation to explore the relationship between what a law intended and what an executive agency has done, it is engaged in *(p. 304)*
   a) oversight.
   b) advice and consent.
   c) appropriations.
   d) executive agreement.
   e) direct patronage.

14. Which of the following statements about impeachment is *not* true? *(p. 305)*
   a) The president is the only official who can be impeached by Congress.
   b) Impeachment means to charge a government official with "Treason, Bribery, or other high Crimes and Misdemeanors."
   c) The House of Representatives decides by simple majority vote whether the accused ought to be impeached.
   d) The Senate decides whether to convict and remove the person from office.
   e) There have only been two instances of presidential impeachment in American history.

Key Terms

agency representation *(p. 278)* a type of representation in which a representative is held accountable to a constituency if he or she fails to represent that constituency properly; this is incentive for the representative to provide good representation when his or her personal backgrounds, views, and interests differ from those of his or her constituency

apportionment *(p. 283)* the process, occurring after every decennial census, that allocates congressional seats among the 50 states

appropriations *(p. 304)* the amounts of money approved by Congress in statutes (bills) that each unit or agency of government can spend

bicameral *(p. 277)* having a legislative assembly composed of two chambers or houses; distinguished from *unicameral*

bill *(p. 293)* a proposed law that has been sponsored by a member of Congress and submitted to the clerk of the House or Senate

caucus (political) *(p. 289)* a normally closed political party business meeting of citizens or lawmakers to select candidates, elect officers, plan strategy, or make decisions regarding legislative matters

cloture *(p. 295)* a rule or process in a legislative body aimed at ending debate on a given bill; in the U.S. Senate, 60 senators (three-fifths) must agree in order to impose a time limit and end debate

conference *(p. 289)* a gathering of House Republicans every two years to elect their House leaders; Democrats call their gathering the *caucus*

conference committees *(p. 291)* joint committees created to work out a compromise on House and Senate versions of a piece of legislation

constituency *(p. 277)* the residents in the area from which an official is elected

filibuster *(p. 295)* a tactic used by members of the Senate to prevent action on legislation they oppose by continuously holding the floor and speaking until the majority backs down; once given the floor, senators have unlimited time to speak, and it requires a vote of three-fifths of the Senate to end a filibuster

gerrymandering *(p. 285)* the apportionment of voters in districts in such a way as to give unfair advantage to one racial or ethnic group or political party

impeachment *(p. 305)* the formal charge by the House of Representatives that a government official has committed "Treason, Bribery, or other high Crimes and Misdemeanors"

incumbency *(p. 282)* holding the political office for which one is running

joint committees *(p. 291)* legislative committees formed of members of both the House and Senate

logrolling *(p. 302)* a legislative practice whereby agreements are made between legislators in voting for or against a bill; vote trading

majority leader *(p. 289)* the elected leader of the majority party in the House of Representatives or in the Senate; in the House, the majority leader is subordinate in the party hierarchy to the Speaker of the House

minority leader *(p. 289)* the elected leader of the minority party in the House or Senate

oversight *(p. 304)* the effort by Congress, through hearings, investigations, and other techniques, to exercise control over the activities of executive agencies

party unity vote *(p. 299)* a roll-call vote in the House or Senate in which at least 50 percent of the members of one party take a particular position and are opposed by at least 50 percent of the members of the other party

patronage *(p. 286)* the resources available to higher officials, usually opportunities to make partisan appointments to offices and to confer grants, licenses, or special favors to supporters

pocket veto *(p. 297)* a presidential veto that is automatically triggered if the president does not act on a given piece of legislation passed during the final 10 days of a legislative session

pork-barrel legislation (or pork) *(p. 286)* appropriations made by legislative bodies for local projects that are often not needed but that are created so that local representatives can win re-election in their home districts

private bill *(p. 287)* a proposal in Congress to provide a specific person with some kind of relief, such as a special exemption from immigration quotas

redistricting *(p. 284)* the process of redrawing election districts and redistributing legislative representatives; this happens every 10 years to reflect shifts in population or in response to legal challenges to existing districts

roll-call vote *(p. 299)* a vote in which each legislator's yes-or-no vote is recorded as the clerk calls the names of the members alphabetically

select committees *(p. 290)* (usually) temporary legislative committees set up to highlight or investigate a particular issue or address an issue not within the jurisdiction of existing committees

seniority *(p. 291)* the ranking given to an individual on the basis of length of continuous service on a committee in Congress

sociological representation *(p. 278)* a type of representation in which representatives have the same racial, gender, ethnic, religious, or educational backgrounds as their constituents. It is based on the principle that if two individuals are similar in background, character, interests, and perspectives, then one can correctly represent the other's views

Speaker of the House *(p. 289)* the chief presiding officer of the House of Representatives; the Speaker is the most important party and House leader and can influence the legislative agenda, the fate of individual pieces of legislation, and members' positions within the House

standing committee *(p. 289)* a permanent committee with the power to propose and write legislation that covers a particular subject, such as finance or agriculture

term limits *(p. 283)* legally prescribed limits on the number of terms an elected official can serve

veto *(p. 297)* the president's constitutional power to prevent a bill from becoming a law; a presidential veto may be overridden by a two-thirds vote of each house of Congress

whip *(p. 289)* a party member in the House or Senate responsible for coordinating the party's legislative strategy, building support for key issues, and counting votes

For Further Reading

Deering, Christopher, and Steven S. Smith. *Committees in Congress*. 3rd ed. Washington, DC: CQ Press, 1997.

Dodd, Lawrence, and Bruce I. Oppenheimer, eds. *Congress Reconsidered*. 11th ed. Washington, DC: CQ Press, 2016.

Dodson, Debra L. *The Impact of Women in Congress*. New York: Oxford University Press, 2006.

Fenno, Richard F. *Homestyle: House Members in Their Districts*. Boston: Little, Brown, 1978.

Fiorina, Morris. *Congress: Keystone of the Washington Establishment*. 2nd ed. New Haven, CT: Yale University Press, 1989.

Fisher, Louis. *On Appreciating Congress*. Boulder, CO: Paradigm Publishers, 2010.

Koger, Gregory. *Filibustering: A Political History of Obstruction in the House and Senate*. Chicago: University of Chicago Press, 2010.

Mann, Thomas E., and Norman J. Ornstein. *It's Even Worse Than It Looks: How the American Constitutional System Collided with the New Politics of Extremism*. New York: Basic Books, 2012.

Mayhew, David R. *Congress: The Electoral Connection*. New Haven, CT: Yale University Press, 1974.

Palmer, Barbara, and Denise Simon. *Breaking the Political Glass Ceiling: Women and Congressional Elections*. 2nd ed. New York: Routledge, 2008.

Sinclair, Barbara. *Unorthodox Lawmaking*. 5th ed. Washington, DC: CQ Press, 2016.

Spitzer, Robert J. *President and Congress*. New York: McGraw-Hill, 1993.

Tate, Katherine. *Concordance: Black Lawmaking in the U.S. Congress from Carter to Obama*. Ann Arbor: University of Michigan Press, 2014.

The Presidency

WHAT GOVERNMENT DOES AND WHY IT MATTERS Kevin Hartley of Tennessee was 21 years old in April 2017 when he collapsed and died from cardiac arrest after using methylene chloride to strip paint from a bathtub during a renovation job. Although the chemical was associated with dozens of deaths dating back to the 1940s, the Environmental Protection Agency, established in 1970, had lacked the regulatory teeth to remove such widely available products from the market. Wendy Cleland-Hamnett, the EPA's top official overseeing pesticides and toxic chemicals, lamented, "How is it possible that you can go to a home improvement store and buy a paint remover that can kill you?"[1]

In summer 2016, Congress passed and President Obama signed a reform of the Toxic Substances Control Act of 1976, giving the EPA more power to regulate toxic chemicals. Passed with bipartisan support, the new law required the EPA to evaluate both new and existing chemicals, including the ten most toxic chemicals in wide use. In the last days of the Obama administration in January 2017, after ten years of research, the

While presidents inherit policies and regulations implemented during previous administrations, they are empowered to reverse or alter them according to their beliefs. As a former businessman, President Trump rejected the regulations put in place by the Obama administration that could put restraints on some businesses.

EPA proposed banning certain uses of methylene chloride, especially by ordinary consumers and non-industrial businesses.

But as presidential administrations switched from Obama to Trump, these new rules remained mere proposals. As a candidate Donald Trump said that he wanted to eliminate two regulations for every one that his agencies enacted. And when the Trump administration took office in January 2017, it froze rules and proposed regulations across government, including those at the EPA. Kevin Hartley died three months later.

The Trump EPA did release new rules about toxic chemicals in the summer of 2017. They were written by Nancy Beck, a toxicologist who, between stints at the EPA under Presidents George W. Bush and Trump, had worked for the American Chemistry Council, contesting EPA regulations over what she called "phantom risks." The new rules reflected changes that had been requested by the chemical industry and did not include a ban on methylene chloride. The new leadership at the EPA also overturned Ms. Hamnett's recommendation to ban the use of the pesticide chlorpyrifos, associated with developmental disabilities in children, and undermined tracking of the health effects of a chemical once used in nonstick pans associated with birth defects and kidney cancer. Recognizing that the agency's leadership was going in a different direction, Hamnett, who had worked for the EPA since 1979, under presidents of both parties, announced her retirement. "It's time for me to go." In the face of continued public concern over toxic paint strippers, then-EPA head Scott Pruitt indicated in May 2018 that the agency would implement the methylene chloride ban. But months of inaction passed, and in October 2018 a coalition of consumer groups threatened to sue the EPA for delaying the ban after four more people died.

In this chapter, we examine the foundations of the American presidency and assess the origins and character of presidential power. Presidents are empowered by democratic political processes and, increasingly, by their ability to control and expand the institutional resources of the office. They sit atop the executive branch, a large bureaucracy of departments and agencies such as the EPA. They influence policy with their appointments to the Cabinet, the White House staff, and to the Executive Office of the President, choosing officials who are sympathetic to their policy goals and using regulatory review as with the EPA and executive orders to make policy. They set the tone for government as well, as the sole elected official representing the entire country. But, as we will see, presidential power is not without limit, nor should it be. The U.S. Constitution emphasizes checks and balances among the branches of government, not unlimited power. The framers thought a powerful and energetic president would make the U.S. government more effective but knew that presidential power needed to be subject to constraints to prevent it from becoming a threat to citizens' liberties.

CHAPTER GOALS

★ Outline the powers the Constitution gives the president (pp. 317–27)

★ Identify the institutional resources presidents have to help them exercise their powers (pp. 327–31)

★ Explain how modern presidents have become even more powerful (pp. 331–40)

Presidential Power Is Rooted in the Constitution

The presidency was established by Article II of the Constitution, which begins by asserting "The executive power shall be vested in a President of the United States of America." The president's executive power is underscored in Section 3 of Article II, which confers upon the president the duty to "take care that the laws be faithfully executed." The president's oath of office at the end of Section 1, moreover, obligates—and thus empowers—the chief executive to "preserve, protect and defend the Constitution of the United States." This language seems to require the president to take action if constitutional government is threatened. President Abraham Lincoln cited his oath of office as justification for suspending the writ of habeas corpus at the start of the Civil War. He declared that his oath would be broken if the government was overthrown. Suspension of the writ, he said, was necessary to prevent that calamity from taking place. By vesting the executive power in the president, Article II also implies that the president serves as America's head of state and is, therefore, entitled to special deference and respect. On the basis of Article II, presidents have three types of powers. These are called the

Abraham Lincoln, like many other presidents, cited the presidential oath of office as providing the president with the authority to take all the necessary actions to protect the nation.

expressed powers of the office, implied powers, and delegated powers. A fourth type of power claimed by presidents does not appear in Article II. This is called the inherent power of the office.

EXPRESSED POWERS COME DIRECTLY FROM THE WORDS OF THE CONSTITUTION

The **expressed powers** of the presidency are those specifically established by the language of the Constitution. These fall into several categories:

1. *Military.* Article II, Section 2, provides for the power as "Commander in Chief of the Army and Navy of the United States, and of the Militia of the several States, when called into the actual Service of the United States."

2. *Judicial.* Article II, Section 2, also provides the power to "grant Reprieves and Pardons for Offenses against the United States, except in Cases of Impeachment."

3. *Diplomatic.* Article II, Section 2, also provides the power "by and with the Advice and Consent of the Senate, to make Treaties." Article II, Section 3, provides the power to "receive Ambassadors and other public Ministers."

4. *Executive.* Article II, Section 3, authorizes the president to see to it that all the laws are faithfully executed; Section 2 gives the chief executive the power to appoint, remove, and supervise all executive officers and to appoint all federal judges.

5. *Legislative.* Article I, Section 7, and Article II, Section 3, give the president the power to participate authoritatively in the legislative process.

Military The president's military powers are among the most important exercised by the chief executive. The position of **commander in chief** makes the president the highest military authority in the United States, with control of the entire defense establishment. The president also directs the nation's intelligence network, which includes not only the Central Intelligence Agency (CIA) but also the National Security Council (NSC), the National Security Agency (NSA), the Federal Bureau of Investigation (FBI), and a host of less well-known but very powerful international and domestic security agencies.

Military Sources of Domestic Power The president's military powers extend into the domestic sphere. Article IV, Section 4, provides that the "United States shall [protect] every State . . . against Invasion . . . and . . . domestic Violence," and Congress has made this an explicit presidential power through statutes directing the president as commander in chief to discharge these obligations.[2] The Constitution restrains the president's use of domestic force by providing that a state legislature (or governor, when the legislature is not in session) must request federal troops before the president can send them into the state to provide public order. Yet this proviso is not absolute. First, presidents are not obligated to deploy national troops merely because the state legislature or governor makes such a request. More important, the

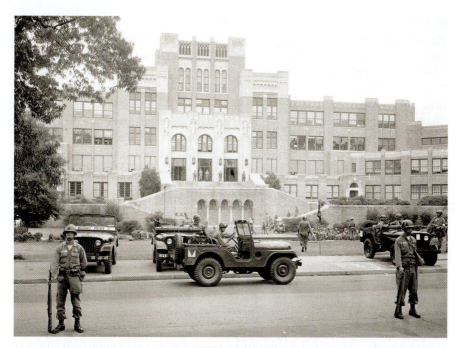

One of the president's responsibilities is the maintenance of public order. President Eisenhower used this to justify sending troops to Little Rock, Arkansas, to enforce racial integration of public schools.

president may deploy troops in a state or city without a specific request from the state legislature or governor if the president considers it necessary to maintain an essential national service during an emergency, enforce a federal judicial order, or protect federally guaranteed civil rights.

One example of the unilateral use of presidential emergency power, even when the state didn't request it, was the decision by President Dwight Eisenhower in 1957 to send troops into Little Rock, Arkansas, to enforce court orders to integrate Little Rock's Central High School. The governor of Arkansas, Orval Faubus, had actually posted the Arkansas National Guard at the entrance of Central High School to prevent the court-ordered admission of nine black students. After an effort to negotiate with Governor Faubus failed, President Eisenhower reluctantly sent 1,000 paratroopers to Little Rock, who stood watch while the black students took their places in the all-white classrooms.

In most instances of domestic disorder, whether from human or from natural causes, presidents sometimes exercise unilateral power by declaring a "state of emergency," as President Trump did in response to the three hurricanes striking the United States in 2017, thereby making available federal grants, insurance, and direct aid.

Judicial The presidential power to grant reprieves, pardons, and amnesty involves the power of life and death over all individuals who may be a threat to the security of the United States. Presidents may use this power on behalf of a particular individual, as did Gerald Ford when he pardoned Richard Nixon in 1974 "for all offenses against the United States which he . . . has committed or may have committed." Or they may use it on a large scale, as did President Andrew Johnson in 1868, when he gave full amnesty to all southerners who had participated in the "Late Rebellion." Presidents' use of the pardon power can be very controversial. President Trump was criticized for pardoning former Arizona sheriff Joe Arpaio in 2017 after Arpaio was found guilty in federal court of criminal contempt for ignoring a court order that directed his office to halt illegal racial profiling practices. The pardon was criticized because Trump did not first consult with the Justice Department's office of pardons, as is customary, and because it was issued before Arpaio had been sentenced.[3]

Diplomatic The president is America's "head of state," its chief representative in dealings with other nations, having the power to make treaties for the United States (with the advice and consent of the Senate) as well as the power to "recognize" other countries. Diplomatic recognition means that the United States acknowledges a government's legitimacy and territorial claims. In 2015, President Obama restored American diplomatic ties with Cuba, which had been severed by President Eisenhower in 1961 after the United States' relations with the Castro regime deteriorated. In 2017, after several staffers at the U.S. embassy in Cuba demonstrated neurological symptoms after being exposed to strange sounds, some blamed these "sonic attacks" on the Cuban government, which prompted President Trump to revisit newly restored American ties with Cuba. In 2018, President Trump met with North Korean leader Kim Jong-un in an effort to defuse tensions on the Korean Peninsula. Earlier in the year North Korea and America had exchanged threats in the wake of North Korean nuclear missile tests.

In recent years, presidents have expanded the practice of using executive agreements instead of treaties to establish relations with other countries.[4] An **executive agreement** is exactly like a treaty because it is a contract between two countries that has the force of a treaty, but it does not require Senate approval. Ordinarily, executive agreements are used to carry out commitments already made in treaties or laws or to arrange for matters well below the level of policy. But when presidents have found it expedient to use an executive agreement in place of a treaty, Congress has typically acquiesced.

As the head of state, the president is America's chief representative in dealings with other countries. Here, President Trump meets with North Korea's Supreme Leader Kim Jong-un in 2018 to discuss nuclear disarmament on the Korean Peninsula.

Executive Power The most important basis of the president's power as chief executive is to be found in Article II, Section 3, which stipulates that the president must see that all the laws are faithfully executed, and

Section 2, which provides that the president will appoint and supervise all executive officers and appoint all federal judges (with Senate approval; after some early controversy, presidents' sole power to remove executive branch officials was accepted). The power to appoint the principal executive officers and to require each of them to report to the president on subjects relating to the duties of their departments makes the president the true chief executive officer (CEO) of the nation. In this manner, the Constitution focuses executive power and legal responsibility on the president. The president is subject to some limitations because the appointment of all such officers, including ambassadors, ministers, and federal judges, is subject to majority approval by the Senate. But these appointments are at the discretion of the president, and these appointees are generally loyal to the president.

Legislative Power Two constitutional provisions are the primary sources of the president's power in the legislative arena. The first of these is the provision in Article II, Section 3, that the president "shall from time to time give to the Congress Information of the State of the Union, and recommend to their Consideration such Measures as he shall judge necessary and expedient."

Delivering a State of the Union address may at first appear to be little more than the president's obligation to make recommendations for Congress's consideration. But as political and social conditions began to favor an increasingly prominent presidential role, each president began to rely on this provision in order to become the primary initiator of proposals for congressional action and the principal source for public awareness of national issues.[5]

The second of the president's legislative powers is the veto power assigned by Article I, Section 7.[6] The **veto** power is the president's constitutional power to prevent a bill from becoming a law (see Figure 10.1). It makes the president the single most important legislative leader.[7] No bill vetoed by the president can become law unless both the House and the Senate override the veto by a two-thirds vote. In the case of a **pocket veto**, Congress does not have the option of overriding the veto but must reintroduce the bill in the new Congress. A pocket veto is a presidential veto that is automatically triggered if the president does not act on a given piece of legislation passed during the final 10 days of a legislative session. Usually, if a president does not sign a bill within 10 days, it automatically becomes law. But this is true only while Congress is in session. If a president chooses not to sign a bill presented within the last 10 days of a legislative session and Congress is out of session when the 10-day limit expires such that returning the bill to Congress is not possible, the bill is vetoed and dies.

Use of the veto varies according to the political situation each president confronts. Ten of President Obama's 12 vetoes occurred during his last two years in office, when Republicans held the majority in both Houses. The veto power is effective: more than 90 percent of all vetoes in history have been upheld.

Although not explicitly stated, the Constitution implies that the president has the power of **legislative initiative**—the president's implied power to bring a legislative agenda before Congress. *Initiative* implies the ability to formulate proposals

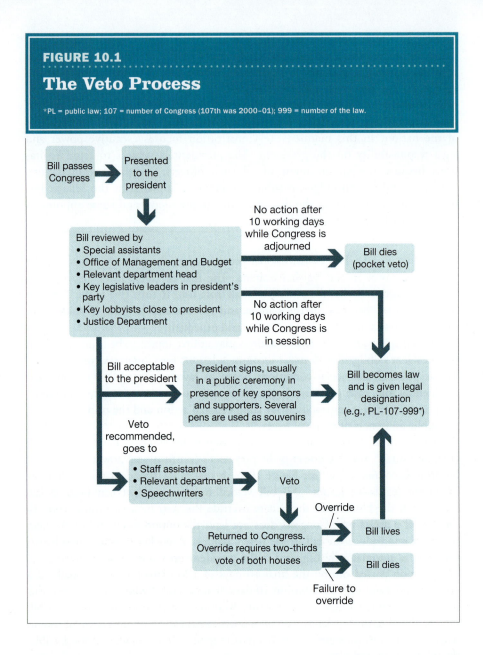

FIGURE 10.1

The Veto Process

*PL = public law; 107 = number of Congress (107th was 2000–01); 999 = number of the law.

Bill passes Congress → Presented to the president

Bill reviewed by
- Special assistants
- Office of Management and Budget
- Relevant department head
- Key legislative leaders in president's party
- Key lobbyists close to president
- Justice Department

No action after 10 working days while Congress is adjourned → Bill dies (pocket veto)

No action after 10 working days while Congress is in session

Bill acceptable to the president → President signs, usually in a public ceremony in presence of key sponsors and supporters. Several pens are used as souvenirs → Bill becomes law and is given legal designation (e.g., PL-107-999*)

Veto recommended, goes to
- Staff assistants
- Relevant department
- Speechwriters
→ Veto

Returned to Congress. Override requires two-thirds vote of both houses

Override → Bill lives

Failure to override → Bill dies

for important policies, and the president, as an individual with a great deal of staff assistance, is able to initiate decisive action more frequently than Congress, with its large assemblies that have to deliberate and debate before taking action. With some important exceptions, Congress depends on the president to set the agenda of public policy. For example, during the weeks following September 11, 2001, George W. Bush took many presidential initiatives to Congress, and each was given nearly unanimous support.

IMPLIED POWERS DERIVE FROM EXPRESSED POWERS

The list of expressed presidential powers is brief, but each expressed power has become the foundation of a second set of presidential powers, the so-called **implied powers** of the office. An implied power is one that can be said to be necessary to allow presidents to exercise their expressed power. For example, the Constitution expressly gives the president the power to appoint "all other officers of the United States . . . which shall be established by law." Article II does not, however, expressly grant the president the power to remove such officials from office. There is no reason to assume that the power to appoint necessarily indicates the power to remove an official. From the earliest years of the Republic, though, presidents claimed that the removal power was implied by the appointment power. The Supreme Court eventually agreed that presidents did have sole removal power.

Presidents have also made much of the very first sentence of Article II, which declares, "The executive power shall be vested in a President of the United States of America." This grant of power along with the subsequent admonition to presidents to see to it that the laws are faithfully executed, as well as the president's oath of office, have been cited by successive White Houses as justifications for actions not expressly sanctioned by the Constitution.

In recent years, the vesting clause has been said by some to support what has come to be known as the "theory of the unitary executive."[8] Unitary executive theory holds that all executive power inheres in the president except as explicitly limited by the Constitution.[9] Thus, according to this view, the president is subject only to expressly stated restraints, such as Congress's control of revenues, its impeachment power, and its power to override presidential vetoes. Proponents of unitary executive theory also maintain that presidents have their own power to interpret the Constitution as it applies to the executive branch and need not necessarily defer to the judiciary. This claim was advanced by President George W. Bush when he signed a Defense Appropriation Bill that included language introduced by Senator John McCain barring the use of torture on terrorist suspects. In his signing statement, Bush declared that he would construe the portion of the Act relating to the treatment of detainees "in a manner consistent with the constitutional authority of the President to supervise the unitary executive branch and as Commander in Chief and consistent with the constitutional limitations on the judicial power."[10] The president was claiming, in other words, that particularly in the military realm, he possessed sole authority to execute acts of Congress according to his own understanding of the law.

Unitary executive theory particularly holds that the president controls all policy making by the executive branch, and that neither Congress nor the courts may intervene. But the principle of constitutional checks and balances would appear to provide Congress with powers over the many important agencies of the executive branch through "congressional oversight" of the executive arising from Congress's Article I powers. Thus, the stage is set for conflict between the implied powers of Congress and those of the president.

DELEGATED POWERS COME FROM CONGRESS

Many of the powers exercised by the president and the executive branch are not found in the Constitution but are **delegated powers**, the products of congressional statutes (laws) and resolutions. Over the past century, Congress has voluntarily delegated a great deal of its own legislative authority to the executive branch. This delegation of power has been an almost inescapable consequence of the expansion of government activity in the United States since the New Deal. Given the vast range of the federal government's responsibilities, Congress cannot execute and administer all the programs it creates and the laws it enacts. Inevitably, Congress must turn to the hundreds of departments and agencies in the executive branch or, when necessary, create new agencies to implement its goals. Thus, for example, in 2002, when Congress sought to protect America from terrorist attacks, it established the Department of Homeland Security with broad powers in the realms of law enforcement, public health, and immigration.

MODERN PRESIDENTS HAVE CLAIMED INHERENT POWERS

Presidents have claimed a fourth source of power beyond expressed, implied, and delegated powers. These are powers not specified in the Constitution but said to stem from the "rights, duties and obligations of the presidency." They are referred to as the **inherent powers** and are most often asserted by presidents in times of war or national emergency.

President Lincoln relied upon a claim of inherent power to raise an army after the fall of Fort Sumter. Similarly, Presidents Roosevelt (World War II), Truman (Korean War), and both Presidents Bush (Persian Gulf and Middle East Wars) claimed inherent powers to defend the nation. Since the Korean War, presidents have used their claim of inherent powers along with their constitutional power as Commander in Chief to bypass the constitutional provision giving Congress the power to declare war. Congress declared war after the Japanese attack on Pearl Harbor on December 7, 1941. Since that time, American forces have been sent to fight foreign wars on more than one hundred occasions but not once was Congress asked for a Declaration of War. In 1973, Congress passed the **War Powers Resolution** designed to restore its role in military policy. Presidents, however, have regarded the resolution as an improper limitation on the inherent powers of the presidency and have studiously ignored the provisions of the War Powers Resolution.

No president has acted so frequently on the basis of inherent powers as President George W. Bush. He claimed that the inherent powers of the presidency gave him the authority to create military commissions, designate U.S. citizens as enemy combatants, engage in "extraordinary renditions" of captured suspects who would be moved to unknown facilities in unnamed countries for interrogation, and authorize the National Security Agency (NSA) to monitor phone conversations between the United States and other nations.[11] When challenged, some but not all of these actions were overturned by the courts. These decisions hardly put to rest the idea of inherent power. Indeed, President Obama continued to rely on the concept of

Executive Branches in Comparison

All democracies have an executive branch, but the specific form it takes varies. In presidential systems such as the United States', the position of the *head of state* (the symbolic leader of a country) and the *head of government* (the leader in charge of the day-to-day running of the government) is combined into one position—the president. In parliamentary systems, these roles are often held by different people, with the head of government being the more powerful position. For example, in Germany, the head of government is the prime minister (called the chancellor), while the head of state is the president, who plays a largely ceremonial role similar to the United Kingdom's queen.

Most democracies use parliamentary executive systems, though presidential systems are common in the Americas, in part due to the historical influence of the United States. A small but growing group of countries use a hybrid "semi-presidential" system. France, for instance, divides the executive between a powerful head of state (the president) and the head of government (the prime minister), who have different but (theoretically) equal powers.

	PRESIDENTIAL	PARLIAMENTARY
Examples	United States, Mexico, Brazil	United Kingdom, India, Germany, Japan
Executive title	President	Prime Minister, Chancellor, etc.
Is the executive the . . .		
Head of state?	Yes	No
Head of government?	Yes	Yes
Executive elected by . . .	voters*	parliament
Term in office	Fixed by law	Subject to support of the parliament
Separation of powers	Yes	No; the PM is a member of the parliament
Executive role in legislating	Veto power	Initiates most bills

*In the United States, the president is elected by the Electoral College, not by the voters directly. Other presidential systems have the voters directly elect the president.

inherent power in ordering drone strikes against suspected terrorists and ordering American air strikes in Libya. In 2017, President Trump's order banning travelers from several Muslim countries was based mainly on a claim that the president had the inherent power to bar any class of immigrants whom he thought to be a threat to the United States.

Congress has endeavored to place some limits on powers that presidents claim to be inherent. One example is the case of emergency powers. Though presidents believe they have the inherent power to deal with emergencies, Congress has, by statute, sought to circumscribe and guide the use of these powers. Under the 1976 National Emergencies Act, the president is authorized to declare a national emergency in the event of major threats to the United States' national security or economy.[12] An emergency declaration relating to foreign threats allows the president to embargo trade, seize foreign assets, and prohibit transactions with whatever foreign nations are involved. During a state of emergency, constitutional rights, including the right of habeas corpus, may be suspended. An emergency declaration, however, remains in force for only one year unless it is renewed by the president. Congress may, by a joint resolution of the two houses, terminate a state of emergency.

A closely related area in which Congress has sought to regulate matters that presidents tend to view as involving their own inherent power is the nation's response to natural disasters. Under the 1988 Stafford Act, the governor of a state affected by a disastrous flood, hurricane, earthquake, or other calamitous event must ask the Federal Emergency Management Agency for a determination that the scope of the

Congress has tried to limit presidential power in the area of disaster relief, however presidents view disaster response as an inherent executive power. President Trump sent troops to Puerto Rico in 2017 in the aftermath of Hurricane Maria.

disaster is beyond the abilities of state and local authorities to handle. The president may then declare a disaster and make the state eligible for federal funds and relief. The purpose of the Stafford Act was to ensure that presidential disaster declarations were governed by statutory criteria. In recent years, however, critics have charged that presidential determinations and funding authorizations seemed, nevertheless, to be driven by political motivations.[13]

Institutional Resources of Presidential Power Are Numerous

> **Identify the institutional resources presidents have to help them exercise their powers**

Constitutional sources of power are not the only resources available to the president. Presidents have at their disposal a variety of other formal and informal resources that have important implications for their ability to govern (see Figure 10.2). Collectively, these individuals could be said to make up the institutional presidency and to give the president a capacity for action that no single individual, however energetic, could duplicate. The first component of the institutional presidency is the president's Cabinet.

THE CABINET IS OFTEN DISTANT FROM THE PRESIDENT

In the American system of government, the **Cabinet** is the traditional but informal designation for the heads of all the major federal government departments. Cabinet secretaries are appointed by the president with the consent of the Senate. The Cabinet has no constitutional status. Unlike in Great Britain and many other parliamentary countries, where the cabinet *is* the government, the American Cabinet meets but makes no decisions as a group. The Senate must approve each appointment, but Cabinet members are responsible to the president, not to the Senate or to Congress at large, although Congress may require cabinet secretaries and their deputies to testify before congressional committees. Since Cabinet appointees generally have not shared political careers with the president or one another and since they may meet literally for the first time only after their selection, the formation of an effective governing group out of this diverse collection of appointments is highly unlikely.

THE WHITE HOUSE STAFF CONSTITUTES THE PRESIDENT'S EYES AND EARS

The **White House staff** is composed mainly of analysts and advisers who are closest to, and most responsive to, the president's needs and preferences.[14] Although many of the top White House staff members hold such titles as "adviser to the president," "assistant to the president," "deputy assistant," and "special assistant" for a particular task or sector, the judgment and advice they are supposed to provide are a good deal broader and more generally political than those coming from the

FIGURE 10.2

The Institutional Presidency

THE WHITE HOUSE STAFF

Includes:
  Chief of Staff
  Press Secretary
  Senior Advisers
  Special Assistants

INDEPENDENT AGENCIES AND GOVERNMENT CORPORATIONS

Includes:
  Central Intelligence Agency
  Environmental Protection Agency
  Federal Labor Relations Authority
  General Services Administration

THE PRESIDENT

THE CABINET

Department of Agriculture
Department of Commerce
Department of Defense
Department of Education
Department of Energy
Department of Health and
    Human Services
Department of Homeland Security
Department of Housing and
    Urban Development
Department of the Interior
Department of Justice
Department of Labor
Department of State
Department of Transportation
Department of the Treasury
Department of Veterans Affairs

EXECUTIVE OFFICE OF THE PRESIDENT

Council of Economic Advisers
Council on Environmental Quality
National Security Council
Office of Administration
Office of Management and
    Budget
Office of National Drug
    Control Policy
Office of Science and Technology Policy
Office of the United States Trade
    Representative
President's Intelligence Advisory Board
    and Intelligence Oversight Board
White House Military Office
White House Office

Executive Office of the President or from the cabinet departments. The members of the White House staff also tend to be more closely associated with the president than are other presidentially appointed officials. They are appointed directly by the president and do not need to win Senate approval.

THE EXECUTIVE OFFICE OF THE PRESIDENT IS A VISIBLE SIGN OF THE MODERN STRONG PRESIDENCY

The **Executive Office of the President (EOP)** is a major part of what is often called the "institutional presidency"—the permanent agencies that perform defined management tasks for the president. Created in 1939, the EOP is composed of between

1,500 and 2,000 highly specialized people who work for EOP agencies. The most important and largest EOP agency is the Office of Management and Budget (OMB). Its roles in preparing the national budget, designing the president's program, reporting on agency activities, and overseeing regulatory proposals make OMB personnel part of virtually every conceivable presidential responsibility. The status and power of the OMB have grown in importance with each successive president. The process of budgeting at one time was a "bottom-up" procedure, with expenditure and program requests passing from the lowest bureaus through the departments to "clearance" in the OMB and hence to Congress, where each agency could be called in to reveal what its "original request" was before the OMB revised it. Now the budgeting process is "top-down": the OMB sets priorities for agencies as well as for Congress.

The staff of the Council of Economic Advisers (CEA) constantly analyzes the economy and economic trends and attempts to give the president the ability to anticipate events rather than waiting for and reacting to them. The Council on Environmental Quality was designed to do for environmental issues what the CEA does for economic issues. The National Security Council (NSC) is composed of designated cabinet officials and others spanning military, diplomatic, and intelligence areas who meet regularly with the president to give advice on national security matters. Other EOP agencies perform more specialized tasks.

THE VICE PRESIDENCY HAS BECOME MORE IMPORTANT SINCE THE 1970S

The vice presidency is a constitutional anomaly even though the Constitution created the office along with the presidency. The vice president exists for two purposes only: to succeed the president in case of death, resignation, or incapacity and to preside over the Senate, casting a tie-breaking vote when necessary.[15]

The main value of the vice president as a political resource for the president is electoral. Traditionally, presidential candidates choose running mates who can win the support of at least one state (preferably a large one) not otherwise likely to support the ticket. It is very doubtful that John Kennedy would have won in 1960 without his vice-presidential candidate, Texan Lyndon Johnson, and the contribution Johnson made to winning his home state. Another rule holds that the vice-presidential nominee should provide some regional balance and, wherever possible, some balance among various ideological or ethnic subsections of the party. In 2016, Donald Trump chose Governor Mike Pence of Indiana as his running mate for a number of reasons. First, Pence, a former host of conservative radio and television talk shows, was well known among conservatives. His radio and television background also meant that Pence was an experienced public speaker. Second, Pence served in Congress for 12 years. He worked to reassure skeptical party leaders that Trump was a qualified candidate. Third and most important, Pence is a devout Christian who is very well regarded by social conservatives. As vice president, Pence is often the person Trump relies on to smooth relations with Republican members of Congress.

Mike Pence, who served as a member of Congress and then governor of Indiana, is devoutly Christian and socially conservative. He helped improve Donald Trump's electoral appeal among social conservatives and establishment Republicans.

The vice president is also important because, in the event of the death or incapacity of the president, he or she will succeed to the nation's highest office. During the course of American history, eight vice presidents have had to replace presidents who died in office. One vice president, Gerald Ford, found himself at the head of the nation when President Richard Nixon was forced to resign as a result of the Watergate scandal.

THE FIRST SPOUSE HAS BECOME IMPORTANT TO POLICY

The president serves as both chief executive and chief of state—the equivalent of Great Britain's prime minister and monarch rolled into one, simultaneously leading the government and representing the nation at official ceremonies and functions.

Because they are generally associated with the head-of-state aspect of America's presidency, presidential spouses are usually not subject to the same degree of media scrutiny or partisan attack as the president. Traditionally, most first ladies have limited their activities to the ceremonial portion of the presidency. First ladies greet foreign dignitaries, visit other countries, and attend important national ceremonies.

Some first spouses, however, have had considerable influence over policy. Franklin Roosevelt's wife, Eleanor, was widely popular but also widely criticized for her active role in many elements of her husband's presidency. During the 1992 campaign, Bill Clinton often implied that his wife would be active in the administration; he joked that voters would get "two for the price of one." After the election, Hillary Clinton took a leading role in many policy areas, most notably heading the administration's health care reform effort. She also became the first first lady to win public office on her own, winning a seat in the U.S. Senate from New York in 2000. She also ran for the presidency in 2008 and 2016, having served in between as Barack Obama's secretary of state. Melania Trump is the first foreign-born first lady in almost 200 years. With no political or public affairs experience, Mrs. Trump said that she would be a traditional first lady. Given the current expectation that the first spouse should assume some public responsibility, however, Mrs. Trump has taken on a limited public role in the Trump administration.

Party, Popular Mobilization, and Administration Make Presidents Stronger

> **Explain how modern presidents have become even more powerful**

During the nineteenth century, Congress was America's dominant institution of government, and members of Congress sometimes treated the president with disdain. Today, however, no one would assert that the presidency is unimportant. Presidents seek to dominate the policy-making process and claim the inherent power to lead the nation in time of war. The expansion of presidential power over the course of the past century has come about not by accident but as the result of an ongoing effort by successive presidents to enlarge the powers of the office.

Generally, presidents can expand their power in two ways: through popular mobilization and through the administration. First, presidents may use popular appeals to create a mass base of support that will allow them to dominate their political foes, a tactic called "going public."[16] Second, presidents may seek to bolster their control of established executive agencies or to create new administrative institutions and procedures that will reduce their dependence on Congress and give them a more independent governing and policy-making capability. Perhaps the most obvious example of this is the use of executive orders to achieve policy goals in lieu of seeking to persuade Congress to enact legislation.

Presidents do have a third possible tool: their political party. Each president has relied on his own party to implement his legislative agenda. In 2009–10, for example, President Obama relied on congressional Democrats to prevent rejection of his agreement with Iran to pass the Affordable Care Act in the face of virtually unanimous Republican opposition. However, the president does not control his party; party members have considerable autonomy. President Trump has often been unable to rally Republican legislators to his cause, and the Republican congressional delegations were so divided that it was unclear whether GOP leaders could mobilize a majority for any set of programs. Moreover, in America's system of separated powers, the president's party may be in the minority in Congress and unable to do much for the chief executive's programs. Consequently, although their party is valuable to chief executives, it has not been a fully reliable presidential tool. As a result, contemporary presidents are more likely to use the two other methods, popular mobilization and executive administration, to achieve their political goals.

GOING PUBLIC MEANS TRYING TO WHIP UP THE PEOPLE

During the nineteenth century, it was considered inappropriate for presidents to engage in personal campaigning on their own behalf or in support of programs and policies. When Andrew Johnson broke this unwritten rule and made a series of speeches vehemently seeking public support for his Reconstruction program, even some of Johnson's most ardent supporters were shocked at what they saw as his lack of decorum and dignity. The president's opponents cited his "inflammatory" speeches in one of the articles of impeachment drafted by the Congress pursuant to the first impeachment trial of a president in history.[17]

In the twentieth century, though, popular mobilization became a favored weapon in the political arsenals of most presidents. Among modern presidents, the one who used public appeals most effectively was Franklin Delano Roosevelt (FDR). FDR was "firmly persuaded of the need to form a direct link between the executive office and the public."[18] He developed a number of tactics aimed at forging such a link. He made important use of the new electronic medium, the radio, to reach millions of Americans. In his famous "fireside chats," the president, or at least his voice, came into every living room in the country to discuss programs and policies and generally to assure Americans that he was aware of their difficulties and working diligently toward solutions.

FDR was also an innovator in the realm of what is now called press relations. When he entered the White House, FDR faced a mainly hostile press typically controlled by conservative members of the business establishment. As the president wrote, "All the fat-cat newspapers—85 percent of the whole—have been utterly opposed to everything the Administration is seeking."[19] FDR hoped to use the press to mold public opinion, but to do so he needed to circumvent the editors and publishers who were generally unsympathetic to his goals. To this end, he worked to cultivate the reporters who covered the White House. FDR made himself available for biweekly press conferences, where he offered candid answers to reporters' questions and made certain to make important policy announcements that would provide the reporters with significant stories for their papers.[20]

Every president since FDR has sought to craft a public-relations strategy that would emphasize the incumbent's strengths and maximize his popular appeal. For John F. Kennedy, handsome and quick-witted, the televised press conference was an excellent public-relations vehicle. Both Bill Clinton and Barack Obama made extensive use of televised town meetings—carefully staged events that gave the presidents an opportunity to appear to consult with rank-and-file citizens about goals and policies without having to face pointed questions preferred by reporters. President Obama was a talented and effective speaker who often relied on his own speaking abilities rather than material crafted by the Communications Office.

Going Public Online President Obama was also the first to make full use of the internet as a communication medium. Drawing on the interactive tools of the web, Obama's 2008 and 2012 campaigns changed the way politicians organize supporters, advertise to voters, defend against attacks, and communicate with their constituents.[21] In the 2016 presidential campaign, candidates Hillary Clinton and especially Donald Trump made particular use of Twitter to communicate with millions of voters, bypassing traditional media.

The internet has changed not only the way modern presidents campaign but also how they govern. The WhiteHouse.gov website keeps the president's constituents abreast of his policy agenda with a weekly streaming video address by the president, press briefings, speeches and remarks, a daily blog, photos of the president, the White House schedule, and other information. Virtually everything the president does is recorded online. YouTube aired Obama's press conferences and public appearances on a daily basis. Every presidential address is now streamed live online.

Donald J. Trump ✔
@realDonaldTrump

Follow ⌄

We must not let #CrookedHillary take her CRIMINAL SCHEME into the Oval Office. #DrainTheSwamp

12:20 PM - 28 Oct 2016 from Manchester, NH

Over the last century, presidents and candidates have made more and more use of direct appeals to the American people. President Franklin Roosevelt made effective use of radio to build public support for his programs. Donald Trump has likewise used Twitter to promote his message, both as a candidate and as president.

Circumventing television and other traditional media, the internet allows the president to reach citizens directly. First as a candidate and then as president, Donald Trump has transformed the use of Twitter. Every Trump legislative initiative and policy direction, as well as political controversy, includes a flurry of tweets endlessly repeated by the broadcast and print media. Trump's language seems tailored to the Twitter age. Calling North Korean leader Kim Jong-un "Little Rocket Man" in his tweets allowed Trump to boil down his sense of contempt and harsh posture toward North Korea into a tweet-sized threat to use force.

The Limits of Going Public Some presidents have been able to make effective use of popular appeals to overcome congressional opposition. Popular support, though, has not been a firm foundation for presidential power. The public is notoriously fickle. President George W. Bush maintained an approval rating of over 70 percent for more than a year following the September 11, 2001, terrorist attacks. By the end of 2005, however, Bush's approval rating had dropped to 39 percent as a result of the growing unpopularity of the Iraq War, the administration's inept handling of hurricane relief, and several White House scandals, including the conviction of Vice President Cheney's chief of staff on charges of lying to a federal grand jury. Between the time President Obama took office in 2009 and May 2016, his public approval ranged from a high of 76 percent in January 2009 to a low of 36 percent in the fall of 2014.[22] Such declines in popular approval during a president's term in office are nearly inevitable and follow a predictable pattern.[23] Presidents generate popular support by promising to undertake important programs that will contribute directly to the well-being of large numbers of Americans. Almost without exception, presidential performance falls short of promises and popular expectations, leading to a decline in public support and the ensuing weakening of presidential influence.[24] It is a rare American president, such as Bill Clinton, who exits the White House more popular than when he went in. President Trump was saddled with unprecedentedly low public approval from the start of his presidency.

THE ADMINISTRATIVE STRATEGY INCREASES PRESIDENTIAL CONTROL

Contemporary presidents have increased the administrative capabilities of their office in four ways. First, they have enhanced the reach and power of the EOP. Second, they have sought to increase White House control over the federal bureaucracy. Third, they have expanded the role of executive orders. Fourth, they have made frequent use of signing statements and other instruments of direct presidential governance. Taken together, these four components of what might be called the White House "administrative strategy" have given presidents a capacity to achieve their programmatic and policy goals even when they are unable to secure congressional approval. Indeed, some recent presidents have been able to accomplish a great deal with remarkably little congressional, partisan, or even public support.

The Executive Office of the President The EOP has grown from six administrative assistants in 1939 to today's several hundred employees working directly for the president in the White House office, along with some 2,500 individuals staffing the divisions of the Executive Office.[25] The creation and growth of the White House staff give the president an enormously enhanced capacity to gather information, plan programs and strategies, communicate with constituencies, and exercise supervision over the executive branch. The staff multiplies the president's eyes, ears, and arms, becoming a critical instrument of presidential power.[26]

In particular, the OMB serves as a potential instrument of presidential control over federal spending and hence a mechanism through which the White House has greatly expanded its power. In addition to its power over the federal budget process (discussed earlier), the OMB has the capacity to analyze and approve all legislative proposals, not only budgetary requests, emanating from all federal agencies before they are submitted to Congress. This procedure, now a matter of routine, greatly enhances the president's control over the entire executive branch. All legislation originating in the White House and all executive orders also go through the OMB.[27] Thus, through one White House agency, the president has the means to exert major influence over the flow of money and the shape and content of national legislation.

Regulatory Review A second tactic that presidents have used to increase their power and reach is the process of regulatory review, through which they have sought to seize control of rule making by the agencies of the executive branch (see also Chapter 11). Whenever Congress enacts a statute, the statute's actual implementation requires the promulgation of hundreds of rules by the agency charged with administering the law and giving effect to the will of Congress. For example, if Congress wishes to improve air quality, it must delegate to an agency—say the Environmental Protection Agency—the power to establish numerous rules and regulations that will govern the actions of the government agencies, firms, and individuals whose conduct may have an impact upon the atmosphere. The agency rule-making process is, itself, governed by a number of statutory requirements concerning public notice, hearings, and appeals, but once completed, administrative rules have the effect of law and will be enforced by the federal courts.

The discretion Congress delegates to administrative agencies has provided recent presidents with an important avenue for expanding their own power. During his administration, President Clinton issued 107 directives to administrators, ordering them to propose specific rules and regulations. In some instances, the language of the rule to be proposed was drafted by the White House staff; in other cases, the president asserted a priority but left it to the agency to draft the precise language of the proposal. President George W. Bush continued the Clinton-era practice of issuing presidential directives to agencies to spur them to issue new rules and regulations. The Obama administration not only issued a number of major regulatory directives to federal agencies but also launched a "look back" program. Under this program, the administration sought to eliminate several hundred existing rules it deemed obsolete.[28] In 2015, Obama sought new regulations governing power plant emissions, overtime pay for workers, the educational practices of career (for-profit) colleges, and a host of other matters. President Trump moved aggressively to reverse these and other directives by issuing new rules or repealing existing ones to roll back environmental regulations, reduce banking regulations, eliminate workplace safety regulations, and remove protections for transgender workers, among others. Most notably, in the first year of his presidency, Trump eliminated nearly 70 environmental regulations.[29]

Governing by Decree: Executive Orders and Memoranda

Another mechanism through which contemporary presidents have sought to enhance their power to govern unilaterally is the use of executive orders and other forms of presidential decrees, including executive agreements, memoranda, national security findings and directives, proclamations, reorganization plans, signing statements, and a host of other tools.[30]

An **executive order** is a direct presidential directive to the bureaucracy to undertake some action, bypassing Congress and the legislative process. Executive orders have a long history in the United States and have been the instruments for a number of important policies including the purchase of Louisiana, the annexation of Texas, the emancipation of the slaves, the wartime internment of Japanese Americans, the desegregation of the military, the initiation of affirmative action, and the creation of a number of federal agencies including the Environmental Protection Agency, the Food and Drug Administration, and the Peace Corps.[31]

Presidential use of executive orders is constrained by law. When presidents issue executive orders, in principle they do so pursuant to the powers granted to them by the Constitution or delegated to them by Congress. When presidents issue orders they generally must state the constitutional or statutory basis for their actions. Historically, executive orders were most often used during times of war or national emergency. In recent years, though, executive orders have become routine instruments of presidential governance rather than emergency wartime measures (Figure 10.3). In the first seven years of his presidency, Barack Obama issued 242 executive orders and 219 presidential memoranda, using some of them to reverse executive orders of his predecessor (just as Bush reversed some of those of the Clinton years). Obama's executive orders authorized stem cell research, restored funding for international family planning organizations, opened access to presidential papers, enhanced federal gun regulations, and barred improper interrogation methods of detainees captured by the United States.[32] In 2014, Obama issued executive orders that would protect some 4 million undocumented immigrants from the threat of deportation. President Trump rescinded most of Obama's orders on immigration and opened the way for the deportation of those who had been protected by Obama's orders. Trump also issued a number of orders, including a controversial "travel ban" decree seeking to prevent travelers from several majority-Muslim countries from entering the United States. Trump's orders led to a number of lawsuits, but the Supreme Court ultimately upheld the ban.

Executive orders are one form of presidential decree. Others include administrative orders, national security directives, presidential memoranda, presidential

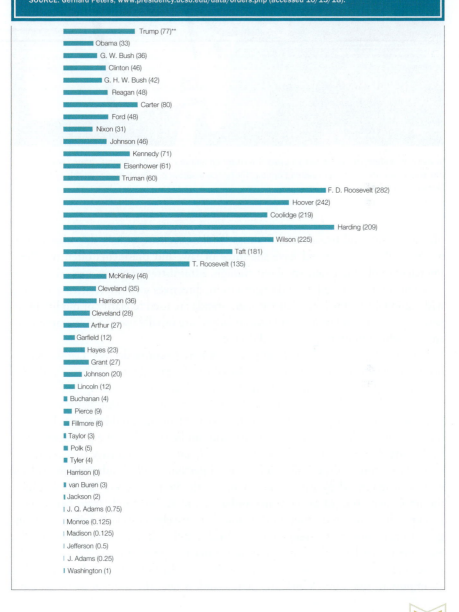

FIGURE 10.3

Presidential Executive Orders*

Executive orders are a tool presidents have for influencing policy. Their use has varied considerably over time. Each bar in the graph shows the average number of executive orders each president issued per year in office. Which presidents issued the most executive orders? What events in U.S. history were occurring when those presidents were in office?

*Does not include memoranda or other forms of executive action
**As of October 2018.
SOURCE: Gerhard Peters, www.presidency.ucsb.edu/data/orders.php (accessed 10/15/18).

Trump (77)**
Obama (33)
G. W. Bush (36)
Clinton (46)
G. H. W. Bush (42)
Reagan (48)
Carter (80)
Ford (48)
Nixon (31)
Johnson (46)
Kennedy (71)
Eisenhower (61)
Truman (60)
F. D. Roosevelt (282)
Hoover (242)
Coolidge (219)
Harding (209)
Wilson (225)
Taft (181)
T. Roosevelt (135)
McKinley (46)
Cleveland (35)
Harrison (36)
Cleveland (28)
Arthur (27)
Garfield (12)
Hayes (23)
Grant (27)
Johnson (20)
Lincoln (12)
Buchanan (4)
Pierce (9)
Fillmore (6)
Taylor (3)
Polk (5)
Tyler (4)
Harrison (0)
van Buren (3)
Jackson (2)
J. Q. Adams (0.75)
Monroe (0.125)
Madison (0.125)
Jefferson (0.5)
J. Adams (0.25)
Washington (1)

In 2017, President Trump signed an Executive Order on health care. The administration claimed this would provide patients expanded options for health insurance, though many felt this order would undermine the stability of Obamacare.

proclamations, and presidential findings.[33] Like executive orders, the other instruments establish policy and have the force of law, and presidents often use them interchangeably. Generally speaking, though, administrative orders apply to matters of administrative procedure and organization; directives seem most often associated with national or homeland security; memoranda are used to clarify or modify presidential positions and orders; and proclamations are usually used to give emphasis to an especially important presidential decree.

Congress is not entirely without power vis à vis executive decrees. Legislators can overturn presidential orders that were based on the president's legislative authority (as opposed to constitutional authority) through legislation declaring that the order "shall not have legal effect," or through actually repealing the statute on which the order was based. Efforts to overturn the orders of sitting presidents are, however, hindered by the fact that any such legislation can be vetoed by the president. Thus, two-thirds of the members of both houses of Congress would have to agree to the move. One study indicates that only about 4 percent of all presidential orders have ever been rescinded by legislation.[34] Usually, the best Congress can do is inhibit the implementation of an executive order by preventing funds from being spent to implement the order, though this, too, is relatively unusual.[35] Failure by Congress to act, moreover, strengthens the legal validity of a presidential order. The Supreme Court has held that congressional inaction tends to validate an order by indicating congressional "acquiescence" in the president's decision.[36] This idea raises an important question. Many presidential orders take the form of secret national security directives and findings of which Congress is unaware. Can Congress be said to acquiesce in presidential decisions made without its knowledge?

Signing Statements To negate congressional actions to which they object, recent presidents have made frequent and calculated use of presidential **signing statements**.[37] The signing statement is an announcement made by the president at the time of signing a congressional enactment into law, often presenting the president's interpretation of the law in addition to the usually innocuous remarks about the many benefits the law will bring the nation. Occasionally presidents have used signing statements to point to sections of the law they deem improper or even unconstitutional and to instruct executive branch agencies how to execute the law.[38] In 2013, for example, President Obama signed a bill containing a provision requiring the president to notify Congress before transferring any prisoner from Guantánamo Bay. In his signing statement, Obama declared that the provision was unconstitutional and ignored the legislation.

PRESIDENTIAL POWER HAS LIMITS

From the Constitution, presidents derive expressed, implied, and delegated powers. Claims of inherent powers are derived from the basic principles of national sovereignty. But, while the framers sought an energetic executive, they were also concerned that executive power could be abused and might stifle citizens' liberties. To guard against this possibility, the framers contrived a number of checks on executive power. The president's term is limited to four years, though with the possibility of reelection (since 1951, presidents may only be elected twice). The Congress is empowered to impeach and remove the president, to reject presidential appointments and refuse to ratify treaties, to refuse to enact laws requested by the president, to deny funding for the president's programs, and to override presidential vetoes of congressional enactments.

The framers viewed the threat of impeachment as an important check upon executive power. The Constitution provides that a president may be impeached for "high crimes and misdemeanors." Such offenses are to be charged by the House and tried in the Senate, with the Chief Justice presiding and a two-thirds vote needed for conviction. Only two presidents, Andrew Johnson and Bill Clinton, have been impeached, though neither was convicted. A third president, Richard Nixon, would almost certainly have been impeached for his misdeeds in the Watergate affair, but Nixon chose to resign to avoid the impeachment process.

The requirement that the Senate concur in treaties and presidential appointments was seen by the framers as another important check on executive power. However, in recent years severe partisan disagreements have led presidents to resort to "recess appointments." These are authorized by Article II, Section 2, which states, "The President shall have power to fill up all Vacancies that may happen during the Recess of the Senate, by granting Commissions which shall expire at the End of their next Session." Until recent years, recess appointments were made only between Senate sessions or when the Senate was adjourned for lengthy periods. In recent years, however, recess appointments have become more frequent and the Senate has resorted to a strategy similar to the one employed to prevent pocket vetoes. One senator is assigned the task of calling the chamber to order for a few moments every day for a pro forma session during periods of recess so that the president cannot claim the Senate was closed for business. This procedure was found constitutional by the Supreme Court.

And, of course, under the Constitution, only the Congress has the power to enact legislation or to levy taxes or to appropriate funds. Indeed, so many were the constitutional checks on executive power that some delegates to the Constitutional Convention feared that the executive would be too weak and the potential energy of executive power lost. As we can see, however, from the many actions of presidents in recent years, presidential power has grown significantly beyond the framers' vision.

The Presidency
WHAT DO WE WANT?

The framers of the Constitution created a system of government in which the Congress and the executive branch were to share power. At least since the New Deal of the 1930s, however, the powers of Congress have waned, whereas those of the presidency have expanded. There is no doubt that Congress continues to be able to confront presidents and even, on occasion, hand the White House a sharp rebuff.

In the larger view, however, presidents' occasional defeats, however dramatic, have to be seen as temporary setbacks in a gradual but decisive shift toward increased presidential power. Louis Fisher, a leading authority on the separation of powers, recently observed that in what are arguably the two most important policy arenas, national defense and the federal budget, the powers of Congress have been in decline for at least the past 50 years.[39]

What might the growth of presidential power mean for students reading this book today? It might mean that policies they favor can more easily become the law of the land. Congress works slowly, while the president can work quickly—making law by the stroke of a pen. Presidential strength works both ways, however: for those who oppose a particular policy or have qualms about some aspect of it, the stroke of the presidential pen might seem hasty and autocratic. The consequences can even be deadly, as we saw in the chapter opener when a ban on a toxic chemical is at stake.

A powerful presidency, a weak Congress, and a partially apathetic electorate make for a dangerous mix. Who we vote into the office of the president matters. The "**Who Participates?**" feature on the facing page shows who voted for Donald Trump in 2016.

Who Voted for Donald Trump in 2016?

Age

18–29	30–44	45–64	65+
37% 55%	42% 50%	53% 44%	53% 45%

Race

White	African American	Hispanic	Asian American	Other
58% 37%	8% 88%	29% 65%	29% 65%	37% 56%

Income

<$50,000	$50,000–$99,999	$100,000+
41% 52%	50% 46%	48% 47%

Sex

Men	Women
53% 41%	42% 54%

Legend:
- Trump
- Clinton
- Other candidates

SOURCE: "2016 Election Exit Polls," *Washington Post*, November 10, 2016, www.washingtonpost.com/graphics/politics/2016-election/exit-polls/ (accessed 11/10/16).

WHAT YOU CAN DO

★ WHAT YOU CAN DO ★

Contact the White House

 After he or she is elected, the president is expected to represent all Americans. Ask a question or share your view on a policy with the president and White House staff via **www.whitehouse.gov/contact**.

 Create a petition at **http://petitions.whitehouse.gov** regarding an issue you care about, and try to get as many signatures as possible.

 Watch a few recent presidential speeches, including this year's State of the Union address, on YouTube. Share your views with your fellow students, friends, and family.

★ STUDY GUIDE ★

Practice Quiz

1. Which article of the Constitution describes the basic powers of the presidency and the means of selecting presidents? *(p. 317)*
   a) Article I
   b) Article II
   c) Article III
   d) Article IV
   e) Article V

2. Executive agreements are exactly like treaties except that *(p. 320)*
   a) executive agreements involve only domestic, not international, affairs.
   b) the Constitution explicitly mentions the president's ability to make executive agreements.
   c) executive agreements do not require the Senate's approval.

   d) executive agreements are ordinarily used to carry out commitments not already made in treaties or laws.
   e) executive agreements require a two-thirds approval vote in the Senate.

3. What are the requirements for overriding a presidential veto? *(p. 321)*
   a) 50 percent plus one vote in both houses of Congress
   b) two-thirds vote in both houses of Congress
   c) two-thirds vote in the Senate only
   d) three-fourths vote in both houses of Congress
   e) A presidential veto cannot be overridden by Congress.

4. The Supreme Court has ruled that
   (p. 323)
   a) the power to remove executive appointees belongs exclusively to the Senate.
   b) the power to remove executive appointees belongs exclusively to the House of Representatives.
   c) the power to remove executive appointees belongs exclusively to the president.
   d) the power to remove executive appointees belongs exclusively to the federal judiciary.
   e) executive appointees cannot be removed from office under any circumstance.

5. The War Powers Resolution of 1973 was an act passed by Congress that *(p. 324)*
   a) required the CIA to collect intelligence on all Americans born in a foreign country.
   b) outlawed presidential use of executive agreements.
   c) created the National Security Council.
   d) granted the president the authority to declare war.
   e) allowed the president to send American troops into action abroad only if Congress had granted an authorization to use force or if military personnel were already under attack.

6. Which of the following statements about presidential declarations of national emergency is *not* accurate? *(p. 326)*
   a) Presidents can only declare a state of national emergency in response to foreign threats after receiving the approval of Congress.
   b) Once the president has declared a state of national emergency, constitutional rights, including the right of habeas corpus, may be temporarily suspended.
   c) A declaration of national emergency in response to foreign threats allows the president to embargo trade, seize foreign assets, and prohibit transactions with whatever foreign nations are involved.

   d) Declarations of national emergency remain in force for only one year unless they are renewed by the president.
   e) Congress may, by a joint resolution of the two houses, terminate a declaration of national emergency.

7. Approximately how many people work for agencies within the Executive Office of the President? *(p. 329)*
   a) 25 to 50
   b) 500 to 750
   c) 1,500 to 2,000
   d) 4,500 to 5,000
   e) over 10,000

8. The EOP agency responsible for preparing the national budget, designing the president's program, and overseeing regulatory proposals is called *(p. 329)*
   a) the Office of Management and Budget.
   b) the National Security Council.
   c) the Council of Economic Advisers.
   d) the Congressional Budget Office.
   e) the Bureau of Economic Analysis.

9. Which of the following statements about vice presidents is not true? *(pp. 329–30)*
   a) The vice president succeeds the president in case of death, resignation, or incapacitation.
   b) The vice president casts the tie-breaking vote in the Senate when necessary.
   c) The vice president also serves as an honorary member of the Supreme Court.
   d) Eight vice presidents have had to replace American presidents who died in office.
   e) Presidential candidates typically select a vice-presidential candidate who is likely to bring the support of a state that would not otherwise support the ticket.

10. What are two primary ways that presidents can expand their power? *(p. 331)*
    a) avoiding popular appeals and loosening their control of executive agencies

b) using popular appeals and bolstering their control of executive agencies

c) using popular appeals and loosening their control of executive agencies

d) avoiding popular appeals and bolstering their control of executive agencies

e) weakening national partisan institutions and bolstering their control of executive agencies

11. The Environmental Protection Agency and the Food and Drug Administration were created through the use of (p. 336)
a) a pocket veto.
b) a signing statement.

c) an executive agreement.
d) an executive order.
e) executive privilege.

12. When the president makes an announcement about his interpretation of a congressional enactment that he is signing into law, it is called (p. 339)
a) a signing statement.
b) a line-item veto.
c) an executive order.
d) legislative initiative.
e) executive privilege.

Key Terms

Cabinet (p. 327) the secretaries, or chief administrators, of the major departments of the federal government; Cabinet secretaries are appointed by the president with the consent of the Senate

commander in chief (p. 318) the role of the president as commander of the national military and the state National Guard units (when called into service)

delegated powers (p. 324) In the Tenth Amendment to the Constitution, delegated powers are described as those granted by the Constitution to the federal government; however, the term has commonly come to be used more broadly to refer to constitutional powers that are assigned to one government agency but exercised by another with the express permission of the first

executive agreement (p. 320) an agreement, made between the president and another country, that has the force of a treaty but does not require the Senate's "advice and consent"

Executive Office of the President (EOP) (p. 328) the permanent agencies that perform defined management tasks for the president; created in 1939, the EOP includes the OMB, the CEA, the NSC, and other agencies

executive order (p. 336) a rule or regulation issued by the president that has the effect and formal status of legislation

expressed powers (p. 318) specific powers granted by the Constitution to Congress (Article I, Section 8) and to the president (Article II); the term *expressed powers* was coined by Chief Justice John Marshall

inherent powers (p. 324) powers claimed by a president that are not expressed in the Constitution but are inferred from it

implied powers (p. 323) powers derived from the necessary and proper clause of Article I, Section 8, of the Constitution; such powers are not specifically expressed but are implied through the expansive interpretation of delegated powers

legislative initiative (p. 321) the president's implied power to bring a legislative agenda before Congress

pocket veto (p. 321) a presidential veto that is automatically triggered if the president does not act on a given piece of legislation passed during the final 10 days of a legislative session

signing statements *(p. 339)* announcements made by the president when signing bills into law, often presenting the president's interpretation of the law

veto *(p. 321)* the president's constitutional power to prevent a bill from becoming a law; a presidential veto may be overridden by a two-thirds vote of each house of Congress

War Powers Resolution *(p. 324)* a resolution of Congress that the president can send troops into action abroad only by authorization of Congress or if American troops are already under attack or serious threat

White House staff *(p. 327)* analysts and advisers to the president, each of whom is often given the title "special assistant"

For Further Reading

Crouch, Jeffrey P. *The Presidential Pardon Power.* Lawrence: University Press of Kansas, 2009.

Dodds, Graham. *Take Up Your Pen: Unilateral Presidential Directives in American Politics.* Philadelphia: University of Pennsylvania Press, 2013.

Fisher, Louis. *Constitutional Conflicts between President and Congress.* 6th ed. Lawrence: University Press of Kansas, 2014.

Fisher, Louis. *The Law of the Executive Branch.* New York: Oxford University Press, 2014.

Genovese, Michael, and Robert J. Spitzer. *The Presidency and the Constitution.* New York: Palgrave/Macmillan, 2005.

Ginsberg, Benjamin. *Presidential Government.* New Haven, CT: Yale University Press, 2016.

Han, Lori Cox, and Diane Heith. *Presidents and the American Presidency*, 2nd ed. New York: Oxford University Press, 2017.

Kernell, Samuel. *Going Public: New Strategies of Presidential Leadership.* 4th ed. Washington, DC: CQ Press, 2006.

Neustadt, Richard E. *Presidential Power: The Politics of Leadership from Roosevelt to Reagan.* Rev. ed. New York: Free Press, 1990.

Spitzer, Robert J. *The Presidential Veto: Touchstone of the American Presidency.* Albany: State University of New York Press, 1988.

Tulis, Jeffrey K. *The Rhetorical Presidency.* Princeton, NJ: Princeton University Press, 2017.

Bureaucracy

WHAT GOVERNMENT DOES AND WHY IT MATTERS Lee Ann Walters couldn't figure out what was wrong with her 4-year-old twins. They had just moved to a new house in Flint, Michigan, and had rashes all over their bodies. One doctor thought it was contact dermatitis, another eczema. Yet another doctor suspected scabies, but tests were negative. Then Walters had an epiphany: every time her sons swam in the kiddie pool in the yard, or took a bath, the rash flared up. She told her family to stop drinking the tap water, which was orange-brown even after running through a filter she had installed.

That was December 2014. Eight months earlier, the cash-strapped city of Flint, under a state-appointed emergency manager, had switched its water supply to save money. Rather than draw water from the Detroit system, the city switched to the Flint River, which had been an industrial dumping ground for years. Walters had the city test her tap water: the lead count was 104 parts per billion; the legal limit is 15. A follow-up test a week later revealed a lead count of 397 parts per billion. Flint's utility administrator told her not to use the water. Lead exposure can cause developmental delays and disability in children. The damage is permanent.

Government bureaucracies affect ordinary Americans in countless ways. The Flint water crisis, exposed by Lee Ann Walters, demonstrates how the failures of bureaucracy on every level of government can affect citizens' lives directly.

Walters discovered from an EPA official that in switching to the Flint River, city officials had failed to add anti-corrosive chemicals to the water despite a federal regulation requiring corrosion control. Running through old pipes, the untreated river water was leaching lead into the drinking supply. An official from Michigan's Department of Environmental Quality assured the EPA official that there was corrosion control in place. Meanwhile, the city had been testing for lead, but telling residents to flush their water before collecting their samples and retesting in houses where the initial lead levels were low, not high.[1]

Finally, in January 2016, in the face of growing outcry from city residents, researchers, and advocates such as the ACLU, the EPA declared a state of emergency in Flint and took over lead testing in the city. In March 2016 the Flint Water Advisory Task Force issued its final report. The report cited a "series of government failures" at all levels: the local water department rushed to switch the water supply without corrosion control; the state departments of environmental quality and health and human services ignored mounting evidence of unsafe water; the federal EPA delayed enforcement of the Safe Water Drinking Act and Lead and Copper Rule; and the governor's office failed to reverse the poor decisions of the emergency manager and state agencies despite the urgings of senior staff members.[2]

When bureaucracies work well, we barely notice. But when they fail, the results can be truly alarming, like the Flint crisis, or the September 11, 2001, terror attacks, widely viewed as a failure of the national security bureaucracy.[3] Such failures play into Americans' ambivalence about the role of government. Some disasters prompt politicians to promise that they will slash the bureaucracy, while others result in an increase in the bureaucracy, like the creation of the federal Department of Homeland Security after September 11, 2001. Each instance raises a number of questions: Should the bureaucracy be smaller or larger? How can it become more efficient and effective? How can the bureaucracy be made more responsive to the needs of the American people?

CHAPTER GOALS

★ Define bureaucracy, and describe the basic features of the executive branch (pp. 349–55)

★ Describe the major goals we expect federal agencies to promote (pp. 355–63)

★ Explain why it is often difficult to control the bureaucracy (pp. 363–67)

Bureaucracy Exists to Improve Efficiency

> **Define bureaucracy, and describe the basic features of the executive branch**

Although Congress, the president, and the courts may garner more attention in the American system as they make policy, the **bureaucracy** plays a crucial role in administering public policy on the ground. Bureaucrats carry out the normal work of government, implementing the policies that Congress and the President have passed and that the court system may have adjudicated. The teachers you had in elementary school, the Social Security officer who approved your grandmother's retirement pension, the air traffic controller who guided the plane on your last vacation, the engineers who designed the roads that carried you to class, and the inspector who approved the meat in this morning's breakfast sausage are all bureaucrats.

Both routine and exceptional tasks require the organization, specialization, and expertise found in bureaucracies. To provide these services, government bureaucracies employ specialists such as meteorologists, doctors, and scientists. To do their job effectively, these specialists require resources and tools (ranging from paper to complex computer software); they have to coordinate their work with others (e.g., traffic engineers must communicate with construction engineers); and there must be effective outreach to the public (e.g., doctors must be made aware of health warnings). Bureaucracy is a means of coordinating the many different parts that must work together to provide useful services.

BUREAUCRATS FULFILL IMPORTANT ROLES

Congress is responsible for making the laws, but in most cases legislation only sets the broad parameters for government action. Bureaucracies are responsible for filling in the blanks by determining how the laws should be implemented. This requires bureaucracies to draw up much more detailed rules that guide the process of **implementation** (the efforts of departments and agencies to translate laws into specific bureaucratic rules and actions) and to play a key role in enforcing the laws. Congress needs the bureaucracy to engage in rule making and implementation for several reasons. One is that bureaucracies employ people who have much more specialized expertise in specific policy areas than do members of Congress. Decisions about how to achieve many policy goals—from managing the national parks to regulating air quality to ensuring a sound economy—rest on the judgment of specialized experts. A second reason that Congress needs bureaucracy is that because updating legislation can take many years, bureaucratic flexibility can ensure that laws are administered in ways that take new conditions into account. Finally, members of Congress often prefer to delegate politically difficult decisions to bureaucrats.

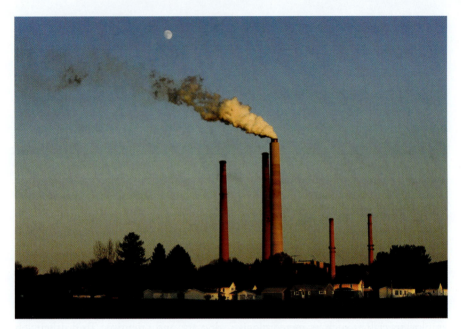

An example of bureaucratic rules that affect Americans both positively and negatively are the regulations set forth by the Environmental Protection Agency (EPA). When President Obama extended the EPA's authority to regulate greenhouse gas emissions in 2014, many people applauded the benefits to the environment, but at the same time, thousands lost jobs because of the new rules.

Bureaucrats Make Rules One of the most important things that government agencies do is issue rules that provide more detailed and specific indications of what a given congressional policy will actually mean. For example, the Clean Air Act empowers the Environmental Protection Agency (EPA) to assess whether current or projected levels of air pollutants pose a threat to public health, to identify whether motor vehicle emissions are contributing to such pollution, and to create rules designed to regulate these emissions. After the Supreme Court ruled in 2007 that the EPA had the authority to regulate auto emissions, including "greenhouse gases" like carbon dioxide that contribute to climate change, the agency in the Obama administration imposed new emission standards for automobiles, which would raise the average per-vehicle fuel economy for new vehicles to 35.5 miles per gallon starting in 2016, a standard later boosted to 54.4 miles per gallon by 2025.[4] In 2014 the EPA extended its reach to regulate factories and power plants that emit greenhouse gases. Especially controversial was the Clean Power Plan, which required power plants to reduce greenhouse gas emissions by 32 percent by 2030. The plan never went into effect due to lawsuits filed by a number of states, and in 2017 the head of the EPA in the Trump administration repealed the plan.[5]

Once a new law is passed, the agency studies the legislation and proposes a set of rules to guide implementation. These proposed rules are then open to comment by anyone who wishes to weigh in. Representatives for the regulated industries and advocates of all sorts commonly submit comments. But anyone who wants to can go to www.regulations.gov to read proposed rules, enter comments, and view the comments of others. Once rules are approved, they are published in the *Federal Register* and have the force of law.

Bureaucrats Enforce Laws In addition to rule making, bureaucracies play an essential role in enforcing the laws. In doing so, bureaucracies exercise considerable power over private actors. In 2015 the EPA charged Volkswagen with cheating on emissions tests of its diesel vehicles. For over seven years, the company had installed software that showed emissions at legal levels during testing conditions but, once the cars were on the road, showed that emissions were actually 10 to 40 percent higher. After the EPA threatened to bar the company from selling some of its 2016 cars in the United States, Volkswagen admitted that it had cheated. The financial repercussions for the company will be long-lasting. In 2016 the company agreed to a $15.8 billion settlement that required it to buy back the faulty vehicles and compensate owners. As part of the settlement, Volkswagen also agreed to fund several clean air programs. Even with these payments, Volkswagen faced additional lawsuits from states and investors.[6]

Who Are Bureaucrats? Bureaucrats are considered members of the "civil service" and work under the **merit system** created by the Civil Service Act of 1883. With this act, the federal government attempted to imitate business by requiring appointees to public office be qualified for the job to which they were appointed. The goal was to end political appointments under the "spoils system," which awarded jobs based on political connections, and to create a system of competitive examinations through which the very best candidates were to be hired for every job. As a further safeguard against political interference, merit-system employees were given legal protection against being fired without a show of cause. Reasonable people may disagree about the value of such job security and how far it should extend in the civil service, but the justifiable objective of this job protection, cleansing bureaucracy of political interference while upgrading performance, cannot be disputed. At the higher levels of government agencies, including such posts as cabinet secretaries and assistant secretaries, many jobs are filled with political appointees and are not part of the merit system.

Today's federal bureaucrats are distributed around the country—nearly 4 out of 5 federal employees work outside of Washington, D.C. Compared to private sector workers, members of the full-time civilian federal workforce are more educated—more hold college and advanced degrees—and are more likely to hold professional occupations in science, engineering, diplomacy, and other advanced fields.[7] Federal workers are more diverse than the private workforce: as of 2017, 36.7 percent were minority group members: 18.2 percent black, 8.8 percent Hispanic, 5.6 percent Asian, 2.2 percent Native Hawaiian/Pacific Islander/American Indian/Alaska Native, and 1.5 percent non-Hispanic multiracial. Federal workers are more likely to be male than private sector workers (57 percent compared to 54 percent in the private sector),[8] and nearly one-third of federal workers are veterans.[9]

THE SIZE OF THE FEDERAL SERVICE HAS ACTUALLY DECLINED

For decades, politicians from both parties including Presidents Reagan, Clinton, and Bush have asserted that the federal government is too big. President Obama struck a different note in his first inaugural address, saying, "The question we ask today is not whether our government is too big or too small, but whether it works."[10] President Trump's first budget proposed major decreases in federal departments outside of Defense and Homeland Security. Despite fears of bureaucratic growth getting out of hand, however, the federal service has hardly grown at all since 1980; it reached its peak postwar level in 1968 with 3.0 million civilian employees plus 3.6 million military personnel (a figure swollen by the war in Vietnam). The number of civilian federal employees has since fallen to fewer than 2.7 million in 2017, and 1.3 million military personnel as of 2017.[11]

The growth of the federal service in the second half of the twentieth century and the beginning of the twenty-first is even less imposing when placed in the context of the total workforce and when compared with the size of state and local public employment. Figure 11.1 indicates that since 1950 the ratio of federal employment to the total workforce has in fact *declined* slightly. Meanwhile, state and local employment has grown: in 1950, there were 4.3 million state and local civil service employees (about 6.5 percent of the country's workforce). In 2015 there were roughly 19.3 million state and local employees (nearly 15 percent of the nation's employed workforce).[12] Federal employment, in contrast, exceeded 6 percent of the workforce only during World War II, and almost all of that temporary growth was military.

Another useful comparison is illustrated in Figure 11.2. Although the dollar increase in federal spending shown by the bars looks impressive, the trend line indicating the relation of federal spending to the gross domestic product (GDP) remained close to what it had been in 1960. This changed in 2009, when the recession pushed spending up dramatically as the federal government sought to stimulate the economy and spending rose on other recession-related programs, such as unemployment insurance. After 2009 the budget also reflected the costs of the wars in Iraq and Afghanistan, which had not been included in the Bush administration's budgets.

In sum, the national government is indeed "very large," but it has not been growing any faster than the economy or society. The same is roughly true of the growth pattern of state and local public personnel. Bureaucracy keeps pace with society, despite people's seeming dislike of it, because the air traffic control towers, the prisons, the Social Security system, and other essential elements of modern-day society cannot operate without bureaucracy.

THE EXECUTIVE BRANCH IS ORGANIZED HIERARCHICALLY

Cabinet departments, agencies, and bureaus are the operating parts of the bureaucratic whole. A **department** is the largest subunit of the executive branch. At the top is the head of the department, who in the United States is called the "secretary"

FIGURE 11.1

Employees in the Federal Service as a Percentage of the National Workforce, 1950–2018

Since 1950, the ratio of federal employment to the total workforce has gradually declined. Today, federal employees make up less than 2 percent of the total workforce in the United States. Even at its height, federal employees made up less than 6 percent. What do these numbers suggest about the size of the federal government today?

NOTE: Employment numbers are for December of each year; 2018 numbers are from September.

SOURCE: Bureau of Labor Statistics, Current Employment Statistics, "Employment, Hours, and Earnings from the Current Employment Statistics survey (National)" for Federal Government and Total Nonfarm (seasonally adjusted)," https://data.bls.gov/timeseries/CES9091000001 (accssed 10/13/18).

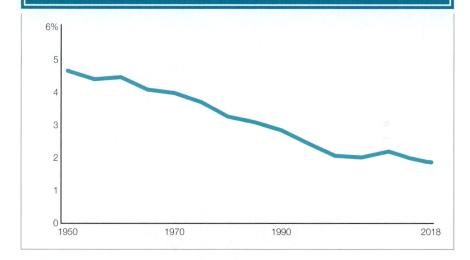

of the department.[13] Below the secretary and the deputy secretary are the "undersecretaries," who have management responsibilities for one or more operating agencies. Those operating agencies are the most directly responsible for shaping the department's actual programs and are called the "bureau level." Each bureau-level agency usually operates under the statute adopted by Congress that set up the agency and gave it its authority and jurisdiction. The names of these bureau-level agencies are often quite well known to the public—the Forest Service and the Agricultural Research Service, for example. These are the so-called line agencies, or agencies that deal directly with the public. Each bureau or agency is subdivided into still other units, known as "divisions," "offices," or "units." All are parts of the bureaucratic hierarchy.

Not all government agencies are part of cabinet departments. Some **independent agencies** are set up by Congress outside the departmental structure altogether, even though the president appoints and directs the heads of these agencies. Independent agencies usually have broad powers to provide public services that are either too

Annual Federal Outlays, 1960–2018*

As the bars in the figure indicate, when measured in dollars, federal government spending has gone up over time, from $423 billion in 1960 to over $3 trillion in 2015. (The amounts here are measured in constant 2009 dollars, which means the numbers have been adjusted for inflation.) But as the red line shows, federal spending as a percent of gross domestic product (GDP) has moved up and down just slightly over time. Thus, while government spending has grown, it has basically kept pace with the growing size of the U.S. economy.

*Data for 2017–18 are estimated.

SOURCE: Office of Management and Budget, "Table 1.3—Summary of Receipts, Outlays, and Surpluses or Deficits in Current Dollars, Constant (FY 2009) Dollars, and as Percentages of GDP: 1940–2023," www.whitehouse.gov/omb/budget/historicals (accessed 10/13/18).

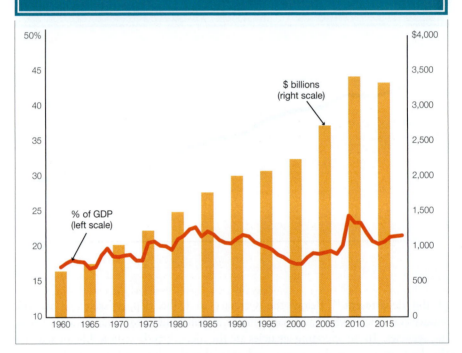

expensive or too important to be left to private initiatives. Some examples of independent agencies are the National Aeronautics and Space Administration (NASA), the Central Intelligence Agency (CIA), and the EPA. **Government corporations** are a third type of government agency but are more like private businesses in performing and charging for a market service, such as transporting railroad passengers (Amtrak).

Yet a fourth type of agency is the independent regulatory commission, given broad discretion to make rules. The first regulatory agencies established by Congress, beginning with the Interstate Commerce Commission in 1887, were set up as independent regulatory commissions because Congress recognized that regulatory

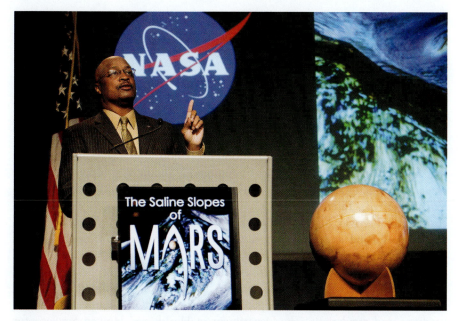

The National Aeronautics and Space Administration (NASA), an independent agency of the federal government, was established by President Eisenhower in 1958. Here, NASA public affairs officer Dwayne Brown announces the presence of water on Mars.

agencies are "mini-legislatures," whose rules are exactly the same as legislation but require the kind of expertise and full-time attention that is beyond the capacity of Congress. Until the 1960s most of the regulatory agencies that were set up by Congress, such as the Federal Trade Commission (1914) and the Federal Communications Commission (FCC; 1934), were independent regulatory commissions. But beginning in the late 1960s and the early 1970s, all new regulatory programs, with two or three exceptions (such as the Federal Election Commission), were placed within existing departments and made directly responsible to the president. The first new major regulatory agency established in decades was approved by Congress in 2010, the Consumer Financial Protection Bureau. It was created to protect consumers by carrying out federal consumer financial protection laws. It functions as an independent unit within the U.S. Federal Reserve.

Federal Bureaucracies Promote Welfare and Security

Describe the major goals we expect federal agencies to promote

The different agencies of the executive branch can be classified into three main groups based on the services they provide to the American public. The first category of agencies provides services and products that seek to promote the public welfare. The second group provides services that help maintain a strong economy. The third group works to promote national security. Let us look more closely at what each set of agencies offers to the public.

FEDERAL BUREAUCRACIES PROMOTE PUBLIC WELL-BEING

One of the most important activities of the federal bureaucracy is to promote the public good by providing services, building infrastructure, and enacting regulations designed to enhance the well-being of the vast majority of citizens. Departments that have important responsibilities for promoting public well-being include the Departments of Housing and Urban Development, Health and Human Services, Veterans' Affairs, Interior, Education, and Labor. Ensuring the public welfare is also the main activity of agencies in other departments, such as the Department of Agriculture's Food and Nutrition Service, which administers the federal school lunch program and the Supplemental Nutrition Assistance Program (SNAP, formerly known as food stamps). In addition, a variety of independent regulatory agencies enforce regulations to safeguard the public health and welfare.

Federal bureaucracies promote public well-being with a diverse set of services, products, and regulations. The Department of Health and Human Services, for example, oversees the National Institutes of Health (NIH), which is responsible for cutting-edge biomedical research and two major health programs provided by the federal government: Medicaid, which provides health care for low-income families and for many elderly and disabled people, and Medicare, which is the health insurance available to most elderly people in the United States.

A different kind of public well-being, but one highly valued by most Americans, is provided by the National Park Service, under the Department of the Interior. Created in 1916, the National Park Service is responsible for the care and upkeep of national parks. Since the nineteenth century, Americans have seen protection of the natural environment as an important public goal and have looked to federal agencies to implement laws and administer programs that preserve natural areas and keep them open to the public.

The federal bureaucracy also promotes the public good through the watchdog activities of many **regulatory agencies**—departments, bureaus, or independent agencies whose primary mission is to impose limits, restrictions, or other obligations on the conduct of individuals or companies in the private sector. These include the FDA within the Department of Health and Human Services, the Occupational Safety and Health Administration (OSHA) in the Department of Labor, and independent regulatory commissions, such as the FCC and the EPA. An agency or commission is regulatory if Congress delegates to it relatively broad powers over a sector of the economy or a type of commercial activity and authorizes it to make rules within that jurisdiction. Rules made by regulatory agencies have the force of law.

As we saw in Chapters 8 and 9, government agencies often develop close ties to the groups in society that they are supposed to regulate. This close political connection is known as an **iron triangle**: the stable, cooperative relationships that often develop among a congressional committee, an administrative agency, and one or

Bureaucracy in Comparison

As one of the world's largest and most populous countries, the United States has a vast bureaucracy to run government programs and services. However, as a percentage of the labor force, the number of government employees in the United States is not especially high. As the first graph below shows, the size of government bureaucracies, relative to each country's work force, varies widely. For example, the Norwegian government employs nearly 30 percent of the labor force, whereas only around 8 percent of Japanese workers work for the government.

We can also see differences in whether most government employees work at the national level or the subnational level in each country. In the United States, most government employees work at the state or local level, rather than the national level. In other countries like Turkey, most bureaucrats work for the national government. What do you think accounts for these differences? How does federalism influence American bureaucracy, and what differences do we see in countries like Turkey or Ireland that do not have federalism?

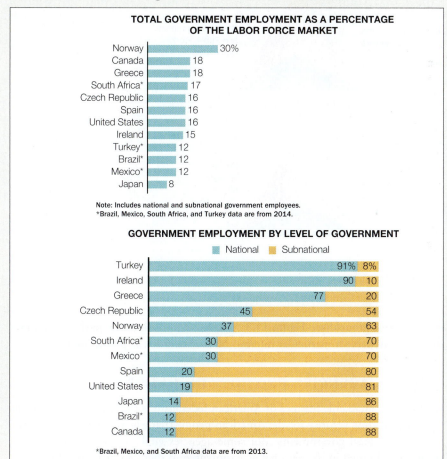

TOTAL GOVERNMENT EMPLOYMENT AS A PERCENTAGE OF THE LABOR FORCE MARKET

Country	Percentage
Norway	30%
Canada	18
Greece	18
South Africa*	17
Czech Republic	16
Spain	16
United States	16
Ireland	15
Turkey*	12
Brazil*	12
Mexico*	12
Japan	8

Note: Includes national and subnational government employees.
*Brazil, Mexico, South Africa, and Turkey data are from 2014.

GOVERNMENT EMPLOYMENT BY LEVEL OF GOVERNMENT

National ■ Subnational ■

Country	National	Subnational
Turkey	91%	8%
Ireland	90	10
Greece	77	20
Czech Republic	45	54
Norway	37	63
South Africa*	30	70
Mexico*	30	70
Spain	20	80
United States	19	81
Japan	14	86
Brazil*	12	88
Canada	12	88

*Brazil, Mexico, and South Africa data are from 2013.

SOURCES: OECD, "Public Employment and Pay," Government at a Glance, 2017, www.stats.oecd.org (accessed 4/16/18).

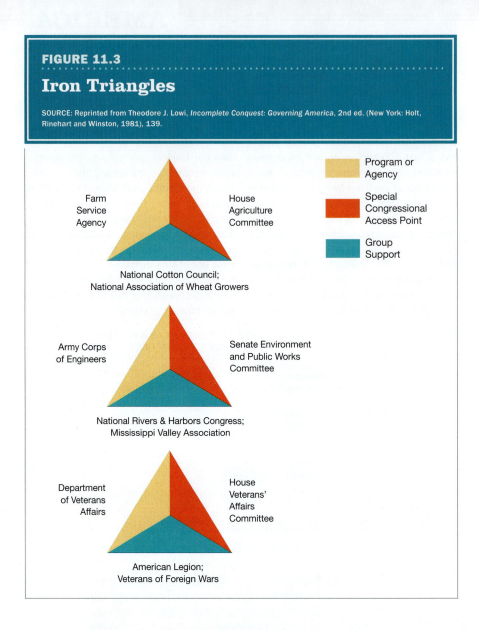

FIGURE 11.3

Iron Triangles

SOURCE: Reprinted from Theodore J. Lowi, *Incomplete Conquest: Governing America*, 2nd ed. (New York: Holt, Rinehart and Winston, 1981), 139.

Program or Agency

Special Congressional Access Point

Group Support

Farm Service Agency

House Agriculture Committee

National Cotton Council; National Association of Wheat Growers

Army Corps of Engineers

Senate Environment and Public Works Committee

National Rivers & Harbors Congress; Mississippi Valley Association

Department of Veterans Affairs

House Veterans' Affairs Committee

American Legion; Veterans of Foreign Wars

more interest groups (see Figure 11.3). These relationships may push policies in a direction favorable to particular interests but inimical to the public interest.

FEDERAL AGENCIES PROVIDE FOR NATIONAL SECURITY

One of the remarkable features of American federalism is that the most vital agencies for providing security for the American people (namely, the police) are located in state and local governments. But some agencies vital to maintaining national security are located in the national government, and they can be grouped into two categories: agencies to confront threats to internal national security and agencies to defend American security from external threats. The departments of greatest influence in these two areas are Homeland Security, Justice, Defense, and State.

Agencies for Internal Security The task of maintaining domestic security changed dramatically after the terrorist attacks of September 11, 2001. The creation of the Department of Homeland Security (DHS) in 2002 signaled the high priority that domestic security would now have. The orientation of domestic agencies also shifted as agencies geared up to prevent terrorism, a task that differed greatly from their former charge of investigating crime. With this shift in responsibility came broad new powers, many of them controversial—including the power to detain terrorist suspects and to engage in extensive domestic intelligence-gathering about possible terrorists. The DHS has also assumed a large role in domestic security, bringing under its umbrella such responsibilities as border safety and security (including immigration and customs); emergency preparedness; science-related concerns pertaining in particular to chemical, biological, and nuclear threats; and information and intelligence analysis and assessment.

Growing pains were evident in the DHS's first years. Different bureaucratic cultures, now part of a single operation, quickly became embroiled in turf battles with one another and with the Federal Bureau of Investigation (FBI, which remained in the Justice Department) as the two departments attempted to sort out their respective responsibilities. These early problems signaled deeper challenges that the DHS has continued to face. Under President Trump DHS has new visibility in implementing the president's travel bans on certain visitors and arresting undocumented immigrants, and his first two budget proposals called for increased funding for the department.[14]

Agencies for External National Security Two departments occupy center stage in maintaining national security: the Departments of State and Defense.

The State Department's primary mission is diplomacy. As the most visible public representative of American diplomacy, the secretary of state works to promote American perspectives and interests in the world. For example, then–Secretary of State Rex Tillerson traveled to Moscow in 2017 in a bid to weaken Russia's support for Syrian president Bashar al-Assad amid concerns about his use of chemical weapons.[15] Although diplomacy is the primary task of the State Department, diplomatic missions are only one of its organizational dimensions. As of 2016 the State Department also included several dozen bureau-level units, each under the direction of an undersecretary, although Tillerson proposed a departmental reorganization. Considering the department too bloated, Tillerson froze hiring, pushed out top career officials, and limited promotions, steps that earned criticism from some in Congress.[16] Secretary of State Mike Pompeo lifted Tillerson's hiring freeze, although many positions remain unfilled.

These bureaus support the responsibilities of the elite foreign service officers, who staff U.S. embassies around the world and who hold almost all of the most powerful positions in the department below the rank of ambassador.[17] The ambassadorial positions, especially the plum positions in the major capitals of the world, are

The Departments of Defense and State are the most important parts of the federal bureaucracy focused on national security. Secretary James Mattis (top) is the civilian head of the military (reporting to the president in his role as commander in chief). Secretary of State Mike Pompeo (bottom right) is the United States' chief diplomat.

filled by presidential appointees, many of whom get their positions by having been important donors to victorious political campaigns.

Despite the importance of the State Department in foreign affairs, fewer than 20 percent of all U.S. government employees working abroad are directly under its authority. By far the largest number of career government professionals working abroad are under the authority of the Defense Department. The Defense Department provides the military forces needed to deter war and protect the nation. Headquartered in the Pentagon, across the Potomac River from Washington, D.C., the DOD is one of the largest bureaucracies in the world, composed of 2 million people across five sets of institutions.[18] The president appoints the Secretary of Defense, whose Office of the Secretary of Defense (OSD) plans and carries out the nation's security policies as directed by the Secretary and president. The OSD provides civilian oversight of the military. The second institution is the Joint Chiefs of Staff, consisting of the Chairman of the Joint Chiefs of Staff, who is the president's principal military adviser, and the five military service chiefs (Army, Navy, Air Force, Marine Corps, and National Guard; the Coast Guard is in the Department of Homeland Security except in wartime). Third, there are three military departments, each with its own civilian secretary and military secretary (Army, Navy, Air Force; the Marine Corps is part of the Department of the Navy). The military departments train and equip military forces. Fourth, the Unified Combatant Commands (COCOMs) execute military operations. There are six regional COCOMs (Africa Command; European Command; Central Command; Northern Command; Southern Command; and Pacific Command) and three functional COCOMS (Strategic Command; Special Operations Command; and Transportation Command). Finally there are the defense agencies that perform supply or service activities that are common to more than one military department. There are currently 20 such defense agencies.[19]

National Security and Democracy Of all the agencies in the federal bureaucracy, those charged with providing national security most often come into conflict with the norms and expectations of American democracy. Two issues in particular arise as these agencies work to ensure national security: (1) the trade-offs between respecting the personal rights of individuals and protecting the general public and (2) the need for secrecy in matters of national security versus the public's right to know what the government is doing.

Protecting national security often requires the government to conduct its activities in secret. Yet, as Americans have come to expect a more open government, many believe that federal agencies charged with national security keep too many secrets from the American public. The effort to make information related to national security more available began in 1966 with the passage of the Freedom of Information Act (FOIA). The information obtained often reveals unflattering or unsuccessful aspects of national security activities. One private organization, the National Security Archive, makes extensive use of FOIA to obtain information about the activities of national security agencies. The website's "The Torture Archive," for example, is a searchable database of documents related to the detention of individuals in the war on terrorism and the authorized use of torture by the American government.

The tension between secrecy and democracy has sharpened dramatically with the threat of terrorism. Since September 11, 2001, the FOIA has been curtailed, and the range of information deemed sensitive has greatly expanded. Although most Americans agreed that enhanced secrecy was needed to ensure domestic security, concerns about excessive secrecy mounted. Some analysts worried that secrecy would prevent Congress from carrying out its basic oversight responsibilities and that much of the secrecy had nothing to do with national security. President Obama ordered federal agencies to administer the FOIA law more liberally and signed an executive order to speed declassification of secret documents.

However, Obama's campaign to make government more transparent was challenged by national security contract worker Edward Snowden's leak of sensitive national security documents in 2013. The Snowden documents exposed the extent, and potential illegality, of the National Security Agency's (NSA's) global surveillance operations. They showed that the NSA was collecting private data on millions of Americans and foreign nationals, including the tracking of phone calls, email messages, web browser histories, and personal contacts. The revelations prompted outrage at home and abroad.[20] President Obama responded by appointing an independent panel of intelligence experts to assess the NSA's activities, which determined that its massive data collection "made only a modest contribution to the nation's security." Among many changes they recommended was that the government stop the collection program and relinquish the files to a third party. Even after these reforms more Americans disapproved than approved of the government's role in collecting internet and telephone data.[21] Congress barred bulk collection of telephone data and instituted other limits on government surveillance in the 2015 USA Freedom Act. The restrictions in the new legislation sought to ensure security without jeopardizing privacy, although critics remain concerned about the scope of government surveillance.[22]

FEDERAL BUREAUCRACIES HELP TO MAINTAIN A STRONG NATIONAL ECONOMY

In our capitalist economic system, the government does not directly run the economy. Yet many federal government activities are critical to maintaining a strong economy. Foremost among these are the agencies that are responsible for fiscal and monetary policy. Other agencies, such as the Internal Revenue Service (IRS), collect private resources into federal funds for public purposes. Tax policy may also strengthen the economy through decisions about whom to tax, how much, and when. Finally, the federal government, through such agencies as the Department of Transportation, the Commerce Department, and the Energy Department, may directly provide services or goods that bolster the economy.

Fiscal and Monetary Agencies Fiscal policy—the government's use of taxing, monetary, and spending powers to manipulate the economy—can refer to any government policy having to do with public finance. However, Americans often reserve the word *fiscal* for taxing and spending policies and use the term *monetary* for policies having to do with banks, credit, and currency.

While the responsibility for making fiscal policy lies with Congress, the administration of fiscal policy occurs primarily in the Treasury Department. In addition to collecting income, corporate, and other taxes, and performing tax and economic policy analysis, the Treasury manages the national debt—over $21 trillion in 2018.[23] The Treasury Department is also responsible for printing the U.S. currency, but currency represents only a tiny proportion of the entire money economy. Most of the trillions of dollars used in the transactions of the private and public sectors of the U.S. economy exist in computerized accounts rather than as actual currency.

A key monetary agency is the **Federal Reserve System**, a system of 12 Federal Reserve banks, headed by the Federal Reserve Board, that facilitates exchanges of cash, checks, and credit; regulates member banks; and uses monetary policies to fight inflation and deflation. The Federal Reserve System (called the Fed) has authority over the interest rates and lending activities of the nation's most important banks. Congress established the Fed in 1913 as a clearinghouse responsible for adjusting the supply of money and credit to the needs of commerce and industry in different regions of the country. The Fed is also responsible for ensuring that banks do not overextend themselves, a policy that guards against bank failures during a sudden economic scare, such as occurred in 1929 and again in 2008. The Treasury and the Federal Reserve took center stage in 2008 when a string of bank failures threatened economic catastrophe. These agencies designed a $700-billion bailout package and persuaded Congress that a rapid response was needed to avert a worldwide depression. Although the Treasury and the Federal Reserve sprang into action when economic calamity loomed, critics charged that the crisis could have been prevented if these agencies had exercised more regulatory oversight over the financial sector during the previous decade. In 2010, Congress and President Obama created the Financial Stability Oversight Council to identify system-wide risks to the financial sector. The financial industry has kept a close eye on these developments, aiming to limit the regulatory reach of the new council.[24]

Revenue Agencies Revenue agencies are responsible for collecting taxes. Examples include the Bureau of Alcohol, Tobacco, Firearms and Explosives for collection of taxes on the sales of those particular products, and federal customs agents (part of the DHS) who oversee the collection of taxes on imports at every U.S. seaport and international airport. But far and away the most important of the revenue agencies is the Internal Revenue Service, which collects income taxes.

The IRS is the government agency that Americans love to hate. Taxpayers complain about the IRS's needless complexity, its lack of sensitivity and responsiveness to individual taxpayers, and its overall lack of efficiency. Such complaints led Congress to pass the IRS Restructuring and Reform Act of 1998, which instituted a number of new protections for taxpayers. Yet Congress continued to cut the IRS budget: $900 million over eight years through 2018 and nearly a quarter of its work force. With the enactment of a major tax overhaul at the end of 2017, worries grew that the IRS would be unable to effectively do its job.[25]

Several Forces Control Bureaucracy

Explain why it is often difficult to control the bureaucracy

By their very nature, bureaucracies pose challenges to democratic governance. Although they provide the expertise needed to implement the public will, they can also become entrenched organizations that serve their own interests. The task is neither to retreat from bureaucracy nor to attack it but to take advantage of its strengths while making it more accountable to the demands of democratic politics and representative government.

THE PRESIDENT AS CHIEF EXECUTIVE CAN DIRECT AGENCIES

In 1937, President Franklin Roosevelt's Committee on Administrative Management officially addressed a plea that had been growing increasingly urgent: "The president needs help." The national government had grown rapidly during the preceding 25 years, but the structures and procedures necessary to manage the burgeoning executive branch had not yet been established. The response to the call for "help" for the president initially took the form of three management policies: (1) all communications and decisions that related to executive policy decisions must pass through the White House; (2) in order to cope with such a flow, the White House must have adequate staffs of specialists in research, analysis, legislative and legal writing, and public affairs; and (3) the White House must have additional staff to ensure that presidential decisions are made, communicated to Congress, and carried out by the appropriate agency.

Making the Managerial Presidency The story of the modern presidency can be told largely as a series of responses to the plea for managerial help as the scope of the federal government—and presidential power—has grown.[26]

The president heads the federal government, which is the largest employer in the country and the largest purchaser of goods and services in the world.[27] As the CEO of this enormous organization, the president may have goals associated with management (striving for efficiency) and control (shaping policy outcomes). Presidents have several tools at their disposal. They have appointment power over the top layer of the executive branch, the political appointees who sit on top of the career civil service. They can issue executive orders, making policy and shaping the executive branch unilaterally. They can also alter an agency's budget or organizational scheme. Indeed, the presidency has been marked by waves of executive branch reorganization by presidents seeking to exert administrative and political control.[28]

President Jimmy Carter's interest in administrative reform and reorganization resulted in his reorganization of the civil service and will long be recognized as one of the most significant contributions of his presidency. The Civil Service Reform Act of 1978 was the first major revamping of the federal civil service since its creation in 1883. The 1978 act created the Merit Systems Protection Board to defend competitive merit recruitment and promotion from political encroachment. The separate Federal Labor Relations Authority was set up to administer collective bargaining and individual personnel grievances. The third new agency, the Office of Personnel Management, was created to manage recruiting, testing, training, and the retirement system. The Senior Executive Service—a top management rank for civil servants—was also created at this time to recognize and foster "public management" as a profession and to facilitate the movement of top, "supergrade" career officials across agencies and departments.[29]

President Bill Clinton was often criticized for the way he managed his administration—his loose approach to administration included all-night "bull sessions" complete with pizza, yet, he inaugurated one of the most systematic efforts "to change the way government does business" in his National Performance Review. Heavily influenced by the theories of management consultants who prized decentralization, customer responsiveness, and employee initiative, Clinton sought to infuse these new practices into government.[30]

Like his predecessors, George W. Bush pursued a strategy different from those of previous presidents, dismantling Clinton's National Performance Review and favoring **privatization**—the transfer of all or part of a program from the public sector to the private sector. Bush was the first president with a degree in business, and his management strategy followed a standard business school dictum: select skilled subordinates and delegate responsibility to them. Bush followed this model closely in his appointment of highly experienced officials to cabinet positions. But critics contended that the Bush administration's distrust of the bureaucracy led it to exercise inappropriate political control.

After Obama took office, his administration sought to reinvigorate federal agencies, which reflected the Democrats' greater support for strong government institutions. Obama's approach to the managerial presidency featured a deep belief in the importance of scientific expertise, which was reflected in his appointments to key regulatory agencies such as the FDA, OSHA, and the EPA. But he had his own critics, who complained about micromanagement and centralization.[31]

President Trump called for deep budget cuts and reorganization in a number of executive branch departments and agencies. His presidency has also raised the specter of a "deep state" of bureaucrats who exert power independent of political control. Political scientist Michael Glennon has used the term "the double state" to describe a phenomenon in which, for example, Bush-era national security policies such as covert drone strikes and use of the Guantánamo Bay prison continued under President Obama, even though Obama as a candidate had criticized them. Glennon raises the possibility of a "double government" of bureaucrats that continues to pursue policies of its preference outside of political or democratic control.[32] Episodes such as EPA employees informing the media about a report on climate change they feared would be suppressed seemed to confirm Trump supporters' fears of the limits of presidential control over the bureaucracy.[33] There is little evidence of the truly rogue bureaucracy that figures in the most extreme versions of conspiracy theories, but questions of who controls the bureaucracy and how much autonomy bureaucrats should have have occupied political scientists and government leaders for decades.

CONGRESS PROMOTES RESPONSIBLE BUREAUCRACY

Another lever of control over the bureaucracy is Congress. Congress passes legislation, which the bureaucracy must then implement. Such delegation derives from the constitutionally mandated roles for each branch of government; the president must "faithfully execute" the laws Congress passes. But because Congress cannot possibly stipulate every detail of every law, the bureaucracy must interpret legislative intent.[34] The delegation of implementation introduces the principal-agent problem: does the bureaucracy (the agent) implement laws in the manner Congress (the principal) intended?

One way Congress can hold the bureaucracy accountable is **oversight.** Congressional committees and subcommittees have jurisdictions roughly parallel to one or more departments and agencies in the executive branch, and members of Congress who sit on these committees can develop expertise equal to that of the bureaucrats.

The most visible indication of Congress's oversight efforts is the use of public hearings, before which bureaucrats and other witnesses are summoned to scrutinize agency budgets and decisions. Concern has grown in recent years about failures of oversight.[35] There appears to be less **"police patrol" oversight**—regular or even preemptive hearings on agency operations—and more **"fire alarm" oversight** prompted by media attention or advocacy group complaints. For example, consumer outrage prompted the House Oversight and Government Reform Committee's 2016 inquiry into a 500-percent price hike on EpiPens used to treat severe allergic reactions.[36] Oversight hearings can also become highly politicized. In 2015 the House Select Committee on Benghazi (a Libyan city where four U.S. diplomats were killed by extremists in 2012), which was the eighth committee to investigate the matter, called former secretary of state Hillary Clinton to appear for a second time. During the televised hearings Republican members of the committee aggressively questioned the former secretary for more

The most visible aspect of congressional oversight is the use of public hearings. Following the 2012 attack on the U.S. embassy in Benghazi, Libya, Congress held multiple highly publicized—and highly politicized—hearings to investigate the matter, focusing on the activities of former secretary of state Hillary Clinton.

than eight hours. Democrats charged that the hearing was designed to harm Clinton's presidential campaign.[37]

In addition, Congress created three agencies whose obligations are to engage in constant research for Congress on problems taking place in or confronted by the executive branch. These are the Government Accountability Office, the Congressional Research Service, and the Congressional Budget Office. Each of these agencies is designed to give Congress information independent of the information it can get directly from the executive branch through hearings and other communications.[38] Another source of information for oversight comes directly from citizens through the FOIA, which, as we have seen, gives ordinary citizens the right of access to agency files and agency data.

CAN THE BUREAUCRACY BE REFORMED?

When citizens complain that government is too bureaucratic, what they often mean is that government bureaucracies seem inefficient, waste money, and perform poorly. Do these frustrations mean that bureaucracy needs to be reformed? In a sense, bureaucracy is always in need of reform. Yet, reforms may be more difficult to implement in the public sector because the government is held to much higher standards of accountability than are private companies. The government has sought various ways to make the federal bureaucracy more efficient. The key strategies used to promote reform include termination, devolution, and privatization. In general, Democratic administrations have aimed to make the existing bureaucracy work more effectively, whereas Republican administrations have sought to sideline or reduce the bureaucracy, especially by contracting out government work to private companies.

The only certain way to reduce the size of the bureaucracy is to eliminate programs. But termination is extraordinarily difficult. Even in the 12 years of the Reagan and George H. W. Bush administrations, both of which proclaimed a strong commitment to the reduction of the national government, not a single national government agency or program was terminated. In the 1990s, Republicans did succeed in eliminating two small agencies.

The next most effective approach to genuinely reducing the size of the federal bureaucracy is **devolution**, downsizing the federal bureaucracy by delegating the implementation of programs to state and local governments. Often the central aim of devolution is to provide more efficient and flexible government services. Yet by its very nature, devolution entails variation across the states. Up to a point, variation can be considered one of the virtues of federalism. But in a democracy, it is inherently dangerous to have large variations in the provision of services and benefits.

Privatization simply means that a formerly public activity is picked up under contract by a private company or companies. But such programs are still government programs—paid for by government and supervised by government. Privatization downsizes the government only in that the workers providing the service are no longer counted as part of the government bureaucracy. When private contractors can perform a task as well as government can but for less money, taxpayers win. But if private firms are less efficient or more costly than government, then taxpayers may lose. In addition, concerns about adequate government oversight and accountability of private contractors have escalated as the scale of contracting has dramatically increased. Congress and presidents have reacted to these concerns in several ways, but conducting adequate oversight of contractors remains a challenge.

Bureaucracy
WHAT DO WE WANT?

Americans' views about the federal government bureaucracy present something of a paradox. On the one hand, the public expresses dislike for "big government," exemplified by bureaucracy. From this perspective, the federal government is too large, inherently wasteful, and at odds with individual freedom. On the other hand, Americans support many government programs and have high expectations for government. Indeed, high expectations lead many Americans to blame bureaucrats when the country faces problems, such as the prolonged economic downturn of recent years. One consequence of these divergent views can be that bureaucracies try to maximize one value but undermine others. As we saw in the chapter opener, the decision to switch the Flint water supply was to save money, but it endangered the health of Flint residents.

Reconciling bureaucracy and democracy requires clear rules and laws, maximum openness in agency decisions, clear rationales for those decisions, and accessible means for questioning and appealing those decisions. One important way for Congress to ensure accountability of the bureaucracy is for it to spend more time clarifying its legislative intent. Bureaucrats are more responsive to clear legislative guidance than to anything else, and when Congress and the president are at odds about the interpretation of laws, bureaucrats can evade responsibility by playing off one branch against another. Moreover, clearer laws from Congress and clearer rules and decisions made by administrative agencies would reduce the need for courts to review those laws and decisions, which is expensive and time-consuming. Adequate congressional oversight is also important because a bureaucracy that is out of the public eye may wind up pursuing its own interests or narrowly focused private interests rather than those of the public. (The "**Who Participates?**" feature on the facing page shows the bureaucracy's response to public concerns about health care accessibility for veterans.) Finding the right balance between bureaucratic autonomy and public scrutiny is a central task of creating an effective government; it requires both presidential and congressional vigilance to build an effective and responsive bureaucracy.

The emergence of "big data" is likely to change the way bureaucracies operate in the future. *Big data* refers to huge data sets that involve information on a wide range of topics including climate, traffic, health, and the NSA's massive database of phone calls and use of social media. Big data has the potential to improve government performance by linking sources of information that were previously unconnected. It also allows the government to analyze information that was stored as text or went uncollected. Advances in government's ability to implement programs in public health, food safety, and transportation are only the beginning of what big data promises. At the same time, however, big data poses a threat to individual privacy, as the revelations about the NSA's data suggest. As bureaucracies tap into the promise of big data to create more effective programs, a close public eye on the implications for the right to privacy will be needed. How might big data improve the government's delivery of services in the future? What additional safeguards might be needed to protect individuals' privacy?

Waiting for a Veterans Affairs Health Care Appointment

After media reports about excessive waits endured by veterans seeking health care appointments, and widespread fraud in reporting those wait times, Congress passed the 2014 Veterans Choice Act, which allows veterans to go to private doctors if they would otherwise have to wait more than 30 days to see a Veterans Affairs provider. This act was supplemented in 2017 by the website, Access to Care (accesstocare.va.gov), which reports wait times at its veterans clinics around the country. The vast majority of veterans seeking health care appointments are now able to schedule one at their local VA within 30 days.

93%
195,604,902 total

Scheduled within 30 days

Total appointments requested in 2017:
208,065,313

4%
7,306,571 total

Scheduled within 31–60 days

1.4%
2,835,626 total

Scheduled within 61–90 days

0.3%
545,582 total

Scheduled within 90+ days

Note: Numbers may not add up to 100% due to rounding.

SOURCES: "Attempted Fix for VA Health Delays Creates New Bureaucracy," npr.org; Patient Access Data, www.va.gov (accessed 3/9/18).

WHAT YOU CAN DO

★ WHAT YOU CAN DO ★

Ask Questions about Federal Agencies

 Find out how veterans access their benefits and more about the U.S. Department of Veterans Affairs by visiting **www.va.gov**. For more information on veterans access to health care, visit **www.accestocare.va.gov**.

 To find more information on how the bureaucracy affects your life, visit **www.usa.gov/federal-agencies** and search by agency.

☑ Ask a question about how federal agencies can help you. Most agencies have FAQ and contact pages on their websites.

★ STUDY GUIDE ★

Practice Quiz

1. Which of the following statements about Congress and the bureaucracy is not true? *(p. 349)*
   a) Bureaucracies employ people who have much more specialized expertise in specific policy areas than do members of Congress.
   b) Members of Congress often prefer to delegate politically difficult decision-making to bureaucrats.
   c) While Congress is responsible for making laws, the bureaucracy is responsible for filling in the blanks by determining how the laws should be implemented.
   d) Congress banned rule making by the federal bureaucracy in 1995.
   e) Congress relies heavily on bureaucratic flexibility in implementing laws because updating legislation can take many years, and bureaucrats can ensure that laws are administered in ways that take new conditions into account.

2. The Civil Service Act of 1883 required that appointees to positions within the federal bureaucracy *(p. 351)*
   a) pledge an oath of loyalty to the United States.
   b) register as independents rather than as members of an organized political party.
   c) be qualified for the job to which they were appointed.
   d) serve for no more than ten years.
   e) serve for no fewer than ten years.

3. Which of the following best describes the size of the federal service? *(p. 352)*
   a) The size of the federal service has grown exponentially since 1980.
   b) The size of the federal service has changed very little since 1980.
   c) The size of the federal service reached its peak in 1955 and has been dramatically declining ever since.
   d) The federal service has employed at least 15 percent of the American workforce every year since 1950.
   e) The federal service was eliminated during the 1990s in order to hire more state government employees.

4. Which of the following is an example of a government corporation? *(p. 354)*
   a) National Aeronautics and Space Administration
   b) Amtrak
   c) Federal Bureau of Investigation
   d) Environmental Protection Agency
   e) Department of Justice

5. A stable relationship between a bureaucratic agency, an interest group, and a legislative committee is called *(p. 356)*
   a) a standing committee.
   b) a conference committee.
   c) a cabinet.
   d) an issue network.
   e) an iron triangle.

6. The State Department's primary mission is *(p. 359)*
   a) gathering intelligence.
   b) unifying the nation's military departments.
   c) engaging in diplomacy.
   d) investigating terrorism.
   e) overseeing domestic security efforts.

7. Which of the following statements about the Freedom of Information Act (FOIA) is most accurate? *(p. 361)*
   a) It was passed following the September 11, 2001, terrorist attacks.
   b) The National Security Archive is legally prohibited from using the FOIA to obtain information about the activities of national security agencies.

c) The range of information deemed sensitive has been heavily reduced in response to the threat of terrorism.
   d) The range of information deemed sensitive has been greatly expanded in response to the threat of terrorism.
   e) President Obama instructed federal agencies that they should reject all FOIA requests made during his term in office.

8. Americans refer to government policy about banks, credit, and currency as *(p. 362)*
   a) monetary policy.
   b) deficit policy.
   c) fiscal policy.
   d) interstate commerce policy.
   e) regulatory policy.

9. Which of the following is an example of a revenue agency? *(p. 363)*
   a) the Office of Management and Budget
   b) the Treasury Department
   c) the Federal Reserve Board
   d) the Internal Revenue Service
   e) the Commerce Department

10. Which president instituted the bureaucratic reform called the National Performance Review? *(p. 364)*
    a) Richard Nixon
    b) Lyndon Johnson
    c) Jimmy Carter
    d) Bill Clinton
    e) George W. Bush

11. When congressional hearings on bureaucratic agency operations are prompted by media attention or advocacy group complaints, it is an example of *(p. 365)*
    a) "police patrol" oversight.
    b) "fire alarm" oversight.
    c) "watchdog" oversight.
    d) devolution.
    e) preemption.

12. *Devolution* refers to *(p. 367)*
    a) the gradual decline in efficiency that always comes when government begins to implement a new program.

b) moving all or part of a program from the public sector to the private sector.

c) a policy of reducing or eliminating regulatory restraints on the conduct of individuals or private institutions.

d) a policy to remove a program from one level of government by passing it down to a lower level of government.

e) reducing the overall number of regulatory agencies in the federal bureaucracy.

Key Terms

bureaucracy (p. 349) the complex structure of offices, tasks, rules, and principles of organization that are employed by all large-scale institutions to coordinate effectively the work of their personnel

department (p. 352) the largest subunit of the executive branch; the secretaries of the 15 departments form the Cabinet

devolution (p. 367) a policy to remove a program from one level of government by delegating it or passing it down to a lower level of government, such as from the national government to the state and local governments

Federal Reserve System (p. 362) a system of 12 Federal Reserve banks that facilitates exchanges of cash, checks, and credit; regulates member banks; and uses monetary policies to fight inflation and deflation

"fire alarm" oversight (p. 365) episodic, as-needed congressional hearings on bureaucratic agency operations, usually prompted by media attention or advocacy group complaints

fiscal policy (p. 362) the government's use of taxing, monetary, and spending powers to manipulate the economy

government corporation (p. 354) government agency that performs a service normally provided by the private sector

implementation (p. 349) the efforts of departments and agencies to translate laws into specific bureaucratic rules and actions

independent agency (p. 353) agency that is not part of a cabinet department

iron triangle (p. 356) the stable, cooperative relationships that often develop among a congressional committee, an administrative agency, and one or more supportive interest groups; not all of these relationships are triangular, but the iron triangle is the most typical

merit system (p. 351) a product of civil service reform, in which appointees to positions in public bureaucracies must objectively be deemed qualified for those positions

oversight (p. 365) the effort by Congress, through hearings, investigations, and other techniques, to exercise control over the activities of executive agencies

"police patrol" oversight (p. 365) regular or even preemptive congressional hearings on bureaucratic agency operations

privatization (p. 364) the transfer of all or part of a program from the public sector to the private sector

regulatory agency (p. 356) a department, bureau, or independent agency whose primary mission is to impose limits, restrictions, or other obligations on the conduct of individuals or companies in the private sector

revenue agency (p. 363) an agency responsible for collecting taxes; examples include the Internal Revenue Service for income taxes, the U.S. Customs Service for tariffs and other taxes on imported goods, and the Bureau of Alcohol, Tobacco, Firearms and Explosives for collection of taxes on the sales of those particular products

For Further Reading

Gormley, William, and Stephen Balla. *Bureaucracy and Democracy: Accountability and Performance*. 3rd ed. Washington, DC: CQ Press, 2012.

Kettl, Donald F. *System under Stress: The Challenge to 21st Century Governance*. 3rd ed. Los Angeles: Sage/CQ Press, 2014.

Kettl, Donald F. *The Politics of the Administrative Process*. 6th ed. Los Angeles: Sage/CQ Press, 2014.

Light, Paul C. *A Government Ill Executed: The Decline of the Federal Service and How to Reverse It*. Cambridge, MA: Harvard University Press, 2008.

Lowi, Theodore J. *The End of Liberalism*. New York: W. W. Norton, 1979.

Moffitt, Susan. *Making Public Policy: Participatory Bureaucracy in American Democracy*. New York: Cambridge University Press, 2014.

Verkuil, Paul. *Outsourcing Sovereignty: Why Privatization of Government Functions Threatens Democracy and What We Can Do about It*. New York: Cambridge University Press, 2007.

Weiner, Tom. *Legacy of Ashes: The History of the CIA*. New York: Doubleday, 2007.

Wildavsky, Aaron, and Naomi Caiden. *The New Politics of the Budgetary Process*. New York: Longman, 2003.

Wood, B. Dan. *Bureaucratic Dynamics: The Role of Bureaucracy in a Democracy*. Boulder, CO: Westview, 1994.

Zegart, Amy B. *Spying Blind: The CIA, The FBI, and the Origins of 9/11*. Princeton, NJ: Princeton University Press, 2009.

The Federal Courts

WHAT GOVERNMENT DOES AND WHY IT MATTERS Mark Janus works for the Illinois Department of Healthcare and Family Services as a child support specialist. He is not a member of the union representing many public-sector workers in the state, the American Federation of State, County, and Municipal Employees (AFSCME). Nonetheless, he is required to pay a "fair-share" fee to the union on the grounds that nonmembers benefit from the union's bargaining activities over issues such as pay and benefits. Nonmembers do not have to contribute to the union's political activities, such as endorsements of political candidates.

Janus argues, however, that all activity that public-sector unions engage in is inherently political. In particular, he disagreed with the union's bargaining for increased benefits when Illinois was facing a budget crisis due in part to mismanagement of the state pension program. "The union's fight is not my fight," he says. "For years it supported politicians who put the state into its current budget and pension crises. . . . That's not public service." He believes that being forced to pay a fee that supports the union's activities violates his

Although the Supreme Court is often viewed as the least political of the three branches, its rulings touch on major political issues that affect Americans in many ways. Here Mark Janus (center) stands with supporters after winning his Supreme Court case that could have a profound effect on how unions operate.

First Amendment rights. His case went to the Supreme Court, which heard oral arguments in February 2018.

After taking office in 2017, Trump nominated conservative appeals court judge Neil Gorsuch to the vacant seat. With the Gorsuch appointment, conservatives once again enjoyed a 5–4 Supreme Court majority. Perhaps not suprisingly, the Gorsuch appointment resulted in a conservative decision in *Janus v. AFSCME*, Mr. Janus's First Amendment rights would be upheld. But union supporters say the decision will have devastating effects on public-sector unions' ability to protect workers, including female, African American, and Hispanic employees, who face a smaller gap in pay in union jobs compared to nonunion jobs, according to the Economic Policy Institute and the National Women's Law Center.[1]

For both Democrats and Republicans, the importance of the Supreme Court's 5–4 decision underscored the significance of President Trump's Supreme Court appointments. Had Obama nominee Merrick Garland, rather than Trump nominee Neil Gorsuch, been seated on the High Court, the mandatory-dues requirement would likely have been upheld. With the *Janus* decision in mind, Democrats and Republicans prepared to redouble their efforts to win subsequent battles over judicial appointments, as President Trump announced the nomination of Brett Kavanaugh, another conservative judge, to take the place of Justice Anthony Kennedy, who announced his retirement in July 2018. After a divisive political battle, Kavanaugh was confirmed by the Senate and joined the Court in October.

Every year, nearly 25 million cases are tried in American courts. Cases can arise from disputes between citizens, from efforts by government agencies to punish wrongdoing, from citizens' efforts to prove that their rights have been infringed on as a result of government action—or inaction—and from efforts by interest groups to promote their agendas. The framers of the Constitution called the Supreme Court the "least dangerous branch" of American government. Today, though, it is not unusual to hear the Court described as an all-powerful "imperial judiciary." But before we can understand this transformation and its consequences, we must look in some detail at America's judicial process.

CHAPTER GOALS

★ Identify the general types of cases and types of courts in our legal system (pp. 377–81)

★ Describe the different levels of federal courts and their functions (pp. 381–85)

★ Explain how the Supreme Court exercises the power of judicial review (pp. 385–90)

★ Describe the process the Supreme Court follows in the exercise of its power of judicial review (pp. 390–97)

★ Consider the personal and political influences on judges and the courts (pp. 397–99)

The Legal System Settles Disputes

Originally, a "court" was the place where a sovereign ruled—where the king or queen governed. Settling disputes between citizens was part of governing. In modern democracies, courts and judges have taken over from monarchs the power to resolve disputes by hearing the facts on both sides, applying the relevant law or principle to the facts, and deciding which side possesses greater merit. But since judges are not monarchs, they must have a basis for their authority. That basis in the United States is the Constitution and the law.

COURT CASES PROCEED UNDER CRIMINAL AND CIVIL LAW

Court cases in the United States proceed under two broad categories of law: criminal law and civil law.

Cases of **criminal law** deal with disputes or actions involving criminal penalties. Criminal law regulates the conduct of individuals, defines crimes, and specifies punishment for acts defined as illegal. The government charges an individual with violating a statute (a law) that has been enacted to protect the public health, safety, morals, or welfare. In criminal cases, the government is always the **plaintiff** (the individual or organization that brings a complaint in court) and alleges that a

In criminal cases, the government charges an individual with violating a statute protecting health, safety, morals, or welfare. Most such cases arise in state and municipal courts. Here, an Illinois county court hears testimony in a murder case.

criminal violation has been committed by a named **defendant** (the one against whom a complaint is brought in a criminal or civil case). Most criminal cases arise in state and municipal courts and involve matters ranging from traffic offenses to robbery and murder. While the great bulk of criminal law is still a state matter, a large and growing body of federal criminal law deals with infringements from tax evasion and mail fraud to acts of terrorism and the sale of narcotics. Defendants found guilty of criminal violations may be fined or sent to prison.

Cases of **civil law** involve disputes among individuals or between individuals and the government that do not involve criminal penalties. Unlike criminal cases, the losers in civil cases cannot be fined or incarcerated, although they may be required to pay monetary damages for their actions. In a civil case, the one who brings a complaint is the plaintiff and the one against whom the complaint is brought is the defendant. The two most common types of civil cases involve contracts and torts. In a typical contract case, an individual or a corporation charges that it has suffered because of another's violation of a specific agreement between the two. For example, the Smith Manufacturing Corporation may charge that Jones Distributors failed to honor an agreement to deliver raw materials at a specified time, causing Smith to lose business. Smith asks the court to order Jones to compensate it for the damage it allegedly suffered. In a typical tort case, one individual charges that he has been injured by another's negligence or malfeasance. Medical malpractice suits are one example of tort cases. Another important area of civil law is administrative law, which involves disputes over the jurisdiction, procedures, or authority of administrative agencies. A plaintiff may assert, for example, that an agency did not follow proper procedures when issuing new rules and regulations. A court will then examine the agency's conduct in light of the Administrative Procedure Act, the legislation that governs agency rule making.

In deciding cases, courts apply statutes (laws) and legal **precedents** (prior cases whose principles are used by judges as the basis for their decisions in present cases). State and federal statutes, for example, often govern the conditions under which contracts are and are not legally binding. Jones Distributors might argue that it was not obliged to fulfill its contract with the Smith Manufacturing Corporation because actions by Smith, such as the failure to make promised payments, constituted fraud under state law. Attorneys for a physician being sued for malpractice, meanwhile, may search for prior instances in which courts ruled that actions similar to those of their client did not constitute negligence. Such precedents are applied under the doctrine of **stare decisis**, a Latin phrase meaning "let the decision stand." It is the doctrine that a previous decision by a court applies as a precedent in similar cases until that decision is overruled.

TYPES OF COURTS INCLUDE TRIAL, APPELLATE, AND SUPREME

In the United States, systems of courts have been established both by the federal government and by the governments of the individual states. Both systems have several levels, as shown in Figure 12.1. More than 97 percent of all court cases in the

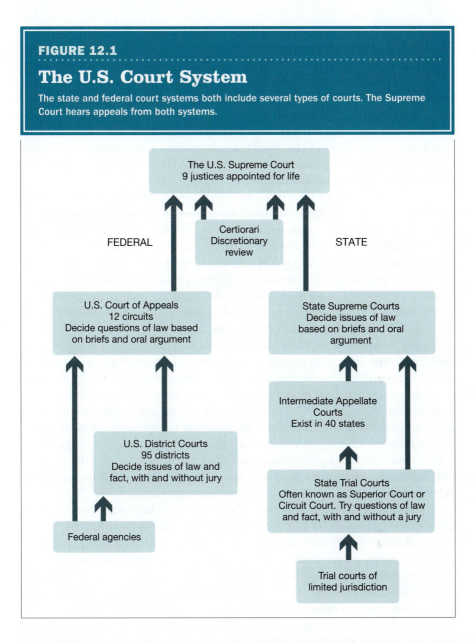

FIGURE 12.1

The U.S. Court System

The state and federal court systems both include several types of courts. The Supreme Court hears appeals from both systems.

The U.S. Supreme Court
9 justices appointed for life

FEDERAL

Certiorari
Discretionary
review

STATE

U.S. Court of Appeals
12 circuits
Decide questions of law based
on briefs and oral argument

State Supreme Courts
Decide issues of law
based on briefs and oral
argument

Intermediate Appellate
Courts
Exist in 40 states

U.S. District Courts
95 districts
Decide issues of law and
fact, with and without jury

State Trial Courts
Often known as Superior Court or
Circuit Court. Try questions of law
and fact, with and without a jury

Federal agencies

Trial courts of
limited jurisdiction

United States are heard in state courts. The overwhelming majority of criminal cases, for example, involve violations of state laws prohibiting such actions as murder, robbery, fraud, theft, and assault. If such a case is brought to trial, it will be heard in a state **trial court** (the first court to hear a criminal or civil case), in front of a judge and sometimes a jury, who will determine whether the defendant violated state law. If the defendant is convicted, she may appeal the conviction to a higher court, such as a state **court of appeals** (a court that hears the appeals of trial court decisions) and from there to a state's **supreme court** (the highest court in a particular state or in the

United States, which primarily serves an appellate function). The government is not entitled to appeal if the defendant is found not guilty in a criminal case.

The party filing an appeal, known as an appellant, usually must show that the trial court made a legal error in deciding the case. Appeals courts do not hear witnesses or examine additional evidence and will only consider new facts under unusual circumstances. Thus, for example, a physician who loses a malpractice case might appeal on the basis that the trial court misapplied the relevant law or incorrectly instructed the jury. It should be noted that most criminal and civil cases are settled before trial through negotiated agreements between the parties. In criminal cases, these agreements are called **plea bargains**.

Cases are heard in the federal courts if they involve federal laws, treaties with other nations, or the U.S. Constitution; these areas are the official **jurisdiction** (the sphere of a court's power and authority) of the federal courts. In addition, any case in which the U.S. government is a party is heard in the federal courts. If, for example, an individual is accused of violating a federal criminal statute, such as evading the payment of income taxes, a federal prosecutor would bring charges before a federal judge. Civil cases involving the citizens of more than one state and in which more than $75,000 is at stake may be heard in either the federal or the state courts, usually depending on the preference of the plaintiff.

Federal courts serve another purpose in addition to trying cases within their jurisdiction: that of hearing appeals from state-level courts. In both civil and criminal cases, a decision of the highest state court can be appealed to the U.S. Supreme Court by raising a federal issue. A defendant who appeals a lower-court decision in federal court might assert, for example, that he was denied the right to counsel or was otherwise deprived of the **due process of law** (the right of every citizen against arbitrary action by national or state governments) guaranteed by the federal Constitution, or that important issues of federal law were at stake in the case. The U.S. Supreme Court is not obligated to accept such appeals and will do so only if it believes that the matter has considerable national significance.

In addition, in criminal cases, defendants who have been convicted in a state court may request a **writ of habeas corpus** from a federal district court. Sometimes known as the "Great Writ," habeas corpus is a court order that the individual in custody be brought into court and shown the cause for her detention. The court then evaluates the sufficiency of the cause and may order the release of a prisoner deemed to be held in violation of his legal rights. Habeas corpus is guaranteed by the Constitution and can be suspended only in cases of rebellion or invasion. In 1867, Congress's distrust of southern courts led it to authorize federal district judges to issue such writs to prisoners who they believed had been deprived of constitutional rights in state court. Generally speaking, state defendants seeking a federal writ of habeas corpus must show that they have exhausted all available state remedies and must raise issues not previously raised in their state appeals. Federal courts of appeal and, ultimately, the U.S. Supreme Court have appellate jurisdiction for federal district court habeas decisions.

Although the federal courts hear only a small fraction of all the civil and criminal cases decided each year in the United States, their decisions are extremely important.

It is in the federal courts that the Constitution and federal laws that govern all Americans are interpreted and their meaning and significance established. Moreover, it is in the federal courts that the powers and limitations of the increasingly powerful national government are tested. Finally, through their power to review the decisions of the state courts, it is ultimately the federal courts that dominate the American judicial system.

The Federal Courts Hear a Small Percentage of All Cases

> **Describe the different levels of federal courts and their functions**

During the year ending in March 2017 federal district courts (the lowest federal level) received 362,028 cases. Though large, this number is less than 1 percent of the number of cases heard by state courts. The federal courts of appeal listened to 58,951 cases during that period, and about 15 percent of the verdicts were appealed to the U.S. Supreme Court. Most of the roughly 9,000 cases filed with the Supreme Court yearly are dismissed without a ruling on their merits. The Court has broad latitude to decide what cases it will hear and generally listens to only those cases it deems raise the most important issues. In recent years, fewer than 80 cases per year have received full-dress Supreme Court review.[2]

THE LOWER FEDERAL COURTS HANDLE MOST CASES

Most of the cases of original federal jurisdiction are handled by the federal district courts. **Original jurisdiction** is the authority to initially consider a case. It is distinguished from *appellate jurisdiction*, which is the authority to hear appeals from a lower court's decision. Courts of original jurisdiction are the courts that are responsible for discovering the facts in a controversy and creating the record on which a judgment is based. In courts that have appellate jurisdiction, judges receive cases after the factual record is established by the trial court. Ordinarily, new facts cannot be presented before appellate courts. Article III of the Constitution gives the Supreme Court original jurisdiction in a limited number of cases including (1) cases between the United States and one of the 50 states, (2) cases between two or more states, (3) cases involving foreign ambassadors or other ministers, and (4) cases brought by one state against citizens of another state or against a foreign country. Article III assigns original jurisdiction in all other federal cases to the lower courts that Congress was authorized to establish. Importantly, the Constitution gives the Supreme Court appellate jurisdiction in *all* federal cases. Almost all cases heard by the Supreme Court are under its appellate jurisdiction.

The 94 federal district courts are staffed by 678 federal district judges. District judges are assigned to district courts according to the workload; the busiest of these courts may have as many as 28 judges. Only one judge is assigned to each case, except where statutes provide for three-judge courts to deal with special issues. The routines and procedures of the federal district courts are essentially the same as those of the lower state courts, except that federal procedural requirements tend to be stricter. States, for example, do not have to provide a grand jury, a 12-member trial jury, or a unanimous jury verdict. Federal courts must follow all these procedures.

THE APPELLATE COURTS HEAR 20 PERCENT OF LOWER-COURT CASES

Roughly 20 percent of all lower-court and federal agency cases are accepted for review by the federal appeals courts and by the Supreme Court in its capacity as an appellate court. There are 13 U.S. Court of Appeals judicial districts, or circuits, with a total of 179 judges. Those districts consist of 11 that divide up the nation geographically plus one for the District of Columbia and one federal circuit that deals with patents, trademarks, international trade, and claims against the federal government (see Figure 12.2).

FIGURE 12.2

Federal Appellate Court Circuits

The 94 federal district courts are organized into 12 regional circuits: the 11 shown here plus the District of Columbia, which has its own circuit. Each circuit court hears appeals from lower federal courts within the circuit. A thirteenth federal circuit court, the U.S. Court of Appeals for the Federal Circuit, hears appeals from a number of specialized courts such as the U.S. Court of Federal Claims.

SOURCE: United States Courts, "Geographic Boundaries," www.uscourts.gov/about-federal-courts/federal-courts-public/court-website-links (accessed 8/23/16).

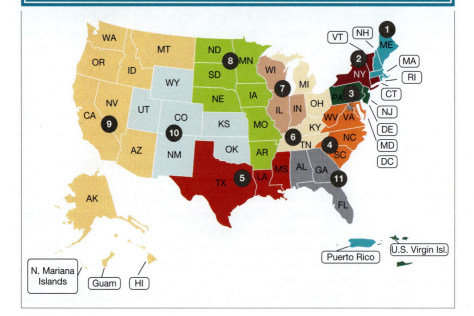

Except for cases selected for review by the Supreme Court, decisions made by the appeals courts are final. Because of this finality, certain safeguards have been built into the system. The most important is the provision of more than one judge for every appeals case. Each court of appeals has from 6 to 28 permanent judgeships, depending on the workload of the circuit. Although normally three judges hear appealed cases, in some instances a larger number of judges sit together en banc.

Another safeguard is provided by the assignment of a Supreme Court justice as the circuit justice for each of the circuits. Since the creation of the appeals court in 1891, the circuit justice's primary duty has been to review appeals arising in the circuit in order to expedite Supreme Court action. The most frequent and best-known action of circuit justices is that of reviewing requests for stays of execution when the full Court is unable to do so—primarily during the summer, when the Court is in recess.

THE SUPREME COURT IS THE COURT OF FINAL APPEAL

The Supreme Court is America's highest court. Article III of the Constitution vests "the judicial power of the United States" in the Supreme Court, and this court is supreme in fact as well as form. The Supreme Court is the only federal court established by the Constitution. The lower federal courts were created by Congress and can be restructured or, presumably, even abolished by the legislative branch. The Supreme Court is made up of a chief justice and eight associate justices (see Table 12.1). The **chief justice** presides over the Court's public sessions and conferences and is the first to speak and vote. Voting then proceeds from most to

TABLE 12.1

Supreme Court Justices, 2019 (in Order of Seniority)

NAME	YEAR OF BIRTH	PRIOR EXPERIENCE	APPOINTED BY	YEAR OF APPOINTMENT
Clarence Thomas	1948	Federal judge	G. H. W. Bush	1991
Ruth Bader Ginsburg	1933	Federal judge	Clinton	1993
Stephen Breyer	1938	Federal judge	Clinton	1994
John Roberts, Jr. (Chief Justice)	1955	Federal judge	G. W. Bush	2005
Samuel Alito	1950	Federal judge	G. W. Bush	2006
Sonia Sotomayor	1954	Federal judge	Obama	2009
Elena Kagan	1960	Solicitor general	Obama	2010
Neil Gorsuch	1967	Federal judge	Trump	2017
Brett Kavanaugh	1965	Federal judge	Trump	2018

least senior. In the Court's actual deliberations and decisions, however, the chief justice has no more authority than the other justices. Each justice casts one vote. To some extent, the influence of the chief justice is a function of her own leadership ability. Some chief justices, such as the late Earl Warren, have been able to lead the Court in a new direction. In other instances, forceful associate justices, such as the late Felix Frankfurter, are the dominant figures on the Court.

The Constitution does not specify the number of justices who should sit on the Supreme Court; Congress has the authority to change the Court's size. In the early nineteenth century, there were six Supreme Court justices; later there were seven. Congress set the number of justices at nine in 1869, and the Court has remained that size ever since.

JUDGES ARE APPOINTED BY THE PRESIDENT AND APPROVED BY THE SENATE

Federal judges are nominated by the president and are generally selected from among the more prominent or politically active members of the legal profession. Many federal judges previously served as state court judges or state or local prosecutors. There are no formal qualifications for service as a federal judge. In general, presidents endeavor to appoint judges who possess legal experience and good character and whose partisan and ideological views are similar to their own. Once the president has formally nominated an individual, the nominee must be considered by the Senate Judiciary Committee and confirmed by a majority vote in the full Senate. In recent years, the judicial appointments process has been affected by increasing partisan conflict. Senate Democrats have sought to prevent Republican presidents from appointing conservative judges, while Senate Republicans have worked to prevent Democratic presidents from appointing liberal judges. During the early months of the Obama administration, Republicans were able to slow the judicial appointment process through filibusters and other procedural maneuvers so that only 3 of the president's 23 nominations for federal judgeships were confirmed by the Senate.[3] Obama's allies urged the president to take a more aggressive stance or risk allowing Republicans to block what had been considered a key Democratic priority. In 2013 the Senate voted 52 to 48 to end the use of the filibuster against all executive branch and judicial nominees except those to the Supreme Court, allowing President Obama to quickly secure the appointment of more than 300 new district court judges and 55 new appeals court judges.

In 2017, as we saw earlier, Republicans turned the tables and extended these rule changes to include Supreme Court nominees, thus blocking Democratic efforts to prevent President Trump from appointing Neil Gorsuch to the High Court. In July 2018, Justice Anthony Kennedy, who had been a swing vote on the Court, announced his resignation. President Trump nominated Judge Brett Kavanaugh to replace Kennedy. Kavanaugh was generally seen as a conservative in the Gorsuch mold. Liberal groups promised an all-out fight to block the nomination but, with Republican control of the Senate and the elimination of filibusters on judicial appointments, there was little chance Democrats could derail the Kavanaugh appointment.

If political factors play an important role in the selection of district and appellate court judges, they are decisive when it comes to Supreme Court appointments. Because the Court has so much influence over law and politics, virtually all presidents have made an effort to select justices who share their political views.

As of 2018, five of the nine current justices were appointed by Republican presidents. With the exception of the months between the passing of Antonin Scalia in February 2016 and the confirmation of Neil Gorsuch in April 2017, the Court had a conservative majority for 45 years. This majority has propelled the Court in a more conservative direction in a variety of areas, including civil rights (Chapter 4) and election law.

After Justice Anthony Kennedy announced his retirement in 2018, Trump nominated Brett Kavanaugh to the Supreme Court. Many feel that Kavanaugh will shift the Court in a more conservative direction.

Supreme Court nominations have come to involve intense partisan struggle in recent decades. The struggle over filling the Scalia vacancy in 2016 reflected the heightened partisanship over court nominees. In eleven past instances when presidents had put forward nominees to fill Supreme Court vacancies in the last years of their terms, the Senate considered and voted on them.[4] In 2016, however, the Republican-controlled Senate refused to even consider President Obama's nominee, Judge Merrick Garland, leaving the seat vacant for a year until President Trump successfully nominated Judge Gorsuch.

The Kavanaugh nomination touched off one of the most intense political struggles in recent American history. Days before the Senate was to vote, Christine Blasey Ford came forward to assert that the judge had attempted to sexually assault her 36 years ago when he was 17 and she was 15. Kavanaugh vehemently denied the accusation as well as accusations of sexual impropriety by two other women who had known him in college. Televised testimony before the Senate Judiciary Committee by Kavanaugh and Ford divided the Senate and the nation, primarily along partisan lines. Democrats argued that Kavanaugh was unfit to serve on the Court while Republicans asserted that the charges against Kavanaugh had been invented for political reasons. An FBI investigation failed to shed light on the allegations, and Kavanaugh was confirmed, receiving the votes of all but one Republican and only one Democrat.[5]

The Power of the Supreme Court Is Judicial Review

Explain how the Supreme Court exercises the power of judicial review

The term **judicial review** refers to the power of the judiciary to review and, if necessary, declare actions of the legislative and executive branches invalid or unconstitutional. It is sometimes also used to describe the scrutiny that appellate courts give to the actions of trial courts, but strictly speaking, this is improper usage. A higher court's examination of a lower court's decisions might be called "appellate review," but it is not judicial review.

JUDICIAL REVIEW COVERS ACTS OF CONGRESS

Because the Constitution does not give the Supreme Court the power of judicial review over congressional enactments, the Court's exercise of it seems like something of a usurpation. But judicial review was debated at the Constitutional Convention. Some delegates expected the courts to exercise this power, while many others were "departmentalists," believing that each branch of the new government would interpret the Constitution as it applied to its own actions, with the judiciary mainly ensuring that individuals did not suffer injustices. Ambiguity over the framers' intentions was settled in 1803 in the case of *Marbury v. Madison*.[6] The Court said,

> It is emphatically the province and duty of the Judicial Department [the judicial branch] to say what the law is. Those who apply the rule to particular cases must, of necessity, expound and interpret that rule. If two laws conflict with each other, the Courts must decide on the operation of each. . . . So, if a law [e.g., a statute or treaty] be in opposition to the Constitution, if both the law and the Constitution apply to a particular case, so that the Court must either decide that case conformably to the law, disregarding the Constitution, or conformably to the Constitution, disregarding the law, the Court must determine which of these conflicting rules governs the case. This is of the very essence of judicial duty.

The Court's legal power to review acts of Congress has not been seriously questioned since 1803 in part because the Supreme Court tends to give acts of Congress an interpretation that will make them constitutional. For example, in its 2012 decision upholding the constitutionality of the ACA, the Court agreed with the many legal scholars who had argued that Congress had no power under the Constitution's commerce clause to order Americans to purchase health insurance. But rather than invalidate the act, the Court declared that the law's requirement that all Americans purchase insurance was actually a tax and, thus, represented a constitutionally acceptable use of Congress's power to levy taxes.[7]

In more than two centuries, the Court has concluded that fewer than 160 acts of Congress directly violated the Constitution.[8] These cases are often highly controversial. For example, in 2007, 2010, and 2014, the high court struck down key portions of the Bipartisan Campaign Reform Act, through which Congress had sought to regulate spending in political campaigns.[9] The Court found that provisions of the act limiting political advertising violated the First Amendment. In the 2017 case of *Matal v. Tam* the Court also cited free speech concerns in striking down a federal law that prohibited trademarks that disparaged people or groups.[10] The decision was cheered by fans of the Washington "Redskins" football team. These cases are important but unusual in that the Court rarely overturns acts of Congress.

Term Limits for High Court Justices

Once appointed, Supreme Court justices "shall hold their Offices during good Behaviour,"[a] which has effectively meant they serve for life. Only once (in 1804) has the Senate started impeachment proceedings against a Supreme Court justice, and this judge was ultimately acquitted.[b]

While the founding fathers may have created life terms with the intention of preserving judicial independence and isolating justices from partisan pressures, the life term limits may have created other political problems. Scholars point out that the extreme partisan nature and tensions that emerge during Supreme Court appointment hearings (as described in this chapter) may be due to the life term rule.[c] After all, appointing a justice favorable to your partisan position is considered a major political coup given that the average Supreme Court justice serves over 25 years.

Constitutional courts (courts with the power of judicial review) aim to preserve judicial independence as they play an important role in guaranteeing democracy by checking executive overreach. Other countries, however, have sought to balance this with the need of also having a more dynamic and changing court. Canada, for instance, sets a mandatory retirement age of 75 for their Supreme Court justices. Other countries have set term limits so that justices serve one long, nonrenewable term. This system insulates justices from political pressures yet still promotes judicial turnover. If the United States used the same rules as Germany (see below), only 3 of the 9 current justices—Sotomayor, Kagan, and the recently-appointed Gorsuch—would still be on the court.

TERM LIMITS		MANDATORY RETIREMENT AGE
Chilean Constitutional Court	9 years	–
French Constitutional Council	9	–
German Constitutional Court	12	68
High Court of Australia	Life	70
India Supreme Court	Life	65
South African Constitutional Court	12	70
South Korean Constitutional Court	6	65
Supreme Court of Canada	Life	75
Supreme Federal Court of Brazil	Life	75
U.S. Supreme Court	Life	–

SOURCE: Central Intelligence Agency, "Judicial Branch," The World Factbook, www.cia.gov/index .html (accessed 4/15/18).

[a] U.S. Constitution, Article III, Section 1.

[b] U.S. Senate, "Senate Prepares for Impeachment Trial," www.senate.gov/artandhistory/history/minute/Senate_Tries_Justice. htm (accessed 4/15/18).

[c] Steven G. Calabresi and James Lindgren, "Term Limits for the Supreme Court: Life Tenure Reconsidered," *Harvard Journal of Law & Public Policy* 29, no. 3 (2005): 769–878.

JUDICIAL REVIEW APPLIES TO PRESIDENTIAL ACTIONS

The federal courts also review presidential actions from time to time. In recent decades, the courts have, more often than not, upheld presidential power in such areas as foreign policy, war and emergency powers, legislative power, and administrative authority. But the Supreme Court ruled on three cases involving President George W. Bush's antiterrorism initiatives and claims of executive power, and in two of the three cases placed some limits on presidential authority.

One important case was *Hamdi v. Rumsfeld*.[11] Yaser Esam Hamdi, apparently a Taliban soldier, was captured by American forces in Afghanistan and brought to the United States, where he was incarcerated at the Norfolk Naval Station. Hamdi was classified as an enemy combatant and denied civil rights, including the right to counsel, despite the fact that he had been born in the United States and was a U.S. citizen. In 2004 the Supreme Court ruled that Hamdi was entitled to a lawyer and "a fair opportunity to rebut the government's factual assertions." Thus, the Court imposed restrictions on the president's power, although it also affirmed the president's most important claim: the unilateral power to declare individuals, including U.S. citizens, "enemy combatants" who could be detained by the United States.

In the 2006 case of *Hamdan v. Rumsfeld*,[12] Salim Hamdan, a Taliban fighter, was captured in Afghanistan and held at the Guantánamo Bay naval base. The Bush administration planned to try Hamdan before a military commission created by a 2002 presidential order. The Supreme Court ruled that this presidentially created commission violated federal law and U.S. treaty obligations. In response,

After President Trump's "travel ban" was implemented in early 2017, many court cases challenged this decision, and eventually one case was tried before the Supreme Court. In a 5–4 decision, the Court upheld the travel ban, sparking outrage from Democratic lawmakers.

Bush pressed Congress to rewrite the law, which it did, enacting the Military Commissions Act. This law gave the president legal authority for his actions. Section 7 of the law said that Guantánamo prisoners could not bring habeas corpus petitions to federal courts to seek their release. In the 2008 case of *Boumediene v. Bush*,[13] however, the Supreme Court struck down Section 7, saying that habeas corpus was a fundamental right.

Judicial review of presidential actions is not limited to presidential war powers and the realm of terrorism. In the 2017 case of *Trump v. International Refugee Assistance Project*, the Court overturned lower court injunctions blocking President Trump's temporary ban on travelers from six majority Muslim countries.[14] The Court's decision at least temporarily allowed the government to enforce the ban with exceptions for some travelers such as those with close family members in the United States. The Court ultimately upheld the ban in *Trump v. Hawaii* in June 2018.[15]

JUDICIAL REVIEW ALSO APPLIES TO STATE ACTIONS

The logic of the **supremacy clause** of Article VI of the Constitution, which states that laws passed by the national government and all treaties "shall be the supreme Law of the Land" and superior to all laws adopted by any state or any subdivision, implies that the Court may review the constitutionality of state laws. Furthermore, in the Judiciary Act of 1789, Congress conferred on the Supreme Court the power to reverse state constitutions and laws whenever they are clearly in conflict with the U.S. Constitution, federal laws, or treaties.[16] This power gives the Supreme Court appellate jurisdiction over all of the millions of cases handled by U.S. courts each year.

The supremacy clause of the Constitution also provides that "the Judges in every State shall be bound thereby, any Thing in the Constitution or Laws of any State to the Contrary notwithstanding." Under this authority, the Supreme Court has frequently overturned state constitutional provisions or statutes and state court decisions it deems contrary to the federal Constitution or federal statutes.

The civil rights arena abounds with examples of state laws that were overturned because the statutes violated guarantees of due process and equal protection contained in the Constitution's Fourteenth Amendment. For example, in the 1954 case of *Brown v. Board of Education*, the Court overturned statutes from Kansas, South Carolina, Virginia, and Delaware that either required or permitted segregated public schools, on the basis that such statutes denied black schoolchildren equal protection of the law.[17] In 2003 the Court ruled that Texas's law criminalizing sodomy violated the right to liberty protected by the due process clause.[18] In the 2017 case of *Pavan v. Smith*, the Court overturned an Arkansas law that denied same-sex couples the right to include a spouse's name on a birth certificate—a right granted to other couples.[19] The Court said the statute denied same-sex couples equal protection of the law.

State statutes in other areas of law are equally subject to challenge. Many of the Supreme Court's recent decisions overturning state law have come in cases concerning election law. In 2015, for example, the Court ruled against an Alabama legislative districting plan that opponents charged was designed to reduce the influence of black voters.[20] During the same year the Court ruled against an

The Supreme Court has the power to review state action. In *Pavan v. Smith*, the Supreme Court overturned Arkansas's law that disallowed same-sex parents to have both of their names listed on their children's birth certificates. Here, Marisa Pavan, the plaintiff in the case, holds her daughter and her birth certificate showing both parents' names.

effort by the Arizona legislature to invalidate a districting plan drawn up by an independent commission created by a voter referendum.[21] In the 2017 case of *Cooper v. Harris*, the Court invalidated a North Carolina legislative districting plan that moved tens of thousands of black voters into congressional districts that already had large black majorities.[22] This tactic is known as "packing," and is designed to reduce the number of seats that might be affected by some group of voters by packing them all into as few districts as possible.

One realm in which the Court constantly monitors state conduct is that of law enforcement. As we saw in Chapter 4, the Supreme Court has developed a number of principles regulating police conduct to ensure that the police do not violate constitutional liberties. These principles, however, must often be updated to keep pace with changes in technology. In the 2012 case of *United States v. Jones*, the Supreme Court found that police use of a Global Positioning System tracker—a device invented more than two centuries after the adoption of the Bill of Rights—constituted a "search" as defined by the Fourth Amendment. In the 2014 case of *Riley v. California*, the Court held that the police could not undertake a warrantless search of the digital contents of a cell phone—another device hardly imagined by the framers.[23]

Most Cases Reach the Supreme Court by Appeal

Describe the process the Supreme Court follows in the exercise of its power of judicial review

Article III of the Constitution and Supreme Court decisions define judicial power as extending only to "cases and controversies." This means that the case before a court must be an actual controversy, not a hypothetical one, with two truly adversarial parties. The courts have interpreted this language to mean that they do not have the power to render advisory opinions to legislatures or agencies about the constitutionality of proposed laws or regulations. Furthermore, even after a law is enacted, the courts will generally refuse to consider its constitutionality until it is actually applied. Even with this provision, given that millions of disputes arise every year, the job of the Supreme Court would be impossible if it were not able to control the flow of cases and its own caseload.

Parties to a case must also have **standing**—that is, they must show that they have a substantial stake in the outcome of the case. The traditional requirement for standing has been to show injury to oneself; that injury can be personal, economic, or even aesthetic, such as a neighbor's building a high fence that blocks one's view of the ocean. In order for a group or class of people to have standing (as in class-action suits), each member must show specific injury. This means that a general interest in the environment, for instance, does not provide a group with sufficient basis for standing.

The Supreme Court also uses a third criterion in determining whether it will hear a case: that of **mootness**. In theory, this requirement disqualifies cases that are brought too late—after the relevant facts have changed or the problem has been resolved by other means. The criterion of mootness, however, is subject to the discretion of the courts, which have begun to relax the rules of mootness, particularly in cases where a situation that has been resolved is likely to come up again.

Most cases reach the Supreme Court through the **writ of certiorari**, which is granted whenever four of the nine justices agree to review a decision of a lower court. (*Certiorari* comes from the Latin for "to make more certain.") The term *certiorari* is sometimes shortened to *cert*, and cases deemed to merit certiorari are referred to as "certworthy." An individual who loses in a lower federal court or state court and wants the Supreme Court to review the decision has 90 days to file a petition for a writ of certiorari with the clerk of the U.S. Supreme Court. Petitions for thousands of cases are filed with the Court every year.

Since 1972 most of the justices have participated in a "certiorari pool" in which their law clerks work together to evaluate the petitions. Each petition is reviewed by one clerk, who writes a memo for all the justices participating in the pool, summarizing the facts and issues and making a recommendation. Clerks for the other justices add their comments to the memo. After the justices have reviewed the memos, any one of them may place any case on the discuss list, which is circulated by the chief justice. If a case is not placed on the discuss list, it is automatically denied certiorari. Cases placed on the discuss list are considered and voted on during the justices' closed-door conference.

For certiorari to be granted, four justices must be convinced that the case satisfies Rule 10 of the Rules of the U.S. Supreme Court. Rule 10 states that certiorari is not a matter of right but is to be granted only when there are special and compelling reasons. These include conflicting decisions by two or more circuit courts, conflicts between circuit courts and state courts of last resort, conflicting decisions by two or more state courts of last resort, decisions by circuit courts on matters of federal law that should be settled by the Supreme Court, a circuit court decision on an important question that conflicts with Supreme Court decisions, cases that present important questions of civil rights or civil liberties, and cases in which the federal government is an appellant. It should be clear from this list that the Court will usually take action under only the most compelling circumstances. Ultimately, however, the question of which cases to accept can come down to the preferences and priorities of the justices.

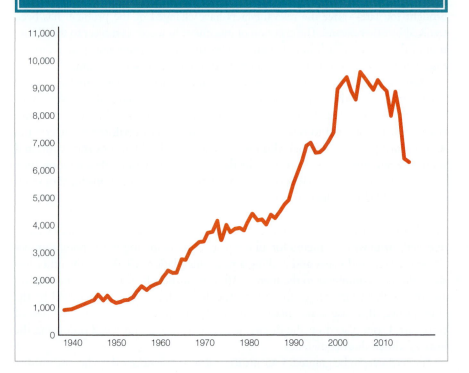

FIGURE 12.3

Number of Cases Filed in the U.S. Supreme Court, 1938–2017 Terms

NOTE: Number of cases filed in term starting in year indicated.

SOURCES: Years 1938–69, 1970–83, 1984–99: *The United States Law Week* (Washington, DC: Bureau of National Affairs), vol. 56, no. 3102; vol. 59, no. 3064; vol. 61, no. 3098; vol. 63, no. 3134; vol. 65, no. 3100; vol. 67, no. 3167; vol. 69, no. 3134 (copyright © Bureau of National Affairs Inc.); 2000–05: U.S. Bureau of the Census, *Statistical Abstract of the United States*; 2006–10: Office of the Clerk, Supreme Court of the United States; and 2011–14: Supreme Court of the United States, Cases on Docket, www.uscourts.gov/statistics-reports/caseload-statistics-data-tables. 2017 Year-End Report on the Federal Judiciary, www.supremecourt.gov/publicinfo/year-end/2017year-endreport.pdf (accessed 4/5/18).

As Figure 12.3 shows, the Court is inundated by appeals, and the number of appeals has skyrocketed over the years, even though the Court actually rules on less than 1 percent of these appeals.

THE SOLICITOR GENERAL, LAW CLERKS, AND INTEREST GROUPS ALSO INFLUENCE THE FLOW OF CASES

In addition to the judges themselves, three other entities play an important role in shaping the flow of cases through the federal courts: the solicitor general, federal law clerks, and interest groups.

The Solicitor General If any single person has greater influence than individual judges over the federal courts, it is the **solicitor general** of the United States. The solicitor general is the third-ranking official in the Justice Department (below the attorney general and the deputy attorney general) but the top government lawyer in virtually all cases before the Supreme Court in which the government is a party. The solicitor general controls the flow of cases by screening them before any agency of the federal government can appeal them to the Supreme Court; indeed, the justices rely on the solicitor general to "screen out undeserving litigation and furnish them with an agenda to government cases that deserve serious consideration."[24] More than half of the Supreme Court's total workload consists of cases under the direct charge of the solicitor general. Typically, more requests for appeals are rejected than are accepted by the solicitor general. Without the solicitor general's support, requests directly from government agencies are seldom reviewed by the Court.

The solicitor general can enter a case even when the federal government is not a direct litigant, by writing an **amicus curiae** ("friend of the court") brief. A "friend of the court" is not a direct party to a case but seeks to assist the Supreme Court in reaching a decision by presenting additional briefs. Other interested parties may file amicus briefs as well.

In addition to exercising substantial control over the flow of cases, the solicitor general can shape the arguments used before the federal courts. Indeed, the Supreme Court tends to give special attention to the way the solicitor general characterizes the issues.

Law Clerks Every federal judge employs law clerks to research legal issues and assist with the preparation of opinions. Each Supreme Court justice is assigned four clerks. The clerks are almost always honors graduates from the nation's most prestigious law schools. A clerkship with a Supreme Court justice is a great honor and generally indicates that the fortunate individual is likely to reach the very top of the legal profession. The work of the Supreme Court clerks is a closely guarded secret, but some justices rely heavily on their clerks for advice in writing opinions and in deciding whether specific cases ought to be heard by the Court. In a recent book, a former law clerk to the late justice Harry Blackmun charged that Supreme Court justices yielded "excessive power to immature, ideologically driven clerks, who in turn use that power to manipulate their bosses."[25]

Lobbying for Access: Interests and the Court At the same time that the Court exercises discretion over which cases it will review, groups and forces in society often seek to persuade the justices to listen to their problems. Lawyers representing interest groups try to choose the proper client and the proper case so that the issues in question are most dramatically and appropriately portrayed. When possible, they also pick a district with a sympathetic judge in which to bring the case. Sometimes they wait for an appropriate political climate.

Group litigants have to plan carefully when to use and when to avoid publicity. They must also attempt to develop a proper record at the trial court level, one that includes some constitutional arguments and even, when possible, errors on the part of the trial court. One of the most effective strategies that litigants use in getting cases accepted for review by the appellate courts is to bring the same type of suit in more than one circuit (that is, to develop a "pattern of cases"), in the hope that inconsistent treatment by two different courts will improve the chance of a Supreme Court review.

The two most notable users of the "pattern of cases" strategy in recent years have been the National Association for the Advancement of Colored People (NAACP) and the American Civil Liberties Union (ACLU). For many years, the NAACP (and its Defense Fund—now a separate group) has worked through local chapters and with many individuals to encourage litigation on issues of racial discrimination and segregation. Sometimes it distributes petitions to be signed by parents and filed with local school boards and courts, deliberately sowing the seeds of future litigation. The NAACP and the ACLU often encourage private parties to bring suit and then join the suit as amici curiae.

THE SUPREME COURT'S PROCEDURES MEAN CASES MAY TAKE MONTHS OR YEARS

Preparation The Supreme Court's decision to accept a case is the beginning of what can be a lengthy and complex process (see Figure 12.4). First, the attorneys on both sides must prepare briefs—written documents that may be several hundred pages long in which the attorneys explain, using case precedents, why the Court should rule in favor of their client. Briefs are filled with referrals to precedents specifically chosen to show that other courts have frequently ruled in the same way that the Supreme Court is being asked to rule. The attorneys for both sides muster the most compelling precedents they can in support of their arguments.

As the attorneys prepare their briefs, they often ask sympathetic interest groups for help. Groups are asked to file amicus curiae briefs that support the claims of one or the other litigant. In a case involving separation of church and state, for example, liberal groups such as the ACLU and Citizens for the American Way are likely to be asked to file amicus briefs in support of strict separation, whereas conservative religious groups are likely to file amicus briefs advocating increased public support for religious ideas. Often, dozens of briefs will be filed on each side of a major case. Amicus filings are a primary method used by interest groups to lobby the Court.

Oral Argument The next stage of a case is oral argument, in which attorneys for both sides appear before the Court to present their positions and answer questions posed by justices. Each attorney has only a half hour to present the case, and this time includes interruptions for questions. Certain members of the Court, such as the late Justice Scalia, are known to interrupt attorneys dozens of times. Others, such as Justice Thomas, seldom ask questions. For an attorney, the opportunity to argue a case before the Supreme Court is a singular honor and a mark of professional distinction. It can also be a harrowing experience as justices interrupt a carefully prepared presentation to ask pointed questions. Oral argument can be very important to the

FIGURE 12.4

Time Line of a Supreme Court Case

This calendar of events in the case of *Janus v. American Federation of State, County, and Municipal Employees*, discussed at the start of this chapter, illustrates the steps of the process as a case moves through the Supreme Court.

SOURCE: www.scotusblog.com/case-files/cases/janus-v-american-federation-state-county-municipal-employees
-council-31/ (accessed 9/26/18).

June 6, 2017

Petition for a writ of certiorari filed.

July 7, 2017

Filing of briefs and amicus curiae briefs in support of the petitioner.

August 11, 2017

Brief of respondent American Federation of State, County, and Municipal Employees, Council 31 in opposition filed.

August 30, 2017

The case is distributed for conference.

September 28, 2017

The petition (certiorari) is granted.

December 20, 2017

Date for oral argument is set for February 26, 2018.

December 2017

Briefs and amicus curiae briefs are filed on behalf of petitioner.

January 2018

Briefs and amicus curiae briefs are filed on behalf of respondent.

February 26, 2018

Oral argument of one hour

June 27, 2018

Decision

outcome of a case. It allows justices to better understand the heart of the case and to raise questions that might not have been addressed in the opposing side's briefs. It is not uncommon for justices to go beyond the strictly legal issues and ask opposing counsel to discuss the implications of the case for the Court and the nation at large.

Conference Following oral argument, the Court discusses the case in its Wednesday or Friday conference, a strictly private meeting that no outsiders are permitted to attend. The chief justice presides over the conference and speaks first; the other justices follow in order of seniority. The justices discuss the case and eventually reach a decision on the basis of a majority vote. If the Court is divided, a number of votes may be taken before a final decision is reached. As the case is discussed, justices may try to influence or change one another's opinions. At times, this may result in compromise decisions.

Opinion Writing After a decision has been reached, one of the members of the majority is assigned to write the **opinion**—the written explanation of the Supreme Court's decision in a particular case. This assignment is made by the chief justice or by the most senior justice in the majority if the chief justice is on the losing side. The assignment of the opinion can make a significant difference to the interpretation of a decision. Lawyers and judges in the lower courts will examine the opinion carefully to ascertain the Supreme Court's intent. Differences in wording and emphasis can have important implications for future litigation. Once the majority opinion is drafted, it is circulated to the other justices. Some members of the majority may decide that they do not agree with all the language of the opinion and therefore write "concurring" opinions that support the decision but offer a different rationale or emphasis. In assigning an opinion, serious thought must be given to the impression the case will make on lawyers and the public and to the probability that one justice's opinion will be more widely accepted than another's.

One of the more dramatic instances of this tactical consideration occurred in 1944, when Chief Justice Harlan F. Stone chose Justice Felix Frankfurter to write the opinion in the "white primary" case *Smith v. Allwright*. The chief justice believed that this sensitive case, which overturned the southern practice of prohibiting black participation in nominating primaries, required the efforts of the most brilliant and scholarly jurist on the Court. But the day after Stone made the assignment, Justice Robert H. Jackson wrote a letter to Stone urging a change of assignment. In his letter, Jackson argued that Frankfurter, a foreign-born Jew from New England, would not win the South with his opinion, regardless of its brilliance. Stone accepted the advice and substituted Justice Stanley Reed, an American-born Protestant from Kentucky and a southern Democrat in good standing.[26]

Dissent Justices who disagree with the majority decision of the Court may choose to publicize their disagreement in the form of a **dissenting opinion** (a decision written by a justice in the minority in a particular case in which the justice wishes to express his reasoning in the case). Dissents can be used to express opposition to an outcome or to signal to defeated political forces in the nation that their position is supported by at least some members of the Court. Because there is no need to please a majority, dissenting opinions can be more eloquent and less guarded than majority opinions. The Supreme Court often produces 5–4 decisions, with dissenters writing long and detailed opinions that, they hope, will help them to persuade a swing justice to join their side on the next round of cases dealing with a similar topic. During the Court's 2006–07 term, Justice Ruth Bader Ginsburg was so unhappy about the majority's decisions in a number of cases that she began to read forceful dissents from the bench, a practice she has continued to underscore her disagreements with several recent decisions and point the way toward other possibilities.

Supreme Court Decisions Are Influenced by Activism and Ideology

Consider the personal and political influences on judges and the courts

The Supreme Court explains its decisions in terms of law and precedent. But although law and precedent do have an effect on the Court's deliberations and eventual decisions, throughout its history, the Court has shaped and reshaped the law. In the late nineteenth and early twentieth centuries, for example, the Supreme Court held that the Constitution, law, and precedent permitted racial segregation in the United States. Beginning in the late 1950s, however, the Court found that the Constitution prohibited segregation on the basis of race and ruled that racial categories in legislation were always suspect. By the 1970s and '80s the Court once again held that the Constitution permitted the use of racial categories—when such categories were needed to help members of minority groups achieve full participation in American society. In the 1990s the Court began to retreat from this position, too, indicating that governmental efforts to provide extra help to racial minorities could represent an unconstitutional infringement on the rights of the majority.

Institutional Interests The Supreme Court's justices are acutely aware of the Court's place in history, and they care about protecting the Court's power and reputation. This desire to protect the institutional integrity of the Court can sometimes influence judicial thinking. Chief Justice John Roberts seemed to have institutional concerns in mind when he surprised fellow conservatives by casting the deciding vote in favor of the constitutionality of the ACA in 2012. Roberts had been widely expected to oppose the president's health care reform effort. However, the Court's conservative majority had come under increasing political fire for its positions on such matters as campaign finance and affirmative action. Roberts, according to one commentator, saw himself as "uniquely entrusted with the custodianship of the court's legitimacy, reputation, and stature" and was determined to show that the Court stood above mere political ideology.[27] Roberts repeated his support of the ACA in 2015 in the case of *King v. Burwell*.

Activism and Restraint The judicial philosophy of judges plays an important role in their decision-making. One element of judicial philosophy is the issue of activism versus restraint. Over the years, some justices have believed that courts should narrowly interpret the Constitution according to the stated intentions of its framers and defer to the views of Congress when interpreting federal statutes. Justice Frankfurter, for example, advocated judicial deference to legislative bodies and avoidance of the "political thicket" in which the Court would entangle itself by deciding questions that were essentially political rather than legal in character. Advocates of **judicial restraint** are sometimes called "strict constructionists" because they refuse to go beyond the clear words of the Constitution in interpreting the document's meaning.

The alternative to restraint is **judicial activism**. Activist judges, such as the former chief justice Earl Warren, believe that the Court should go beyond the words of the Constitution or a statute to consider the broader societal implications of its decisions. Activist judges sometimes strike out in new directions, promulgating new interpretations or inventing new legal and constitutional concepts when they believe these to be socially desirable. For example, Justice Harry Blackmun's opinion in *Roe v. Wade* was based on a constitutional right to privacy that is not found in the words of the Constitution but was, rather, from the Court's prior decision in *Griswold v. Connecticut*.[28] Blackmun and the other members of the majority in the *Roe* case argued that the right to privacy was implied by other constitutional provisions. In this instance of judicial activism, the Court knew the result it wanted to achieve and was not afraid to make the law conform to the desired outcome.

Activism and restraint can overlap with but are not necessarily the same as liberalism and conservatism. For example, conservative politicians often castigate "liberal activist" judges and call for the appointment of conservative jurists who will refrain from reinterpreting the law. Indeed, the Rehnquist Court, dominated by conservatives, was among the most activist courts in American history, striking out in new directions in such areas as federalism and election law. The Roberts Court is continuing along the same route. As the examples of these conservative courts illustrate, a judge may be philosophically conservative and believe in strict construction of the Constitution but also be jurisprudentially activist and believe that the courts must play an active and energetic role in policy making, if necessary striking down acts of Congress to ensure that the intent of the framers is fulfilled.

Political Ideology and Partisanship The philosophy of activism versus restraint is sometimes a smokescreen for political ideology, and indeed, the liberal or conservative attitudes or partisan leanings of justices play an important role in their decisions.[29] In the past, liberal judges have often been activists, willing to use the law to achieve social and political change, whereas conservatives have been associated with judicial restraint. Interestingly, however, in recent years some conservative justices who have long called for restraint have actually become activists in seeking to undo some of the work of liberal jurists. From the 1950s to the '80s, the Supreme Court took an activist role in such areas as civil rights, civil liberties, abortion, voting rights, and police procedures. For example, the Supreme Court was more responsible than any other governmental institution for breaking down America's system of racial segregation. The Supreme Court virtually prohibited states from interfering with the right of a woman to seek an abortion and sharply curtailed state restrictions on voting rights. And it was the Supreme Court that placed restrictions on the behavior of local police and prosecutors in criminal cases. In a series of decisions since 1989, however, the conservative justices appointed by Ronald Reagan, George H. W. Bush, and George W. Bush were able to swing the Court to a more conservative position on civil rights, affirmative action, abortion rights, property rights, criminal procedure, voting rights, desegregation, and the power of the national government.

The political struggles of recent years amply illustrate the importance of judicial ideology. Is abortion a fundamental right or a criminal activity? How much separation must there be between church and state? Does application of the Voting Rights Act to increase minority representation constitute a violation of the rights of whites? The answers to these and many other questions cannot be found in the words of the Constitution. They must be located, instead, in the hearts and minds of the judges who interpret that text.

In a historic decision in 2015, the Supreme Court declared same-sex marriage a fundamental right protected by the due process and equal protection clauses of the Fourteenth Amendment to the Constitution.

The Federal Courts
WHAT DO WE WANT?

In the original conception of the framers, the judiciary was to be the institution that would protect individual liberty from the government. As we saw in Chapter 2, the framers believed that in a democracy the great danger was what they termed "tyranny of the majority"—the possibility that a popular majority, "united or actuated by some common impulse or passion," would "trample on the rules of justice."[30] The framers hoped that the courts would protect liberty from the potential excesses of democracy. And for most of American history, this was precisely the role played by the federal courts. The courts' most important decisions were those that protected the freedoms—to speak, worship, publish, vote, and attend school—of groups and individuals whose political views, religious beliefs, or racial or ethnic backgrounds made them unpopular.

Today, Americans of all political persuasions seem to view the courts as useful instruments through which to pursue their political and policy goals. Conservatives want to ban abortion and help business maintain its profitability, whereas liberals want to protect the environment and help enhance the power of workers in the workplace. (The "**Who Participates?**" feature on the facing page looks at efforts to influence the Supreme Court through amicus briefs). These may all be noble goals, but they present a basic dilemma for students of American government. If the courts are simply one more set of policy-making institutions, then who is left to protect the liberty of individuals?

Students should realize that the decisions made by the Supreme Court today will have important consequences for their lives and futures. The Court's campaign finance decisions will have consequences for who will govern the nation you inherit. The Court's decisions on health care influence your access to health insurance, the type of care you receive, and its cost. The Court's decisions in the realm of equal protection do and will impact your life (in particular, gays and lesbians with respect to marriage) and career chances. The Court's decisions in the realm of immigration will affect who will and will not be able to call themselves Americans. The Court's decision in Mark Janus's case against public sector unions could influence your future job and taxes. The Supreme Court is not an abstract entity in far-off Washington. It reaches directly into your life.

Influencing the Supreme Court?

Average Amicus Briefs per Case

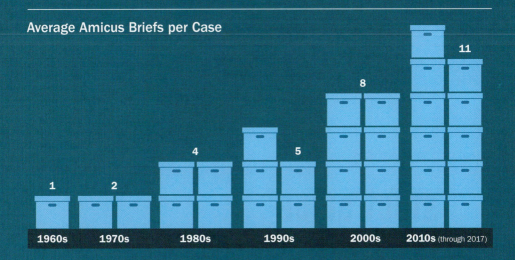

1960s	1970s	1980s	1990s	2000s	2010s (through 2017)
1	2	4	5	8	11

Amicus Briefs for Selected Landmark Cases

Brown v. Board of Education, 1954
(racial segregation)
6

Grutter v. Bollinger, 2003
(affirmative action admissions policy)
107

National Federation of Independent Business v. Sebelius, 2012
(Affordable Care Act, individual mandate)
136

Obergefell v. Hodges, 2015
(marriage equality)
147

SOURCES: Anthony J. Franze and R. Reeves Anderson, "Record Breaking Term for Amicus Curiae in Supereme Court Reflects New Norm," *The National Law Journal*, www.nationallawjournal.com/supremecourtbrief/id=202735095655/ Record-Breaking-Term-for-Amicus-Curiae-Reflects-New-Norm (accessed 12/8/15); Thomas G. Hansford and Kristen Johnson, "The Supply of Amicus Curiae Briefs in the Market for Information at the U.S. Supreme Court," *Justice System Journal*, 35, no. 4 (2014): 362–82; and Anthony J. Franze and R. Reeves Anderson, "In Quiet Term, Drop in Amicus Curiae at the Supreme Court," *Supreme Court Brief*, September 6, 2017, www.law.com (accessed 12/23/17).

WHAT YOU CAN DO

★ WHAT YOU CAN DO ★

Look inside the Federal Courts

✓ Find which groups filed amicus briefs for U.S. Supreme Court cases at **www.scotusblog.com**, and read a few of the briefs.

✓ Click on the "Court Locator" tab at **www.uscourts.gov** to find which federal courts are near you and to view their calendar of oral arguments. Court dockets and some case files are available about **www.pacer.gov**.

✓ Watch videos of cases from the Cameras in Courts pilot project at **www.uscourts.gov/about-federal-courts/cameras-courts**.

★ STUDY GUIDE ★

Practice Quiz

1. What is the name for the body of law that deals with disputes not involving criminal penalties? *(p. 378)*
   a) civil law
   b) privacy law
   c) plea bargains
   d) household law
   e) common law

2. The doctrine that previous court decisions should apply as precedents in similar cases is known as *(p. 378)*
   a) habeas corpus.
   b) a writ of certiorari.
   c) stare decisis.
   d) rule of four.
   e) senatorial courtesy.

3. Where do most trials in America take place? *(p. 378)*
   a) state courts
   b) appellate courts
   c) federal courts
   d) federal circuit courts
   e) the Supreme Court

4. The term *writ of habeas corpus* refers to *(p. 380)*
   a) a short, unsigned decision by an appellate court that rejects a petition to review the decision of a lower court.
   b) a criterion used by courts to screen cases that no longer require resolution.
   c) a decision of at least four of the nine Supreme Court justices to review a decision of a lower court.
   d) a court order that an individual in custody be brought into court and shown the cause for his or her detention.
   e) a brief filed by the solicitor general when the federal government is not a direct litigant in a Supreme Court case.

5. Which of the following is not included in the original jurisdiction of the Supreme Court? *(p. 381)*
   a) cases between the United States and one of the 50 states
   b) cases brought by one state against citizens of another state or against a foreign country
   c) cases involving challenges to the constitutionality of state laws
   d) cases between two or more states
   e) cases involving foreign ambassadors or other ministers

6. The size of the Supreme Court is determined by *(p. 384)*
   a) the president.
   b) the chief justice.
   c) the Department of Justice.
   d) Congress.
   e) the Constitution.

7. The Supreme Court's decision in *Marbury v. Madison* was important because *(p. 386)*
   a) it invalidated state laws prohibiting interracial marriage.
   b) it ruled that the recitation of prayers in public schools is unconstitutional under the establishment clause of the First Amendment.
   c) it established that arrested people have the right to remain silent, the right to be informed that anything they say can be held against them, and the right to counsel before and during police interrogation.
   d) it provided an expansive definition of *commerce* under the interstate commerce clause.
   e) it established the power of judicial review.

8. Which of the following is *not* included as a "special and compelling" reason to hear a case under Rule 10 of the Rules of the Supreme Court of the United States? *(p. 391)*
   a) The president of the United States authors an amicus curiae brief on the issue in question.
   b) A circuit court decision on the issue in question conflicts with previous Supreme Court decisions.

   c) There are conflicting decisions by two or more state courts of last resort on the issue in question.
   d) There are conflicting decisions between circuit courts and state courts of last resort on the issue in question.
   e) There are conflicting decisions by two or more circuit courts on the issue in question.

9. Which of the following play an important role in shaping the flow of cases heard by the Supreme Court? *(p. 393)*
   a) the attorney general, the secretary of state, and the American Bar Association
   b) the solicitor general, federal law clerks, and interest groups
   c) the president, Congress, and the Department of Justice
   d) state legislatures
   e) the federal district and circuit courts

10. Which of the following is a brief submitted to the Supreme Court by someone other than one of the parties in the case? *(p. 393)*
    a) amicus curiae
    b) habeas corpus
    c) writ of certiorari
    d) ex post brief
    e) de jure brief

11. A dissenting opinion is written by *(p. 396)*
    a) the chief justice of the Supreme Court.
    b) a Supreme Court justice who agrees with the majority's ultimate decision but wishes to offer a different rationale or emphasis.
    c) a Supreme Court justice who disagrees with the majority decision.
    d) the solicitor general.
    e) a Supreme Court justice assigned by the chief justice.

12. If a justice refuses to go beyond the clear words of the Constitution in interpreting the document's meaning, he or she would be considered an advocate of which judicial philosophy? *(p. 398)*
    a) judicial restraint
    b) judicial activism
    c) *stare decisis*
    d) judicial liberalism
    e) judicial conservatism

Key Terms

amicus curiae *(p. 393)* literally, "friend of the court"; individuals or groups who are not parties to a lawsuit but who seek to assist the Supreme Court in reaching a decision by presenting additional briefs

briefs *(p. 394)* written documents in which attorneys explain, using case precedents, why the court should find in favor of their client

chief justice *(p. 383)* justice on the Supreme Court who presides over the Court's public sessions and whose official title is chief justice of the United States

civil law *(p. 378)* the branch of law that deals with disputes that do not involve criminal penalties

court of appeals *(p. 379)* a court that hears the appeals of trial court decisions

criminal law *(p. 377)* the branch of law that regulates the conduct of individuals, defines crimes, and specifies punishment for acts defined as illegal

defendant *(p. 378)* the one against whom a complaint is brought in a criminal or civil case

dissenting opinion *(p. 396)* a decision written by a justice in the minority in a particular case in which the justice wishes to express his or her reasoning in the case

due process of law *(p. 380)* the right of every citizen against arbitrary action by national or state governments

judicial activism *(p. 398)* judicial philosophy that posits that the Court should go beyond the words of the Constitution or a statute to consider the broader societal implications of its decisions

judicial restraint *(p. 398)* judicial philosophy whose adherents refuse to go beyond the clear words of the Constitution in interpreting the document's meaning

judicial review *(p. 385)* the power of the courts to review and, if necessary, declare actions of the legislative and executive branches invalid or unconstitutional; the Supreme Court asserted this power in *Marbury v. Madison*

jurisdiction *(p. 380)* the sphere of a court's power and authority

mootness *(p. 391)* a criterion used by courts to screen cases that no longer require resolution

opinion *(p. 396)* the written explanation of the Supreme Court's decision in a particular case

oral argument *(p. 394)* the stage in Supreme Court procedure in which attorneys for both sides appear before the Court to present their positions and answer questions posed by justices

original jurisdiction *(p. 381)* the authority to initially consider a case; distinguished from *appellate jurisdiction*, which is the authority to hear appeals from a lower court's decision

plaintiff *(p. 377)* the individual or organization that brings a complaint in court

plea bargain *(p. 380)* a negotiated agreement in a criminal case in which a defendant agrees to plead guilty in return for the state's agreement to reduce the severity of the criminal charge the defendant is facing

precedent *(p. 378)* prior case whose principles are used by judges as the basis for their decisions in present cases

solicitor general *(p. 393)* the top government lawyer in all cases before the Supreme Court in which the government is a party

standing *(p. 391)* the right of an individual or organization to initiate a court case, on the basis of having a substantial stake in the outcome

stare decisis *(p. 378)* literally, "let the decision stand"; the doctrine that a previous decision by a court applies as a precedent in similar cases until that decision is overruled

supremacy clause *(p. 389)* Article VI of the Constitution, which states that laws passed by the national government and all treaties "shall be the supreme Law of the Land" and superior to all laws adopted by any state or any subdivision

supreme court *(p. 379)* the highest court in a particular state or in the United States; this court primarily serves an appellate function

trial court *(p. 379)* the first court to hear a criminal or civil case

writ of certiorari *(p. 391)* a decision of at least four of the nine Supreme Court justices to review a decision of a lower court; *certiorari* is Latin, meaning "to make more certain"

writ of habeas corpus *(p. 380)* a court order that the individual in custody be brought into court and shown the cause for detention; habeas corpus is guaranteed by the Constitution and can be suspended only in cases of rebellion or invasion

For Further Reading

Baum, Lawrence. *The Supreme Court*. 12th ed. Washington, DC: CQ Press, 2015.

Breyer, Stephen. *The Court and the World: American Law and the New Global Realities*. New York: Knopf, 2015.

Chemerinsky, Erwin. *Closing the Courthouse Door: How Your Constitutional Rights Became Unenforceable*. New Haven, CT: Yale University Press, 2017.

Epstein, Lee, and Thomas G. Walker. *Constitutional Law for a Changing America*. 8th ed. Washington, DC: CQ Press, 2013.

Fisher, Louis. *Constitutional Dialogues*. Princeton, NJ: Princeton University Press, 1988.

Greenberg, Jan Crawford. *Supreme Conflict: The Inside Story of the United States Supreme Court*. New York: Penguin, 2008.

Hall, Kermit L., James Ely, and Joel Grossman. *The Oxford Companion to the Supreme Court*. New York: Oxford University Press, 2005.

Hirshman, Linda. *Sisters in Law: How Sandra Day O'Conner and Ruth Bader Ginsburg Went to the Supreme Court and Changed the World*. New York: Harper, 2015.

Irons, Peter. *A People's History of the Supreme Court*. New York: Penguin, 2006.

Johnson, Timothy R. *Oral Arguments and Decision Making on the U.S. Supreme Court*. Albany: State University of New York Press, 2004.

O'Brien, David M. *Storm Center: The Supreme Court in American Politics*. 11th ed. New York: W. W. Norton, 2017.

Spitzer, Robert J. *Saving the Constitution from Lawyers*. New York: Cambridge University Press, 2008.

Toobin, Jeffrey. *The Oath: The Obama White House and the Supreme Court*. New York: Anchor, 2013.

Domestic Policy

WHAT GOVERNMENT DOES AND WHY IT MATTERS

Marcella Wagner was a promising student in a nursing program at a public university. She was driving to class one day when the driver next to her swerved into her path, causing her car to roll over, crushing the roof. The hit-and-run accident left her paralyzed from the chest down.[1]

No longer able to care for herself without assistance, Wagner was eligible for Medicaid, the government health insurance program for low-income people, which also provides long-term care to the disabled. Wagner is eligible for Medicaid as a disabled person, but she still has to meet the income and asset limits that determine eligibility, because Medicaid is a means-tested program for the poor. After her accident, she and her husband Dave had to spend down their assets to meet California's eligibility limit, which is $3,150 (excluding their house and one vehicle), and they must keep their income below 133 percent of the poverty level (just over $27,000 in 2017 dollars for a family of three; they have a child). Medicaid provides fairly comprehensive health insurance, but payments to doctors and hospitals are low compared to

The crafting of social policies leads to challenging trade-offs, the outcomes of which deeply affect people's lives. Upon being permanently disabled after a horrible accident, Marcella Wagner and her family faced difficult choices as they navigated America's complicated system of social programs and government benefits.

other forms of insurance, and Wagner sometimes has difficulty finding doctors willing to see her as a patient.

Wagner's mother-in-law, Mary Ann, now lives in Minnesota but often goes to California to help out Marcella and Dave. As a senior citizen she gets health insurance through Medicare, the government health insurance program for older Americans. Medicare is a contributory social insurance program for which Mary Ann is qualified as a retiree who paid a payroll tax during her working years that helps fund the program. Most doctors and hospitals accept Medicare, which pays more than Medicaid.

Marcella Wagner is the sister-in-law and Mary Ann the mother of one of this book's authors, Andrea Campbell. Campbell's interaction with American social policy is different still from her mother's or sister-in-law's. Like many Americans working full-time, Campbell has private health insurance through her employer. Government still plays a role by subsidizing her insurance: she and her employer share the cost of her health insurance, but neither is taxed on the portion of the monthly premium they pay. Campbell's private health insurance covers some benefits that her mother's Medicare does not, such as vision and hearing, but she has to use doctors within her plan's network or pay more, unlike her mother, whose Medicare insurance works the same nationwide.

As Campbell's family's experience shows, American social policy has three main goals. It provides opportunity: in the hopes of a stable, well-paying career in nursing, Wagner had pursued training at a public university with the help of government-provided student loans. It addresses the risks that people might face in their everyday lives that are expensive and difficult to meet: illness, unemployment, loss of income due to aging, or, as in Wagner's case, disability. And it seeks to alleviate poverty, the most controversial goal. American social policy pursues these goals along three tracks: social insurance (like Mary Ann's Medicare), social assistance (Marcella's Medicaid), and tax expenditures (Andrea's private health insurance, subsidized through the tax code).

In the last several chapters, we examined the parts of the government that make policy: Congress, the presidency, the bureaucracy, and the courts. In this chapter, we will examine the different approaches to achieving policy goals. We will then examine one broad area of domestic public policy: social policy. We focus on social policy because much of the government's annual budget goes to social programs, because such spending is often controversial, and because this process illustrates how the government tries to accomplish its goals.

CHAPTER GOALS

★ **Explain how different kinds of public policies achieve their goals using different means (pp. 409–16)**

★ **Trace the history of government programs designed to promote economic security (pp. 416–22)**

★ **Describe how education, health, and housing policies try to advance equality of opportunity (pp. 423–32)**

★ **Explain how contributory, noncontributory, and tax expenditure programs benefit different groups of Americans (pp. 432–37)**

The Tools for Making Policy Are Techniques of Control

Explain how different kinds of public policies achieve their goals using different means

Most of this book has focused on how government gets things done. This chapter and Chapter 14 will focus on what the government produces, called **public policy**. *Public policy* can be defined simply as a law, a rule, a statute, or an edict that expresses the government's goals and provides for rewards and punishments to promote those goals' attainment. Public policy can include a law passed by Congress, a presidential directive, a Supreme Court ruling, or a rule issued by a bureaucratic agency.

In trying to achieve some purpose, public policy is inherently coercive, even when motivated by the best and most benign intentions. Note that the word *policy* shares a root with the word *police*. Both terms come from the Greek words *polis* and *politeia*, which refer to the political community and the sources of public authority. So it is important to remember that although the idea of coercion seems inherently negative, it is in fact a vital and necessary part of governing. (If overused or misused, however, coercion can obviously be harmful.)

Techniques of control are to policy makers what tools are to a carpenter. There are a limited number of techniques that the government can use, each with its own logic and limitations. An accumulation of experience helps us to understand when a certain technique is likely to work. Still, just as carpenters will have different ideas about the best tool for a job, so policy makers will disagree about which techniques work best and when. What we offer here is a workable elementary handbook of techniques that will be useful for analyzing policy.

Table 13.1 lists some important techniques of control available to policy makers. These techniques can be grouped into three categories: promotional, regulatory, and redistributive policies.

PROMOTIONAL POLICIES GET PEOPLE TO DO THINGS BY GIVING THEM REWARDS

Promotional policies use positive incentives to encourage behavior. Their purpose is to encourage people to do something they might not otherwise do or to get people to do more of what they are already doing. Sometimes the purpose is merely to compensate people for something done in the past. Promotional techniques can be classified into at least two separate types: subsidies and contracting.

Subsidies Subsidies are simply government grants of cash or other valuable commodities, such as land, to individuals or an organization that are used to promote activities desired by the government, to reward political support, or to buy off political opposition. Subsidies were the dominant form of public policy of the national government and the state and local governments throughout the nineteenth century. They continue to be an important category of public policy at all levels of government.

TABLE 13.1

Techniques of Public Control

TYPE OF POLICY	TECHNIQUES	DEFINITIONS AND EXAMPLES
Promotional	Subsidies and grants of cash, land, etc.	"Patronage"—the promotion of private activity through what recipients consider "benefits" (example: in the nineteenth century the government encouraged westward settlement by granting land to those who went west)
	Contracts	Agreements with individuals or firms in the "private sector" to purchase goods or services
	Licenses	Unconditional permission to do something that is otherwise illegal (franchise, permit)
Regulatory	Criminal penalties	Heavy fines or imprisonment, loss of citizenship
	Civil penalties	Less onerous fines, probation, public exposure, restitution
	Administrative regulations	The setting of interest rates, maintenance of health and safety standards, and the investigation and publicizing of wrongdoing
	Subsidies and contracts	Can be considered regulatory when certain conditions are attached (example: the government refuses to award a contract to firms that show no evidence of affirmative action in hiring)
	Regulatory taxes	Taxes that keep down consumption or production (liquor, gas, cigarette taxes)
Redistributive	Expropriation	"Eminent domain"—the power to take private property for public use
	Taxes	Alteration of the redistribution of money by changing taxes or tax rules
	Budgeting and spending through subsidies and contracts	Deficit spending to pump money into the economy when it needs a boost; creation of a budget surplus by cutting spending or increasing taxes to discourage consumption in inflationary times
	Fiscal use of credit and interest (monetary techniques)	Change in interest rates to affect both demand for money and consumption (example: the Federal Reserve Board raises interest rates to slow economic growth and ward off inflation)

Economic sectors receiving substantial subsidies include agriculture, energy, transportation, health, and national defense. Policies using the subsidy technique have continued to be plentiful in the modern era, even after the 1990s, when there was widespread public and official hostility toward subsidies. For example, in 2017 the annual value of corporate subsidies, not including agriculture, was estimated at $110 billion.[2]

Subsidies have always been a technique favored by politicians because they can be treated as benefits that can be spread widely in response to many demands that might otherwise produce profound political conflict. Subsidies can, in other words, be used to buy off the opposition.

Contracting Like any corporation, a government agency must purchase goods and services by contract. The law requires open bidding for a substantial proportion of these contracts because government contracts are extremely valuable to businesses in the private sector and because the opportunities and incentives for abuse are very great. Yet contracting is more than a method of buying goods and services. It is also an important technique of policy because government agencies are often authorized to use their **contracting power** (the power of government to set conditions on companies seeking to sell goods or services to government agencies) as a means of encouraging corporations to improve themselves, helping to build up whole sectors of the economy, and encouraging certain desirable goals or behavior, such as equal employment opportunity.

Military contracting has long been a major element in government spending. So tight was the connection between defense contractors and the federal government during the Cold War that as he was leaving office President Eisenhower warned the nation to beware of the powerful "military–industrial complex." After the Cold War, as military spending and production declined, major defense contractors began to look for alternative business activities to supplement the reduced demand for weapons. Since the terrorist attacks of 2001, however, the military budget has been awash in new funds, and military contractors are flooded with business. President George W. Bush increased the Pentagon budget by more than 7 percent a year, requesting so many weapons systems that one observer called the budget a "weapons smorgasbord."[3] Military contractors geared up to produce not only weapons for foreign warfare but also surveillance systems to enhance domestic security.

REGULATORY POLICIES ARE RULES BACKED BY PENALTIES

Regulation is a technique of control in which the government adopts rules that impose restrictions on the conduct of private citizens. The conduct may be regulated because people feel it is harmful to others, or threatens to be, such as drunk driving or false advertising. Or the conduct may be regulated because people think it's immoral, whether it harms others or not, such as prostitution, gambling, or drinking. Because there are many forms of regulation, we have subdivided them here: (1) police regulation, through civil and criminal penalties; (2) administrative regulation; (3) regulatory taxation; and (4) expropriation.

Police Regulation "Police regulation" comes closest to the traditional exercise of police power—a power traditionally reserved to the states to regulate the health, safety, and morals of its citizens. After a person's arrest and conviction, these techniques are administered by courts and, where necessary, penal institutions. They are regulatory techniques.

Civil penalty usually refers to a fine or some other form of material restitution (such as public service) as a sanction for violating civil laws or common law principles or committing negligence. Civil penalties can range from a five-dollar fine for a parking violation to a more onerous penalty for late payment of income taxes to the much more onerous penalties for violating antitrust laws against unfair competition or environmental protection laws against pollution. *Criminal penalty* usually refers to imprisonment but can also involve heavy fines and the loss of certain civil rights and liberties, such as the right to vote.

Administrative Regulation Police regulation addresses conduct considered immoral. But what about conduct that is not considered morally wrong but that may have harmful consequences? For example, there is nothing morally wrong with radio or television broadcasting. But government regulates broadcasting on a particular frequency or channel because there would be virtual chaos if everybody could broadcast on any frequency at any time.

This kind of conduct is thought of less as *policed* conduct and more as *regulated* conduct. This type of regulation is sometimes called *administrative regulation* because the controls are given over to civilian agencies rather than to the police and the rules are made by regulatory agencies and commissions. Each regulatory agency has extensive powers to keep a sector of the economy under surveillance and to make rules dealing with the behavior of individual companies and people. But these administrative agencies have fewer powers of punishment than the police and the courts have, and the administrative agencies generally rely on the courts to issue orders enforcing the rules and decisions.

Table 13.1 lists subsidies and contracts as examples of both promotional and regulatory policies; although these techniques might normally be thought of as strictly promotional policies, they can also be used for administrative regulation. It all depends on whether the law sets serious conditions on eligibility for the subsidy or contract. To put it another way, the government can use the threat of losing a valuable subsidy or contract to improve compliance with the goals of regulation. For example, social welfare subsidies (benefits) can be lowered to encourage or force people to take low-paying jobs, or they can be increased to calm political unrest when people are engaging in political protest.[4]

Regulatory Taxation In many instances, the primary purpose of a tax is not to raise revenue but to influence conduct, often to discourage or eliminate an activity altogether by making it too expensive for most people. Such taxes are called regulatory taxes. For example, since the end of Prohibition, although there has been no penalty for the production or sale of alcoholic beverages, the alcohol industry has not been free from regulation. First, all alcoholic beverages have to be licensed, allowing only those companies that are "bonded" to put their product on the market. Beyond that, federal and state taxes on alcohol are made disproportionately high, on the theory that, in addition to the revenue gained, less alcohol will be consumed. The same is true of cigarette taxes.

Expropriation Confiscation of property with or without compensation for a public use, or *expropriation*, is a widely used technique of control in the United States, especially in land-use regulation. Almost all public works, from highways to parks to government office buildings, involve the forceful taking of some private property in order to acquire sufficient land for the necessary construction.

We generally call the power to expropriate *eminent domain* (the right of government to take private property for public use), a power that is recognized as inherent in any government. The Fifth Amendment of the U.S. Constitution provides an important safeguard against abuse, saying that private property cannot be taken for public use "without just compensation." Thus, the government is not permitted to use that power except through a strict due process, and it must offer "fair market value" for the land sought.

Forcing individuals to work for a public purpose is another form of expropriation. The draft of young men for the armed forces, court orders to strikers to return to work, and sentences for convicted felons to do community service are examples of the regular use of expropriation in the United States.

REDISTRIBUTIVE POLICIES AFFECT BROAD CLASSES OF PEOPLE

Redistributive policies are usually of two types, monetary and fiscal; but they have a common purpose: to control people by manipulating the entire economy rather than by regulating *people* directly. Whereas regulatory policies focus on individual conduct, redistributive policies seek to control conduct more indirectly by altering the conditions of conduct or manipulating the environment of conduct.

Monetary Policies Monetary policies allow government to regulate the economy through the manipulation of the supply of money and credit. America's most powerful institution in this area of monetary policy is the Federal Reserve Board (the Fed), the governing board of the **Federal Reserve System**, consisting of a chair and six other members, all appointed by the president with the consent of the Senate. The Fed can affect the total amount of credit available through the interest (called the federal funds rate) that member banks charge one another for loans. If the Fed significantly decreases the federal funds rate, it can give a boost to a sagging economy. In the steep recession that began in 2008, the Fed acted aggressively. By December 2008 it had cut rates nine times, from a high in September 2007 of 4.75 percent to a historically low zero percentage rate. Moreover, the Federal Reserve kept interest rates at or near that level well into 2017, in an attempt to encourage new lending and thus economic growth.[5] If the Fed raises the federal funds rate, it can put a brake on the economy because the higher rates make it more expensive to borrow money. This makes it more difficult for new businesses to get loans,

Financial markets closely watch the statements of the Federal Reserve. Here, Fed Chair Jerome Powell speaks about the necessity of raising interest rates to fight inflation.

for instance. The Federal Reserve is responsible for ensuring high employment as well as price stability, but it has been particularly important in fighting inflation. During the late 1970s and early '80s, with inflation at record-high levels, Federal Reserve chair Paul Volcker aggressively raised interest rates in order to dampen inflation. Although his actions provoked a sharp recession, they raised the stature of the Fed, demonstrating its ability to manage the economy.

Fiscal Policies Fiscal policies are the government's use of taxing, monetary, and spending powers to manipulate the economy. Personal and corporate income taxes, which raise most of the U.S. government's revenues, are the most prominent examples. While the direct purpose of an income tax is to raise revenue, each tax has a different impact on the economy; and government can plan for that impact. Although the primary purpose of the graduated income tax is, of course, to raise revenue, an important second objective is to collect revenue in such a way as to reduce the disparities of wealth between the lowest and the highest income brackets. We call this a policy of **redistribution**. Another policy objective of the income tax is the encouragement of the capitalist economy by rewarding investment. The tax laws allow individuals or companies to deduct from their taxable income any money they can justify as an investment or a "business expense"; this gives an incentive to individuals and companies to spend money to expand their production, their advertising, or their staff and reduces the income taxes that businesses have to pay.

Americans have long debated the appropriate levels of taxation on individual and corporate income. After passing major income tax cuts in 2001, President Bush proposed and Congress passed a sweeping new round of cuts in 2003. Bush's plan was intended to promote investment by reducing taxes on most stock dividends, to spur business activity by offering tax breaks to small businesses, and to stimulate the economy by reducing the tax rates for all taxpayers. In 2006, Congress extended the rate reductions on dividends and capital gains, a move that estimates showed would cost the treasury $70 billion over five years.

President Obama and the Democratic leadership proposed extending the tax cuts for everyone with annual incomes under $250,000; those making more would have their income taxes revert back to the rates in the 1990s. Republicans and some Democrats preferred to extend the tax cuts for everyone. In 2010, Obama and Congress reached a deal to extend the Bush tax cuts for two years, when they were extended again and made permanent. In 2017, Congress enacted President Trump's major tax cut package that was estimated to add $1.5 trillion to the national debt.

Spending Power as Fiscal Policy Perhaps the most important redistributive technique of all is the most familiar one: the "spending power," which is a combination of subsidies and contracts. Government can use these techniques to achieve policy goals far beyond buying goods and services and regulating individual conduct. This is why subsidies and contracts show up yet again in Table 13.1 as redistributive techniques.

Agricultural subsidies are one example of the national government's use of its purchasing power as a fiscal or redistributive technique. Since the 1930s the federal government has attempted to raise and to stabilize the prices of several important agricultural products, such as corn and wheat, by authorizing the Department of Agriculture to buy enormous amounts of these commodities if prices on the market fall below a fixed level.

SHOULD THE GOVERNMENT INTERVENE IN THE ECONOMY?

Until 1929 most Americans believed that government had little to do with actively managing the economy. The world was guided by the theory that the economy, if left to its own devices, would produce full employment and maximum production. This traditional view of the relationship between government and the economy crumbled in 1929 before the stark reality of the Great Depression of 1929–39. When President Franklin Delano Roosevelt took office in 1933, he energetically threw the federal government into the business of fighting the depression. One of the main ways that the federal government sought to keep the economy healthy was through decisions about taxing and spending in accordance with the ideas of the British economist John Maynard Keynes. Keynesians argue that by pumping money into the economy, particularly by running deficits during periods of recession, government can stimulate demand and create a cycle of increased production and jobs that will pull the economy out of recession.

In the 1980s growing numbers of Republicans began to reject the idea that government could help ensure economic prosperity. Instead, they argued that freeing markets from government intervention would produce the best economic results. Many Democrats, on the other hand, continued to believe that government has an important role to play in promoting a strong economy. This fundamental disagreement between the parties over the appropriate role of government underlies the fierce contemporary political debates over the government's role in the economy. Today, some of the most intense conflicts between Democrats and Republicans concern taxes. This conflict came to a head when Congress passed President Trump's sweeping tax cut bill in 2017. Passed along party-line votes in both houses (most Republicans for, Democrats against), the bill sought to stimulate economic growth by enacting tax cuts for all, with the biggest share going to the wealthy. The law dropped the corporate tax rate from 35 percent to 21 percent; reduced the top individual tax rate from 39.6 percent to 37 percent; and doubled the standard deduction and child tax credit. It also capped the amount of state and local taxes that filers could claim as a deduction, and eliminated personal exemptions. In all, the cuts would add $1.5 trillion to the national debt over ten years.[6]

Social Policy and the Welfare System Buttress Equality

Trace the history of government programs designed to promote economic security

For much of American history, local governments and private charities were in charge of caring for the poor. During the 1930s, when this largely private system of charity collapsed in the face of widespread economic destitution, the federal government created the beginnings of an American welfare state. The idea of the welfare system was new; it meant that the national government would oversee programs designed to promote economic security for all Americans—not just for the poor. Today, the American system of social welfare includes many different policies enacted over the years since the Great Depression. Because each program is governed by distinct rules, the type and level of assistance available vary widely.

THE HISTORY OF THE GOVERNMENT WELFARE SYSTEM DATES ONLY TO THE 1930S

There has always been a welfare system in America, but until 1935 it was almost entirely private, composed of an extensive system of voluntary philanthropy through churches and other religious groups, ethnic and fraternal societies, communities and neighborhoods, and philanthropically inclined rich individuals. Most often it was called *charity*, and although it was private and voluntary, it was thought of as a public obligation.

The traditional approach of charity crumbled in the face of the stark reality of the Great Depression. During the depression, misfortune became so widespread and private wealth shrank so drastically that private charity was out of the question and the distinction between deserving and undeserving became impossible to draw. Following the crash of 1929 around 20 percent of the workforce immediately became

During the Great Depression, the government took a more active role in helping poor and struggling Americans. Here, people line up to receive free bread.

unemployed; this figure grew as the depression stretched into years. Moreover, few of the unemployed had any monetary resources or any family farm on which to fall back. Banks failed, wiping out the savings of millions who had been prudent enough or fortunate enough to have any savings at all. Thousands of businesses failed as well, throwing middle-class Americans onto the bread lines along with unemployed laborers, dispossessed farmers, and those who had never worked in any capacity. The Great Depression proved to Americans that poverty could be a result of imperfections in the economic system as well as of individual irresponsibility. It also forced Americans to drastically alter their standards regarding who was deserving and who was not.

Once poverty and dependency were accepted as problems inherent in the economic system, a large-scale public policy approach was not far away. By the time President Franklin Delano Roosevelt took office in 1933, the question was not whether there was to be a public welfare system but how generous or restrictive that system would be.

THE MODERN WELFARE SYSTEM HAS THREE PARTS

The modern welfare state in the United States consists of three separate categories of welfare: contributory and noncontributory programs, many created by the Social Security Act of 1935; and the tax expenditure system, first established by the new federal income tax in 1913 and expanded over time.

Contributory Programs The category of welfare programs that are financed by taxation or other mandatory contributions by their present or future recipients can justifiably be called "forced savings" because these programs force working Americans to contribute a portion of their earnings to provide income and benefits during their retirement years. These **contributory programs** are what most people have in mind when they refer to **Social Security** or social insurance, a contributory welfare program into which working Americans contribute a percentage of their wages and from which they receive cash benefits after retirement. Under the original contributory program, old-age insurance, the employer and the employee were each required to pay an equal amount, which in 1937 was set at 1 percent of the first $3,000 of wages, to be deducted from the paycheck of each employee and matched by the same amount from the employer. This percentage has increased over the years; the contribution in 2018 was 7.65 percent subdivided as follows: 6.2 percent on the first $128,400 of income for Social Security benefits, plus 1.45 percent on all earnings for Medicare.[7] Starting in 2014, households earning over $250,000 a year paid an extra 0.9 percent in Medicare taxes as a result of a provision in the Affordable Care Act.

The formula by which Social Security benefits are calculated is redistributive, aiming to provide lower-income workers with a higher proportion of their contributions than higher-income workers receive. This is because the goal of Social Security is to ensure a basic income to all workers once they retire. Research has shown, however, that due to different mortality rates and other factors, the system does not end up redistributing from well-off to less well-off workers as much as intended by the formula. The system does redistribute to women, who on average earn less than men, have fewer years in the workforce (and hence tend to contribute less to Social Security than do men), and live longer than men.[8] In the short term, Social Security redistributes money from the young to the old: the taxes of current workers are paying for the benefits received by current retirees. But Social Security also plays a vital role for young people by providing survivor benefits to those whose parents die, retire, or become disabled. Surviving spouses also receive survivor benefits. In addition, in 1956 Social Security Disability Insurance (SSDI) was created to provide a monthly cash benefit to the permanently disabled.[9]

The biggest single expansion in contributory programs since 1935 was the establishment in 1965 of **Medicare**, a form of national health insurance for the elderly and the disabled that provides substantial medical services to elderly persons who are already eligible to receive old-age, survivors', and disability insurance under the original Social Security system. In 2003, Congress added a prescription drug benefit to the package of health benefits for the elderly. Social Security benefits and costs are adjusted through **indexing**, whereby benefits paid out under contributory programs are modified annually by **cost-of-living adjustments (COLAs)**—changes made to the level of benefits of a government program based on the rate of inflation. Of course, Social Security taxes (contributions) also increased after almost every benefit increase.

Unemployment insurance is another contributory program that is funded by a combination of federal and state taxes. States set benefit levels and eligibility criteria for receiving unemployment insurance and tax employers to fund the program. In most states, benefits last for a maximum of 26 weeks. Such benefits are generally funded by federal taxes. Unemployment benefits are meant to help replace lost wages, but they do so at a low level: most workers receive only half of their wages. Moreover, because states impose criteria about how long people must work or how much they must earn to become eligible for unemployment insurance, only about half of workers who lose their jobs receive unemployment benefits.[10]

Noncontributory Programs Social programs that provide assistance to people based on demonstrated need rather than any contribution they have made—**noncontributory programs**—are also known as "social assistance programs" or, more commonly, as "welfare." Eligibility for social assistance is determined by **means testing**, a procedure that requires applicants to show a financial need for assistance. The 1935 Social Security Act founded cash assistance to families with children (later known as AFDC) and cash assistance to the poor, elderly, blind, and disabled (later changed to Supplemental Security Income or SSI). In the ensuing decades the government also created programs to provide housing assistance, food stamps, and school lunches.

The largest single category of expansion was the establishment in 1965 of **Medicaid**, a federally and state-funded, state-operated program that provides extended medical services to low-income Americans. Noncontributory programs underwent another major transformation in the 1970s in the level of benefits they provide. Besides being means-tested, noncontributory programs are state-based; grants-in-aid are provided by the federal government to the states as incentives to establish the programs, but states retain considerable leeway to establish eligibility criteria (see Chapter 3). Thus, from the beginning there were considerable disparities in benefits from state to state. The national government sought to rectify the disparities in levels of old-age benefits in 1974 by creating the Supplemental Security Income (SSI) program to augment benefits for the aged, the blind, and the disabled. SSI provides uniform minimum benefits across the entire nation and includes mandatory COLAs.

The TANF program is also administered by the states, and, as with the old-age benefits just discussed, benefit levels vary widely from state to state (see Figure 13.1). In 2017 the states' monthly TANF benefits for a family of three varied from $170 in Mississippi to $1,021 in New Hampshire.[11] Most TANF payments are much lower than New Hampshire's and well below the federal poverty line, which was $20,420 per year or $1,702 per month in 2017.[12]

The number of people receiving AFDC benefits expanded in the 1970s, in part because new welfare programs had been established in the mid-1960s: Medicaid and the **Supplemental Nutrition Assistance Program (SNAP)**, which is still sometimes called by its old name, *food stamps*. SNAP is the largest antipoverty program, which provides recipients with a debit card for food at most grocery stores. Collectively, these programs provide what are called **in-kind benefits**—noncash goods and services provided by the government that the beneficiary would otherwise have to pay for in cash. At the time, AFDC recipients were automatically eligible for Medicaid and food stamps (a linkage later broken by the 1996 welfare reform).

Tax Expenditures In addition to contributory and noncontributory programs, the United States provides social welfare benefits through tax breaks—credits, deductions, and preferential tax rates that subsidize social welfare through what some analysts call the shadow welfare state. The **tax expenditure** system includes benefits that employers may offer to their workers, such as medical insurance and retirement plans—both

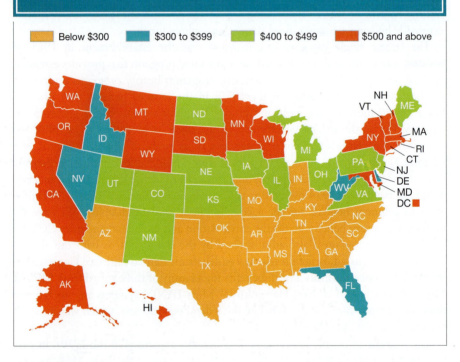

FIGURE 13.1

Monthly Spending on TANF Benefits

Spending on TANF benefits varies widely across the country. In 14 states, monthly benefits for a single-parent family of three are below $300; in 17 states, they are above $500. In which regions does spending on TANF benefits tend to be highest? In which regions is it generally lower?

SOURCE: Ife Floyd and Liz Schott, "TANF Cash Benefits Have Fallen by More Than 20 Percent in Most States and Continue to Erode," Center for Budget and Policy Priorities, October 13, 2017, www.cbpp.org/research/family -income-support/tanf-cash-benefits-have-fallen-by-more-than-20-percent-in-most-states (accessed 8/19/18).

Below $300 | $300 to $399 | $400 to $499 | $500 and above

traditional pensions and 401(k)s (whether employers offer these "fringe benefits" is optional). The federal government subsidizes such benefits by not taxing the payments that employers and employees make for health insurance and pensions.

The shadow welfare state also includes tax breaks that individuals can file for when they prepare their federal tax returns. For example, taxpayers can deduct the amount they paid in interest on a home mortgage from the income they report on their tax returns, as well as state and local taxes they paid up to a $10,000 cap. There are also tax deductions for out-of-pocket medical expenses, child care, charitable contributions, and so on. There are dozens of such tax breaks in the tax code. By reducing taxes, these tax breaks lower the effective cost of home ownership, health insurance, child-rearing, and other subsidized activities. But such benefits are concentrated among middle- and upper-income people who are most likely to have employer-provided benefits at work and to engage in subsidized activities such as buying a house. People often do not think

The Supplemental Nutrition Assistance Program (SNAP), formerly known as "food stamps," helps people in need buy food. Today recipients use a government-provided debit card that is accepted at most grocery stores. In 2017, 42.9 million Americans were enrolled in SNAP.

of these tax expenditures as part of social policy because they are not as visible as the programs that provide direct payments or services to beneficiaries. But tax expenditures represent a significant federal investment that mostly benefit middle- and upper-income people: although the 2017 tax bill signed by President Trump alters some tax expenditures, they still cost the national treasury over $1 trillion in forgone revenue each year—about the amount collected by the personal income tax, and greater than the amount spent on Social Security, the largest federal program.

WELFARE REFORM HAS DOMINATED THE WELFARE AGENDA IN RECENT YEARS

From the 1960s to the 1990s, opinion polls consistently showed that the public viewed welfare beneficiaries as "undeserving."[13] Underlying that judgment was the belief that welfare recipients did not want to work. These negative assessments were amplified by racial stereotypes. By 1973, 46 percent of welfare recipients were African American. Although the majority of recipients were white, media portrayals helped to create the widespread perception that the vast majority of welfare recipients were black. A careful study by Martin Gilens has shown how racial stereotypes of blacks as uncommitted to the work ethic reinforced public opposition to welfare.[14]

During the recession of the early 1990s welfare rolls reached an all-time high. Sensing continuing public frustration with welfare, when Bill Clinton was a presidential candidate he vowed "to end welfare as we know it," an unusual promise for a Democrat. When Republicans gained control of Congress in the 1994 midterm election, they proposed a dramatic reform of welfare, which Clinton, facing a campaign for re-election in 1996, signed. The Personal Responsibility and Work Opportunity Reconciliation Act (PRWORA) repealed AFDC and replaced it with the TANF program. In place of the individual entitlement to assistance, the new law created block grants to the states and allowed states much more discretion in designing their cash-assistance programs to needy families. The new law also established time limits, restricting recipients to two years of assistance and creating a lifetime limit of five years. It imposed new work requirements on those receiving welfare, and it restricted most legal immigrants from receiving benefits. The aim of the new law was to reduce welfare caseloads, promote work, and reduce out-of-wedlock births. Notably, reducing poverty was not one of its stated objectives.

After this law was enacted, the number of families receiving assistance dropped by 60 percent nationwide. The sharp decline in the number of recipients was widely hailed as a sign that welfare reform was working. Indeed, former welfare recipients have been more successful at finding and keeping jobs than many critics of the law predicted. One important indicator of how welfare has changed is the proportion of funds it provides in cash assistance. Before the 1996 reform, assistance was provided largely in the form of a cash grant. After the reform, 64 percent of welfare funds were allocated for noncash services and 36 percent for cash assistance.[15] This means that an increasing proportion of welfare funds is spent on such costs as assistance with transportation to work, temporary shelter, or one-time payments for emergencies so that people do not end up on the welfare rolls. The orientation of assistance has shifted away from subsidizing people who are not in the labor force and toward addressing temporary problems that low-income people face and providing assistance that facilitates work.[16] But critics point out that most former welfare recipients are not paid enough to pull their families out of poverty. While the 1996 law has helped reduce welfare caseloads, it has done little to reduce the underlying problem of poverty.[17]

Because the TANF block grants to the states were not adjusted to inflation, federal funds for welfare have fallen in real terms. TANF was unable to keep pace with the growth of poverty caused by the Great Recession that started in 2008.[18] Advocates for the poor contrasted it to the growth of the supplemental nutrition program (SNAP, or food stamps), whose growth closely tracked the rise in unemployment and poverty during the recession. In 2007, before the recession took hold, approximately 26.3 million individuals received SNAP benefits. By 2015 that number had risen to approximately 45 million people a month, close to 15 percent of all Americans.[19] In 2018, close to 42 million Americans per month received SNAP.[20]

In April 2018, President Trump signed an executive order requesting cabinet secretaries review assistance programs, such as TANF, SNAP, and housing assistance, and strengthen or add work requirements for benefits. In January 2018 the administration allowed states to impose work requirements for Medicaid for the first time in the program's history.

The Cycle of Poverty Can Be Broken by Education, Health, and Housing Policies

Describe how education, health, and housing policies try to advance equality of opportunity

The welfare state not only supplies a measure of economic security but also provides opportunity. The American belief in equality of opportunity makes such programs particularly important. Programs that provide opportunity keep people from falling into poverty, and they offer a hand up to those who are poor. At their best, opportunity policies allow all individuals to rise as high as their talents will take them. Three types of policies are most significant in opening opportunity: education policies, health policies, and housing policies.

EDUCATION POLICIES PROVIDE LIFE TOOLS

Those who understand American federalism (see Chapter 3) already are aware that most of the education of the American people is provided by the public policies of state and local governments. What may be less obvious is that these education policies—especially the policy of universal compulsory public education—are the most important single force in the distribution and redistribution of opportunity in America.

Compared to state and local efforts, the role of national government education policy has been limited for most of American history. After World War II the federal government stepped up its role in education policy with the enactment of the GI Bill of Rights of 1944. The GI Bill, however, was aimed almost entirely at postsecondary schooling; the national government did not enter the field of elementary education until after 1957.[21]

What finally brought the national government into elementary education was embarrassment over the fact that the Soviet Union had beaten the United States into space with the launching of the world's first satellite, *Sputnik*, in 1957. As a result, in 1958 the federal government adopted the policy under the National Defense Education Act of improving education in science and mathematics. The federal government recognized the role of education in promoting equal opportunity. In 1965 the Elementary and Secondary Education Act offered federal aid for education by allocating funds to school districts with substantial numbers of children from families who were unemployed or earning less than $2,000 a year. Today, the federal government spends $79 billion, 10 percent of all spending, on K–12 education; states and localities each account for 45 percent of spending. Over time, however, federal education funds have become less targeted on low-income districts as Congress has failed to update the formula for allocating funds.[22]

The federal government also pursued the goal of equal opportunity in education through its support for racial desegregation. This meant dismantling the system of "separate but equal" education in the South and challenging de facto racial segregation in the North. Throughout the 1960s the Justice Department played a major role in pressing for desegregation and in monitoring progress of school integration. Yet, more than 50 years after the Civil Rights Act, this goal has remained elusive. Segregated patterns in housing create segregated schools unless vigorous policy interventions are implemented. However, such policies, including requirements for cross-district busing and provisions for affordable housing in affluent suburbs, have been struck down by the courts.

The Republican administrations of Ronald Reagan and George H. W. Bush refocused the goal of federal education policy away from equal opportunity and toward higher standards. The Department of Education's influential 1983 report, "A Nation at Risk," identified low education standards as the cause of America's declining international economic competitiveness. A new era emphasizing standards and testing began, although at first the federal role was primarily advisory to the states.

The federal role was substantially increased in 2001 by President George W. Bush's signature education initiative, No Child Left Behind (NCLB). Supported by Democrats and Republicans, the law sought to combine the goals of higher standards and equality of opportunity. It aimed to improve standards through stronger federal requirements for student testing and school accountability. Every child in grades 3 through 8 had to be tested yearly for proficiency in math and reading. The law aimed to promote equality of opportunity with two provisions: first, for a school to be judged a success, it had to show positive test results for all subcategories of children—minority race and ethnicity, English learners, and disability—not just overall averages. Second, parents with children in schools whose scores were poor had the right to transfer their children to a better school or to get funds for tutoring and summer programs. Because of strong congressional opposition to creating a national test, the states were made responsible for setting standards and devising appropriate tests.

NCLB soon generated considerable controversy. Many states branded it an "unfunded mandate," noting that the law placed expensive new obligations on schools to improve their performance but provided woefully inadequate resources. Teachers objected that "teaching to the test" undermined critical-thinking skills. In some states, up to half of the schools failed to meet the new standards, which resulted in a costly challenge to get more students up to speed. Under the federal law, they were required to improve student performance by providing such new services as supplemental tutoring, longer school days, and additional summer school. Critics also charged that NCLB actually undermined equal opportunity because it ended up punishing underperforming schools that bear the greatest burden for teaching the neediest students.[23]

The Obama administration sought a major overhaul of NCLB. By 2015 most states had received waivers from NCLB.[24] Later that year, Congress passed a bipartisan bill replacing NCLB, creating a new program called the Every Student Succeeds Act. The new law returned control to the states for school performance and made them responsible for devising their own methods of ensuring accountability. Controversial federal requirements for teachers' evaluations and mandated standards were eliminated. Every Student Succeeds continues to mandate testing and disaggregation of testing results by minority race and ethnicity, English learners, and disability. It also requires states to intervene to correct problems in the lowest 5 percent of schools but it leaves the specific remedies up to the states. While many people hailed the new law, others charged that it would do little to alter the achievement gap between richer and poorer schools.[25]

The Obama administration also supported charter schools—publicly funded schools that are free from the bureaucratic rules and regulations of the school district in which they are located and free to design specialized curricula and to use resources in ways they think most effective. One of the Obama administration's legislative initiatives, the American Recovery and Reinvestment Act, included a new $4.3-billion program called Race to the Top, which offered competitive grants to state education systems. The administration awarded sizable grants to 11 states and to Washington, D.C., for proposing bold new programs for assessing teachers and overhauling failing schools.[26] Several years after the program began, however, it was clear that states had promised more than they could do in the limited time that the funds were provided.[27]

The Secretary of Education under Donald Trump, Betsy DeVos, came to office a strong proponent of charter schools and vouchers, which allow students to use public funds to attend private schools. After a year in office, DeVos planned to focus much of her effort on reducing the size of the Education Department, hoping to free up more resources to fund school choice and a free-market approach to education. Supporters of public education, including teacher unions, worried that her policies would undercut support for the public school system.[28]

HEALTH POLICIES MEAN FEWER SICK DAYS

Until recent decades, no government in the United States—national, state, or local—concerned itself directly with individual health. But public responsibility was always accepted for *public* health. After New York City's newly created Board of Health was credited with holding down a cholera epidemic in 1867, most states created statewide public health agencies, recognizing that government can play an important role in preventing the spread of disease and reducing the likelihood of injury.

The U.S. Public Health Service (USPHS) has been in existence since 1798 but was only a small part of public-health policy until after World War II. It is headed by the U.S. Surgeon General. It includes, among other agencies, the National Institutes of Health (NIH), dedicated to biomedical research, and the Centers for Disease Control and Protection, which monitors outbreaks of disease and implements prevention measures and awareness campaigns about HIV/AIDS, Ebola, Zika, and other public health threats.

Additional federal commitments to the improvement of public health include the numerous laws aimed at cleaning up and defending the environment (including the creation in 1970 of the Environmental Protection Agency) and laws attempting to improve the health and safety of consumer products (regulated by the Consumer Product Safety Commission, created in 1972). Health policies aimed directly at the poor include nutritional programs, such as SNAP and the school lunch

Protecting public health has always been a focus of federal, state, and local governments. Here, Florida Surgeon General and Secretary Celeste Philip speaks to residents about protecting themselves against the 2015–16 outbreak of the Zika virus.

program, and Medicaid. In 2016 federal grants to states for Medicaid totaled an estimated $392 billion, up from $41 billion in 1990.[29] Medicaid covers the poor and people who are disabled; it also assists the elderly poor who cannot pay Medicare premiums. Because there is no provision for long-term care in the United States, Medicaid has become the de facto program financing nursing home residents when they have exhausted their savings. In fact, the disabled and elderly account for 65 percent of all Medicaid spending.[30] Medicaid is the single largest medical insurance program in the United States, covering 72.4 million people, a number that rose by 24 percent after the ACA's expansion provisions (discussed below) were put into place.[31]

As Figure 13.2 shows, the government has committed large resources to health care programs. While they yield great benefits by providing health care to millions, these programs have seen their costs rise dramatically in recent years—far more than the rate of inflation—prompting growing calls for major changes in spending and funding.[32]

After the 2008 election, the Obama administration and the Democratic Congress pressed forward with comprehensive health care reform. The administration aimed to cover most Americans who lacked health insurance with a reform strategy that built on the existing system. The plan enacted in 2010, the Affordable Care Act (ACA), had three key features: the first was the creation of new state-based insurance exchanges where individuals could buy health insurance, along with insurance regulation that would prohibit insurers from denying benefits for a variety of

U.S. Health Care: High Cost, Poor Outcomes

Countries that spend more on health care see better health outcomes—except for the United States. Americans spend more on health care than almost any other country, yet life expectancy remains low in comparison. A 2017 report cites three reasons why the United States lags in health outcomes: a highly fragmented system that leaves many people uninsured, poor health-related behaviors (e.g., higher levels of obesity, drug usage, traffic accidents, homicide), and higher rates of poverty and income inequality.[a]

In addition the United States' fragmented health care system contributes to health care inefficiencies, which undermine the quality of care while increasing costs.[b] If the U.S. government wants to reduce medical costs and improve the quality of health care, what would be the best policies to tackle these problems?

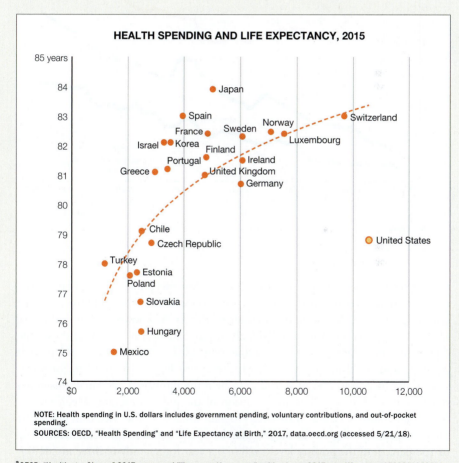

HEALTH SPENDING AND LIFE EXPECTANCY, 2015

NOTE: Health spending in U.S. dollars includes government pending, voluntary contributions, and out-of-pocket spending.

SOURCES: OECD, "Health Spending" and "Life Expectancy at Birth," 2017, data.oecd.org (accessed 5/21/18).

[a]OECD, "Health at a Glance," 2017, www.oecd-ilibrary.org/docserver/health_glance-2017-en.pdf?expires=1526931082&id=id&accname=guest&checksum=30893EF283DD3E267220A7DA219DEF49, p. 48 (accessed 5/21/18).

[b]N.F. Hanna, *Dying of Health Care: How the System Harms Americans Physically and Financially, and How to Change It* (Friday Harbor, WA: Copernicus Healthcare, 2016).

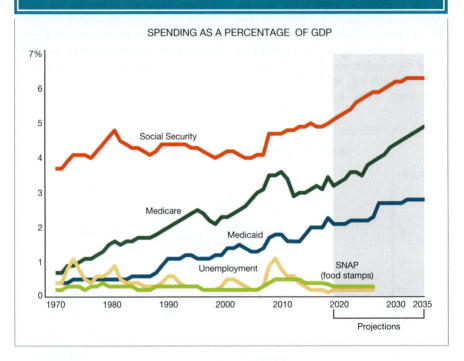

FIGURE 13.2

The Size of the Welfare State

Spending on Medicare, Medicaid, and Social Security is projected to rise as a percent of gross domestic product (GDP). Social Security, a contributory program that provides income to the elderly, is by far the largest welfare program in the United States. Which program is the smallest?

SOURCES: Congressional Budget Office, www.cbo.gov (accessed 8/19/18); and Office of Management and Budget, www.whitehouse.gov/omb/budget/Historicals (accessed 8/19/18). See endnote 30 for specific reports.

SPENDING AS A PERCENTAGE OF GDP

Social Security

Medicare

Medicaid

Unemployment

SNAP
(food stamps)

Projections

reasons such as preexisting conditions. With a few exceptions, the legislation also makes insurers cover preventive care, such as vaccinations, mammograms, and other screenings, in full. The second provision of the ACA, known as "the individual mandate," required uninsured individuals to purchase health insurance; those who do not have insurance are subject to a fine (scheduled to rise over time) of 1 percent of yearly household income or $95, whichever was larger. The third major provision of the ACA was a set of subsidies to help the uninsured and small businesses purchase insurance as well as an expansion of the public programs Medicaid and the State Children's Health Insurance Program (SCHIP). The Medicaid expansion made more people eligible for the program by opening it to people with incomes up to 138 percent of the poverty level ($28,676 a year for a family of three in 2018).[33]

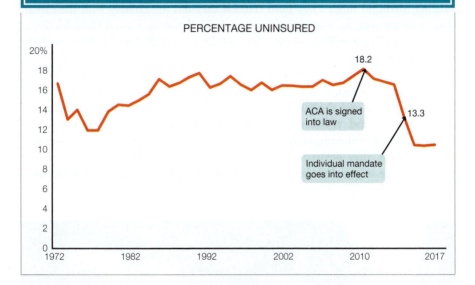

FIGURE 13.3

Health Insurance Coverage, 1972–2017

The percentage of Americans under 65 without health insurance reached 18.2 percent in 2010, when the ACA was enacted. With implementation beginning in 2014, the uninsurance rate fell to 10 percent in 2016. The Congressional Budget Office predicts that the repeal of the individual mandate, effective 2019, will increase the number of uninsured by 4 million in 2019 and 13 million in 2027.

SOURCES: 1995–2015 Kaiser Family Foundation, Key Facts about the Uninsured Population, September 2016, Figure 1, http://files.kff.org/attachment/Fact-Sheet-Key-Facts-about-the-Uninsured-Population (accessed 6/12/17).

PERCENTAGE UNINSURED

18.2

ACA is signed into law

13.3

Individual mandate goes into effect

The reform also allowed working-aged adults without dependent children to qualify for the program for the first time. Figure 13.3 shows the percentage of Americans without health insurance over time.

The new health care reform law faced challenges from state governments soon after it was enacted. Twenty-one states filed lawsuits against the legislation on the grounds that the provision requiring individuals to purchase health insurance expanded the commerce clause beyond its constitutional limits. The states also objected to provisions that required them to expand their Medicaid programs to cover more poor people or lose the Medicaid funds that they received from the federal government. Even though the federal government initially paid for 100 percent of the expansion and starting in 2016 would cover 90 percent of new costs, the states argued that the federal government had overstepped its powers in withdrawing all federal Medicaid funds if states did not comply with new coverage requirements.

The Supreme Court decided these suits in 2012, ruling that most of the act was constitutional.[34] Chief Justice John Roberts, regarded as a conservative, surprised many observers by writing the decision that declared the individual mandate constitutional. However, the decision found that the mandate could not be justified as constitutional under the commerce clause, which the administration relied on in its arguments before the Court. Because the mandate regulated economic *inactivity* (i.e., failure to purchase health insurance), Roberts argued that it could not be justified under the commerce clause, which regulates economic *activity*. Instead, the Court ruled that the requirement to purchase insurance was legal under Congress's taxing powers (since, under the law, failure to purchase insurance results in a penalty). The Court also ruled that Congress did not have the power to take existing Medicaid funds away from states if they did not comply with the expansion requirements. In response, 19 states decided not to expand their Medicaid programs, leaving 3 million people who would have qualified for Medicaid without access to health care.[35]

The politics of health care reform remain a focus of partisan contention. By 2016 Republican members of the House of Representatives had voted 62 times to repeal the act and the public remained split.[36] President Trump campaigned on the repeal and replacement of Obamacare, and after Republicans won unified control of the presidency and both houses of Congress in the November 2016 election, they devised an Obamacare replacement bill. The measure met stiff resistance as it ended the Medicaid entitlement by turning the program into

Because of their large population and strength in voting and organizing, the elderly in America receive many benefits from the federal government. Medicare and Social Security are two of America's most popular social policies.

a block grant to the states, and it permitted states to apply for waivers that would have effectively ended some regulatory protections for people with pre-existing conditions, among other changes. By fall 2017, Republicans had ended their efforts to repeal the ACA entirely, but did succeed in repealing the individual mandate to purchase health insurance in the Tax Cut and Jobs Act, enacted in December 2017. The Trump administration also cut the ACA enrollment period in half in late 2017 and reduced funds for advertising. Nonetheless, nearly as many Americans signed up for ACA health plans for 2018 as had enrolled for 2017.[37]

HOUSING POLICIES PROVIDE RESIDENTIAL STABILITY

Opportunity is also closely connected to housing. Access to quality, affordable housing gives individuals and families stability and freedom from pollution, infectious disease, chronic disease, injury, and anxiety and depression. The effects of quality housing are especially strong for children.[38] The United States has one of the highest rates of home ownership in the world, and the central thrust of federal housing policy has been to promote home ownership. The federal government has traditionally done much less to provide housing for low-income Americans who cannot afford to buy homes.

Federal housing programs were first created in the 1930s, when many Americans found themselves unable to afford housing. Through public housing for low-income families, which originated in 1937 with the Wagner-Steagall National Housing Act, and subsidized private housing after 1950, the percentage of American families living in overcrowded conditions was reduced from 20 percent in 1940 to 9 percent in 1970. Federal policies made an even greater contribution to reducing "substandard" housing, defined by the U.S. Census Bureau as dilapidated houses without hot running water and without some other plumbing. In 1940 almost 50 percent of American households lived in substandard housing. By 1950 this had been reduced to 35 percent; by 1975 the figure was reduced further, to 8 percent.[39]

Despite these improvements in housing standards, federal housing policy through the 1970s was largely seen as a failure. Restricted to the poorest of the poor and marked by racial segregation and inadequate spending, public housing contributed to the problems of the poor by isolating them from shopping, jobs, and urban amenities. Dilapidated high-rise housing projects stood as a symbol of the failed American policy of "warehousing the poor."

By the 1980s, the orientation of housing policy had changed. Federal housing assistance for low-income Americans shifted toward housing vouchers (now called housing choice vouchers) that provide recipients with support to rent in the private market. Although this program does not promote the same kind of isolation of the poor, most cities and suburbs have long waiting lists to receive vouchers; only one-quarter of eligible individuals and families receive them.[40] Another concern is that vouchers provide too little money to cover rental costs in very active housing markets.

Beginning in 2007 and 2008, a home loan crisis presented the government with a different kind of housing problem. During the housing boom of the early 2000s, many homeowners had received loans that they later could not afford to repay. This was caused in part by the deregulation of the mortgage industry in 1999, which allowed many new mortgage companies to form, offering loans that cost little at first but required large payments from homeowners later. This "predatory lending" targeted unsophisticated buyers and made it very hard for borrowers to understand the terms of the loans. Lending standards were relaxed to the point that rising numbers of borrowers were offered "no-doc" loans, which required no documentation of the borrowers' income. As more and more Americans took out such loans, demand for housing rose, and housing prices skyrocketed. This was the housing bubble—a bubble that was bound to burst because so many borrowers would not be able to pay back their loans. As growing numbers of homeowners began to default on their loans in 2007, banks foreclosed on their houses, and the value of housing began to drop. This downward spiral set off the major recession that began in 2008. As borrowers defaulted, banks holding that debt—including the biggest banks in America—teetered on the edge of failure and threatened to destabilize the entire economy. Many of the new mortgage companies went bankrupt. As unemployment rose, more families, unable to pay their mortgages, lost their homes. Many homeowners found that their homes were "underwater," meaning that the homeowners owed more on their mortgages than the homes were now worth. By 2015 over 5 million homes had been lost to foreclosure.[41]

Social Policy Spending Benefits the Middle Class More Than the Poor

Explain how contributory, noncontributory, and tax expenditure programs benefit different groups of Americans

The three categories of social policy, contributory, noncontributory, and tax expenditure programs, generally serve different groups of people. We can understand much about the development of social policy by examining which constituencies benefit from different policies.

The strongest and most generous programs are those in which the beneficiaries are widely perceived as deserving of assistance and are politically powerful. Because Americans prize work, constituencies who have "earned" their benefits in some way or those who cannot work because of a disability are usually seen as most deserving of government assistance. Politically powerful constituencies are those who vote as a group, lobby effectively, and mobilize to protect the programs from which they benefit.

When we study social policies from a group perspective, we can see that senior citizens and the middle class receive the most benefits from the government's social policies and that children and the working poor receive the fewest. In addition, America's social policies do little to change the fact that minorities and women are more likely to be poor than white Americans and men.

SENIOR CITIZENS RECEIVE OVER A THIRD OF ALL FEDERAL DOLLARS

The elderly are the beneficiaries of the two strongest and most generous social policies: retirement pensions (what we call Social Security) and health insurance for older Americans (Medicare). As these programs have grown, they have provided most elderly Americans with economic security and have dramatically reduced the poverty rate among the elderly. In 1959, before very many people over the age of 65 received social insurance, the poverty rate for the elderly was 35 percent; by 2016 it had dropped to 9.3 percent.[42] Because of this progress, many people call Social Security the most effective antipoverty program in the United States.[43] This does not mean that the elderly are rich, however; in 2016 the median income of elderly households was $39,823, well below the national median income. The aim of these programs is to provide security and prevent poverty.[44]

Even with the success of these programs at reducing poverty among the elderly, older African Americans and Latinos are much more likely to be poor than are white seniors. In 2016 the poverty rate for African Americans over age 65 was 18.5 percent and for Latinos over age 65 was 17.4 percent, compared to only 7.1 percent of non-Hispanic whites over 65. The difference is due in part to the lower wages of these groups during their working years since Social Security benefits are pegged to wages. Social Security may do less to pull immigrants out of poverty depending on the number of years they have worked in the United States.[45]

One reason that Social Security and Medicare are politically strong is that senior citizens are widely seen as a deserving population. Because of their age, they are not expected to work. Moreover, both programs are contributory, and a work history is a requirement for receiving a Social Security pension. But these programs are also strong because they serve a constituency that has become quite powerful. The elderly are a very large group: in 2016 there were 49.2 million Americans aged 65 and over. The size of this group is of such political importance also because the elderly turn out to vote in higher numbers than the rest of the population.

In addition, the elderly have developed strong and sophisticated lobbying organizations that can influence policy making and mobilize elderly Americans to defend these programs against proposals to cut them. One important and influential organization is AARP (formerly the American Association of Retired Persons). AARP had 38 million members in 2016, amounting to one-fourth of all voters. It also has a sophisticated lobbying organization in Washington that employs 51 lobbyists and a staff of nearly 50 policy analysts.[46]

When government has tried to reform Social Security or Medicare, beneficiaries of these programs have rallied together—often successfully—in opposition.

THE MIDDLE AND UPPER CLASSES BENEFIT FROM SOCIAL POLICIES

Americans don't usually think of the middle and upper classes as benefiting from social policies, but government action promotes the social welfare of these groups in a variety of ways. First, health insurance and pensions for the elderly help the middle class by relieving them of the burden of caring for elderly relatives. Before these programs existed, old people were more likely to live with and depend financially on their adult children. Many middle-class families whose parents and grandparents are in nursing homes rely on Medicaid to pay nursing home bills.

Second, the middle and upper classes are the chief beneficiaries of the shadow welfare state of tax expenditures.[47] Beyond the Earned Income Tax Credit (or EITC, described below), which principally benefits the working poor, the great majority of tax expenditure benefits go to middle- and upper-income households. For example, while households with incomes under $30,000 receive 70 percent of the EITC, households with incomes over $200,000 claim 40 percent of the property tax deduction, 46 percent of the home mortgage deduction, and 71 percent each of the state and local tax deduction and the deduction for charitable contributions.[48]

THE WORKING POOR RECEIVE FEWER BENEFITS

People who are working but are poor or are just above the poverty line receive only limited assistance from government social programs. This is somewhat surprising, given that Americans value work so highly. But the working poor are typically employed in jobs that do not provide pensions or health insurance; often, they are renters because they cannot afford to buy homes. This means they cannot benefit from the shadow welfare state that subsidizes the social benefits enjoyed by most middle-class Americans. Because the wages of less educated workers have declined significantly since the 1980s and minimum wages have not kept pace with inflation, the problems of the working poor remain acute.

Government programs that assist the working poor include the ACA (discussed earlier), the EITC, and SNAP. The EITC was implemented in 1976 to provide poor workers some relief from increases in the taxes that pay for Social Security. As it has expanded, the EITC has provided a modest wage supplement for the working poor, allowing them to catch up on utility bills or pay for children's clothing.

Poor workers can also receive benefits from the SNAP program. To be eligible, households must earn below 130 percent of the poverty line (about $26,600 a year for a three-person family in 2018). The average monthly benefit for a family of three is $376 a month.[49] Food advocates such as Feeding America have encouraged people to take "the SNAP Challenge," in which people who do not need SNAP spend $1.50 a meal (the average for SNAP recipients) for a week. In the words of one high-profile participant, "I was hungry last week—laser-focused on how much food was left in the fridge and how many dollars were left in my wallet. I was scared about eating portions that were too big, and wasn't sure what to do if my food ran out."[50]

The working poor are more likely to be in jobs that do not provide health benefits from their employers. By expanding Medicaid to cover workers who earn up to 138 percent of the poverty line ($28,676 for a family of three in 2018), the ACA sought to ensure coverage for this group. However, the decision of 19 states to opt out of Medicaid expansion left a gap in coverage. Latinos and African Americans were more likely to be harmed by this gap than whites: 27 percent of Hispanics and 16 percent of blacks lacked access to health insurance as a result of these state decisions, but only 11 percent of whites were affected in this way.[51] Even though the working poor may be seen as deserving, they lack political power because they are not organized.

SPENDING FOR THE NONWORKING POOR IS DECLINING

The only nonworking, able-bodied poor people who receive federal cash assistance are parents who are caring for children. The primary source of cash assistance for these families is the state-run TANF program; such families also rely on the SNAP program and Medicaid. Able-bodied adults who are not caring for children are not eligible for federal assistance other than SNAP. Many states provide small amounts of cash assistance to such individuals through programs called "general assistance," but most states have abolished or greatly reduced their general-assistance programs in an effort to encourage these adults to work. Americans don't like to subsidize adults who are not working, but they do not want to harm children.

AFDC was the most unpopular social spending program, and as a result, it was vulnerable to change. Under its replacement, TANF, states receive a fixed amount of federal funds (no adjustment for inflation), whether the welfare rolls rise or fall. Welfare recipients have little political power to resist cuts to their benefits. During the late 1960s and early 1970s, the short-lived National Welfare Rights Organization sought to represent the interests of welfare recipients. But keeping the organization in operation proved difficult because its members and its constituents had few resources and were difficult to organize.[52] Because welfare recipients are widely viewed as undeserving and are not politically organized, they have played little part in debates about welfare.

The deep recession that started in 2008 meant that record numbers of Americans were without work. In part because of eligibility expansions during the George W. Bush administration, the numbers of people receiving SNAP benefits during this period soared. At the height in 2013, over 47 million people (more than one in seven Americans) received SNAP benefits. As the unemployment rate declined, the number of SNAP beneficiaries began to decline as well, although in 2018, 42.3 million people continued to rely on SNAP.[53] These numbers reflect the high levels of need that persisted long after the recession.

MINORITIES, WOMEN, AND CHILDREN ARE MOST LIKELY TO FACE POVERTY

Minorities, women, and children are disproportionately poor. Much of this poverty is the result of disadvantages rooted in the position of these groups in the labor market. In 2016 the poverty rate for African Americans was 22 percent, and for Latinos it was 19.4 percent. For non-Hispanic whites, it was 8.8 percent.[54] Much of this economic inequality stems from the fact that minority workers tend to have low-wage jobs. Minorities are also more likely to become unemployed and to remain unemployed for longer periods of time than are white Americans. African Americans, for example, typically have experienced twice as much unemployment as have other Americans. The combination of low-wage jobs and unemployment often means that minorities are less likely to have jobs that give them access to the shadow welfare state. They are more likely to fall into the precarious categories of the working poor or the nonworking poor.

Policy analysts have increasingly examined the "feminization of poverty," or the fact that women are more likely than men to be poor. This problem is particularly acute for single mothers, who are more than twice as likely as the average American to fall below the poverty line (see Figure 13.4). When the Social Security Act was passed in 1935, the main programs for poor women were Aid to Dependent Children (ADC) and survivors' insurance for widows. The framers of the act

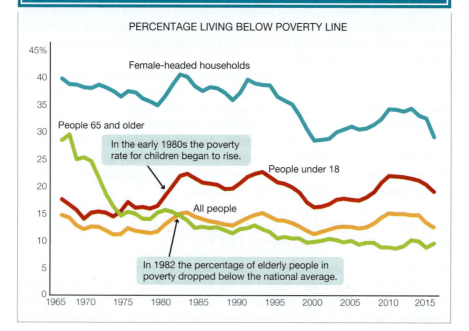

FIGURE 13.4

Poverty Levels in the United States, 1966–2016

Poverty rates in the U.S. population vary considerably. The rate of poverty among female-headed households declined significantly in the 1990s, increased since 2000, and declined again after 2000. Which group has seen the greatest reduction in its poverty level since 1966?

SOURCES: U.S. Census Bureau, Historical Poverty Tables, "Table 2. Poverty Status of People by Family Relationship, Race, and Hispanic Origin: 1959 to 2016" and "Table 3. Poverty Status of People, by Age, Race, and Hispanic Origin," www.census.gov/data/tables/time-series/demo/income-poverty/historical-poverty-people.html (accessed 9/7/18).

PERCENTAGE LIVING BELOW POVERTY LINE

Female-headed households

People 65 and older

In the early 1980s the poverty rate for children began to rise.

People under 18

All people

In 1982 the percentage of elderly people in poverty dropped below the national average.

believed that ADC would gradually disappear as more women became eligible for survivors' insurance. The social model behind the Social Security Act was that of a male breadwinner with a wife and children. Women were not expected to work, and if a woman's husband died, ADC or survivors' insurance would help her stay at home and raise her children. The framers of Social Security did not envision today's large number of single women heading families. At the same time, they did not envision that so many women with children would also be working. This combination of changes helped make AFDC (the successor program to ADC) more controversial. Many people asked why welfare recipients shouldn't work, if the majority of women who were not on welfare worked. Such questions led to the welfare reform of 1996, which created TANF.

One of the most troubling issues related to American social policy is the number of American children who live in poverty. The rate of child poverty in 2016 was 18 percent—5.3 percentage points higher than that of the population as a whole. African American and Latino children experience much higher rates of poverty than do whites. In 2016 the rate of child poverty for white children was 10.8 percent, while 26.6 percent of Latino children and 30.8 percent of black children lived in poverty.[55] High rates of child poverty stem in part from the design of American social policies. Because these policies do not generously assist able-bodied adults who aren't working and because these policies offer little help to the working poor, the children of these adults are likely to be poor as well.

As child poverty has grown, several lobbying groups have emerged to represent children's interests; the best known of these is the Children's Defense Fund. But even with a sophisticated lobbying operation and although their numbers are large, poor children do not vote and therefore wield little political power.

Domestic Policy
WHAT DO WE WANT?

Public policy encompasses many different ways for the government to achieve its objectives. All public policies are tools of government control, but the means chosen to achieve their goals can have a major effect on how the public feels about those policies. After all, who wouldn't rather be encouraged to do something by being paid to do it instead of being told that failure to do the very same thing may result in jail time? This might lead you to think that the government should do everything by relying on payments or subsidies, but for many areas of public life, this is simply not possible—not to mention incredibly expensive.

Economic policy has changed dramatically in recent decades. The American economy is now far more open to the rest of the world, and many American firms do most of their production in China and other developing economies. At the same time, the distribution of economic gains in the United States has shifted upward. As the debate about more or less government has led to a series of policy stalemates among politicians, the income of the American middle class has mostly stagnated and the gains going to the top 1 percent have soared. Some Americans think the government should do more to address income inequality through tax policy, for example by taxing the wealthy at higher rates.

Social policies, established in the 1930s, have stirred up much controversy. Liberals often argue that more generous social policies are needed if the United States is truly to ensure equality of opportunity, saying that the government needs to go beyond simply providing opportunity and should ensure more equal conditions, especially where children are concerned. Conservatives, on the other hand, often argue that social policies that offer income support take the ideal of equality too far and, in the process, do for individuals what those individuals should be doing for themselves. From this perspective, social policies make the government too big, and big government is seen as a fundamental threat to Americans' liberties.

Where do average Americans fit in these debates? Americans are often said to be philosophical conservatives and operational liberals.[56] When asked about government social policy in the abstract, they say they disapprove of activist government—a conservative view. But when they must evaluate particular programs, Americans generally express support—a liberal perspective. Some programs are more popular than others. Policies in which the recipients are regarded as deserving, such as programs for the elderly, receive more support than those that assist working-age people. Programs that have a reputation for effectiveness and those that require people to help themselves through work are also viewed favorably.[57] In sum, most Americans take a pragmatic approach to social welfare policies: they favor programs that work, and they want to reform those that seem not to work.

One way to think about the role of social policy is to consider what you would do if you faced a threat to your ability to support yourself and those around you. Imagine if you had difficulty paying for school. The "**Who Participates?**" feature on the facing page looks at the growth in student loans and describes some government programs to help students pay off their loans. Or imagine you experienced a catastrophic accident like we saw with Marcella Wagner at the beginning of the chapter, or had a parent fall ill, or had a job that did not pay enough to make ends meet. What strategies would you use to overcome those risks? Are there government policies in place to help in these situations? What do you think about government playing such a role for you or for other individuals? Does current government policy reflect your views, and if not, what could you as an individual do to make your voice heard?

Growing Student Debt Burden

Student Loan Balances (in billions of dollars)

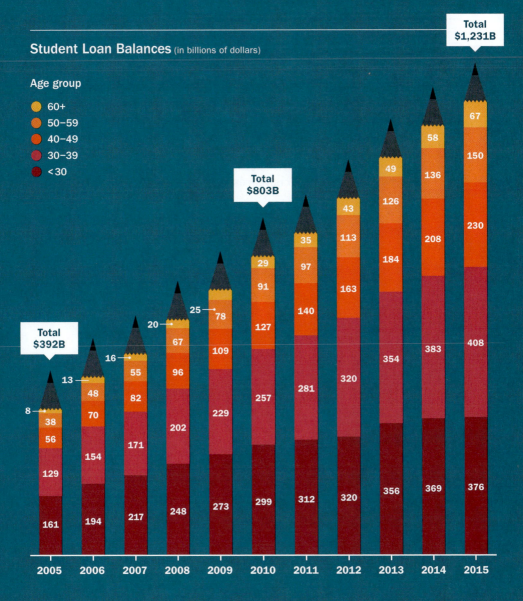

Total $1,231B

Total $803B

Total $392B

Age group

- 60+
- 50–59
- 40–49
- 30–39
- < 30

Year	60+	50–59	40–49	30–39	< 30	Total
2005	8	38	56	129	161	$392B
2006	13	48	70	154	194	
2007	16	55	82	171	217	
2008	20	67	96	202	248	
2009	25	78	109	229	273	
2010	29	91	127	257	299	$803B
2011	35	97	140	281	312	
2012	43	113	163	320	320	
2013	49	126	184	354	356	
2014	58	136	208	383	369	
2015	67	150	230	408	376	$1,231B

SOURCE: Federal Reserve Bank of New York Consumer Credit Panel, "2016 Student Loan Update," newyorkfed.org (accessed 12/26/17).

WHAT YOU CAN DO

Contact the Government about Student Loan Issues

☑ Contact your member of Congress with your opinion on how government agencies should regulate student loans.

☑ If your employer is a government organization, a 501(c)(3) nonprofit, or a private company that provides public services, you may qualify to get your federal loans forgiven through the Public Service Loan Forgiveness (PSLF) program: **www.studentaid.ed.gov/sa/repay-loans/ forgiveness-cancellation/public-service**.

☑ If you have Perkins Loans and go to work in public service, including the active-duty military, education, health services, and public safety, you might be eligible for Perkins Loans cancellation: **https://studentaid .ed.gov/sa/repay-loans/forgiveness-cancellation**.

★ STUDY GUIDE ★

Practice Quiz

1. Monetary policy seeks to influence the economy through *(p. 413)*
  a) taxing and spending.
  b) privatizing and nationalizing selected industries.
  c) the availability of credit and money.
  d) foreign exchange of currency.
  e) administrative regulation.

2. The most powerful institution in determining America's monetary policy is *(p. 413)*
  a) the Department of Commerce.
  b) the Department of the Treasury.
  c) the federal judiciary.
  d) the Federal Reserve Board.
  e) the president.

3. Government attempts to manipulate the economy by using its taxing and spending powers are called *(p. 414)*
  a) antitrust policies.
  b) expropriation policies.
  c) monetary policies.
  d) fiscal policies.
  e) redistributive policies.

4. A policy whose objective is to tax or spend in such a way as to reduce the disparities of wealth between the highest and lowest income brackets is called *(p. 414)*
  a) antitrust policy.
  b) deregulation.
  c) discretionary spending.
  d) equalization.
  e) redistribution.

5. The United States' welfare state was constructed initially in response to *(p. 416)*
   a) the Civil War.
   b) World War II.
   c) political reforms of the Progressive era.
   d) the Great Depression.
   e) the growth of the military–industrial complex.

6. Which of the following is an example of a contributory program? *(p. 418)*
   a) Medicaid
   b) Medicare
   c) Temporary Assistance for Needy Families
   d) Supplemental Nutrition Assistance Program
   e) Aid to Families with Dependent Children

7. Means testing requires that applicants for welfare benefits show *(p. 419)*
   a) that they are capable of getting to and from their workplace.
   b) that they have the ability to store and prepare food.
   c) a financial need for assistance.
   d) that they have the time and resources to take full advantage of federal educational opportunities.
   e) that they are natural-born citizens who have never been convicted of a felony.

8. Which of the following are examples of in-kind benefits? *(p. 419)*
   a) Medicaid and the Supplemental Nutrition Assistance Program
   b) Social Security and the Troubled Assets Relief Program
   c) Medicare and unemployment compensation
   d) the GI Bill of Rights and the Equal Rights Amendment
   e) the Earned Income Tax Credit and No Child Left Behind

9. What event prompted the federal government to enter the field of elementary education? *(p. 423)*
   a) the Civil War
   b) the Great Depression
   c) World War II

   d) the Soviet Union's launching of *Sputnik*
   e) the civil rights movement

10. Which of the following was *not* part of the No Child Left Behind Act of 2001? *(p. 424)*
    a) a provision allowing parents whose child is attending a failing school to transfer the child to a better school
    b) a requirement that states failing to meet national standards improve student performance by providing supplemental tutoring, longer school days, and additional summer school
    c) a requirement that schools show positive results for all subcategories of students and not just positive overall averages
    d) a requirement that a national test be used to evaluate every student around the country
    e) a requirement that every child in grades 3 through 8 be tested yearly for proficiency in math and reading

11. Who are the chief beneficiaries of the "shadow welfare state"? *(p. 434)*
    a) children
    b) the elderly
    c) the nonworking poor
    d) the working poor
    e) the middle class

12. Which three government programs provide assistance to the working poor? *(p. 434)*
    a) Temporary Assistance for Needy Families, Medicare, and the Supplemental Nutrition Assistance Program
    b) the Affordable Care Act, the Earned Income Tax Credit, and the Supplemental Nutrition Assistance Program
    c) Temporary Assistance for Needy Families, Social Security, and the Earned Income Tax Credit
    d) Temporary Assistance for Needy Families, Medicare, and the Affordable Care Act
    e) Social Security, Medicaid, and Medicare

Key Terms

contracting power *(p. 411)* the power of government to set conditions on companies seeking to sell goods or services to government agencies

contributory programs *(p. 418)* social programs financed in whole or in part by taxation or other mandatory contributions by their present or future recipients

cost-of-living adjustments (COLAs) *(p. 418)* changes made to the level of benefits of a government program based on the rate of inflation

Federal Reserve System *(p. 413)* a system of 12 Federal Reserve banks that facilitates exchanges of cash, checks, and credit; regulates member banks; and uses monetary policies to fight inflation and deflation

fiscal policy *(p. 414)* the government's use of taxing, monetary, and spending powers to manipulate the economy

indexing *(p. 418)* periodic process of adjusting of social benefits or wages to account for increases in the cost of living

in-kind benefits *(p. 419)* noncash goods and services provided to needy individuals and families by the federal government

means testing *(p. 419)* a procedure by which potential beneficiaries of a public-assistance program establish their eligibility by demonstrating a genuine need for the assistance

Medicaid *(p. 419)* a federally and state-financed, state-operated program providing medical services to low-income people

Medicare *(p. 418)* a form of national health insurance for the elderly and the disabled

monetary policies *(p. 413)* efforts to regulate the economy through the manipulation of the supply of money and credit; America's most powerful institution in this area of monetary policy is the Federal Reserve Board

noncontributory programs *(p. 419)* social programs that provide assistance to people based on demonstrated need rather than any contribution they have made

public policy *(p. 409)* a law, a rule, a statute, or an edict that expresses the government's goals and provides for rewards and punishments to promote those goals' attainment

redistribution *(p. 414)* collecting revenue in such a way as to reduce the disparities of wealth between the lowest and the highest income brackets

Social Security *(p. 418)* a contributory welfare program into which working Americans contribute a percentage of their wages and from which they receive cash benefits after retirement or if they become disabled

subsidies *(p. 409)* government grants of cash or other valuable commodities, such as land, to individuals or an organization; used to promote activities desired by the government, to reward political support, or to buy off political opposition

Supplemental Nutrition Assistance Program (SNAP) *(p. 419)* the largest antipoverty program, which provides recipients with a debit card for food at most grocery stores; formerly known as *food stamps*

tax expenditures *(p. 419)* government subsidies provided to employers and employees through tax deductions for amounts spent on health insurance and other benefits

For Further Reading

Baldwin, Robert, Martin Cave, and Martin Lodge. *Understanding Regulation*. New York: Oxford University Press, 2012.

Campbell, Andrea Louise. *Trapped in America's Safety Net*. Chicago: University of Chicago Press, 2014.

Cohen, David K., and Susan L. Moffitt. *The Ordeal of Equality: Did Federal Regulation Fix the Schools?* Cambridge, MA: Harvard University Press, 2009.

Desmond, Matthew. *Evicted: Poverty and Profit in the American City*. New York: Crown, 2016.

Edin, Kathryn J., and Luke Shafer. *$2.00 a Day: Living on Almost Nothing in America*. New York: Houghton Mifflin Harcourt, 2015.

Hacker, Jacob S. *The Great Risk Shift: Why American Jobs, Families, Health Care, and Retirement Aren't Secure—And How We Can Fight Back*. New York: Oxford University Press, 2006.

Howard, Christopher. *The Welfare State Nobody Knows: Debunking Myths about U.S. Social Policy*. Princeton, NJ: Princeton University Press, 2007.

Mettler, Suzanne. *Degrees of Inequality: How the Politics of Higher Education Sabotaged the American Dream*. New York: Basic Books, 2014.

Ravitch, Diane. *Reign of Error: The Hoax of the Privatization Movement and the Danger to America's Public Schools*. New York: Knopf, 2013.

Soss, Joe, Richard C. Fording, and Sanford F. Schramm. *Disciplining the Poor: Neoliberal Paternalism and the Persistent Power of Race*. Chicago: University of Chicago Press, 2011.

Wailoo, Keith, Alan Cohen, Julian Zelizer, and David Colby, eds. *Medicare and Medicaid at 50*. New York: Oxford University Press, 2015.

Weir, Margaret, Ann Orloff, and Theda Skocpol, eds. *The Politics of Social Policy in the United States*. Princeton, NJ: Princeton University Press, 1988.

Foreign Policy

WHAT GOVERNMENT DOES AND WHY IT MATTERS

Foreign policy may seem like a distant or abstract matter, but it carries tremendous consequences for ordinary people. In January 2017, President Trump signed an executive order banning travel to the United States for people from Iran, Iraq, Libya, Somalia, Sudan, Syria, and Yemen. The president's purpose was to protect U.S. borders and prohibit entry from countries with lax security standards. As with any public policy, views on the travel ban varied. Amanda Patrick of Georgia, a 38-year-old tax associate with a young son, supported the ban, saying, "The biggest thing for me, especially with having a child now, is the safety factor. Just people coming in that we aren't properly vetting." Susan Richardson, a 74-year-old artist and entrepreneur from Florida and an immigrant from England, believes countries have a right to defend their borders: "When I came to this country, if you didn't have the right visa, if you didn't have somebody who sponsored you, you were turned back at the airport."[1]

For yet others, the travel ban has meant personal turmoil. Mohamed Iye, an American citizen born in Somalia, was about to be reunited with his Somali

America's foreign policy can have profound effects on the lives of individuals here and abroad. President Trump's decision to ban immigration from certain countries put many lives in limbo, like that of Mohamed Iye (pictured here). Iye was reunited with his family after being stranded in Kenya when the ban was declared.

wife and two American daughters after a two-year separation when the travel ban was issued, stranding his family in Nairobi. He and many others joined lawsuits against the ban. "It was never my intention to go against the president of the United States. I was just following the law and doing everything the way it's in the books. And it came to this." Ali Asaei, a 27-year-old originally from Iran who holds a master's degree and works at a psychiatric research institute in New York, also joined a lawsuit against the travel ban. He hadn't seen his family in four years, and their visa applications to visit him were rejected after the travel ban went into effect. He said that in Iran, "There is no freedom of speech, no freedom of press.... One of the reasons I came here was because I thought, here we're going to have the freedom of speech and religion and all these. But if I don't have those freedoms, then what would be the point of staying here?"[2]

The Trump administration's travel ban was challenged in the federal courts and was finally upheld by the U.S. Supreme Court in the 2018 case of *Trump v. Hawaii*.[3] The issue illustrates just one of the complexities of foreign policy.

A government's first duty is to protect its citizens, but should protection mean the exclusion of citizens of foreign countries from America's shores? What about foreign trade? America's interests and those of foreign countries are so closely intertwined that the Trump administration's tariffs against foreign auto companies, and subsequent retaliation from America's trading partners, hurt workers in South Carolina where BMWs (a German car) are assembled and then shipped all over the world. In the realm of security interests, when dealing with America's rivals such as Russia, China, and North Korea, what is the proper mix of such foreign policy tools as diplomacy, economic pressure, and the threat of force? To make matters even more complicated, some threats require international rather than national responses, but achieving international cooperation is sometimes problematic. President Trump has demanded that America's NATO allies pay a larger share of the collective cost of defense, though his demands threaten to undermine the NATO alliance. The United States, like other nations, struggles to strike the right balance between competition and cooperation in the international arena.

CHAPTER GOALS

★ Explain how foreign policy is designed to promote security, prosperity, and humanitarian goals (pp. 447–53)

★ Identify the major players in foreign-policy making, and describe their roles (pp. 453–58)

★ Describe the means the United States uses to carry out foreign policy today (pp. 458–64)

★ Analyze the foreign policy problems facing American policy makers today (pp. 464–68)

Foreign Policy Goals Are Related

Explain how foreign policy is designed to promote security, prosperity, and humanitarian goals

The term *foreign policy* refers to the programs and policies that determine America's relations with other nations and foreign entities. Foreign policy includes diplomacy, military and security policy, international human rights policies, and various forms of economic policy such as trade policy and international energy policy. Of course, foreign policy and domestic policy are not completely separate categories: domestic politics affects foreign policy and foreign policy certainly affects domestic politics. Take security policy, for example. Defending the nation requires the design and manufacture of tens of billions of dollars in military hardware. The manufacture of this military equipment provides jobs in American communities where the equipment is built, while paying for it involves raising taxes or choosing not to fund other programs.

Although U.S. foreign policy has a number of purposes, three main, interrelated goals stand out. These are security, prosperity, and the creation of a better world.

SECURITY IS BASED ON MILITARY STRENGTH

To many Americans, the chief purpose of the nation's foreign policy is protection of U.S. security in an often hostile world. Traditionally, the United States has been concerned about threats that might emanate from other countries, such as Nazi Germany during the 1940s and then Soviet Russia until the Soviet Union's collapse in 1991. Today, American security policy is concerned not only with the actions of other nations but also with the activities of terrorist groups and other hostile **non-state actors**.[4] To protect the nation's security from foreign threats, the United States has built an enormous military apparatus and a complex array of intelligence-gathering institutions, such as the Central Intelligence Agency (CIA), charged with evaluating and anticipating challenges from abroad.[5]

During the eighteenth and nineteenth centuries, American security was based mainly on the geographic isolation of the United States. We were separated by two oceans from European and Asian powers, and many Americans thought that our security would be best preserved by remaining aloof from international power struggles. This policy of avoiding involvement in the affairs of other nations was known as **isolationism**. In his 1796 Farewell Address, President George Washington warned Americans to avoid permanent alliances with foreign powers; and in 1823, President James Monroe warned foreign powers not to meddle in the Western Hemisphere. Washington's warning and what came to be called the Monroe Doctrine were the cornerstones of the U.S. foreign policy of isolationism until the end of the nineteenth century. The United States saw itself as the dominant power in the Western Hemisphere and, indeed, believed that its "manifest destiny" was to expand from sea to sea. The rest of the world, however, should remain at arm's length.

In the twentieth century, technology made oceans less a barrier to foreign threats, and the world's growing economic interdependence meant that the nation could no longer ignore events abroad. Early in the twentieth century, the United States entered World War I on the side of Great Britain and France when the Wilson administration concluded that a German victory would adversely affect America's economic and security interests. In 1941 the United States was drawn into World War II when Japan attacked the U.S. Pacific fleet anchored at Pearl Harbor, Hawaii. Even before the attack, the Roosevelt administration had concluded that the United States needed to act to prevent a victory by the German–Japanese–Italian Axis alliance.

Following World War II, the United States developed a new security policy known as **containment** to check or "contain" the growing power of the Soviet Union, which by the end of the 1940s had built a huge empire, enormous military forces, and nuclear weapons and bombers capable of attacking the United States. The United States was committed to maintaining its own military might as a means of **deterrence**, to discourage the Soviets from attacking the United States or its allies. Some Americans wanted a more aggressive policy and argued that we should attack the Soviets before it was too late, a policy known as **preventive war**. Others said that we should show our peaceful intentions and attempt to placate the Soviets. This policy is called **appeasement**.

The policies that the United States adopted, deterrence and containment, could be seen as midway between aggression and appeasement. A nation pursuing a policy of deterrence, on the one hand, signals its peaceful intentions but, on the other hand, indicates its willingness and ability to fight if attacked. Thus, during the era of confrontation with the Soviet Union between the late 1940s and 1990, known as the **Cold War**, the United States frequently asserted that it had no intention of attacking the Soviet Union but at the same time built a huge military force, including a vast arsenal of nuclear weapons and intercontinental missiles, and frequently asserted that in the event of a Soviet attack it would respond with overwhelming force. The Soviet Union announced that its nuclear weapons were also intended for deterrent purposes. Eventually, the two sides possessed such enormous arsenals of nuclear missiles that each had the ability to destroy the other in the event of war. This heavily armed standoff came to be called a posture of mutually assured

During the Cold War, the United States and the Soviet Union engaged in an arms race, each acquiring nuclear weapons to deter the other from attacking.

destruction. During the 1962 Cuban missile crisis, the United States and the Soviet Union came to the brink of war when President Kennedy declared that the Soviet Union must remove its nuclear missiles from Cuba and threatened to use force if the Soviets refused. After an extremely intense several weeks, the crisis was defused by a negotiated compromise in which the Soviets agreed to remove their missiles in exchange for a guarantee from the United States that it would not invade Cuba. The two superpowers had come so close to nuclear war that afterward the leaders of both nations sought ways to reduce tensions. This effort led to a period of détente, in which a number of arms control agreements were signed and the threat of war was reduced.

In 1991 the Soviet Union collapsed, partly because its huge military expenditures undermined its inefficient, centrally planned economy. The new Russia, though still a formidable power, posed less of a threat to the United States. Within several years, however, new security threats emerged, requiring new policy responses. The September 11, 2001, terrorist attacks demonstrated a threat against which some security scholars had long warned: that non-state actors and so-called rogue states might acquire significant military capabilities, including nuclear weapons, and would not be affected by America's deterrent capabilities.

Unlike **nation-states** (political entities consisting of a people with some common cultural experience who also share a common political authority, recognized by other sovereignties), which have governments and fixed borders, terrorist groups are non-state actors having no fixed geographic location that can be attacked. Terrorists may believe that they can attack and melt away, leaving the United States with no one against whom to retaliate. Hence, the threat of massive retaliation does not deter them. Rogue states are nations with unstable and erratic leaders who seem to pursue policies driven by ideological or religious fervor rather than careful consideration of economic or human costs. The United States considers North Korea to be a rogue state.

To counter these new security threats, the George W. Bush administration shifted from a policy of deterrence to one of preventive war—the willingness to strike first in order to prevent an enemy attack. The United States declared that, if necessary, it would take action to disable terrorist groups and rogue states before they could develop the ability to do it harm. This idea gained important support after the September 11, 2001, attacks. The Bush administration's "global war on terror" was an expression of this notion of prevention, as was the U.S. invasion of Iraq. This policy has also been advanced by the Trump administration. The United States has refused to rule out the possibility that it would attack North Korea or Iran if it deemed those nations' nuclear programs to be an imminent threat to American security interests. Accompanying this shift in military doctrine was a significant increase in overall U.S. military spending (see Figure 14.1).

President Obama took a less aggressive line, saying that the United States would rely on diplomacy and economic sanctions. President Trump, however, said that the United States was prepared to use overwhelming force against its adversaries. Trump called North Korean leader Kim Jong-un "Little Rocket Man" and declared

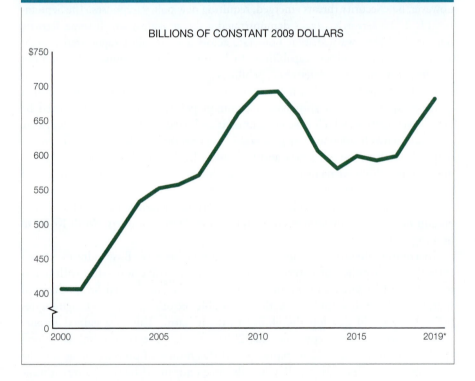

FIGURE 14.1

U.S. Spending on National Defense since 2000

During the 1990s the budget for national defense declined as the country enjoyed a "peace dividend" following the conclusion of the Cold War. After the attacks of September 11, 2001, and the commencement of the war on terrorism, however, national defense spending rose steadily; in a decade, spending increased by 70 percent. Since that time defense spending has fallen.

*Data for 2019 are estimated.

SOURCE: Office of Management and Budget, "Table 3.1—Outlays by Superfunction and Function: 1940–2023," www.whitehouse.gov/omb/historical-tables/ (accessed 7/23/18).

BILLIONS OF CONSTANT 2009 DOLLARS

that only force would thwart Kim's ambitions. Nevertheless, in April 2018, Trump agreed to a meeting with Kim to discuss ways of reducing tensions on the Korean Peninsula. After the two leaders met in June 2018, Trump declared that progress had been made toward a more peaceful resolution of the Korean conflict. In July 2018, Trump met with Russian president Vladimir Putin. Trump called the meeting a great success but critics charged that the president had not been sufficiently aggressive in demanding an accounting for Russian attempts to influence the 2016 American election.

ECONOMIC PROSPERITY HELPS ALL NATIONS

A second major goal of U.S. foreign policy is to promote American prosperity. America's international economic policies are intended to expand employment opportunities in the United States, to maintain access to foreign energy supplies at a reasonable cost, to promote foreign investment in the United States, and to lower the prices Americans pay for goods and services.

The most important international organization for promoting free trade is the **World Trade Organization (WTO)**, established in 1995. The WTO grew out of the **General Agreement on Tariffs and Trade (GATT)**, established in 1947, which set many of the rules governing international trade. Since World War II, GATT had brought together a wide range of nations for regular negotiations designed to reduce barriers to trade. Such barriers, many believed, had contributed to the breakdown of the world economy in the 1930s and had helped cause World War II. The WTO has 164 members worldwide, including the United States. Similar policy goals are pursued in regional arrangements, such as the **United States–Mexico–Canada Agreement (USMCA)**, formerly known as NAFTA, a trade treaty among the United States, Canada, and Mexico to lower and eliminate tariffs among the three countries.

The United States is the world's largest importer and exporter of goods and services. In 2013 the United States exported more than $1.5 trillion in goods and services while importing $2.2 trillion in goods and services. Roughly 11 million jobs in the United States are directly tied to international trade. Accordingly, America has a vital interest in maintaining international trade and monetary practices that promote American prosperity.

AMERICA SEEKS A MORE HUMANE WORLD

A third goal of American policy is to make the world a better place for all its inhabitants. Many Americans believe that the United States has an obligation to protect human rights and to provide assistance to needy groups throughout the world. Other Americans say we should spend our resources at home and let other nations look after their own people. A third group of Americans view human rights and humanitarian policies as a form of "soft power," serving American interests and winning friends by demonstrating our concern for the less fortunate throughout the world. This third group has generally been dominant within the American foreign policy community.

The main forms of policy that address this goal are international environmental policy, international human rights policy, and international peacekeeping. The United States also contributes to international organizations that work for global health and against hunger, such as the World Health Organization. These policies are often seen as secondary to the other goals of American foreign policy and are forced to give way if they interfere with security or foreign economic policy. Moreover, while the United States spends billions annually on security policy and hundreds of millions on trade policy, it spends relatively little on environmental, human rights, and peacekeeping efforts.

In the realm of international environmental policy, the United States supports various international efforts to protect the environment. These include the United

Building Influence through International Connections

Since World War II, the United States has been considered the leading global hegemon: an international actor so powerful that it can spread its influence across continents. When thinking of U.S. hegemony, most people focus on the dominant military power of the United States. However, the military is only one tool for expanding a country's interest, and we might consider a country's level of globalization to be another measure of influence. Globalization is the process of increasing interactions across country borders and between societies and economies; countries that are more globalized have built multiple connections and influence.

Comparing the United States to two main international challengers, Russia and China, we can see how highly integrated the United States is into the global system. While all three countries are close on political globalization, the United States has a clear lead in social and economic globalization. This means that in terms of international negotiations, the United States has more tools at its disposal than any other country.

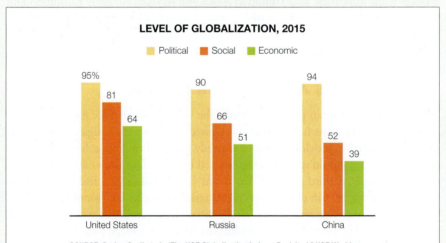

LEVEL OF GLOBALIZATION, 2015

Political Social Economic

United States: Political 95%, Social 81, Economic 64
Russia: Political 90, Social 66, Economic 51
China: Political 94, Social 52, Economic 39

SOURCE: Savina Gygli et al., "The KOF Globalization Index—Revisited," KOF Working Paper, No. 439, 2018, www.kof.ethz.ch (accessed 5/29/18).

Nations (UN) Framework Convention on Climate Change, an international agreement to study and ameliorate harmful changes in the global environment, and the Montreal Protocol, an agreement signed by more than 150 countries to limit the production of substances potentially harmful to the world's ozone layer. The United States has a long-standing commitment to human rights and is a party to most major international human rights agreements. This commitment, though, has a lower priority in American foreign policy than the nation's security concerns and economic interests. Thus, the United States is likely to overlook human rights violations by its major trading partners, such as China, and remain silent in the face of human rights violations by such allies as Saudi Arabia. Nevertheless, human rights concerns do play a role in American foreign policy. For example, beginning in 2007 the United States has annually made available several million dollars in small grants to pay medical and legal expenses incurred by individuals who have been the victims of retaliation in their own countries for working against their governments' repressive practices. In this small way, the United States is backing its often-asserted principles.

Another form of U.S. policy designed to improve the condition of the world is support for international peacekeeping efforts. At any point in time, a number of border wars, civil wars, and guerrilla conflicts are flaring somewhere in the world, usually in its poorer regions. These wars often generate humanitarian crises in the form of casualties, disease, and refugees. In cooperation with international agencies and other nations, the United States funds a number of efforts to keep the peace in volatile regions and to deal with the health care and refugee problems associated with conflict. In 2015 the United States provided nearly $2 billion in humanitarian assistance to help Syrian refugees displaced by the civil war in that nation and by the end of 2016 had donated over $5 billion to the cause.[6]

As the world's wealthiest nation, the United States also recognizes an obligation to render assistance to nations facing crises and emergencies. In 2014, for example, the United States pledged $300 million in humanitarian aid to the people of South Sudan, a population at grave risk of famine caused by military conflict between government and rebel forces.

American Foreign Policy Is Shaped by Government and Nongovernment Actors

> **Identify the major players in foreign-policy making, and describe their roles**

As we have seen, domestic policies are made by governmental institutions and influenced by a variety of interest groups, political movements, and even the mass media. The same is true in the realm of foreign policy. The president and his chief advisers are the principal architects of U.S. foreign policy. However, the Congress, the bureaucracy, the courts, political parties, interest groups, and trade associations also play important roles in this realm. Often, the president and Congress are at odds over foreign policy.

THE PRESIDENT LEADS FOREIGN POLICY

The president is the leading figure in the conduct of American foreign policy. The president's foreign policy powers today, particularly in the military realm, are far greater than the Constitution's framers had thought wise. The framers gave the power to declare war to Congress and made the president the nation's top military commander if and when Congress chose to go to war. Today, presidents both command the troops and decide when to go to war.

All four recent presidents, like most of their predecessors, were faced with momentous challenges to American security and to America's international interests. George W. Bush, in particular, was compelled to develop a response to the September 11, 2001, terror attacks. By 2002 foreign policy had become the centerpiece of the Bush administration's agenda. In a June 1, 2002, speech at West Point, the president announced a policy of unilateral action and preemptive war—what came to be called the **Bush Doctrine**. Bush said, "...our security will require all Americans...to be ready for preemptive action when necessary to defend our liberty and to defend our lives." In his 2014 West Point speech, President Obama appeared to articulate a different policy when he said the United States must reduce its reliance on military force and make more use of diplomacy. But even though Obama expressed reservations about unilateral preemption, during the Obama years the United States continued to launch many attacks against suspected terrorists before they were able to strike. President Trump rattled America's allies by declaring an "America first" foreign policy and adopting a confrontational posture toward North Korea and Iran. In terms of actions, however, as of July 2018, Trump

The president meets with many foreign leaders, often after key agreements have been hammered out by the president's staff. In a highly controversial move, President Trump met alone with Russian president Vladimir Putin in July 2018, leaving many staffers and observers wondering what the two said.

seemed to have given diplomacy a greater emphasis as evidenced by his meetings with North Korea's leader and Russian president Putin.

As the dominant figure in the realm of American foreign and military policy, the president exercises substantial control over the nation's diplomatic and military institutions and, as a result, is in a position to decide with whom, when, and how the United States will interact in the international arena. Since World War II, American military forces have fought in many parts of the world. In every instance, the decision to commit troops to battle was made by the president, often without much consultation with the Congress. When President Obama ordered special operations soldiers to attack Osama bin Laden's compound in Pakistan, members of Congress learned of the operation and bin Laden's death from news broadcasts—just like other Americans. And it is the president and his emissaries who conduct negotiations with Russia, Iran, North Korea—and a host of other nations—to deal with international problems and crises.

Presidents can also make use of **executive agreements** to partially bypass congressional power in the realm of foreign relations. Executive agreements are presidential orders enforceable by the courts that do not require Senate ratification. Since presidents seem free to use executive agreements as they see fit, the importance of the Senate's constitutional treaty power has sharply diminished. Since 1947 the United States has entered into more than 17,000 different agreements with other nations and international entities. Of these, only 6 percent were submitted to the Senate for approval.[7]

THE BUREAUCRACY IMPLEMENTS AND INFORMS POLICY DECISIONS

The major foreign policy actors in the bureaucracy are the secretaries of the departments of State, Defense, and the Treasury; the Joint Chiefs of Staff, especially the chair; and the director of the CIA. Since 1947, a separate unit in the White House has overseen the vast foreign policy establishment for the purpose of synthesizing all the messages arising out of the bureaucracy and helping the president make his own foreign policy. This is the National Security Council. It is a "subcabinet" made up of the major players just listed plus others whom each president appoints. Since the profound shake-up of September 11, 2001, two key players have been added: the secretary of the Department of Homeland Security, created in 2002, and the director of national intelligence, established in 2005, to collate and coordinate intelligence coming in from multiple sources and to report a synthesis of all this to the president on a daily basis.

Since the creation of the CIA and the Department of Defense in 1947, the secretary of defense and the director of the CIA have often been rivals engaged in power struggles for control of the intelligence community.[8] For the most part, secretaries of defense have prevailed in these battles, and the Defense Department today controls more than 80 percent of the nation's intelligence capabilities and funds. The creation of the position of director of national intelligence to coordinate all intelligence activities set off new Washington power struggles as the "intelligence czar" faced opposition from both the CIA and the Department of Defense.

In the wake of September 11, 2001, military and law-enforcement agencies increased their role in America's foreign-policy making.[9] In recent years, American ambassadors have complained that they have been relegated to secondary status as the White House has looked to military commanders for information, advice, and policy implementation. For every region of the world, the U.S. military has assigned a "combatant commander," usually a senior general or admiral, to take charge of operations in that area. In many instances, these combatant commanders, who control troops, equipment, and intelligence capabilities, have become the real eyes, ears, and voices for American foreign policy in their designated regions.

CONGRESS'S LEGAL AUTHORITY CAN BE DECISIVE

Although the Constitution gives Congress the power to declare war (see Table 14.1), Congress has exercised this power on only five occasions: the War of 1812, the Mexican War (1846), the Spanish–American War (1898), World War I (1917), and World War II (1941). For the first 150 years of American history, Congress's role in foreign policy was limited because the United States' role in world affairs was limited. The treaty power was and is an important entrée of the Senate into foreign-policy making. But since World War II and the continual involvement of the United States in international security and foreign aid, Congress as a whole has become a major foreign-policy maker because most modern foreign policies require financing. Since Congress controls the "power of the purse," the appropriation of money requires action by both the House of Representatives and the Senate. For example,

TABLE 14.1

Principal Foreign Policy Powers Granted by the Constitution

	PRESIDENT	CONGRESS
War power	Commander in chief of armed forces	Provide for the common defense; declare war
Treaties	Negotiate treaties	Ratification of treaties by two-thirds majority (Senate)
Appointments	Nominate high-level government officials	Confirm president's appointments (Senate)
Foreign commerce	No explicit powers, but treaty negotiation and appointment powers pertain	Explicit power "to regulate foreign commerce"
General powers	Executive power; veto	Legislative power; power of the purse; oversight and investigation

Congress's first act after the September 11, 2001, attacks was to authorize the president to use "all necessary and appropriate force," coupled with a $40-billion emergency appropriations bill for homeland defense. Although President Bush believed he possessed the constitutional authority to invade Iraq, he still sought congressional approval, which he received in October 2002.

Not only does the president need Congress to provide funding for foreign and military policy initiatives but also, under the Constitution, many presidential agreements with foreign nations have to be approved by Congress. Article II, Section 2 of the Constitution declares that proposed treaties with other nations must be submitted by the president to the Senate and approved by a two-thirds vote. Because this "supermajority" is usually difficult to achieve, presidents generally prefer executive agreements, discussed above, with other nations.

Another aspect of Congress's role in foreign policy is the Senate's power to confirm the president's nominations of cabinet members, ambassadors, and other high-ranking officials (such as the director of the CIA, but not the director of the National Security Council). A final constitutional power of Congress is the regulation of "commerce with foreign nations."

Other congressional players are the foreign policy, military policy, and intelligence committees: in the Senate, these are the Foreign Relations Committee, the Armed Services Committee, the Intelligence Committee, and the Homeland Security and Governmental Affairs Committee; in the House, these are the Foreign Affairs Committee, the Intelligence Committee, the Homeland Security Committee, and the Armed Services Committee. Usually, a few members of these committees who have spent years specializing in foreign affairs become trusted members of the foreign policy establishment and are influential makers of foreign policy. In fact, several members of Congress have left the legislature to become key foreign affairs cabinet members.

INTEREST GROUPS PRESSURE FOREIGN POLICY DECISION MAKERS

Although the president, the executive branch "bureaucracy," and Congress are the true makers of foreign policy, the "foreign policy establishment" is a much larger arena, including what can properly be called the shapers of foreign policy: a host of unofficial, informal players who possess varying degrees of influence depending on their prestige, reputation, socioeconomic standing, and, most important, the party and ideology that are dominant at a given moment.

By far the most important category of nonofficial player is the interest group—that is, the interest group to which one or more foreign policy issues are of long-standing and vital relevance. Most of these are "single-issue" economic groups, such as the tobacco industry and the computer hardware and software industries, which become most active when their particular issue is on the agenda.

Another type of interest group with a well-founded reputation for influence in foreign policy comprises people who strongly identify with a particular country. For example, many Jewish Americans and Evangelical Protestants possess strong emotional ties to Israel. In 2015 some Jewish groups lobbied heavily but ultimately

Cuban Americans have strong voices in Congress in Senator Marco Rubio (R-Fla.), among others.

unsuccessfully against the Obama administration's agreement with Iran to limit its nuclear program, which they argued posed a threat to both the United States and Israel. In 2018 these groups strongly supported President Trump's decision to move the American embassy from Tel Aviv to Jerusalem, over the strenuous objection of most in the Middle East and American allies. Similarly, Americans of Irish heritage still maintain vigilance about American policies toward Ireland and Northern Ireland. Cuban Americans have long been a powerful voice in support of maintaining sanctions against Cuba. This helps explain why relations with Cuba were not normalized until 2015, and remain tenuous.

A third type of interest group is devoted to human rights or other global causes, such as protection of the environment. Such groups are made up of people who, instead of having self-serving economic or ethnic interests in foreign policy, are genuinely concerned about the welfare and treatment of people throughout the world—particularly those who suffer under harsh political regimes. One quite influential example is Amnesty International, whose exposés of human rights abuses have altered the practices of many regimes around the world. Ecological and environmental groups, have staged major protests to support the reduction in global greenhouse gases and other environmental causes.

A final actor in the realm of foreign policy is public opinion. For the most part, the public is not as engaged in foreign policy issues as they are with domestic issues. However, public opinion does begin to count when the nation is at war. Americans are often impatient with military actions that seem long and drawn out, producing costs and casualties for reasons that no longer seem clear. Fear of public opinion is one reason that presidents have favored professional military forces and technologies like drones that would reduce the immediacy of war to America's general public.

Tools of American Foreign Policy Include Diplomacy, Force, and Money

Describe the means the United States uses to carry out foreign policy today

We will deal here with those instruments of American foreign policy most important in the modern epoch: diplomacy, the United Nations, the international monetary structure, economic aid and sanctions, collective security, military deterrence, and arbitration. Each of these instruments will be evaluated in this section for its utility in the conduct of American foreign policy, and each will be assessed in light of the history and development of American values.

DIPLOMACY

We begin this treatment of instruments with **diplomacy**. Diplomacy is the representation of a government to other foreign governments. Its purpose is to promote national values or interests by peaceful means. The United States maintains diplomatic missions throughout the world. American ambassadors are tasked with maintaining good relations with foreign governments, promoting a positive view of the United States abroad, and securing information about foreign governments that might be helpful to the United States in its international dealings. When it comes to major diplomatic initiatives, however, such as new international agreements, presidents or their personal representatives usually take charge.

Diplomacy, by its very nature, is overshadowed by spectacular international events, dramatic initiatives, and meetings among heads of state or their direct personal representatives. The traditional American distrust of diplomacy continues today, albeit in weaker form. Impatience with or downright distrust of diplomacy has been built not only into all the other instruments of foreign policy but also into the modern presidential system itself.[10] So much personal responsibility has been heaped on the presidency that it is difficult for presidents to entrust any of their authority or responsibility in foreign policy to professional diplomats in the State Department and other bureaucracies.

THE UNITED NATIONS IS THE WORLD'S CONGRESS

The utility of the **United Nations (UN)** to the United States as an instrument of foreign policy can be too easily underestimated because the UN is a very large and unwieldy institution with few powers and no armed forces to implement its rules and resolutions. It is an organization of nations founded in 1945 to be a channel for negotiation and a means of settling international disputes peaceably. The UN can serve as a useful forum for international discussions and an instrument for multilateral action. Most peacekeeping efforts to which the United States contributes, for example, are undertaken under UN auspices.

The UN's supreme body is the General Assembly, comprising one representative of each of the 192 member states; each member representative has one vote, regardless of the size of the country. Important issues require a two-thirds majority vote, and the annual session of the General Assembly runs only from September to December (although it can call extra sessions). The General Assembly has little organization that can make it an effective decision-making body, with only six standing committees, few tight rules of procedure, and no political parties to provide priorities and discipline. Its defenders are quick to add that although it lacks armed forces, it relies on the power of world opinion—and this is not to be taken lightly. The powers of the UN devolve mainly to the organization's "executive committee," the UN Security Council, which alone has the real power to make decisions and rulings that member states are obligated by the UN Charter to implement. The Security Council may be called into session at any time, and each member (or a designated alternate) must be present at UN headquarters in New York at all times. The council is composed of 15 members: 5 are permanent (the victors of World War II), and 10 are elected by the General Assembly for unrepeatable two-year terms. The 5 permanent members are China, France, Russia, the United Kingdom, and the United States. Each of the 15 members has only one vote, and a 9-vote majority of the 15 is required on all substantive matters. But each of the 5 permanent members also has a negative vote, a "veto"; and one veto is sufficient to reject any substantive proposal.

THE INTERNATIONAL MONETARY STRUCTURE HELPS PROVIDE ECONOMIC STABILITY

Fear of a repeat of the economic devastation that followed World War I brought the United States together with its allies (except the Soviet Union) to Bretton Woods, New Hampshire, in 1944 to create a new international economic structure for the postwar world. One major goal of this structure was to prevent economic instability that might, in turn, lead to political instability and war. Participants in the Bretton Woods conference were mindful of the economic collapse in Germany that opened the way for Nazism. At the same time, the structure would give the United States and its allies greater leverage in the economic and political affairs of developing countries.

The Bretton Woods Conference resulted in two institutions: the International Bank for Reconstruction and Development (commonly called the World Bank) and the International Monetary Fund. The World Bank's chief mission is development aid to poor countries through long-term capital investments.

The World Bank was set up to finance long-term capital. Leading nations took on the obligation of contributing funds to enable the World Bank to make loans to capital-hungry countries. (The U.S. quota has been about one-third of the total.) The **International Monetary Fund (IMF)** was set up to provide for the short-term flow of money. It provides loans and facilitates international monetary exchanges. After the war, the dollar, instead of gold, was the chief means by which the currencies of one country would be "changed into" currencies of another country for purposes of making international transactions. To permit debtor countries with no international balances to make purchases and investments, the IMF was set up to lend dollars or other appropriate currencies to such needy member countries to help them overcome temporary trade deficits.

During the 1990s the importance of the IMF increased through its efforts to reform some of the largest debtor nations and formerly communist countries, to bring them more fully into the global capitalist economy. The future of the IMF, the World Bank, and all other private sources of international investment will depend in part on extension of more credit to the developing world because credit means investment and productivity. But the future may depend even more on reducing existing debt from previous extensions of credit.

ECONOMIC AID HAS TWO SIDES

Every year, the United States provides nearly $30 billion in economic assistance to other nations. Some aid has a humanitarian purpose, such as helping to provide health care, shelter for refugees, or famine relief. Much American aid, however, is designed to promote American security interests or economic concerns. For example, the United States provides military assistance to a number of its allies in the form of advanced weapons or loans to help them purchase such weapons. These loans generally stipulate that the recipient must purchase the designated weapons from American firms. In this way the United States hopes to bolster its security and economic interests with one grant. The two largest recipients of American military assistance are Israel and Egypt, American allies that fought two wars against each other. The United States believes that its military assistance allows both countries to feel sufficiently secure to remain at peace with each other.

Aid is an economic carrot. Sanctions are an economic stick. Economic sanctions that the United States employs against other nations include trade embargoes, bans on investment, and efforts to prevent the World Bank or other international institutions from extending credit to a nation against which the United States has a grievance. Sanctions are most often employed when the United States seeks to weaken what it considers a hostile regime or when it is attempting to compel some particular action by another regime. In 2014, for example, the United States imposed economic sanctions against Russia in response to the Russian annexation of Crimea, which the United States regards as part of Ukraine. In 2017 the United States tightened its already existing economic sanctions against North Korea in response to that nation's missile tests. The United States also uses economic sanctions to advance its international humanitarian policy goals by imposing them against governments with records of serious violations of civil and political rights.[11]

COLLECTIVE SECURITY IS DESIGNED TO DETER WAR

Collective security means the development of alliances and agreements among a group of nations that pledge to aid one another in fending off or confronting security threats. In 1947 most Americans hoped that the United States could meet its world obligations through the UN and economic structures alone. But most foreign-policy makers anticipated the need for military entanglements at the time of drafting the original UN Charter by insisting on language that recognized the right of all nations to provide for their mutual defense independent of the UN. Almost immediately after enactment of the Marshall Plan, designed to promote European economic recovery, the White House and other top officials urgently requested the Senate to ratify and both houses of Congress to finance mutual defense alliances.

The first collective security agreement was the Rio Treaty (ratified by the Senate in 1947), which created the Organization of American States. This was the model treaty, anticipating all succeeding collective security treaties by providing that an armed attack against any of its members "shall be considered as an attack against all the American States," including the United States. A more significant break with U.S. tradition of avoiding peacetime entanglements came with the North Atlantic Treaty (signed in 1949), which created the **North Atlantic Treaty Organization (NATO)**. Comprising the United States, Canada, and most of Western Europe, NATO was formed to counter the perceived threat from the Soviet Union.

In 1998 the expansion of NATO took its first steps toward including former Warsaw Pact members, extending membership to the Czech Republic, Hungary, and Poland.[12] Most of Washington embraced this expansion as the true and fitting end of the Cold War, and the U.S. Senate echoed this with a resounding 80–19 vote to induct these three former Soviet satellites into NATO. After the collapse of the Soviet Union, the importance of NATO as a military alliance seemed to wane. However, since 2014 the resurgence of Russia as a military power forced NATO members once again to look to one another for support. In 2014, Russia seized the Crimean Peninsula from Ukraine and appeared to pose a threat to the Baltic states and other portions of the old Soviet empire. Russia also sent military forces to support the Assad regime in Syria. Facing an aggressive new Russia, NATO's period of relative quiet seemed to be coming to a close.

The attack on the United States on September 11, 2001, was the first time in its more than 50-year history that Article 5 of the North Atlantic Treaty was invoked; it provides that an attack on one country is an attack on all the member countries. In fighting "the war on terror," the Bush administration recognized that no matter how preponderant American power was, some aspects of U.S. foreign policy could not be achieved without multilateral cooperation. On the other hand, the United States did not want to be constrained by its alliances. The global coalition initially forged after September 11, 2001, numbered more than 170 countries. Not all joined the war effort in Afghanistan, but most, if not all, provided some form of support for some aspect of "the war on terror," such as economic sanctions and intelligence.

MILITARY FORCE IS "POLITICS BY OTHER MEANS"

The most visible instrument of foreign policy is military force. The United States has built the world's most imposing military, with army, navy, marine, and air force units stationed around the globe. The United States is responsible for one-third of

Often military efforts abroad do not turn out as the government or the public expected. Although most Americans were in favor of U.S. involvement in Iraq and Afghanistan following September 11, 2001, public opinion on the issue has shifted.

the world's total military expenditures. The Prussian military strategist Carl von Clausewitz famously called war "politics by other means." By this he meant that nations used force or the threat of force not simply to demonstrate their capacity for violence but to achieve their foreign policy goals. Military force may be needed to protect a nation's security interests and economic concerns. Ironically, force may also be needed to achieve humanitarian goals. For example, in 2014 and 2015, international military force was required to protect tens of thousands of Yazidi refugees threatened by ISIS forces in Iraq. Without the use of military force, humanitarian assistance to the Yazidis would have been irrelevant.

Military force is generally seen as a last resort to be avoided if possible because a number of problems are commonly associated with its use. First, the use of military force is extremely costly in both human and financial terms. In the past 50 years, tens of thousands of Americans have been killed and hundreds of billions of dollars spent in America's military operations. Second, the use of military force is inherently risky. However carefully policy makers and generals plan for military operations, results can seldom be fully anticipated. For example, American policy makers expected, accurately, to defeat the Iraqi army quickly and easily in 2003. Policy makers did not anticipate, however, that American forces would still be struggling years later to defeat the insurgency that arose in the war's aftermath. Finally, in a democracy, any government that chooses to address policy problems through military means is almost certain to encounter political difficulties. Generally speaking, the American public will support relatively short and decisive military engagements. If, however, a conflict drags on, producing casualties and expenses with no clear outcome, the public loses patience and opposition politicians point to the government's lies and ineptitude.

SOFT POWER USES PERSUASION

The term *soft power* refers to efforts by one nation to influence the people and governments of other nations by persuasion rather than coercion. The instruments of soft power include development aid, cultural diplomacy, student exchange programs, and other mechanisms designed to shape perceptions. Cultural programs that send American actors, athletes, and musicians around the world are thought to offer a positive view of the United States that will encourage foreign governments and their citizens to see America as the "good guy" in international disputes. Exchange programs that bring foreign students to the United States serve a similar purpose. The effects of soft power are difficult to measure but the United States makes an effort to promote its "brand" of freedom and democracy throughout the world. Other nations do the same. Chinese development projects in Africa, for example, are partly intended to promote a favorable image of China on the continent.

ARBITRATION RESOLVES DISPUTES

The final foreign policy tool is dispute arbitration. Arbitration is the resolution of a disagreement by a neutral third party. International arbitration is sometimes seen as a form of "soft power" as distinguished from military force, economic sanctions, and other coercive foreign policy instruments. The United States will occasionally turn to international tribunals to resolve disputes with other countries. For example, in 2008 the U.S. government asked the International Court of Justice to resolve a long-standing dispute with Italy over American property confiscated by the Italian government decades earlier.

More important, the United States relies heavily on the work of arbitral panels to maintain the flow of international trade on which the U.S. economy depends. U.S. firms would be reluctant to do business abroad if they could not be certain that their property and contractual rights would be honored by other nations. Arbitration helps produce that certainty. Almost every international contract contains an arbitration clause requiring that disputes between the parties will be resolved not by foreign governments but by impartial arbitral panels accepted by both sides. By the terms of the New York Convention, virtually every nation in the world has agreed to accept and enforce arbitral verdicts. The United States has incorporated the terms of the New York Convention into federal law, and U.S. courts vigorously enforce arbitral judgments. The United States may not be happy with the outcome of every arbitral proceeding, but the arbitral system is essential to America's economic interests.

Current Foreign Policy Issues Facing the United States

Analyze the foreign policy problems facing American policy makers today

The United States currently faces many foreign policy problems, but a few stand out: relations with China and Russia; relations with Iran and North Korea; the global environment; and international trade policy. Each reveals how the key players in foreign policy use the tools at their disposal to achieve their policy goals.

A POWERFUL CHINA AND A RESURGENT RUSSIA

After the United States, China and Russia are the world's greatest military powers. China is an economic power as well, with an economy that in some respects already outpaces America's and continues to grow. China seems determined to expand its military capabilities and to replace the United States as the dominant power in Asia. The United States has no desire to engage in a military conflict with China but, at the same time, would prefer to blunt Chinese ambitions. The relationship between the United States and China is not at a point of crisis but represents a growing concern for American policy makers.

While relations with China are a long-term problem, the United States' interactions with Russia present a more immediate set of issues. Once a global superpower and America's chief rival in the world, Russia remains heavily armed but economically weak. Under its current leader, Vladimir Putin, Russia has challenged the United States in Europe and in the Middle East, and has even meddled in American politics.[13]

The first in this series of direct Russian challenges to the United States came in 2014, when Russian forces seized control of the Crimean Peninsula, an area that had been part of Ukraine, though many of the peninsula's inhabitants were ethnic Russians. Russian president Vladimir Putin said Russia's actions were necessary to prevent disorder and bloodshed and to reassert Russia's historic rights to the region. Russian troops next massed along other portions of the Ukrainian border. The Obama administration urged the Russians to withdraw, announced a program of economic sanctions, and sought through diplomacy to encourage NATO allies to impose sanctions as well. The result illustrated the difficulties inherent in collective action and the use of sanctions. Many of the United States' European allies depend on Russian energy supplies and engage in a good deal of trade with the Russians. As a result, while all agreed in principle that Russia should withdraw from Crimea, none were prepared to follow the American lead of imposing sanctions, and it seemed that nothing would be done to dislodge the Russians from the area.

In 2015, Russia challenged the United States in another part of the world when Russian forces entered the Syrian civil war in support of the Assad regime, which the United States had sought to oust. Russia claimed that its military actions were aimed at the Islamic State of Iraq and Syria (ISIS) and other terrorist groups, but in reality Russian attacks seemed to be directed at anti-Assad rebels. With American military advisers fighting alongside some of these same rebel groups, there was danger of a direct clash between Russia and the United States. President Obama called for Russian withdrawal and for negotiations to prevent an accidental confrontation between Russian and American military forces. In 2016, Russia claimed to have withdrawn its forces, but it was unclear whether this action had, in fact, occurred. During the course of the year, the United States and Russia continued to negotiate—and violate—new agreements as the fighting continued.

To counter Russia's actions, the United States has worked to strengthen and enlarge NATO to include Eastern European nations that feel threatened by Russia, including Poland, Lithuania, Albania, Bulgaria, and Slovenia. Russia, for its part, views NATO's expansion into its former satellite empire as a provocative action and has sought to enhance its own military capabilities in the region.

In 2016 Russia also sought to intrude into American presidential politics. Russian agents purchased ads on Facebook and other social media designed to cause dissention in the United States, and to exploit ethnic and economic tensions. For the most part, Russian efforts seemed to favor Donald Trump and oppose Hillary Clinton. What effect these efforts had is open to question.

Both the Chinese and the Russians have made use of extensive electronic "hacking" to break into the computer systems of American government agencies and American firms. Both countries deny these allegations—as does the United States when accused of hacking into Russian and Chinese systems.[14]

NUCLEAR PROLIFERATION IN IRAN AND NORTH KOREA

Unlike China and Russia, Iran and North Korea are not great powers, but both present challenges to the United States, especially in the realm of nuclear proliferation. For years the United States has worried that Iran is working toward obtaining nuclear weapons with which it could threaten Saudi Arabia and Israel—both close U.S. allies—and bring Middle Eastern oil fields under its control. To prevent Iran from obtaining nuclear weapons, U.S. presidents have used a mix of carrots (in the form of diplomacy) and sticks (in the form of sanctions). In 2015 the United States and Iran signed an agreement; the Iranians pledged not to build nuclear weapons in exchange for a lifting of the economic sanctions. Critics of the agreement expressed fears that it would not deter the Iranians from continuing with their nuclear program, and during his presidential campaign Donald Trump promised to abrogate the agreement.

With North Korea, U.S. diplomacy has thus far been futile, because North Korea's major backer and trading partner—China—will not cooperate with efforts by the United States to undermine the North Korean regime. China regards North Korea as a useful pawn on the geopolitical chessboard, preventing the United States and two of its allies, Japan and South Korea, from dominating the Sea of Japan. As a result, the North Koreans have continued to build nuclear warheads and to test missiles capable of carrying them. The current North Korean leader, Kim Jong-un, angered the Chinese by arresting and killing several members of North Korea's leadership, including members of Kim's own family, whom he deemed too closely associated with China. With his actions, Kim reduced Chinese influence over North Korea's policies, leaving the country's Chinese patrons unsure of how to proceed.

The Secretary of State is America's chief diplomat. Here, Secretary of State Mike Pompeo meets with North Korean leader Kim Jong-un.

President Trump met with North Korean leader Kim Jong-un in June 2018 seeking to improve America's relations with North Korea and, perhaps, to move that nation out of the Chinese orbit.

TRADE POLICY

Trade is one of the most contentious issues in contemporary international relations. The United States has accused China and other nations of unfair trade practices that limit the sale of goods in their markets while they export billions of dollars in goods to the United States. Trade also affects job growth in the United States, which has been low for several years. Populist politicians like Donald Trump charge that this is the result of trade policies that allowed American jobs to be exported to Asia and Mexico where labor is cheaper. Trade, as we saw above, supports many millions of jobs in the United States. However, U.S. workers whose jobs were lost when industries moved abroad call for tariffs and other remedies they hope might bring their jobs back to the United States.

Many workers voted for Donald Trump, who criticized U.S. trade policies during his campaign and promised to bring these jobs back. One of Trump's first acts in office was to withdraw from the Trans-Pacific Partnership (TPP), a free-trade agreement between the United States and 11 Pacific Rim nations. Trump said the TPP would allow foreign countries to profit at America's expense.

Trade disputes have especially complicated America's relationship with China. In 2010 the United States accused China of manipulating trade rules to its own advantage, and China, in return, accused the United States of mismanaging its own economy. In 2012, China announced that it would reduce its purchases of U.S. government securities in order to become less vulnerable to fluctuations in the value of the dollar. The United States pointed out that this might result in a reduction of its imports of Chinese goods. President Trump has declared that the Chinese trade unfairly and has promised to change the rules in America's favor—a move sure to increase Chinese enmity toward the United States. In 2018, President Trump announced the imposition of $50 billion in tariffs on Chinese steel, aluminum, and electronic goods sold to the United States. China quickly announced that it would retaliate with tariffs on U.S. farm products, seafoods, and autos sold in China. These moves raised the prospect of an all-out trade war between the world's two largest economies.

GLOBAL ENVIRONMENTAL POLICY

A final trouble spot for American policy makers is international environmental policy. The environment is a global matter. Pollutants produced in one country affect all others. Generally speaking, the United States supports various international efforts to protect the environment. These include the United Nations Framework Convention on Climate Change, an international agreement to study and ameliorate harmful changes in the global environment, and the Montreal Protocol, an agreement signed by over 150 countries to limit the production of substances potentially harmful to the world's ozone layer. Other nations have criticized the United States for withdrawing from the 1997 Kyoto Protocol, an agreement setting limits on industrial countries' emissions of greenhouse gases. The United States asserted that the Kyoto Protocol would harm American economic interests. The Kyoto Protocol expired in 2012, but 37 of the original signatories signed the Doha Amendment to renew their commitment to reduce greenhouse gas emissions. The United States refrained from signing this new agreement as well.

In 2015, however, the United States did signed on to the Paris Agreement to reduce greenhouse gas emissions. Each country agreed to reduce emissions but would set its own contribution to the effort. Many Republicans, including Donald Trump, opposed the agreement, and as president, Trump ended U.S. participation in the Paris Agreement, stating that strict environmental controls would undermine American manufacturing interests and cause more jobs to leave the United States in favor of developing nations without such standards. America's western European allies, on the other hand, remain committed to the Paris Agreement and view the American administration as uninformed and reckless.

Foreign Policy and Democracy
WHAT DO WE WANT?

The harsh realities of foreign policy often clash with the United States' history and ideals. U.S. democratic and liberal traditions lead Americans to hope for a world in which ideals rather than naked interests govern foreign policy and in which U.S. leaders follow those ideals. American ideals are what attracted many of those affected by the 2017 travel ban (and generations of immigrants before them) to the United States in the first place. Traditional American values assert that our foreign policies should have a higher purpose than narrow self-interest and that America would use force only as a last resort. But the realities of foreign policy often collide with these historical ideals, leaving U.S. policy makers to struggle to explain their actions and avoid admitting to motivations that might not sit well with the public.

International events can make it difficult to pursue those ideals. The forces of globalization mean that it is easier than ever for small groups of extremists with violent intentions to travel to American shores and carry out their plans. (The "**Who Participates?**" feature on the facing page shows public opinion on security issues and reflects strong concern about international terrorism among all age groups.) On the other hand, those same forces of globalization have been the source of many positive outcomes. Greater trade reduces the price of many products for American consumers as well as for those abroad. Furthermore, many scholars believe that the increasing global economic interdependence is a force for peace: nations that trade heavily with each other are less likely to go to war with each other. What can U.S. leaders do in the future to make sure that globalization is a positive force that promotes U.S. security and prosperity?

Public Opinion on Security Issues

As we learned in this chapter, public opinion can influence foreign policy. However, many Americans are not engaged with or knowledgeable about foreign policy. Moreover, public opinion varies by political party. These figures show what percentage of members of each major political party think each issue is a major threat to the United States.

Percentage who think each is a major threat to the well-being of the United States

🐎 Democrats
🐘 Republicans

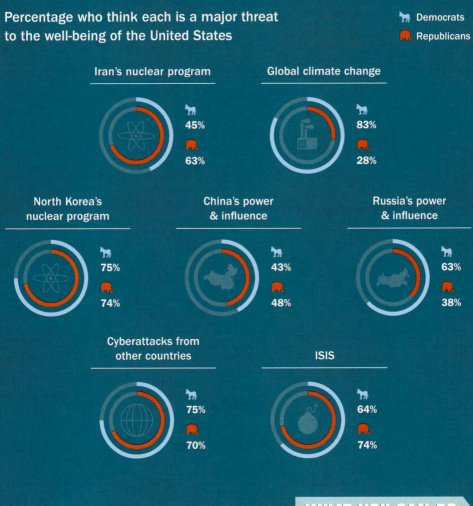

Iran's nuclear program
🐎 45%
🐘 63%

Global climate change
🐎 83%
🐘 28%

North Korea's nuclear program
🐎 75%
🐘 74%

China's power & influence
🐎 43%
🐘 48%

Russia's power & influence
🐎 63%
🐘 38%

Cyberattacks from other countries
🐎 75%
🐘 70%

ISIS
🐎 64%
🐘 74%

SOURCE: Pew Research Center, "Partisans Have Starkly Different Opinions about How the World Views the U.S.," pewresearch.org (accessed 1/11/18).

WHAT YOU CAN DO ▶

★ WHAT YOU CAN DO ★

Stay Informed about International News

 Learn more about the issues above and others through coverage in major U.S. newspapers such as the *New York Times* (**www.nytimes.com**) and the *Wall Street Journal* (**www.wsj.com**).

 For in-depth conversations about world affairs, watch videos at the World Affairs Council (**www.worldaffairs.org**) or the Council on Foreign Relations (**www.cfr.org**).

✓ Consider working with an interest group on a foreign policy issue you care about, such as Amnesty International (human rights), Move America Forward (supporting American troops), or Just Foreign Policy (equality and justice from a nonpartisan perspective).

★ STUDY GUIDE ★

Practice Quiz

1. Which of the following terms best describes the American posture toward the world prior to the twentieth century? *(p. 447)*
   a) interventionist
   b) isolationist
   c) appeasement
   d) humanitarian
   e) internationalist

2. Which of the following terms describes an effort to forestall war by giving in to the demands of a hostile power? *(p. 448)*
   a) appeasement
   b) deterrence
   c) détente
   d) containment
   e) "Minuteman" theory of defense

3. The World Trade Organization is *(p. 451)*
   a) an agency in the federal executive branch that analyzes trade deficits.
   b) an American interest group that lobbies Congress for the passage of agricultural and manufacturing tariffs.
   c) an American interest group that lobbies Congress for the passage of so-called Fair Trade laws.
   d) an international organization composed of Western European countries that oppose free trade.
   e) an international organization promoting free trade that grew out of the General Agreement on Tariffs and Trade.

4. The *Bush Doctrine* refers to *(p. 454)*
   a) the idea that the United States should not allow foreign powers to meddle in the Western Hemisphere.
   b) the idea that the United States should avoid future wars by giving in to the demands of hostile foreign powers.
   c) the idea that the United States should take preemptive action against threats to its national security.
   d) the idea that the United States should never take preemptive action against threats to its national security.
   e) the idea that the United States should always secure international approval before taking any military action.

5. An agreement made between the president and another country that has the force of a treaty but does not require the Senate's "advice and consent" is called *(p. 454)*
   a) an executive order.
   b) an executive privilege.
   c) an executive agreement.
   d) a diplomatic decree.
   e) arbitration.

6. The Constitution assigns the power to declare war to *(p. 456)*
   a) the National Security Council.
   b) the president.
   c) the chief justice of the United States.
   d) the secretary of defense.
   e) Congress.

7. Which of the following statements about the United Nations is *not* true? *(p. 459)*
   a) It has a powerful army to implement its decisions.
   b) It gives every country one vote in the General Assembly.
   c) The five permanent members of the UN Security Council are China, France, Russia, the United Kingdom, and the United States.

d) It was designed to be a channel for negotiation and a means of settling international disputes peaceably.
   e) Important issues require a two-thirds majority vote.

8. Which of the following were founded during the 1940s in order to create a new international monetary structure for the postwar world? *(p. 460)*
   a) the Federal Reserve System and the Council of Economic Advisors
   b) the North Atlantic Treaty Organization and the Southeast Asia Treaty Organization
   c) the International Monetary Fund and the World Bank
   d) the International Court of Justice and the Warsaw Pact
   e) the Office of Management and Budget and the General Agreement on Tariffs and Trade

9. Cultural programs that send American actors, athletes, and musicians around the world in order to promote a positive view of the United States are examples of the use of *(p. 463)*
   a) soft power.
   b) star power.
   c) arbitration.
   d) détente.
   e) hard power.

10. In 2015 the United States entered into an international agreement to reduce greenhouse gas emissions called the *(p. 468)*
   a) Kyoto Protocol.
   b) Doha Amendment.
   c) Trans-Pacific Partnership.
   d) Montreal Protocol.
   e) Paris Agreement.

Key Terms

appeasement *(p. 448)* the effort to forestall war by giving in to the demands of a hostile power

Bush Doctrine *(p. 454)* foreign policy based on the idea that the United States should take preemptive action against threats to its national security

Cold War *(p. 448)* the period of struggle between the United States and the former Soviet Union lasting from the late 1940s to about 1990

containment *(p. 448)* a policy designed to curtail the political and military expansion of a hostile power

deterrence *(p. 448)* the development and maintenance of military strength as a means of discouraging attack

diplomacy *(p. 459)* the representation of a government to foreign governments

executive agreement *(p. 455)* an agreement, made between the president and another country, that has the force of a treaty but does not require the Senate's "advice and consent"

General Agreement on Tariffs and Trade (GATT) *(p. 451)* international trade organization, in existence from 1947 to 1995, that set many of the rules governing international trade

International Monetary Fund (IMF) *(p. 460)* an institution established in 1944 that provides loans and facilitates international monetary exchange

isolationism *(p. 447)* avoidance of involvement in the affairs of other nations

nation-states *(p. 449)* political entities consisting of people with some common cultural experience (nation) who also share a common political authority (state), recognized by other sovereignties (nation-states)

non-state actors *(p. 447)* groups other than nation-states that attempt to play a role in the international system; terrorist groups are one type of non-state actor

North Atlantic Treaty Organization (NATO) *(p. 461)* an organization, comprising the United States, Canada, and most of Western Europe, formed in 1949 to counter the perceived threat from the Soviet Union

preventive war *(p. 448)* policy of striking first when a nation fears that a foreign foe is contemplating hostile action

United Nations (UN) *(p. 459)* an organization of nations founded in 1945 to be a channel for negotiation and a means of settling international disputes peacefully; the UN has had frequent successes in providing a forum for negotiation and on some occasions a means of preventing international conflicts from spreading; on a number of occasions, the UN has supported U.S. foreign policy goals

United States–Mexico–Canada Agreement (USMCA) *(p. 451)* trade treaty among the United States, Canada, and Mexico to lower and eliminate tariffs among the three countries

World Trade Organization (WTO) *(p. 451)* international organization promoting free trade that grew out of the General Agreement on Tariffs and Trade

For Further Reading

Art, Robert. *The Use of Force: Military Power and International Politics*. New York: Rowman and Littlefield, 2009.

Gaddis, John L. *The Cold War: A New History*. New York: Penguin, 2005.

Ginsberg, Benjamin. *The Worth of War*. Amherst, NY: Prometheus Books, 2014.

Haass, Richard. *A World in Disarray: Foreign Policy and the Crisis of the Old Order*. New York: Penguin, 2017.

Hook, Steven W., and John Spanier. *American Foreign Policy since World War II*. 20th ed. Washington, DC: CQ Press, 2016.

Ikenberry, John. *American Foreign Policy*. New York: Wadsworth, 2010.

Jentleson, Bruce. *American Foreign Policy: The Dynamics of Choice in the 21st Century*. 5th ed. New York: W. W. Norton, 2013.

Mandelbaum, Michael. *The Case for Goliath: How America Acts as the World's Government in the 21st Century*. Washington, DC: Public Affairs Press, 2005.

Mearsheimer, John J., and Stephen M. Walt. *The Israel Lobby and U.S. Foreign Policy*. New York: Farrar, Straus and Giroux, 2008.

Nasr, Vali. *The Dispensable Nation: American Foreign Policy in Retreat*. New York: Anchor Books, 2014.

Appendix

The Declaration of Independence

In Congress, July 4, 1776

The unanimous Declaration of the thirteen united States of America,

When in the Course of human events, it becomes necessary for one people to dissolve the political bands which have connected them with another, and to assume among the powers of the earth, the separate and equal station to which the Laws of Nature and of Nature's God entitle them, a decent respect to the opinions of mankind requires that they should declare the causes which impel them to the separation.

We hold these truths to be self-evident, that all men are created equal, that they are endowed by their Creator with certain unalienable Rights, that among these are Life, Liberty and the pursuit of Happiness.—That to secure these rights, Governments are instituted among Men, deriving their just powers from the consent of the governed.—That whenever any Form of Government becomes destructive of these ends, it is the Right of the People to alter or to abolish it, and to institute new Government, laying its foundation on such principles and organizing its powers in such form, as to them shall seem most likely to effect their Safety and Happiness. Prudence, indeed, will dictate that Governments long established should not be changed for light and transient causes; and accordingly all experience hath shewn, that mankind are more disposed to suffer, while evils are sufferable, than to right themselves by abolishing the forms to which they are accustomed. But when a long train of abuses and usurpations, pursuing invariably the same Object evinces a design to reduce them under absolute Despotism, it is their right, it is their duty, to throw off such Government, and to provide new Guards for their future security.—Such has been the patient sufferance of these Colonies; and such is now the necessity which constrains them to alter their former Systems of Government. The history of the present King of Great Britain is a history of repeated injuries and usurpations, all having in direct object the establishment of an absolute Tyranny over these States. To prove this, let Facts be submitted to a candid world.

He has refused his Assent to Laws, the most wholesome and necessary for the public good.

He has forbidden his Governors to pass Laws of immediate and pressing importance, unless suspended in their operation till his Assent should be obtained; and when so suspended, he has utterly neglected to attend to them.

He has refused to pass other Laws for the accommodation of large districts of people, unless those people would relinquish the right of Representation in the Legislature, a right inestimable to them and formidable to tyrants only.

He has called together legislative bodies at places unusual, uncomfortable, and distant from the depository of their public Records, for the sole purpose of fatiguing them into compliance with his measures.

He has dissolved Representative Houses repeatedly, for opposing with manly firmness his invasions on the rights of the people.

He has refused for a long time, after such dissolutions, to cause others to be elected; whereby the Legislative powers, incapable of Annihilation, have returned to the People at large for their exercise; the State remaining in the mean time exposed to all the dangers of invasion from without, and convulsions within.

He has endeavoured to prevent the population of these States; for that purpose obstructing the Laws for Naturalization of Foreigners; refusing to pass others to encourage their migrations hither, and raising the conditions of new Appropriations of Lands.

He has obstructed the Administration of Justice, by refusing his Assent to Laws for establishing Judiciary powers.

He has made Judges dependent on his Will alone, for the tenure of their offices, and the amount and payment of their salaries.

He has erected a multitude of New Offices, and sent hither swarms of Officers to harrass our people, and eat out their substance.

He has kept among us, in times of peace, Standing Armies without the Consent of our legislatures.

He has affected to render the Military independent of and superior to the Civil power.

He has combined with others to subject us to a jurisdiction foreign to our constitution, and unacknowledged by our laws; giving his Assent to their Acts of pretended Legislation:

For Quartering large bodies of armed troops among us:

For protecting them, by a mock Trial, from punishment for any Murders which they should commit on the Inhabitants of these States:

For cutting off our Trade with all parts of the world:

For imposing Taxes on us without our Consent:

For depriving us in many cases, of the benefits of Trial by Jury:

For transporting us beyond Seas to be tried for pretended offences:

For abolishing the free System of English Laws in a neighboring Province, establishing therein an Arbitrary government, and enlarging its Boundaries so as to render it at once an example and fit instrument for introducing the same absolute rule into these Colonies:

For taking away our Charters, abolishing our most valuable Laws, and altering fundamentally the Forms of our Governments:

For suspending our own Legislatures, and declaring themselves invested with power to legislate for us in all cases whatsoever.

He has abdicated Government here, by declaring us out of his Protection and waging War against us.

He has plundered our seas, ravaged our Coasts, burnt our towns, and destroyed the lives of our people.

He is at this time transporting large Armies of foreign Mercenaries to compleat the works of death, desolation and tyranny, already begun with circumstances of Cruelty & perfidy scarcely paralleled in the most barbarous ages, and totally unworthy the Head of a civilized nation.

He has constrained our fellow Citizens taken Captive on the high Seas to bear Arms against their Country, to become the executioners of their friends and Brethren, or to fall themselves by their Hands.

He has excited domestic insurrections amongst us, and has endeavoured to bring on the inhabitants of our frontiers, the merciless Indian Savages, whose known rule of warfare, is an undistinguished destruction of all ages, sexes and conditions.

In every stage of these Oppressions We have Petitioned for Redress in the most humble terms: Our repeated Petitions have been answered only by repeated injury. A Prince whose character is thus marked by every act which may define a Tyrant, is unfit to be the ruler of a free people.

Nor have We been wanting in attentions to our Brittish brethren. We have warned them from time to time of attempts by their legislature to extend an unwarrantable jurisdiction over us. We have reminded them of the circumstances of our emigration and settlement here. We have appealed to their native justice and magnanimity, and we have conjured them by the ties of our common kindred to disavow these usurpations, which, would inevitably interrupt our connections and correspondence. They too have been deaf to the voice of justice and of consanguinity. We must, therefore, acquiesce in the necessity, which denounces our Separation, and hold them, as we hold the rest of mankind, Enemies in War, in Peace Friends.

We, Therefore, the Representatives of the United States of America, in General Congress, Assembled, appealing to the Supreme Judge of the world for the rectitude of our intentions, do, in the Name, and by Authority of the good People of these Colonies, solemnly publish and declare, That these United Colonies are, and of Right ought to be Free and Independent States; that they are Absolved from all Allegiance to the British Crown, and that all political connection between them and the State of Great Britain, is and ought to be totally dissolved; and that as Free and Independent States, they have full Power to levy War, conclude Peace, contract Alliances, establish Commerce, and to do all other Acts and Things which Independent States may of right do. And for the support of this Declaration, with a firm reliance on the protection of divine Providence, we mutually pledge to each other our Lives, our Fortunes and our sacred Honor.

The foregoing Declaration was, by order of Congress, engrossed, and signed by the following members:

John Hancock

NEW HAMPSHIRE
Josiah Bartlett
William Whipple
Matthew Thornton

MASSACHUSETTS BAY
Samuel Adams
John Adams
Robert Treat Paine
Elbridge Gerry

RHODE ISLAND
Stephen Hopkins
William Ellery

CONNECTICUT
Roger Sherman
Samuel Huntington
William Williams
Oliver Wolcott

NEW YORK
William Floyd
Philip Livingston
Francis Lewis
Lewis Morris

NEW JERSEY
Richard Stockton
John Witherspoon
Francis Hopkinson
John Hart
Abraham Clark

PENNSYLVANIA
Robert Morris
Benjamin Rush
Benjamin Franklin
John Morton
George Clymer
James Smith
George Taylor
James Wilson
George Ross

DELAWARE
Caesar Rodney
George Read
Thomas M'Kean

MARYLAND
Samuel Chase
William Paca
Thomas Stone
Charles Carroll,
*   of Carrollton*

VIRGINIA
George Wythe
Richard Henry Lee
Thomas Jefferson
Benjamin Harrison
Thomas Nelson, Jr.
Francis Lightfoot Lee
Carter Braxton

NORTH CAROLINA
William Hooper
Joseph Hewes
John Penn

SOUTH CAROLINA
Edward Rutledge
Thomas Heyward, Jr.
Thomas Lynch, Jr.
Arthur Middleton

GEORGIA
Button Gwinnett
Lyman Hall
George Walton

Resolved, That copies of the Declaration be sent to the several assemblies, conventions, and committees, or councils of safety, and to the several commanding officers of the continental troops; that it be proclaimed in each of the United States, at the head of the army.

The Articles of Confederation

Agreed to by Congress November 15, 1777;
ratified and in force March 1, 1781

To all whom these Presents shall come, we the undersigned Delegates of the States affixed to our Names, send greeting. Whereas the Delegates of the United States of America, in Congress assembled, did, on the fifteenth day of November, in the Year of Our Lord One thousand Seven Hundred and Seventy seven, and in the Second Year of the Independence of America, agree to certain articles of Confederation and perpetual Union between the States of Newhampshire, Massachusetts-bay, Rhodeisland and Providence Plantations, Connecticut, New-York, New-Jersey, Pennsylvania, Delaware, Maryland, Virginia, North-Carolina, South-Carolina and Georgia in the words following, viz. "Articles of Confederation and perpetual Union between the states of Newhampshire, Massachusettsbay, Rhodeisland and Providence Plantations, Connecticut, New-York, New-Jersey, Pennsylvania, Delaware, Maryland, Virginia, North-Carolina, South-Carolina and Georgia.

Art. I. The Stile of this confederacy shall be "The United States of America."

Art. II. Each state retains its sovereignty, freedom and independence, and every Power, Jurisdiction and right, which is not by this confederation expressly delegated to the United States, in Congress assembled.

Art. III. The said states hereby severally enter into a firm league of friendship with each other, for their common defence, the security of their Liberties, and their mutual and general welfare, binding themselves to assist each other, against all force offered to, or attacks made upon them, or any of them, on account of religion, sovereignty, trade, or any other pretence whatever.

Art. IV. The better to secure and perpetuate mutual friendship and intercourse among the people of the different states in this union, the free inhabitants of each of these states, paupers, vagabonds and fugitives from Justice excepted, shall be entitled to all privileges and immunities of free citizens in the several states; and the people of each state shall have free ingress and regress to and from any other state, and shall enjoy therein all the privileges of trade and commerce, subject to the same duties, impositions and restrictions as the inhabitants thereof respectively, provided that such restriction shall not extend so far as to prevent the removal of property imported into any state, to any other state, of which the Owner is an inhabitant; provided also that no imposition, duties or restriction shall be laid by any state, on the property of the united states, or either of them.

If any Person guilty of, or charged with treason, felony, or other high misdemeanor in any state, shall flee from Justice, and be found in any of the united states, he shall, upon demand of the Governor or executive power, of the state from which he fled, be delivered up and removed to the state having jurisdiction of his offence.

Full faith and credit shall be given in each of these states to the records, acts and judicial proceedings of the courts and magistrates of every other state.

Art. V. For the more convenient management of the general interests of the united states, delegates shall be annually appointed in such manner as the legislature of each state shall direct, to meet in Congress on the first Monday in November, in every year, with a power reserved to each state, to recall its delegates, or any of them, at any time within the year, and to send others in their stead, for the remainder of the Year.

No state shall be represented in Congress by less than two, nor by more than seven Members; and no person shall be capable of being a delegate for more than three years in any term of six years; nor shall any person, being a delegate, be capable of holding any office under the united states, for which he, or another for his benefit receives any salary, fees or emolument of any kind.

Each state shall maintain its own delegates in a meeting of the states, and while they act as members of the committee of the states.

In determining questions in the united states, in Congress assembled, each state shall have one vote.

Freedom of speech and debate in Congress shall not be impeached or questioned in any Court, or place out of Congress, and the members of congress shall be protected in their persons from arrests and imprisonments, during the time of their going to and from, and attendance on congress, except for treason, felony, or breach of the peace.

Art. VI. No state without the Consent of the united states in congress assembled, shall send any embassy to, or receive any embassy from, or enter into any conference, agreement, or alliance or treaty with any King, prince or state; nor shall any person holding any office or profit or trust under the united states, or any of them, accept of any present, emolument, office or title of any kind whatever from any king, prince or foreign state; nor shall the united states in congress assembled, or any of them, grant any title of nobility.

No two or more states shall enter into any treaty, confederation or alliance whatever between them, without the consent of the united states in congress assembled, specifying accurately the purposes for which the same is to be entered into, and how long it shall continue.

No state shall lay any imposts or duties, which may interfere with any stipulations in treaties, entered into by the united states in congress assembled, with any king, prince or state, in pursuance of any treaties already proposed by congress, to the courts of France and Spain.

No vessels of war shall be kept up in time of peace by any state, except such number only, as shall be deemed necessary by the united states in congress assembled, for the defence of such state, or its trade; nor shall any body of forces be kept up by any state, in time of peace, except such number only, as in the judgment of the united states, in congress assembled, shall be deemed requisite to garrison the forts necessary for the defence of such state; but every state shall always keep up a well regulated and disciplined militia, sufficiently armed and accoutred, and shall provide and constantly have ready for use, in public stores, a due number of field pieces and tents, and a proper quantity of arms, ammunition and camp equipage.

No state shall engage in any war without the consent of the united states in congress assembled, unless such state be actually invaded by enemies, or shall have received certain advice of a resolution being formed by some nation of Indians to invade such state, and the danger is so imminent as not to admit of a delay, till the united states in congress asssembled can be consulted; nor shall any state grant commissions to any ships or vessels of war, nor letters of marque or reprisal, except it be after a declaration of war by the united states in congress assembled, and then only against the kingdom or state and the subjects thereof, against which war has been so declared, and under such regulations as shall be established by the united states in congress assembled, unless such state be infested by pirates; in which case vessels of war may be fitted out for that occasion, and kept so long as the danger shall continue, or until the united states in congress assembled shall determine otherwise.

Art. VII. When land-forces are raised by any state for the common defence, all officers of or under the rank of colonel, shall be appointed by the legislature of each state respectively, by whom such forces shall be raised, or in such manner as such state shall direct, and all vacancies shall be filled up by the state which first made the appointment.

Art. VIII. All charges of war, and all other expences that shall be incurred for the common defence or general welfare, and allowed by the united states in congress assembled, shall be defrayed out of a common treasury, which shall be supplied by the several states in proportion to the value of all land within each state, granted to or surveyed for any Person, as such land and the buildings and improvements thereon shall be estimated according to such mode as the united states in congress assembled, shall from time to time direct and appoint.

The taxes for paying that proportion shall be laid and levied by the authority and direction of the legislatures of the several states within the time agreed upon by the united states in congress assembled.

Art. IX. The united states in congress assembled, shall have the sole and exclusive right and power of determining on peace and war, except in the cases mentioned in the sixth article—of sending and receiving ambassadors—entering into treaties and alliances, provided that no treaty of commerce shall be made whereby the legislative power of the respective states shall be restrained from imposing such imposts and duties on foreigners, as their own people are subjected to, or from prohibiting the exportation of any species of goods or commodities whatsoever—of establishing rules for deciding in all cases, what captures on land or water shall be legal, and in what manner prizes taken by land or naval forces in the service of the united states shall be divided or appropriated—of granting letters of marque and reprisal in times of peace—appointing courts for the trial of piracies and felonies committed on the high seas and establishing courts for receiving and determining finally appeals in all cases of captures, provided that no member of congress shall be appointed a judge of any of the said courts.

The united states in congress assembled shall also be the last resort on appeal in all disputes and differences now subsisting or that hereafter may arise between two or more states concerning boundary, jurisdiction or any other cause whatever; which authority shall always be exercised in the manner following. Whenever the legislative or executive authority or lawful agent of any state in controversy with another shall present a petition to congress stating the matter in question and praying for a hearing, notice thereof shall be given by order of congress to the legislative or executive authority of the other state in controversy, and a day assigned for the appearance of the parties by their lawful agents, who shall then be directed to appoint by joint consent, commissioners or judges to constitute a court for hearing and determining the matter in question: but if they cannot agree, congress shall name three persons out of each of the united states, and from the list of such persons each party shall alternately strike out one, the petitioners beginning, until the number shall be reduced to thirteen; and from that number not less than seven, nor more than nine names as congress shall direct, shall in the presence of congress be drawn out by lot, and the persons whose names shall be so drawn or any five of them, shall be commissioners or judges, to hear and finally determine the controversy, so always as a major part of the judges who shall hear the cause shall agree in the determination: and if either party shall neglect to attend at the day appointed, without shewing reasons, which congress shall judge sufficient, or being present shall refuse to strike, the congress shall proceed to nominate three persons out of each state, and the secretary of congress shall strike in behalf of such party absent or refusing; and the judgment and sentence of the court to be appointed, in the manner before prescribed, shall be final and conclusive; and if any of the parties shall refuse to submit to the authority of such court, or to appear to defend their claim or cause, the court shall nevertheless proceed to pronounce sentence, or judgment, which shall in like manner be final and decisive, the judgment or sentence and other proceedings being in either case transmitted to congress, and lodged among the acts of congress for the security of the parties concerned: provided that every commissioner, before he sits in judgment, shall take an oath to be administered by one of the judges of the supreme or superior court of the state, where the cause shall be tried, "well and truly to hear and determine the matter in question, according to the best of his judgment, without favour, affection or hope of reward:" provided also, that no state shall be deprived of territory for the benefit of the united states.

All controversies concerning the private right of soil claimed under different grants of two or more states, whose jurisdictions as they may respect such lands, and the states which passed such grants are adjusted, the said grants or either of them being at the same time claimed to have originated antecedent to such settlement of jurisdiction, shall on the petition of either party to the congress of the united states, be finally determined as near as may be in the same manner as is before prescribed for deciding disputes respecting territorial jurisdiction between different states.

The united states in congress assembled shall also have the sole and exclusive right and power of regulating the alloy and value of coin struck by their own authority, or by that of the respective states—fixing the standard of weights and measures throughout the united states—regulating the trade and managing all affairs with the Indians, not members of any of the states, provided that the legislative right of any state within its own limits be not infringed or violated—establishing and regulating post-offices from one state to another, throughout all the united states, and exacting such postage on the papers passing thro' the same as may be requisite to defray the expences of the said office—appointing all officers of the land forces, in the service of the united states, excepting regimental officers—appointing all the officers of the naval forces, and commissioning all officers whatever in the service of the united states—making rules for the government and regulation of the said land and naval forces, and directing their operations.

The united states in congress assembled shall have authority to appoint a committee, to sit in the recess of congress, to be denominated "A Committee of the States," and to consist of one delegate from each state; and to appoint such other committees and civil officers as may be necessary for managing the general affairs of the united states under their direction—to appoint one of their number to preside, provided that no person be allowed to serve in the office of president more than one year in any term of three years; to ascertain the necessary sums of Money to be raised for the service of the united states, and to appropriate and apply the same for defraying the public expenses—to borrow money, or emit bills on the credit of the united states, transmitting every half year to the respective states an account of the sums of money so borrowed or emitted,—to build and equip a navy—to agree upon the number of land forces, and to make requisitions from each state for its quota, in proportion to the number of white inhabitants in such state; which requisition shall be binding, and thereupon the legislature of each state shall appoint the regimental officers, raise the men and cloath, arm and equip them in a soldier like manner, at the expense of the united states; and the officers and men so cloathed, armed and equipped shall march to the place appointed, and within the time agreed on by the united states in congress assembled: But if the united states in congress assembled shall, on consideration of circumstances judge proper that any state should not raise men, or should raise a smaller number than its quota, and that any other state should raise a greater number of men than the quota thereof, such extra number shall be raised, officered, cloathed, armed and equipped in the same manner as the quota of such state, unless the legislature of such state shall judge that such extra number cannot be safely spared out of the same, in which case they shall raise officer, cloath, arm and equip as many of such extra number as they judge can be safely spared. And the officers and men so cloathed, armed and equipped, shall march to the place appointed, and within the time agreed on by the united states in congress assembled.

The united states in congress assembled shall never engage in a war, nor grant letters of marque and reprisal in time of peace, nor enter into any treaties or alliances, nor coin money, nor regulate the value thereof, nor ascertain the sums and expenses necessary for the defence and welfare of the united states, or any of them, nor emit bills, nor borrow money on the credit of the united states, nor appropriate money, nor agree upon the number of vessels of war, to be built or purchased, or the number of land or sea forces to be raised, nor appoint a commander in chief of the army or navy, unless nine states assent to the same: nor shall a question on any other point, except for adjourning from day to day be determined, unless by the votes of a majority of the united states in congress assembled.

The congress of the united states shall have power to adjourn to any time within the year, and to any place within the united states, so that no period of adjournment be for a longer duration than the space of six Months, and shall publish the Journal of their proceedings monthly, except such parts thereof relating to treaties, alliances or military operations, as in their judgment require secrecy; and the yeas and nays of the delegates of each state on any question shall be entered on the Journal, when it is desired by any delegate; and the delegates of a state, or any of them, at his or their request shall be furnished with a transcript of the said Journal, except such parts as are above excepted, to lay before the legislatures of the several states.

Art. X. The committee of the states, or any nine of them, shall be authorised to execute, in the recess of congress, such of the powers of congress as the united states in congress assembled, by the consent of nine states, shall from time to time think expedient to vest them with; provided that no power be delegated to the said committee, for the exercise of which, by the articles of confederation, the voice of nine states in the congress of the united states assembled is requisite.

Art. XI. Canada acceding to this confederation, and joining in the measures of the united states, shall be admitted into, and entitled to all the advantages of this union: but no other colony shall be admitted into the same, unless such admission be agreed to by nine states.

Art. XII. All bills of credit emitted, monies borrowed and debts contracted by, or under the authority of congress, before the assembling of the united states, in pursuance of the present confederation, shall be deemed and considered as a charge against the united states, for payment and satisfaction whereof the said united states and the public faith are hereby solemnly pledged.

Art. XIII. Every state shall abide by the determinations of the united states in congress assembled, on all questions which by this confederation are submitted to them. And the Articles of this confederation shall be inviolably observed by every state, and the union shall be perpetual; nor shall any alteration at any time hereafter be made in any of them; unless such alteration be agreed to in a congress of the united states, and be afterwards confirmed by the legislatures of every state.

And Whereas it hath pleased the Great Governor of the World to incline the hearts of the legislatures we respectively represent in congress, to approve of, and to authorize us to ratify the said articles of confederation and perpetual union. Know Ye that we the undersigned delegates, by virtue of the power and authority to us given for that purpose, do by these presents, in the name and in behalf of our respective constituents, fully and entirely ratify and confirm each and every of the said articles of confederation and perpetual union, and all and singular the matters and things therein contained: And we do further solemnly plight and engage the faith of our respective constituents, that they shall abide by the determinations of the united states in congress assembled, on all questions, which by the said confederation are submitted to them. And that the articles thereof shall be inviolably observed by the states we respectively represent, and that the union shall be perpetual. In Witness whereof we have hereunto set our hands in Congress. Done at Philadelphia in the state of Pennsylvania the ninth day of July, in the Year of our Lord one Thousand seven Hundred and Seventy-eight, and in the third year of the independence of America.

The Constitution of the United States of America

We the People of the United States, in Order to form a more perfect Union, establish Justice, insure domestic Tranquility, provide for the common defence, promote the general Welfare, and secure the Blessings of Liberty to ourselves and our Posterity, do ordain and establish this Constitution for the United States of America.

ARTICLE I

SECTION 1
[LEGISLATIVE POWERS]

All legislative Powers herein granted shall be vested in a Congress of the United States, which shall consist of a Senate and House of Representatives.

SECTION 2
[HOUSE OF REPRESENTATIVES, HOW CONSTITUTED, POWER OF IMPEACHMENT]

The House of Representatives shall be composed of Members chosen every second Year by the People of the several States, and the Electors in each State shall have the Qualifications requisite for Electors of the most numerous Branch of the State Legislature.

No Person shall be a Representative who shall not have attained to the Age of twenty five Years, and been seven Years a Citizen of the United States, and who shall not, when elected, be an Inhabitant of that State in which he shall be chosen.

Representatives and *direct Taxes*[1] shall be apportioned among the several States which may be included within this Union, according to their respective Numbers, *which shall be determined by adding to the whole Number of free Persons, including those bound to Service for a Term of Years, and excluding Indians not taxed, three fifths of all other Persons.*[2] The actual Enumeration shall be made within three Years after the first Meeting of the Congress of the United States, and within every subsequent Term of ten Years, in such Manner as they shall by Law direct. The Number of Representatives shall not exceed one for every thirty Thousand, but each State shall have at Least one Representative; *and until such enumeration shall be made, the State of New Hampshire shall be entitled to chuse three, Massachusetts eight, Rhode-Island and Providence Plantations one, Connecticut five, New-York six, New Jersey four, Pennsylvania eight, Delaware one, Maryland six, Virginia ten, North Carolina five, South Carolina five, and Georgia three.*[3]

When vacancies happen in the Representation from any State, the Executive Authority thereof shall issue Writs of Election to fill such Vacancies.

The House of Representatives shall chuse their Speaker and other Officers; and shall have the sole Power of Impeachment.

---

[1]Modified by Sixteenth Amendment.

[2]Modified by Fourteenth Amendment.

[3]Temporary provision.

SECTION 3
[THE SENATE, HOW CONSTITUTED, IMPEACHMENT TRIALS]

The Senate of the United States shall be composed of two Senators from each State, *chosen by the Legislature thereof,*[4] for six Years; and each Senator shall have one Vote.

Immediately after they shall be assembled in Consequence of the first Election, they shall be divided as equally as may be into three Classes. The Seats of the Senators of the first Class shall be vacated at the Expiration of the second Year, of the second Class at the Expiration of the fourth Year, and of the third Class at the Expiration of the sixth Year, so that one third may be chosen every second Year; *and if Vacancies happen by Resignation, or otherwise, during the Recess of the Legislature of any State, the Executive thereof may make temporary Appointments until the next Meeting of the Legislature, which shall then fill such Vacancies.*[5]

No Person shall be a Senator who shall not have attained to the Age of thirty Years, and been nine Years a Citizen of the United States, and who shall not, when elected, be an Inhabitant of that State for which he shall be chosen.

The Vice President of the United States shall be President of the Senate, but shall have no Vote, unless they be equally divided.

The Senate shall chuse their other Officers, and also a President pro tempore, in the Absence of the Vice President, or when he shall exercise the Office of President of the United States.

The Senate shall have the sole Power to try all Impeachments. When sitting for that Purpose, they shall be on Oath or Affirmation. When the President of the United States is tried, the Chief Justice shall preside: And no Person shall be convicted without the Concurrence of two thirds of the Members present.

Judgment in Cases of Impeachment shall not extend further than to removal from Office, and disqualification to hold and enjoy any Office of honor, Trust or Profit under the United States: but the Party convicted shall nevertheless be liable and subject to Indictment, Trial, Judgment and Punishment, according to Law.

SECTION 4
[ELECTION OF SENATORS AND REPRESENTATIVES]

The Times, Places and Manner of holding Elections for Senators and Representatives, shall be prescribed in each State by the Legislature thereof; but the Congress may at any time by Law make or alter such Regulations, except as to the Places of chusing Senators.

The Congress shall assemble at least once in every Year, and such Meeting shall be on the first Monday in December, unless they shall by Law appoint a different Day.[6]

SECTION 5
[QUORUM, JOURNALS, MEETINGS, ADJOURNMENTS]

Each House shall be the Judge of the Elections, Returns and Qualifications of its own Members, and a Majority of each shall constitute a Quorum to do Business; but a smaller Number may adjourn from day to day, and may be authorized to compel the Attendance of absent Members, in such Manner, and under such Penalties as each House may provide.

---

[4]Modified by Seventeenth Amendment.

[5]Modified by Seventeenth Amendment.

[6]Modified by Twentieth Amendment.

Each House may determine the Rules of its Proceedings, punish its Members for disorderly Behaviour, and, with the Concurrence of two thirds, expel a Member.

Each House shall keep a Journal of its Proceedings, and from time to time publish the same, excepting such Parts as may in their Judgment require Secrecy; and the Yeas and Nays of the Members of either House on any questions shall, at the Desire of one fifth of those Present, be entered on the Journal.

Neither House, during the Session of Congress, shall, without the Consent of the other, adjourn for more than three days, nor to any other Place than that in which the two Houses shall be sitting.

SECTION 6
[COMPENSATION, PRIVILEGES, DISABILITIES]

The Senators and Representatives shall receive a Compensation for their Services, to be ascertained by Law, and paid out of the Treasury of the United States. They shall in all Cases, except Treason, Felony and Breach of the Peace, be privileged from Arrest during their Attendance at the Session of their respective Houses, and in going to and returning from the same; and for any Speech or Debate in either House, they shall not be questioned in any other Place.

No Senator or Representative shall, during the Time for which he was elected, be appointed to any civil Office under the Authority of the United States, which shall have been created, or the Emoluments whereof shall have been encreased during such time; and no Person holding any Office under the United States, shall be a Member of either House during his Continuance in Office.

SECTION 7
[PROCEDURE IN PASSING BILLS AND RESOLUTIONS]

All Bills for raising Revenue shall originate in the House of Representatives; but the Senate may propose or concur with Amendments as on other Bills.

Every Bill which shall have passed the House of Representatives and the Senate, shall, before it become a Law, be presented to the President of the United States: If he approve he shall sign it, but if not he shall return it, with his Objections to that House in which it shall have originated, who shall enter the Objections at large on their Journal, and proceed to reconsider it. If after such Reconsideration two thirds of that House shall agree to pass the Bill, it shall be sent, together with the Objections, to the other House, by which it shall likewise be reconsidered, and if approved by two thirds of that House, it shall become a Law. But in all such Cases the Votes of both Houses shall be determined by yeas and Nays, and the Names of the Persons voting for and against the Bill shall be entered on the Journal of each House respectively. If any Bill shall not be returned by the President within ten Days (Sundays excepted) after it shall have been presented to him, the Same shall be a Law, in like Manner as if he had signed it, unless the Congress by their Adjournment prevent its Return, in which Case it shall not be a Law.

Every Order, Resolution, or Vote to which the Concurrence of the Senate and House of Representatives may be necessary (except on a question of Adjournment) shall be presented to the President of the United States; and before the Same shall take Effect, shall be approved by him, or being disapproved by him, shall be repassed by two thirds of the Senate and House of Representatives, according to the Rules and Limitations prescribed in the Case of a Bill.

SECTION 8

The Congress shall have Power

To lay and collect Taxes, Duties, Imposts and Excises, to pay the Debts and provide for the common Defence and general Welfare of the United States; but all Duties, Imposts and Excises shall be uniform throughout the United States;

To borrow Money on the credit of the United States;

To regulate Commerce with foreign Nations, and among the several States, and with the Indian Tribes;

To establish an uniform Rule of Naturalization, and uniform Laws on the subject of Bankruptcies throughout the United States;

To coin Money, regulate the Value thereof, and of foreign Coin, and fix the Standard of Weights and Measures;

To provide for the Punishment of counterfeiting the Securities and current Coin of the United States;

To establish Post Offices and post Roads;

To promote the Progress of Science and useful Arts, by securing for limited Times to Authors and Inventors the exclusive Right to their respective Writings and Discoveries;

To constitute Tribunals inferior to the supreme Court;

To define and punish Piracies and Felonies committed on the high Seas, and Offences against the Law of Nations;

To declare War, grant Letters of Marque and Reprisal, and make Rules concerning Captures on Land and Water;

To raise and support Armies, but no Appropriation of Money to that Use shall be for a longer Term than two Years;

To provide and maintain a Navy;

To make Rules for the Government and Regulation of the land and naval Forces;

To provide for calling forth the Militia to execute the Laws of the Union, suppress Insurrections and repel Invasions;

To provide for organizing, arming, and disciplining, the Militia, and for governing such Part of them as may be employed in the Service of the United States, reserving to the States respectively, the Appointment of the Officers, and the Authority of training the Militia according to the discipline prescribed by Congress;

To exercise exclusive Legislation in all Cases whatsoever, over such District (not exceeding ten Miles square) as may, by Cession of particular States, and the Acceptance of Congress, become the Seat of the Government of the United States, and to exercise like Authority over all Places purchased by the Consent of the Legislature of the State in which the Same shall be, for the Erection of Forts, Magazines, Arsenals, dock-Yards, and other needful Buildings;—And

To make all Laws which shall be necessary and proper for carrying into Execution the foregoing Powers, and all other Powers vested by this Constitution in the Government of the United States, or in any Department or Officer thereof.

SECTION 9

The Migration or Importation of such Persons as any of the States now existing shall think proper to admit, shall not be prohibited by the Congress prior to the Year one thousand eight hundred

and eight, but a Tax or duty may be imposed on such Importation, not exceeding ten dollars for each Person.[7]

The Privilege of the Writ of Habeas Corpus shall not be suspended, unless when in Cases of Rebellion or Invasion the public Safety may require it.

No Bill of Attainder or ex post facto Law shall be passed.

No Capitation, or other direct, Tax shall be laid, unless in Proportion to the Census or Enumeration herein before directed to be taken.[8]

No Tax or Duty shall be laid on Articles exported from any State.

No Preference shall be given by any Regulation of Commerce or Revenue to the Ports of one State over those of another; nor shall Vessels bound to, or from, one State, be obliged to enter, clear, or pay Duties in another.

No Money shall be drawn from the Treasury, but in Consequence of Appropriations made by Law; and a regular Statement and Account of the Receipts and Expenditures of all public Money shall be published from time to time.

No Title of Nobility shall be granted by the United States: And no Person holding any Office of Profit or Trust under them, shall, without the Consent of the Congress, accept of any present, Emolument, Office, or Title, of any kind whatever, from any King, Prince, or foreign State.

SECTION 10
[RESTRICTIONS UPON POWERS OF STATES]

No State shall enter into any Treaty, Alliance, or Confederation; grant Letters of Marque and Reprisal; coin Money; emit Bills of Credit; make any Thing but gold and silver Coin a Tender in Payment of Debts; pass any Bill of Attainder, ex post facto Law, or Law impairing the Obligation of Contracts, or grant any Title of Nobility.

No State shall, without the Consent of the Congress, lay any Imposts or Duties on Imports or Exports, except what may be absolutely necessary for executing its inspection Laws: and the net Produce of all Duties and Imposts, laid by any State on Imports or Exports, shall be for the Use of the Treasury of the United States; and all such Laws shall be subject to the Revision and Control of the Congress.

No State shall, without the Consent of Congress, lay any Duty of Tonnage, keep Troops, or Ships of War in time of Peace, enter into any Agreement or Compact with another State, or with a foreign Power, or engage in War, unless actually invaded, or in such imminent Danger as will not admit of delay.

ARTICLE II

SECTION 1
[EXECUTIVE POWER, ELECTION, QUALIFICATIONS OF THE PRESIDENT]

The executive Power shall be vested in a President of the United States of America. *He shall hold his Office during the Term of four Years, and, together with the Vice President, chosen for the same Term, be elected, as follows*[9]

---

[7]Temporary provision.

[8]Modified by Sixteenth Amendment.

[9]Number of terms limited to two by Twenty-Second Amendment.

Each State shall appoint, in such Manner as the Legislature thereof may direct, a Number of Electors, equal to the whole Number of Senators and Representatives to which the State may be entitled in the Congress: but no Senator or Representative, or Person holding an Office of Trust or Profit under the United States, shall be appointed an Elector.

The electors shall meet in their respective States, and vote by ballot for two Persons, of whom one at least shall not be an Inhabitant of the same State with themselves. And they shall make a List of all the Persons voted for, and of the Number of Votes for each; which List they shall sign and certify, and transmit sealed to the Seat of the Government of the United States, directed to the President of the Senate. The President of the Senate shall, in the Presence of the Senate and House of Representatives, open all the Certificates, and the Votes shall then be counted. The Person having the greatest Number of Votes shall be the President, if such Number be a Majority of the whole Number of Electors appointed; and if there be more than one who have such Majority, and have an equal Number of Votes, then the House of Representatives shall immediately chuse by Ballot one of them for President; and if no Person have a Majority, then from the five highest on the List the said House shall in like Manner chuse the President. But in chusing the President, the Votes shall be taken by States, the Representation from each State having one Vote; A quorum for this Purpose shall consist of a Member or Members from two thirds of the States, and a Majority of all the States shall be necessary to a Choice. In every Case, after the Choice of the President, the person having the greatest Number of Votes of the Electors shall be the Vice President. But if there should remain two or more who have equal Votes, the Senate shall chuse from them by Ballot the Vice President.[10]

The Congress may determine the Time of chusing the Electors, and the Day on which they shall give their Votes; which Day shall be the same throughout the United States.

No Person except a natural born Citizen, or a Citizen of the United States, at the time of the Adoption of this Constitution, shall be eligible to the Office of President; neither shall any Person be eligible to that Office who shall not have attained to the Age of thirty five Years, and been fourteen Years a Resident within the United States.

In Case of the Removal of the President from Office, or his Death, Resignation, or Inability to discharge the Powers and Duties of the said Office, the Same shall devolve on the Vice President, and the Congress may by Law provide for the Case of Removal, Death, Resignation or Inability, both of the President and Vice President, declaring what Officer shall then act as President, and such Officer shall act accordingly, until the Disability be removed, or a President shall be elected.

The President shall, at stated Times, receive for his Services, a Compensation, which shall neither be increased nor diminished during the Period for which he shall have been elected, and he shall not receive within that Period any other Emolument from the United States, or any of them.

Before he enter on the Execution of his Office, he shall take the following Oath or Affirmation:—"I do solemnly swear (or affirm) that I will faithfully execute the Office of President of the United States, and will to the best of my Ability, preserve, protect and defend the Constitution of the United States."

SECTION 2
[POWERS OF THE PRESIDENT]

The President shall be Commander in Chief of the Army and Navy of the United States, and of the Militia of the several States, when called into the actual Service of the United States;

---

[10]Modified by Twelfth and Twentieth Amendments.

he may require the Opinion, in writing, of the principal Officer in each of the executive Departments, upon any Subject relating to the Duties of their respective Offices, and he shall have Power to grant Reprieves and Pardons for Offences against the United States, except in Cases of Impeachment.

He shall have Power, by and with the Advice and Consent of the Senate, to make Treaties, provided two thirds of the Senators present concur; and he shall nominate, and by and with the Advice and Consent of the Senate, shall appoint Ambassadors, other public Ministers and Consuls, Judges of the supreme Court, and all other Officers of the United States, whose Appointments are not herein otherwise provided for, and which shall be established by Law: but the Congress may by Law vest the Appointment of such inferior Officers, as they think proper, in the President alone, in the Courts of Law, or in the Heads of Departments.

The President shall have Power to fill up all Vacancies that may happen during the Recess of the Senate, by granting Commissions which shall expire at the End of their next Session.

SECTION 3
[POWERS AND DUTIES OF THE PRESIDENT]

He shall from time to time give to the Congress Information of the State of the Union, and recommend to their Consideration such Measures as he shall judge necessary and expedient; he may, on extraordinary Occasions, convene both Houses, or either of them, and in Case of Disagreement between them, with Respect to the Time of Adjournment, he may adjourn them to such Time as he shall think proper; he shall receive Ambassadors and other public Ministers; he shall take Care that the Laws be faithfully executed, and shall Commission all the Officers of the United States.

SECTION 4
[IMPEACHMENT]

The President, Vice President and all civil Officers of the United States, shall be removed from Office on Impeachment for, and Conviction of, Treason, Bribery, or other high Crimes and Misdemeanors.

ARTICLE III

SECTION 1
[JUDICIAL POWER, TENURE OF OFFICE]

The judicial Power of the United States, shall be vested in one supreme Court, and in such inferior Courts as the Congress may from time to time ordain and establish. The Judges, both of the supreme and inferior Courts, shall hold their Offices during good Behaviour, and shall, at stated Times, receive for their Services, a Compensation, which shall not be diminished during their Continuance in Office.

SECTION 2
[JURISDICTION]

The judicial Power shall extend to all Cases, in Law and Equity, arising under this Constitution, the Laws of the United States, and Treaties made, or which shall be made, under their Authority;—to all Cases affecting Ambassadors, other public Ministers and Consuls;—to all Cases of admiralty and maritime Jurisdiction;—to Controversies to which the United States shall be a Party;—to Controversies between two or more States;—*between a State and Citizens of another State;*—between Citizens of different States,—between Citizens of the same State claiming Lands under Grants of different States, *and between a State,* or the Citizens thereof, *and foreign States, Citizens or Subjects.*[11]

In all Cases affecting Ambassadors, other public Ministers and Consuls, and those in which a State shall be Party, the supreme Court shall have original Jurisdiction. In all the other Cases before mentioned, the supreme Court shall have appellate Jurisdiction, both as to Law and Fact, with such Exceptions, and under such Regulations as the Congress shall make.

The Trial of all Crimes, except in Cases of Impeachment, shall be by Jury; and such Trial shall be held in the State where the said Crimes shall have been committed; but when not committed within any State, the Trial shall be at such Place or Places as the Congress may by Law have directed.

SECTION 3
[TREASON, PROOF, AND PUNISHMENT]

Treason against the United States, shall consist only in levying War against them, or in adhering to their Enemies, giving them Aid and Comfort. No Person shall be convicted of Treason unless on the Testimony of two Witnesses to the same overt Act, or on Confession in open Court.

The Congress shall have Power to declare the Punishment of Treason, but no Attainder of Treason shall work Corruption of Blood, or Forfeiture except during the Life of the Person attainted.

ARTICLE IV

SECTION 1
[FAITH AND CREDIT AMONG STATES]

Full Faith and Credit shall be given in each State to the public Acts, Records, and judicial Proceedings of every other State. And the Congress may by general Laws prescribe the Manner in which such Acts, Records and Proceedings shall be proved, and the Effect thereof.

SECTION 2
[PRIVILEGES AND IMMUNITIES, FUGITIVES]

The Citizens of each State shall be entitled to all Privileges and Immunities of Citizens in the several States.

A Person charged in any State with Treason, Felony or other Crime, who shall flee from Justice, and be found in another State, shall on Demand of the executive Authority of the State from which he fled, be delivered up, to be removed to the State having Jurisdiction of the Crime.

No person held to Service or Labour in one State, under the Laws thereof, escaping into another, shall, in Consequence of any Law or Regulation therein, be discharged from such Service or Labour, but shall be delivered up on Claim of the Party to whom such Service or Labour may be due.[12]

---

[11]Modified by Eleventh Amendment.

[12]Repealed by the Thirteenth Amendment.

SECTION 3

[ADMISSION OF NEW STATES]

New States may be admitted by the Congress into this Union; but no new State shall be formed or erected within the Jurisdiction of any other State; nor any State be formed by the Junction of two or more States, or Parts of States, without the Consent of the Legislatures of the States concerned as well as of the Congress.

The Congress shall have Power to dispose of and make all needful Rules and Regulations respecting the Territory or other Property belonging to the United States; and nothing in this Constitution shall be so construed as to Prejudice any Claims of the United States, or of any particular State.

SECTION 4

[GUARANTEE OF REPUBLICAN GOVERNMENT]

The United States shall guarantee to every State in this Union a Republican Form of Government, and shall protect each of them against Invasion; and on Application of the Legislature, or of the Executive (when the Legislature cannot be convened), against domestic Violence.

ARTICLE V

[AMENDMENT OF THE CONSTITUTION]

The Congress, whenever two thirds of both Houses shall deem it necessary, shall propose Amendments to this Constitution, or, on the Application of the Legislatures of two thirds of the several States, shall call a Convention for proposing Amendments, which, in either Case, shall be valid to all Intents and Purposes, as Part of this Constitution, when ratified by the Legislatures of three fourths of the several States, or by Conventions in three fourths thereof, as the one or the other Mode of Ratification may be proposed by the Congress; *Provided that no Amendment which may be made prior to the Year One thousand eight hundred and eight shall in any Manner affect the first and fourth Clauses in the Ninth Section of the first Article;*[13] and that no State, without its Consent, shall be deprived of its equal Suffrage in the Senate.

ARTICLE VI

[DEBTS, SUPREMACY, OATH]

All Debts contracted and Engagements entered into, before the Adoption of this Constitution, shall be as valid against the United States under this Constitution, as under the Confederation.

This Constitution, and the Laws of the United States which shall be made in Pursuance thereof; and all Treaties made, or which shall be made, under the Authority of the United States, shall be the supreme Law of the Land; and the Judges in every State shall be bound thereby, any Thing in the Constitution or Laws of any State to the Contrary notwithstanding.

The Senators and Representatives before mentioned, and the Members of the several State Legislatures, and all executive and judicial Officers, both of the United States and of the

---

[13]Temporary provision.

several States, shall be bound by Oath or Affirmation, to support this Constitution; but no religious Test shall be required as a Qualification to any Office or public Trust under the United States.

ARTICLE VII

[RATIFICATION AND ESTABLISHMENT]

The Ratification of the Conventions of nine States, shall be sufficient for the Establishment of this Constitution between the States so ratifying the Same.[14]

Done in Convention by the Unanimous Consent of the States present the Seventeenth Day of September in the Year of our Lord one thousand seven hundred and Eighty seven and of the Independence of the United States of America the Twelfth. *In Witness* whereof We have hereunto subscribed our Names,

G:⁰ WASHINGTON—
Presidt. and deputy from Virginia

NEW HAMPSHIRE
John Langdon
Nicholas Gilman

MASSACHUSETTS
Nathaniel Gorham
Rufus King

CONNECTICUT
Wm. Saml. Johnson
Roger Sherman

NEW YORK
Alexander Hamilton

NEW JERSEY
Wil: Livingston
David Brearley
Wm. Paterson
Jona: Dayton

PENNSYLVANIA
B Franklin
Thomas Mifflin
Robt. Morris
Geo. Clymer
Thos. FitzSimons
Jared Ingersoll
James Wilson
Gouv Morris

DELAWARE
Geo: Read
Gunning Bedford jun
John Dickinson
Richard Bassett
Jaco: Broom

MARYLAND
James McHenry
Dan of St Thos. Jenifer
Danl. Carroll

VIRGINIA
John Blair—
James Madison Jr.

NORTH CAROLINA
Wm. Blount
Richd. Dobbs Spaight
Hu Williamson

SOUTH CAROLINA
J. Rutledge
Charles Cotesworth
    Pinckney
Charles Pinckney
Pierce Butler

GEORGIA
William Few
Abr Baldwin

---

[14]The Constitution was submitted on September 17, 1787, by the Constitutional Convention, was ratified by the conventions of several states at various dates up to May 29, 1790, and became effective on March 4, 1789.

Amendments to the Constitution

Proposed by Congress and Ratified by the Legislatures of the Several States, Pursuant to Article V of the Original Constitution.

Amendments I–X, known as the Bill of Rights, were proposed by Congress on September 25, 1789, and ratified on December 15, 1791.

AMENDMENT I

[FREEDOM OF RELIGION, OF SPEECH, AND OF THE PRESS]

Congress shall make no law respecting an establishment of religion, or prohibiting the free exercise thereof; or abridging the freedom of speech, or of the press; or the right of the people peaceably to assemble, and to petition the Government for a redress of grievances.

AMENDMENT II

[RIGHT TO KEEP AND BEAR ARMS]

A well regulated Militia, being necessary to the security of a free State, the right of the people to keep and bear Arms, shall not be infringed.

AMENDMENT III

[QUARTERING OF SOLDIERS]

No Soldier shall, in time of peace be quartered in any house, without the consent of the Owner, nor in time of war, but in a manner to be prescribed by law.

AMENDMENT IV

[SECURITY FROM UNWARRANTABLE SEARCH AND SEIZURE]

The right of the people to be secure in their persons, houses, papers, and effects, against unreasonable searches and seizures, shall not be violated, and no Warrants shall issue, but upon probable cause, supported by Oath or affirmation, and particularly describing the place to be searched, and the persons or things to be seized.

AMENDMENT V

[RIGHTS OF ACCUSED PERSONS IN CRIMINAL PROCEEDINGS]

No person shall be held to answer for a capital, or otherwise infamous crime, unless on a presentment or indictment of a Grand Jury, except in cases arising in the land or naval forces, or in the Militia, when in actual service in time of War or in public danger; nor shall any person be subject for the same offence to be twice put in jeopardy of life or limb; nor shall be compelled in any criminal case to be a witness against himself, nor be deprived of life, liberty, or property, without due process of law; nor shall private property be taken for public use, without just compensation.

AMENDMENT VI

[RIGHT TO SPEEDY TRIAL, WITNESSES, ETC.]

In all criminal prosecutions, the accused shall enjoy the right to a speedy and public trial, by an impartial jury of the State and district wherein the crime shall have been committed, which district shall have been previously ascertained by law, and to be informed of the nature and cause of the accusation; to be confronted with the witnesses against him; to have compulsory process for obtaining witnesses in his favor, and to have the Assistance of Counsel for his defence.

AMENDMENT VII

[TRIAL BY JURY IN CIVIL CASES]

In suits at common law, where the value in controversy shall exceed twenty dollars, the right of trial by jury shall be preserved, and no fact tried by a jury, shall be otherwise reexamined in any Court of the United States, than according to the rules of the common law.

AMENDMENT VIII

[BAILS, FINES, PUNISHMENTS]

Excessive bail shall not be required, nor excessive fines imposed, nor cruel and unusual punishments inflicted.

AMENDMENT IX

[RESERVATION OF RIGHTS OF PEOPLE]

The enumeration in the Constitution, of certain rights, shall not be construed to deny or disparage others retained by the people.

AMENDMENT X

[POWERS RESERVED TO STATES OR PEOPLE]

The powers not delegated to the United States by the Constitution, nor prohibited by it to the States, are reserved to the States respectively, or to the people.

AMENDMENT XI

[PROPOSED BY CONGRESS ON MARCH 4, 1794; DECLARED RATIFIED ON JANUARY 8, 1798.]

[RESTRICTION OF JUDICIAL POWER]

The Judicial power of the United States shall not be construed to extend to any suit in law or equity, commenced or prosecuted against one of the United States by Citizens of another State, or by Citizens or Subjects of any Foreign State.

AMENDMENT XII

[PROPOSED BY CONGRESS ON DECEMBER 9, 1803; DECLARED RATIFIED ON SEPTEMBER 25, 1804.]

[ELECTION OF PRESIDENT AND VICE PRESIDENT]

The Electors shall meet in their respective states and vote by ballot for President and Vice-President, one of whom, at least, shall not be an inhabitant of the same state with themselves; they shall name in their ballots the person voted for as President, and in distinct ballots the person voted for as Vice-President, and they shall make distinct lists of all persons voted for as President, and of all persons voted for as Vice-President, and of the number of votes for each, which lists they shall sign and certify, and transmit sealed to the seat of the government of the United States, directed to the President of the Senate;—the President of the Senate shall, in presence of the Senate and House of Representatives, open all the certificates and the votes shall then be counted;—The person having the greatest number of votes for President, shall be the President, if such number be a majority of the whole number of Electors appointed; and if no person have such majority, then from the persons having the highest numbers not exceeding three on the list of those voted for as President, the House of Representatives shall choose immediately, by ballot, the President. But in choosing the President, the votes shall be taken by states, the representation from each state having one vote; a quorum for this purpose shall consist of a member or members from two-thirds of the states, and a majority of all the states shall be necessary to a choice. And if the House of Representatives shall not choose a President whenever the right of choice shall devolve upon them, before the fourth day of March next following, then the Vice-President shall act as President, as in the case of the death or other constitutional disability of the President.—The person having the greatest number of votes as Vice-President, shall be the Vice-President, if such number be a majority of the whole number of Electors appointed, and if no person have a majority, then from the two highest numbers on the list, the Senate shall choose the Vice-President; a quorum for the purpose shall consist of two-thirds of the whole number of Senators, and a majority of the whole number shall be necessary to a choice. But no person constitutionally ineligible to the office of President shall be eligible to that of Vice-President of the United States.

AMENDMENT XIII

[PROPOSED BY CONGRESS ON JANUARY 31, 1865; DECLARED RATIFIED ON DECEMBER 18, 1865.]

SECTION 1
[ABOLITION OF SLAVERY]

Neither slavery nor involuntary servitude, except as a punishment for crime whereof the party shall have been duly convicted, shall exist within the United States, or any place subject to their jurisdiction.

SECTION 2
[POWER TO ENFORCE THIS ARTICLE]

Congress shall have power to enforce this article by appropriate legislation.

AMENDMENT XIV

[PROPOSED BY CONGRESS ON JUNE 13, 1866; DECLARED RATIFIED ON JULY 28, 1868.]

SECTION 1
[CITIZENSHIP RIGHTS NOT TO BE ABRIDGED BY STATES]

All persons born or naturalized in the United States, and subject to the jurisdiction thereof, are citizens of the United States and of the State wherein they reside. No State shall make or enforce any law which shall abridge the privileges or immunities of citizens of the United States; nor shall any State deprive any person of life, liberty, or property, without due process of law; nor deny to any person within its jurisdiction the equal protection of the laws.

SECTION 2

Representatives shall be apportioned among the several States according to their respective numbers, counting the whole number of persons in each State, excluding Indians not taxed. But when the right to vote at any election for the choice of electors for President and Vice-President of the United States, Representatives in Congress, the Executive and Judicial officers of a State, or the members of the Legislature thereof, is denied to any of the male inhabitants of such State, being twenty-one years of age, and citizens of the United States, or in any way abridged, except for participation in rebellion, or other crime, the basis of representation therein shall be reduced in the proportion which the number of such male citizens shall bear to the whole number of male citizens twenty-one years of age in such State.

SECTION 3
[PERSONS DISQUALIFIED FROM HOLDING OFFICE]

No person shall be a Senator or Representative in Congress, or elector of President and Vice-President, or hold any office, civil or military, under the United States, or under any State, who, having previously taken an oath, as a member of Congress, or as an officer of the United States, or as a member of any State legislature, or as an executive or judicial officer of any State, to support the Constitution of the United States, shall have engaged in insurrection or rebellion against the same, or given aid or comfort to the enemies thereof. But Congress may by a vote of two-thirds of each House, remove such disability.

SECTION 4
[WHAT PUBLIC DEBTS ARE VALID]

The validity of the public debt of the United States, authorized by law, including debts incurred for payment of pensions and bounties for services in suppressing insurrection or rebellion, shall not be questioned. But neither the United States nor any State shall assume or pay any debt or obligation incurred in aid of insurrection or rebellion against the United States, or any claim for the loss or emancipation of any slave; but all such debts, obligations and claims shall be held illegal and void.

SECTION 5
[POWER TO ENFORCE THIS ARTICLE]

The Congress shall have power to enforce, by appropriate legislation, the provisions of this article.

AMENDMENT XV

[PROPOSED BY CONGRESS ON FEBRUARY 26, 1869; DECLARED RATIFIED ON MARCH 30, 1870.]

SECTION 1
[NEGRO SUFFRAGE]

The right of citizens of the United States to vote shall not be denied or abridged by the United States or by any State on account of race, color, or previous condition of servitude.

SECTION 2
[POWER TO ENFORCE THIS ARTICLE]

The Congress shall have power to enforce this article by appropriate legislation.

AMENDMENT XVI

[PROPOSED BY CONGRESS ON JULY 2, 1909; DECLARED RATIFIED
ON FEBRUARY 25, 1913.]

[AUTHORIZING INCOME TAXES]

The Congress shall have power to lay and collect taxes on incomes, from whatever source derived, without apportionment among the several States, and without regard to any census or enumeration.

AMENDMENT XVII

[PROPOSED BY CONGRESS ON MAY 13, 1912; DECLARED RATIFIED ON MAY 31, 1913.]

[POPULAR ELECTION OF SENATORS]

The Senate of the United States shall be composed of two Senators from each State, elected by the people thereof, for six years; and each Senator shall have one vote. The electors in each State shall have the qualifications requisite for electors of the most numerous branch of the State legislatures.

When vacancies happen in the representation of any State in the Senate, the executive authority of such State shall issue writs of election to fill such vacancies: *Provided,* That the legislature of any State may empower the executive thereof to make temporary appointments until the people fill the vacancies by election as the legislature may direct.

This amendment shall not be so construed as to affect the election or term of any Senator chosen before it becomes valid as part of the Constitution.

AMENDMENT XVIII

[PROPOSED BY CONGRESS DECEMBER 18, 1917; DECLARED RATIFIED
ON JANUARY 29, 1919.]

SECTION 1
[NATIONAL LIQUOR PROHIBITION]

After one year from the ratification of this article the manufacture, sale, or transportation of intoxicating liquors within, the importation thereof into, or the exportation thereof from the United States and all territory subject to the jurisdiction thereof for beverage purposes is hereby prohibited.

SECTION 2
[POWER TO ENFORCE THIS ARTICLE]

The Congress and the several States shall have concurrent power to enforce this article by appropriate legislation.

SECTION 3
[RATIFICATION WITHIN SEVEN YEARS]

This article shall be inoperative unless it shall have been ratified as an amendment to the Constitution by the legislatures of the several States, as provided in the Constitution, within seven years from the date of the submission hereof to the States by the Congress.[1]

---

[1]Repealed by the Twenty-First Amendment.

AMENDMENT XIX

[PROPOSED BY CONGRESS ON JUNE 4, 1919; DECLARED RATIFIED ON AUGUST 26, 1920.]
[WOMAN SUFFRAGE]

The right of citizens of the United States to vote shall not be denied or abridged by the United States or by any State on account of sex.

Congress shall have power to enforce this article by appropriate legislation.

AMENDMENT XX

[PROPOSED BY CONGRESS ON MARCH 2, 1932; DECLARED RATIFIED ON FEBRUARY 6, 1933.]

SECTION 1
[TERMS OF OFFICE]

The terms of the President and Vice President shall end at noon on the 20th day of January, and the terms of Senators and Representatives at noon on the 3rd day of January, of the years in which such terms would have ended if this article had not been ratified; and the terms of their successors shall then begin.

SECTION 2
[TIME OF CONVENING CONGRESS]

The Congress shall assemble at least once in every year, and such meeting shall begin at noon on the 3rd day of January, unless they shall by law appoint a different day.

SECTION 3
[DEATH OF PRESIDENT-ELECT]

If, at the time fixed for the beginning of the term of the President, the President elect shall have died, the Vice President elect shall become President. If a President shall not have been chosen before the time fixed for the beginning of his term, or if the President elect shall have failed to qualify, then the Vice President elect shall act as President until a President shall have qualified; and the Congress may by law provide for the case wherein neither a President elect nor a Vice President elect shall have qualified, declaring who shall then act as President, or the manner in which one who is to act shall be selected, and such person shall act accordingly until a President or Vice President shall have qualified.

SECTION 4
[ELECTION OF THE PRESIDENT]

The Congress may by law provide for the case of the death of any of the persons from whom the House of Representatives may choose a President whenever the right of choice shall have devolved upon them, and for the case of the death of any of the persons from whom the Senate may choose a Vice President whenever the right of choice shall have devolved upon them.

SECTION 5
[AMENDMENT TAKES EFFECT]

Sections 1 and 2 shall take effect on the 15th day of October following the ratification of this article.

SECTION 6
[RATIFICATION WITHIN SEVEN YEARS]

This article shall be inoperative unless it shall have been ratified as an amendment to the Constitution by the legislatures of three-fourths of the several States within seven years from the date of its submission.

AMENDMENT XXI

[PROPOSED BY CONGRESS ON FEBRUARY 20, 1933; DECLARED RATIFIED ON DECEMBER 5, 1933.]

SECTION 1
[NATIONAL LIQUOR PROHIBITION REPEALED]

The eighteenth article of amendment to the Constitution of the United States is hereby repealed.

SECTION 2
[TRANSPORTATION OF LIQUOR INTO "DRY" STATES]

The transportation or importation into any State, Territory, or Possession of the United States for delivery or use therein of intoxicating liquors, in violation of the laws thereof, is hereby prohibited.

SECTION 3
[RATIFICATION WITHIN SEVEN YEARS]

This article shall be inoperative unless it shall have been ratified as an amendment to the Constitution by conventions in the several States, as provided in the Constitution, within seven years from the date of the submission hereof to the States by the Congress.

AMENDMENT XXII

[PROPOSED BY CONGRESS ON MARCH 21, 1947; DECLARED RATIFIED ON FEBRUARY 27, 1951.]

SECTION 1
[TENURE OF PRESIDENT LIMITED]

No person shall be elected to the office of President more than twice, and no person who has held the office of President or acted as President, for more than two years of a term to which some other person was elected President shall be elected to the office of the President more than once. But this Article shall not apply to any person holding the office of President when this Article was proposed by the Congress, and shall not prevent any person who may be holding the office of President, or acting as President, during the term within which this Article becomes operative from holding the office of President or acting as President during the remainder of such term.

SECTION 2
[RATIFICATION WITHIN SEVEN YEARS]

This article shall be inoperative unless it shall have been ratified as an amendment to the Constitution by the legislatures of three-fourths of the several States within seven years from the date of its submission to the States by the Congress.

AMENDMENT XXIII

[PROPOSED BY CONGRESS ON JUNE 16, 1960; DECLARED RATIFIED ON MARCH 29, 1961.]

SECTION 1
[ELECTORAL COLLEGE VOTES FOR THE DISTRICT OF COLUMBIA]

The District constituting the seat of Government of the United States shall appoint in such manner as the Congress may direct:

A number of electors of President and Vice President equal to the whole number of Senators and Representatives in Congress to which the District would be entitled if it were a State, but in no event more than the least populous State; they shall be in addition to those appointed by the States, but they shall be considered, for the purposes of the election of President and Vice President, to be electors appointed by a State; and they shall meet in the District and perform such duties as provided by the twelfth article of amendment.

SECTION 2
[POWER TO ENFORCE THIS ARTICLE]

The Congress shall have power to enforce this article by appropriate legislation.

AMENDMENT XXIV

[PROPOSED BY CONGRESS ON AUGUST 27, 1962; DECLARED RATIFIED ON JANUARY 23, 1964.]

SECTION 1
[ANTI-POLL TAX]

The right of citizens of the United States to vote in any primary or other election for President or Vice President, for electors for President or Vice President, or for Senator or Representative of Congress, shall not be denied or abridged by the United States or any State by reason of failure to pay any poll tax or other tax.

SECTION 2
[POWER TO ENFORCE THIS ARTICLE]

The Congress shall have power to enforce this article by appropriate legislation.

AMENDMENT XXV

[PROPOSED BY CONGRESS ON JULY 6, 1965; DECLARED RATIFIED ON FEBRUARY 10, 1967.]

SECTION 1
[VICE PRESIDENT TO BECOME PRESIDENT]

In case of the removal of the President from office or his death or resignation, the Vice President shall become President.

SECTION 2
[CHOICE OF A NEW VICE PRESIDENT]

Whenever there is a vacancy in the office of the Vice President, the President shall nominate a Vice President who shall take the office upon confirmation by a majority vote of both houses of Congress.

SECTION 3

Whenever the President transmits to the President pro tempore of the Senate and the Speaker of the House of Representatives his written declaration that he is unable to discharge the powers and duties of his office, and until he transmits to them a written declaration to the contrary, such powers and duties shall be discharged by the Vice President as Acting President.

SECTION 4

[ALTERNATE PROCEDURES TO DECLARE AND TO END PRESIDENTIAL DISABILITY]

Whenever the Vice President and a majority of either the principal officers of the executive departments, or of such other body as Congress may by law provide, transmit to the President pro tempore of the Senate and the Speaker of the House of Representatives their written declaration that the President is unable to discharge the powers and duties of his office, the Vice President shall immediately assume the powers and duties of the office as Acting President.

Thereafter, when the President transmits to the President pro tempore of the Senate and the Speaker of the House of Representatives his written declaration that no inability exists, he shall resume the powers and duties of his office unless the Vice President and a majority of either the principal officers of the executive department, or of such other body as Congress may by law provide, transmit within four days to the President pro tempore of the Senate and the Speaker of the House of Representatives their written declaration that the President is unable to discharge the powers and duties of his office. Thereupon Congress shall decide the issue, assembling within forty eight hours for that purpose if not in session. If the Congress, within twenty one days after receipt of the latter written declaration, or, if Congress is not in session, within twenty one days after Congress is required to assemble, determines by two-thirds vote of both Houses that the President is unable to discharge the powers and duties of his office, the Vice President shall continue to discharge the same as Acting President; otherwise, the President shall resume the powers and duties of his office.

AMENDMENT XXVI

[PROPOSED BY CONGRESS ON MARCH 23, 1971; DECLARED RATIFIED ON JULY 1, 1971.]

SECTION 1

[EIGHTEEN-YEAR-OLD VOTE]

The right of citizens of the United States, who are eighteen years of age or older, to vote shall not be denied or abridged by the United States or by any State on account of age.

SECTION 2

[POWER TO ENFORCE THIS ARTICLE]

The Congress shall have power to enforce this article by appropriate legislation.

AMENDMENT XXVII

[PROPOSED BY CONGRESS ON SEPTEMBER 25, 1789; DECLARED RATIFIED ON MAY 8, 1992.]

[CONGRESS CANNOT RAISE ITS OWN PAY]

No law varying the compensation for the services of the Senators and Representatives, shall take effect, until an election of representatives shall have intervened.

The Federalist Papers

NO. 10: MADISON

Among the numerous advantages promised by a well constructed Union, none deserves to be more accurately developed than its tendency to break and control the violence of faction. The friend of popular governments never finds himself so much alarmed for their character and fate, as when he contemplates their propensity to this dangerous vice. He will not fail therefore to set a due value on any plan which, without violating the principles to which he is attached, provides a proper cure for it. The instability, injustice, and confusion introduced into the public councils have, in truth, been the mortal diseases under which popular governments have everywhere perished, as they continue to be the favorite and fruitful topics from which the adversaries to liberty derive their most specious declamations. The valuable improvements made by the American constitutions on the popular models, both ancient and modern, cannot certainly be too much admired; but it would be an unwarrantable partiality to contend that they have as effectually obviated the danger on this side, as was wished and expected. Complaints are everywhere heard from our most considerate and virtuous citizens, equally the friends of public and private faith and of public and personal liberty, that our governments are too unstable, that the public good is disregarded in the conflicts of rival parties, and that measures are too often decided, not according to the rules of justice and the rights of the minor party, but by the superior force of an interested and overbearing majority. However anxiously we may wish that these complaints had no foundation, the evidence of known facts will not permit us to deny that they are in some degree true. It will be found, indeed, on a candid review of our situation, that some of the distresses under which we labor have been erroneously charged on the operation of our governments; but it will be found, at the same time, that other causes will not alone account for many of our heaviest misfortunes; and, particularly, for that prevailing and increasing distrust of public engagements and alarm for private rights which are echoed from one end of the continent to the other. These must be chiefly, if not wholly, effects of the unsteadiness and injustice with which a factious spirit has tainted our public administration.

By a faction I understand a number of citizens, whether amounting to a majority or minority of the whole, who are united and actuated by some common impulse of passion, or of interest, adverse to the rights of other citizens, or to the permanent and aggregate interests of the community.

There are two methods of curing the mischiefs of faction: the one, by removing its causes; the other, by controlling its effects.

There are again two methods of removing the causes of faction: the one, by destroying the liberty which is essential to its existence; the other, by giving to every citizen the same opinions, the same passions, and the same interests.

It could never be more truly said than of the first remedy, that it is worse than the disease. Liberty is to faction what air is to fire, an aliment without which it instantly expires. But it could not be a less folly to abolish liberty, which is essential to political life, because it nourishes faction, than it would be to wish the annihilation of air, which is essential to animal life, because it imparts to fire its destructive agency.

The second expedient is as impracticable, as the first would be unwise. As long as the reason of man continues fallible, and he is at liberty to exercise it, different opinions will be formed. As long as the connection subsists between his reason and his self-love, his opinions and his passions will have a reciprocal influence on each other; and the former will be objects to which the latter will attach themselves. The diversity in the faculties of men, from which the rights of property originate, is not less an insuperable obstacle to a uniformity of interests. The protection of these faculties is the first object of Government. From the protection of different and unequal faculties of acquiring property, the possession of different degrees and kinds of property immediately results; and from the influence of these on the sentiments and views of the respective proprietors, ensues a division of the society into different interests and parties.

The latent causes of faction are thus sown in the nature of man; and we see them everywhere brought into different degrees of activity, according to the different circumstances of civil society. A zeal for different opinions concerning religion, concerning Government, and many other points, as well of speculation as of practice; an attachment to different leaders ambitiously contending for pre-eminence and power; or to persons of other descriptions whose fortunes have been interesting to the human passions, have in turn divided mankind into parties, inflamed them with mutual animosity, and rendered them much more disposed to vex and oppress each other, than to co-operate for their common good. So strong is this propensity of mankind to fall into mutual animosities, that where no substantial occasion presents itself, the most frivolous and fanciful distinctions have been sufficient to kindle their unfriendly passions, and excite their most violent conflicts. But the most common and durable source of factions has been the various and unequal distribution of property. Those who hold and those who are without property have ever formed distinct interests in society. Those who are creditors, and those who are debtors, fall under a like discrimination. A landed interest, a manufacturing interest, a mercantile interest, a moneyed interest, with many lesser interests, grow up of necessity in civilized nations, and divide them into different classes, actuated by different sentiments and views. The regulation of these various and interfering interests forms the principal task of modern Legislation, and involves the spirit of party and faction in the necessary and ordinary operations of Government.

No man is allowed to be judge in his own cause, because his interest would certainly bias his judgment and, not improbably, corrupt his integrity. With equal, nay with greater reason, a body of men are unfit to be both judges and parties at the same time; yet what are many of the most important acts of legislation but so many judicial determinations, not indeed concerning the rights of single persons, but concerning the rights of large bodies of citizens; and what are the different classes of legislators but advocates and parties to the causes which they determine? Is a law proposed concerning private debts? It is a question to which the creditors are parties on one side and the debtors on the other. Justice ought to hold the balance between them. Yet the parties are, and must be, themselves the judges; and the most numerous party, or in other words, the most powerful faction must be expected to prevail. Shall domestic manufacturers be encouraged, and in what degree, by restrictions on foreign manufacturers? are questions which would be differently decided by the landed and the manufacturing classes, and probably by neither with a sole regard to justice and the public good. The apportionment of taxes on the various descriptions of property is an act which seems to require the most exact impartiality; yet there is, perhaps, no legislative act in which greater opportunity and temptation are given to a predominant party to trample on the rules of justice. Every shilling with which they overburden the inferior number is a shilling saved to their own pockets.

It is in vain to say that enlightened statesmen will be able to adjust these clashing interests and render them all subservient to the public good. Enlightened statesmen will not always be at the helm. Nor, in many cases, can such an adjustment be made at all without taking into view indirect and remote considerations, which will rarely prevail over the immediate interest which one party may find in disregarding the rights of another or the good of the whole.

The inference to which we are brought is that the *causes* of faction cannot be removed and that relief is only to be sought in the means of controlling its *effects*.

If a faction consists of less than a majority, relief is supplied by the republican principle, which enables the majority to defeat its sinister views by regular vote. It may clog the administration, it may convulse the society; but it will be unable to execute and mask its violence under the forms of the Constitution. When a majority is included in a faction, the form of popular government, on the other hand, enables it to sacrifice to its ruling passion or interest both the public good and the rights of other citizens. To secure the public good and private rights against the danger of such a faction, and at the same time to preserve the spirit and the form of popular government, is then the great object to which our enquiries are directed. Let me add that it is the great desideratum by which alone this form of government can be rescued from the opprobrium under which it has so long labored and be recommended to the esteem and adoption of mankind.

By what means is this object attainable? Evidently by one of two only. Either the existence of the same passion or interest in a majority at the same time must be prevented, or the majority, having such co-existent passion or interest, must be rendered, by their number and local situation, unable to concert and carry into effect schemes of oppression. If the impulse and the opportunity be suffered to coincide, we well know that neither moral nor religious motives can be relied on as an adequate control. They are not found to be such on the injustice and violence of individuals, and lose their efficacy in proportion to the number combined together, that is, in proportion as their efficacy becomes needful.

From this view of the subject it may be concluded that a pure Democracy, by which I mean a Society consisting of a small number of citizens, who assemble and administer the Government in person, can admit of no cure for the mischiefs of faction. A common passion or interest will, in almost every case, be felt by a majority of the whole; a communication and concert results from the form of Government itself; and there is nothing to check the inducements to sacrifice the weaker party or an obnoxious individual. Hence it is that such Democracies have ever been spectacles of turbulence and contention; have ever been found incompatible with personal security or the rights of property; and have in general been as short in their lives as they have been violent in their deaths. Theoretic politicians, who have patronized this species of Government, have erroneously supposed that by reducing mankind to a perfect equality in their political rights, they would at the same time be perfectly equalized and assimilated in their possessions, their opinions, and their passions.

A Republic, by which I mean a Government in which the scheme of representation takes place, opens a different prospect and promises the cure for which we are seeking. Let us examine the points in which it varies from pure Democracy, and we shall comprehend both the nature of the cure and the efficacy which it must derive from the Union.

The two great points of difference between a Democracy and a Republic are: first, the delegation of the Government, in the latter, to a small number of citizens elected by the rest; secondly, the greater number of citizens and greater sphere of country over which the latter may be extended.

The effect of the first difference is, on the one hand, to refine and enlarge the public views by passing them through the medium of a chosen body of citizens, whose wisdom may best discern the true interest of their country and whose patriotism and love of justice will be least likely to sacrifice it to temporary or partial considerations. Under such a regulation it may well happen that the public voice, pronounced by the representatives of the people, will be more consonant to the public good than if pronounced by the people themselves, convened for the purpose. On the other hand, the effect may be inverted. Men of factious tempers, of local prejudices, or of sinister designs, may, by intrigue, by corruption, or by other means, first obtain the suffrages, and then betray the interests of the people. The question resulting is, whether small or extensive Republics are most favorable to the election of proper guardians of the public weal; and it is clearly decided in favor of the latter by two obvious considerations.

In the first place it is to be remarked that however small the Republic may be, the Representatives must be raised to a certain number in order to guard against the cabals of a few; and that however large it may be they must be limited to a certain number in order to guard against the confusion of a multitude. Hence, the number of Representatives in the two cases not being in proportion to that of the Constituents, and being proportionally greatest in the small Republic, it follows that if the proportion of fit characters be not less in the large than in the small Republic, the former will present a greater option, and consequently a greater probability of a fit choice.

In the next place, as each Representative will be chosen by a greater number of citizens in the large than in the small Republic, it will be more difficult for unworthy candidates to practise with success the vicious arts by which elections are too often carried; and the suffrages of the people being more free, will be more likely to centre on men who possess the most attractive merit and the most diffusive and established characters.

It must be confessed that in this, as in most other cases, there is a mean, on both sides of which inconveniencies will be found to lie. By enlarging too much the number of electors, you render the representative too little acquainted with all their local circumstances and lesser interests; as by reducing it too much, you render him unduly attached to these, and too little fit to comprehend and pursue great and national objects. The Federal Constitution forms a happy combination in this respect; the great and aggregate interests being referred to the national, the local and particular to the State legislatures.

The other point of difference is the greater number of citizens and extent of territory which may be brought within the compass of Republican than of Democratic Government; and it is this circumstance principally which renders factious combinations less to be dreaded in the former than in the latter. The smaller the society, the fewer probably will be the distinct parties and interests composing it; the fewer the distinct parties and interests, the more frequently will a majority be found of the same party; and the smaller the number of individuals composing a majority, and the smaller the compass within which they are placed, the more easily will they concert and execute their plans of oppression. Extend the sphere and you take in a greater variety of parties and interests; you make it less probable that a majority of the whole will have a common motive to invade the rights of other citizens; or if such a common motive exists, it will be more difficult for all who feel it to discover their own strength and to act in unison with each other. Besides other impediments, it may be remarked, that where there is a consciousness of unjust or dishonorable purposes, communication is always checked by distrust in proportion to the number whose concurrence is necessary.

Hence, it clearly appears that the same advantage which a Republic has over a Democracy in controlling the effects of faction is enjoyed by a large over a small republic—is enjoyed by the Union over the States composing it. Does this advantage consist in the substitution of representatives whose enlightened views and virtuous sentiments render them superior to local prejudices and to schemes of injustice? It will not be denied that the representation of the Union will be most likely to possess these requisite endowments.

Does it consist in the greater security afforded by a greater variety of parties, against the event of any one party being able to outnumber and oppress the rest? In an equal degree does the increased variety of parties comprised within the Union increase this security? Does it, in fine, consist in the greater obstacles opposed to the concert and accomplishment of the secret wishes of an unjust and interested majority? Here again the extent of the Union gives it the most palpable advantage.

The influence of factious leaders may kindle a flame within their particular States but will be unable to spread a general conflagration through the other States: a religious sect may degenerate into a political faction in a part of the Confederacy; but the variety of sects dispersed over the entire face of it must secure the national Councils against any danger from that source: a rage for paper money, for an abolition of debts, for an equal division of property, or for any other improper or wicked project, will be less apt to pervade the whole body of the Union than a particular member of it; in the same proportion as such a malady is more likely to taint a particular county or district than an entire State.

In the extent and proper structure of the Union, therefore, we behold a republican remedy for the diseases most incident to Republican Government. And according to the degree of pleasure and pride we feel in being republicans ought to be our zeal in cherishing the spirit and supporting the character of federalist.

PUBLIUS
November 22, 1787

NO. 51: MADISON

To what expedient, then, shall we finally resort, for maintaining in practice the necessary partition of power among the several departments as laid down in the constitution? The only answer that can be given is that as all these exterior provisions are found to be inadequate the defect must be supplied, by so contriving the interior structure of the government as that its several constituent parts may, by their mutual relations, be the means of keeping each other in their proper places. Without presuming to undertake a full development of this important idea I will hazard a few general observations which may perhaps place it in a clearer light, and enable us to form a more correct judgment of the principles and structure of the government planned by the convention.

In order to lay a due foundation for that separate and distinct exercise of the different powers of government, which to a certain extent is admitted on all hands to be essential to the preservation of liberty, it is evident that each department should have a will of its own; and consequently should be so constituted that the members of each should have as little agency as possible in the appointment of the members of the others. Were this principle rigorously adhered to, it would require that all the appointments for the supreme executive, legislative, and judiciary magistracies should be drawn from the same fountain of authority, the people, through channels having no communication whatever with one another. Perhaps such a plan of constructing the several departments would be less difficult in practice than it may in contemplation appear. Some difficulties, however, and some additional expense would attend the execution of it. Some deviations, therefore, from the principle must be admitted. In the constitution of the judiciary department in particular, it might be inexpedient to insist rigorously on the principle: first, because peculiar qualifications being essential in the members, the primary consideration ought to be to select that mode of choice which best secures these qualifications; second, because the permanent tenure by which the appointments are held in that department must soon destroy all sense of dependence on the authority conferring them.

It is equally evident that the members of each department should be as little dependent as possible on those of the others for the emoluments annexed to their offices. Were the executive magistrate, or the judges, not independent of the legislature in this particular, their independence in every other would be merely nominal.

But the great security against a gradual concentration of the several powers in the same department consists in giving to those who administer each department the necessary constitutional means and personal motives to resist encroachments of the others. The provision for defence must in this, as in all other cases, be made commensurate to the danger of attack. Ambition must be made to counteract ambition. The interest of the man must be connected with the constitutional rights of the place. It may be a reflection on human nature that such devices should be necessary to control the abuses of government. But what is government itself but the greatest of all reflections on human nature? If men were angels, no government would be necessary. If angels were to govern men, neither external nor internal controls on government would be necessary. In framing a government which is to be administered by men over men, the great difficulty lies in this: You must first enable the government to control the governed; and in the next place oblige it to control itself. A dependence on the people is, no doubt, the primary control on the government; but experience has taught mankind the necessity of auxiliary precautions.

This policy of supplying, by opposite and rival interests, the defect of better motives, might be traced through the whole system of human affairs, private as well as public. We see it particularly displayed in all the subordinate distributions of power, where the constant aim is to divide and arrange the several offices in such a manner as that each may be a check on the other; that the private interest of every individual may be a sentinel over the public rights. These inventions of prudence cannot be less requisite in the distribution of the supreme powers of the State.

But it is not possible to give to each department an equal power of self-defense. In republican government, the legislative authority necessarily predominates. The remedy for this inconveniency is to divide the legislature into different branches; and to render them, by different modes of election and different principles of action, as little connected with each other as the nature of their common functions and their common dependence on the society will admit. It may even be necessary to guard against dangerous encroachments by still further precautions. As the weight of the legislative authority requires that it should be thus divided, the weakness of the executive may require, on the other hand, that it should be fortified. An absolute negative on the legislature appears, at first view, to be the natural defense with which the executive magistrate should be armed. But perhaps it would be neither altogether safe nor alone sufficient. On ordinary occasions it might not be exerted with the requisite firmness, and on extraordinary occasions it might be perfidiously abused. May not this defect of an absolute negative be supplied by some qualified connection between this weaker branch of the stronger department, by which the latter may be led to support the constitutional rights of the former, without being too much detached from the rights of its own department?

If the principles on which these observations are founded be just, as I persuade myself they are, and they be applied as a criterion to the several State constitutions, and to the federal Constitution, it will be found that if the latter does not perfectly correspond with them, the former are infinitely less able to bear such a test.

There are, moreover, two considerations particularly applicable to the federal system of America, which place that system in a very interesting point of view.

First. In a single republic, all the power surrendered by the people is submitted to the administration of a single government; and usurpations are guarded against by a division of the government into distinct and separate departments. In the compound republic of America, the power surrendered by the people is first divided between two distinct governments, and then the portion allotted to each subdivided among distinct and separate departments. Hence a double security arises to the rights of the people. The different governments will control each other, at the same time that each will be controlled by itself.

Second. It is of great importance in a republic not only to guard the society against the oppression of its rulers, but to guard one part of the society against the injustice of the other part. Different interests necessarily exist in different classes of citizens. If a majority be united by a common interest, the rights of the minority will be insecure. There are but two methods of providing against this evil: The one by creating a will in the community independent of the majority—that is, of the society itself; the other, by comprehending in the society so many separate descriptions of citizens as will render an unjust combination of a majority of the whole very improbable, if not impracticable. The first method prevails in all governments possessing an hereditary or self-appointed authority. This, at best, is but a precarious security; because a power independent of the society may as well espouse the unjust views of the major as the rightful interests of the minor party, and may possibly be turned against both parties. The second method will be exemplified in the federal republic of the United States. Whilst all authority in it will be derived from and dependent on the society, the society itself will be broken into so many parts, interests and classes of citizens, that the rights of individuals, or of the minority, will be in little danger from interested combinations of the majority. In a free government the security for civil rights must be the same as that for religious rights. It consists in the one case in the multiplicity of interests, and in the other in the multiplicity of sects. The degree of security in both cases will depend on the number of interests and sects; and this may be presumed to depend on the extent of country and number of people comprehended under the same government. This view of the subject must particularly recommend a proper federal system to all the sincere and considerate friends of republican government: Since it shows that in exact proportion as the territory of the Union may be formed into more circumscribed Confederacies, or States, oppressive combinations of a majority will be facilitated; the best security, under the republican form, for the rights of every class of citizens, will be diminished; and consequently the stability and independence of some member of the government, the only other security, must be proportionally increased. Justice is the end of government. It is the end of civil society. It ever has been and ever will be pursued until it be obtained, or until liberty be lost in the pursuit. In a society under the forms of which the stronger faction can readily unite and oppress the weaker, anarchy may as truly be said to reign as in a state of nature, where the weaker individual is not secured against the violence of the stronger: And as, in the latter state, even the stronger individuals are prompted, by the uncertainty of their condition, to submit to a government which may protect the weak as well as themselves: So, in the former state, will the more powerful factions or parties be gradually induced, by a like motive, to wish for a government which will protect all parties, the weaker as well as the more powerful. It can be little doubted that if the State of Rhode Island was separated from the Confederacy and left to itself, the insecurity of rights under the popular form of government within such narrow limits would be displayed by such reiterated oppressions of factious majorities that some power altogether independent of the people would soon be called for by the voice of the very factions whose misrule had proved the necessity of it. In the extended republic of the United States, and among the great variety of interests, parties, and sects which it embraces, a coalition of a majority of the whole society could seldom take place on any other principles than those of justice and the general good; and there being thus less danger to a minor from the will of the major party, there must be less pretext, also, to provide for the security of the former, by introducing into the government a will not dependent on the latter, or, in other words, a will independent of the society itself. It is no less certain than it is important, notwithstanding the contrary opinions which have been entertained, that the larger the society, provided it lie within a practicable sphere, the more duly capable it will be of self-government. And happily for the *republican cause,* practicable sphere may be carried to a very great extent by a judicious modification and mixture of the *federal principle.*

PUBLIUS
February 6, 1788

The Anti-Federalist Papers

Essay by Brutus in the *New York Journal*

When the public is called to investigate and decide upon a question in which not only the present members of the community are deeply interested, but upon which the happiness and misery of generations yet unborn is in great measure suspended, the benevolent mind cannot help feeling itself peculiarly interested in the result.

In this situation, I trust the feeble efforts of an individual, to lead the minds of the people to a wise and prudent determination, cannot fail of being acceptable to the candid and dispassionate part of the community. Encouraged by this consideration, I have been induced to offer my thoughts upon the present important crisis of our public affairs.

Perhaps this country never saw so critical a period in their political concerns. We have felt the feebleness of the ties by which these United-States are held together, and the want of sufficient energy in our present confederation, to manage, in some instances, our general concerns. Various expedients have been proposed to remedy these evils, but none have succeeded. At length a Convention of the states has been assembled, they have formed a constitution which will now, probably, be submitted to the people to ratify or reject, who are the fountain of all power, to whom alone it of right belongs to make or unmake constitutions, or forms of government, at their pleasure. The most important question that was ever proposed to your decision, or to the decision of any people under heaven, is before you, and you are to decide upon it by men of your own election, chosen specially for this purpose. If the constitution, offered to your acceptance, be a wise one, calculated to preserve the invaluable blessings of liberty, to secure the inestimable rights of mankind, and promote human happiness, then, if you accept it, you will lay a lasting foundation of happiness for millions yet unborn; generations to come will rise up and call you blessed. You may rejoice in the prospects of this vast extended continent becoming filled with freemen, who will assert the dignity of human nature. You may solace yourselves with the idea, that society, in this favoured land, will fast advance to the highest point of perfection; the human mind will expand in knowledge and virtue, and the golden age be, in some measure, realised. But if, on the other hand, this form of government contains principles that will lead to the subversion of liberty—if it tends to establish a despotism, or, what is worse, a tyrannic aristocracy; then, if you adopt it, this only remaining assylum for liberty will be shut up, and posterity will execrate your memory.

Momentous then is the question you have to determine, and you are called upon by every motive which should influence a noble and virtuous mind, to examine it well, and to make up a wise judgment. It is insisted, indeed, that this constitution must be received, be it ever so imperfect. If it has its defects, it is said, they can be best amended when they are experienced. But remember, when the people once part with power, they can seldom or never resume it again but by force. Many instances can be produced in which the people have voluntarily increased the powers of their rulers; but few, if any, in which rulers have willingly abridged their authority. This is a sufficient reason to induce you to be careful, in the first instance, how you deposit the powers of government.

With these few introductory remarks, I shall proceed to a consideration of this constitution:

The first question that presents itself on the subject is, whether a confederated government be the best for the United States or not? Or in other words, whether the thirteen United States should be reduced to one great republic, governed by one legislature, and under the direction of one executive and judicial; or whether they should continue thirteen confederated republics, under the direction and controul of a supreme federal head for certain defined national purposes only?

This enquiry is important, because, although the government reported by the convention does not go to a perfect and entire consolidation, yet it approaches so near to it, that it must, if executed, certainly and infallibly terminate in it.

This government is to possess absolute and uncontroulable power, legislative, executive and judicial, with respect to every object to which it extends, for by the last clause of section 8th, article 1st, it is declared "that the Congress shall have power to make all laws which shall be necessary and proper for carrying into execution the foregoing powers, and all other powers vested by this constitution, in the government of the United States; or in any department or office thereof." And by the 6th article, it is declared "that this constitution, and the laws of the United States, which shall be made in pursuance thereof, and the treaties made, or which shall be made, under the authority of the United States, shall be the supreme law of the land; and the judges in every state shall be bound thereby, any thing in the constitution, or law of any state to the contrary notwithstanding." It appears from these articles that there is no need of any intervention of the state governments, between the Congress and the people, to execute any one power vested in the general government, and that the constitution and laws of every state are nullified and declared void, so far as they are or shall be inconsistent with this constitution, or the laws made in pursuance of it, or with treaties made under the authority of the United States.—The government then, so far as it extends, is a complete one, and not a confederation. It is as much one complete government as that of New-York or Massachusetts, has as absolute and perfect powers to make and execute all laws, to appoint officers, institute courts, declare offences, and annex penalties, with respect to every object to which it extends, as any other in the world. So far therefore as its powers reach, all ideas of confederation are given up and lost. It is true this government is limited to certain objects, or to speak more properly, some small degree of power is still left to the states, but a little attention to the powers vested in the general government, will convince every candid man, that if it is capable of being executed, all that is reserved for the individual states must very soon be annihilated, except so far as they are barely necessary to the organization of the general government. The powers of the general legislature extend to every case that is of the least importance—there is nothing valuable to human nature, nothing dear to freemen, but what is within its power. It has authority to make laws which will affect the lives, the liberty, and property of every man in the United States; nor can the constitution or laws of any state, in any way prevent or impede the full and complete execution of every power given. The legislative power is competent to lay taxes, duties, imposts, and excises;—there is no limitation to this power, unless it be said that the clause which directs the use to which those taxes, and duties shall be applied, may be said to be a limitation: but this is no restriction of the power at all, for by this clause they are to be applied to pay the debts and provide for the common defence and general welfare of the United States; but the legislature have authority to contract debts at their discretion; they are the sole judges of what is necessary to provide for the common defence, and they only are to determine what is for the general welfare; this power therefore is neither more nor less, than a power to lay and collect taxes, imposts, and excises, at their pleasure; not only [is] the power to lay taxes unlimited, as to the amount they may require, but it is perfect and absolute to raise them in any mode they please. No state legislature, or any power in the state governments, have any more to do in carrying this into effect, than the authority of one state has to do with that of another. In the business therefore of laying and collecting taxes, the idea of confederation is totally lost, and that of one entire republic is embraced. It is proper here to remark, that the authority to lay and collect taxes is the most important of any power that can be granted; it connects with it almost all other powers, or at least will in process of time draw all other after it; it is the great mean of protection, security, and defence, in a good government, and the great engine of oppression and tyranny in a bad one. This cannot fail of being the case, if we consider the contracted limits which are set by this constitution, to the late [state?] governments, on this article of raising money. No state can emit paper money—lay any duties, or imposts, on imports, or exports, but by consent of the Congress; and then the net produce shall be for the benefit of the United States: the only mean therefore left, for any state to support its government and discharge its debts, is by direct taxation; and the United States have also power to lay and collect taxes, in any way they please. Every one who has thought on the subject, must be convinced that but small sums of money can be collected in any country, by direct taxe[s], when the foederal government begins to exercise the right of taxation in all its parts, the legislatures of the several states will find it impossible to raise monies to support their governments. Without money they cannot be supported, and they must dwindle away, and, as before observed, their powers absorbed in that of the general government.

It might be here shewn, that the power in the federal legislative, to raise and support armies at pleasure, as well in peace as in war, and their controul over the militia, tend, not only to a consolidation of the government, but the destruction of liberty.—I shall not, however, dwell upon these, as a few observations upon the judicial power of this government, in addition to the preceding, will fully evince the truth of the position.

The judicial power of the United States is to be vested in a supreme court, and in such inferior courts as Congress may from time to time ordain and establish. The powers of these courts are very extensive; their jurisdiction comprehends all civil causes, except such as arise between citizens of the same state; and it extends to all cases in law and equity arising under the constitution. One inferior court must be established, I presume, in each state, at least, with the necessary executive officers appandant thereto. It is easy to see, that in the common course of things, these courts will eclipse the dignity, and take away from the respectability, of the state courts. These courts will be, in themselves, totally independent of the states, deriving their authority from the United States, and receiving from them fixed salaries; and in the course of human events it is to be expected, that they will swallow up all the powers of the courts in the respective states.

How far the clause in the 8th section of the 1st article may operate to do away all idea of confederated states, and to effect an entire consolidation of the whole into one general government, it is impossible to say. The powers given by this article are very general and comprehensive, and it may receive a construction to justify the passing almost any law. A power to make all laws, which shall be *necessary and proper*, for carrying into execution, all powers vested by the constitution in the government of the United States, or any department or officer thereof, is a power very comprehensive and definite [indefinite?], and may, for ought I know, be exercised in a such manner as entirely to abolish the state legislatures. Suppose the legislature of a state should pass a law to raise money to support their government and pay the state debt, may the Congress repeal this law, because it may prevent the collection of a tax which they may think proper and necessary to lay, to provide for the general welfare of the United States? For all laws made, in pursuance of this constitution, are the supreme lay of the land, and the judges in every state shall be bound thereby, any thing in the constitution or laws of the different states to the contrary notwithstanding.—By such a law, the government of a particular state might be overturned at one stroke, and thereby be deprived of every means of its support.

It is not meant, by stating this case, to insinuate that the constitution would warrant a law of this kind; or unnecessarily to alarm the fears of the people, by suggesting, that the federal legislature would be more likely to pass the limits assigned them by the constitution, than that of an individual state, further than they are less responsible to the people. But what is meant is, that the legislature of the United States are vested with the great and uncontroulable powers, of laying and collecting taxes, duties, imposts, and excises; of regulating trade, raising and supporting armies, organizing, arming, and disciplining the militia, instituting courts, and other general powers. And are by this clause invested with the power of making all laws, *proper and necessary*, for carrying all these into execution; and they may so exercise this power as entirely to annihilate all the state governments, and reduce this country to one single government. And if they may do it, it is pretty certain they will; for it will be found that the power retained by individual states, small as it is, will be a clog upon the wheels of the government of the United States; the latter therefore will be naturally inclined to remove it out of the way. Besides, it is a truth confirmed by the unerring experience of ages, that every man, and every body of men, invested with power, are ever disposed to increase it, and to acquire a superiority over every thing that stands in their way. This disposition, which is implanted in human nature, will operate in the federal legislature to lessen and ultimately to subvert the state authority, and having such advantages, will most certainly succeed, if the federal government succeeds at all. It must be very evident then, that what this constitution wants of being a complete consolidation of the several parts of the union into one complete government, possessed of perfect legislative, judicial, and executive powers, to all intents and purposes, it will necessarily acquire in its exercise and operation.

Let us now proceed to enquire, as I at first proposed, whether it be best the thirteen United States should be reduced to one great republic, or not? It is here taken for granted, that all agree in this, that whatever government we adopt, it ought to be a free one; that it should be so framed as to secure the liberty of the citizens of America, and such an one as to admit of a full, fair, and equal representation of the people. The question then will be, whether a government thus constituted, and founded on such principles, is practicable, and can be exercised over the whole United States, reduced into one state?

If respect is to be paid to the opinion of the greatest and wisest men who have ever thought or wrote on the science of government, we shall be constrained to conclude, that a free republic cannot succeed over a country of such immense extent, containing such a number of inhabitants, and these encreasing in such rapid progression as that of the whole United States. Among the many illustrious authorities which might be produced to this point, I shall content myself with quoting only two. The one is the baron de Montesquieu, spirit of laws, chap. xvi. vol. I [book VIII]. "It is natural to a republic to have only a small territory, otherwise it cannot long subsist. In a large republic there are men of large fortunes, and consequently of less moderation; there are trusts too great to be placed in any single subject; he has interest of his own; he soon begins to think that he may be happy, great and glorious, by oppressing his fellow citizens; and that he may raise himself to grandeur on the ruins of his country. In a large republic, the public good is sacrificed to a thousand views; it is subordinate to exceptions, and depends on accidents. In a small one, the interest of the public is easier perceived, better understood, and more within the reach of every citizen; abuses are of less extent, and of course are less protected." Of the same opinion is the marquis Beccarari.

History furnishes no example of a free republic, any thing like the extent of the United States. The Grecian republics were of small extent; so also was that of the Romans. Both of these, it is true, in process of time, extended their conquests over large territories of country; and the consequence was, that their governments were changed from that of free governments to those of the most tyrannical that ever existed in the world.

Not only the opinion of the greatest men, and the experience of mankind, are against the idea of an extensive republic, but a variety of reasons may be drawn from the reason and nature of things, against it. In every government, the will of the sovereign is the law. In despotic governments, the supreme authority being lodged in one, his will is law, and can be as easily expressed to a large extensive territory as to a small one. In a pure democracy the people are the sovereign, and their will is declared by themselves; for this purpose they must all come together to deliberate, and decide. This kind of government cannot be exercised, therefore, over a country of any considerable extent; it must be confined to a single city, or at least limited to such bounds as that the people can conveniently assemble, be able to debate, understand the subject submitted to them, and declare their opinion concerning it.

In a free republic, although all laws are derived from the consent of the people, yet the people do not declare their consent by themselves in person, but by representatives, chosen by them, who are supposed to know the minds of their constituents, and to be possessed of integrity to declare this mind.

In every free government, the people must give their assent to the laws by which they are governed. This is the true criterion between a free government and an arbitrary one. The former are ruled by the will of the whole, expressed in any manner they may agree upon; the latter by the will of one, or a few. If the people are to give their assent to the laws, by persons chosen and appointed by them, the manner of the choice and the number chosen, must be such, as to possess, be disposed, and consequently qualified to declare the sentiments of the people; for if they do not know, or are not disposed to speak the sentiments of the people, the people do not govern, but the sovereignty is in a few. Now, in a large extended country, it is impossible to have a representation, possessing the sentiments, and of integrity, to declare the minds of the people, without having it so numerous and unwieldly, as to be subject in great measure to the inconveniency of a democratic government.

The territory of the United States is of vast extent; it now contains near three millions of souls, and is capable of containing much more than ten times that number. Is it practicable for a country, so large and so numerous as they will soon become, to elect a representation, that will speak their sentiments, without their becoming so numerous as to be incapable of transacting public business? It certainly is not.

In a republic, the manners, sentiments, and interests of the people should be similar. If this be not the case, there will be a constant clashing of opinions; and the representatives of one part will be continually striving against those of the other. This will retard the operations of government, and prevent such conclusions as will promote the public good. If we apply this remark to the condition of the United States, we shall be convinced that it forbids that we should be one government. The United States includes a variety of climates. The productions of the different parts of the union are very variant, and their interests, of consequence, diverse. Their manners and habits differ as much as their climates and productions; and their sentiments are by no means coincident. The laws and customs of the several states are, in many respects, very diverse, and in some opposite; each would be in favor of its own interests and customs, and, of consequence, a legislature, formed of representatives from the respective parts, would not only be too numerous to act with any care or decision, but would be composed of such heterogenous and discordant principles, as would constantly be contending with each other.

The laws cannot be executed in a republic, of an extent equal to that of the United States, with promptitude.

The magistrates in every government must be supported in the execution of the laws, either by an armed force, maintained at the public expence for that purpose; or by the people turning out to aid the magistrate upon his command, in case of resistance.

In despotic governments, as well as in all the monarchies of Europe, standing armies are kept up to execute the commands of the prince or the magistrate, and are employed for this purpose when occasion requires: But they have always proved the destruction of liberty, and [are] abhorrent to the spirit of a free republic. In England, where they depend upon the parliament for their annual support, they have always been complained of as oppressive and unconstitutional, and are seldom employed in executing of the laws; never except on extraordinary occasions, and then under the direction of a civil magistrate.

A free republic will never keep a standing army to execute its laws. It must depend upon the support of its citizens. But when a government is to receive its support from the aid of the citizens, it must be so constructed as to have the confidence, respect, and affection of the people. Men who, upon the call of the magistrate, offer themselves to execute the laws, are influenced to do it either by affection to the government, or from fear; where a standing army is at hand to punish offenders, every man is actuated by the latter principle, and therefore, when the magistrate calls, will obey: but, where this is not the case, the government must rest for its support upon the confidence and respect which the people have for their government and laws. The body of the people being attached, the government will always be sufficient to support and execute its laws, and to operate upon the fears of any faction which may be opposed to it, not only to prevent an opposition to the execution of the laws themselves, but also to compel the most of them to aid the magistrate; but the people will not be likely to have such confidence in their rulers, in a republic so extensive as the United States, as necessary for these purposes. The confidence which the people have in their rulers, in a free republic, arises from their knowing them, from their being responsible to them for their conduct, and from the power they have of displacing them when they misbehave: but in a republic of the extent of this continent, the people in general would be acquainted with very few of their rulers: the people at large would know little of their proceedings, and it would be extremely difficult to change them. The people in Georgia and New-Hampshire would not know one another's mind, and therefore could not act in concert to enable them to effect a general change of representatives. The different parts of so extensive a country could not possibly be made acquainted with the conduct of their representatives, nor be informed of the reasons upon which measures were founded. The consequence will be, they will have no confidence in their legislature, suspect them of ambitious views, be jealous of every measure they adopt, and will not support the laws they pass. Hence the government will be nerveless and inefficient, and no way will be left to render it otherwise, but by establishing an armed force to execute the laws at the point of the bayonet—a government of all others the most to be dreaded.

In a republic of such vast extent as the United-States, the legislature cannot attend to the various concerns and wants of its different parts. It cannot be sufficiently numerous to be acquainted with the local condition and wants of the different districts, and if it could, it is impossible it should have sufficient time to attend to and provide for all the variety of cases of this nature, that would be continually arising.

In so extensive a republic, the great officers of government would soon become above the controul of the people, and abuse their power to the purpose of aggrandizing themselves, and oppressing them. The trust committed to the executive offices, in a country of the extent of the United-States, must be various and of magnitude. The command of all the troops and navy of the republic, the appointment of officers, the power of pardoning offences, the collecting of all the public revenues, and the power of expending them, with a number of other powers, must be lodged and exercised in every state, in the hands of a few. When these are attended with great honor and emolument, as they always will be in large states, so as greatly to interest men to pursue them, and to be proper objects for ambitious and designing men, such men will be ever restless in their pursuit after them. They will use the power, when they have acquired it, to the purposes of gratifying their own interest and ambition, and it is scarcely possible, in a very large republic, to call them to account for their misconduct, or to prevent their abuse of power.

These are some of the reasons by which it appears, that a free republic cannot long subsist over a country of the great extent of these states. If then this new constitution is calculated to consolidate the thirteen states into one, as it evidently is, it ought not to be adopted.

Though I am of opinion, that it is a sufficient objection to this government, to reject it, that it creates the whole union into one government, under the form of a republic, yet if this objection was obviated, there are exceptions to it, which are so material and fundamental, that they ought to determine every man, who is a friend to the liberty and happiness of mankind, not to adopt it. I beg the candid and dispassionate attention of my countrymen while I state these objections—they are such as have obtruded themselves upon my mind upon a careful attention to the matter, and such as I sincerely believe are well founded. There are many objections, of small moment, of which I shall take no notice—perfection is not to be expected in any thing that is the production of man—and if I did not in my conscience believe that this scheme was defective in the fundamental principles—in the foundation upon which a free and equal government must rest—I would hold my peace.

BRUTUS
October 18, 1787

Presidents and Vice Presidents

PRESIDENT	VICE PRESIDENT
1 George Washington *(Federalist 1789)*	John Adams *(Federalist 1789)*
2 John Adams *(Federalist 1797)*	Thomas Jefferson *(Dem.-Rep. 1797)*
3 Thomas Jefferson *(Dem.-Rep. 1801)*	Aaron Burr *(Dem.-Rep. 1801)*
	George Clinton *(Dem.-Rep. 1805)*
4 James Madison *(Dem.-Rep. 1809)*	George Clinton *(Dem.-Rep. 1809)*
	Elbridge Gerry *(Dem.-Rep. 1813)*
5 James Monroe *(Dem.-Rep. 1817)*	Daniel D. Tompkins *(Dem.-Rep. 1817)*
6 John Quincy Adams *(Dem.-Rep. 1825)*	John C. Calhoun *(Dem.-Rep. 1825)*
7 Andrew Jackson *(Democratic 1829)*	John C. Calhoun *(Democratic 1829)*
	Martin Van Buren *(Democratic 1833)*
8 Martin Van Buren *(Democratic 1837)*	Richard M. Johnson *(Democratic 1837)*
9 William H. Harrison *(Whig 1841)*	John Tyler *(Whig 1841)*
10 John Tyler *(Whig and Democratic 1841)*	
11 James K. Polk *(Democratic 1845)*	George M. Dallas *(Democratic 1845)*
12 Zachary Taylor *(Whig 1849)*	Millard Fillmore *(Whig 1849)*
13 Millard Fillmore *(Whig 1850)*	
14 Franklin Pierce *(Democratic 1853)*	William R. D. King *(Democratic 1853)*

PRESIDENT	VICE PRESIDENT
15 James Buchanan *(Democratic 1857)*	John C. Breckinridge *(Democratic 1857)*
16 Abraham Lincoln *(Republican 1861)*	Hannibal Hamlin *(Republican 1861)* Andrew Johnson *(Unionist 1865)*
17 Andrew Johnson (Unionist 1865)	
18 Ulysses S. Grant *(Republican 1869)*	Schuyler Colfax *(Republican 1869)* Henry Wilson *(Republican 1873)*
19 Rutherford B. Hayes *(Republican 1877)*	William A. Wheeler *(Republican 1877)*
20 James A. Garfield *(Republican 1881)*	Chester A. Arthur *(Republican 1881)*
21 Chester A. Arthur *(Republican 1881)*	
22 Grover Cleveland *(Democratic 1885)*	Thomas A. Hendricks *(Democratic 1885)*
23 Benjamin Harrison *(Republican 1889)*	Levi P. Morton *(Republican 1889)*
24 Grover Cleveland *(Democratic 1893)*	Adlai E. Stevenson *(Democratic 1893)*
25 William McKinley *(Republican 1897)*	Garret A. Hobart *(Republican 1897)* Theodore Roosevelt *(Republican 1901)*
26 Theodore Roosevelt *(Republican 1901)*	Charles W. Fairbanks *(Republican 1905)*
27 William H. Taft *(Republican 1909)*	James S. Sherman *(Republican 1909)*
28 Woodrow Wilson *(Democratic 1913)*	Thomas R. Marshall *(Democratic 1913)*
29 Warren G. Harding *(Republican 1921)*	Calvin Coolidge *(Republican 1921)*
30 Calvin Coolidge *(Republican 1923)*	Charles G. Dawes *(Republican 1925)*

PRESIDENT	VICE PRESIDENT
31 Herbert Hoover *(Republican 1929)*	Charles Curtis *(Republican 1929)*
32 Franklin D. Roosevelt *(Democratic 1933)*	John Nance Garner *(Democratic 1933)*
	Henry A. Wallace *(Democratic 1941)*
	Harry S. Truman *(Democratic 1945)*
33 Harry S. Truman *(Democratic 1945)*	Alben W. Barkley *(Democratic 1949)*
34 Dwight D. Eisenhower *(Republican 1953)*	Richard M. Nixon *(Republican 1953)*
35 John F. Kennedy *(Democratic 1961)*	Lyndon B. Johnson *(Democratic 1961)*
36 Lyndon B. Johnson *(Democratic 1963)*	Hubert H. Humphrey *(Democratic 1965)*
37 Richard M. Nixon *(Republican 1969)*	Spiro T. Agnew *(Republican 1969)*
	Gerald R. Ford *(Republican 1973)*
38 Gerald R. Ford *(Republican 1974)*	Nelson Rockefeller *(Republican 1974)*
39 James E. Carter *(Democratic 1977)*	Walter Mondale *(Democratic 1977)*
40 Ronald Reagan *(Republican 1981)*	George H. W. Bush *(Republican 1981)*
41 George H. W. Bush *(Republican 1989)*	J. Danforth Quayle *(Republican 1989)*
42 William J. Clinton *(Democratic 1993)*	Albert Gore, Jr. *(Democratic 1993)*
43 George W. Bush *(Republican 2001)*	Richard Cheney *(Republican 2001)*
44 Barack H. Obama *(Democratic 2009)*	Joseph R. Biden, Jr. *(Democratic 2009)*
45 Donald J. Trump *(Republican 2017)*	Michael R. Pence *(Republican 2017)*

Endnotes

CHAPTER 1

1. Lindsey Bever, "Meet Saira Blair, 18, Soon to Be the Nation's Youngest Lawmaker," *Washington Post,* November 7, 2014, www.washingtonpost.com/news/morning-mix/wp/2014/11/07/meet-saira-blair-18-soon-to-be-the-nations-youngest-lawmaker/?utm_term=.708303648d03 (accessed 1/16/18); Lucy McCalmont, "Conservative, Lawmaker, Student," *Politico,* November 5, 2014, www.politico.com/story/2014/11/saira-blair-west-virginia-112602 (accessed 11/16/18); Jae Jones, "This Texas City Just Elected the Youngest City Council Member in the State," *The Nation,* June 1, 2017, www.thenation.com/article/texas-city-just-elected-youngest-person-hold-office-state/ (accessed 1/16/18); City of Prairie View, TX, Kendric Jones website, www.prairieviewtexas.gov/departments/kendric_jones_-_pos_3.php (accessed 1/16/18).
2. Arch Puddington and Tyler Roylance, *Freedom in the World,* 2016, Essay: Democratic Breakthroughs in the Balance," Freedom House, www.freedomhouse.org/sites/default/files/FH_FITW_Report_2016.pdf (accessed 4/10/16).
3. Eugen Weber, *Peasants into Frenchmen: The Modernization of Rural France, 1870–1914* (Stanford, CA: Stanford University Press, 1976), chap. 5.
4. Harold Lasswell, *Politics: Who Gets What, When, How* (New York: Meridian Books, 1958).
5. Abby Goodnough, "Maine Voters Approve Medicaid Expansion, a Rebuke of Gov. LePage," *New York Times,* November 7, 2017, www.nytimes.com/2017/11/07/us/maine-medicaid-healthcare.html (accessed 12/27/17).
6. This definition is taken from Norman H. Nie, Jane Junn, and Kenneth Stehlik-Barry, *Education and Democratic Citizenship in America* (Chicago: University of Chicago Press, 1996).
7. Kyle Dropp and Brendan Nyhan, "One-Third Don't Know Obamacare and Affordable Care Act Are The Same," *New York Times,* The Upshot, February 7, 2017, www.nytimes.com/2017/02/07/upshot/one-third-dont-know-obamacare-and-affordable-care-act-are-the-same.html?_r=0 (accessed 12/28/17).
8. John B. Horrigon and Lee Rainie, "Americans' Views on Open Government Data," Pew Research Center, April 21, 2015, www.pewinternet.org/2015/04/21/open-government-data/ (accessed 7/22/15).
9. Carroll Doherty, Jocelyn Kiley, Alec Tyson, and Bridget Jameson, Pew Research Center, "Beyond Distrust: How Americans View Their Government" November 23, 2015, http://assets.pewresearch.org/wp-content/uploads/sites/5/2015/11/11-23-2015-Governance-release.pdf (accessed 4/15/18).
10. Pew Research Center, "Beyond Distrust."
11. U.S. Census Bureau, Population Clock, April 15, 2018, www.census.gov/popclock/ (accessed 4/15/18).

12. Susan B. Carter et al., eds., *Historical Statistics of the United States: Millennial Edition Online* (New York: Cambridge University Press, 2006), Table Aa145–184, Population, by Sex and Race: 1790–1990, 23. Current data available at U.S. Census Bureau, www.census.gov (accessed 2/25/12).

13. Carter et al., *Historical Statistics of the United States*, Table Aa145–184, Population, by Sex and Race: 1790–1990, 23.

14. Carter et al., *Historical Statistics of the United States*, Table Aa145–184, Population, by Sex and Race: 1790–1990, 23; Table Aa2189–2215, Hispanic Population Estimates.

15. U.S. Census Bureau, "Statistical Abstract of the United States," www.census.gov (accessed 11/13/07); Claude S. Fischer and Michael Hout, *A Century of Difference: How America Changed in the Last One Hundred Years* (New York: Russell Sage Foundation, 2006), 36.

16. Carter et al., *Historical Statistics of the United States*, Table Aa22–35, Selected Population Characteristics.

17. Michael B. Katz and Mark J. Stern, *One Nation Divisible: What America Was and What It Is Becoming* (New York: Russell Sage Foundation, 2006), 16.

18. Carter et al., *Historical Statistics of the United States*, Table Aa145–184, Population, by Sex and Race: 1790–1990, 23; Karen R. Humes, Nicholas A. Jones, and Roberto R. Ramirez, "Overview of Race and Hispanic Origin: 2010. 2010 Census Briefs," no. C210BR-02 (Washington, DC: U.S. Census Bureau, March 2011), 4, www.census.gov/prod/cen2010/briefs/c2010br-02.pdf (accessed 10/14/2011).

19. U.S. Census Bureau, "2016 American Community Survey 1-Year Estimates: Selected Characteristics of the Native and Foreign-Born Populations."

20. U.S. Census Bureau, "2014 American Community Survey 1-Year Estimates," www.census.gov/popest/data/counties/asrh/2014/PEPSR6H.html (accessed 4/11/16).

21. Bryan Baker and Nancy Rytina, "Estimates of the Unauthorized Immigrant Population Residing in the United States: January 2012," *Population Estimates*, Office of Immigration Statistics, Department of Homeland Security, March 2013, www.dhs.gov/sites/default/files/publications/Unauthorized%20Immigrant%20Population%20Estimates%20in%20the%20US%20January%202012_0.pdf (accessed 12/26/17).

22. Robert P. Jones and Daniel Cox, "America's Changing Religious Identity, 2016," Public Religion Research Institute, September 6, 2017, www.prri.org/wp-content/uploads/2017/09/PRRI-Religion-Report.pdf (accessed 11/4/17).

23. Jones and Cox, "America's Changing Religious Identity."

24. U.S. Census Bureau, "Demographic Trends in the 20th Century, Table 5: Population by Age and Sex for the United States: 1900 to 2000," www.census.gov/prod/2002pubs/censr-4.pdf (accessed 4/11/16); U.S. Census Bureau, "Population Estimates, Age and Sex," www.census.gov/quickfacts/fact/table/US/PST045217 (accessed 12/26/17).

25. Central Intelligence Agency, "World Factbook: Urbanization," 2017, www.cia.gov/library/publications/the-world-factbook/fields/2212.html (accessed 4/15/18).

26. Thomas Piketty and Emmanuel Saez, "Income Inequality in the United States, 1913–1998," *Quarterly Journal of Economics* 18, no. 1 (2003), 1–39 (tables and figures updated to 2014, June 2015), elsa.berkeley.edu/~saez/TabFig2014prel.xls (accessed 4/11/16).

27. U.S. Census Bureau, "Income: Historical Income Data, Tables F-2, F-3, and F-6," www.census.gov/hhes/www/income/data/historical/index.html (accessed 4/12/16).

28. U.S. Census Bureau, "Historical Poverty Tables, Table 2: Poverty Status of People by Family Relationship, Race, and Hispanic Origin: 1959 to 2014," www.census.gov/hhes/www/poverty/data/historical/hstpov2.xls (accessed 4/11/16).

29. Jesse Sussell and James A. Thomson, "Are Changing Constituencies Driving Rising Polarization in the U.S. House of Representatives?" RAND Corporation Research

Report RR-396-RC, 2015, www.rand.org/pubs/research_reports/RR896.html (accessed 1/15/18).

30. Herbert McClosky and John Zaller, *The American Ethos: Public Attitudes toward Capitalism and Democracy* (Cambridge, MA: Harvard University Press, 1984), 19.

31. J. R. Pole, *The Pursuit of Equality in American History* (Berkeley: University of California Press, 1978), 19.

32. New York Times/CBS News Poll, "Americans' Views on Income Inequality and Workers' Rights," www.nytimes.com/interactive/2015/06/03/business/income -inequality-workers-rights-international-trade-poll.html (accessed 12/27/17); Frank Newport, "Majority Say Wealthy Americans, Corporations Taxed Too Little," April 18, 2017, news.gallup.com/poll/208685/majority-say-wealthy-americans -corporations-taxed-little.aspx (accessed 12/27/17).

33. Pew Research Center, "Public Trust in Government, 1958–2017," www.people-press .org/2017/05/03/public-trust-in-government-1958-2017/ (accessed 12/27/17).

34. Pew Research Center, "Public Trust in Government, 1958–2017."

35. Joseph S. Nye, Jr., "Introduction: The Decline of Confidence in Government," in *Why People Don't Trust Government*, ed. Joseph S. Nye, Philip D. Zelikow, and David C. King (Cambridge, MA: Harvard University Press, 1999), 4.

CHAPTER 2

1. "Jim Obergefell," *Biography*, 2015, www.biography.com/people/jim-obergefell (accessed 3/4/18).

2. *Obergefell v. Hodges* 576 U.S. __ (2015).

3. Richard E. Neustadt, *Presidential Power and the Modern Presidents: The Politics of Leadership from Roosevelt to Reagan* (New York: Simon & Schuster, 1991), 29

4. The social makeup of colonial America and some of the social conflicts that divided colonial society are discussed in Jackson Turner Main, *The Social Structure of Revolutionary America* (Princeton, NJ: Princeton University Press, 1965).

5. George B. Tindall and David E. Shi, *America: A Narrative History*, 8th ed. (New York: W. W. Norton, 2010), 202.

6. For a discussion of events leading up to the Revolution, see Charles M. Andrews, *The Colonial Background of the American Revolution* (New Haven, CT: Yale University Press, 1924).

7. See Carl Becker, *The Declaration of Independence* (New York: Knopf, 1942).

8. See Merrill Jensen, *The Articles of Confederation* (Madison: University of Wisconsin Press, 1970).

9. Reported in Samuel E. Morrison, Henry Steele Commager, and William Leuchtenburg, *The Growth of the American Republic*, vol. 1 (New York: Oxford University Press, 1969), 244.

10. Quoted in Morrison, Commager, and Leuchtenburg, *Growth of the American Republic*, 242.

11. Charles A. Beard, *An Economic Interpretation of the Constitution of the United States* (New York: Macmillan, 1913).

12. Max Farrand, ed., *The Records of the Federal Convention of 1787*, 4 vols., rev. ed., vol. 1 (New Haven, CT: Yale University Press, 1966).

13. Farrand, *Records of the Federal Convention of 1787*, 476.

14. Alexander Hamilton, James Madison, and John Jay, *The Federalist Papers*, ed. Clinton L. Rossiter (New York: New American Library, 1961), no. 71.

15. *The Federalist Papers*, no. 62.

16. *Marbury v. Madison*, 5 U.S. 137 (1803).

17. Max Farrand, *The Framing of the Constitution of the United States* (New Haven, CT: Yale University Press, 1962), 49.

18. Melancton Smith, quoted in Herbert J. Storing, *What the Anti-Federalists Were For* (Chicago: University of Chicago, 1981), 17.
19. *The Federalist Papers*, no. 57.
20. "Essays of Brutus," no. 15, in *The Complete Anti-Federalist*, ed. Herbert Storing (Chicago: University of Chicago Press, 1981).
21. *The Federalist Papers*, no. 10.
22. *The Federalist Papers*, no. 51.

CHAPTER 3

1. Steph Sherer, "Medical Marijuana Users Caught in State-Federal Conflict," CNN, November 10, 2014, www.cnn.com/2014/09/05/opinion/sherer-medical -marijuana-prosecutions/index.html (accessed 7/31/17).
2. National Council of State Legislatures, "State Medical Marijuana Laws," October 17, 2018, www.ncsl.org/research/health/state-medical-marijuana-laws.aspx (accessed 10/23/18); "33 Legal Medical Marijuana States and DC," November 7, 2018, https:// medicalmarijuana.procon.org/view.resource.php?resourceID=000881 (accessed 11/7/18).
3. Sherer, "Medical Marijuana Users."
4. John Hudak, "The Disorienting Effect of Marijuana on the Trump Administration," Brookings Institution, April 20, 2017, www.brookings.edu/blog/fixgov/2017/04/20/ disorienting-effects-of-marijuana-on-the-trump-administration/ (accessed 7/31/17).
5. ProCon.org, "35 States with Legal Gay Marriage and 15 States with Same-Sex Marriage Bans," updated November 20, 2014, http://gaymarriage.procon.org/view .resource.php?resourceID=004857 (accessed 5/11/16).
6. *United States v. Windsor*, 570 U.S. __ (2013).
7. *Hicklin v. Orbeck*, 437 U.S. 518 (1978).
8. *Sweeny v. Woodall*, 344 U.S. 86 (1952).
9. A good discussion of the constitutional position of local governments is in York Willbern, *The Withering Away of the City* (Bloomington: Indiana University Press, 1971). For more on the structure and theory of federalism, see Thomas R. Dye, *American Federalism: Competition among Governments* (Lexington, MA: Lexington Books, 1990), chap. 1, and Martha Derthick, "Up-to-Date in Kansas City: Reflections on American Federalism," 1992 John Gaus Lecture, *PS: Political Science and Politics* 25 (December 1992): 671–75.
10. For a good treatment of the contrast between national political stability and social instability, see Samuel P. Huntington, *Political Order in Changing Societies* (New Haven, CT: Yale University Press, 1968), chap. 2.
11. *McCulloch v. Maryland*, 17 U.S. 316 (1819).
12. *Gibbons v. Ogden*, 22 U.S. 1 (1824).
13. The Sherman Antitrust Act, adopted in 1890, for example, was enacted not to restrict commerce but rather to protect it from monopolies, or trusts, so as to prevent unfair trade practices and to enable the market again to become self-regulating. Moreover, the Supreme Court sought to uphold liberty of contract to protect businesses. For example, in *Lochner v. New York*, 198 U.S. 45 (1905), the Court invalidated a New York law regulating the sanitary conditions in bakeries and the hours of labor for bakers on the grounds that the law interfered with liberty of contract.
14. Kenneth T. Palmer, "The Evolution of Grant Policies," in *The Changing Politics of Federal Grants*, ed. Lawrence D. Brown, James W. Fossett, and Kenneth T. Palmer (Washington, DC: Brookings Institution Press, 1984), 15.
15. The key case in this process of expanding the power of the national government is generally considered to be *NLRB v. Jones & Laughlin Steel Corporation*, 301 U.S. 1

(1937), in which the Supreme Court approved federal regulation of the workplace and thereby virtually eliminated interstate commerce as a limit on the national government's power.

16. *United States v. Darby Lumber Co.*, 312 U.S. 100 (1941).
17. W. John Moore, "Pleading the 10th," *National Journal*, July 29, 1996, 1940.
18. *United States v. Lopez*, 514 U.S. 549 (1995).
19. *Printz v. United States*, 521 U.S. 898 (1997).
20. Morton Grodzins, *The American System*, ed. Daniel J. Elazar (Chicago: Rand McNally, 1966).
21. See Terry Sanford, *Storm over the States* (New York: McGraw-Hill, 1967).
22. James L. Sundquist, *Making Federalism Work*, with David W. Davis (Washington, DC: Brookings Institution Press, 1969), 271. Wallace was mistrusted by the architects of the War on Poverty because he was a strong proponent of racial segregation. He believed in "states' rights," which meant that states, not the federal government, should decide what liberty and equality meant.
23. See Don Kettl, *The Regulation of American Federalism* (Baton Rouge: Louisiana State University Press, 1983).
24. Eliza Newlin Carney, "Power Grab," *National Journal*, April 11, 1998, 798.
25. Philip Rucker, "Obama Curtails Bush's Policy of 'Preemption,'" *Washington Post*, May 22, 2009, A3.
26. See Advisory Commission on Intergovernmental Relations, *Federal Regulation of State and Local Governments: The Mixed Record of the 1980s* (Washington, DC: Advisory Commission on Intergovernmental Relations, July 1993).
27. Robert Jay Dilger and Richard S. Beth, "Unfunded Mandates Reform Act: History, Impact, and Issues" (Washington, DC: Congressional Research Service, April 19, 2011), 40, http://digital.library.unt.edu/ark:/67531/metadc40084/m1/1/high_res_d/R40957_2011Apr19.pdf (accessed 11/16/13).
28. Advisory Commission on Intergovernmental Relations, *Federal Regulation of State and Local Governments*, iii.
29. Advisory Commission on Intergovernmental Relations, *Federal Regulation of State and Local Governments*, 51.
30. Robert Frank, "Proposed Block Grants Seem Unlikely to Cure Management Problems," *Wall Street Journal*, May 1, 1995, 1.
31. Sarah Kershaw, "U.S. Rule Limits Emergency Care for Immigrants," *New York Times*, September 22, 2007, A1.
32. *National Federation of Independent Businesses v. Sebelius*, 567 U.S. __ (2012). Adam Liptak, "In Health Law, Asking Where U.S. Power Stops," *New York Times*, November 14, 2011, A1.
33. *King v. Burwell*, 576 U.S. __ (2015). Robert Barnes, "Affordable Care Act Survives Supreme Court Challenge," *Washington Post*, June 25, 2015, www.washingtonpost.com/politics/courts_law/obamacare-survives-supreme-court-challenge/2015/06/25/af87608e-188a-11e5-93b7-5eddc056ad8a_story.html (accessed 8/16/15).
34. National Conference of State Legislatures, "2013 Report on State Immigration Laws," www.ncsl.org/research/immigration/immgration-report-august-2013.aspx (accessed 11/3/13).
35. Terry Frieden, "Justice Department Sues Utah over State Immigration Law," CNN, November 22, 2011, www.cnn.com/2011/11/22/us/utah-immigration-law/ (accessed 4/21/16).
36. *Arizona v. United States*, 567 U.S. __ (2012).
37. *United States v. Texas,* 579 U.S. __ (2016).

38. Alexander Bolton, "GOP Looks for Plan B after Failure of Immigration Measures," The Hill, February 16, 2018, www.thehill. com/homenews/senate/374143-gop-looks -for-plan-b-after -failure-of-immigration-measures (accessed 2/18/18).

39. "Enhancing Public Safety in the Interior of the United States," Executive Order 13768, January 25, 2017, www.federalregister.gov/documents/2017/01/30/ 2017-02102/enhancing-public-safety-in-the-interior-of-the-united-states (accessed 7/27/17).

40. Vivian Yee and Rebecca R. Ruiz, "Sessions Once Again Threatens Sanctuary Cities," *New York Times*, July 26, 2017, www.nytimes.com/2017/07/26/us/politics/ sessions-sanctuary-cities.html?_r=0 (accessed 7/27/2017).

41. Rafael Bernal, "Momentum Builds for Bill to Help 'Dreamers'," The Hill, July 29, 2017, http://thehill.com/latino/344421-momentum-builds-for-bill-to-help-dreamers (accessed 7/30/2017).

CHAPTER 4

1. This account taken from: April Baer, "The Slants: Trading in Stereotypes," NPR, June 11, 2008, www.npr.org/templates/story/story.php?storyId=90278746; Katy Steinmetz, "'The Slants' Suit: Asian-American Band Goes to Court over Name," *TIME*, October 23, 2013, http://entertainment.time.com/2013/10/23/the-slants-suit -asian-american-band-goes-to-court-over-name/; Kat Chow, "The Slants: Fighting for the Right to Rock a Racial Slur," NPR, January 19, 2017, www.npr.org/sections/ codeswitch/2017/01/19/510467679/the-slants-fighting-for-the-right-to-rock-a-racial -slur; *Matal v. Tam*, 582 U.S. __ (2017), https://supreme.justia.com/cases/federal/ us/582/15-1293/opinion3.html; Ian Shapira and Ann E. Marimow, "Washington Redskins Win Trademark Fight over the Team's Name," *Washington Post,* June 29, 2017, www.washingtonpost.com/local/public-safety/2017/06/29/a26f52f0-5cf6-11e7 -9fc6-c7ef4bc58d13_story.html?utm_term=.22ed3bf39917 (accessed 2/4/18).

2. Alexander Hamilton, James Madison, and John Jay, *The Federalist Papers*, ed. Clinton Rossiter (New York: New American Library, 1961), no. 84, 513.

3. *The Federalist Papers*, no. 84, 513.

4. Let there be no confusion about the words *liberty* and *freedom*. They are synonymous and interchangeable. *Freedom* comes from the German *Freiheit. Liberty* is from the French *liberté*. Although people sometimes try to make them appear to be different, both of them have equal concern with the absence of restraints on individual choices of action.

5. *Barron v. Baltimore*, 32 U.S. 7 Peters 243, 246 (1833).

6. The Fourteenth Amendment also seems designed to introduce civil rights. The final clause of the all-important Section 1 provides that no state can "deny to any person within its jurisdiction the equal protection of the laws." It is reasonable to conclude that the purpose of this provision was to obligate the state governments as well as the national government to take positive actions to protect citizens from arbitrary and discriminatory actions, at least those based on race.

7. For example, *The Slaughter-House Cases*, 83 U. S. 36 (1873).

8. *Chicago, Burlington and Quincy Railroad Company v. Chicago,* 166 U.S. 226 (1897).

9. *Gitlow v. New York*, 268 U.S. 652 (1925).

10. *Near v. Minnesota*, 283 U.S. 697 (1931); *Hague v. C.I.O.*, 307 U.S. 496 (1939).

11. *McDonald v. Chicago*, 561 U.S. 742 (2010).

12. *Palko v. Connecticut*, 302 U.S. 319 (1937).

13. *Abington School District v. Schempp*, 374 U.S. 203 (1963).

14. *Engel v. Vitale*, 370 U.S. 421 (1962).

15. *Doe v. Santa Fe Independent School District*, 530 U.S. 290 (2000).
16. *Wallace v. Jaffree*, 472 U.S. 38 (1985).
17. *Lynch v. Donnelly*, 465 U.S. 668 (1984).
18. *Van Orden v. Perry*, 545 U.S. 677 (2005).
19. *McCreary v. ACLU of Kentucky*, 545 U.S. 844 (2005).
20. *West Virginia State Board of Education v. Barnette*, 319 U.S. 624 (1943). The case it reversed was *Minersville School District v. Gobitus*, 310 U.S. 586 (1940).
21. *Holt v. Hobbs*, 574 U.S. __ (2015); *Equal Employment Opportunity Commission v. Abercrombie and Fitch Stores, Inc.*, 575 U.S. __ (2015); *Burwell v. Hobby Lobby Stores*, 573 U.S. __ (2014).
22. *Abrams v. United States*, 250 U.S. 616 (1919).
23. *United States v. Carolene Products Company*, 304 U.S. 144 (1938), 4n. This footnote is one of the Court's most important doctrines. See Alfred H. Kelly, Winfred A. Harbison, and Herman Belz, *The American Constitution: Its Origins and Development*, 7th ed., vol. 2 (New York: W. W. Norton, 1991), 519–23.
24. *Schenk v. United States*, 249 U.S. 47 (1919).
25. *Hague v. Committee for Industrial Organization*, 307 U.S. 496 (1939).
26. *Stromberg v. California*, 283 U.S. 359 (1931).
27. *Texas v. Johnson*, 491 U.S. 397 (1989).
28. *Snyder v. Phelps*, 562 U.S. __ (2011).
29. For a good general discussion of "speech plus," see Louis Fisher, *American Constitutional Law* (New York: McGraw-Hill, 1990), 544–6. The case upholding the buffer zone against the abortion protesters is *Madsen v. Women's Health Center*, 512 U.S. 753 (1994).
30. *Bethel School District v. Fraser*, 478 U.S. 675 (1986).
31. *Hazelwood v. Kuhlmeier*, 484 U.S. 260 (1988).
32. *Morse v. Frederick*, 551 U.S. 393 (2007).
33. *Near v. Minnesota*, 283 U.S. 697 (1931).
34. *New York Times v. United States*, 403 U.S. 713 (1971).
35. *Branzburg v. Hayes*, 408 U.S. 665 (1972).
36. *New York Times v. Sullivan*, 376 U.S. 254 (1964).
37. See *Zeran v. America Online*, 129 F.3d 327 (4th Cir. 1997).
38. *Roth v. United States*, 354 U.S. 476 (1957).
39. Concurring opinion in *Jacobellis v. Ohio*, 378 U.S. 184 (1964).
40. *Miller v. California*, 413 U.S. 15 (1973).
41. *Reno v. American Civil Liberties Union*, 521 U.S. 844 (1997).
42. *United States v. Williams*, 553 U.S. 285 (2008).
43. *United States v. Playboy Entertainment Group*, 529 U.S. 803 (2000).
44. *Brown v. Entertainment Merchants Association*, 564 U.S. __ (2011).
45. *Chaplinsky v. State of New Hampshire*, 315 U.S. 568 (1942).
46. *Dennis v. United States*, 341 U.S. 494 (1951).
47. *Broadcasting Company v. Acting Attorney General*, 405 U.S. 1000 (1972).
48. *City Council v. Taxpayers for Vincent*, 466 U.S. 789 (1984).
49. *44 Liquormart, Inc. and Peoples Super Liquor Stores Inc., Petitioners v. Rhode Island and Rhode Island Liquor Stores Association*, 517 U.S. 484 (1996).
50. *Lorillard Tobacco v. Reilly*, 533 U.S. 525 (2001).
51. *United States v. Miller*, 307 U.S. 174 (1939).
52. *District of Columbia v. Heller*, 554 U.S. 570 (2008).
53. *McDonald v. Chicago*, 561 U.S. 742 (2010).
54. *Horton v. California*, 496 U.S. 128 (1990).

55. *Mapp v. Ohio*, 367 U.S. 643 (1961). Although Mapp went free in this case, she was later convicted in New York on narcotics trafficking charges and served 9 years of a 20-year sentence.
56. For a good discussion of the issue, see Fisher, *American Constitutional Law*, 884–9.
57. *Florida v. Jardines*, 569 U.S. __ (2013).
58. *United States v. Jones*, 565 U.S. __ (2012).
59. *Maryland v. King*, 569 U.S. __ (2013).
60. *Riley v. California*, 573 U.S. __ (2014).
61. Marjorie Cohn, "NSA Metadata Collection: Fourth Amendment Violation," JURIST, January 15, 2014, www.jurist.org/forum/2014/01/marjorie-cohn-nsa-metadata.php (accessed 4/19/16).
62. *Palko v. Connecticut*, 302 U.S. 319 (1937).
63. *Miranda v. Arizona*, 384 U.S. 436 (1966).
64. *Gideon v. Wainwright*, 372 U.S. 335 (1963). For a full account of the story of the trial and release of Clarence Earl Gideon, see Anthony Lewis, *Gideon's Trumpet* (New York: Random House, 1964). See also David O'Brien, *Storm Center*, 8th ed. (New York: W. W. Norton, 2008).
65. *Furman v. Georgia*, 408 U.S. 238 (1972).
66. *Gregg v. Georgia*, 428 U.S. 153 (1976).
67. *Kennedy v. Louisiana*, 554 U.S. 407 (2008).
68. *Snyder v. Louisiana*, 522 U.S. 472 (2008).
69. *Glossip v. Gross*, 576 U.S. __ (2015).
70. *Griswold v. Connecticut*, 381 U.S. 479 (1965).
71. *Griswold v. Connecticut*, concurring opinion. In 1972 the Court extended the privacy right to unmarried women: *Eisenstadt v. Baird*, 405 U.S. 438 (1972).
72. *Roe v. Wade*, 410 U.S. 113 (1973).
73. *Lawrence v. Texas*, 539 U.S. 558 (2003).
74. *Plessy v. Ferguson*, 163 U.S. 537 (1896).
75. *Missouri ex rel. Gaines v. Canada*, 305 U.S. 337 (1938).
76. The District of Columbia case came up, too, but since the District of Columbia is not a state, this case did not directly involve the Fourteenth Amendment and its "equal protection" clause. It confronted the Court on the same grounds, however—that segregation is inherently unequal. Its victory in effect was "incorporation in reverse," with equal protection moving from the Fourteenth Amendment to become part of the Bill of Rights. See *Bolling v. Sharpe*, 347 U.S. 497 (1954).
77. *Brown v. Board of Education of Topeka, Kansas*, 347 U.S. 483 (1954).
78. The Supreme Court first declared that race was a suspect classification requiring strict scrutiny in the decision *Korematsu v. United States*, 323 U.S. 214 (1944). In this case, the Court upheld President Roosevelt's executive order of 1941 allowing the military to exclude persons of Japanese ancestry from the West Coast and to place them in internment camps. It is one of the few cases in which classification based on race survived strict scrutiny.
79. For good treatments of this long stretch of the struggle of the federal courts to integrate the schools, see Paul Brest and Sanford Levinson, *Processes of Constitutional Decision-Making: Cases and Materials*, 2nd ed. (Boston: Little, Brown, 1983), 471–80; and Alfred H. Kelly, Winfred A. Harbison, and Herman Belz, *The American Constitution: Its Origins and Development*, 6th ed. (New York: W. W. Norton, 1983), 610–16.
80. Pierre Thomas, "Denny's to Settle Bias Cases," *Washington Post*, May 24, 1994, A1.
81. *Parents Involved in Community Schools v. Seattle School District No. 1*, 551 U.S. 701 (2007).

82. John A. Powell, "Segregated Schools Ruling Not All Bad: In Rejecting Seattle's Integration Bid Top Court Majority Also Held that Avoiding Racial Isolation Is a Legitimate Public Goal," *Newsday*, July 16, 2007, A33.
83. See especially *Katzenbach v. McClung*, 379 U.S. 294 (1964). Almost immediately after passage of the Civil Rights Act of 1964, a case was brought challenging the validity of Title II, which covered discrimination in public accommodations. Ollie's Barbecue was a neighborhood restaurant in Birmingham, Alabama. It was located 11 blocks away from an interstate highway and even farther from railroad and bus stations. Its table service was for whites only; there was only take-out service for blacks. The Supreme Court agreed that Ollie's was strictly an intrastate restaurant, but since a substantial proportion of its food and other supplies were bought from companies outside the state of Alabama, there was a sufficient connection to interstate commerce; therefore, racial discrimination at such restaurants would "impose commercial burdens of national magnitude upon interstate commerce." Although this case involved Title II, it had direct bearing on the constitutionality of Title VII.
84. In 1970 this act was amended to outlaw for five years literacy tests as a condition for voting in all states.
85. See Douglas S. Massey and Nancy A. Denton, *American Apartheid: Segregation and the Making of the Underclass* (Cambridge, MA: Harvard University Press, 1993), chap. 7.
86. Michael Powell, "Bank Accused of Pushing Mortgage Deals on Blacks," *New York Times*, June 6, 2009, A16; Office of the Illinois Attorney General, "Madigan Sues Wells Fargo for Discriminatory and Deceptive Mortgage Lending Practices," press release, July 31, 2009, www.illinoisattorneygeneral.gov/pressroom/2009_07/20090731.html (accessed 10/23/09).
87. The Department of Health, Education, and Welfare (HEW) was the cabinet department charged with administering most federal social programs. In 1980, when education programs were transferred to the newly created Department of Education, HEW was renamed the Department of Health and Human Services.
88. *Regents of the University of California v. Bakke*, 438 U.S. 265 (1978).
89. *Grutter v. Bollinger*, 539 U.S. 306 (2003).
90. *Gratz v. Bollinger*, 539 U.S. 244 (2003).
91. *Fisher v. University of Texas*, 570 U.S. __ (2013).
92. *Fisher v. University of Texas*, No. 14-981 __ (2016).
93. See Jane J. Mansbridge, *Why We Lost the ERA* (Chicago: University of Chicago Press, 1986); and Gilbert Steiner, *Constitutional Inequality* (Washington, DC: Brookings Institution Press, 1985).
94. See *Frontiero v. Richardson*, 411 U.S. 677 (1973).
95. *Meritor Savings Bank v. Vinson*, 477 U.S. 57 (1986).
96. *Franklin v. Gwinnett County Public Schools*, 503 U.S. 60 (1992).
97. *United States v. Virginia*, 518 U.S. 515 (1996).
98. *Ledbetter v. Goodyear Tire and Rubber Co.*, 550 U.S. 618 (2007).
99. Claire Zillman, "Barnes & Noble Is Latest Retailer to Face Transgender Discrimination Lawsuit," *Fortune*, May 7, 2015, http://fortune.com/2015/05/07/barnes-noble-transgender-lawsuit/ (accessed 1/10/16).
100. Helene Cooper, "Transgender People Will Be Allowed to Enlist in the Military as a Court Case Advances," *New York Times*, December 11, 2017, www.nytimes.com/2017/12/11/us/politics/transgender-military-pentagon.html (accessed 7/26/18).
101. *Lau v. Nichols*, 414 U.S. 563 (1974).
102. Dick Kirschten, "Not Black and White," *National Journal*, March 2, 1991, 497.
103. *R.A.V. v. City of St. Paul*, 506 U.S. 377 (1992).
104. *United States v. Texas*, 579 U.S. __ (2016).

105. See the discussion in Robert A. Katzmann, *Institutional Disability: The Saga of Transportation Policy for the Disabled* (Washington, DC: Brookings Institution Press, 1986).

106. For example, after pressure from the Justice Department, one of the nation's largest rental-car companies agreed to make special hand controls available to any customer requesting them. See "Avis Agrees to Equip Cars for Disabled," *Los Angeles Times*, September 2, 1994, D1.

107. For more, see Dale Carpenter, *Flagrant Conduct: The Story of* Lawrence v. Texas (New York: W. W. Norton & Co., 2012).

108. *Bowers v. Hardwick*, 478 U.S. 186 (1986).

109. *Romer v. Evans*, 517 U.S. 620 (1996).

110. *Obergefell v. Hodges*, 576 U.S. __ (2015).

CHAPTER 5

1. Suzanna Hupp, "In Their Own Words: The Gun Rights Advocate," *Texas Monthly*, March 23, 2016, www.texasmonthly.com/list/in-their-own-words/the-gun-rights -advocate/ (accessed 3/3/18).

2. Brianna Sacks, "After Florida School Shooting, Several Survivors and Victims' Parents Pan Trump's Idea to Arm Teachers," BuzzFeed News, February 24, 2018, www.buzzfeed.com/briannasacks/students-and-parents-react-to-armed-teacher -proposal?utm_term=.rtNPqM580#.xrVbnry1A (accessed 3/3/8).

3. Samantha Smith, "Young people less likely to view Iraqi, Syrian refugees as major threat to U.S.," Pew Research, February 3, 2017, www.pewresearch.org/fact-tank/ 2017/02/03/young-people-less-likely-to-view-iraqi-syrian-refugees-as-major-threat-to -u-s/ (accessed 6/26/18).

4. M. Lodge and C. S. Taber, "Three Steps toward a Theory of Motivated Political Reasoning," in *Elements of Reason: Cognition, Choice, and the Bounds of Rationality*, ed. A. Lupia, M. McCubbins, and S. Popkin (London: Cambridge University Press, 2000); George E. Marcus, W. Russell Neuman, and Michael MacKuen, *Affective Intelligence and Political Judgment* (Chicago: University of Chicago Press, 2000); David Redlawsk, "Hot Cognition or Cool Consideration? Testing the Effects of Motivated Reasoning on Political Decision Making," *Journal of Politics* 64 (2002): 1021–44; David Redlawsk, Andrew Civettini, and Karen Emmerson, "The Affective Tipping Point: Do Motivated Reasoners Ever 'Get It'?" *Political Psychology* 31, no. 4 (2010): 563–93.

5. Caroline J. Tolbert, David P. Redlawsk, and Kellen J. Gracey, "Racial Attitudes and Emotional Responses to the 2016 Republican Candidates," *Journal of Election, Public Opinion and Parties* 28, no. 2 (2018): 245–62.

6. Marcus, Neuman, and MacKuen, *Affective Intelligence and Political Judgment*.

7. See Karen Mossberger, Caroline Tolbert, and Ramona McNeal, *Digital Citizenship: The Internet, Society and Participation* (Cambridge, MA: MIT Press, 2008).

8. See Harry Holloway and John George, *Public Opinion* (New York: St. Martin's, 1986). See also Paul R. Abramson, *Political Attitudes in America* (San Francisco: Freeman, 1983).

9. Lydia Saad, "Conservative Lead in U.S. Ideology Down to Single Digits," Gallup, January 11, 2018, https://news.gallup.com/poll/225074/conservative-lead-ideology -down-single-digits.aspx (accessed 10/10/18); Jocelyn Kiley and Michael Dimock, "The GOP's Millennial Problem Runs Deep," September 25, 2014, www.pewresearch .org/fact-tank/2014/09/25/the-gops-millennial-problem-runs-deep/ (accessed 3/4/16).

10. Pippa Norris, ed., *Critical Citizens: Global Support for Democratic Government* (New York: Oxford University Press, 1999); Robert Putnam, *Bowling Alone: The Collapse and Revival of American Community* (New York: Simon and Schuster, 2000).

11. Todd Donovan and Shaun Bowler, *Reforming the Republic: Democratic Institutions for the New America* (New York: Prentice Hall, 2004).
12. Pew Research Center, "Public Trust in Government: 1958–2017," May 3, 2017, www.people-press.org/2017/05/03/public-trust-in-government-1958-2017/ (accessed 2/2/18).
13. See Angus Campbell et al., *The American Voter* (New York: Wiley, 1960), 147.
14. Omid Aziz, Derrick McMillen, and Tony Liu, "72 Hours to Launch Celebrate Pride," July 2, 2015, https://code.facebook.com/posts/778505998932780/72-hours-to-launch-celebrate-pride/ (accessed 3/2/16).
15. "Changing Attitudes on Gay Marriage," www.gallup.com/poll/183272/record-high-americans-support-sex-marriage.aspx, and Pew Research Center, "Changing Attitudes on Gay Marriage," July 29, 2015, www.pewforum.org/2015/07/29/graphics-slideshow-changing-attitudes-on-gay-marriage/ (accessed 2/23/16).
16. Jennifer A. Heerwig and Brian J. McCabe, "Education and Social Desirability Bias: The Case of a Black Presidential Candidate," *Social Science Quarterly* 90, no. 3 (2009): 674–86.
17. Raymond E. Wolfinger and Steven J. Rosenstone, *Who Votes?* (New Haven, CT: Yale University Press, 1980). See also Steven J. Rosenstone and John Mark Hansen, *Mobilization, Participation, and Democracy in America* (New York: Macmillan, 1993).
18. Katherine Tate, *Black Faces in the Mirror* (Princeton, NJ: Princeton University Press, 1993).
19. Brakkton Booker, "How Equal Is American Opportunity? Survey Shows Attitudes Vary by Race," NPR, September 21, 2015, www.npr.org/sections/thetwo-way/2015/09/21/442068004/how-equal-is-american-opportunity-survey-shows-attitudes-vary-by-race (accessed 2/24/16).
20. Pew Research Center, "Across Racial Lines, More Say Nation Needs to Make Changes to Achieve Racial Equality," U.S. Politics & Policy, August 5, 2015, www.people-press.org/2015/08/05/across-racial-lines-more-say-nation-needs-to-make-changes-to-achieve-racial-equality/8-4-2015_02a/ (accessed 2/24/16).
21. Matt Barreto and Gary M. Segura, *Latino America: How America's Most Dynamic Population Is Poised to Transform the Politics of the Nation* (New York: Public Affairs, 2014).
22. "Trump Gets Negative Ratings for Many Personal Traits, but Most Say He Stands Up for His Beliefs," Pew Research Center, October 1, 2018, www.people-press.org/2018/10/01/trump-gets-negative-ratings-for-many-personal-traits-but-most-say-he-stands-up-for-his-beliefs/ (accessed 10/10/18).
23. Michael Lipka, "Religious 'Nones' Are Not Only Growing, They're Becoming More Secular," Pew Research Center, Fact Tank, November 11, 2015, www.pewresearch.org/fact-tank/2015/11/11/religious-nones-are-not-only-growing-theyre-becoming-more-secular/ (accessed 11/11/15).
24. 2014 Cooperative Comparative Election Study.
25. Donald Green, Bradley Palmquist, and Eric Schickler, *Partisan Hearts and Minds: Political Parties and the Social Identities of Voters* (New Haven, CT: Yale University Press, 2002).
26. See Richard Lau and David Redlawsk, *How Voters Decide: Information Processing during an Election Campaign* (New York: Cambridge University Press, 2006).
27. Cooperative Comparative Election Study 2014, Harvard University, released February 2015, http://projects.iq.harvard.edu/cces/home (accessed 12/16/15).
28. John R. Zaller, *The Nature and Origins of Mass Opinion* (New York: Cambridge University Press, 1992).

29. Carol Glynn et al., *Public Opinion*, 2nd ed. (Boulder, CO: Westview, 2004), 293. See also Michael X. Delli Carpini and Scott Keeter, *What Americans Know about Politics and Why It Matters* (New Haven, CT: Yale University Press, 1996).

30. Delli Carpini and Keeter, *What Americans Know about Politics*.

31. Adam J. Berinsky, "Assuming the Costs of War: Events, Elites and American Support for Military Conflict," *Journal of Politics* 69, no. 4 (2007): 975–97; Zaller, *Nature and Origins of Mass Opinion*.

32. Richard R. Lau and David P. Redlawsk, "Advantages and Disadvantages of Cognitive Heuristics in Political Decision Making," *American Journal of Political Science* 45 (October 2001): 951–71; Lau and Redlawsk, *How Voters Decide*.

33. James Druckman, Erik Petersen, and Rune Slothuus, "How Elite Partisan Polarization Affects Public Opinion Formation," *American Political Science Review* 107, no. 1 (February 2013): 57–79.

34. Tony Dokoupil, "Is the Internet Making Us Crazy? What the New Research Says," *Newsweek,* July 9, 2012, www.newsweek.com/internet-making-us-crazy-what-new -research-says-65593; Nicholas Carr, *The Shallows: What the Internet Is Doing to Our Brains* (New York: W. W. Norton, 2011).

35. Benjamin Ginsberg, *The American Lie: Government by the People and Other Political Fables* (Boulder, CO: Paradigm, 2007).

36. Peter Marks, "Adept in Politics and Advertising, 4 Women Shape a Campaign," *New York Times*, November 11, 2001, B6.

37. Jason Gainous and Kevin Wagner, *Tweeting to Power: The Social Media Revolution in American Politics* (New York: Oxford University Press, 2013).

38. *Roe v. Wade*, 410 U.S. 113 (1973).

39. See Gillian Peele, *Revival and Reaction* (Oxford: Clarendon, 1985). See also Connie Paige, *The Right-to-Lifers* (New York: Summit, 1983).

40. David W. Moore, "Support for Invasion of Iraq Remains Contingent on U.N. Approval," Gallup, November 12, 2002, www.gallup.com/poll/7195/support -invasion-iraq-remains-contigent-un-approval.aspx; Pew Research Center, "Public Attitudes toward the War in Iraq: 2003–2008," March 19, 2008, www.pewresearch .org/2008/03/19/public-attitudes-toward-the-war-in-iraq-20032008 (accessed 2/19/14).

41. Benjamin I. Page and Robert Y. Shapiro, "Effects of Public Opinion on Policy," *American Political Science Review* 77, no.1 (1983): 175–90.

42. Page and Shapiro, "Effects of Public Opinion on Policy."

43. Pew Research Center, "Mixed Views of Economic Policies and Health Care Reform Persist," U.S. Politics & Policy, October 8, 2009, www;people-press.org/2009/10/08/ mixed-views-of-economic-policies-and-health-care-reform-persist (accessed 3/18/14).

44. Christopher Wlezien, "The Public as Thermostat: Dynamics of Preferences for Spending," *American Journal of Political Science* 39, no. 4 (1995): 981–1000.

45. Malcolm E. Jewell, *Representation in State Legislatures* (Lexington: University Press of Kentucky, 1982).

46. Lawrence R. Jacobs and Robert Y. Shapiro, *Politicians Don't Pander: Political Manipulation and the Loss of Democratic Responsiveness* (Chicago: University of Chicago Press, 2000).

47. Herbert Asher, *Polling and the Public* (Washington, DC: CQ Press, 2001), 64.

48. Drew DeSilver and Scott Keeter, "The Challenges of Polling when Fewer People Are Available to Be Polled," Fact Tank, July 21, 2015, www.pewresearch.org/fact -tank/2015/07/21/the-challenges-of-polling-when-fewer-people-are-available-to-be -polled/ (accessed 3/1/16).

49. Michael Kagay and Janet Elder, "Numbers Are No Problem for Pollsters, Words Are," *New York Times*, August 9, 1992, E6.

50. See Adam Berinsky, "The Two Faces of Public Opinion," *American Journal of Political Science* 43, no. 4 (1999): 1209–30. See also Adam Berinsky, "Political Context and the Survey Response: The Dynamics of Racial Policy Opinion," *Journal of Politics* 64, no. 2 (2002): 567–84.
51. Christopher Wlezien and Stuart Soroka, "The Relationship between Public Opinion and Policy," in *Oxford Handbook of Political Behavior*, ed. Russell Dalton and Hans-Dieter Klingemann (New York: Oxford University Press, 2009), 799–817.
52. Martin Gilens, "Inequality and Democratic Responsiveness," *Public Opinion Quarterly* 69, no. 5 (2005): 778–96; Larry Bartels, *Unequal Democracy*. Princeton, NJ: Princeton University Press, 2008.
53. Ryan Claassen and Benjamin Highton, "Does Policy Debate Reduce Information Effects in Public Opinion? Analyzing the Evolution of Public Opinion on Health Care," *Journal of Politics* 68, no. 2 (2006): 410–20.

CHAPTER 6

1. Julian P. Boyd et al., ed., *The Papers of Thomas Jefferson* (Princeton, NJ: Princeton University Press), www.jeffersonpapers.princeton.edu/ (accessed 5/30/14).
2. Rodney Tiffen, "Journalism in the Trump Era," *Inside Story*, February 24, 2017, http://insidestory.org.au/journalism-in-the-trump-era (accessed 6/26/18).
3. Columbia Journalism Review, "Covering Trump," http://archives.cjr.org/resources/index.php, (accessed 7/3/18).
4. For a criticism of the increasing consolidation of the media, see the essays in Patricia Aufderheide et al., *Conglomerates and the Media* (New York: New Press, 1997).
5. Pew Research Center, "2017 Pew Research Center's American Trends Panel," March 27, 2017, http://assets.pewresearch.org/wp-content/uploads/sites/13/2017/05/09125944/PJ_2017.05.10_Media-Attitudes_TOPLINE.pdf (accessed 1/22/18).
6. Pew Research Center, "Amid Criticism, Support for Media's 'Watchdog' Role Stands Out," August 8, 2013, www.people-press.org/2013/08/08/amid-criticism-support-for-medias-watchdog-role-stands-out (accessed 4/27/14).
7. Pew Research Center, "Digital News Fact Sheet" August 7, 2017, www.journalism.org/fact-sheet/digital-news/ (accessed 1/22/18).
8. Clay Shirky, *Here Comes Everybody: The Power of Organizing without Organizations* (New York: Penguin Books, 2008).
9. Amy Mitchell, Jesse Holcomb, Rachel Weisel, "State of the News Media 2016," Pew Research Center, June 15, 2016, www.journalism.org/2016/06/15/state-of-the-news-media-2016/?utm_content=buffer6871f&utm_medium=social&utm_source=twitter.com&utm_campaign=buffer (accessed 6/29/18).
10. Shirky, *Here Comes Everybody*, 2008; Mitchell et al., "State of the News Media 2016."
11. Robert McChesney and John Nichols, *The Death and Life of American Journalism: The Media Revolution That Will Begin the World Again* (New York: Nation Books, 2010).
12. "Newspapers Fact Sheet," Pew Research Center, June 13, 2018, www.journalism.org/fact-sheet/newspapers/ (accessed 10/10/18).
13. Darrell West, *The Next Wave: Using Digital Technology to Further Social and Political Innovation* (Washington, DC: Brookings Institution Press, 2011).
14. Laura Wamsley, "Big Newspapers Are Booming: 'Washington Post' to Add 60 Newsroom Jobs," NPR, December 27, 2016, www.npr.org/sections/thetwo-way/2016/12/27/507140760/big-newspapers-are-booming-washington-post-to-add-sixty-newsroom-jobs (accessed 1/22/18).

15. Michael Barthel, "Circulation and Revenue Fall for Industry Overall," Pew Research Center, June 1, 2017, www.pewresearch.org/fact-tank/2017/06/01/circulation-and-revenue-fall-for-newspaper-industry/(accessed 1/22/18).

16. Mitchell, Holcomb, and Weisel, "State of the News Media 2016."

17. Mitchell, Holcomb, and Weisel, "State of the News Media 2016."

18. Pew Research Center, "Audio and Podcasting Fact Sheet," July 12, 2018, www.journalism.org/fact-sheet/audio-and-podcasting/ (accessed 10/12/18).

19. Mitchell, Holcomb, and Weisel, "State of the News Media 2016."

20. Pew Research Center, "The Internet's Broader Role in Campaign 2008," January 11, 2008, www.people-press.org/2008/01/11/internets-broader-role-in-campaign-2008/; and Pew Research Center, "Journalism, Satire or Just Laughs? 'The Daily Show with Jon Stewart' Examined," May 8, 2008, www.journalism.org/2008/05/08/journalism-satire-or-just-laughs-the-daily-show-with-jon-stewart-examined/ (both accessed 7/3/18).

21. West, *The Next Wave*; Edward Glaeser, *Triumph of the City: How Our Greatest Invention Makes Us Richer, Smarter, Greener, Healthier, and Happier* (New York: Penguin Press, 2011).

22. Pew Research Center, "Internet Use over Time," 2014, www.pewinternet.org/datatrend/internet-use/internet-use-over-time (accessed 4/29/2014).

23. Amy Mitchell, Jeffrey Gottfried, and Katerina Eva Matsa, "Millennials and Political News: Social Media—The Local TV for the Next Generation?" June 1, 2015, Pew Research Center, www.journalism.org/2015/06/01/millennials-political-news/ (accessed 1/14/16).

24. Jeffrey Gottfried and Elisa Shearer, "News Use across Social Media Platforms 2016," Pew Research Center, May 26, 2016, www.journalism.org/2016/05/26/news-use-across-social-media-platforms-2016/ (accessed 6/17/16).

25. Antony Wilhelm, *Digital Nation: Toward an Inclusive Information Society* (Cambridge, MA: MIT Press, 2006); Paul DiMaggio et al., "Social Implications of the Internet," *Annual Review of Sociology* 27, no. 1 (2001): 307–36.

26. Karen Mossberger, Caroline J. Tolbert, and Allison Hamilton, "Measuring Digital Citizenship: Mobile Access and Broadband," *International Journal of Communication 6* (2012): 2492–528; Brian A. Krueger, "A Comparison of Conventional and Internet Political Mobilization," *American Politics Research* 34, no. 6 (2006): 759–76.

27. Karen Mossberger, Caroline J. Tolbert, and Mary Stansbury, *Virtual Inequality: Beyond the Digital Divide* (Washington, DC: Georgetown University Press, 2003); Pippa Norris, *Digital Divide: Civic Engagement, Information Poverty, and the Internet Worldwide* (New York: Cambridge University Press, 2001).

28. Karen Mossberger, Caroline J. Tolbert, and Ramona S. McNeal, *Digital Citizenship* (Cambridge, MA: MIT Press, 2008); Pew Research Center, "Internet Broadband Fact Sheet," February 5, 2018, www.pewinternet.org/fact-sheet/internet-broadband/ (accessed 3/19/18).

29. National Telecommunications & Information Administration, *Digital Nation: 21st Century America's Progress towards Universal Broadband Access* (Washington, DC: U.S. Department of Commerce, 2011).

30. Thom File, "Voting in America: A Look at the 2016 Presidential Election," U.S. Census, May 20, 2017, www.census.gov/newsroom/blogs/random-samplings/2017/05/voting_in_america.html (accessed 3/19/18).

31. Aaron Smith and Monica Anderson, "Social Media Use in 2018," Pew Research Center, March 1, 2018, www.pewinternet.org/2018/03/01/social-media-use-in-2018/ (accessed 3/19/18).

32. Michael Barthel et al., "The Evolving Role of News on Twitter and Facebook," Pew Research Center, July 14, 2015, www.journalism.org/2015/07/14/the-evolving -role-of-news-on-twitter-and-facebook/ (accessed 1/14/16).

33. Jason Gainous and Kevin Wagner, *Tweeting to Power: The Social Media Revolution in American Politics* (New York: Oxford University Press, 2013).

34. Richard Davis, "Interplay: Political Blogging and Journalism," in *iPolitics: Citizens, Elections, and Governing in the New Media Era*, ed. Richard L. Fox and Jennifer M. Ramos (Cambridge: Cambridge University Press, 2012), 76–99.

35. Pew Research Center Publications, "State of the News Media 2010," March 15, 2010, http://pewresearch.org/pubs/1523/state-of-the-news-media-2010 (accessed 9/11/12); West, *The Next Wave*.

36. Matthew A. Baum, "Preaching to the Choir or Converting the Flock: Presidential Communication Strategies in the Age of Three Medias," in *iPolitics: Citizens, Elections, and Governing in the New Media Era*, ed. Richard L. Fox and Jennifer M. Ramos (Cambridge: Cambridge University Press, 2012), 183–205.

37. Eli Pariser, *The Filter Bubble: What the Internet Is Hiding from You* (New York: Penguin Press, 2011).

38. Larry Bartels, *Unequal Democracy: The Political Economy of the New Gilded Age* (Princeton, NJ: Princeton University Press, 2008).

39. Shanto Iyengar and Donald R. Kinder, *News That Matters: Television and American Opinion* (Chicago: University of Chicago Press, 1987), 63.

40. *New York Times v. United States*, 403 U.S. 713 (1971).

41. *Red Lion Broadcasting Company v. Federal Communications Commission*, 395 U.S. 367 (1969).

42. United Nations General Assembly, "Report of the Special Rapporteur on the Promotion and Protection of the Right to Freedom of Opinion and Expression, 2011," www2.ohchr .org/english/bodies/hrcouncil/docs/17session/A.HRC.17.27_en.pdf (accessed 3/14/16).

43. See Martin Linsky, *Impact: How the Press Affects Federal Policymaking* (New York: W. W. Norton, 1986).

CHAPTER 7

1. "Meet Keli Carender, Tea Party Organizer in Seattle, Washington," Taxdayteaparty .com, March 15, 2009, http://taxdayteaparty.com/2009/03/meet-keli-carender-tea -party-organizer-in-seattle-washington/ (accessed 1/26/18).

2. Alan Greenblatt, "With Major Issues Fading, Capitol Life Lures Fewer," *Congressional Quarterly Weekly Report*, October 25, 1997, 2625.

3. For a discussion of third parties in the United States, see Daniel Mazmanian, *Third Parties in Presidential Elections* (Washington, DC: Brookings Institution Press, 1974).

4. Rolfe, Meredith, *Voter Turnout: A Social Theory of Political Participation* (New York: Cambridge University Press, 2012).

5. Jeffrey Gottfried and Elisa Shearer, "News Use across Social Media Platforms 2016," Pew Research Center, Journalism & Media, May 26, 2016, www.journalism .org/2016/05/26/news-use-across-social-media-platforms-2016/ (accessed 6/25/16).

6. Katerina Eva Matsa and Amy Mitchell, "8 Key Takeaways about Social Media and News," Pew Research Center, Journalism & Media, March 26, 2014, www .journalism.org/2014/03/26/8-key-takeaways-about-social-media-and-news/ (accessed 1/12/16).

7. Helen Margetts, Peter John, Scott Hale, and Taha Yasseri, *Political Turbulence: How Social Media Shape Collective Action* (New York: Oxford University Press, 2017).

8. Amy Mitchell and Emily Guskin, "Twitter News Consumers Young, Mobile and Educated," Pew Research Center, Journalism & Media, November 4, 2013, www .journalism.org/2013/11/04/twitter-news-consumers-young-mobile-and-educated/ (accessed 4/12/16).

9. Caroline J. Tolbert, David P. RedLawsk and Kellen J. Gracey, "Racial Attitudes and Emotional Responses to the 2016 Republican Candidates," *Journal of Election, Public Opinion and Parties* 28, no. 2 (2018): 245–62.

10. For a discussion of the decline in voter turnout over time, see Ruy A. Teixeria, *The Disappearing American Voter* (Washington, DC: Brookings Institution Press, 1992). See also Michael McDonald and Samuel Popkin, "The Myth of the Vanishing Voter," *American Political Science Review* 95 (2001): 963–74; and Michael McDonald, "2012 November General Election Turnout Rates," United States Election Project, www .electproject.org/2012g (accessed 9/14/12).

11. Robert Jackman, "Political Institutions and Voter Turnout in the Democracies," *American Political Science Review* 81 (June 1987): 420.

12. Angus Campbell et al., *The American Voter* (New York: Wiley, 1960); Steven Rosenstone and John Mark Hansen, *Mobilization, Participation, and Democracy in America* (New York: Macmillan, 1993).

13. Sidney Verba and Norman H. Nie, *Participation in America: Political Democracy and Social Equality* (New York: Harper and Row, 1972).

14. Jan E. Leighley and Jonathan Nagler, "Socioeconomic Class Bias in Turnout, 1964–1988: The Voters Remain the Same," *American Political Science Review* 86, no. 3 (1992): 725–36.

15. Rosenstone and Hansen, *Mobilization, Participation, and Democracy*, 59.

16. Michael P. McDonald and John Samples, eds., *The Marketplace of Democracy: Electoral Competition and American Politics* (Washington, DC: Brookings Institution Press, 2006).

17. Mark N. Franklin, "Electoral Participation," in *Comparing Democracies: Elections and Voting in Global Perspective*, ed. Lawrence LeDuc, Richard G. Niemi, and Pippa Norris (Thousand Oaks, CA: Sage, 1996), 216–35; G. Bingham Powell, "American Voter Turnout in Comparative Perspective," *American Political Science Review* 80, no. 1 (1986): 17–43.

18. National Conference of State Legislatures, "Voter Identification Requirements," www.ncsl.org/research/elections-and-campaigns/voter-id.aspx (accessed 4/11/16).

19. Matt Barreto, Stephen Nuño, and Gabriel Sanchez, "The Disproportionate Impact of Voter-ID Requirements on the Electorate—New Evidence from Indiana," *PS: Political Science & Politics* 42 (2009): 111–16.

20. See Morris Fiorina, "Parties and Partisanship: A Forty Year Retrospective," *Political Behavior* 24, no. 2 (June 2002): 93–115.

21. On the limited polarization among ordinary voters, see Morris P. Fiorina, *Culture War? The Myth of a Polarized America*, with Samuel J. Abrams and Jeremy C. Pope (New York: Pearson Longman, 2004); on growing partisan attachment among a subset of voters, see Alan Abramowitz and Kyle Saunders, "Why Can't We Just Get Along? The Reality of a Polarized America," *The Forum* 3, no. 2 (2005): 1–22.

22. *League of United Latin American Citizens v. Wilson*, CV-94-7569 (C.D. Calif. 1995); Adam Nagourney, "Court Strikes Down Ban on Gay Marriage in California," *New York Times*, February 7, 2012, www.nytimes.com/2012/02/08/us/marriage-ban -violates-constitution-court-rules.html (accessed 8/21/12).

23. State legislatures determine the system by which electors are selected. Almost all states use this "winner-take-all" system. Maine and Nebraska, however, provide that one electoral vote goes to the winner in each congressional district and two electoral votes go to the winner statewide.

24. *Bush v. Gore*, 531 U.S. 98 (2000). In the presidential election of 1824, no candidate received a majority of the electoral vote, so the election was thrown into the House of Representatives. It chose John Quincy Adams, even though Andrew Jackson won the nationwide popular vote.

25. GDELT Project, "Presidential Campaign 2016: Candidate Television Tracker," television.gdeltproject.org/cgi-bin/iatv_campaign2016/iatv_campaign2016 (accessed 11/11/16).

26. Nancy Scola, "Massive Twitter Data Release Sheds Light on Russia Trump Strategy," Politico, October 17, 2018, www.politico.com/story/2018/10/17/twitter-foreign-influence-operations-910005

27. Tim Craig, "Democrats' Gains in State Capitols Mark a Significant Turnaround for Party," *Washington Post*, November 8, 2018, A27.

28. Center for Responsive Politics, "Behind the Candidates: Campaign Committees and Outside Groups," www.opensecrets.org/pres16/raised-summ (accessed 11/12/16).

29. *McCutcheon et al. v. Federal Election Commission*, 572 U.S. __ (2014).

30. *Citizens United v. Federal Election Commission*, 558 U.S. 50 (2010); *SpeechNow v. FEC*, 558 U.S. __ (2010).

31. *McCutcheon et al.*

32. *Buckley v. Valeo*, 424 U.S. 1 (1976).

CHAPTER 8

1. Matt Miller, "Young Americans Get the Shaft," *Washington Post,* June 13, 2012, www.washingtonpost.com/opinions/young-americans-get-the-shaft/2012/06/13/gJQAeHp4ZV_story.html?utm_term=.4a68ebb3076f 9 (accessed 1/26/18).

2. This account drawn from Araz Hachadourian, "Who's Lobbying for Millennial Interests? Meet the 'AARP for Young People,'" *Yes! Magazine,* May 19, 2016, www.yesmagazine.org/people-power/millennials-have-the-numbers-to-move-our-politics-and-theyre-about-to-get-their-own-lobbyists-20160519 (accessed 1/26/18); and Association of Young Americans, joinaya.com/ (accessed 1/26/18).

3. Alexis de Tocqueville, *Democracy in America*, ed. J. P. Mayer and trans. George Lawrence (New York: Harper Collins, [1835–40] 1988), 513.

4. Alexander Hamilton, James Madison, and John Jay, *The Federalist Papers*, ed. Clinton L. Rossiter (New York: New American Library, 1961), no. 10, 83.

5. *The Federalist Papers*, no. 10.

6. The best statement of the pluralist view is in David Truman, *The Governmental Process* (New York: Knopf, 1951), chap. 2.

7. Beth L. Leech, National Survey of Governmental Relations, 2012; Center for Responsive Politics, "Political Action Committees," www.opensecrets.org/pacs/; Lobbyists.Info, www.lobbyists.info/ (accessed 12/2/15).

8. Megan R. Wilson, "Lobbying's Top 50: Who's Spending Big," The Hill, February 7, 2017, www.thehill.com/business-a-lobbying/business-a-lobbying/318177-lobbyings-top-50-whos-spending-big (accessed 4/5/18).

9. Frank R. Baumgartner et al., *Lobbying and Policy Change: Who Wins, Who Loses, and Why* (Chicago: University of Chicago Press, 2009).

10. Erika Falk, Erin Grizard, and Gordon McDonald, "Legislative Issue Advertising in the 108th Congress: Pluralism or Peril?" *Harvard International Journal of Press/Politics* 11, no. 4 (Fall 2006): 148–64.

11. Truman, *Governmental Process.*

12. For an exploration of lower-class interest groups and social movements, see Frances Piven and Richard Cloward, *Poor People's Movements* (New York: Vintage, 1978).

13. Piven and Cloward, *Poor People's Movements.*

14. E. E. Schattschneider, *The Semisovereign People: A Realist's View of Democracy in America* (New York: Holt, Rinehart and Winston, 1960).

15. Kay Lehman Schlozman and John T. Tierney, *Organized Interests and American Democracy* (New York: Harper and Row, 1986), 60.

16. Clay Shirky, *Here Comes Everybody: The Power of Organizing without Organizations* (New York: Penguin, 2008).

17. Mancur Olson, *The Logic of Collective Action* (Cambridge, MA: Harvard University Press, 1965).

18. Lisa Stiffler, "How Connected Students Are Wielding the Internet to Fight for Gun Control and Climate Protection," *GeekWire,* March 23, 2018, www.geekwire .com/2018/vocal-students-wielding-internet-powerful-weapon-fight-gun-control -climate-protection/ (accessed 4/24/18).

19. John Herbers, "Special Interests Gaining Power as Voter Disillusionment Grows," *New York Times*, November 14, 1978.

20. For discussions of lobbying, see Allan J. Cigler and Burdett A. Loomis, eds., *Interest Group Politics* (Washington, DC: CQ Press, 1983). See also Jeffrey M. Berry, *Lobbying for the People* (Princeton, NJ: Princeton University Press, 1977).

21. Andrew Chin, "A Case of Insecure Browsing," Newsobserver.com, September 30, 2004, www.unclaw.com/chin/scholarship/nando.pdf (accessed 3/30/16).

22. David Kirkpatrick, "Congress Finds Ways of Avoiding Lobbyist Limits," *Washington Post*, February 11, 2007, 1.

23. *Brown v. Board of Education of Topeka, Kansas*, 347 U.S. 483 (1954).

24. *Roe v. Wade*, 410 U.S. 113 (1973).

25. *Webster v. Reproductive Health Services*, 492 U.S. 490 (1989).

26. *Obergefell v. Hodges*, 576 U.S. __ (2015).

27. "How the NRA Relies More on Grassroots Mobilization Rather Than Lobbying," *U.S. News and World Report*, December 18, 2012, http://usnews.tumblr.com/post/38229308383/how-the-nra-relies-more-on-grassroots-mobilization (accessed 12/11/15).

28. *Citizens United v. Federal Election Commission*, 558 U.S. 310 (2010).

29. *Citizens United v. Federal Election Commission.*

30. Center for Responsive Politics, "Behind the Candidates: Campaign Committees and Outside Groups," December 6, 2017, www.opensecrets.org/pres16/raised-summ (accessed 4/6/18).

31. Center for Responsive Politics, "2016 Outside Spending, by Super PAC," www.opensecrets.org/outsidespending/summ.php?chrt=V&type=S (accessed 11/10/16).

32. Center for Responsive Politics, "2018 Outside Spending, by Super PAC," November 8, 2018, www.opensecrets.org/outsidespending/summ.php?chrt=V&type=S (accessed 11/8/18).

33. Elisabeth R. Gerber, *The Populist Paradox* (Princeton, NJ: Princeton University Press, 1999), 6.

34. *The Federalist Papers*, no. 10.

35. Olson, *Logic of Collective Action.*

CHAPTER 9

1. "Small Business Owners Praise GOP Tax Bill," Fox Business, December 20, 2017, www.foxbusiness.com/politics/2017/12/20/small-business-owners-praise-gop-tax-bill.html (accessed 2/3/18).

2. Erin Dooley and Meridith McGraw, "Program That Provides Low-Cost Health Care to 9M Children Set to Expire," ABC News, September 29, 2017, abcnews.go.com/US/program-low-cost-health-care-9m-children-set/story?id=50188069 (accessed 2/4/18).

3. Juliette Cubanski and Tricia Neuman, "The Facts of Medicare Spending and Financing," Kaiser Family Foundation Issue Brief, July 18, 2017, www.kff.org/medicare/issue-brief/the-facts-on-medicare-spending-and-financing/ (accessed 2/4/18).

4. Jennifer E. Manning, "Membership of the 114th Congress," Congressional Research Service, September 7, 2016 www.senate.gov/CRSpubs/c527ba93-dd4a-4ad6-b79d-b1c9865ca076.pdf (accessed 11/10/16); Ballotpedia, "U.S. Senate" and "U.S. House," www.ballotpedia.org (accessed 11/10/16); and U.S. Census Quick Facts, www.census.gov/quickfacts/table/PST045215/00 (accessed 11/10/16).

5. Jennifer E. Manning, *Membership of the 112th Congress: A Profile*, Congressional Research Service 7-5700, September 20, 2011, 2, http://fpc.state.gov/documents/organization/174246.pdf (accessed 1/23/12).

6. For some interesting empirical evidence, see Angus Campbell et al., *Elections and the Political Order* (New York: Wiley, 1966), chap. 11.

7. Partnership for a More Perfect Union at the Congressional Management Foundation, "Communicating with Congress: How Citizen Advocacy Is Changing Mail Operations on Capitol Hill," 2011, http://congressfoundation.org/storage/documents/CMF_Pubs/cwc-mail-operations.pdf (accessed 1/23/12).

8. John S. Saloma, *Congress and the New Politics* (Boston: Little, Brown, 1969), 184–85. A 1977 official report using less detailed categories came up with almost the same impression of Congress's workload. Commission on Administrative Review, "Administrative Reorganization and Legislative Management," H.R. Doc. No. 95-232 (September 28, 1977), vol. 2, especially 17–19.

9. Dan Balz, "Dodd, Dorgan, and Ritter to Retire as Democrats Face a Difficult Mid-Term Year," *Washington Post*, January 7, 2010, www.washingtonpost.com/wp-dyn/content/article/2010/01/06/AR2010010602543.html (accessed 9/17/18).

10. Simone Pathe, "Democrats Identify Vulnerable Incumbent Members for 2018," Roll Call, March 6, 2017, www.rollcall.com/politics/democrats-identify-vulnerable-members-2018 (accessed 3/22/18).

11. See Barbara C. Burrell, *A Woman's Place Is in the House: Campaigning for Congress in the Feminist Era* (Ann Arbor: University of Michigan Press, 1994); and David Broder, "Key to Women's Political Parity: Running," *Washington Post*, September 8, 1994, A17.

12. Mark Hugo Lopez and Paul Taylor, "The 2010 Congressional Reapportionment and Latinos," Pew Research Center, Hispanic Trends, January 5, 2011, www.pewhispanic.org/2011/01/05/the-2010-congressional-reapportionment-and-latinos (accessed 2/24/14).

13. R. E. Cohen, "Did Redistricting Sink the Democrats?" *National Journal*, December 17, 1994, 2984.

14. *Miller v. Johnson*, 515 U.S. 900 (1995).

15. Bernie Becker, "Reapportionment Roundup," *New York Times*, December 24, 2009, http://thecaucus.blogs.nytimes.com/2009/12/24/reapportionment-roundup/ (accessed 1/31/10).

16. L. Paige Whitaker, "Congressional Redistricting and the Voting Rights Act: A Legal Overview," Congressional Research Service, April 13, 2015, www.fas.org/sgp/crs/misc/R42482.pdf (accessed 7/1/16).

17. Chris Cillizza, "What the Supreme Court's Voting Rights Act Decision Means for Politics," *Washington Post*, June 25, 2013, www.washingtonpost.com/blogs/the-fix/wp/2013/06/25/what-the-voting-rights-act-decision-means-for-politics (accessed 12/2/13).
18. Tarini Parti, "High Court Reasserts Voting Rights Act in Alabama Decision," *Politico*, March 25, 2015, www.politico.com/story/2015/03/supreme-court-alabama-redistricting-ruling-116384 (accessed 9/14/15).
19. Tom Hamburger and Richard Simon, "Everybody Will Know If It's Pork," *Los Angeles Times*, January 6, 2007, A1.
20. Don Seymour, "House Republicans Renew Earmark Ban for 113th Congress," website of the Speaker of the House, November 16, 2012, www.speaker.gov/general/house-republicans-renew-earmark-ban-113th-congress (accessed 12/1/13).
21. Aaron Blake, "Trump Wants to Bring Earmarks Back," *Washington Post*, January 10, 2018, www.washingtonpost.com/news/the-fix/wp/2018/01/10/trump-wants-to-bring-earmarks-back-heres-why-its-not-so-crazy/?utm_term=.5748db2288a1 (accessed 3/22/18).
22. Martin Frost and Tom Davis, "How to Fix What Ails Congress; Bring Back Earmarks," *Los Angeles Times*, February 8, 2015, www.latimes.com/opinion/op-ed/la-oe-frost-earmark-spending-20150209-story.html (accessed 9/14/15).
23. Associated Press, "Congress Passes Rare Private Immigration Bills," December 15, 2010, www.huffingtonpost.com/huff-wires/20101215/us-private-immigration-bills/ (accessed 2/1/12).
24. Richard Fenno, Jr., *Home Style: House Members in Their Districts* (Boston: Little, Brown, 1978).
25. Edward Epstein, "Dusting Off Deliberation," *CQ Weekly*, June 14, 2010, 1436–42; Sarah Binder, "Where Have All the Conference Committees Gone?" *The Monkey Cage* (blog), December 21, 2011, themonkeycage.org/blog/2011/12/21/where-have-all-the-conference-committees-gone (accessed 2/7/12).
26. Rebecca Kimitch, "CQ Guide to the Committees: Democrats Opt to Spread the Power," *Congressional Quarterly Weekly*, April 16, 2007, 1080.
27. U.S. Senate, Senate Action on Cloture Motions, www.senate.gov/pagelayout/reference/cloture_motions/clotureCounts.htm (accessed 11/9/18).
28. Jeremy W. Peters, "Senate Vote Curbs Filibuster Power to Stall Nominees," *New York Times*, November 22, 2013, A1.
29. Sean Sullivan and Mike DeBonis, "Congress Averts Homeland Security Shutdown with One-Week Extension," *Washington Post*, February 28, 2015, www.washingtonpost.com/politics/house-gop-hopes-to-pass-stopgap-dhs-funding-before-midnight-shutdown/2015/02/27/22021530-be88-11e4-b274-e5209a3bc9a9_story.html (accessed 9/21/15).
30. See John W. Kingdon, *Congressmen's Voting Decisions* (New York: Harper & Row, 1973), chap. 3; and R. Douglas Arnold, *The Logic of Congressional Action* (New Haven, CT: Yale University Press, 1990).
31. Eric Lipton and Ben Protess, "Banks' Lobbyists Help in Drafting Financial Bills," *New York Times*, May 23, 2013, dealbook.nytimes.com/2013/05/23/banks-lobbyists-help-in-drafting-financial-bills/; Michael Corkery, "Citigroup Becomes the Fall Guy in the Spending Bill Battle," *New York Times*, December 12, 2014, dealbook.nytimes.com/2014/12/12/citigroup-becomes-the-fall-guy-in-the-spending-bill-battle/ (accessed 9/21/15).
32. Thomas E. Mann and Norman J. Ornstein, "Vital Statistics," The Brookings Institution, May 21, 2018, www.brookings.edu/multi-chapter-report/vital-statistics-on-congress/ (accessed 7/1/18).
33. Center for Responsive Politics, Open Secrets.org, www.opensecrets.org/pacs/pacgot.php?cmte=C00525600&cycle=2016 (accessed 10/13/16).
34. Daniel Newhauser, "Three Booted from GOP Whip Team as Leaders Crack Down," *National Journal*, June 16, 2015, www.nationaljournal.com/congress/2015/06/16/Three-Booted-From-GOP-Whip-Team-Leaders-Crack-Down (accessed 9/21/15).

35. Mann and Ornstein, "Vital Statistics," Table 6-4.
36. Frank Newport, "Congressional Approval Sinks to Record Low," Gallup, Politics, November 12, 2013, www.gallup.com/poll/165809/congressional-approval-sinks-record-low.aspx (accessed 4/17/14).
37. See Geoffrey C. Layman, Thomas M. Carsey, and Juliana Menasce Horowitz, "Party Polarization in American Politics: Characteristics, Causes, and Consequences," *Annual Review of Political Science* 9 (2006): 83–110.
38. Michael S. Schmidt and Maggie Haberman, "Aides for Hillary Clinton and Benghazi Committee Dispute Testimony Plan," *New York Times*, July 25, 2015, www.nytimes.com/2015/07/26/us/clinton-to-testify-publicly-before-house-committee-investigating-benghazi-attacks.html (accessed 9/21/15).
39. Gregory Krieg, "FBI Boss Comey's 7 Most Damning Lines on Clinton," CNN, July 5, 2016, www.cnn.com/2016/07/05/politics/fbi-clinton-email-server-comey-damning-lines/ (accessed 9/21/16).
40. Carroll J. Doherty, "Impeachment: How It Would Work," *Congressional Quarterly Weekly Report*, January 31, 1998, 222.

CHAPTER 10

1. This account is drawn from Amy Nixon, "Community Raises Funds to Support Hartley Family after Son Dies in Work Accident," *Tennessean,* May 4, 2017, www.tennessean.com/story/news/local/cheatham/2017/05/04/community-raises-funds-support-hartley-family-after-son-dies-work-accident/101283588/ (accessed 3/2/18); Eric Lipton, "Why Has the E.P.A. Shifted on Toxic Chemicals? An Industry Insider Helps Call the Shots," *New York Times,* October 21, 2017, www.nytimes.com/2017/10/21/us/trump-epa-chemicals-regulations.html (accessed 3/2/18); and Jamie Smith Hopkins, "EPA Wants to Restrict Sometimes-Deadly Paint Stripper Chemical," The Center for Public Integrity, January 12, 2017, www.publicintegrity.org/2017/01/12/20589/epa-wants-restrict-sometimes-deadly-paint-stripper-chemical (accessed 3/2/18).
2. These statutes are contained mainly in Title 10 of the U.S. Code, Sections 331, 332, and 333.
3. Devlin Barrett and Abby Phillip, "Trump Pardons Former Arizona Sheriff Joe Arpaio," *Washington Post,* August 25, 2017, www.washingtonpost.com/world/national-security/trump-pardons-former-arizona-sheriff-joe-arpaio/2017/08/25/afbff4b6-86b1-11e7-961d-2f373b3977ee_story.html?utm_term=.a1ee89306fef (accessed 2/20/18).
4. In *United States v. Pink*, 315 U.S. 203 (1942), the Supreme Court confirmed that an executive agreement is the legal equivalent of a treaty, despite the absence of Senate approval. This case approved the executive agreement that was used to establish diplomatic relations with the Soviet Union in 1933. An executive agreement, not a treaty, was used in 1940 to exchange "50 overage destroyers" for 99-year leases on some important military bases.
5. For a different perspective, see William F. Grover, *The President as Prisoner: A Structural Critique of the Carter and Reagan Years* (Albany: State University of New York Press, 1988).
6. There is a third source of presidential power implied from the provision for "faithful execution of the laws." This is the president's power to impound funds—that is, to refuse to spend money Congress has appropriated for certain purposes. One author referred to this as a "retroactive veto power" (Robert E. Goosetree, "The Power of the President to Impound Appropriated Funds," *American University Law Review*

[January 1962]). Many modern presidents used this impoundment power freely and to considerable effect, and Congress has occasionally delegated such power to the president by statute. But in reaction to the Watergate scandal, Congress adopted the Budget and Impoundment Control Act of 1974, which was designed to circumscribe the president's ability to impound funds by requiring that the president spend all appropriated funds unless both houses of Congress consented to an impoundment within 45 days of a presidential request. Therefore, since 1974, the use of impoundment has declined significantly. Presidents have had to either bite their tongues and accept unwanted appropriations or revert to the older and more dependable but politically limited method of vetoing the entire bill.

7. For more on the veto, see Robert J. Spitzer, *The Presidential Veto: Touchstone of the American Presidency* (Albany: State University of New York Press, 1988).

8. John Yoo, *The Powers of War and Peace* (Chicago: University of Chicago Press, 2003). See also Dana Nelson, "The Unitary Executive Question: What Do McCain and Obama Think of the Concept?" *Los Angeles Times*, October 11, 2008, www.latimes.com/opinion/la-oe-nelson11-2008oct11-story.html (accessed 7/30/18).

9. See Eric Posner and Adrian Vermeule, *The Executive Unbound: After the Madisonian Republic* (Chicago: University of Chicago Press, 2011); Robert J. Spitzer, "The Unitary Executive and the Bush Presidency," in *The George W. Bush Presidency*, ed. Meena Bose (New York: Nova Publishers, 2016).

10. "Unchecked Abuse," *Washington Post*, January 11, 2006, www.washingtonpost.com/wp-dyn/content/article/2006/01/10/AR2006011001536.html (accessed 7/30/18).

11. Louis Fisher, "Invoking Inherent Powers: A Primer," *Presidential Studies Quarterly* 37, no. 1 (March 2007): 1–22.

12. Harold C. Relyea, "National Emergency Powers," Congressional Research Service, 2007, http://fas.org/sgp/crs/natsec/98-505.pdf (accessed 3/27/18).

13. Andrew Reeves, "Political Disaster: Unilateral Powers, Electoral Incentives, and Presidential Disaster Declarations," *Journal of Politics* 73, no. 4 (October 2011): 1142–51.

14. A substantial portion of this section is taken from Theodore J. Lowi, *The Personal President* (Ithaca, NY: Cornell University Press, 1985), 141–50.

15. Article I, Section 3, provides that "The Vice-President . . . shall be President of the Senate, but shall have no Vote, unless they be equally divided." This is the only vote the vice president is allowed.

16. Samuel Kernell, *Going Public: New Strategies of Presidential Leadership*, 4th ed. (Washington, DC: CQ Press, 2006); also, Jeffrey K. Tulis, *The Rhetorical Presidency* (Princeton, NJ: Princeton University Press, 1987).

17. Tulis, *The Rhetorical Presidency*, 91.

18. Sidney M. Milkis, *The President and the Parties* (New York: Oxford University Press, 1993), 97.

19. James MacGregor Burns, *Roosevelt: The Lion and the Fox* (New York: Harcourt, Brace, 1956), 317.

20. Kernell, *Going Public*, 79.

21. Claire Cain Miller, "How Obama's Internet Campaign Changed Politics," *New York Times*, November 7, 2008; David Plouffe, *The Audacity to Win: The Inside Story and Lessons of Barack Obama's Historic Victory* (New York: Penguin, 2009).

22. Gallup, "Presidential Job Approval Center," www.gallup.com/poll/124922/presidential-approval-center.aspx (accessed 3/14/14).

23. Lowi, *The Personal President*.

24. Lowi, *The Personal President*, 11.

25. Harold W. Stanley and Richard G. Niemi, *Vital Statistics on American Politics, 2001–2002* (Washington, DC: CQ Press, 2001), 250–51.

26. Milkis, *The President and the Parties*, 128.

27. Milkis, *The President and the Parties*, 160.

28. John M. Broder, "Powerful Shaper of U.S. Rules Quits, with Critics in Wake," *New York Times*, August 4, 2012, A1.

29. Nadja Popovich, "67 Environmental Rules on the Way Out under Trump," *New York Times*, January 31, 2018, www.nytimes.com/interactive/2017/10/05/climate/trump-environment-rules-reversed.html (accessed 2/20/18).

30. A complete inventory is provided in Harold C. Relyea, "Presidential Directives: Background and Review," Congressional Research Service Report 98-611 (Washington, DC: Library of Congress, November 9, 2001).

31. Terry M. Moe and William G. Howell, "The Presidential Power of Unilateral Action," *Journal of Law, Economics and Organization* 15, no. 1 (January 1999): 133–34.

32. Peter Baker, "Obama Is Making Plans to Use Executive Power for Action on Several Fronts," *New York Times*, February 13, 2010, A12.

33. Harold C. Relyea, "Presidential Directives: Background and Overview," Congressional Research Service, November 26, 2008, http://fas.org/sgp/crs/misc/98-611.pdf (accessed 7/30/18)

34. Adam L. Warber, *Executive Orders and the Modern Presidency* (Boulder, CO: Lynne Rienner Publishers, 2006), 118–20.

35. Vivian S. Chu and Ted Garvey, "Executive Orders: Issuance, Modification, and Revocation," Congressional Research Service, April 16, 2014, http://fas.org/sgp/crs/misc/RS20846.pdf (accessed 3/25/18).

36. *Dames & Moore v. Regan,* 453 U.S. 654 (1981).

37. Mark Killenbeck, "A Matter of Mere Approval: The Role of the President in the Creation of Legislative History," *University of Arkansas Law Review* 239, no. 48 (1995).

38. Philip Cooper, *By Order of the President* (Lawrence: University Press of Kansas, 2002), 201.

39. Louis Fisher, *Congressional Abdication on War and Spending* (College Station: Texas A&M Press, 2000).

CHAPTER 11

1. This account draws from Abby Goodnough, Monica Davey, and Mitch Smith, "When the Water Turned Brown," *New York Times,* January 23, 2016, www.nytimes.com/2016/01/24/us/when-the-water-turned-brown.html; Amy Davidson, "The Contempt That Poisoned Flint's Water," *New Yorker,* January 22, 2016, www.newyorker.com/news/amy-davidson/the-contempt-that-poisoned-flints-water; and Lindsey Smith, "This Mom Helped Uncover What Was Really Going On with Flint's Water," Michigan Public Radio, December 4, 2015, http://michiganradio.org/post/mom-helped-uncover-what-was-really-going-flint-s-water (accessed 8/11/17).

2. Flint Water Advisory Task Force, Final Report, March 2016, www.michigan.gov/documents/snyder/FWATF_FINAL_REPORT_21March2016_517805_7.pdf (accessed 8/11/17).

3. Amy B. Zegart, *Spying Blind: The CIA, the FBI, and the Origins of 9/11* (Princeton, NJ: Princeton University Press, 2009).

4. John M. Broder, "U.S. Issues Limits on Greenhouse Gas Emissions from Cars," *New York Times*, April 2, 2010, B1.

5. Lisa Friedman and Brad Plumer, "E.P.A. Announces Repeal of Major Obama-Era Carbon Emissions Rule," *New York Times,* October 9, 2017, www.nytimes.com/2017/10/09/climate/clean-power-plan.html (accessed 10/24/17).

6. Margaret Cronin Fisk, Kartikay Mehrotra, Alan Katz, and Jeff Plungis, "Volkswagen Agrees to $15 Billion Diesel-Cheating Settlement," Bloomberg News, June 28, 2016, www.bloomberg.com/news/articles/2016-06-28/volkswagen-to-pay-14-7-billion-to-settle-u-s-emissions-claims (accessed 7/8/16).

7. Congressional Budget Office, "Comparing the Compensation of Federal and Private-Sector Employees, 2011–2015," April 2017, www.cbo.gov/system/files/115th-congress-2017-2018/reports/52637-federalprivatepay.pdf (accessed 12/20/17).

8. Office of Personnel Management, "Profile of Federal Civilian Non-Postal Employees," September 30, 2017, www.opm.gov/policy-data-oversight/data-analysis-documentation/federal-employment-reports/reports-publications/profile-of-federal-civilian-non-postal-employees/ (accessed 10/13/18).

9. The President's Budget FY18, Analytical Perspectives, www.whitehouse.gov/omb/budget (accessed 8/10/17).

10. President Barack Obama, First Inaugural Address, January 21, 2009, https://obamawhitehouse.archives.gov/blog/2009/01/21/president-barack-obamas-inaugural-address (accessed 8/5/17).

11. Lisa Rein and Andrew Ba Tran, "How the Trump Era Is Changing the Federal Bureaucracy," *Washington Post,* December 30, 2017, www.washingtonpost.com/politics/how-the-trump-era-is-changing-the-federal-bureaucracy/2017/12/30/8d5149c6-daa7-11e7-b859-fb0995360725_story.html?utm_term=.c60128f90c6f (accessed 9/11/18); U.S. Department of Defense, "About the Department of Defense," www.defense.gov/About/ (accessed 12/20/17). The DOD also employs about 750,000 civilians.

12. Bureau of Labor Statistics, "Table B-1. Employees on Nonfarm Payrolls by Industry Sector and Selected Industry Detail," www.bls.gov/webapps/legacy/cesbtab1.htm (accessed 7/15/16).

13. There are historical reasons that American cabinet-level administrators are called "secretaries." During the Second Continental Congress and the subsequent confederal government, standing committees were formed to deal with executive functions related to foreign affairs, military and maritime issues, and public financing. The heads of those committees were called "secretaries" because their primary task was to handle all correspondence and documentation related to their areas of responsibility.

14. Morgan Chalfant, "Homeland Security Sees Power Grow under Trump," The Hill, October 19, 2017, http://thehill.com/policy/national-security/356131-homeland-security-sees-power-grow-under-trump (accessed 11/10/17).

15. Laura Koran, Elise Labott, and Nicole Gaouette, "Tillerson Visits Russia as Tensions over Syria Flare," CNN, April 11, 2017, www.cnn.com/2017/04/11/politics/rex-tillerson-putin-russia-g7/index.html (accessed 8/11/17).

16. U.S. Department of State, "Department Organization Chart: November 2016," www.state.gov/r/pa/ei/rls/dos/99484.htm (accessed 8/5/17); Robbie Gramer, "Lawmakers Slam Tillerson's Bungled State Department Reforms," *Foreign Policy,* November 15, 2017, http://foreignpolicy.com/2017/11/15/lawmakers-slam-tillersons-bungled-state-department-reforms-diplomacy-foreign-service-trump-administration-redesign-congress-corker-cardin/ (accessed 1/5/18).

17. For more detail, consult John E. Harr, *The Professional Diplomat* (Princeton, NJ: Princeton University Press, 1972), 11; and Nicholas Horrock, "The CIA Has Neighbors in the 'Intelligence Community,'" *New York Times*, June 29, 1975, sec. 4, 2.

See also Roger Hilsman, *The Politics of Policy Making in Defense and Foreign Affairs*, 3rd ed. (Englewood Cliffs, NJ: Prentice Hall, 1993).

18. In 2017 the Department of Defense had over 1.3 million active duty personnel and nearly 750,000 civilian employees. U.S. Department of Defense, "About the Department of Defense," www.defense.gov/About/ (accessed 12/20/17).

19. Congressional Research Service, "Defense Primer: The Department of Defense," December 13, 2016, https://fas.org/sgp/crs/natsec/IF10543.pdf (accessed 8/10/17).

20. Louise Osborne, "Europeans Outraged over NSA Spying, Threaten Action," *USA Today*, October 29, 2013, www.usatoday.com/story/news/world/2013/10/28/report -nsa-spain/3284609/ (accessed 1/24/14).

21. Mary Madden and Lee Rainie, "Americans' Views about Data Collection and Security," Pew Research Center, Internet, Science & Tech, May 20, 2015, www.pewinternet.org/ 2015/05/20/americans-views-about-data-collection-and-security/ (accessed 9/30/15).

22. David Cole, "Here's What's Wrong with the USA Freedom Act," *The Nation*, May 6, 2015, www.thenation.com/article/heres-whats-wrong-usa-freedom-act/ (accessed 11/10/17).

23. U.S. Department of the Treasury, "The Debt to the Penny and Who Holds It," www .treasurydirect.gov/NP/debt/current (accessed 7/7/16).

24. For an account of the Financial Stability Oversight Council and the passage of the Dodd-Frank financial regulatory legislation, see John T. Woolley and J. Nicholas Ziegler, "The Two-Tiered Politics of Financial Reform in the United States," in *Crisis and Control: Institutional Change in Financial Market Regulation*, ed. Renate Mayntz (Frankfurt, Germany: Campus Verlag, 2012); the council's early activities are described in Financial Stability Oversight Council, "2011 Annual Report," www.treasury.gov/initiatives/fsoc/Documents/FSOCAR2011.pdf, and in Edward V. Murphy and Michael B. Bernier, *Financial Stability Oversight Council: A Framework to Mitigate Systemic Risk* (Washington, DC: Congressional Research Service, November 15, 2011), www.llsdc.org/assets/DoddFrankdocs/crs-r42083.pdf (accessed 1/3/12).

25. The Editorial Board, "Don't Cheer as the I.R.S. Grows Weaker," *New York Times*, December 29, 2017, www.nytimes.com/2017/12/29/opinion/dont-cheer-as-the-irs -grows-weaker.html (accessed 7/30/18).

26. The title of this section was inspired by Peri Arnold, *Making the Managerial Presidency* (Princeton, NJ: Princeton University Press, 1986).

27. Daniel P. Gitterman, *Calling the Shots: The President, Executive Orders, and Public Policy* (Washington, DC: Brookings, 2017).

28. Paul C. Light, *A Government Ill Executed: The Decline of the Federal Service and How to Revive It* (Cambridge, MA: Harvard University Press, 2008).

29. For more details and evaluations, see David Rosenbloom, *Public Administration* (New York: Random House, 1986), 186–221; Charles H. Levine and Rosslyn Kleeman, "The Quiet Crisis in the American Public Service," in *Agenda for Excellence: Public Service in America*, ed. Patricia Ingraham and Donald Kettl (Chatham, NJ: Chatham House, 1992); and Patricia Ingraham and David Rosenbloom, "The State of Merit in the Federal Government," in *Agenda for Excellence*.

30. John Micklethwait, "Managing to Look Attractive," *New Statesman* 125, November 8, 1996, 24.

31. Robert M. Gates, *Duty: Memoirs of a Secretary at War* (New York: Alfred A. Knopf, 2014); Leon Panetta, *Worthy Fights: A Memoir of Leadership in War and Peace* (New York: Penguin, 2014).

32. Michael J. Glennon, *National Security and Double Government* (New York: Oxford University Press, 2015).

33. Michael Crowley, "The Deep State Is Real. But It Might Not Be What You Think," *Politico Magazine,* September/October 2017, www.politico.com/magazine/story/2017/09/05/deep-state-real-cia-fbi-intelligence-215537 (accessed 11/10/17).

34. David Epstein and Sharyn O'Halloran, *Delegating Powers: A Transaction Cost Politics Approach to Policymaking under Separate Powers* (Cambridge: Cambridge University Press, 1999).

35. Thomas E. Mann and Norman J. Ornstein, *The Broken Branch: How Congress Is Failing America and How to Get It Back on Track* (New York: Oxford University Press, 2006).

36. Linette Lopez and Lydia Ramsey, "'You Asked for It'—Congress Railed on the Maker of EpiPen," *Business Insider,* September 21, 2016, www.businessinsider.com/mylan-ceo-heather-bresch-house-oversight-committee-hearing-epipen-2016-9 (accessed 11/9/17); see Mathew D. McCubbins and Thomas Schwartz, "Congressional Oversight Overlooked: Police Patrols versus Fire Alarms," *American Journal of Political Science* 28, no. 1 (1984): 165–79.

37. Michael D. Shear and Michael S. Schmidt, "Benghazi Panel Engages Clinton in Tense Session," *New York Times*, October 22, 2015, www.nytimes.com/2015/10/23/us/politics/hillary-clinton-benghazi-committee.html?_r50 (accessed 10/29/15).

38. The Office of Technology Assessment was a fourth research agency serving Congress until 1995. It was one of the first agencies scheduled for elimination by the 104th Congress. Until 1983, Congress had still another tool of legislative oversight: the legislative veto. Agencies were obliged to submit to Congress every proposed decision or rule, which would then lie before both chambers for 30 to 60 days. If Congress took no action by a one-house or two-house resolution explicitly to veto the proposed measure during the prescribed period, the measure became law. In 1983 the Supreme Court declared the legislative veto unconstitutional on the grounds that it violated the separation of powers—that is, the resolutions Congress passed to exercise its veto were not subject to presidential veto, as required by the Constitution. See *Immigration and Naturalization Service v. Chadha*, 462 U.S. 919 (1983).

CHAPTER 12

1. This account draws from Austin Berg, "Meet the Man Who Could End Forced Union Fees for Government Workers," Illinois Policy, 2018, www.illinoispolicy.org/story/meet-the-man-who-could-end-forced-union-fees-for-government-workers/ (accessed 3/3/18); and P. R. Lockhart, "What the Latest Union Case Before the Supreme Court Could Mean for Workers of Color," Vox, February 26, 2018, www.vox.com/policy-and-politics/2018/2/26/17053328/janus-afscme-supreme-court-unions-minorities (accessed 3/3/18).

2. United States Courts, "Judicial Business 2014," www.uscourts.gov/statistics-reports/judicial-business-2014 (accessed 9/19/15).

3. Michael A. Fletcher, "Obama Criticized as Too Cautious, Slow on Judicial Posts," *Washington Post*, October 16, 2009, www.washingtonpost.com/wp-dyn/content/article/2009/10/15/AR2009101504083.html (accessed 3/1/10).

4. Timothy S. Huebner, "In Election Years, a History of Confirming Court Nominees," *New York Times,* February 16, 2016, www.nytimes.com/2016/02/16/opinion/in-election-years-a-history-of-confirming-court-nominees.html (accessed 3/15/18).

5. John Bowden, "Timeline: Brett Kavanaugh's Nomination to the Supreme Court," The Hill, October 6, 2018, https://thehill.com/homenews/senate/410217-timeline -brett-kavanaughs-nomination-to-the-supreme-court (accessed 10/16/18).
6. *Marbury v. Madison*, 5 U.S. 137 (1803).
7. *National Federation of Independent Businesses v. Sebelius*, 567 U.S. 519 (2012).
8. U.S. Government Printing Office, "Acts of Congress Held Unconstitutional in Whole or in Part by the Supreme Court of the United States," www.gpo.gov/fdsys/ pkg/GPO-CONAN-2013/pdf/GPO-CONAN-2013-11.pdf (accessed 4/20/14).
9. *Federal Election Commission v. Wisconsin Right to Life*, 551 U.S. 449 (2007); *Citizens United v. Federal Election Commission*, 558 U.S. 310 (2010); *McCutcheon v. Federal Election Commission*, 572 U.S. __ (2014).
10. *Matal v. Tam*, 582 U.S. __ (2107).
11. *Hamdi v. Rumsfeld*, 542 U.S. 507 (2004).
12. *Hamdan v. Rumsfeld*, 548 U.S. 557 (2006).
13. *Boumediene v. Bush*, 553 U.S. 723 (2008).
14. *Trump v. International Refugee Assistance Project* 582 U.S. __ (2017).
15. *Trump v. Hawaii*, 585 U.S. __ (2018).
16. The Supreme Court affirmed this review power in *Martin v. Hunter's Lessee*, 1 Wheat. 304 (1816).
17. *Brown v. Board of Education*, 347 U.S. 483 (1954).
18. *Lawrence v. Texas*, 539 U.S. 558 (2003).
19. *Pavan v. Smith*, 582 U.S. __ (2017).
20. *Alabama Legislative Black Caucus v. Alabama*, 575 U.S. __ (2015).
21. *Arizona State Legislature v. Arizona Independent Redistricting Commission*, 576 U.S. __ (2015).
22. *Cooper v. Harris* 581 U.S. __ (2017).
23. *United States v. Jones*, 565 U.S. __ (2012); *Riley v. California*, 573 U.S. __ (2014).
24. Robert Scigliano, *The Supreme Court and the Presidency* (New York: Free Press, 1971), 161. For an interesting critique of the solicitor general's role during the Reagan administration, see Lincoln Caplan, "Annals of the Law," *New Yorker*, August 17, 1987, 30–62.
25. Edward Lazarus, *Closed Chambers* (New York: Times Books, 1998), 6.
26. *Smith v. Allwright*, 321 U.S. 649 (1944).
27. Charles Krauthammer, "Why Roberts Did It," *Washington Post*, June 29, 2012, www .washingtonpost.com/opinions/charles-krauthammer-why-roberts-did-it/2012/06/28/ gJQA4X0g9V_story.html (accessed 4/22/14).
28. *Roe v. Wade*, 410 U.S. 113 (1973); *Griswold v. Connecticut*, 381 U.S. 479 (1965).
29. R. W. Apple, Jr., "A Divided Government Remains, and with It the Prospect of Further Combat," *New York Times*, November 7, 1996, B6.
30. Alexander Hamilton, James Madison, and John Jay, *The Federalist Papers*, ed. Clinton Rossiter (New York: New American Library, 1961), no. 10, 78.

CHAPTER 13

1. See Andrea Louise Campbell, *Trapped in America's Safety Net* (Chicago: University of Chicago Press, 2014).
2. David Brunori, "Where Is the Outrage Over Corporate Welfare?" *Forbes*, March 14, 2014, www.forbes.com/sites/taxanalysts/2014/03/14/where-is-the-outrage-over -corporate-welfare/#3f4a0aa727dd (accessed 1/1/18); Michael B. Tanner, "No to Coal Subsidies, No to Corporate Welfare," Cato Institute, August 16, 2017, www.cato.org/ publications/commentary/no-coal-subsidies-no-corporate-welfare, (accessed 10/25/17).

3. James Dao, "The Nation; Big Bucks Trip Up the Lean New Army," *New York Times*, February 10, 2002, sec. 4, 5.

4. For an evaluation of the policy of withholding subsidies to carry out desegregation laws, see Gary Orfield, *Must We Bus?* (Washington, DC: Brookings Institution Press, 1978). For an evaluation of the use of subsidies to encourage work or to calm political unrest, see Frances Fox Piven and Richard Cloward, *Regulating the Poor: The Functions of Public Welfare* (New York: Random House, 1971).

5. Federal Reserve Board, "Open Market Operations," www.federalreserve.gov/ monetarypolicy/openmarket.htm (accessed 8/1/16).

6. Thomas Kaplan, "House Gives Final Approval to Sweeping Tax Overhaul," *New York Times,* December 20, 2017, www.nytimes.com/2017/12/20/us/politics/tax-bill -republicans.html (accessed 7/31/18).

7. Social Security Administration, www.ssa.gov/policy/docs/quickfacts/prog_highlights/ RatesLimits2018.html (accessed 4/15/18).

8. C. Eugene Steuerle, Adam Carasso, and Lee Cohen, *How Progressive Is Social Security and Why?* (Washington, DC: Urban Institute, 2004), www.urban.org/research/ publication/how-progressive-social-security-and-why (accessed 5/3/14).

9. John R. Kearney, "Social Security and the 'D' in OASDI: The History of a Federal Program Insuring Earners against Disability," *Social Security Bulletin* 66 (3): 2005–6, www.ssa.gov/policy/docs/ssb/v66n3/v66n3p1.html (accessed 6/7/17).

10. Workers must have lost their job through no fault of their own. For a full description of the program see Chad Stone and William Chen, "Introduction to Unemployment Insurance," Center on Budget and Policy Priorities, July 30, 2014, www.cbpp.org/ research/introduction-to-unemployment-insurance (accessed 11/18/15).

11. Ife Floyd and Liz Schott, "TANF Cash Benefits Have Fallen by More Than 20 Percent in Most States and Continue to Erode," Center on Budget and Policy Priorities, October 13, 2017, www.cbpp.org/research/family-income-support/tanf-cash-benefits -have-fallen-by-more-than-20-percent-in-most-states (accessed 8/19/18).

12. This poverty threshold is for a household of three persons that includes two children. Department of Health and Human Services, Office of the Assistant Secretary for Planning and Evaluation, Poverty Guidelines, January 13, 2018, http://aspe.hhs.gov/ poverty-guidelines (accessed 7/10/18).

13. See Martin Gilens, *Why Americans Hate Welfare* (Chicago: University of Chicago Press, 1999), chaps. 3, 4.

14. Gilens, *Why Americans Hate Welfare.*

15. U.S. Government Accountability Office, "Temporary Assistance for Needy Families," December 2012, www.gao.gov/assets/660/650635.pdf (accessed 10/31/15).

16. Center for Law and Social Policy, "Analysis of Fiscal Year 2006 TANF and MOE Spending by States," http://clasp.org (accessed 4/9/08).

17. See the discussion of the law and the data presented in House Ways and Means Committee, *Background Material and Data on Programs within the Jurisdiction of the Committee on Ways and Means (Green Book)*, Section 7, "Temporary Assistance for Needy Families (TANF)," WMCP 106-14, http://frwebgate.access.gpo.gov (accessed 3/26/08); Rebecca M. Blank, "Evaluating Welfare Reform in the United States," *Journal of Economic Literature* 40 (December 2002): 1105–66.

18. LaDonna Pavetti and Liz Schott, "TANF's Inadequate Response to Recession High-lights Weakness of Block-Grant Structure," Center on Budget and Policy Priorities, July 14, 2011, www.cbpp.org/research/family-income-support/tanfs-inadequate -response-to-recession-highlights-weakness-of-block (accessed 6/1/16).

19. Center for Budget and Policy Priorities, "Chartbook: SNAP Helps Struggling Families Put Food on the Table," April 18, 2012, www.cbpp.org/research/food-assistance/

chart-book-snap-helps-struggling-families-put-food-on-the-table (accessed 6/1/16); U.S. Department of Agriculture, Food and Nutrition Service, "Supplemental Nutrition Assistance Program (SNAP)," www.fns.usda.gov/pd/34SNAPmonthly.htm (accessed 5/3/14)

20. Center for Budget and Policy Priorities, "Chartbook: SNAP Helps Struggling Families Put Food on the Table," April 18, 2012, www.cbpp.org/research/food-assistance/chart-book-snap-helps-struggling-families-put-food-on-the-table (accessed 6/1/16); U.S. Department of Agriculture, Food and Nutrition Service, "National and/or State Level Monthly and/or Annual Data," April 6, 2018, https://fns-prod.azureedge.net/sites/default/files/pd/34SNAPmonthly.pdf (accessed 4/15/18).

21. There were a couple of minor precedents. One was the Smith-Hughes Act of 1917, which made federal funds available to the states for vocational education at the elementary and secondary levels. Another was the Lanham Act of 1940, which made federal funds available to schools in "federally impacted areas," that is, areas with an unusually large number of government employees and/or where the local tax base was reduced by large amounts of government-owned property.

22. New America Foundation, "PreK–12 Financing Overview," June 29, 2015, atlas.newamerica.org/school-finance (accessed 7/10/16).

23. David K. Cohen and Susan L. Moffitt, *The Ordeal of Equality: Did Federal Regulation Fix the Schools?* (Cambridge, MA: Harvard University Press, 2009).

24. Rich Motoko, "'No Child' Law Whittled Down by White House," *New York Times*, July 6, 2012, A1; U.S. Department of Education, Elementary and Secondary Education, "ESEA Flexibility," www2.ed.gov/policy/elsec/guid/esea-flexibility/index.html (accessed 5/11/14).

25. Valerie Strauss, "The Successor to No Child Left Behind Has, It Turns Out, Big Problems of Its Own," *Washington Post*, December 7, 2015, www.washingtonpost.com/news/answer-sheet/wp/2015/12/07/the-successor-to-no-child-left-behind-has-it-turns-out-big-problems-of-its-own/ (accessed 7/11/16).

26. Sam Dillon, "Obama Proposes Sweeping Change in Education Law," *New York Times*, March 14, 2010, A1; Veronica DeVore, "'Race to the Top' Education Funds Awarded to 9 States and D.C.," August 24, 2010, www.pbs.org/newshour/rundown/2010/08/round-two-results-announced-for-race-to-the-top.html (accessed 11/13/12).

27. Elaine Weiss, "Mismatches in Race to the Top Limit Educational Improvement: Lack of Time, Resources, and Tools to Address Opportunity Gaps Puts Lofty State Goals Out of Reach," Economic Policy Institute, September 12, 2013, www.epi.org/publication/race-to-the-top-goals/ (accessed 5/11/14).

28. Tim Alberta, "The Education of Betsy DeVos," *Politico*, November/December 2017, www.politico.com/magazine/story/2017/11/01/betsy-devos-secretary-education-profile-2017-215768 (accessed 1/4/18).

29. Office of Management and Budget, Fiscal Year 2017, Historical Tables, "Table 12.3, Total Outlays for Grants to State and Local Governments, by Function, Agency, and Program: 1940–2017," www.whitehouse.gov/sites/default/files/omb/budget/fy2017/assets/hist.pdf (accessed 7/11/18).

30. Henry J. Kaiser Family Foundation, "Medicaid: A Primer—Key Information on the Nation's Health Coverage Program for Low-Income People," March 1, 2013, https://kaiserfamilyfoundation.files.wordpress.com/2010/06/7334-05.pdf (see p. 26) (accessed 6/2/16).

31. Henry J. Kaiser Family Foundation, "Total Monthly Medicaid and CHIP Enrollment," http://kff.org/health-reform/state-indicator/total-monthly-medicaid-and-chip-enrollment/ (accessed 11/4/15).

32. Congressional Budget Office, Long-Term Budget Projections (July 2016), "Table 1. Summary Data for the Extended Baseline," www.cbo.gov/about/products/budget_economic_data (accessed 7/16/16); Congressional Budget Office, Updated Budget Projections: 2016 to 2026, "Table 4. Mandatory Outlays Projected in CBO's Baseline," www.cbo.gov/sites/default/files/114th-congress-2015-2016/reports/51384-MarchBaseline_OneCol.pdf (accessed 7/16/16); Congressional Budget Office, Historical Budget Data (March 2016), "Table 5. Mandatory Outlays," www.cbo.gov/about/products/budget_economic_data (accessed 7/16/16); Congressional Budget Office, Baseline Projections for Selected Programs, Medicaid (Mar 2016), "Detail of Spending and Enrollment for Medicaid for CBO's March 2016 Baseline," www.cbo.gov/sites/default/files/51301-2016-03-Medicaid.pdf (accessed 7/16/16); Office of Management and Budget, Historical Tables, "Table 11.3—Outlays for Payments for Individuals by Category and Major Program: 1940–2021," www.whitehouse.gov/omb/budget/Historicals (accessed 7/16/16).

33. Henry J. Kaiser Family Foundation, "The Coverage Gap: Uninsured Poor Adults in States that Do Not Expand Medicaid—An Update," June 12, 2018, kff.org/health-reform/issue-brief/the-coverage-gap-uninsured-poor-adults-in-states-that-do-not-expand-medicaid-an-update/ (accessed 9/10/18).

34. *National Federation of Independent Business v. Sebelius*, 567 U.S. __ (2012). The ACA survived another major challenge when the Supreme Court upheld the law in *King v. Burwell* in 2015.

35. Henry J. Kaiser Family Foundation, "The Coverage Gap."

36. Jennifer Steinhauer, "House Votes to Send Bill to Repeal Health Law to Obama's Desk," *New York Times*, January 6, 2016, www.nytimes.com/2016/01/07/us/politics/house-votes-to-send-bill-to-repeal-health-law-to-obamas-desk.html (accessed 7/11/16).

37. Amy Goldstein, "ACA Enrollment for 2018 Nearly Matches Last Year's, Despite Trump Administration Efforts to Undermine It," *Washington Post*, December 21, 2017, www.washingtonpost.com/news/to-your-health/wp/2017/12/21/aca-enrollment-for-2018-nearly-matches-last-years-despite-trump-administration-efforts-to-undermine-it/?utm_term=.71fd6fc2204e (accessed 4/15/18).

38. James Krieger and Donna L. Higgins, "Housing and Health: Time Again for Public Health Action," *American Journal of Public Health* 92, no. 5 (May 2002): 758–68.

39. John E. Schwarz, *America's Hidden Success*, 2nd ed. (New York: W. W. Norton, 1988), 41–42.

40. Congressional Budget Office, "Federal Housing Assistance for Low-Income Households," September 2015, www.cbo.gov/sites/default/files/114th-congress-2015-2016/reports/50782-lowincomehousing-onecolumn.pdf (accessed 5/29/17).

41. ATTOM Data, "U.S. Foreclosure Activity Drops to 12-Year Low in 2017," January 16, 2018, www.attomdata.com/news/foreclosure-trends/2017-year-end-u-s-foreclosure-market-report/ (accessed 3/29/18).

42. U.S. Census Bureau, "Income and Poverty in the United States: 2016," Table 5, www.census.gov/content/dam/Census/library/publications/2016/demo/p60-256.pdf (accessed 9/10/18).

43. See, for example, Theodore R. Marmor, Jerry L. Mashaw, and Philip L. Harvey, *America's Misunderstood Welfare State* (New York: Basic Books, 1990), 156; U.S. Census Bureau, "Income and Poverty in the United States: 2016," www.census.gov/content/dam/Census/library/publications/2016/demo/p60-256.pdf (accessed 4/16/18).

44. U.S. Census Bureau, "Income and Poverty in the United States: 2016," www.census.gov/content/dam/Census/library/publications/2016/demo/p60-256.pdf (accessed 9/10/18).

45. U.S. Census Bureau, "Income and Poverty in the United States: 2015," Table B-2, www.census.gov/content/dam/Census/library/publications/2016/demo/p60-256.pdf (accessed 5/29/17).

46. See Andrea Louise Campbell, *How Policies Make Citizens: Senior Political Activism and the American Welfare State* (Princeton, NJ: Princeton University Press, 2005).

47. Christopher Howard, *The Hidden Welfare State: Tax Expenditures and Social Policy in the United States* (Princeton, NJ: Princeton University Press, 1999); Jacob S. Hacker, *The Divided Welfare State: The Battle over Public and Private Benefits in the United States* (New York: Cambridge University Press, 2002).

48. U.S. Congress Joint Committee on Taxation, "Estimates of Federal Tax Expenditures for Fiscal Years 2016–2020," www.jct.gov/publications.html?func=startdown& id=4971 (accessed 5/29/2017).

49. U.S. Department of Agriculture, Food and Nutrition Service, "Supplemental Nutrition Assistance Program (SNAP)," www.fns.usda.gov/snap/eligibility#Income (accessed 7/11/16); Center on Budget and Policy Priorities, "Policy Basics: Introduction to the Supplemental Nutrition Assistance Program (SNAP)," updated February 7, 2018, www.cbpp.org/research/policy-basics-introduction-to-the -supplemental-nutrition-assistance-program-snap (accessed 9/10/18).

50. "Panera CEO: On Food Stamps, I Can't Eat in My Own Restaurant," September 25, 2013, https://cnneatocracy.wordpress.com/2013/09/25/panera-ceo-on-food-stamps -i-cant-eat-in-my-own-restaurant/ (accessed 5/12/14).

51. Samantha Artiga, Anthony Damico, and Rachel Garfield, "The Impact of the Coverage Gap for Adults in States not Expanding Medicaid by Race and Ethnicity," October 26, 2015, http://kff.org/disparities-policy/issue-brief/the-impact-of-the -coverage-gap-in-states-not-expanding-medicaid-by-race-and-ethnicity/ (accessed 11/11/15).

52. Frances Fox Piven and Richard Cloward, *Poor People's Movements* (New York: Pantheon, 1977), chap. 5.

53. U.S. Department of Agriculture, Food and Nutrition Service, "National and/or State Level Monthly and/or Annual Data," April 6, 2018, www.fns.usda.gov/pd/ supplemental-nutrition-assistance-program-snap (accessed 9/10/18).

54. U.S. Census Bureau, "Income and Poverty in the United States: 2016."

55. U.S. Census Bureau, "Income and Poverty in the United States: 2016," Table B-2.

56. L. Free and Hadley Cantril, *The Political Beliefs of Americans* (New York: Simon and Schuster, 1968).

57. Fay Lomax Cook and Edith Barrett, *Support for the American Welfare State* (New York: Columbia University Press, 1992); and Hugh Heclo, "The Political Foundations of Antipoverty Policy," in *Fighting Poverty*, ed. Sheldon H. Danziger and Daniel H. Weinberg (Cambridge, MA: Harvard University Press, 1986), 312–40.

CHAPTER 14

1. Lyric Lewin, "In Support of a Travel Ban," CNN Politics, March 2017, www.cnn .com/interactive/2017/03/politics/travel-ban-supporters-cnnphotos/ (accessed 2/1/18).

2. Vivian Yee, "Meet the Everyday People Who Have Sued Trump. So Far, They've Won," *New York Times*, March 29, 2017, www.nytimes.com/2017/03/29/us/trump -travel-ban.html (accessed 4/12/18).

3. *Trump v. Hawaii*, 585 U.S. __ (2018).

4. Rupert Smith, *The Utility of Force: The Art of War in the Modern World* (New York: Vintage, 2008).

5. D. Robert Worley, *Shaping U.S. Military Forces: Revolution or Relevance in a Post–Cold War World* (Westport, CT: Praeger Security International, 2006).

6. Better World Campaign, "How the U.S. Funds the UN," https://betterworldcampaign .org/us-un-partnership/how-the-us-funds-the-un/ (accessed 9/19/14).

7. U.S. Senate, "Treaties," www.senate.gov/artandhistory/history/common/briefing/ Treaties.htm (accessed 4/15/18).

8. Benjamin Ginsberg, *The American Lie: Government by the People and Other Political Fables* (Boulder, CO: Paradigm, 2007).

9. Paul R. Pillar, *Terrorism and American Foreign Policy* (Washington, DC: Brookings Institution Press, 2003).

10. See Theodore Lowi, *The Personal President: Power Invested, Promise Unfulfilled* (Ithaca, NY: Cornell University Press, 1985), 167–9.

11. For information on current U.S. sanctions programs, visit U.S. Department of the Treasury, "Sanctions Programs and Country Information," www.treasury.gov/ resource-center/sanctions/Programs/Pages/Programs.aspx (accessed 6/11/14).

12. The Warsaw Pact was signed in 1955 by Albania, Bulgaria, Czechoslovakia, Hungary, the German Democratic Republic (East Germany), Poland, Romania, and the Soviet Union. Albania later dropped out. The Warsaw Pact was terminated in 1991.

13. Scott Shane and Mark Mazzetti, "Inside a Three-Year Russian Campaign to Influence U.S. Voters, *New York Times*, February 16, 2018, www.nytimes.com/2018/02/16/us/ politics/russia-mueller-election.html (accessed 4/15/18).

14. Elias Groll, "Feds Quietly Reveal Chinese State-Backed Hacking Operation," *Foreign Policy*, November 30, 2017, www.foreignpolicy.com/2017/11/30/feds-quietly-reveal -chinese-state-backed-hacking-operation/ (accessed 4/15/18).

Answer Key

Chapter 1
1. C
2. D
3. B
4. D
5. D
6. A
7. D
8. A
9. E
10. D
11. C
12. C
13. C
14. D

Chapter 2
1. B
2. A
3. B
4. C
5. C
6. E
7. D
8. E
9. E
10. A
11. D
12. A

Chapter 3
1. B
2. C
3. C
4. E
5. A
6. A
7. D
8. B
9. B

10. D
11. D
12. B

Chapter 4
1. E
2. B
3. A
4. E
5. B
6. D
7. A
8. A
9. C
10. D
11. C

Chapter 5
1. C
2. C
3. A
4. D
5. E
6. E
7. A
8. C
9. B
10. A
11. B

Chapter 6
1. B
2. A
3. B
4. D
5. D
6. A
7. B
8. C
9. C

10. C
11. B

Chapter 7
1. A
2. E
3. D
4. E
5. B
6. D
7. C
8. C
9. B
10. D
11. C

Chapter 8
1. A
2. B
3. E
4. D
5. C
6. B
7. B
8. E
9. D
10. E
11. C
12. D

Chapter 9
1. B
2. A
3. D
4. B
5. C
6. D
7. B
8. D
9. D

10. E
11. C
12. B
13. A
14. A

Chapter 10
1. B
2. C
3. B
4. C
5. E
6. A
7. C
8. A
9. C
10. B
11. D
12. A

Chapter 11
1. D
2. C
3. B
4. B
5. E
6. C
7. D
8. A
9. D
10. D
11. B
12. D

Chapter 12
1. A
2. C
3. A
4. D
5. C

6. D
7. E
8. A
9. B
10. A
11. C
12. A

Chapter 13
1. C
2. D

3. D
4. E
5. D
6. B
7. C
8. A
9. D
10. D
11. E
12. B

Chapter 14
1. B
2. A
3. D
4. C
5. C
6. E

7. A
8. C
9. A
10. E

Credits

PHOTOGRAPHS

Front Matter: Page vii: AP Photo/Cliff Owen; p. viii (top): Alex Wong/Getty Images; p. ix (top): Rob Hotakainen/MCT/Newscom; (bottom) Anthony Pidgeon/Redferns/Getty Images; p. x: Jay Mallin/ZUMAPRESS.com/Alamy live news; p. xi: Lyndon French/The New York Times/Redux; p. xii: Rod Lamkey/Getty Images; p. xiii (top): American Benefits Council; (bottom): Courtesy Guy Berkebile; p. xiv: Cheriss May/ZUMA Press/Newscom; p. xv (top): © G92, MJ3, F31/Zuma Press; (bottom): AP Photo/Andrew Harnik; p. xvi: AP Photo/Record Searchlight, Andreas Fuhrmann; p. xvii: Jerry Holt/Star Tribune/ZUMA Press.

Chapter 1: Page 2: Shutterstock; p. 3 (left): AP Photo/Cliff Owen; (right): Courtesy Kendric Jones; p. 8: Erik McGregor/Pacific Press/Newscom; p. 11: Rue des Archives/Granger, NYC—All rights reserved; p. 14: Jim West/Alamy Stock Photo; p. 18: Peter Casolino/Alamy Stock Photo; p. 20: Screenshot 2016 U.S. Department of Education Office of Federal Student Aid; p. 21: Ethan Miller/Getty Images.

Chapter 2: Page 30: Shutterstock; p. 31: Alex Wong/Getty Images; p. 36: Bettmann/Corbis via Getty Images; p. 37: Paul J. Richards/AFP/Getty Images; p. 40: Sarin Images/Granger, NYC—All rights reserved; p. 43: Samuel Jennings (active 1789–1834) *Liberty Displaying the Arts and Sciences, or The Genius of America Encouraging the Emancipation of the Blacks, 1792.* Oil on canvas. 60 1/4" × 74." Library Company of Philadelphia. Gift of the artist, 1792; p. 54: Paul J. Richards/AFP/Getty Images.

Chapter 3: Page 66: Sergey Pykhonin/Alamy Stock Vector; p. 67: Rob Hotakainen/MCT/Newscom; p. 71: AP Photo/Adam Beam; p. 77: Library of Congress; p. 78: Library of Congress; p. 84: Ilene MacDonald/Alamy Stock Photo; p. 85: AP Photo; p. 89: Ethan Miller/Getty Images.

Chapter 4: Page 96: Shutterstock; p. 97: Anthony Pidgeon/Redferns/Getty Images; p. 105: Chip Somodevilla/Getty Images; p. 107: Michael S. Williamson/The Washington Post via Getty Images; p. 115: AP Photo/Matt York; p. 118: Tracy A. Woodward/The Washington Post via Getty Images; p. 120: Win McNamee/Getty Images; p. 122: Library of Congress; p. 124: Bettmann/Getty Images; p. 132: AP Photo/Ron Edmonds; p. 133: Kent Sievers/The World-Herald via AP; p. 137: Drew Angerer/CNP/AdMedia/Newscom.

Chapter 5: Page 144: Shutterstock; p. 145 (left): Jay Mallin/ZUMAPRESS.com/Alamy live news; (right): Tom Brenner/The New York Times/Redux; p. 148: AP Photo/Evan Vucci; p. 153: Shelly Rivoli/Alamy Stock Photo; p. 159 (top): Saul Loeb/AFP/Getty Images; (bottom): Twitter/@realDonaldTrump; p. 162 CALVIN AND HOBBES © 1994 Watterson. Reprinted with permission of Andrews McMeel Syndication. All rights reserved; p. 168 (top): Bettmann/Getty Images; (bottom): Lionel Hahn/ABACAPRESS.com/Sipa via AP Images.

Chapter 6: Page 176 (both): Shutterstock; p. 177: Lyndon French/The New York Times/Redux; p. 181: (left): Paul Marotta/Getty Images; (right): AP Photo/Richard Drew; p. 191: Melina Mara/The Washington Post via Getty Images; p. 194: Kyodo via AP Images; p. 195: AP Photo/Mary Altaffer.

Chapter 7: Page 204: Shutterstock; p. 205 (photo): Rod Lamkey/Getty Images; (illustration):

Shutterstock; p. 209: Mario Tama/Getty Images; p. 214: Granger, NYC—All rights reserved; p. 225: Scott Olson/Getty Images; p. 230: Smith Collection/Gado/Getty Images; p. 235: Whitney Curtis/Getty Images.

Chapter 8: Page 246: Shutterstock; p. 247: American Benefits Council; p. 251: AP Photo/ Sue Ogrocki; p. 265: Justin Sullivan/Getty Images.

Chapter 9: Page 274: Shutterstock; p. 275: (left): Courtesy Guy Berkebile; (right): Scott Olson/ Getty Images; p. 280: Chip Somodevilla/Getty Images; P. 285: AP Photo/Ross D. Franklin; p. 290: Tom Williams/CQ Roll Call/Getty Images; p. 298: Rachel Mummey for The Washington Post via Getty Images; p. 302: DPA Picture Alliance/ Alamy Stock Photo.

Chapter 10: Page 314: Shutterstock; p. 315: Cheriss May/ZUMA Press/Newscom; p. 317: Bettmann/Getty Images; p. 319: AP Photo/ File; p. 320: Anthony Wallace/AFP/Getty Images; p. 326: U.S. Army photo by Capt. Tyson Friar; p. 330: Tom Williams/CQ Roll Call/Getty Images; p. 333: Twitter/@realDonaldTrump; p. 338: T.J. Kirkpatrick/Bloomberg via Getty Images.

Chapter 11: Page 346: Shutterstock; p. 347: © G92, MJ3, F31/Zuma Press; p. 350: Michael Williamson/The Washington Post via Getty Images; p. 355: NG Images/Alamy Stock Photo; p. 360 (both): Yasin Ozturk/Anadolu Agency/ Getty Images; p. 366: Andrew Harrer/Bloomberg via Getty Images.

Chapter 12: Page 374: Shutterstock; p. 375: AP Photo/Andrew Harnik; p. 377: AP Photo/ Michael Tarm; p. 388: Mark Wilson/Getty Images; p. 390: Michael Hibblen/KUAR News; p. 399: Alex Wong/Getty Images.

Chapter 13: Page 406: LEO crafts/iStock/ Getty Images; p. 407: AP Photo/Record Searchlight, Andreas Fuhrmann; p. 414: Drew Angerer/ Getty Images; p. 417: Joseph Barnell/SuperStock; p. 421: Derek Davis/Portland Press Herald via Getty Images; p. 426: Education & Exploration 1/ Alamy Stock Photo; p. 430: Bryan R. Smith/ AFP/Getty Images; p. 433: Saul Loeb/Getty Images.

Chapter 14: Page 444 (both): Shutterstock; p. 445: Jerry Holt/Star Tribune/ZUMA Press; p. 448: Bettmann/Getty Images; p. 454: Mikhail Metzel/TASS via Getty Images; p. 458: Michele Eve Sandberg/Corbis via Getty Images; p. 462: Adek Berry/Stringer/Getty Images; p. 466: Korean Central News Agency/Korea News Service via AP, File.

TEXT

Figure 5.1: Graph from "Large Majorities See Checks and Balances, Right to Protest as Essential for Democracy," Pew Research Center, Washington, DC (May 2017) http://www.people -press.org/2017/03/02/large-majorities-see-checks -and-balances-right-to-protest-as-essential-for -democracy/democracy_11/. Reprinted with permission.

Figure 11.3: "Iron Triangles" republished with permission of Wadsworth, a division of Cengage Learning from *Incomplete Conquest: Governing America*, 2nd ed. by Theodore J. Lowi (New York: Holt, Rinehart and Winston, 1981), p. 139. © 1981 by CBS College.

Glossary/Index

agents of socialization, 152–57 social institutions, including families and schools, that help to shape individuals' basic political beliefs and values

Agricultural Research Service, 353
agricultural subsidies, 415
AIDS, 425
Aid to Dependent Children (ADC), 436–37
Aid to Families with Dependent Children (AFDC), 419, 435, 437
Air America, 180
Alabama
    and comity clause, 72
    immigration law in, 133
    legislative districting, 389
    Montgomery bus boycott, 124
Alabama syndrome, 81
Alaska, 72
Alien and Sedition Acts, 106
ambassadors, 454, 455

amendments, 56–60, *58–59* a change added to a bill, law, or constitution; *see also* Bill of Rights
    as "higher law," 57–60
    list of, *58–59*
    methods for creating, 56–57, *57*
    process for creating, 48
    proposed, 56–57

American Chemistry Council, 315
American Civil Liberties Union (ACLU), 110, 394
American Federation of State, County, and Municipal Employees (AFSCME), 374
American Medical Association, 250
American population
    changes over time in, 10–16
    political knowledge of, 157–60
American Recovery and Reinvestment Act, 425
American Revolution (1776), 6
    and balance of power among states, 37–38
    forces contributing to, 34
Americans with Disabilities Act of 1990 (ADA), *84,* 87, 136

amicus curiae, 393, 394 literally, "friend of the court"; individuals or groups who are not parties to a lawsuit but who seek to assist the Supreme Court in reaching a decision by presenting additional briefs

Amtrak, 354
Andrus, Ethel Percy, 257
Annapolis Convention, 39

Antifederalists those who favored strong state governments and a weak national government and were opponents of the constitution proposed at the American Constitutional Convention of 1787
    and bill of rights, 99, 100
    Federalists vs., *52*
    as outsiders, 211

primary base of, 207
and ratification of Constitution, 51–56

appeals, filing, 380

appeasement, 448 the effort to forestall war by giving in to the demands of a hostile power

appellant, 380
appellate courts, *382,* 382–83
Apple, *54*
Apple Corporation, 115
appointments, political, 384–85

apportionment, 283–86, *284, 285* the process, occurring after every decennial census, that allocates congressional seats among the 50 states

appropriations, 304 the amounts of money approved by Congress in statutes (bills) that each unit or agency of government can spend

arbitration, 463–64
Arizona
    districting plan in, 390
    immigration law in, 89, 133–34
    and 2010 reapportionment, 284
Arizona v. United States, 89
Arkansas, 319, 389
Arpaio, Joe, 320
Arthur, John, 30–31
Article III (U.S. Constitution), 381, 390–91

Articles of Confederation, 37–38, *45* America's first written constitution; served as the basis for America's national government until 1789

Asaei, Ali, 445
Asia, ethnic and racial diversity in, 17
Asian Americans
    civil rights of, 132–34
    as digital citizens, 188
    as proportion of population, 11, *13*
Asians, ban on naturalization of, 11
Assad, Bashar al-, 465
assembly, freedom of, 106–8
Associated Press, 180, 181
Association of Young Americans (AYA), 246–47
AT&T, 250

attitude (or opinion) a specific preference on a particular issue
    about politics, 147–52
    defined, 147
    political, 147

Australia, *226*

authoritarian government, 5 a system of rule in which the government recognizes no formal limit but may nevertheless be restrained by the power of other social institutions

automobile emission standards, 350

B

background checks, for firearm sales, *113*

Bakke, Allan, 129

Bakke case, 129

balance of powers, 43–51, *50*

ballot initiative, 7, 230, 267   a proposed law or policy change that is placed on the ballot by citizens or interest groups for a popular vote

ballots, bilingual, 126

bandwagon effect, 169   a shift in electoral support to the candidate whom public-opinion polls report as the front-runner

banks, Federal Reserve, 362

Barron v. Baltimore, 101

bear arms, right to, 112–13

Beard, Charles, 40

Beck, Nancy, 315

Bedford, Gunning, 41

beliefs, 147

Berkebile, Guy, 274, 306

biases

in interest groups, 253–54

in media, *181*

in polling, 165

bicameral, 44, 277   having a legislative assembly composed of two chambers or houses; distinguished from *unicameral*

big data, bureaucracy and, 368

bill   a proposed law that has been sponsored by a member of Congress and submitted to the clerk of the House or Senate

in conference committees, 296–97

debate on, 293, 295

private, 287

that die in committee, 293

bill of attainder   a law that declares a person guilty of a crime without a trial

Bill of Rights, 16, 44, 48, 51   the first 10 amendments to the Constitution, ratified in 1791; they ensure certain rights and liberties of the people; *see also individual amendments*

First Amendment, 103–11

Second Amendment, 112–13

Fourth Amendment, 114–15

Fifth Amendment, 115–17

Sixth Amendment, 117

Eighth Amendment, 118–19

and civil rights, 99–103

origin of, 99, 100

and right to privacy, 119–20

bin Laden, Osama, 187, 455

Bipartisan Campaign Reform Act of 2002, 238, 266, 386

Black Lives Matter movement, *8*, 124, 265, *265*

Blackmun, Harry, 393, 398

Blades, Joan, 254

Blair, Saira, 2–4, *3*

block grants, 85, 86   federal grants-in-aid that allow states considerable discretion in how the funds are spent

blogs

of Congress members, 281

as news source, 182, 188

Bloomberg News, 188

Blue Cross Blue Shield, 250

Boehner, John, *290, 302, 302,* 306

Boeing, 250

Boston Massacre (1770), 35

Boston Tea Party, 35, *36*

Boumediene v. Bush, 389

bourgeoisie, 6

Bowers v. Hardwick, 136

Boyd, Wes, 254

Brady Handgun Violence Prevention Act, 80

Brazil, *55*

government employment in, *357*

voter turnout in, *226*

Brennan, William, 110

Bretton Woods agreement, 460

Breyer, Stephen, 104

briefs, 394   written documents in which attorneys explain, using case precedents, why the court should find in favor of their client

British taxes, 34–35

broadcast media, 184–85, 194–97   television, radio, or other media that transmit audio and/or video content to the public

Brown, Ben, 246–47, *247*

Brown, Dwayne, *355*

Brown, Linda, 122–23

Brown, Oliver, 122–23

***Brown v. Board of Education*, 123–24, 263, 390**   the 1954 Supreme Court decision that struck down the "separate but equal" doctrine as fundamentally unequal; this case eliminated state power to use race as a criterion for discrimination in law and provided the national government with the power to intervene by exercising strict regulatory policies against discriminatory actions

Brown v. Entertainment Merchants Association, 111

Bryan, William Jennings, 213, 218

Buckley v. Valeo, 239

budgeting, zero-base, 360

bureaucracy, 346–69   the complex structure of offices, tasks, rules, and principles of organization that are employed by all large-scale institutions to coordinate effectively the work of their personnel

control of, 363–67

defined, 349

Chairman of the Joint Chiefs of Staff, 360
Chamber of Commerce v. Environmental Protection Agency, 395
Charlottesville, Virginia, white nationalist rally, *148*
charter schools, 425

checks and balances, 44, 49–50, *50*
   mechanisms through which each branch
   of government is able to participate in and
   influence the activities of the other branches.
   Major examples include the presidential veto
   power over congressional legislation, the
   power of the Senate to approve presidential
   appointments, and judicial review of
   congressional enactments
   on presidential power, 339–40
   and unitary executive theory, 323

Cheney, Dick, 334
Chicago Tribune, 184

chief justice, 383–84   justice on the Supreme
   Court who presides over the Court's public
   sessions and whose official title is chief justice
   of the United States

children, poverty among, 437
Children's Defense Fund, 437
Children's Health Insurance Program (CHIP),
   275, 306
China, 453, 460
   foreign policy with, 464, 465
   influence and international connections of, 452
   and North Korea, 466–67
   trade policy with, 467
Chinese Exclusion Act of 1882, 11
chlorpyrifos, 315–16
Christian Broadcasting Network, 161
Christian Coalition, 253
CIA. *See* Central Intelligence Agency
Citadel, 131
cities
   direct legislation in, 7
   home rule for, 72
Citigroup, 298
citizen interest groups, 251

citizen journalism, 189–90   news reported
   and distributed by citizens, rather than by
   professional journalists and for-profit news
   organizations

citizens
   civil liberties as protection for, 100–101
   digital, 187–88; *see also* digital citizen
   naturalized, 11
   political participation by, 2–4
Citizens for the American Way, 394

citizenship, 8–9   informed and active
   membership in a political community
   for African Americans, 12
   digital. *See* digital citizen
   for immigrants, 157
   and political knowledge, 157–60

Citizens United v. Federal Election Commission, 238,
   266–67
civic engagement, on social media, 199
Civil Aeronautics Act, 82
civil cases, 378

civil law, 378   the branch of law that deals
   with disputes that do not involve criminal
   penalties

civil liberties, 99–103   areas of personal freedom
   constitutionally protected from government
   interference
   Bill of Rights, 99–103, *102*
   defined, 98, 99
   and Doctrine of Incorporation, 101–3, *102*
   due process of law, 113–19
   freedom of religion, 103–11, *140*
   freedom of speech and of the press, 105–6
   global, 135
   as protection against government, 100–101
   right to own a gun, 112–13
   right to privacy, 119–20

civil penalties, 412

civil rights, 120–30   obligation imposed on
   government to take positive action to protect
   citizens from any illegal action of government
   agencies and of other private citizens
   and affirmative action, 128–30
   defined, 98, 99
   for disabled Americans, 136
   gender equality, 130–32
   and immigration laws, 132–34
   for language minorities, 133
   for Native Americans, 134
   and New Deal coalition, 215
   as protection by government, 120–30
   racial equality, 120–30
   and sexual orientation, 136–37
   Supreme Court cases related to, 389

Civil Rights Act of 1875, 121
Civil Rights Act of 1964, 123–24, 130, 131
civil rights movement
   after *Brown v. Board of Education,* 123–24
   goals of, 99
   and school segregation, 123–24
   Southern Manifesto, 79–80
Civil Service Act of 1883, 351
civil service reform, 364
Civil Service Reform Act of 1978, 364
civil society, 252
Civil War, 213
Clausewitz, Carl von, 463
Clean Air Act, 350
Clean Power Plan, 350

"clear and present danger" test, 106   test to
   determine whether speech is protected or
   unprotected, based on its capacity to present a
   "clear and present danger" to society

Cleveland, Grover, 232

independent regulatory commissions
established by, 354–55
interest groups' access to, 262–63
interest groups' influence on, 260
judicial review of acts of, 385, 388–89
non-lawmaking tasks of, 303–5
organization of, 288–93
oversight by, 365–66
parties and organization of power in, 210
party leadership in, 289
party polarization in, 303
powers of, 47, 50
and the presidency, 331
public opinion of, 306
reapportioning of seats, 14
as representatives of American people,
277–88, 288
rules of lawmaking in, 293–97
social composition of, 278–81, 279
sociological vs. agency representation,
278–81
sources of information on, 308
staff system of, 291
tax cut bills, 416
unfunded mandates of, 82, 84
and unitary executive theory, 323
Congressional Budget Office, 366
Congressional Research Service, 366
Connecticut, 119
Connecticut Compromise, 42
conservatism, 150–51, 151, 398, 438

conservative, 87 today this term refers to
those who generally support the social and
economic status quo and are suspicious of
efforts to introduce new political formulae and
economic arrangements; conservatives believe
that a large and powerful government poses a
threat to citizens' freedom

constituency the residents in the area from
which an official is elected
of branches of government, 50
of Congress, 280–81
and congressional decision making, 297, 298
defined, 277

constituents, 298
Constitution, U.S., 43–51
Amendments to, 56–60, 58–59
Annapolis Convention, 39
Articles of Confederation vs., 45
balance of powers in, 43–51, 50
changing, 54–60
expressed powers from, 318–22
foreign policy provisions of, 456
future of, 60
original jurisdiction in, 381
powers of president in, 317–27, 454
preamble of, 16
presidential power limited by, 339
purpose of government under, 32
ratification of, 48, 51–56

rights in, 62, 100
and weakness of Articles of Confederation,
38–39
Constitutional Amendments, 56–60, 58–59, 61
Constitutional Convention of 1787, 39–40, 386
constitutional democracies, 5

constitutional government, 5 a system of rule
in which formal and effective limits are placed
on the powers of the government

Consumer Financial Protection Bureau, 355
Consumer Product Safety Commission, 425

containment, 448 a policy designed to
curtail the political and military expansion
of a hostile power

Continental Congress
First, 36
Second, 36–37
contract cases, 378

contracting power, 411 the power of
government to set conditions on companies
seeking to sell goods or services to government
agencies

contributory programs, 417–19, 432 social
programs financed in whole or in part by
taxation or other mandatory contributions by
their present or future recipients

control, public policy as means of, 409–16, 410

cooperative federalism, 80–81, 81, 83 a
type of federalism existing since the New
Deal era in which grants-in-aid have been
used strategically to encourage states and
localities (without commanding them) to
pursue nationally defined goals; also known as
"intergovernmental cooperation"

Cooper v. Harris, 390

cost-of-living adjustments (COLAs), 418
changes made to the level of benefits of a
government program based on the rate of
inflation

Council of Economic Advisers (CEA), 329
Council on Environmental Quality, 329
counsel, right to, 117
court cases, 377–78
Courtney, Joe, 282

court of appeals, 379–80 a court that hears the
appeals of trial court decisions

court-related rights, 115–17
courts, 379
and balance of values, 23
interest groups' use of, 263–64
state, 378–81
Crimean Peninsula, Russia and, 462, 465
criminal justice system, 72, 154

criminal law, 377–78   the branch of law that regulates the conduct of individuals, defines crimes, and specifies punishment for acts defined as illegal

criminally accused, due process for, 113–19
cruel and unusual punishment, *118,* 118–19
Cuba, 320, 458
Cuban missile crisis, 449
cultural exchange programs, 463
Cunningham, Randy "Duke," 287
cyberporn, 110
Czech Republic, *357*

D

Daily Show, The, 186
"dark money," 237–38
Dasari, Anooha, 177, *177*
Davids, Sharice, *235*
Davie, William R., 42
Davis, Gray, 231
death-penalty laws, *118,* 118–19
decision making, in Congress, 297–303
Declaration of Independence, 36–37, *37*
    consent of governed in, 145
    on equality, 18–19
    inalienable rights in, 16

defendant, 378   the one against whom a complaint is brought in a criminal or civil case

Defense, Department of, 318, *360*
    and external national security, 359–60
    and foreign policy, 455
    Pentagon Papers, 193
    security function of, 359–60
Defense of Marriage Act of 1996 (DOMA), 30–32, 71, 136–37, *137*
defense spending, *450*
Deferred Action for Childhood Arrivals (DACA) program, 89, *89, 133*
Deferred Action for Parents of Americans (DAPA), 89
Delaware, 122

delegated powers, 324   in the Tenth Amendment to the Constitution, delegated powers are described as those granted by the Constitution to the federal government; however, the term has commonly come to be used more broadly to refer to constitutional powers that are assigned to one government agency but exercised by another with the express permission of the first

democracy   a system of rule that permits citizens to play a significant part in the governmental process, usually through the election of key public officials
    bureaucracy controlled in, 368
    and campaign funding, 238–39
    and conflicts among values, 19–20
    constitutional, 5
    defined, 5

education on virtues of, 153
    "excessive," 44
    as fundamental value, 19–20
    importance of media in, 178
    and inadequate political knowledge, 159–60
    interest groups' impact on, 268
    and internet, 196
    and liberty, 60
    public opinion in, 169
    representative, 7
    as shared value, 149

democratic institutions, confidence in, 164
Democratic Party; *see also* political parties
    on citizenship for immigrants, 157
    and congressional polarization, 303
    on environmental protection, 157
    fundraising by, 237
    internal disagreements in, 217
    membership of, 207
    party identification, 220
    and party system, 210–20
    policy positions of, 207
    and political orientation, 156–57
    roots of, 207
    and second party system, 213
    socialists and, 151
    third parties' effects on, 218–20
    trust of government among, 153
demographic change(s)
    and political organization, 268
    and political values, 24
demonstrations, 264–65
Dennis v. United States, 111
Denny's restaurant, 125

department, 352   the largest subunit of the executive branch; the secretaries of the 15 departments form the Cabinet; *see also individual departments*

détente, 449

deterrence, 448   the development and maintenance of military strength as a means of discouraging attack

devolution, 367   a policy to remove a program from one level of government by delegating it or passing it down to a lower level of government, such as from the national government to the state and local governments

DeVos, Betsy, 425
Dewey, Thomas, *168*
digital cameras, 189

digital citizen, 169–70, 187–88   a daily internet user with high-speed home internet access and the technology and literacy skills to go online for employment, news, politics, entertainment, commerce, and other activities; *see also* internet
    defined, 187–88
    and internet access, 187–88

participation by, 9
skills for, 187–88

digital divide, 188   the gap in access to the
internet among demographic groups based on
education, income, age, geographic location,
and race/ethnicity

digital media; *see also* new media; online media;
    online news
  bias of, 183
  concerns about, 190
  media habits and, 186–89
  as news source, 178
  political fact-checking websites, 182
  political influence of, 191–97
  as political networking tool, 222
  subscriptions to digital newspapers, 184
digital-only news organizations, 188
digital political participation, 221–22

diplomacy, 459   the representation of a
government to foreign governments

diplomatic powers, 320
diplomatic recognition, 320

direct democracy   a system of rule that permits
citizens to vote directly on laws and policies

direct legislation, 7
direct lobbying, 261
Director of National Intelligence, 455
direct patronage, 286–88
Disability Rights Education and Defense Fund,
    136
disabled Americans, civil rights for, 136
disaster relief, *326,* 326–27
discrimination
  based on disability, *84*
  employment, 72, 126, 132
  gender, 130–32
  housing, 128
  national origin, 133
  racial, 122–23
  religious, 105
  in school desegregation, 125–26
  sex, 132
  sexual orientation, 136–37
dispute arbitration, 463–64

dissenting opinion, 396–97   a decision written
by a justice in the minority in a particular case
in which the justice wishes to express his or her
reasoning in the case

district courts, 381
District of Columbia
  firearms law in, 112
  Medicaid expansion, 84
  regulation of marijuana use in, 66
  and school segregation, 122
  voter registration in, 225
District of Columbia v. Heller, 112

diversity
  ethnic, 10
  global, 17
  of new media, 190
  as strength, 23

divided government, 218   the condition in
American government wherein the presidency
is controlled by one party while the opposing
party controls one or both houses of Congress

DNA testing, 115
Doctrine of Incorporation, 101–3, *102*
Dodd-Frank Wall Street Reform and Consumer
    Protection Act of 2010, 298
dogs, police, 114–15
Doha Amendment, 468
Dole, Bob, 80
DOMA. *See* Defense of Marriage Act of 1996
domestic policy, 406–39
  education policies, 423–25
  and foreign policy, 447
  health policies, 425–31
  housing policies, 431–32
  social policy and the welfare system, 416–22,
      432–37
  as techniques of control, 409–16
domestic power, military sources of, 318–19

double jeopardy, 116   the Fifth Amendment
right providing that a person cannot be tried
twice for the same crime

double state, 365
Douglas, William O., 119
DREAM Act, *133*
Drudge Report, 184
Drug Enforcement Administration, 67

dual federalism, 73, *81*   the system of
government that prevailed in the United
States from 1789 to 1937 in which most
fundamental governmental powers were shared
between the federal and state governments

due process of law, 380, 389, *399*   the right
of every citizen against arbitrary action by
national or state governments
  for the criminally accused, 113–19
  defined, 100
  and property rights, 101
  search and seizure, 114–15

E

early voting, *225,* 227
earmarks, 286–88
Earned Income Tax Credit (EITC), 434
East India Company, 35–36, *36*
economic aid, 460, 461
economic equality, 18–19
economic freedom, 16, 18, *18*
economic interest groups, 250
economic interests, Kyoto Protocol and, 451

nonprofits can spend unlimited amounts on political campaigns and not disclose their donors as long as their activities are not coordinated with the candidate campaigns and political activities are not their primary purpose

527 committees (Super PACs), 237–38
nonprofit independent groups that receive and disburse funds to influence the nomination, election, or defeat of candidates; named after Section 527 of the Internal Revenue Code, which defines and provides tax-exempt status for nonprofit advocacy groups

framing, 192   the power of the media to influence how events and issues are interpreted

free exercise clause, 104–5   the First Amendment clause that protects a citizen's right to believe and practice whatever religion he or she chooses

free riders, 255   those who enjoy the benefits of collective goods but did not participate in acquiring them

full faith and credit clause, 71   provision from Article IV, Section 1, of the Constitution requiring that the states normally honor the public acts and judicial decisions that take place in another state

gender gap, 156   a distinctive pattern of voting behavior reflecting the differences in views between women and men

General Agreement on Tariffs and Trade (GATT), 451 international trade organization, in existence from 1947 to 1995, that set many of the rules governing international trade

general election, 230 a regularly scheduled election involving most districts in the nation or state, in which voters decide who wins office; in the United States, general elections for national office and most state and local offices are held on the first Tuesday following the first Monday in November in even-numbered years (every four years for presidential elections)

general revenue sharing, 85 the process by which one unit of government yields a portion of its tax income to another unit of government, according to an established formula; revenue sharing typically involves the national government providing money to state governments

geography, in population shifts, 14
George Washington, 210
Georgia, 42, 133, 284
Germany, 5, 447
    cooperative federalism, 83
    government employment in, *357*
    heads of state and of government in, 325
    voter turnout in, *226*

gerrymandering, 285 the apportionment of voters in districts in such a way as to give unfair advantage to one racial or ethnic group or political party

Gibbons v. Ogden, 75–76
Gideon, Clarence Earl, 117
Gideon v. Wainwright, 117
Gilens, Martin, 421
Gillibrand, Kirsten, 301
Gingrich, Newt, 291
Ginsburg, Ruth Bader, 397
Glennon, Michael, 365
globalization, 452, 468
global security, 461–62
Global War on Terror, 449
"going public," 332–34
Goldberg, Arthur, 119
Goldwater, Barry, 215
Google, 159
Gore, Al, 232
Gorsuch, Neil, 296, 375, 384, 385, 387

government, 2–23 institutions and procedures through which a territory and its people are ruled; *see also* federal government; local governments; state governments
    and changes in identity of Americans, 10–16
    and citizenship, 8–9
    comparing systems of, 55
    created by country's founders, 33
    daily life affected by, 20–22

    defined, 5
    divided, 218
    economic interventions of, 415–16
    expansion of American participation in, 7
    forms of, 5–6
    functions and value of, 66–68
    fundamental values underlying, 16–20
    institutions and procedures of, 5–7
    interest groups and expansion of, 258–59
    limited, 16, 53
    limits on, 6
    and political efficacy, 9
    and politics, 11
    protection against, 100–101; *see also* civil
        liberties
    public opinion influenced by, 160
    separation of church and state, 103–4
    under "traditional system," 73–75
    trust in, 21, 23, 152
    types and numbers of, *72*

Government Accountability Office, 366

government corporation, 354 government agency that performs a service normally provided by the private sector

government policies, public opinion and, 162–63
government spending, 83, 411
government surveillance programs, 193

grand jury, 116 jury that determines whether sufficient evidence is available to justify a trial; grand juries do not rule on the accused's guilt or innocence

grants-in-aid, 77, *79*, 82 programs through which Congress provides money to state and local governments on the condition that the funds be employed for purposes defined by the federal government

Grassley, Chuck, *298*

grassroots mobilization, 258, 265 a lobbying campaign in which a group mobilizes its membership to contact government officials in support of the group's position

Gratz v. Bollinger, 130
Great Britain
    government structure in, 33
    taxes levied on colonies, 34–35

Great Compromise, 42–44 the agreement reached at the Constitutional Convention of 1787 that gave each state an equal number of senators regardless of its population but linked representation in the House of Representatives to population

Great Depression, 77–78, 215, 415–17, *417*
Great Recession. *See* financial crisis of 2008–2009
Greece, *357*
Greeks, ancient, 8

H

I

implementation, 349, 351 the efforts of departments and agencies to translate laws into specific bureaucratic rules and actions

implied powers, 69, 323–24 powers derived from the necessary and proper clause of Article I, Section 8, of the Constitution; such powers are not specifically expressed but are implied through the expansive interpretation of delegated powers

inalienable rights, 16
income
    and internet access, 187–88
    of middle class, 438
    in the United States, *15*
    voters compared to population by, *307*
    of voters in 2016 election, *341*
    of wealthy Americans, 438
income inequality, 144

incumbency, 282 holding the political office for which one is running

incumbency advantage, 281–86

incumbent, 208 a candidate running for re-election to a position that he or she already holds

independent agency, 353 agency that is not part of a cabinet department

Independent Redistricting Commission (Arizona), *285*
independent regulatory commissions, 354–55

indexing, 418 periodic process of adjusting of social benefits or wages to account for increases in the cost of living

India, *55, 226*
information
    consumption of, 159
    ways of getting/sharing, 182

informational benefits, 256, *256* special newsletters, periodicals, training programs, conferences, and other information provided to members of groups to entice others to join

inherent powers, 324 powers claimed by a president that are not expressed in the Constitution but are inferred from it

in-kind benefits noncash goods and services provided to needy individuals and families by the federal government

Instagram, *187*

institutional advertising, 264 advertising designed to create a positive image of an organization

institutional presidency, 327–31, *328*
insurance coverage, *429*
intelligence agencies, 447, 455

interest group, 246–70 individuals who organize to influence the government's programs and policies
    active members of, 252
    advocation by, 249–54
    for children, 437
    and congressional decision making, *260, 298–99*
    cultivation of access by, *262, 262–63*
    defined, 249–50
    direct lobbying by, 261
    electoral politics used by, 266–67
    and flow of cases to Supreme Court, 393–94
    and foreign policy, 457–58
    in the Founding of America, 34
    impact on democracy, 268
    increasing number of, 258–59
    litigation by, 263–64
    lobbying expenditures of, *269*
    mobilization of public opinion by, 265
    organizational components of, 254–58
    "pattern of cases" strategy of, 393–94
    pluralist and elitist views of, 249–50
    public opinion influenced by, 161
    for senior citizens, 433
    strategies used by, 259–67

Internal Revenue Service (IRS), 362, 363
international arbitration, 463–64
International Bank for Reconstruction and Development (World Bank), 460
international benefits, U.S. foreign policy for, 451
International Court of Justice, 464
international environmental policy, 451–52, 467–68
international human rights policy, 453

International Monetary Fund (IMF), 460 an institution established in 1944 that provides loans and facilitates international monetary exchange

international monetary structure, 460
international news sources, 470
international peacekeeping efforts, 453, 459
internet; *see also* social media
    access to, 188, 197
    attempts to regulate content of, 197
    cyberporn on, 110
    and global democracy, 196
    "going public" on, 333, 334
    and information consumption, 159
    and interest groups, 257–58
    and libel laws, 109
    as news source, 182
    online news, 186–89
    and organization of interest groups, 254–55
    political participation on, 221–22
    politics changed by, 240
    politics on, 169–70
    public opinion surveys on, 166
    quality of information on, 190
interstate commerce, 76
Interstate Commerce Commission, 354–55
intervention, of government, 415–16

iPhone, *54*
Iran, 449
    and negotiations with Syria, 359
    nuclear weapons agreement with, 331,
        457–58, 466
Iraq
    ISIS in, 463
    U.S. involvement in, *462*
Iraq War
    aftermath of, 463
    costs of, 352
    as preventive war, 449
    public opinion on, 162
Ireland, *357, 458*

iron triangle, 262, *262*, 356, 358, *358*   the
    stable, cooperative relationships that often
    develop among a congressional committee,
    an administrative agency, and one or more
    supportive interest groups; not all of these
    relationships are triangular, but the iron
    triangle is the most typical

IRS (Internal Revenue Service), 362, 363
IRS Restructuring and Reform Act of 1998, 363
Islamic State of Iraq and Syria (ISIS), 359, 463, 465

isolationism, 447   avoidance of involvement in
    the affairs of other nations

Israel, *55,* 457–58, 461
Italy, 464
Iye, Mohamed, 444–45, *445*

J
Jackson, Andrew, 211
Jackson, Robert H., 396
Jacksonian Democrats, *200*
Janus, Mark, 374–75, *375*
Janus v. AFSCME, 375–76
Japan, 357
    government employment in, *357*
    immigrant assimilation in, 17
    racial homogeneity of, 17
    voter turnout in, *226*
Jay, John, 52
Jefferson, Thomas
    and bill of rights, 97–100
    and Declaration of Independence, 36–37
    on freedom of the press, 178
    and Locke's work, 33
    on newspapers, 179
    and separation of church and state, 104
Jeffersonian Republicans, 211, 217–18
Jeffersonians (Antifederalists), 207
Jehovah's Witnesses, 104
Jewish Americans, 12, 457–58
Jewish immigrants, 10–11
Johnson, Andrew, 320, 332, 339
Johnson, Gary, *219*
Johnson, Lyndon
    election of 1964, 215
    as vice president, 329

Joint Chiefs of Staff, 360, 455

joint committees, 291   legislative committees
    formed of members of both the House and
    Senate

Jones, Kendric D., 2–4, *3*
journalists
    as news-gathering professionals, 179–80
    professional and citizen, 189–90
judges
    appointed to federal courts, 384–85
    for district courts, 381
    federal, 384–85
    Supreme Court justices, 47–48, *383,* 383–84

judicial activism   judicial philosophy that
    posits that the Court should go beyond the
    words of the Constitution or a statute to
    consider the broader societal implications of
    its decisions

judicial branch, 47–48
judicial powers, of the president, 319–20

judicial restraint, 398   judicial philosophy
    whose adherents refuse to go beyond the clear
    words of the Constitution in interpreting the
    document's meaning

judicial review, 47, 385–90   the power of the
    courts to review and, if necessary, declare
    actions of the legislative and executive branches
    invalid or unconstitutional. The Supreme
    Court asserted this power in *Marbury v.*
    Madison (1803)
    of acts of Congress, 385, 388–89
    of state actions, 389–90

Judiciary Act of 1789, 389

jurisdiction, 380, 381   the sphere of a court's
    power and authority

Justice Department, 67–68, 88–89
    and Arizona civil rights, 133–34
    and discrimination against transgender
        people, 132
    and employment discrimination, 126
    Microsoft lobbying and, 261
    and school desegregation, 125–26, 424
    security function of, 359
    and state immigration laws, 133–34

K
Kagan, Elena, 385, 387
Kaine, Tim, *228*
Kansas, 122
Kavanaugh, Brett, 376, 384, *385*
Kennedy, Anthony, 376, 384, *385*
Kennedy, John F., 329, 332, 449
Kentucky, 104
Kenya, 196
Kerry, John, 359

regulation of, 263
by senior citizens, 433

local broadcast media, 184–85
local governments, 351
local politics, participation in, 91, 92
Locke, John, 33, 36–37

logrolling, 302 a legislative practice whereby agreements are made between legislators in voting for or against a bill; vote trading

lower federal courts, 381

M

Maddow, Rachel, *181*
Madison, James
    on Congress, 46
    Federalist Papers, 52
    on interest groups, 249
    on liberty, 268
    on limited government, 54
    on representation, 52
    on slavery, 42
mail, voting by, *225*
Maine, 7

majority leader, 289 the elected leader of the majority party in the House of Representatives or in the Senate; in the House, the majority leader is subordinate in the party hierarchy to the Speaker of the House

majority party, 210 the party that holds the majority of legislative seats in either the House or the Senate

majority rule/minority rights the democratic principle that a government follows the preferences of the majority of voters but protects the interests of the minority
    check on, 19–20
    Federalists vs. Antifederalists on, 53
    with minority rights, 19–20

Malik, Tashfeen, 115
Malkin, Michelle, 205
managerial presidency, 363–65
manifest destiny, 447
Mapp, Dollree, 114
Mapp v. Ohio, 114
Marbury v. Madison, 47–48, 386
March for Our Lives movement, 257, 265
March on Washington (1963), 124
margin of error, 165
marijuana
    medical, 66–68, 87
    recreational, 67, 87–88
    regulation of use of, 67–68, 90
Marine Corps, 360
Marjory Stoneman Douglas High School, 145, 169

marketplace of ideas, 105, 160 the public forum in which beliefs and ideas are exchanged and compete

marriage, same-sex. *See* same-sex marriage
Marshall, John, 75
Marshall Plan, 461
Martin, Lockheed, 411
Martin, Luther, 42
Maryland
    public accommodation settlements in, 125
    slaves in, 42
Maryland v. King, 115
Massachusetts
    ban on cigarette advertising in, 111
    provincial government of, 35–36
    same-sex marriage in, 71
    Shays's Rebellion, 39–40
Matal v. Tam, 386

material benefits, 256, *256* special goods, services, or money provided to members of groups to entice others to join

Mattis, James, *360*
McCain, John, 168–69, 239, 323
McCain-Feingold bill, 266
McClatchy Corporation, 181
McConnell, Mitch, 281
McCreary v. ACLU of Kentucky, 104
McCulloch, v. Maryland, 75–76
McCutcheon, Shaun, *239*
McCutcheon et al. v. Federal Election Commission, 238
McDonald v. Chicago, 112
McKinley, William, 213

means testing, 419 a procedure by which potential beneficiaries of a public-assistance program establish their eligibility by demonstrating a genuine need for the assistance

media, 176–99 print and digital forms of communication, including television, newspapers, radio, and the internet, intended to convey information to large audiences
    adversarial journalism, 194
    as business, 180
    and candidate characteristics, 229
    in a democracy, 179
    informed consumption of, 198
    investigations by, 190
    leaked information sources, 193–94
    online news, 186–89
    ownership of, 180–82
    partisan nature of, *181*
    and political power relations, 191–97
    political role of, 178
    and public opinion, 158, 161–62, 191–93
    regulation of, 194–97
    rise of new media, 186–89
    roles of, 179
    traditional, 179–82

Medicaid, 419, 426 a federally and state-financed, state-operated program providing medical services to low-income people
    as categorical grant, 78
    as domestic policy, 406–8

expansion of, 7, 84, 428–31
middle class benefits from, 434
for the nonworking poor, 435
oversight of, 356
spending on, *428*
for the working poor, 434–35
work requirements for, 422

medical marijuana, 66–68, 87

Medicare, 418   a form of national health
insurance for the elderly and the disabled
contributions for, 418
as domestic policy, 407–8, *430*
oversight of, 356
senior citizens' benefits from, 433
spending on, *428*

membership association, 255   an organized
group in which members actually play a
substantial role, sitting on committees and
engaging in group projects

merit system, 351   a product of civil service
reform, in which appointees to positions
in public bureaucracies must objectively be
deemed qualified for those positions

Merit Systems Protection Board, 364
methylene chloride, 314, 315
Mexican War, 456
Mexico, 451
government employment in, *357*
voter turnout in, *226*
Michigan, 129
Michigan Department of Environmental
Quality, 347
Microsoft, 261

micro-targeting, 209–10   when political
campaigns tailor messages to individuals in
small homogeneous groups based on their
group interests to support a candidate or
policy issue

middle class, 432, 434, 438
military
expressed powers of, 318–19
and foreign policy, 455–56
gays in, 137
and national security, 447–50
transgender people in, 132
Military Commissions Act, 389
military contracting, 411
military force, 462–63
military spending, *450*
militias, 112
Miller, Judith, 109
Miller v. Johnson, 285–86
minimum wage, 434
minorities, poverty among, 435–36

minority leader, 289   the elected leader of the
minority party in the House or Senate

minority party, 210   the party that holds the
minority of legislative seats in either the House
or the Senate

minority rights, majority rule with, 19–20
Miranda, Ernesto, 116–17

Miranda rule, 117   the requirement, articulated
by the Supreme Court in *Miranda v. Arizona*
(1966), that persons under arrest must be
informed prior to police interrogation of their
rights to remain silent and to have the benefit
of legal counsel

Mississippi, 86
Missouri, 122
mixed regime, 50

mobilization   the process by which large
numbers of people are organized for a political
activity
external, 207
in forming political parties, 207
internal, 207
and political participation, 224
by presidents, 332–34
of public opinion, 265
via social media, 188–90
of voters, *209,* 209–10

moderates, 151, *151*
monetary agencies, 362

monetary policies, 413–14   efforts to
regulate the economy through the
manipulation of the supply of money and
credit; America's most powerful institution
in this area of monetary policy is the Federal
Reserve Board

monetary structure, international, 460
money, in politics, 240
Monroe, James, 447
Monroe Doctrine, 447
Montesquieu, Baron de la Brède et de, 33, 48, 50
Montgomery bus boycott, 124
Montreal Protocol, 452, 467
Moonves, Les, 180

mootness, 391   a criterion used by courts to
screen cases that no longer require resolution

Morse v. Frederick, 108
mortgage crisis, 128, 431–32
MoveOn.org, 254
MSNBC, 184
multiracial Americans, 12
Muslim, 12
mutual defense alliances, 461

N
NAACP. *See* National Association for the
Advancement of Colored People
Nader, Ralph, 219, 259

National Aeronautics and Space Administration (NASA), 354, *355*
National Association for the Advancement of Colored People (NAACP), 122, 263, 394
National Defense Education Act of 1958, 423
National Emergencies Act, 326
National Federation of Independent Business v. Sebelius, 88
national government. *See* federal government
National Institutes of Health (NIH), 356, 425
National Opinion Research Center, University of Chicago, 165
National Organization for Women (NOW), 130
national origin discrimination, 126, 133
national origin interest groups, 457–58
National Origins Quota System, 11
National Park Service, 356
National Performance Review (NPR), 364
National Public Radio (NPR), 185–86
National Rifle Association (NRA), 247, 265, 268
National Right to Life Committee, 251–53
national security
    clear and present danger to, 106
    federal agencies maintaining, 358–61
    foreign policy for, 447–50
National Security Agency (NSA), 115, 193, 318, 361, 368
National Security Council (NSC), 318, 329, 455
national standards, 81–84
national-state balance, 86–89
National Taxpayers Union, 253
National Welfare Rights Organization, 435

nation-states, 449   political entities consisting of people with some common cultural experience (nation) who also share a common political authority (state), recognized by other sovereignties (nation-states)

Native Americans, 11
    affirmative action points for, 129
    civil rights for, 134
    voting rights for, 11
    Washington Redskins (NFL) and freedom of speech, 137–38
NATO. *See* North Atlantic Treaty Organization
naturalized citizens, 11
Near v. Minnesota, 108

necessary and proper clause, 69   provision from Article I, Section 8, of the Constitution providing Congress with the authority to make all laws necessary and proper to carry out its expressed powers

net neutrality, 176–78, *195,* 198
Nevada, 284
Never Again MSD, 145
New Deal
    and federalism, 77–78
    party system, 214–15

New Federalism, 85–86, *86*   attempts by presidents Nixon and Reagan to return power to the states through block grants

New Jersey Plan, 41   a framework for the Constitution, introduced by William Paterson, that called for equal state representation in the national legislature regardless of population

new media, 186–89; *see also* digital media

New Politics movement, 259   a political movement that began in the 1960s and '70s, made up of professionals and intellectuals for whom the civil rights and antiwar movements were formative experiences; the New Politics movement strengthened public interest groups

news
    fake, 159, 190
    online, 190
    sources of, *185,* 198

news aggregator, 186   an application or feed that collects web content such as news headlines, blogs, podcasts, online videos, and more in one location for easy viewing

newsmagazines, 197
news media
    new, 186–89
    online, 186–89
    traditional, 179–82
newspapers, 183–84
New York (state), 109
New York City Board of Health, 425
New York Times, 130, 161, 182, 184
New York Times v. United States, 108
New York v. Sullivan, 109
New Zealand, *357*

niche journalism, 188   news reporting devoted to a targeted portion (subset) of a journalism market sector or for a portion of readers or viewers based on content or ideological presentation

niche media, 188
NIH (National Institutes of Health), 356, 425
Nineteenth Amendment, *61*
Ninth Amendment, 119
Nixon, Richard, and administration
    and block grants, 85
    election of 1968, 215
    Ford's pardon of, 319–20
    resignation of, 339
    "southern strategy" of, 215
No Child Left Behind Act of 2001, 87, 424

nomination   the process by which political parties select their candidates for election to public office
    confirmation of, 457
    defined, 208
    of federal judges, 384
    by political parties, 208

opinion, 147 the written explanation of the Supreme Court's decision in a particular case; *see also* public opinion
    dissenting, 396–97
    emotional underpinnings of, 147–48
    writing, 396

opinion polls. *See* public-opinion polls
opportunity, equality of, 18, 148–49

oral argument, 394, 396 the stage in Supreme Court procedure in which attorneys for both sides appear before the Court to present their positions and answer questions posed by justices

Oregon, 225
Organization of American States, 461

original jurisdiction, 381 the authority to initially consider a case; distinguished from *appellate jurisdiction,* which is the authority to hear appeals from a lower court's decision

OSHA (Occupational Safety and Health Administration), 356
"outsider" candidates, 240

oversight, 304, 365–66 the effort by Congress, through hearings, investigations, and other techniques, to exercise control over the activities of executive agencies

P
PAC. *See* political action committee
packing technique, 390
Page, Benjamin, 162
Paj, Ajit, 176, 179
Palko, Frank, 116
Palko v. Connecticut, 116
Parents Involved in Community Schools v. Seattle School District No. 1, 125–26
Paris Agreement, 468
Parkland, Florida, shooting, 145, 257
Parks, Rosa, 124
parliamentary system
    bicameral body vs., 306
    executive branch in, 325
parliaments, 6
partisan politics, 210
partisanship
    in Benghazi hearings, 365
    and congressional decision making, 302
    in media reporting, *181,* 183, 190
    in public opinion, 147
    and Supreme Court, 397–99
    of voters, 227
Partnership to Protect Consumer Credit, 251

party identification, *216, 220, 221, 228* an individual voter's psychological ties to one party or another

party leadership, in Congress, 289
party loyalty, political participation and, 227
party system, 210–20, *212*

party unity vote, 299, *300* a roll-call vote in the House or Senate in which at least 50 percent of the members of one party take a particular position and are opposed by at least 50 percent of the members of the other party

Paterson, William, 41
Patient Protection and Affordable Care Act of 2010. *See* Affordable Care Act (ACA)
Patrick, Amanda, 444

patronage, 286–88 the resources available to higher officials, usually opportunities to make partisan appointments to offices and to confer grants, licenses, or special favors to supporters

Paul, Rand, 303
Pavan, Marisa, *390*
Pavan v. Smith, 389, *390*
Paxton, Ken, 72
pay discrimination, 132
PBS (Public Broadcasting System), 184
peacekeeping efforts, 453, 459
Pelosi, Nancy, *290,* 301
Pence, Michael, *228,* 329–30, *330*

penny press, 186 cheap, tabloid-style newspaper produced in the nineteenth century, when mass production of inexpensive newspapers first became possible due to the steam-powered printing press; a penny press newspaper cost one cent compared with other papers, which cost more than five cents

Pentagon Papers, 108, 161, 193
Perot, Ross, 218, 239
personal freedom, 16; *see also* liberty
Personal Responsibility and Work Opportunity Reconciliation Act (PRWORA), 422
petition(s)
    freedom of, 107
    right of, 261
Pew Research Center, 152, 167
Philip, Celeste, *426*
philosophy, political, 33
physician-assisted suicide, 120

plaintiff, 377 the individual or organization that brings a complaint in court

Plame, Valerie, 109

plea bargain, 380 a negotiated agreement in a criminal case in which a defendant agrees to plead guilty in return for the state's agreement to reduce the severity of the criminal charge the defendant is facing

Plessy, Homer, 121
Plessy v. Ferguson, 121, *122*

pluralism, 249 the theory that all interests are and should be free to compete for influence in the government; the outcome of this competition is compromise and moderation plurality rules, in elections, 232

pocket veto, 297, 321   a presidential veto that is automatically triggered if the president does not act on a given piece of legislation passed during the final 10 days of a legislative session

podcasts, 185–86

polarization
    of Congress, 303
    of politics, 158

police
    misconduct by, 124
    public opinion concerning, 154

police dogs, 114–15

"police patrol" oversight, 365   regular or even preemptive congressional hearings on bureaucratic agency operations

police power, 70, 76   power reserved to the state government to regulate the health, safety, and morals of its citizens

police regulation, 412

political action committee (PAC)   a private group that raises and distributes funds for use in election campaigns
    campaign funding from, 237–39
    defined, 250
    as interest group strategy, 266–67
    interest groups vs., 250
    leadership, 300–301
    purpose of, 208
    Super PACs, 237–38, 267, 299

political campaigns. *See* election campaigns

political efficacy, 9   the ability to influence government and politics

political environment
    as agent of political socialization, 157
    and political participation, 224

political equality, 19   the right to participate in politics equally, based on the principle of "one person, one vote"

political ideology, 149–51, *151*   a cohesive set of beliefs that forms a general philosophy about the role of government
    conservatism, 150–51
    liberalism, 150
    of Supreme Court, 398–99

political knowledge   possessing information about the formal institutions of government, political actors, and political issues
    for citizenship, 8–9
    shaping public opinion, 157–60

political mobilization, 188–89; *see also* mobilization

political opinions, expression of, *171*

political outlook, education and, 153

political participation, 60
    in 2008 and 2016 primary campaigns, *21*
    in 2012 presidential election, *25*
    and candidate characteristics, 229
    by citizens, 2–4, 8–9
    digital, 221–22
    electoral process, 229–32
    expansion of, 7
    forms of, 220
    issues in, 228
    and online news, 186–88
    and party loyalty, 227
    in state and local politics, 91
    and strength of democracy, 159–60
    through digital citizenship, 9
    via social media, 198, 199
    by voting, 220, 222, 225, 227

political parties, 204–41, *221*   organized groups that attempt to influence the government by electing their members to important government offices
    congressional organization by, 289
    defined, 207
    and electoral realignments, 217–18
    formation of, 60
    functions of, 207–8
    identification with, *216, 220, 221*
    interest groups vs., 250
    internal disagreements for, 217
    microtargeting messages of, 209–10
    party loyalty, 227
    and political orientation, 156–57
    presidents supported by, 331
    psychological ties to, 220
    purpose of, 204–6
    third parties, 218–20
    two-party system, 210–20
    voter turnout, 209–10, 223–24

political philosophy, 33

political socialization, 152–57   the induction of individuals into the political culture; learning the underlying beliefs and values on which the political system is based

political speech, 106

political system, urban areas representation in, 14

political values, 147–48
    and demographic changes, 24
    and diversity, 17
    in future, 23

politicians, Americans' suspicions of, 21, 23

Politico, 184, 188

politics   conflict over the leadership, structure, and policies of governments
    colonial, 34
    defined, 7
    electoral, 266–67
    goal of, 7
    and government, 7
    importance of media in, 179

prior restraint, 108 an effort by a governmental agency to block the publication of material it deems libelous or harmful in some other way; censorship; in the United States, the courts forbid prior restraint except under the most extraordinary circumstances

prisoners, freedom of worship for, 105
privacy
 right to, 115, 119–20, 398
 and unreasonable search, 114–15

private bill, 287 a proposal in Congress to provide a specific person with some kind of relief, such as a special exemption from immigration quotas

private property, 59
 and eminent domain, 117, 413
 state definitions of, 70

privatization, 364, 366 the transfer of all or part of a program from the public sector to the private sector

privileges and immunities clause, 72 provision, from Article IV, Section 2, of the Constitution, that a state cannot discriminate against someone from another state or give its own residents special privileges

probability sample, 163
pro-business conservatives, 217
professional associations, 250–51
profits, in media business, 180
Progressive Party, 7, 218–19
property rights, 101, 114; *see also* private
 property

proportional representation, 219 a multiple-member district system in which many competing political parties are awarded legislative seats in rough proportion to the percentage of popular votes that each party wins.

prospective voting, 228
Protestants
 and abortion, 161
 immigrants as, 10–11
 political opinions of, 156
 as proportion of Americans, 12
protests, 124, 264–65
PRWORA (Personal Responsibility and Work Opportunity Reconciliation Act), 422
public accommodations, 125
public broadcasting, 180
Public Broadcasting System (PBS), 184
public health, 425–31
public housing, 431

public interest groups, 251 groups that claim they serve the general good rather than only their own particular interest

public opinion, 144–71 citizens' attitudes about political issues, leaders, institutions, and events
 defined, 147
 in a democracy, 169
 disapproval of Congress, 303, 306
 and dominant political ideologies, 149–51, *151*
 education's influence on, 153–54
 and foreign policy, 458
 and government policies, 162–63
 government's influence on, 160–63, 192–93
 interest groups' mobilization of, 265
 measuring, 163–69
 media's influence on, 160–63, 191–93
 political knowledge shaping, 157–60
 political socialization shaping, 152–57
 private groups shaping, 161
 representing attitudes about politics, 147–52
 on security, *469*
 shared political values, 148–49, *149*

public-opinion polls, 163–66, 172 scientific instruments for measuring public opinion
 design and wording of, 165–66, *166*
 inaccurate results of, 165–66
 samples for, 163, 165

public policy, 409 a law, a rule, a statute, or an edict that expresses the government's goals and provides for rewards and punishments to promote those goals' attainment; *see also* domestic policy; foreign policy
 gender and opinions about, *156*
 implementation of, 349–51
 as techniques of control, 409–16, *410*

public-relations strategies, 332–34
public school students, speech by, 108
public school teachers, *251*
public-sector groups, 253
Puerto Rico, *326*

purposive benefits, *256*, 257 selective benefits of group membership that emphasize the purpose and accomplishments of the group

push polling, 168–69 a polling technique in which the questions are designed to shape the respondent's opinion

Putin, Vladimir, 450, *454*, 454–55, 464–65

R
race
 and public opinion differences, 154, *155*
 and redistricting, 283–86
 voters compared to population by, *307*
 of voters in 2016 election, *341*
 "whiteness," 12
Race to the Top program, 425
racial classifications in population, 12
 diversity of, 17
 global, 17

racial discrimination
  Black Lives Matter movement, 265, *265*
  and death-penalty cases, 118
  in employment, 126
  in housing, 128
  post–World War II, 122–23
  school segregation, 123–24
racial equality, 120–30
racial immigration criteria, 11–12
racial integration, *319*
racial minorities, tolerance for, 154
racial profiling, 124
racial segregation, 81
  in public accommodations, 125
  in schools, 123–24, 423–24
  and Southern Manifesto, 79–80
racism, 154, *155*
radio news, 183, 185–86
Randolph, Edmund, 41, 42

random digit dialing, 163   a polling method
  in which respondents are selected at random
  from a list of 10–digit telephone numbers,
  with every effort made to avoid bias in the
  construction of the sample

ratification of the Constitution, 48, 51–56
Reagan, Ronald, and administration
  education policies, 424
  fiscal policy of, 415
  on government as a problem, 352
  New Federalism, 85–86
  Republican coalition under, 215–17
  Supreme Court justices appointed by, 399
reapportionment, *284*
rebuttal, right of, 197

recall, 231   a procedure to allow voters to remove
  state officials from office before their terms
  expire by circulating petitions to call a vote

recess appointments, 339–40
Reconstruction, 213, 332
recreational marijuana, 67, 87–88
Reddit, *187,* 222

redistribution, 413–15   collecting revenue
  in such a way as to reduce the disparities of
  wealth between the lowest and the highest
  income brackets

redistricting, 283–86, *284, 285,* **389–90**   the
  process of redrawing election districts and
  redistributing legislative representatives; this
  happens every 10 years to reflect shifts in
  population or in response to legal challenges to
  existing districts

Red Lion Broadcasting Company v. FCC, 197
Redskins (NFL), 137–38, 386
Reed, Stanley, 396

referendum, 7, 231   the practice of referring a
  measure proposed or passed by a legislature

to the vote of the electorate for approval or
rejection

Reform Party, 218
regional population shifts, 14
Regulated Federalism, *86*
regulation
  of commerce, 76
  debate over scope of, 18–19
  of financial transactions, 298–99
  of media, 194–97
  and preemption, 82, 84

regulatory agency, 356, 358   a department,
  bureau, or independent agency whose primary
  mission is to impose limits, restrictions, or
  other obligations on the conduct of individuals
  or companies in the private sector

regulatory policies, 411–13
regulatory review, by presidents, 335–36
regulatory taxation, 412–13
Rehabilitation Act of 1973, 136
Reid, Harry, 295
religion(s), *140*
  and employment discrimination, 126
  freedom of, 103–11
  free exercise of, 104–5, *107*
  of immigrants, 14–15
  and Latinos' political decisions, 154
  and political opinions, 156
  separation of church and state, 103–4
religious conservatives, 217
Religious Freedom Restoration Act, 105
religiously unaffiliated, 12
Reno v. ACLU, 110
representation
  in Congress, 277, *288*
  Federalists vs. Antifederalists on, 53
  and population, 15–16
  proportional, 219
  and shifts in population, 15–16
  sociological vs. agency, 278–81
  and writing of Constitution, 41–42

representative democracy (republic), 7   a system
  of government in which the populace selects
  representatives, who play a significant role in
  governmental decision making

Republican Congressional Campaign Committee
  (RCCC), 282
Republican Party; *see also* political parties
  2016 presidential nominations, 208
  on citizenship for immigrants, 157
  and congressional polarization, 303
  divisions within, 303
  on environmental protection, 157
  external mobilization in building, 207
  fundraising by, 237
  internal disagreements in, 217
  membership of, 207
  nomination of Trump, 208

and Obama's judicial appointments, 384–85
and party identification, 220
and party system, 213
policy positions of, 207
and political orientation, 156–57
and preemption, 82
roots of, 207
Southern resentment of, 213
Tea Party movement and, *205*
third parties' effects on, 218–20
as third party, 218–20
trust of government among, 153
and voting rights for slaves, 7
"research" lobby, 253

reserved powers, 70 powers, derived from the Tenth Amendment to the Constitution, that are not specifically delegated to the national government or denied to the states

retrospective voting, 228

revenue agency, 363 an agency responsible for collecting taxes; examples include the Internal Revenue Service for income taxes, the U.S. Customs Service for tariffs and other taxes on imported goods, and the Bureau of Alcohol, Tobacco, Firearms and Explosives for collection of taxes on the sales of those particular products

Revolutionary War. *See* American Revolution
Rhode Island, 111
right(s), 62
    to bear arms, 112–13
    to counsel, 117
    inalienable, 16
    of petition, 261
    to privacy, 119–20, 398

right of rebuttal, 197 a Federal Communications Commission regulation giving individuals the right to have the opportunity to respond to personal attacks made on a radio or television broadcast

right to die movement, 120
Riley v. California, 115
Rio Treaty, 461
Roberts, John, 397, 430
Roberts, Pat, 296
Roe v. Wade, 120, *120,* 161, 263, 398
rogue states, 449

roll-call vote, 299 a vote in which each legislator's yes-or-no vote is recorded as the clerk calls the names of the members alphabetically

Romer v. Evans, 136
Roosevelt, Eleanor, 330
Roosevelt, Franklin Delano
    election of 1932, 214–15
    election of 1936, 167
    and electoral realignment, 218

fireside chats of, 332
fiscal policy of, 415
New Deal, 77–78, 214–15
powers used by, 321, 324
press relations of, 332
public appeals of, *333*
welfare system, 417
Rubio, Marco, *458*
rural areas, shift of population away from, 14
Russia, 304, 438, 454–55, 460, 462
    economic sanctions against, 461
    elections influenced by, 196
    foreign policy with, 464–65
    influence and international connections of, 452
    and negotiations with Syria, 359
Ryan, Paul, 302, 306

S

Safe Drinking Water Act, 347
same-sex marriage, 71, 136–37, 159, 264, 389
    legalization of, 30–32
    nationwide legalization of, 153
    states on, 71–72, 137
    Supreme Court on, *71,* 71–72, *137,* 153, *399,* 400

sample, 163 a small group selected by researchers to represent the most important characteristics of an entire population

sampling error (or margin of error), 165 polling error that arises based on the small size of the sample

San Bernardino, California, terrorist attack, *54*
sanctions, 461
sanctuary cities and states, 89
Sanders, Bernie, 23, 151, 217, 222
Santelli, Rick, 206
Saudi Arabia, 453
Scalia, Antonin, 89, 385, 394
Scalise, Steve, 302
Schattschneider, E. E., 253
SCHIP (State Child Health Insurance Program), 86
school desegregation, 125–26, 129, 423–24
schools, shootings at, 112
school segregation, 123–24
search and seizure, 114–15, *115*
Second Amendment, 112–13, *113*
Second Continental Congress, 36–37
Second Founding, 38–43
Second Treatise of Civil Government (Locke), 33
secretaries, federal, 352–53
secrets, government, 360–61
security
    collective, 461–62
    domestic. *See* national security
    public opinion on, *469*
segregation, 79–80
    housing, 128
    school, 123–24, *124,* 129
    voting, 126–28

Select Committee on Benghazi, 304, 365–66, *366*

select committees, 290   (usually) temporary legislative committees set up to highlight or investigate a particular issue or address an issue not within the jurisdiction of existing committees

selection bias, 167–68, 192   the tendency to focus news coverage on only one aspect of an event or issue, avoiding coverage of other aspects

selection bias (surveys)   polling error that arises when the sample is not representative of the population being studied, which creates errors in overrepresenting or underrepresenting some opinions

selective incorporation, 102, *102*   the process by which different protections in the Bill of Rights were incorporated into the Fourteenth Amendment, thus guaranteeing citizens protection from state as well as national governments

self-incrimination, 116–17
self-selection bias, 190
Senate; *see also* Congress
    advice and consent by, 305
    differences between House and, *277*, 277–78
    funding candidates' campaigns for, 208
    under Great Compromise, 42
    and mutual defense alliances, 461
    oversight hearings in, 365
    party unity in, 299–300, *300*
    power to confirm nominations, 457
    under Three-Fifths Compromise, 43
senior citizens, 433
Senior Executive Service, 364

seniority, 291   the ranking given to an individual on the basis of length of continuous service on a committee in Congress

"separate but equal" rule, 121   doctrine that public accommodations could be segregated by race but still be considered equal

separation of church and state, 103–4

separation of powers, 44, *49*, 49–50   the division of governmental power among several institutions that must cooperate in decision-making

September 11, 2001, terrorist attacks, 161–62, 449
    bureaucracy after, 348
    and Bush's foreign policy, 454
    congressional response to, 456–57
    federalism after, 73
    foreign policy following, 456
    national security after, 361
    North Atlantic Treaty after, 462
    trust in government and, 21

services, federal, 351
sex discrimination, 132
sexual harassment, 131
sexual orientation; *see also* same-sex marriage
    and civil rights, 136–37
    and right to privacy, 120
shadow welfare state, 420
Shapiro, Robert, 162
shared political values, 148–49, *149*
Shays, Daniel, 39, *40*
Shays's Rebellion, 39–40, *40*
Shelby County v. Holder, 286
Shepard, Matthew, 137
Sherman, Roger, 36
shield laws, 109
Shirky, Clay, 254–55
Sierra Club, 259

signing statements, 339   announcements made by the president when signing bills into law, often presenting the president's interpretation of the law

simple random sample (or probability sample), 163   a method used by pollsters to select a representative sample in which every individual in the population has an equal probability of being selected as a respondent

Simpson, Alan, 246
single-issue interest groups, 457
Sixth Amendment, 117

slander, 109   an oral statement made in "reckless disregard of the truth" that is considered damaging to the victim because it is "malicious, scandalous, and defamatory"

Slants, The, 96–98, *97,* 137
slavery
    laws concerning, 74
    Thirteenth Amendment, 121
    Three-Fifths Compromise, 42–43
Smith v. Allwright, 396
SNAP. *See* Supplemental Nutrition Assistance
        Program
Snopes, 159
Snowden, Edward, 193–94, *194,* 361
Snyder v. Phelps, 106–8

social desirability effect, 166–67   the effect that results when respondents in a survey report what they expect the interviewer wishes to hear rather than what they believe

social groups, as agent of socialization, 154

socialist, 151   someone who generally believes in social ownership, strong government, free markets, and reducing economic inequality

socialization, 152–57

social media, 178   web-based and mobile-based technologies that are used to turn communication

into interactive dialogue between organizations, communities, and individuals; social media technologies take on many different forms including blogs, Wikis, podcasts, pictures, video, Facebook, and Twitter
  as agent of socialization, 153–54
  civic engagement on, 199
  Congress members on, 281
  demographics of users, 188
  government use of, 160–61, 222
  interest group mobilization through, 264
  and interest group participation, 258
  as news source, 184, 186–89
  political knowledge from, 158–59
  as political networking tool, 222
  political participation via, 198, 199, 221–22
  role of, in elections, 196

social policy, 416–22
  education policies, 423–25
  health policies, 425–31
  housing policies, 431–32
  and the welfare system, 416–22

Social Security, **418, 422, *430*, 433**   a contributory welfare program into which working Americans contribute a percentage of their wages and from which they receive cash benefits after retirement or if they become disabled

Social Security Act of 1935, 417–21, 436–37
Social Security Disability Insurance (SSDI), 418

socioeconomic status   status in society based on level of education, income, and occupational prestige
  of American population, 14–15
  and bias in interest groups, 254
  and voting, 224

sociological representation, 278–81   a type of representation in which representatives have the same racial, gender, ethnic, religious, or educational backgrounds as their constituents. It is based on the principle that if two individuals are similar in background, character, interests, and perspectives, then one can correctly represent the other's views

soft power, 451, 463

solicitor general, 392–94   the top government lawyer in all cases before the Supreme Court in which the government is a party

solidary benefits, 256, *256*   selective benefits of group membership that emphasize friendship, networking, and consciousness-raising

Sotomayor, Sonia, 385, 387
South
  school segregation in, 123
  Three-Fifths Compromise, 42–43
  treatment of African Americans in, 81
  voter registration in, *127*

South Africa, *55*
  government employment in, *357*
  voter turnout in, *226*
South Carolina
  immigration law in, 133
  and school segregation, 122
  slaves in, 42
  and 2010 reapportionment, 284
Southern Christian Leadership Conference, 124, 264
Southern Manifesto, 79–80
South Sudan, 453
Soviet Union, 5, 423, 447–49, *448,* 462–63
Spain, *357*
Spanish-American War, 456

Speaker of the House, 210, 289   the chief presiding officer of the House of Representatives; the Speaker is the most important party and House leader and can influence the legislative agenda, the fate of individual pieces of legislation, and members' positions within the House

speech
  commercial, 111
  freedom of, 101, 105–6, *107,* 197
  political, 106
  by public school students, 108
  symbolic, 106–8
speech plus, 108
speed limit controls, *85*
spending power, 415
Spirit of the Laws, The (Montesquieu), 33, 49
spoils system, 351
SSDI (Social Security Disability Insurance), 418
SSI (Supplemental Security Income) program, 419
Stafford Act, 326

staff organization, 255   type of membership group in which a professional staff conducts most of the group's activities

staff system (Congress), 291, 293
Stalin, Joseph, 5
Stamp Act, 34

standing, 391   the right of an individual or organization to initiate a court case, on the basis of having a substantial stake in the outcome

standing committee, 289–91   a permanent committee with the power to propose and write legislation that covers a particular subject, such as finance or agriculture

stare decisis, 378   literally, "let the decision stand"; the doctrine that a previous decision by a court applies as a precedent in similar cases until that decision is overruled

"state, the," 5
state actions, judicial review of, 389–90
State Child Health Insurance Program (SCHIP), 86

unitary system, 69 a centralized government system in which lower levels of government have little power independent of the national government, 8

United Kingdom, 460
  false news in, 196
  system of government in, *55*
  voter turnout in, *226*

United Nations (UN), 197, 459–60 an organization of nations founded in 1945 to be a channel for negotiation and a means of settling international disputes peaceably; the UN has had frequent successes in providing a forum for negotiation and on some occasions a means of preventing international conflicts from spreading; on a number of occasions, the UN has supported U.S. foreign policy goals

United Nations Framework Convention on
      Climate Change, 451–52, 467
United States
  government employment in, *357*
  income in, *15*
  as member of UN Security Council, 459–60
  system of government in, *55*
  voter turnout in, *226*

**United States–Mexico–Canada Agreement
(USMCA), 451** trade treaty between the United States, Canada, and Mexico to lower and eliminate tariffs among the three countries

United States v. Lopez, 80
United States v. Playboy Entertainment Group,
    110–11
University of California–Davis, 129
University of Michigan, 129
University of Missouri protest, 189
UN Security Council, 459
upper class, 434
urban areas, shift of population to, 14
U.S. Chamber of Commerce, 250
U.S. Court of Appeals, 382, *382*
U.S. Patent and Trademark Office, 97
U.S. Public Health Service (USPHS), 425
USA Freedom Act, 361
USMCA, 451
USPHS (U.S. Public Health Service), 425
Utah, 133, 284

V

values (or beliefs) basic principles that shape a person's opinions about political issues and events
  Americans' support for, *149*
  conflict of, 23
  defined, 147
  democracy, 23
  equality, 18–19
  liberty, 16, 17

  political, 23, 147–48
  shared, 148–49, *149*
  underlying government, 5, 16–20

Van Ordern v. Perry, 104
Verizon, 176–77

veto, 47, 50, 297, 321–22, *322* the president's constitutional power to prevent a bill from becoming a law; a presidential veto may be overridden by a two-thirds vote of each house of Congress

vice presidency, 329–30
Vietnam War, 157, 193, 215
violent broadcast content, 111
Virginia
  and Annapolis Convention, 39
  and school segregation, 122
  slaves in, 42
Virginia Military Institute (VMI), 131

Virginia Plan, 41 a framework for the Constitution, introduced by Edmund Randolph, that called for representation in the national legislature based on the population of each state

Volcker, Paul, 414
Volkswagen, 351
voter ID laws, 126–28, 225
voter registration, 26, 209, 225
voting, 242
  on bills, 296
  and candidate characteristics, 229
  early, *225,* 227
  factors influencing, 225, 227
  issues in, 228
  by mail, *225*
  party loyalty in, 227, *228*
  as political participation, 220–22, 225, 227
  prospective, 228
  retrospective, 228
  turnout. *See* turnout
voting rights
  Amendments for, *61*
  as civil right, 126–28, *127*
  expansion of, 7
  for Native Americans, 11
  state, 60
  and voter ID laws, 126–28
Voting Rights Act amendments of 1970, 133
Voting Rights Act amendments of 1975, 134
Voting Rights Act of 1965 (VRA), 127, *127,* 286

W

Wagner, Dave, 406
Wagner, Kevin, 189
Wagner, Marcella, 406–8, *407*
Wagner-Steagall National Housing Act of 1937,
    431
Wallace, George, 81
Wall Street Journal, 181, 184

Walt Disney Company, 181
Walters, Lee Ann, 346–48, *347*
war(s)
    deterring, 461–62
    as politics by other means, 462–63
    power to declare, 456
    preventive, 449
    public opinion on, 458
War of 1812, 456
War on Poverty, 80–81
war on terror/terrorism, 449

War Powers Resolution, 324   a resolution of
    Congress that the president can send troops
    into action abroad only by authorization of
    Congress or if American troops are already
    under attack or serious threat

Warren, Earl, 384, 398
Washington (state)
    regulation of marijuana use in, 66
    and 2010 reapportionment, 284
Washington, D.C. *See* District of Columbia
Washington, George, 207
    on foreign nations, 447
    on Shays's Rebellion, 40
Washington Post, 161, 182
Watergate, 161, 266
websites, as news source, 187
Webster v. Reproductive Health Services, 263–64
welfare, bureaucracies promoting, 356, 358, *358*
welfare reform, 421–22
welfare state, 78
welfare system, 416–22
    history of, 416–17
    reform of, 421–22
    size of, *428*
    Social Security Act of 1935, 417–21
Westboro Baptist Church demonstrations, 107, *107*
West Virginia House of Delegates, 2
West Virginia State Board of Education v. Barnette, 104
Whig Party, 211–13

whip, 289   a party member in the House or
    Senate responsible for coordinating the party's
    legislative strategy, building support for key
    issues, and counting votes

whip system, 301–2
whistle-blowers, 193
white Americans
    as digital citizens, 188
    European Americans as proportion of
        population, 12
    Medicaid gap for, 435
    naturalized, 12
    poverty rate for, 435–36
    and racism, 154, *155*
White House, contacting, 342

White House staff, 327   analysts and advisers to
    the president, each of whom is often given the
    title "special assistant"

"whiteness," 12
white non-Hispanics, as digital citizens, 188
WikiLeaks, 194
Wikipedia, 254
Wilson, James, 41, 42
Wilson, Joseph, 109
Wilson, Woodrow, 447
Windsor, Edith, *137*
women
    in Congress, *277,* 280
    and gender discrimination, 130–32
    parlimentary representation for, 292
    poverty among, 436–37
    voter support for candidacies of, 229
    voting rights for, 7
Women's Equity Action League, 130
women's rights movement, 130–32
working poor, social benefits for, 434–35
World Bank, 460
World Health Organization, 451

World Trade Organization (WTO), 451
    international organization promoting free
    trade that grew out of the General Agreement
    on Tariffs and Trade

World War I, 448, 456
World War II, 448, 456

writ of certiorari, 391   a decision of at
    least four of the nine Supreme Court
    justices to review a decision of a lower court;
    certiorari is Latin, meaning "to make more
    certain"

writ of habeas corpus, 317, 380   a court
    order that the individual in custody be
    brought into court and shown the cause for
    detention; habeas corpus is guaranteed by the
    Constitution and can be suspended only in
    cases of rebellion or invasion

writs, 391
WTO (World Trade Organization), 451
Wyoming, 112

Y
Yates, Robert, 42, 52
YouTube
    as news source, *187*
    presidential presence on, 333

Z
Zika virus outbreak, *426*

Voter Registration Information

State	Registration Deadline before Election*	Early Voting Permitted?**	Identification Required to Vote?**	More Information
Alabama	14 days	No	Photo ID requested	alabamavotes.gov
Alaska	30 days	Yes	ID requested; photo not required	elections.alaska.gov
Arizona	29 days	Yes	ID required; photo not required	azsos.gov/election
Arkansas	30 days	Yes	Photo ID requested	sos.arkansas.gov
California	15 days; election-day registration permitted	Yes	No	sos.ca.gov
Colorado	8 days by mail or online; no in-person deadline	Yes (all voting by mail)	ID requested; photo not required	sos.state.co.us
Connecticut	14 days by mail; 7 days in person; election-day registration permitted	No	ID requested; photo not required	ct.gov/sots
Delaware	24 days	No	ID requested; photo not required	elections.delaware.gov
District of Columbia	30 days by mail or online; no in-person deadline	Yes	No	dcboee.org
Florida	29 days	Yes	Photo ID requested	dos.myflorida.com/elections
Georgia	28 days	Yes	Photo ID required	sos.ga.gov
Hawaii	30 days; no in-person deadline	Yes	Photo ID requested	hawaii.gov/elections
Idaho	25 days; election-day registration permitted	Yes	Photo ID requested	idahovotes.gov
Illinois	27 days; 16 days online	Yes	No	elections.il.gov
Indiana	29 days	Yes	Photo ID required	in.gov/sos/elections
Iowa	10 days; election-day registration permitted	Yes	Photo ID required	sos.iowa.gov
Kansas	21 days	Yes	Photo ID required	kssos.org
Kentucky	27 days	No	ID requested; photo not required	elect.ky.gov
Louisiana	30 days; 20 days online	Yes	Photo ID requested	sos.la.gov
Maine	21 days by mail; no in-person deadline	Yes	No	maine.gov/sos
Maryland	21 days	Yes	No	elections.state.md.us
Massachusetts	20 days	No	No	www.sec.state.ma.us
Michigan	30 days	No	Photo ID requested	michigan.gov/sos
Minnesota	21 days; election-day registration permitted	Yes	No	mnvotes.org
Mississippi	30 days	No	Photo ID required	sos.ms.gov
Missouri	Fourth Wednesday prior to election	No	ID requested; photo not required	sos.mo.gov
Montana	30 days by mail; no in-person deadline	Yes	ID requested; photo not required	sos.mt.gov
Nebraska	Third Friday prior to election by mail; second Friday prior to election in person	Yes	No	www.sos.ne.gov
Nevada	31 days by mail; 21 days in person	Yes	No	nvsos.gov

State	Registration Deadline before Election*	Early Voting Permitted?**	Identification Required to Vote?**	More Information
New Hampshire	10 days; election-day registration permitted	No	ID requested; photo not required	sos.nh.gov
New Jersey	21 days	Yes	No	njelections.org
New Mexico	28 days	Yes	No	sos.state.nm.us
New York	25 days	No	No	www.elections.ny.gov
North Carolina	25 days	Yes	No	ncsbe.gov
North Dakota	No voter registration required	Yes	ID required; photo not required	vote.nd.gov
Ohio	30 days	Yes	ID required; photo not required	sos.state.oh.us
Oklahoma	24 days	Yes	ID requested; photo not required	ok.gov/elections
Oregon	21 days	Yes (all voting by mail)	No	sos.oregon.gov
Pennsylvania	30 days	No	No	votespa.com
Rhode Island	30 days; election-day registration permitted	No	Photo ID requested	www.elections.state.ri.us
South Carolina	30 days	No	ID requested; photo not required	scvotes.org
South Dakota	15 days	Yes	Photo ID requested	sdsos.gov
Tennessee	30 days	Yes	Photo ID required	tn.gov/sos/election
Texas	30 days	Yes	Photo ID requested	votetexas.gov
Utah	30 days by mail; 7 days in person; election-day registration permitted	Yes	ID requested; photo not required	elections.utah.gov
Vermont	Wednesday before the election; no in-person deadline	Yes	No	www.sec.state.vt.us/elections
Virginia	22 days	Yes	Photo ID required	sbe.virginia.gov
Washington	30 days by mail and online; 8 days in person	Yes (all voting by mail)	ID requested; photo not required	sos.wa.gov/elections/
West Virginia	21 days	Yes	ID requested; photo not required	sos.wv.gov
Wisconsin	20 days by mail; election-day registration permitted	Yes	Photo ID required	www.sos.state.wi.us
Wyoming	14 days; election-day registration permitted	Yes	No	soswy.state.wy.us

* Information collected from Project Vote Smart, votesmart.org/elections/voter-registration (accessed 11/1/18).
** Information collected from National Conference of State Legislatures, www.ncsl.org (accessed 11/1/18). In states where an ID is "requested," voters who do not bring ID to the polls may be required to sign an affidavit of identity, vote on a provisional ballot, have a poll worker vouch for their identity, or take additional steps after Election Day to make sure their vote is counted.
Note: In November 2018, Arkansas and North Carolina passed ballot measures requiring a photo ID to vote. Michigan passed ballot measures to implement same-day and automatic voter registration.